10/00
DECISION MAKING

DECISION MAKING

DESCRIPTIVE, NORMATIVE, AND PRESCRIPTIVE INTERACTIONS

EDITED BY DAVID E. BELL, HOWARD RAIFFA,
AND AMOS TVERSKY

CAMBRIDGE
UNIVERSITY PRESS

Published by the Press Syndicate of the University of Cambridge
The Pitt Building, Trumpington Street, Cambridge CB2 1RP
40 West 20th Street, New York, NY 10011-4211 USA
10 Stamford Road, Oakleigh, Melbourne 3166, Australia

First published 1988
Reprinted 1989, 1991, 1995
Transferred to digital printing 1998

Printed in the United Kingdom by
Antony Rowe Ltd,
Chippenham, Wiltshire

British Library cataloguing in publication data
Decision making: descriptive, normative,
and prescriptive interactions.
1. Decision making: descriptive,
normative, and prescriptive interactions
I. Bell, David E.   II. Raiffa, Howard
III. Tversky, Amos
153.8´3 HD30.23

Library of Congress cataloguing in publication data
Decision making.
Includes index.
1. Decision-making. I. Bell, David E., 1949 –
2. Raiffa, Howard, 1924   III. Tversky, Amos.
T57.95.D394   1988   658.4´03   87-25698

ISBN 0 521 36851 0 paperback

CONTENTS

V   AREAS OF APPLICATION

Contents

PREFACE

This book is a collection of papers presented at a conference, "Decision Making: Descriptive, Normative, and Prescriptive Interactions," held in Boston at the Harvard Business School during June 16–18, 1983. The conference was one of several celebrating the 75th anniversary of the Harvard Business School. It might equally have been held as a celebration of the renaissance of interest in the analysis of decision making under uncertainty that has occurred in recent years. Not since the early 1950s, in the aftermath of the pathbreaking work by von Neumann and Morgenstern, has so much intellectual enthusiasm been directed at the question of how people should, and do, behave when called upon to take action in the face of uncertainty.

When Amos Tversky visited Harvard in the spring of 1982, the three of us had long discussions about the philosophy behind the contribution made by various disciplines to research on decision making. It was clear that mathematicians (decision theorists) are interested in proposing rational procedures for decision making – how people *should* make decisions if they wish to obey certain fundamental laws of behavior. Psychologists are interested in how people *do* make decisions (whether or not rational) and in determining the extent to which their behavior is compatible with any rational model. They are also interested in learning the cognitive capacities and limitations of ordinary people to process the information required of them if they do not naturally behave rationally, but wish to.

But there is a third interest group, the methodologists, the consultants, call them what you will. Some of us are concerned with the bottom line: how do you improve the quality of decisions in practice? It is one thing to talk of axioms and proofs and paradoxes and cognitive limitations – but how can you really help? A number of researchers are concerned with devising methods that incorporate the insights gained from normative theories, but in a way that recognizes the cognitive limitations of the decision maker. There are those who try to find ways to explain the rational models so that they become appealing to the ordinary person. There are those who have learned, by applying the theory, when certain tricks of the trade work, and when various approximations are valid.

It was our view that the lack of cohesion in the field of decision making was due in part to the fact that these three branches of endeavor – normative, descriptive, and prescriptive – had different disciplinary backgrounds: statistics, mathematics, and economics; psychology and behavioral sciences; operations research and management science, respectively. We thought that by bringing together a cross-section of individuals representing these disciplines we could begin a process of communication that would allow each discipline to understand the philosophy of the others. In addition we brought in scholars from fields such as law, education, and medicine, who had no intrinsic interest in decision theory other than its usefulness to them (and the fact that they had used it).

And so it happened. As the conference began, conversation in the plenary sessions was polite but restrained. Coffee break conversation was animated but intra- rather than interdisciplinary. By the third day communication was in full swing. The discussion of health applications was so stimulating that we have preserved some of the flavor of it in this book.

Our hope in producing this book is to provide researchers and students with a collection of current research work that cuts across these various disciplines. The book could be used as background reading for a decision theory course, or as the central material for a research seminar. Many of the papers have appeared in research journals; our contribution in collecting them here is simply that, by doing so, we provide a convenient compendium for the researcher. However, there are many papers that are new, some of them specifically written for the conference. It is our hope that the collection will provide inspiration and unification to the field of decision analysis.

INTRODUCTION

The papers in this volume are organized according to a few guiding principles. The first dichotomy is between theory (20 papers) and application (8 papers).

Within the domain of theory we organized the papers into the following trichotomy:

(a) conceptions of choice (9 papers)
(b) beliefs and judgments about uncertainties (4 papers)
(c) values and utilities (7 papers)

Within each of these categories we arranged the papers according to the following sequence:

(a) decisions people make and how they decide
(b) logically consistent decision procedures and proposals of how people should decide
(c) behavioral objections to normative proposals
(d) how to help people to make better decisions in the light of behavioral realities and normative ideals
(e) how to train people to make better decisions, for example, by providing heuristics and, possibly, therapy

This sequence is motivated and elaborated in the overview paper by the editors (chapter 1).

In the application section, the papers are arranged by fields: economics, management, education, and medicine.

We, the organizers of this conference and its proceedings, in discussions among ourselves about our domain of concern – individual decision making under uncertainty – have found the following taxonomy helpful:

Descriptive

1. Decisions people make
2. How people decide

Normative

1. Logically consistent decision procedures
2. How people should decide

Prescriptive
1. How to help people to make good decisions
2. How to train people to make better decisions

Observe that we have moved from the usual dichotomy (descriptive and normative) to a trichotomy by adding a "prescriptive" category. We have done this primarily because so much of what two of us (David and Howard) do professionally is not adequately captured in the usual descriptive/normative breakdown. One of us (Amos) feels, however, that, although the prescriptive category has been useful for our internal discussions, it may not be necessary to proselytize for this more elaborative breakdown if we were to clarify further the normative category.

The three of us were of one mind, however, in organizing this Conference. We wanted to foster interactions among a community of researchers pursuing the three orientations of description, normative theory, and prescription. Of course, the lines are blurred and even in our own minds we do not clearly know how to classify certain papers and certain activities. It is just because we want to foster integration among these all-too-often separate strands of inquiry that we have not tried to organize the conference papers into descriptive, normative, and prescriptive parts. Had we done so we would have run into trouble with many of our contributors who do not view the world of decision making through our lenses. But still we think that it will be instructive to you, as it has been for us, to preview the papers in this volume in a sequence that reflects our perception of their descriptive, normative, and prescriptive intents.

DESCRIPTIVE PAPERS

McNeil, Pauker, and Tversky (chapter 26), Slovic, Fischhoff, and Lichtenstein (chapter 8), and Tversky and Kahneman (chapter 9) all produce startling evidence that suggests people may arrive at opposite conclusions when data are presented in different, but mathematically equivalent, ways. Such behavior is strictly ruled out by normative models, though these results are of tremendous significance to those who try to understand how people think (description) and to those who try to apply normative principles in the face of such potential distortions (prescription).

Isenberg (chapter 24) reports on observations he has made of managers in action and cites a dearth of instances of formal decision making, let alone applications of normative principles.

March, Simon, Einhorn and Hogarth and Schelling all question whether the traditional normative paradigms really capture the essence of what is important in making a decision. March (chapter 2) draws attention to the dynamic nature of the world, especially to a decision maker's uncertainty about his own future preferences. He explains apparent (normative) anomalies by the need for people to be resilient in the real world. Simon (chapter 3) discusses his famous premise that people aim to achieve satisfactory rather than optimal results from their decisions. Einhorn and Hogarth give a comprehensive review (which includes March and Simon!) of critiques of traditional normative paradigms. They conclude with implications for methodological (our prescriptive) work.

Schelling (chapter 15) cites (anecdotal but compelling) evidence that suggests people may derive pleasure they will pay for from experiences in which the brain (temporarily) suspends logical analysis. We may cry when a movie character dies even though logic tells us the actor is still alive and that the script is fiction. This and other examples lead him to question "who's in charge?"; if the mind is the ultimate consumer of our actions, should we be trying to frustrate its desires via logical thinking?!

Argyris (chapter 25) looks at the impediments, created by social upbringing, to the identification by decision makers and decision scientists alike of nontraditional (and optimal) solutions to problems. He argues that, when decision makers dislike the outcome of a decision, they infer that something was wrong about their decision and ignore the possibility that there might be something wrong about the values and process that produced their decision. While Argyris's declared aim is to improve the chances of helping people to make better decisions (prescriptive), the majority of his article is descriptive in illustrating how people think.

NORMATIVE PAPERS

Quite a number of papers fall in the normative category, though all of them are clearly motivated by earlier descriptive or prescriptive findings. Fishburn (chapter 4) reviews the traditional theories of von Neumann and Morgenstern, and Ramsey and Savage. In addition he surveys recent attempts to adapt these theories in order to accommodate mounting evidence that many (otherwise rational!) people find the older theories too restrictive. Bell and Raiffa (chapter 5) set themselves the goal of "explaining" the axioms of von Neumann and Morgenstern in such a way as to leave all readers lifelong devotees of expected utility, at least for decisions under risk (using Fishburn's terminology).

Shafer (chapter 10) makes a normative contribution in that he presents a constructive procedure for making decisions. His complaint about subjective expected utility is that it is doomed to failure in a prescriptive mode because it requires as inputs concepts such as probability and utility which are not natural to a decision maker. He builds a theory around goals rather than values, and beliefs rather than probabilities, which, even if aesthetically less pleasing to purists, has the prospect of achieving more success in practice. Shafer and Tversky (chapter 11) explain the belief function approach more thoroughly. They state quite clearly that their work is intended neither as a description nor (yet) as a prescription (in our terminology). Rather, they are investigating the normative implications of their ideas. Hence the article is largely a discussion of a number of illuminating examples.

3

Diaconis and Zabell (chapter 12) look at the normative implications of a descriptive habit: people do not calculate priors in the requisite Bayesian fashion, at least not in the exhaustive manner required in principle, rather than construct (or recalculate) a new prior *in light of the evidence*. This paper is essential reading for those card-carrying Bayesians who feel guilty when doing exploratory data analysis.

Dempster (chapter 13) captures much of the spirit of the conference by examining the various roles possible for a quantitative theory of evidence by distinguishing, as Jevons before him, between a truthful theory and a truthful application of the theory. He reasons that we should not expect one normative theory to be most useful in all situations, and that normative theorists do well to supply a range of tools for applied use.

Russell and Thaler (chapter 23) demonstrate that, much as normativists may hate to admit it, market forces may not eliminate irrational behavior. They use a normative model to investigate the implications for economics of the existence of such "quasi-rational" people and consider whether any of a number of government policy alternatives could help such people avoid exploitation.

Bell (chapter 16), in a similar vein to Schelling, takes as a premise that people suffer (in a way that they would be prepared to pay to avoid) from being disappointed. People are disappointed when the outcome of a decision under uncertainty is lower than their expectations. The paper shows how a normative model may be constructed to take account of the detrimental (and positive) effects of disappointment and uses the model to derive implications for human behavior.

Bell and Raiffa (chapter 17) consider whether the traditional concepts of diminishing marginal economic value and risk aversion are really equivalent, as so often is assumed. They argue that the usual measure of risk aversion confounds two concepts, decreasing marginal value and "intrinsic risk aversion." While a person's value curve may quite properly vary with the commodity over which it is measured (thus altering the measure of risk aversion), the authors hypothesize that a person's intrinsic aversion to risk (dislike of uncertainty) remains constant across situations. Regret and disappointment were two ideas that arose from consideration of factors that might contribute to intrinsic risk aversion.

PRESCRIPTIVE PAPERS

The paper by Edwards, von Winterfeldt, and Moody (chapter 20) falls squarely in the prescriptive category. They describe an application in which multiple objective analysis is used to rank research projects. Along the way they tell many of the lessons they have learned over years of using decision analysis in the field.

Keeney (chapter 21) has also spent many years applying decision analysis, especially multiattribute utility theory. He too relates a number of tips for would-be prescriptivists but the main thrust of this paper is in suggesting a way for people to think more constructively. He suggests that people would do well to analyze their value systems as a means for identifying decisions that could be made. The reverse, as he notes, is more usually the case; a decision situation compels an analysis of values. By pursuing value-focused thinking, Keeney argues, a person may derive greater incremental benefit from opportunities for decisions.

Fischhoff, Slovic, and Lichtenstein (chapter 18) describe a number of difficulties that stand in the way of an analyst who attempts to measure the values of a decision maker. While alerting the reader to the potential pitfalls, they argue it may be mistaken as a premise, both in reality and as a practical matter, to assume that people have values that await quantification. Decision aids might be developed that exploit the insights to be gleaned from the inherent instability of values.

Hershey, Kunreuther, and Schoemaker (chapter 19) identify five sources of distortion in the assessment of utility functions. This is a descriptive contribution to a normative theory with prescriptive implications!

Fong, Krantz, and Nisbett (chapter 14) question whether formal statistical training helps people to avoid common reasoning errors in everyday life. While their results do support such a conclusion it is somewhat alarming to see how often even trained people fall into such traps. The difficulty of the task ahead of those wishing to make prescriptive contributions is clearly underlined by this article.

Arrow (chapter 22) contemplates the implications of recent behavioral evidence for public policy decision making where decision analysis has already had a considerable impact.

This volume ends with a series of papers dealing with medical decision making. We have two applications of decision analysis, the first, Gottlieb and Pauker (chapter 27), on the question of appropriate treatment for a particular patient and the second, Pauker, Pauker, and McNeil (chapter 28), which (via a sample of respondents) estimates the value of permitting a particular prenatal test.

The final chapter by Weinstein, Fineberg, McNeil, and Pauker (chapter 29) lists some of the research questions facing those wishing to use decision analysis in medicine. It becomes clear from examining the list that decision analysis has provided a service in causing these problems to be identified, for they are of concern whether one wishes to use decision analysis for on-line advice or for the solution of generic problems.

It was our intent to produce edited transcripts of some of the many discussions that took place at the conference, but due to technical and, we confess, administrative difficulties, much of the taping was of no use. We were able to rescue portions of the closing discussions on medical decision analysis and this is included in chapter 29. We are grateful to Robert J. Quinn for these transcriptions.

I

OVERVIEW PAPER

1

DESCRIPTIVE, NORMATIVE, AND PRESCRIPTIVE INTERACTIONS IN DECISION MAKING

DAVID E. BELL, HOWARD RAIFFA, AND AMOS TVERSKY

The focus of our attention is the individual decision maker facing a choice involving uncertainty about outcomes. We will consider how people do make decisions, how "rational" people should make decisions, and how we might help less rational people, who nevertheless aspire to rationality, to do better. When we speak of nonrational people, we do not mean those with diminished capacities; we refer instead to normal people who have not given thought to the process of decision making or, even if they have, are unable, cognitively, to implement the desired process. Our decision makers are not economic automatons; they make mistakes, have remorse, suffer anxieties, and cannot make up their minds. We start with a premise, not that people have well thought out preferences, but that they may be viewed as having divided minds with different aspirations, that decision making, even for the individual, is an act of compromise among the different selves.

For our purposes we shall augment the usual dichotomy that distinguishes between the normative and descriptive sides (the "ought" and the "is") of decision making, by adding a third component: the *prescriptive* side. We do this because much of our concern in this paper addresses the question: "How can real people – as opposed to imaginary, idealized, super-rational people without psyches – make better choices in a way that does not do violence to their deep cognitive concerns?" And we find that much that we have to say on these matters does not fit conveniently into the usual normative or descriptive niches. Loosely speaking, prescriptive analyses exploit some of the logical consequences of normative theories and the empirical findings of descriptive studies but, in addition, something else has to be added that is far from the spirit of normative or descriptive analyses.

In order to contrast the three modes of analysis let us consider the concept of transitivity. Insofar as decision makers have opinions about alternatives most (but not all) normative models posit that if the decision agent prefers alternative A to B, and prefers B to C, then he will also have a preference for A over C. This is a common axiom or desideratum of many normative systems. When the transitivity axiom is added to other axioms in a given normative framework, the analyst can generate a superstructure of logical implications. This is the familiar world of the mathematician. Axioms are not God-given but are chosen by the mathematical creator who has one eye on the real world for inspiration. In the case of transitivity the plausibility is self-evident; people, by and large and most of the time, make choices in a transitive fashion.

But describers of reality point out that most individuals occasionally exhibit intransitive (or cyclical) preferences: A over B, B over C, and C over A. There are lots of ways to explain why this might be the case. Preferences might be nonstationary; or they might be stochastic; or they might involve a balancing of attributes. When A and B are compared, the decision maker might highlight certain underlying attributes. Then when the choice set changes from (A, B) to (A, C) or to (B, C) different attributes might be emphasized. Or perhaps the decision maker has consulted three experts in order to make up his own mind and the experts have exhibited the classical cyclical pattern: A over B over C for expert 1, B over C over A for expert 2, and C over A over B for expert 3. When the decision maker combines his advice using a majority rule principle, the intransitivity becomes manifest: A over B, B over C, and C over A. Or perhaps there are no external experts but within the psyche of the single decision maker we can imagine that there are three selves (self', self'', self''') whose aggregate preferences are cyclic. The point of all this is that, descriptively speaking, people are often intransitive and there is a divergence between those normative conceptions of choice that posit transitivity and observed behavior. The normatively oriented analyst can try to accommodate some degree of intransitivity in his mathematical, axiomatic abstractions and attempt to fuse a better concordance between idealistic theorizing and empirical behavior. But perhaps even though some individuals exhibit intransitivities they wish to act otherwise. Is this the case? Well, this again is an empirical proposition that psychologically minded decision theorists may wish to investigate.

Now let us add the prescriptive viewpoint. Mr Johnson has racked his mind and has eliminated a lot of alternatives but is now perplexed about whether he should choose alternative A or C. Choose he must. The trouble is that the alternatives are so different in so many different dimensions and, in addition, uncertainties complicate the picture. Now let us suppose that Johnson (or his consulting decision analyst), after examining aspects of A and C, ingeniously invents a new alternative B for which Johnson finds it comfortable to say that he prefers A to B and B to C. Johnson might also think it is reasonable that his preference involving A, B, and C should be transitive. So the creation of hypothetical alternative B might help Johnson to believe that deep down he really prefers A to C. Alternatively, instead of the introduction of B, there might be the introduction of B', B'', and B''' such that $A > B'$, $B' > B''$, $B'' > B'''$, and $B''' > C$, where $>$ means "is preferred to."

Is this decision-aiding device descriptive? If it were, Johnson would do this for himself. Is it normative (A is preferred to C if and only if there exists B, etc.)? No, we do not think so. What the decision analyst did was find a way to help Johnson by calling on a normative device, in this case transitivity. A prescriptive analyst should also be sophisticated enough to know that Johnson might not really prefer A to C deep down but he might have been led by magic mirrors into believing that he does. Can the same trick be played in reverse? Can an alternative D be concocted such that $C > D$, and $D > A$, which, by transitivity, would lead to the conclusion that Johnson really prefers C to A? Well, it is worth a try. This is the spirit of the art of prescriptive analysis; it is a curious mixture of normative and descriptive analysis but a lot more.

Another example will elucidate the distinctions between the normative, descriptive, and prescriptive viewpoints. McNeil *et al.* (chapter 26 in this volume)

> investigated how variations in the way information is presented to patients influence their choices between alternative therapies. Data were presented summarizing the results of surgery and radiation therapy for lung cancer to 238 ambulatory patients with different chronic medical conditions and to 491 graduate students and 424 physicians.

The subjects were asked to imagine that they had lung cancer and had to choose between two therapies on the basis of given probabilistic assessments. The relevant question (repeated below) was presented to one subset of individuals in terms of survival.

> Of 100 people having treatment A, 90 live through the treatment. A total of 70 people are alive by the end of the first year and a total of 38 people are alive by the end of five years.
>
> Of 100 people having treatment B, all live through the treatment. A total of 79 people are alive by the end of the first year and a total of 26 people are alive by the end of five years.

A second group of individuals was presented with the same choice, except that the data were described in terms of mortality rates rather than survival rates (e.g., "of 100 people having treatment A, 10 die during treatment," etc.).

The data, using the appropriate frame of survival or mortality, are also tabulated and shown to each subject, who is then asked to choose treatment A or B (see table 1.1, frames 1.1 and 1.2). Each subject is shown either frame 1.1 or 1.2 but not both. Observe that the data given to the subjects are identical in informational content whether they are given in terms of survival or mortality.

The punch line is dramatic. There are vast differences in the responses of subjects depending on whether the data are presented in terms of survival or in terms of mortality. The format seems to influence the thought process. The proportion of subjects that preferred treatment B to A was 61% when the data were presented in terms of mortality and was only 37% when presented in terms of survivability. These are the descriptive realities. Choices can be influenced by the framing of the question, a major concern that is not incorporated in the usual normative theory, but is well known among students of the field.

Prescribers, allegedly helpful intervenors in the decision-making process, have

11

Table 1.1. *Alternate frames for a choice selection*

	(Frame 1.1) Cumulative chance of death		(Frame 1.2) Cumulative chance of survival	
	Treatment *A*	Treatment *B*	Treatment *A*	Treatment *B*
During treatment	10%	0%	90%	100%
By year 1	30%	21%	70%	79%
By year 5	62%	74%	38%	26%

Outcome	(Frame 1.3)		Treatment *A*	Treatment *B*
(0)	Not surviving treatment (i.e., dying during treatment)		10%	0%
(0, 1)	Surviving treatment but dying before end of first year		20%	21%
(1, 5)	Surviving 1 year but dying before end of fifth year		32%	53%
(5+)	Surviving at least 5 years		38%	26%
			100%	100%

to be continually aware that they can bias the responses of subjects by the mere wording of questions. In the above example, one possibility is to join the two frames together in the description of a consequence (e.g., "90 live through the treatment and therefore 10 die"). McNeil, Pauker, and Tversky (chapter 26 in this volume) presented some subjects with both versions of the questionnaire and examined subjects' responses to the combined frame and their reactions to their own inconsistencies. The effect of the combined frame was much closer to the mortality frame than to the survival frame, perhaps because the mortality data are more salient than the survival data. When presented with their inconsistencies most subjects are inclined to modify their choices, but are not clear as to which preference should be changed. These observations are descriptively interesting and prescriptively important if we are going to give advice to real people, but they are hardly relevant in most normative conceptions.

Let us continue with this illustration from a prescriptive orientation. The data can also be summarized in a composite version in table 1.1 (frame 1.3) that gives the relative frequency (chance) of each outcome.

Now let us use some more prescriptive magic on a hypothetical decision maker Ms Jones who is faced with frame 1.3. Imagine that we have an urn with 100 balls, each ball having an *A* label on it and a *B* label on it. The *A* labels may be marked in red and the *B* labels in blue. In table 1.2 we indicate possible markings on the 100 balls that correspond to the frequencies in table 1.1. For example, 20 balls

Table 1.2

Number of balls	A-label	B-label
20	(0, 1)	(0, 1)
32	(1, 5)	(1, 5)
26	(5+)	(5+)
1	(0)	(0, 1)
9	(0)	(1, 5)
12	(5+)	(1, 5)

Table 1.3

Event	Original Treatments		Reduction Treatments		Modification Treatments	
	A	B	A'	B'	A''	B''
(0)	10	0	10	0	11	0
(0, 1)	20	21	0	1	0	0
(1, 5)	32	53	0	21	0	22
(5+)	38	26	12	0	11	0
	100	100	22	22	22	22

have a common A and B label, namely (0, 1); and in the last row, 12 balls have an A label of (5+) and a B label of (1, 5). The problem can be viewed as follows: Ms Jones must make a choice of A or B and then draw a ball at random that will determine the outcome.

But there are 78 balls that have identical A and B labels and these balls, so it can be argued, are just cluttering up the problem. So let us get rid of them in order to concentrate on the essence of the choice problem: the choice between the labels on the remaining 22 balls. The original and reduced problems are shown in table 1.3. The argument goes that the choice between A and B should be the same as the choice between A' and B'. Of course, by and large people might choose differently between these two versions, but should they? Would you? Suppose Ms Jones says on reflection that she would want her choice between A and B to be governed by her choice between A' and B' and that she would like to think hard about her choice in the latter problem. Furthermore, let us assume that she is tilting toward favoring A' over B', but is not sure. To test her preference let us pose the following question to Ms Jones. Let us make A' a bit worse to yield A'' and improve B' a bit to yield B'' (see the last two columns of table 1.3). Now let us ask Ms Jones: "Suppose you are told that you can be certain of the outcome (1, 5); would you take a 50–50 chance of getting (0) or (5+)?"

Ms Jones thinks: "Sure, I would do it." Therefore she prefers A'' to B'' and therefore she *should* prefer A' to B' and therefore she *should* prefer A to B. There are a lot of "shoulds" lined up. Is this bit of trickery of help to Jones? Well, it might help us to think deeper about the problem but Jones might think otherwise. She might ask, "If I announce *A* and pick a ball would I be told the outcome on the *B*-label as well?" After all the comparison of what she got and could have got might have an effect on her psyche. Should it? Well even if it *should not* in your opinion, what happens if it *does* in her opinion? This, and a lot more, is what the prescriptive intervenor must wrestle with.

When problems are recast in supposedly equivalent forms there may be subtle psychological nuances that are omitted that on cognitive reflection should not be omitted. Prescriptive intervenors should be especially sensitive to these nuances and they can be sensitized somewhat to understand these nuances by comparing descriptive and normative behaviors. It is much more difficult, however, to know what to do about these nuances in prescriptive interventions.

It is our aim in this chapter to highlight discrepancies between real and idealized behavior such as previewed in the above two motivating examples and to throw out the challenge: what should be done to improve behavior of real people? That is not the aim of those who think of themselves as normative modelers, nor the aim of most empiricists who investigate real-world behavior. Decision analysts who are interested in prescriptive interventions must rise to the challenge if on balance they are to do more good than harm.

Before we attempt a little more systematically to describe potential interactions among descriptive, normative, and prescriptive perspectives, with the purpose of highlighting an identifiable niche for the prescriptive category, we will in the next section put aside questions of prescription and discuss the very fuzzy line separating descriptive and normative analyses.

NORMATIVE IDEALIZATIONS USED AS DESCRIPTIVE APPROXIMATIONS

Mathematical economics – or should we say simply "economics" because so much of economics is mathematical these days – makes extensive use of models that posit utility maximization behavior on the parts of individual agents. A typical example is of the form: let $\underline{x}_i = (x_{1i}, \ldots, x_{ji}, \ldots, x_{Ji})$ represent the allocation of J resources enjoyed by individual i. Let $u_i(\underline{x}_i)$ be i's utility evaluation for $\underline{x}_i$, where u_i is assumed to be strictly monotonic in each variable, concave, and twice differentiable; let . . . etc. Then the abstraction continues by letting the I individuals of this "economy" interact, i.e., trade commodities and information; it posits that each agent seeks to maximize his own expected utility given some rational expectations of what others might do. Is this abstraction normative or descriptive? Or perhaps neither? For the most part researchers who write in this genre are not doing it to help guide or prescribe behavior for agent i. Rather such models are usually formulated as first-cut approximations of the descriptive behavior of individuals. Even though the vast majority, if not all, of the subjects do not behave coherently enough to satisfy the implied behavior of the assumptions of the model, the feeling is that the model might yield empirically meaningful insights because if real-world behavior deviated too far from the equilibrium behavior suggested by the model, a few individuals would exploit such aberrant behavior to their own advantage, and through learning and adaptation the economy would settle down to some distinguishable equilibrium state predicted by the model. In this manner, the normative character of the model is used as an argument to reinforce its descriptive value. A second-cut descriptive model, a far more difficult modeling exercise, would be to posit quasi-rational motives for individual actors and make the model dynamic with adaptive learning feedbacks. A third-cut descriptive model might try to better understand a much richer panoply of human motivations and emotions so that what is deemed "quasi-rational" behavior might indeed be more fully rationalized.

The theoretical results emanating from the simpler model that posits the existence of utility functions only over physical commodity bundles could be more robust than the assumptions themselves. Much of this modeling effort is descriptive – not descriptively accurate in the small but descriptively suggestive or approximative in the large. More realistic and descriptively plausible micro-behavior can be grafted onto the model, although this is not commonly done.

Some researchers who design and analyze such abstract models of economies with idealized agents might have a macro-prescriptive motivation in mind, such as: how should information flows among the agents be modified to make this small economy perform more efficiently? But very often that prescriptive orientation is left unexpressed in the model. The supra-decision maker, the rules manipulator, is not introduced in the model, not given a utility function over the multi-attributed societal concerns; the model is used in its formal structure as an approximation of descriptive reality and is used in a casual, informal manner for a diffuse macro-prescriptive purpose.

Economics textbooks, for pedagogical purposes, assume that economic agents have indifference curves in n-space. These indifference maps are just assumed to exist and no serious attempt is made at establishing a protocol for eliciting such indifference maps as would be necessary if the purpose of the analysis were really prescriptive – prescriptive in the sense of trying to guide reflective behavior. The purpose of the textbook writers really is first-cut descriptive behavior and not prescriptive behavior. For some purposes it may be helpful to foster the myth that deep down in all of us there is an orderly, coherent, n-dimensional preference function and that, when we elicit manifest, phenotypic responses from this latent, genotypic preference function, errors are made. That myth, however, may not be helpful for prescribing (guiding) behavior of the individual. We believe that such orderly representations (such as n-dimensional utility functions and multi-variate subjective probability distributions) do not really exist but in some circumstances their existence might be usefully fabricated and constructively developed in order to guide behavior.

15

David E. Bell, Howard Raiffa, and Amos Tversky

DESCRIPTIVE, PRESCRIPTIVE, AND NORMATIVE ANALYSES

We have refrained up to now from defining just what we mean by descriptive, prescriptive, and normative analyses because it is a bit easier for us to back into a clarification of the distinctions we wish to make. Some authors use "normative" and "prescriptive" interchangeably but we propose to treat these terms quite distinctly.* Our emphasis in this chapter will largely be on prescriptive analysis and therefore it is important for us to distinguish it clearly from normative analysis.

Let us start with *descriptive* analysis because this is easiest. How do real people think and behave? How do they perceive uncertainties, accumulate evidence, learn and update perceptions? How do they learn and adapt their behavior? What are their hang-ups, biases, internal conflicts? How do they talk about their perceptions and choices? Do they really do as they say they do? Can they articulate the reasons for their actions? How do they resolve their internal conflicts or avoid such resolutions? Do they decompose complex problems, think separately about component parts of problems, and then recompose or integrate these separate analyses? Or do they think more holistically and intuitively? What are the differences in types of thought patterns for people of different cultures, of different experience levels? What is the role of tradition, imitation, superstition in decision making (or nonmaking)? How can "approximate" real behavior be described? How good are various mathematical models in predicting future behavior?

In short, descriptive analysis is concerned with how and why people think and act the way they do. At times it may involve intricate mathematical modeling and require sophisticated statistical analysis. It is a highly empirical and clinical activity that falls squarely in the province of the social sciences concerned with individual behavior. Scholars can study this domain without any concern whatsoever of trying to modify behavior, influence behavior, or moralize about such behavior.

Now for the normative side. This activity is harder to characterize because it involves several facets. First, there is the notion that normative theory has something to do with how idealized, rational, super-intelligent people should think and should act. Such analyses abstract away known cognitive concerns of real people, their internal turmoils, their shifting values, their anxieties and lingering post-decisional disappointments and regrets, their repugnance (or zest) for ambiguity or danger, their inabilities to do intricate calculations, and their limited attention span. The hallmarks of such normative analyses are coherence and rationality as captured usually in terms of precisely specified desiderata or axioms of the form: if the decision maker believes so and so, he should do such and such. As usual in any mathematical system, the power of any set of desiderata comes from their logical, synergistic, joint implications.

Axioms, basic principles, and fundamental desiderata are motivated by what

---

* For the purposes of this chapter only; we are not attempting to change common usage.

16

some investigator thinks is logical, rational, intelligent behavior. Then like any mathematical axiom system (such as sets of axioms for geometry) the academic researchers play variations on the themes: what happens if this axiom is dropped, or if this axiom is modified in such and such a way? This exercise is rewarding if the mathematical implications are profound or aesthetically pleasing. The exercise can also be rewarding if the researcher can see a better concordance between the abstract system and some aspects of behavior that is empirically verifiable or that the researcher imagines is verifiable. Thus there is a dynamic interaction between the real world, imaginations about the real world, and the abstract mathematical system. There are extant a host of abstract models of decision making bearing some relation to decision making as it is, or as it is perceived to be, or as it should be in someone's mind.

In the usual parlance, an abstract system that purports to describe or predict behavior is called a descriptive model; an abstract system that attempts to capture how ideal people might behave is called a normative model. There is little difficulty in categorizing some models as clearly descriptive or normative. One trouble is that some normatively motivated models are often used, as mentioned above, as first-cut descriptive models. Other clearly normatively motivated models go through successive modifications that try to make them more useful for descriptive and predictive purposes and then it may be difficult to say whether these modifications should be classified as normative or descriptive. On the other hand, some descriptively motivated models are occasionally modified to come a bit closer to what some analyst believes is a proper norm for wise behavior. And then the model falls into the grey area. Is it descriptive or is it normative?

Now we move on to prescription. What should an individual do to make better choices? What modes of thought, decision aids, conceptual schemes are useful – useful not for idealized, mythical, de-psychologized automata – but for real people? And since real people are different, with differing psyches and emotions, capabilities, and needs, good advice has to be tuned to the needs, capabilities, and emotional makeups of the individuals for whom the prescriptive advice is intended. It becomes even more complicated when individuals who think one way have to interact with experts who think along different paradigmatic lines, as, for example, between a rational decomposer and a holistic intuiter.

For some individuals a wise prescriptive might be: "Behave as you normally do. You're doing well and any new mode of analysis might inhibit your creative thinking." For others the advice might be: "It's important that you decompose your problem and get external advice from experts on such-and-such a component part, because otherwise you will not be able to constructively integrate and synthesize what you know together with what others know."

The differences among the three functions – descriptive, normative, and prescriptive – of choice models can be illuminated by examining the criteria by which they are evaluated. Descriptive models are evaluated by their *empirical validity*, that is, the extent to which they correspond to observed choices.

17

Normative models are evaluated by their *theoretical adequacy*, that is, the degree to which they provide acceptable idealizations or rational choice. Prescriptive models are evaluated by their *pragmatic value*, that is, by their ability to help people make better decisions. To be sure, all three criteria are difficult to define and evaluate, as any student of the philosophy of science knows too well. It is evident, nevertheless, that the criteria are different; an argument against a normative model need not be an argument against a descriptive model and vice versa.

For example, consider the property of stochastic dominance. Because this condition is regarded as a cornerstone of rational choice, any theory that does not obey it can be regarded as unsatisfactory from a normative standpoint. A descriptive theory, on the other hand, is expected to account for observed violations of stochastic dominance (e.g., problems 2 and 8 in Tversky and Kahneman, 1986). A prescriptive analysis may develop procedures designed to eliminate and reduce such violations. A failure of dominance, therefore, can serve as a counter-example to a normative model, as an observation to be explained by a descriptive model, and as a challenge for a prescriptive model.

CONCEPTIONS OF CHOICE

James March (1978) questions the usefulness of choice as a pervasive metaphor for describing and interpreting human behavior and he questions what we shall call the *canonical paradigm* of decision making that posits:

an identified decision agent;

a prespecification of alternative choices in the purview of the decision agent;

a set of potential consequences that can be anticipated and evaluated (ranked) in terms of stable, well-defined objectives;

a partition of the possible states of the world – an articulation of mutually exclusive, collectively exhaustible, possible resolutions of uncertainty with no unanticipated surprises;

information and evidence that can be accumulated for the relevance it has for the choice process.

March observes that the way decisions are talked about is not necessarily the way decisions are made. He asserts that, "Our theoretical ideas about choice are partly inconsistent with what we know about human processes of decision and that as a result we sometimes fail to understand what is going on in decision making, *and that as a consequence we sometimes offer less than perfect counsel to decision makers*" (italics added).

We certainly concur with the sentiments he expresses in *describing* what is happening out there, even though we may not know what to do about it; we also believe that March's observations are pertinent to prescribers or intervenors who want to influence the way decisions might be made better or more wisely.

What we call the "canonical paradigm of choice behavior" – an identified decision maker with prespecified alternatives, consequences, states-of-the-world, preferences, and beliefs – March refers to as a "willful-choice model." He observes and bemoans the fact that such models are omnipresent not only in modern economics but in large parts of anthropology, psychology, political science, and sociology as well as the applied fields that build upon them.

Willful-choice models may not answer questions about what happened in an organization or in society – "Why did it happen?" or "Why did you do it?" – but they might address the question posed by some perplexed actor of that society at a critical juncture in his or her life, "What should I do next?" Societal outcomes result usually from a concatenation of actions, a few taken willfully but others by tradition, by obligation, by duty, by inaction or default, and some taken by chance or God. A single individual rarely makes a grandiose choice for society. But all of us make less grandiose micro-choices: to buy or not to buy, to vote for X or Y, to take job Q or S, and so on. Perhaps each of us, over the course of a lifetime, make a dozen or so critical, deliberative, serious choices. That would add to a vast pool of potential applications for the prescriptive uses of the willful-choice paradigm. But, granted, it would still be a terrible distortion to describe the dénouement of most lifetime careers in terms of these deliberative choices. A lot else happens that can be better described in other ways.

It is alleged that willful-choice models posit the prior specification of *all* alternatives and only rarely does one have all the alternatives. Well, that is not such a serious problem. It still may be helpful to choose as wisely as we can among just those two or three alternatives we can think of *a priori* even though there may be other better alternatives that we are not wise enough to think about. A much more serious objection may be that the decision agent may concentrate so much time on choosing among preconceived alternatives that not enough time or effort goes towards devising new alternatives. That may be the case, but formalizing that meta-dilemma may not be prescriptively productive. It also should be noted, however, that a systematic, deliberative analysis of a set of preconceived alternatives may itself spark creative insights that could generate other more imaginative alternatives.

Herbert Simon and others stress that complex problem solving involves a search process and, descriptively speaking, intelligent decision agents adaptively set up aspirations for this search process. They satisfice. Descriptively this may be the way most individuals behave. Normative models might attempt to rationalize the search-and-quitting process in terms of subjective expected utility maximization in which time and physical and emotional effort are included as components of the utility calculus. This is an old debate between students with normative and descriptive persuasions. This problem is, however, critical for the prescribers: how best to give advice about the search process. A prescriber might believe that satisficing behavior could be adequately rationalized by the maximization of a suitably complex objective function but, if it is too horrendously complicated to constructively formulate such an objective function, then the prescriber's operational advice might be better organized by a satisficing heuristic.

In willful-choice models, preferences for consequences are usually posited to be stable, consistent, precise, and exogenous to the problem. The truth of the matter is that they are often ill-formed, labile, shifting, and endogenous to the problem. Anecdotes galore can be cited where a decision agent feels for some amorphous, nonarticulatable reason that decision A is better than B. It just feels better. His articulated preferences for consequences are not antecedent to his action but rather are derivatives from his action preference. But this is not always the case, and when it is not the case a decision maker might want to think systematically about his basic preferences and base his choice on the implications of these deliberations. Keeney and Raiffa (1976) cite an example in which a decision maker, having already decided what action was best, nevertheless chose to investigate systematically his values and beliefs in order to help develop an advocacy document for his preferred alternative. Surprisingly, an analysis that systematically probed his preferences shifted his opinion. There is no shortage of anecdotes on both sides of this debate.

It is not our aim in this chapter to make an exhaustive list of all the objections to the canonical willful-choice model. We want to underscore, however, our belief that most objections to the use of willful-choice models for the selection of actions yet to be made pose deep intellectual challenges that fall more in the domain of prescriptive analysis than in normative analysis.

THE SUBJECTIVE EXPECTED UTILITY (SEU) MODEL OF CHOICE BEHAVIOR

We now turn our attention to one of several models of willful-choice behavior, the one that is most extensively applied and most often maligned: the subjective expected utility (SEU) model. It is often the case that specific criticisms leveled against the SEU model should more appropriately be directed against the broader class of willful-choice models.

In the SEU model it is assumed that any action chosen by the decision maker will result in some consequences whose specification involves no uncertainties – all the uncertainties of the problem are loaded into what is generally termed "states" or "states-of-the-world." Thus the decision maker confronts an array of states-of-the-world, one of which will ultimately prevail and, given his usually vague information about which of these states will prevail, he must choose an action. It is assumed that the action he chooses will yield some consequence depending on the state that providence, so to speak, selects. In looser parlance, the choice of an act results in a lottery that will yield one consequence depending on which state prevails. The decision maker thus has a choice over lotteries. Consequences and states-of-the-world can often be artfully defined to adapt the SEU model to problems that seem, at first, not to fit. The structure as stated might appear to be static and not to incorporate sequential choice possibilities with appropriate adaptive feedback mechanisms, but these complexities are conceptually accommodated by identifying an action with a dynamic strategy over time.

In the SEU model one assumes that the decision maker can always make up his mind; he has a complete set of transitive preferences for consequences and for lotteries over those consequences. If we keep in mind that consequences can involve a multiplicity of attributes and that action alternatives may incorporate adaptive feedback features, then this assumption of complete comparability – i.e., that the decision maker can always make up his mind in a coherent fashion – is mind boggling. The assumptions imply that the decision maker can accomplish this bit of magic by (a) assessing probabilities for the states-of-the-world, (b) assigning a utility value (real number) to each (complex) consequence, (c) calculating the expected utility value (i.e., the sum of probabilities times utilities) of each lottery associated with each alternative action, and (d) comparing actions by their SEU numbers.

Actually it can be proven as a theorem rather than stated as an axiom that any decision maker who can "consistently" compare actions must behave as if he had embedded within himself a probabilistic assessment over states and a utility function over consequences, and had calculated expected utility values for comparisons. These probabilities and utilities come tumbling out as logical implications of more primitive logical constructs such as full comparability of alternatives, transitivity, and a so-called substitution or sure-thing principle.

Although the SEU model has been treated by many as a descriptive model, it is used primarily as a normative system that captures in a crisp and elegant fashion, the formal properties that characterize one idealized sense of rational choice under uncertainty.

In limited domains the SEU model may also be used as a prescriptive tool in order to guide behavior, but this conscious effort involves a reflective thought process that is far more complex than the bare bones of the SEU model seems to indicate. Real people, in real situations, do not naturally act coherently and one usually cannot discover via their past revealed real behavior their latent probability distributions and utility functions. Rather, the way the SEU model is put to prescriptive use turns the model upside down. We do not start by assuming that the decision maker can, in an unaided fashion, compare any two alternatives but rather we test whether we can compare a few simple hypothetical consequences. Already in this limited domain he might exhibit intransitivities among the few consequences that he is willing initially to compare, but he then must be willing to reflect upon these inconsistencies and modify his preferences so that they line up transitively. In an iterative fashion he must be willing, in a particular instance, to act quite unnaturally: to deliberately police his choices in hypothetical simple situations, one by one, and force to conform to the desideratum of consistency. Gradually, if he is successful, a probability distribution over states and a utility function over consequences will emerge. These will literally have to be constructed bit by bit, and it is a Platonic myth that latently these probabilities and utilities really exist deep down and that the analyst merely has to cut away the fat in order to display the pre-existing structure. Next a leap of faith is required: the decision maker must be willing to use his probability and utility functions that he has laboriously constructed to calculate SEUs that will guide his selection of real-world alternatives.

Why should anyone behave in such an unnatural fashion? Well, first of all, in some simple situations for which probabilities are crisply given and based on relative frequency data, and for which consequences can be adequately described by a single numeraire, like money, the SEU prescriptive process is reasonably transparent and natural. Secondly, there is always the nagging question: is there a better alternative? Remember we are assuming that there is a decision maker who is confused about what he should do in his own best interests. (This in no way implies that these interests have to be hedonistically self-serving.) Thirdly, the prescriptive use of the SEU model is appealing to a lot of people who have thought hard about these problems. The same of course, could be said of other prescriptive procedures. Unfortunately, for those of us who are emotionally and intellectually wedded to the SEU prescriptive process, we cannot cite statistical evidence of the form: 100 decision makers were randomly selected; 50 were instructed in the intricacies of the SEU prescriptive process; 50 others in a control group were not. Of the 50 so instructed, 42 became rich and beloved, whereas 7 of the control group were so indicated. It is hard to accumulate descriptive data on the real use of this prescriptive process. Some favorable laboratory data could be cited, but to the skeptics such data are not very convincing.

A decision maker who constructively employs the SEU model to guide his choice must decompose his judgments about uncertainties from his preferences for consequences. After a separate analysis of each component is made, the analyst fuses these elements together to arrive at a choice. But contaminating influences will often permeate across a boundary that is meant to keep the component activities separate and pure. A decision maker's concerns about utilities might influence his assessments of probabilities and vice versa. In addition, before any analysis is done he may have preferences for actions that might influence his assessments of both beliefs and values.

We can be glib in normative theories by hypothesizing the existence of decision agents who can think separately and distinctly about uncertainties and values and who can then integrate these deliberations jointly to determine preferences for actions. However, real behavior often does not conform to such an ideal, especially in complex, highly emotional choice situations. The sophisticated prescriptive intervenor, who wants to help a real client to decide wisely, must be cognizant of these realities. The prescriptive analyst and client must work carefully to ameliorate some of these potential distortions. Sometimes it might be best to give up: to discard as nonimplementable a formal structuring and decomposition of the problem. But let us not go too far and assume that every case presents insurmountable practical difficulties. In prescriptive analyses, especially when inputs are required from diverse experts, each of whose expertise pertains to only part of the problem, there may not be any other recourse than to decompose the problem into component parts. The point of all this is that the complications alluded to above are real and must be addressed in prescriptive analyses and this is one feature that makes prescriptive analysis so different from normative analysis.

Let us return to an earlier observation that preferences for consequences are not stable, not consistent, and not precise. In descriptive empirical studies these observations are repeatedly documented. Abstract models could try to capture this reality by positing an error theory. A preference value for a consequence could, at any instance, be considered a random drawing from some distribution. Distributions might overlap and therefore at one instance consequence A might be preferred to B and an instance later it might shift. Descriptive modelers have developed a host of other accounts to accommodate the empirical data. In normative analyses one can posit that an accumulation of information or a slight change in one's external environment can account for these shifting preferences even over short periods of time. In prescriptive analysis the spirit is often different than either the normative or the descriptive analysis. A subject may be gently confronted with the observation that some of his responses are seemingly inconsistent and he may be invited to think more deeply about these inconsistencies. Ideally, of course, one might hope that with deeper reflection, with a clarification of the descriptions of consequences, with a better comprehension of the relevant attributes that should be contemplated, the subject would settle down to a set of coherent preferences that could be articulated. Anecdotes can be cited where this state occurs. But, in some cases where preferences shift into a coherent mode, there is the obvious danger that the subject might only be misleading herself and her analyst; she may be generating consistent but not "intrinsically truthful" responses. Anecdotes can also be cited where deeper reflection exacerbates the confusion and coherence is never achieved. It is not generally understood, especially by critics who interpret the SEU model literally, that in a given choice situation it is rarely necessary to have a full articulation of the decision agent's full set of preferences. Occasionally a simple break-even analysis or a sensitivity analysis centered around some crude approximation of the subject's preference structure will suffice. A decision maker may not be sure whether a parameter should be 10, 15, or 20 and in successive probings he may register labile values; but a simple break-even analysis might show that it really does not matter: the break-even point may be 40, way out of the hazy range. At other times an analysis can proceed without obtaining any definitive trade-offs between objectively incommensurable qualities; the answer might be obvious by a simple dominance argument. At other times the prescriptive intervenor might be able to employ an incomplete description of the client's preference structure to eliminate some but not all contending alternatives. In an iterative fashion, the analyst might learn what incremental information should be elicited from the client in order to help the client arrive at a wise choice. This type of intellectual activity is not adequately captured in the usual descriptive or normative literature. The art and science of elicitation of values (about consequences) and judgments (about uncertainties) lies at the heart of prescriptive endeavors.

As we noted above, individuals, by and large, do not follow the precepts of the SEU model. They do not naturally decompose their choice problems into concerns about beliefs and values; they do not base their choices in real situations on consideration of what they think they would want to do in simple hypothetical situations. These observations are readily acknowledged by the "prescribers" and they respond, "If people behaved naturally as we wish they would behave, there would be no need for our services." The discrepancy between theory and behavior is the *raison d'être* of prescriptive interventions.

In the next section we examine discrepancies between descriptive and normative perceptions in choices where probabilities are crystal clear. Afterwards we grapple with cases where distortions about probabilities are the heart of the matter.

PSYCHOLOGICAL CONSIDERATIONS

Tversky and Kahneman (1986) show that most individuals violate the implications of the SEU model even in very simple choice situations where there is absolutely no vagueness about uncertainties – i.e., where probabilities are identifed with known relative frequencies. They go on to catalog the types of discrepancies between the SEU model and descriptive behavior and then they indicate how the SEU model can be modified to better predict actual behavior. Their descriptive, empirically based, model is called "prospect theory."

Prospect theory is a description of how people make decisions between simple lotteries. Three systematic differences between prospect theory and SEU are demonstrated convincingly by them. First of all, people think of consequences as increments (or decrements) to current wealth and have aversion to losses. Loosely speaking, most individuals exhibit an inflection point at their status quo reference point: they are concave (i.e., risk averse) above it and convex (i.e., risk seeking) below it. Secondly, they do not distinguish adequately between large numbers. Twenty thousand dollars sounds a lot like twenty-five thousand dollars. Thirdly, people give unlikely events more weight than they deserve, and give correspondingly less weight to very likely events.

In decision-tree analysis the usual prescription is to accumulate financial flows along the path of the tree and register their total at the end of the tree before working backwards. If a flow totals $1,000, it is irrelevant if the component summands are $500 and $500 or if they are minus $200 and $1,200. But it is not relevant according to the findings of prospect theory where subjects view sequential choices in terms of their reference positions along the way. That is descriptive reality!

In SEU analysis most utility functions are taken to be concave so that a gamble is less preferred to its mean. But in prospect theory more subtle distinctions are shown. For desirable payoffs above the reference point there is a strong certainty effect; if subjects are pleased with an outcome that is certain, they hate to gamble it away. But, if the payoffs are undesirable relative to the reference point, subjects have a reversal effect: they become risk seeking.

For those of us who want to help people make better decisions – better for them, not for us – these results pose dilemmas. We can deftly structure problems to avoid such tendencies. For example, in teaching decision analysis at the Harvard Business School, the instructors insist that analyses be made in terms of final financial asset positions rather than in terms of increments or decrements from a present asset position because, in terms of that accounting, the students will fall prey to a psychological trap, to a cognitive illusion. But the problem persists: are we doing right to force students to think one way if they feel another way? That cannot be right. A better way would be to lead subjects to become consciously aware of those behavioral tendencies that contradict the desiderata of coherence. If a subject behaves in a way that makes it possible for someone to make a book against him, then he might choose to live with that behavioral anomaly or to revise his thinking and feeling. How far should we push this indoctrination? These concerns – and they are troublesome – do not fall in the province of descriptive or normative analysis as normally interpreted. They are at the heart of the craft of a discipline that could be called "prescriptive decision analysis."

A deeper question lurks in the background. If a subject mechanically uses the SEU model, many of these so-called behavioral anomalies are eliminated. But is this in the decision maker's best interests? Of course we may construct situations in which decision makers, by following their natural tendencies, are led into obvious errors, but people do not spend their lives entering into deals with devious decision analysts. They deal with the world as it is. People may have learned by experience that unlikely events happen more often than they should, that adverse selection causes alternatives with the potential for loss to produce losses more often than an objective analysis would suggest. Does the SEU model deal with real life decisions, or only with objectively verifiable decisions?

Prospect theory does not answer these questions; it merely poses them. From the perspective of a person wedded to the SEU model, prospect theory confirms the need for such a model to guide behavior. For the "Darwinian School" (that believes 40 million years of evolution have produced humans with an effective capacity for decision making that should not be tampered with) prospect theory confirms the ivory tower nature of SEU.

There certainly are discrepancies between the tenets of SEU theory and descriptive behavior. Should we be changing the analytical procedures we propose for guiding real behavior or should we be applying a bit of psychological therapy? Or both? But before we consider those questions let us first reflect on discrepancies between theory and behavior on the probabilistic (as opposed to the utility) side of the ledger. We will see that on the probabilistic side

25

we will be more inclined to be more paternalistic: we theorists are not going to change, let the subjects shape up!

BELIEFS OR JUDGMENTS ABOUT UNCERTAINTY

The SEU model asserts that the decision maker should hold beliefs about uncertainties that are in accordance with some subjective probabilistic measure. But copious examples show that most individuals do not "believe" as the SEU theory says they should believe.

Ellsberg (1964) and others have shown that subjectively scaled probability assessments do not always obey the usual probabilistic axioms. Dramatic examples have been concocted for which subjectively assessed probabilities for an event E and for not-E do not sum to unity. Loosely speaking, there is a manifest bias against vagueness, and this discrepancy can lead to choices that are not in conformity with SEU behavior. "That's fine," say the normative analysts, "this shows that we have something to teach."

Tversky and Kahneman (1983) demonstrate empirically that many individuals register beliefs that imply, for them, that the joint event (A and B) is "more probable" than event A alone, the "conjunction fallacy." For example, the probability of a nuclear war starting by a terrorist act is assessed as being more likely than a nuclear war starting. Normative analysts are not disturbed at this: "Oh, that's just a mistake; mention of a terrorist act just helps the imagination." Prescriptive analysts must be aware, however, of these common "mistakes" in the elicitation of judgments about uncertainties.

There are a host of examples where untutored individuals, and even many "tutored" ones as well, have poor intuitions about probability. They might use heuristics developed for one class of problems for another class, such as: information from sample sizes less than 30 should be ignored. Most individuals have poor intuition about how information should modify judgments about uncertainties. Examples abound where even experts neglect base rates, where doctors confuse $P(A/B)$ and $P(B/A)$, where optimism or fatalism or guilt or religious fervor affects deep beliefs about uncertainties. A Peanuts cartoon depicts wishful thinking: "Can this happen?" "Yes, one chance in a million." "Well then let's play." They play; they lose; they become angry for having lost. This is reality.

It is hard to shake most individuals' strong beliefs about the gambler's fallacy: "I've had a couple of successes and therefore I am due for a failure." And there is also the countervailing fallacy: "The dice are running hot. I better get into the act."

The above examples illustrate that often people's beliefs about uncertainty are not in accord with empirical relevant frequencies of plausible physical models – e.g., "a die hath neither memory nor conscience." Normative analysts can remain aloof: "Probability theory does not describe how people think but how they should think." But prescriptive analysts must beware lest they build a so-called logical superstructure on a nonsensical subjective base. Responsible, professional prescribers must be cognizant of such behavioral anomalies and guide their clients around the common pitfalls.

There is another class of common errors where probabilities get linked with outcomes and alternatives. Let p be the probability of an adverse outcome in the population (e.g., a particular form of cancer). An action is contemplated that will reduce this probability from p to $(p - \Delta p)$ and thus save $N\Delta p$ potential victims (where N is the population size). But administrators and the public might evaluate the efficacy of the proposed action not on Δp but on $\Delta p/p$. A reduction from $p = .18$ to $p = .14$ may be deemed much less desirable than a reduction of $p = .04$ to $.02$, say. "Oh well," someone might retort, "this might not be such a mistake if one includes public anxiety as a reality of the problem – even if this anxiety is based on misperceptions of the public's own interest." These examples raise the question of what concerns and possible misperceptions should and should not be included in prescriptive analyses.

If the SEU model is to be applied to guide behavior, then someone will have to supply the basic inputs: probabilities and utilities. Let us continue with the probabilistic side. Many, if not most, real decision problems cannot be analyzed adequately using purely objective probabilities. Subjective assessments must be introduced and this once again leads us into a confrontation between abstract theory and realistic behavior. Real people just do not behave like the models say they should, but still they might need and want help. Descriptive theorists happily demonstrate that people are incoherent in their probabilistic assessments; normative analysts generally remain aloof and do not get involved in empirical measurements; it is the prescriptive analysts who must learn how to elicit judgments and make sense out of them, if there is some sense to be gleaned from those judgments.

We have learned that many experts are willing to answer hypothetical questions about uncertain quantities, such as: Do you think it is more likely that X will fall in the interval from a to b or outside that interval? We have learned that lay people and experts alike do not calibrate well: by and large assessed probability distributions are too tight; people think they know more than they really know and are surprised far too often. We know that some assessment methods lead to less distortions than others. We know that it is devilishly hard to assess small probabilities. We know that subjects can learn to calibrate better if they are given systematic feedback. We know that there is a need to develop better methods for elicitation and that the describers and abstracters are not going to provide the impetus for this development. It is the prescribers who must take the lead.

On the probabilistic side we tend to view incoherent responses as errors in perception that should be monitored and corrected. The matters are more complicated on the utility side. Incoherent utility judgments may also result from fallible thinking but there are other possibilities as well: the analysts may be using an inappropriate analytical framework, or the analysts might have abstracted

27

away too much of reality. We have left the discussion of this problem to the last section because the contrast between probabilities and utilities is instructive.

PSYCHOLOGICAL CONCERNS AS CARRIERS OF VALUE

The study of risky choice began with the study lotteries where all outcomes are simply monetary gains or losses and this paradigm is still the major focus of research in the field. However, the axioms of utility are also applicable for decisions involving nonmonetary and multidimensional outcomes such as health, the environment, or social welfare. In multi-attribute utility theory, the decision maker is asked to identify the dimensions of an outcome that are important determinants of preference. There are few normative guidelines covering what attributes are legitimate and how they should be traded off.

Let us examine the choice of a lottery from the perspective of multi-attribute utility theory. What are some of the concerns of a decision maker faced with a risky choice? A somewhat different question may make the issue clearer: why do many people wish to avoid risk? Bell (1982) has looked at the implications of two *ex post* psychological conditions: regret and disappointment. Regret may occur when a risky choice turns out to be "wrong" after the fact: an alternate choice would have been better given the state-of-the-world that occurred. It is a great frustration to take a chance on a shortcut to the airport only to find that you would have caught the plane had you only kept to your usual route. Not only have you missed your plane but you must live with the fact that it was you, and not providence, who were responsible for the error (see, e.g., Kahneman and Tversky, 1982). Many people anticipate the possible (post-decisional) regret in such situations and trade off a higher chance of making the plane in favor of reducing the possibility of such regret.

Disappointment is a psychological reaction to an outcome that is below expectations. Many people would rather not be told they are being short-listed for an important promotion because this would raise their expectations and lead to great disappointment should they not, in fact, be given the position (see Bell, 1985).

We all recognize that the feelings of anxiety, joy in anticipation, regret, disappointment, elation, envy, and others are a constant part of our lives, but what role should they play in prescriptive analysis? Natural questions for study are (1) To what extent do these psychological concerns actively affect the decisions that are made? (Descriptive.) (2) Should they affect decisions that are made? How can these cognitive concerns be incorporated into more complex models? (Normative.) (3) What are the implications of these cognitive concerns for the way we help people make risky decisions? (Prescriptive.)

It has been argued by many that behavior is always rational; apparent violations of the canons of rationality stem from a too restrictive view of human motivations. Normative modelers might want to embellish the canonical model of willful-choice behavior to include psychological concerns such as envy, anxiety, joy in suspense, regret, disappointment, elation. Certainly the SEU model can be extended to capture some of these nuances by merely elaborating the description of consequences. But does this capture the essence of the problem? Once research modelers move into this psychological domain they would have to sort out what is fundamental from what is derivative, and they would have to grapple with deep problems of the "divided self."

Economists like to point out that any trade-offs that are made to mitigate or exaggerate psychological satisfaction will diminish real economic benefits. If people behave coherently in an extended psychological sense but not coherently in terms of economic payoffs, then a "book" can be made against them. In social poker, for example, a player might choose not to maximize his expected winnings but rather to bluff more than is empirically profitable, or "stay in" too often merely for the fun of it; he may be maximizing his satisfaction, which may not be congruent with maximizing monetary payoffs. Other players, of course, can exploit these behavioral motivations.

Not all deviations from the restrictive SEU model deserve to be rationalized and made legitimate in an elaborated model. Perhaps an analyst might want to incorporate regret and disappointment but how about errors that are made in subjectively updating probabilities? How about enriching a normative model to accommodate the behavior of individuals who enter into contracts which will purposely restrict their future choices because they now know what they later will want to do is not what they (now know is what they) should do. If a researcher decides to extend the classical normative model to include such concerns, what meta-criteria should be used to decide which embellishments should be included? Can we order heuristics and biases as to "eligibility" or normative status? Are any of these questions empirically answerable?

Or maybe the research agenda should be pitched the other way, not towards the reform of the underlying conceptual model but towards the reform of subjects. Perhaps they need education and/or therapy. In some cases therapy might be achieved by an explicit recognition that some cognitive concerns should be acknowledged and once explicitly analyzed these concerns might turn out not to be so important after all. Take the following example. We have explored Smith's preferences for money and have determined that she should prefer a 50–50 gamble on $10,000 or nothing to the certainty of $2,000. But Smith says, if the chips were down, she would take the $2,000 despite her earlier responses to utility questions. When pressed it appears that she is terribly concerned about the anticipation of the possible post-decision regret she would have if the gamble yielded the $0 payoff. "I would feel terrible ending up with this zero value, knowing that I could have had $2,000." Yes, she undoubtedly would feel terrible, but how terrible? She should also consider that there would also be post-decision delight if she ended up with $10,000 and some ambivalence if she accepted $2,000 knowing that she was giving up a gamble with an expected value of $5,000. In other words, each monetary consequence carries along with it some psychological baggage. If we came to grips with these psychological concerns by trying to cost them out – e.g., how much would you be willing to pay in dollars to be able to wave a magical wand and get rid of guilt feelings? – the subject might discover that those concerns left unanalyzed were magnified in her mind and once analyzed were not as important as she thought. Such analysis might alter feelings as well as actions. Therapy through analysis.

The reader can hardly fail to notice that we have raised many questions and answered very few. The message is simply that the art and science of decision analysis require many skills not readily classifiable as either normative and descriptive, but which nonetheless have a legitimate and important role in both research and practice.

REFERENCES

Bell, David E. (1982). "Regret in decision making under uncertainty," *Operations Research* 30, 961–81.

(1985). "Disappointment in decision making under uncertainty," *Operations Research* 33, 1–27 (chapter 16, this volume).

Ellsberg, Daniel (1964). "Risk, ambiguity, and the Savage axioms," *Quarterly Journal of Economics* 75, 643–69.

Kahneman, Daniel, and Tversky, Amos (1982). "The psychology of preferences," *Scientific American* 246, 160–73.

Keeney, Ralph, and Raiffa, Howard (1976). *Decisions With Multiple Objectives*. Wiley, New York.

March, James (1978). "Bounded rationality, ambiguity and the engineering of choice," *Bell Journal of Economics*, 9 (2), 587–608 (chapter 2, this volume).

Tversky, Amos, and Kahneman, Daniel (1983). "Extensional v. intuitive reasoning: the conjunction fallacy in probability judgment," *Psychological Review* 90, 293–315.

(1986). "Rational choice and the framing of decisions," *Journal of Business* 59 (4), part 2, 5251–78 (chapter 9, this volume).

II

CONCEPTIONS OF CHOICE

2

BOUNDED RATIONALITY, AMBIGUITY, AND THE ENGINEERING OF CHOICE

JAMES G. MARCH

THE ENGINEERING OF CHOICE AND ORDINARY CHOICE BEHAVIOR

Recently I gave a lecture on elementary decision theory, an introduction to rational theories of choice. After the lecture, a student asked whether it was conceivable that the practical procedures for decision making implicit in theories of choice might make actual human decisions worse rather than better. What is the empirical evidence, he asked, that human choice is improved by knowledge of decision theory or by application of the various engineering forms of rational choice? I answered, I think correctly, that the case for the usefulness of decision engineering rested primarily not on the kind of direct empirical confirmation that he sought, but on two other things: on a set of theorems proving the superiority of particular procedures in particular situations if the situations are correctly specified and the procedures correctly applied, and on the willingness of clients to purchase the services of experts with skills in decision sciences.

The answer may not have been reasonable, but the question clearly was. It articulated a classical challenge to the practice of rational choice, the possibility that processes of rationality might combine with properties of human beings to produce decisions that are less sensible than the unsystematized actions of an intelligent person, or at least that the way in which we might use rational procedures intelligently is not self-evident. Camus (1951) argued, in effect, that man was not smart enough to be rational, a point made in a different way at about the same time by Herbert A. Simon (1957). Twenty years later, tales of horror have become contemporary clichés of studies of rational analysis in organizations (Wildavsky, 1971; Wildavsky and Pressman, 1973; Warwick, 1975).

I do not share the view of some of my colleagues that microeconomics, decision science, management science, operations analysis, and the other forms of rational decision engineering are mostly manufacturers of massive mischief when they are put into practice. It seems to me likely that these modern technologies of reason have, on balance, done more good than harm, and that students of organizations, politics, and history have been overly gleeful in their compilations of disasters. But I think there is good sense in asking how the practical implementation of theories of choice combines with the ways people behave when they make decisions, and whether our ideas about the engineering of choice might be improved by greater attention to our descriptions of choice behavior.

At first blush, pure models of rational choice seem obviously appropriate as guides to intelligent action, but more problematic for predicting behavior. In practice, the converse seems closer to the truth for much of economics. So long as we use individual choice models to predict the behavior of relatively large numbers of individuals or organizations, some potential problems are avoided by the familiar advantages of aggregation. Even a small signal stands out in a noisy message. On the other hand, if we choose to predict about small numbers of individuals or organizations or give advice to a single individual or organization, the saving graces of aggregation are mostly lost. The engineering of choice depends on a relatively close articulation between choice as it is comprehended in the assumptions of the model and choice as it is made comprehensible to individual actors.

This relation is reflected in the historical development of the field. According to conventional dogma, there are two kinds of theories of human behavior: descriptive (or behavioral) theories that purport to describe actual behavior of individuals or social institutions, and prescriptive (or normative) theories that purport to prescribe optimal behavior. In many ways, the distinction leads to an intelligent and fruitful division of labor in social science, reflecting differences in techniques, objectives, and professional cultures. For a variety of historical and intellectual reasons, however, such a division has not characterized the development of the theory of choice. Whether one considers ideas about choice in economics, psychology, political science, sociology, or philosophy, behavioral and normative theories have developed as a dialectic rather than as separate domains. Most modern behavioral theories of choice take as their starting point some simple ideas about rational human behavior. As a result, new developments in normative theories of choice have quickly affected behavioral theories. Contemplate, for example, the impact of game theory, statistical decision theory, and information theory on behavioral theories of human problem-solving, political decision making, bargaining, and organizational behavior (Rapoport, 1960; Vroom, 1964; Binkley, Bronaugh, and Marras, 1971; Tversky and Kahneman, 1974; Mayhew, 1974). It is equally obvious that prescriptive theories of choice have been affected by efforts to understand actual choice behavior. Engineers of artificial intelligence have modified their perceptions of efficient problem solving procedures by studying the actual behavior of human problem solvers (Simon, 1969; Newell and Simon, 1972). Engineers of organizational decision making have modified their models of rationality on the basis of studies of actual organizational behavior (Charnes and Cooper, 1963; Keen, 1977).

Rationality, ambiguity, and the engineering of choice

Modern students of human choice frequently assume, at least implicitly, that actual human choice behavior in some way or other is likely to make sense. It can be understood as being the behavior of an intelligent being or a group of intelligent beings. Much theoretical work searches for the intelligence in apparently anomalous human behavior. This process of discovering sense in human behavior is conservative with respect to the concept of rational man and to behavioral change. It preserves the axiom of rationality; and it preserves the idea that human behavior is intelligent, even when it is not obviously so. But it is not conservative with respect to prescriptive models of choice. For, if there is sense in the choice behavior of individuals acting contrary to standard engineering procedures for rationality, then it seems reasonable to suspect that there may be something inadequate about our normative theory of choice or the procedures by which it is implemented.

Rational choice involves two kinds of guesses: guesses about future consequence of current actions and guesses about future preference for those consequences (Savage, 1954; Thompson, 1967). We try to imagine what will happen in the future as a result of our actions and we try to imagine how we shall evaluate what will happen. Neither guess is necessarily easy. Anticipating future consequences of present decisions is often subject to substantial error. Anticipating future preferences is often confusing. Theories of rational choice are primarily theories of these two guesses and how we deal with their complications. Theories of choice under uncertainty emphasize the complications of guessing future consequences. Theories of choice under conflict or ambiguity emphasize the complications of guessing future preferences.

Students of decision making under uncertainty have identified a number of ways in which a classical model of how alternatives are assessed in terms of their consequences is neither descriptive of behavior nor a good guide in choice situations. As a result of these efforts, some of our ideas about how the first guess is made and how it ought to be made have changed. Since the early writings of Herbert A. Simon (1957), for example, bounded rationality has come to be recognized widely, though not universally, both as an accurate portrayal of much choice behavior and as a normatively sensible adjustment to the costs and character of information gathering and processing by human beings (Radner, 1975a, b; Radner and Rothschild, 1975; Connolly, 1977).

The second guess has been less considered. For the most part, theories of choice have assumed that future preferences are exogenous, stable, and known with adequate precision to make decisions unambiguous. The assumptions are obviously subject to question. In the case of collective decision making, there is the problem of conflicting objectives representing the values of different participants (March, 1962; Olson, 1965; M. Taylor, 1975; Pfeffer, 1977). In addition, individual preferences often appear to be fuzzy and inconsistent, and preferences appear to change over time, at least in part as a consequence of actions taken. Recently, some students of choice have been examining the ways individuals and organizations confront the second guess under conditions of

35

ambiguity (i.e., where goals are vague, problematic, inconsistent, or unstable) (Cohen and March, 1974; Weick, 1976; March and Olsen, 1976; Crozier and Friedberg, 1977). Those efforts are fragmentary, but they suggest that ignoring the ambiguities involved in guessing future preferences leads both to misinterpreting choice behavior and to misstating the normative problem facing a decision maker. The doubts are not novel; John Stuart Mill (1838) expressed many of them in his essay on Bentham. They are not devastating; the theory of choice is probably robust enough to cope with them. They are not esoteric; Hegel (1832) is relevant, but may not be absolutely essential.

BOUNDED RATIONALITY

There is a history. A little over twenty years ago, Simon published two papers that became a basis for two decades of development in the theory of choice (1955, 1956). The first of these examined the informational and computational limits on rationality by human beings. The paper suggested a focus on step-function utility functions and a process of information gathering that began with a desired outcome and worked back to a set of antecedent actions sufficient to produce it. The second paper explored the consequences of simple payoff functions and search rules in an uncertain environment. The two papers argued explicitly that descriptions of decision making in terms of such ideas conformed more to actual human behavior than did descriptions built upon classical rationality, that available evidence designed to test such models against classical ones tended to support the alternative ideas.

Because subsequent developments were extensive, it is well to recall that the original argument was a narrow one. It started from the proposition that all intendedly rational behavior is behavior within constraints. Simon added the idea that the list of technical constraints on choice should include some properties of human beings as processors of information and as problem solvers. The limitations were limitations of computational capability, the organization and utilization of memory, and the like. He suggested that human beings develop decision procedures that are sensible, given the constraints, even though they might not be sensible if the constraints were removed. As a shorthand label for such procedures, he coined the term "satisficing."

Developments in the field over the past twenty years have expanded and distorted Simon's original formulation. But they have retained some considerable flavor of his original tone. He emphasized the theoretical difficulty posed by self-evident empirical truths. He obscured a distinction one might make between individual and organizational decision making, proposing for the most part the same general ideas for both. He obscured a possible distinction between behavioral and normative theories of choice, preferring to view differences between perfect rationality and bounded rationality as explicable consequences of constraints. Few of the individual scholars who followed had precisely the same interests or commitments as Simon, but the field has generally maintained

36

the same tone. Theoretical puzzlement with respect to the simplicity of decision behavior has been extended to puzzlement with respect to decision inconsistencies and instabilities, and the extent to which individuals and organizations do things without apparent reason (March and Olsen, 1976). Recent books on decision making move freely from studies of organizations to studies of individuals (Janis and Mann, 1977). And recent books on normative decision making accept many standard forms of organizational behavior as sensible (Keen, 1977).

Twenty years later, it is clear that we do not have a single, widely accepted, precise behavioral theory of choice. But I think it can be argued that the empirical and theoretical efforts of the past twenty years have brought us closer to understanding decision processes. The understanding is organized in a set of conceptual vignettes rather than a single, coherent structure; and the connections among the vignettes are tenuous. In effect, the effort has identified major aspects of some key processes that appear to be reflected in decision making; but the ecology of those processes is not well captured by any current theory. For much of this development, Simon bears substantial intellectual responsibility.

Simon's contributions have been honored by subsumption, extension, elaboration, and transformation. Some writers have felt it important to show that aspiration level goals and goal-directed search can be viewed as special cases of other ideas, most commonly classical notions about rational behavior (Riker and Ordeshook, 1974). Others have taken ideas about individual human behavior and extended them to organizations (both business firms and public bureaucracies) and to other institutions, for example, universities (Bower, 1968; Allison, 1969; Steinbruner, 1974; Williamson, 1975). Simon's original precise commentary on specific difficulties in rational models has been expanded to a more general consideration of problems in the assumptions of rationality, particularly the problems of subjective understanding, perception, and conflict of interest (Cyert and March, 1963; Porat and Haas, 1969; Carter, 1971; R. N. Taylor, 1975; Slovic, Fischhoff, and Lichtenstein, 1977). The original articles suggested small modifications in a theory of economic behavior, the substitution of bounded rationality for omniscient rationality. But the ideas ultimately have led to an examination of the extent to which theories of choice might subordinate the idea of rationality altogether to less intentional conceptions of the causal determinants of action (March and Olsen, 1976).

ALTERNATIVE RATIONALITIES

The search for intelligence in decision making is an effort to rationalize apparent anomalies in behavior. In a general way, that effort imputes either calculated or systemic rationality to observed choice behavior. Action is presumed to follow either from explicit calculation of its consequences in terms of objectives, or from rules of behavior that have evolved through processes that are sensible but which obscure from present knowledge full information on the rational justification for any specific rule.

Most efforts to rationalize observed behavior have attempted to place that behavior within a framework of calculated rationality. The usual argument is that a naive rational model is inadequate either because it focuses on the wrong unit of analysis, or because it uses an inaccurate characterization of the preferences involved. As a result, we have developed ideas of limited rationality, contextual rationality, game rationality, and process rationality.

Ideas of *limited rationality* emphasize the extent to which individuals and groups simplify a decision problem because of the difficulties of anticipating or considering all alternatives and all information (March and Simon, 1958; Lindblom, 1959; 1965; Radner, 1975a, b). They introduce, as reasonable responses, such things as step-function tastes, simple search rules, working backward, organizational slack, incrementalism and muddling through, uncertainty avoidance, and the host of elaborations of such ideas that are familiar to students of organizational choice and human problem solving.

Ideas of *contextual rationality* emphasize the extent to which choice behavior is embedded in a complex of other claims on the attention of actors and other structures of social and cognitive relations (Long, 1958; Schelling, 1971; Cohen, March, and Olsen, 1972; Weiner, 1976; Sproull, Weiner, and Wolf, 1978). They focus on the way in which choice behavior in a particular situation is affected by the opportunity costs of attending to that situation and by the apparent tendency for people, problems, solutions, and choices to be joined by the relatively arbitrary accidents of their simultaneity rather than by their prima facie relevance to each other.

Ideas of *game rationality* emphasize the extent to which organizations and other social institutions consist of individuals who act in relation to each other intelligently to pursue individual objectives by means of individual calculations of self-interest (Farquharson, 1969; Harsanyi and Selten, 1972; Brams, 1975). The decision outcomes of the collectivity in some sense amalgamate those calculations, but they do so without imputing a super-goal to the collectivity or invoking collective rationality. These theories find reason in the process of coalition formation, sequential attention to goals, information bias, and interpersonal gaming, and the development of mutual incentives.

Ideas of *process rationality* emphasize the extent to which decisions find their sense in attributes of the decision process, rather than in attributes of decision outcomes (Edelman, 1960; Cohen and March, 1974; Kreiner, 1976; Christensen, 1976). They explore those significant human pleasures (and pains) found in the ways we act while making decisions, and in the symbolic content of the idea and procedures of choice. Explicit outcomes are viewed as secondary and decision making becomes sensible through the intelligence of the way it is orchestrated.

All of these kinds of ideas are theories of intelligent individuals making calculations of the consequences of actions for objectives, and acting sensibly to achieve those objectives. Action is presumed to be consequential, to be connected consciously and meaningfully to knowledge about personal goals and future outcomes, to be controlled by personal intention.

Although models of calculated rationality continue to be a dominant style, students of choice have also shown considerable interest in a quite different kind of intelligence, systemic rather than calculated. Suppose we imagine that knowledge, in the form of precepts of behavior, evolves over time within a' system and accumulates across time, people, and organizations without complete current consciousness of its history. The sensible action is taken by actors without comprehension of its full justification. This characterizes models of adaptive rationality, selected rationality, and posterior rationality.

Ideas of *adaptive rationality* emphasize experiential learning by individuals or collectivities (Cyert and March, 1963; Day and Groves, 1975). Most adaptive models have the property that, if the world and preferences are stable and the experience prolonged enough, behavior will approach the behavior that would be chosen rationally on the basis of perfect knowledge. Moreover, the postulated learning functions normally have properties that permit sensible adaptation to drifts in environmental or taste attributes. By strong information on past experiences in some simple behavioral predilections, adaptive rationality permits the efficient management of considerable experiential information; but it is in a form that is not explicitly retrievable – particularly across individuals or long periods of time. As a result, it is a form of intelligence that tends to separate current reasons from current actions.

Ideas of *selected rationality* emphasize the process of selection among individuals or organizations through survival or growth (Winter, 1964, 1971, 1975; Nelson and Winter, 1973). Rules of behavior achieve intelligence not by virtue of conscious calculation of their rationality by current role players but by virtue of the survival and growth of social institutions in which such rules are followed and such roles are performed. Selection theories focus on the extent to which choice is dominated by standard operating procedures and the social regulation of social roles.

Ideas of *posterior rationality* emphasize the discovery of intentions as an interpretation of action rather than as a prior position (Hirschman, 1967; Weick, 1969; March, 1973). Actions are seen as being exogenous and as producing experiences that are organized into an evaluation after the fact. The valuation is in terms of preferences generated by the action and its consequences, and choices are justified by virtue of their posterior consistency with goals that have themselves been developed through a critical interpretation of the choice. Posterior rationality models maintain the idea that action should be consistent with preferences, but they conceive action as being antecedent to goals.

These explorations into elements of systemic rationality have, of course, a strong base in economics and behavioral science (Wilson, 1975; Becker, 1976); but they pose special problems for decision engineering. On the one hand, systemic rationality is not intentional. That is, behavior is not understood as following from a calculation of consequences in terms of prior objectives. If such a calculation is asserted, it is assumed to be an interpretation of the behavior but not a good predictor of it. On the other hand, these models claim, often explicitly, that there is intelligence in the suspension of calculation. Alternatively, they suggest that whatever sense there is in calculated rationality is attested not by its formal properties but by its survival as a social rule of behavior, or as an experientially verified personal propensity.

In a general way, these explications of ordinary behavior as forms of rationality have considerably clarified and extended our understanding of choice. It is now routine to explore aspects of limited, contextual, game, process, adaptive, selected, and posterior rationality in the behavioral theory of choice. We use such ideas to discover and celebrate the intelligence of human behavior. At the same time, however, this discovery of intelligence in the ordinary behavior of individuals and social institutions is an implicit pressure for reconstruction of normative theories of choice, for much of the argument is not only that observed behavior is understandable as a human phenomenon, but that it is, in some important sense, intelligent. If behavior that apparently deviates from standard procedures of calculated rationality can be shown to be intelligent, then it can plausibly be argued that models of calculated rationality are deficient not only as descriptors of human behavior but also as guides to intelligent choice.

THE TREATMENT OF TASTES

Engineers of intelligent choice sensibly resist the imputation of intelligence to all human behavior. Traditionally, deviations of choice behavior from the style anticipated in classical models were treated normatively as errors, or correctable faults, as indeed many of them doubtless were. The objective was to transform subjective rationality into objective rationality by removing the needless informational, procedural, and judgmental constraints that limited the effectiveness of persons proceeding intelligently from false or incomplete informational premises (Ackoff and Sasieni, 1968). One of Simon's contributions to the theory of choice was his challenge of the self-evident proposition that choice behavior necessarily would be improved if it were made more like the normative model of rational choice. By asserting that certain limits on rationality stemmed from properties of the human organism, he emphasized the possibility that actual human choice behavior was more intelligent than it appeared.

Normative theories of choice have responded to the idea. Substantial parts of the economics of information and the economics of attention (or time) are tributes to the proposition that information gathering, information processing, and decision making impose demands on the scarce resources of a finite capacity human organism (Stigler, 1961; Becker, 1965; McGuire and Radner, 1972; Marschak and Radner, 1972; Rothschild and Stiglitz, 1976). Aspiration levels, signals, incrementalism, and satisficing rules for decision making have been described as sensible under fairly general circumstances (Hirschman and Lindblom, 1962; Spence, 1974; Radner, 1975a, b; Radner and Rothschild, 1975).

These developments in the theory of rational choice acknowledge important aspects of the behavioral critique of classical procedures for guessing the future consequences of present action. Normative response to behavioral discussions of the second guess, the estimation of future preferences, has been similarly conservative but perceptible. That standard theories of choice and the engineering procedures associated with them have a conception of preferences that differs from observations of preferences has long been noted (Johnson, 1968). As in the case of the informational constraints on rational choice, the first reaction within decision engineering was to treat deviations from well-defined, consistent preference functions as correctable faults. If individuals had deficient (i.e., inconsistent, incomplete) preference functions, they were to be induced to generate proper ones, perhaps through revealed preference techniques and education. If groups of organizations exhibited conflict, they were to be induced to resolve that conflict through prior discussion, prior side payments (e.g., an employment contract), or prior bargaining. If individuals or organizations exhibited instability in preferences over time, they were to be induced to minimize that instability by recognizing a more general specification of the preferences so that apparent changes became explicable as reflecting a single, unchanging function under changing conditions or changing resources.

Since the specific values involved in decision making are irrelevant to formal models of choice, both process rationality and contextual rationality are, from such a perspective, versions of simple calculated rationality. The criterion function is changed, but the theory treats the criterion function as any arbitrary set of well-ordered preferences. So long as the preferences associated with the process of choice or the preferences involved in the broader context are well defined and well behaved, there is no deep theoretical difficulty. But, in practice, such elements of human preference functions have not filtered significantly into the engineering of choice.

The record with respect to problems of goal conflict, multiple, lexicographic goals, and loosely coupled systems is similar. Students of bureaucracies have argued that a normative theory of choice within a modern bureaucratic structure must recognize explicitly the continuing conflict in preferences among various actors (Tullock, 1965; Downs, 1967; Allison and Halperin, 1972; Halperin, 1974). Within such systems "decisions" are probably better seen as strategic first-move interventions in a dynamic internal system than as choices in a classical sense. Decisions are not expected to be implemented, and actions that would be optimal if implemented are suboptimal as first moves. This links theories of choice to game-theoretic conceptions of politics, bargaining, and strategic actions in a productive way. Although in this way ideas about strategic choice in collectivities involving conflict of interest are well established in part of the choice of literature (Elster, 1977a), they have had little impact on such obvious applied domains as bureaucratic decision making or the design of organizational control systems. The engineering of choice has been explicitly concerned with multiple criteria decision procedures for dealing with multiple, lexicographic, or political goals (Lee, 1972; Pattanaik, 1973). In some cases these efforts have considerably changed the spirit of decision analysis, moving it toward a role of exploring the implications of constraints and away from a conception of solution.

Behavioral inquiry into preferences has, however, gone beyond the problems of interpersonal conflict of interest in recent years and into the complications of ambiguity. The problems of ambiguity are partly problems of disagreement about goals among individuals, but they are more conspicuously problems of the relevance, priority, clarity, coherence, and stability of goals in both individual and organizational choice. Several recent treatments of organizational choice behavior record some major ways in which explicit goals seem neither particularly powerful predictors of outcomes nor particularly well represented as either stable, consistent preference orders or well-defined political constraints (Cohen and March, 1974; Weick, 1976; March and Olsen, 1976; Sproull, Weiner, and Wolf, 1978).

It is possible, of course, that such portrayals of behavior are perverse. They may be perverse because they systematically misrepresent the actual behavior of human beings or they may be perverse because the human beings they describe are, insofar as the description applies, stupid. But it is also possible that the description is accurate and the behavior is intelligent, that the ambiguous way human beings sometimes deal with tastes is, in fact, sensible. If such a thing can be imagined, then its corollary may also be imaginable: perhaps we treat tastes inadequately in our engineering of choice. When we start to discover intelligence in decision making where goals are unstable, ill-defined, or apparently irrelevant, we are led to asking some different kinds of questions about our normative conceptions of choice and walk close not only to some issues in economics but also to some classical and modern questions in literature and ethics, particularly the role of clear prior purpose in the ordering of human affairs.

Consider the following properties of tastes as they appear in standard prescriptive theories of choice:

Tastes are *absolute*. Normative theories of choice assume a formal posture of moral relativism. The theories insist on morality of action in terms of tastes; but they recognize neither discrimination among alternative tastes, nor the possibility that a person reasonably might view his own preferences and actions based on them as normally distressing.

Tastes are *relevant*. Normative theories of choice require that action be taken in terms of tastes, that decisions be consistent with preferences in the light of information about the probable consequences of alternatives for valued outcomes. Action is willful.

Tastes are *stable*. With few exceptions, normative theories of choice require that tastes be stable. Current action is taken in terms of current tastes. The implicit assumption is that tastes will be unchanged when the outcomes of current actions are realized.

Tastes are *consistent*. Normative theories of choice allow mutually inconsistent tastes only insofar as they can be made irrelevant by the absence of scarcity or reconcilable by the specification of trade-offs.

Tastes are *precise*. Normative theories of choice eliminate ambiguity about the extent to which a particular outcome will satisfy tastes, at least insofar as possible resolutions of that ambiguity might affect the choice.

Tastes are *exogenous*. Normative theories of choice presume that tastes, by whatever process they may be created, are not themselves affected by the choices they control.

Each of these features of tastes seems inconsistent with observations of choice behavior among individuals and social institutions. Not always, but often enough to be troublesome. Individuals commonly find it possible to express both a taste for something and a recognition that the taste is something that is repugnant to moral standards they accept. Choices are often made without respect to tastes. Human decision makers routinely ignore their own, fully conscious, preferences in making decisions. They follow rules, traditions, hunches, and the advice or actions of others. Tastes change over time in such a way that predicting future tastes is often difficult. Tastes are inconsistent. Individuals and organizations are aware of the extent to which some of their preferences conflict with other of their preferences; yet they do nothing to resolve those inconsistencies. Many preferences are stated in forms that lack precision. It is difficult to make them reliably operational in evaluating possible outcomes. While tastes are used to choose among actions, it is often also true that actions and experience with their consequences affect tastes. Tastes are determined partly endogenously.

Such differences between tastes as they are portrayed by or models and tastes as they appear in our experience produce ordinary behavioral phenomena that are not always well accommodated within the structure of our prescriptions.

We manage our preferences. We select actions now partly in terms of expectations about the effect of those actions upon future preferences. We do things now to modify our future tastes. Thus, we know that if we engage in some particularly tasty, but immoral, activity, we are likely to come to like it more. We know that if we develop competence in a particular skill, we shall often come to favor it. So we choose to pursue the competence, or not, engage in an activity, or not, depending on whether we wish to increase or decrease our taste for the competence or activity.

We construct our preferences. We choose preferences and actions jointly, in part, to discover – or construct – new preferences that are currently unknown. We deliberately specify our objectives in vague terms to develop an understanding of what we might like to become. We elaborate our tastes as interpretations of our behavior.

We treat our preferences strategically. We specify goals that are different from the outcomes we wish to achieve. We adopt preferences and rules of actions that if followed literally would lead us to outcomes we do not wish, because we believe that the final outcome will only partly reflect our initial intentions. In effect, we consider the choice of preferences as part of an infinite game with ourselves in which we attempt to deal with our propensities for acting badly by anticipating them and outsmarting ourselves. We use deadlines and make commitments.

We confound our preferences. Our deepest preferences tend often to be paired. We find the same outcome both attractive and repulsive, not in the sense that the two sentiments cancel each other and we remain indifferent, but precisely that we simultaneously want and do not want an outcome, experience it as both pleasure and pain, love and hate it (Catullus, 58 BC, 1.1).

We avoid our preferences. Our actions and our preferences are only partly linked. We are prepared to say that we want something, yet should not want it, or wish we did not want it. We are prepared to act in ways that are inconsistent with our preferences, and to maintain that inconsistency in the face of having it demonstrated. We do not believe that what we do must necessarily result from a desire to achieve preferred outcomes.

We expect change in our preferences. As we contemplate making choices that have consequences in the future, we know that our attitudes about possible outcomes will change in ways that are substantial but not entirely predictable. The subjective probability distribution over possible future preferences (like the subjective probability distribution over possible future consequences) increases its variance as the horizon is stretched. As a result, we have a tendency to want to take actions now that maintain future options for acting when future preferences are clearer.

We suppress our preferences. Consequential argument, the explicit linking of actions to desires, is a form of argument in which some people are better than others. Individuals who are less competent at consequential rationalization try to avoid it with others who are more competent, particularly others who may have a stake in persuading them to act in a particular way. We resist an explicit formulation of consistent desires to avoid manipulation of our choices by persons cleverer than we at that special form of argument called consistent rationality.

It is possible, on considering this set of constrasts between decision making as we think it ought to occur and decision making as we think it does occur to trivialize the issue into a "definitional problem." By suitably manipulating the concept of tastes, one can save classical theories of choice as "explanations" of behavior in a formal sense, but probably only at the cost of stretching a good idea into a doubtful ideology (Stigler and Becker, 1977). More importantly from the present point of view, such a redefinition pays the cost of destroying the practical relevance of normative prescriptions for choice. For prescriptions are useful only if we see a difference between observed procedures and desirable procedures.

Alternatively, one can record all of the deviations from normative specifications as stupidity, errors that should be corrected; and undertake to transform the style of existing humans into the styles anticipated by the theory.

This has, for the most part, been the strategy of operations and management analysis for the past twenty years; and it has had its successes. But it has also had failures.

It is clear that the human behavior I have described may, in any individual case, be a symptom of ignorance, obtuseness, or deviousness. But the fact that such patterns of behavior are fairly common among individuals and institutions suggests that they might be sensible under some general kinds of conditions – that global ambiguity, like limited rationality, is not necessarily a fault in human choice to be corrected but often a form of intelligence to be refined by the technology of choice rather than ignored by it.

Uncertainty about future consequences and human limitations in dealing with them are relatively easily seen as intrinsic in the decision situation and the nature of the human organisms. It is much harder to see in what way ambiguous preferences are a necessary property of human behavior. It seems meaningful in ordinary terms to assert that human decision makers are driven to techniques of limited rationality by the exigencies of the situation in which they find themselves. But what drives them to ambiguous and changing goals? Part of the answer is directly analogous to the formulations of limited rationality. Limitations of memory organization and retrieval and of information capacity affect information processing about preferences just as they affect information processing about consequences (March and Simon, 1958; Cyert and March, 1963; Simon, 1973; March and Romelaer, 1976). Human beings have unstable, inconsistent, incompletely evoked, and imprecise goals at least in part because human abilities limit preference orderliness. If it were possible to be different at reasonable cost, we probably would want to be.

But viewing ambiguity as a necessary cost imposed by the information processing attributes of individuals fails to capture the extent to which similar styles in preferences would be sensible, even if the human organism were a more powerful computational system. We probably need to ask the more general question: Why might a person or institution intelligently choose to have ambiguous tastes? The answer, I believe, lies in several things, some related to ideas of bounded rationality, others more familiar to human understanding as it is portrayed in literature and philosophy than to our theories of choice.

First, human beings recognize in their behavior that there are limits to personal and institutional integration in tastes. They know that, no matter how much they may be pressured both by their own prejudices for integration and by the demands of others, they will be left with contradictory and intermittent desires partially ordered but imperfectly reconciled. As a result, they engage in activities designed to manage preferences or game preferences. These activities make little sense from the point of view of a conception of human choice that assumes people know what they want and will want, or a conception that assumes wants are morally equivalent. But ordinary human actors sense that they might come to want something that they should not, or that they might

45

make unwise or inappropriate choices under the influence of fleeting, but powerful desires if they do not act now either to control the development of tastes or to buffer action from tastes (Elster, 1977b).

Secondly, human beings recognize implicitly the limitations of acting rationally on current guesses. By insisting that action, to be justified, must follow preferences and be consistent both with those preferences and with estimates of future states, we considerably exaggerate the relative power of a choice based consistently upon two guesses compared to a choice that is itself a guess. Human beings are both proponents for preferences and observers of the process by which their preferences are developed and acted upon. As observers of the process by which their beliefs have been formed and consulted, they recognize the good sense in perceptual and moral modesty (Williams, 1973; Elster, 1977c).

Thirdly, human beings recognize the extent to which tastes are constructed, or developed, through a more or less constant confrontation between preferences and actions that are inconsistent with them, and among conflicting preferences. As a result, they appear to be comfortable with an extraordinary array of unreconciled sources of legitimate wants. They maintain a lack of coherence both within and among personal desires, social demands, and moral codes. Though they seek some consistency, they appear to see inconsistency as a normal, and necessary, aspect of the development and clarification of tastes (March, 1973).

Fourthly, human beings are conscious of the importance of preferences as beliefs independent of their immediate action consequences. They appear to find it possible to say, in effect, that they believe something is more important to good action than they are able (or willing) to make it in a specific case. They act as though some aspects of their beliefs are important to life without necessarily being consistent with actions, and important to the long-run quality of choice behavior without controlling it completely in the short run. They accept a degree of personal and social wisdom in ordinary hypocrisy (Chomsky, 1968; March, 1973; Pondy and Olson, 1977).

Fifthly, human beings know that some people are better at rational argument than others, and that those skills are not particularly well correlated with either morality or sympathy. As a result, they recognize the political nature of argumentation more clearly, and more personally, than the theory of choice does. They are unwilling to gamble that God made clever people uniquely virtuous. They protect themselves from cleverness by obscuring the nature of their preferences; they exploit cleverness by asking others to construct reasons for actions they wish to take.

TASTES AND THE ENGINEERING OF CHOICE

These characteristics of preference processing by individual human beings and social institutions seem to me to make sense under rather general circumstances. As a result, it seems likely to me that our engineering of choice behavior does not make so much sense as we sometimes attribute to it. The view of human tastes and their proper role in action that we exhibit in our normative theory of choice is at least as limiting to the engineering applicability of that theory as the perfect knowledge assumptions were to the original formulations.

Since it has taken us over twenty years to introduce modest elements of bounded rationality and conflict of interest into prescriptions about decision making, there is no particular reason to be sanguine about the speed with which our engineerings of choice will accept and refine the intelligence of ambiguity. But there is hope. The reconstruction involved is not extraordinary, and in some respects has already begun. For the doubts I have expressed about engineering models of choice to be translated into significance changes, they will have to be formulated a bit more precisely in terms that are comprehensible within such theories, even though they may not be consistent with the present form of the theories or the questions the theories currently address. I cannot accomplish such a task in any kind of complete way, but I think it is possible to identify a few conceptual problems that might plausibly be addressed by choice theorists and a few optimization problems that might plausibly be addressed by choice engineers.

The conceptual problems involve discovering interesting ways to reformulate some assumptions about tastes, particularly about the stability of tastes, their exogenous character, their priority, and their internal consistency.

Consider the problem of *intertemporal comparison* of preferences (Strotz, 1956; Koopmans, 1964; Bailey and Olson, 1977; Shefrin and Thaler, 1977). Suppose we assume that the preferences that will be held at every relevant future point in time are known. Suppose further that those preferences change over time but are, at any given time, consistent. If action is to be taken now in terms of its consequences over a period of time during which preferences change, we are faced with having to make intertemporal comparisons. As long as the changes are exogenous, we can avoid the problem if we choose to do so. If we can imagine an individual making a complete and transitive ordering over possible outcomes over time, then intertemporal comparisons are implicit in the preference orderings and cause no particular difficulty beyond the heroic character of the assumption about human capabilities. If, on the other hand, we think of the individual as having a distinct, complete, and consistent preference relation defined over the outcomes realized in a particular time period, and we imagine that those preferences change over time, then the problem of intertemporal comparisons is more difficult. The problem is technically indistinguishable from the problem of interpersonal comparison of utilities. When we compare the changing preferences of a single person over time to make trade-offs across time, we are in the identical position to when we attempt to make comparisons across different individuals at a point in time. The fact that the problems are identical has the advantage of immediately bringing to bear on the problems of intertemporal comparisons the apparatus developed to deal with interpersonal comparisons (Meuller, 1976). It has the disadvantage that that apparatus allows

47

a much weaker conception of solution than is possible within a single, unchanging set of preferences. We are left with the weak theorems of social welfare economics, but perhaps with a clearer recognition that there is no easy and useful way to escape the problem of incomparable preference functions by limiting our attention to a single individual, as long as tastes change over time and we think of tastes as being defined at a point in time.

Consider the problem of *endogenous change* in preferences (Von Weiszäcker, 1971; Olson, 1976). Suppose we know that future tastes will change in a predictable way as a consequence of actions taken now and the consequences of those actions realized over time. Then we are in the position of choosing now the preferences we shall have later. If there is risk involved, we are choosing now a probability distribution over future preferences. If we can imagine some "super goal," the problem becomes tractable. We evaluate alternative preferences in terms of their costs and benefits for the "super goal." Such a strategy preserves the main spirit of normal choice theory but allows only a modest extension into endogenous change. This is the essential strategy adopted in some of the engineering examples below. In such cases desirable preferences cannot always be deduced from the "super goal," but alternative preferences can be evaluated. In somewhat the same spirit, we can imagine adaptive preferences as a possible decision procedure and examine whether rules for a sequence of adaptations in tastes can be specified that lead to choice outcomes better in some easily recognized sense than those obtained through explicit calculated rationality at the start of the process. One possible place is the search for cooperative solutions in games in which calculated rationality is likely to lead to outcomes desired to no one (Cyert and de Groot, 1973, 1975). Also in the same general spirit, we might accept the strict morality position and attempt to select a strategy for choice that will minimize change in values. Or we might try to select a strategy that maximizes value change. All of these are possible explorations, but they are not fully attentive to the normative management of adaptation in tastes. The problem exceeds our present concepts: how do we act sensibly now to manage the development of preferences in the future when we do not have now a criterion for evaluating future tastes that will not itself be affected by our actions? There may be some kind of fixed-point theorem answer to such a problem, but I suspect that a real conceptual confrontation with endogenous preferences will involve some reintroduction of moral philosophy into our understanding of choice (Freidman, 1967; Williams, 1973; Beck, 1975).

Consider the problem of *posterior preferences* (Schutz, 1967; Hirschman, 1967; Weick, 1969; Elster, 1976). The theory of choice is built on the idea of prior intentions. Suppose we relax the requirement of priority, allow preferences to rationalize action after the fact in our theories as well as our behavior. How do we act in such a way that we conclude, after the fact, that the action was intelligent, and also are led to an elaboration of our preferences that we find fruitful? Such a formulation seems closer to a correct representation of choice problems in politics, for example, than is conventional social welfare theory. We find meaning and merit in our actions after they are taken and the consequences are observed and interpreted. Deliberate efforts to manage posterior constructions of preferences are familiar to us. They include many elements of child rearing, psychotherapy, consciousness raising, and product advertising. The terms are somewhat different. We talk of development of character in child rearing, of insight in psychotherapy, of recognition of objective reality in political, ethnic, or sexual consciousness raising, and of elaboration of personal needs in advertising. But the technologies are more similar than their ideologies. These techniques for the construction (or excavation) of tastes include both encouraging a reinterpretation of experience and attempting to induce current behavior that will facilitate posterior elaboration of a new understanding of personal preferences. I have tried elsewhere to indicate some of the possibilities this suggests for intelligent foolishness and the role of ambiguity in sensible action (March, 1973, 1977). The problem is in many ways indistinguishable from the problem of poetry and the criticism of poetry (or art and art criticism). The poet attempts to write a poem that has meanings intrinsic in the poem but not necessarily explicit at the moment of composition (Ciardi, 1960). In this sense, at least, decisions, like poems, are open; and good decisions are those that enrich our preferences and their meanings. But to talk in such a manner is to talk the language of criticism and aesthetics, and it will probably be necessary for choice theory to engage that literature in some way (Eliot, 1933; Cavell, 1969; Steinberg, 1972; Rosenberg, 1975).

Finally, consider the problem of *inconsistency* in preferences (Elster, 1977c). From the point of view of ordinary human ideas about choice, as well as many philosophical and behavioral conceptions of choice, the most surprising thing about formal theories of choice is the tendency to treat such terms as values, goals, preferences, tastes, wants, and the like as either equivalent or as reducible to a single objective function with properties of completeness and consistency. Suppose that instead of making such an assumption, we viewed the decision maker as confronted simultaneously with several orderings of outcomes. We could give them names, calling one a moral code, another a social role, another a personal taste, or whatever. From the present point of view what would be critical would be that the several orderings were independent and irreducible. That is, they could not be deduced from each other, and they could not be combined into a single order. Then, instead of taking the conventional step of imputing a preference order across these incomparables by some kind of revealed preference procedures, we treat them as truly incomparable and examine solutions to internal inconsistency that are more in the spirit of our efforts to provide intelligent guidance to collectivities in which we accept the incomparability of preferences across individuals. Then we could give better advice to individuals who want to treat their own preferences strategically, and perhaps move to a clearer recognition of the role of contradiction and paradox in human choice (Farber, 1976; Elster, 1977c). The strategic problems are amenable to relatively straightforward modifications of our views of choice under conflict of interest; the other problems probably require a deeper understanding of contradiction as it appears in philosophy and literature (Elster, 1977c).

Formulating the conceptual problems in these ways is deliberately conservative *vis-à-vis* the theory of choice. It assumes that thinking about human behavior in terms of choice on the basis of some conception of intention is useful, and that the tradition of struggle between normative theories of choice and behavioral theories of choice is a fruitful one. There are alternative paradigms for understanding human behavior that are in many situations likely to be more illuminating. But it is probably unwise to think that every paper should suggest a dramatic paradigm shift, particularly when the alternative is seen only dimly.

Such strictures become even more important when we turn to the engineering of choice. Choice theorists have often discussed complications in the usual abstract representation of tastes. But those concerns have had little impact on ideas about the engineering of choice, perhaps because they pose the problems at a level of philosophic complexity that is remote from decision engineering. Thus, although I think the challenges that ambiguity makes to our models of choice are rather fundamental, my engineering instincts are to sacrifice purity to secure tractability. I suspect we should ask the engineers of choice not initially to reconstruct a philosophy of tastes but to reexamine, within a familiar framework, some presumptions of our craft, and to try to make the use of ambiguity somewhat less of a mystery, somewhat more of a technology. Consider, for example, the following elementary problems in engineering.

The optimal ambition problem. The level of personal ambition is not a decision variable in most theories of choice; but, as a result of the work by Simon and others on satisficing, there has been interest in optimal levels of aspiration. These efforts consider an aspiration level as a trigger that either begins or ends the search for new alternatives. The optimization problem is one of balancing the expected costs of additional search with the expected improvements to be realized from the effort (March and Simon, 1958).

But there is another, rather different, way of looking at the optimum ambition problem. Individuals and organizations form aspirations, goals, targets, or ambitions for achievement. These ambitions are usually assumed to be connected to outcomes in at least two ways: they affect search (either directly or through some variable like motivation) and thereby performance; they affect (jointly with performance) satisfaction (March and Simon, 1958). Suppose we wish to maximize some function of satisfaction over time by selecting among alternative ambitions over time, alternative initial ambitions, or alternatives defined by some other decision variable that affects ambition. Examples of the latter might be division of income between consumption and savings, tax policies, or choice among alternative payment schemes. In effect, we wish to select a preference function for achievement that will, after the various behavioral consequences of that selection are accounted for, make us feel that we have selected the best ambition. It is a problem much more familiar to the real world of personal and institutional choice than it is to the normative theory of choice, but it is something about which some things could be said.

The optimal clarity problem. Conventional notions about intelligent choice often begin with the presumption that good decisions require clear goals, and that improving the clarity of goals unambiguously improves the quality of decision making. In fact, greater precision in the statement of objectives and the measurement of performance with respect to them is often a mixed blessing. There are arguments for moderating an unrestrained enthusiasm for precise performance measures: Where contradiction and confusion are essential elements of the values, precision misrepresents them. The more precise the measure of performance, the greater the motivation to find ways of scoring well on the measurement index without regard to the underlying goals. And precision in objectives does not allow creative interpretation of what the goal might mean (March, 1978). Thus, the introduction of precision into the valuation of performance involves a trade-off between the gains in outcomes attributable to closer articulation between action and performance on an index of performance and the losses in outcomes attributable to misrepresentation of goals, reduced motivation to development of goals, and concentration of effort on irrelevant ways of beating the index. Whether one is considering developing a performance evaluation scheme for managers, a testing procedure for students, or an understanding of personal preferences, there is a problem of determining the optimum clarity in goals.

The optimal sin problem. Standard notions of intelligent choice are theories of strict morality. That is, they presume that a person should do what he believes right and believe that what he does is right. Values and actions are to be consistent. Contrast that perspective with a view, somewhat more consistent with our behavior (as well as some theology), that there is such a thing as sin, that individuals and institutions sometimes do things even while recognizing that what they do is not what they wish they did, and that saints are a luxury to be encouraged only in small numbers. Or contrast a theory of strict morality with a view drawn from Nietzsche (1918) or Freud (1927) (see also Jones, 1926) of the complicated contradiction between conscience and self-interest. Although the issues involved are too subtle for brief treatment, a reasonably strong case can be made against strict morality and in favor of at least some sin, and therefore hypocrisy. One of the most effective ways of maintaining morality is through the remorse exhibited and felt at immoral action. Even if we are confident that our moral codes are correct, we may want to recognize human complexities. There will be occasions on which humans will be tempted by desires that they recognize as evil. If we insist that they maintain consistency between ethics and actions, the ethics will often be more likely to change than the actions. Hypocrisy is a long-run investment in morality made at some cost (the chance that, in action might otherwise adjust to morals). To encourage people always to take responsibility for their actions is to encourage them to deny that bad things are bad – to make evil acceptable. At the same time, sin is an experiment with an alternative morality. By recognizing sin, we make it easier for persons to experiment with the possibility of having different tastes. Moral systems need those experiments, and regularly grant licenses to experiment to drunks, lovers, students, or sinners. These gains from sin are purchased by its costs. Thus, the optimization problem.

The optimal rationality problem. Calculated rationality is a technique for making decisions. In standard versions of theories of choice it is the only legitimate form of intelligence, each with claims to legitimacy. Learned behavior, with its claim to summarize an irretrievable but relevant personal history, or conventional behavior and rules, with their claims to capture the intelligence of survival over long histories of experience more relevant than the susceptible to immediate calculation, are clear alternative contenders. There are others: revelation or intuition, by which we substitute one guess for two; or imitation, or expertise, by which we substitute the guess of someone else for our own. Among all of these, only calculated rationality really uses conscious preferences of a current actor as a major consideration in making decisions. It is easy to show that there exist situations in which any one of these alternative techniques will make better decisions than the independent calculation of rational behavior by ordinary individuals or institutions. The superiority of learned or conventional behavior depends, in general, on the amount of experience it summarizes and the similarity between the world in which the experience was accumulated and the current world. The superiority of imitation depends, in general, on the relative competence of actor and expert and the extent to which intelligent action is reproducible but not comprehensible. At the same time, each form of intelligence exposes an actor to the risks of corruption. Imitation risks a false confidence in the neutrality of the process of diffusion; calculated rationality risks a false confidence in the neutrality of rational argument; and so on. It is not hard to guess that the relative sizes of these risks vary from individual to individual, or institution to institution. What are harder to specify in any very precise way are the extent and occasions on which a sensible person would rely on calculated rationality rather than the alternatives.

A ROMANTIC VISION

Prescriptive theories of choice are dedicated to perfecting the intelligence of human action by imagining that action stems from reason and by improving the technology of decision. Descriptive theories of choice are dedicated to perfecting the understanding of human action by imagining that action makes sense. Not all behavior makes sense; some of it is unreasonable. Not all decision technology is intelligent; some of it is foolish. Over the past twenty years, the contradiction between the search for sense in behavior and the search for improvement in behavior has focused on our interpretation of the way information about future consequences is gathered and processed. The effort built considerably on the idea of bounded rationality and a conception of human decision making as limited by the cognitive capabilities of human beings. Over the next twenty years, I suspect the contradiction will be increasingly concerned with an interpretation of how beliefs about future preferences are generated and utilized. The earlier confrontation led theories of choice to a slightly clearer understanding of information processing and to some modest links with the technologies of computing, inference, and subjective probability. So perhaps the newer confrontation will lead theories of choice to a slightly clearer understanding of the complexities of preference processing and to some modest links with the technologies of ethics, criticism, and aesthetics. The history of theories of choice and their engineering applications suggests that we might appropriately be pessimistic about immediate, major progress. The intelligent engineering of tastes involves questions that encourage despair over their difficulty (Savage, 1954). But though hope for minor progress is a romantic vision, it may not be entirely inappropriate for a theory built on a romantic view of human destiny.

NOTE

Presented at a conference on the new industrial organization at Carnegie-Mellon University, October 14–15, 1977. The conference was organized to honor the contributions of Herbert A. Simon to economics, and his contribution to this paper is obvious. In addition, I profited from comments by Richard M. Cyert, Jon Elster, Alexander L. George, Elisabeth Hansot, Nannerl O. Keohane, Robert O. Keohane, Tjalling Koopmans, Mancur Olson, Louis R. Pondy, Roy Radner, Giovanni Sartori, and Oliver E. Williamson. This research was supported by a grant from the Spencer Foundation. First published in *The Bell Journal of Economics*, 9 (1978), 587–608. Copyright © 1978, American Telephone and Telegraph Company.

REFERENCES

Ackoff, R. L. and Sasieni, M. W. (1968). *Fundamentals of Operations Research*. New York: Wiley.
Allison, G. T. (1969). *Essence of Decision: Explaining the Cuban Missile Crisis*. Boston: Little, Brown.
Allison, G. T. and Halperin, M. H. (1972). "Bureaucratic politics: paradigm and some policy implications," in R. Tanter and R. H. Ullman, eds., *Theory and Policy in International Relations*, Princeton University Press.
Bailey, M. J. and Olson, M. (1977). "Pure time preference, revealed marginal utility, and Friedman–Savage gambles." Unpublished manuscript.
Beck, L. W. (1975). *The Actor and the Spectator*. New Haven: Yale University Press.
Becker, G. S. (1965). "A theory of the allocation of time," *Economic Journal*, 75, 493–517.
(1976). "Altruism, egoism, and genetic fitness: economics and sociobiology," *Journal of Economic Literature*, 14, 817–26.
Binkley, R., Bronaugh, R., and Marras, A., eds. (1971). *Agent, Action, and Reason*. University of Toronto Press.

James G. March

Bower, J. L. (1968). "Descriptive decision theory from the 'administrative viewpoint'," in R. A. Bauer and K. J. Gergen, eds., *The Study of Policy Formation*, New York: Free Press.

Brams, S. J. (1975). *Game Theory and Politics*. New York: Free Press.

Camus, A. (1951). *L'Homme révolté*. Paris: Gallimard. (Published in English as *The Rebel*.)

Carter, E. E. (1971). "The behavioral theory of the firm and top-level corporate decisions," *Administrative Science Quarterly*, 16, 413–29.

Catullus, G. V. (58 BC). *Carmina*, 85. Rome.

Cavell, S. (1969). *Must We Mean What We Say?* New York: Scribner.

Charnes, A. and Cooper, W. W. (1963). "Deterministic equivalents for optimizing and satisficing under chance constraints," *Operations Research*, 11, 18–39.

Christensen, S. (1976). "Decision making and socialization," in J. G. March and J. P. Olsen, eds., *Ambiguity and Choice in Organizations*. Bergen: Universitetsforlaget.

Chomsky, N. (1968). *Language and Mind*. New York: Harcourt, Brace & World.

Ciardi, J. (1960). *How Does a Poem Mean?* Cambridge: Houghton Mifflin.

Cohen, M. D. and March, J. G. (1974). *Leadership and Ambiguity: The American College President*. New York: McGraw-Hill.

Cohen, M. D., March, J. G., and Olsen, J. P. (1972). "A garbage can model of organizational choice," *Administrative Science Quarterly*, 17, 1–25.

Connolly, T. (1977). "Information processing and decision making in organizations," in B. M. Staw and G. R. Salancik, eds., *New Directions in Organizational Behavior*, Chicago: St. Clair.

Crozier, M. and Friedberg, E. (1977). *L'Acteur et le système*. Paris: Seuil.

Cyert, R. M. and de Groot, M. H. (1973). "An analysis of cooperation and learning in a duopoly context," *The American Economic Review*, 63 (1), 24–37.

(1975). "Adaptive utility," in R. H. Day and T. Groves, eds., *Adaptive Economic Models*, New York: Academic Press.

Cyert, R. M. and March, J. G. (1963). *A Behavioral Theory of the Firm*. Englewood Cliffs, N.J.: Prentice-Hall.

Day, R. H. and Groves, T., eds. (1975). *Adaptive Economic Models*. New York: Academic Press.

Downs, A. (1967). *Inside Bureaucracy*. Boston: Little, Brown.

Edelman, M. (1960). *The Symbolic Uses of Politics*. Champaign, Ill.: University of Illinois Press.

Eliot, T. S. (1933). *The Use of Poetry and the Use of Criticism*. Cambridge: Harvard University Press.

Elster, J. (1976). "A note on hysteresis in the social sciences," *Synthese*, 33, 371–91.

(1977a). *Logic and Society*. London: Wiley.

(1977b). "Ulysses and the sirens: a theory of imperfect rationality," *Social Science Information*, 16 (5), 469–526.

(1977c). "Some unresolved problems in the theory of rational behavior." Unpublished manuscript.

Farber, L. (1976). *Lying, Despair, Jealousy, Envy, Sex, Suicide, Drugs, and the Good Life*. New York: Basic Books.

Farquharson, R. (1969). *Theory of Voting*. New Haven: Yale University Press.

Freud, S. (1927). *The Ego and the Id*. London: Hogarth.

Friedman, M. (1967). *To Deny Our Nothingness: Contemporary Images of Man*. New York: Delacorte.

Halperin, M. H. (1974). *Bureaucratic Politics and Foreign Policy*. Washington, DC: The Brookings Institution.

Harsanyi, J. C. and Selten, R. (1972). "A generalized Nash solution for two-person bargaining games with incomplete information," *Management Science*, 18, 80–106.

Hegel, G. W. F. (1832). *G. W. F. Hegel's Werke*. Berlin: Duncker und Humblot.

Hirschman, A. O. (1967). *Development Projects Observed*. Washington, DC: The Brookings Institution.

Hirschman, A. and Lindblom, C. E. (1962). "Economic development, research and development, policy making: some converging views," *Behavioral Science*, 7, 211–22.

Janis, I. L. and Mann, L. (1977). *Decision Making*. New York: Free Press.

Johnson, E. (1968). *Studies in Multiobjective Decision Models*. Lund: Studentlitteratur.

Jones, E. (1926). "The origin and structure of the superego," *International Journal of Psychoanalysis*, 7, 303–11.

Keen, P. G. W. (1977). "The evolving concept of optimality," *TIMS Studies in the Management Sciences*, 6, 31–57.

Koopmans, T. C. (1964). "On flexibility of future preferences," in M. W. Shelly and G. L. Bryan, eds., *Human Judgments and Optimality*, New York: Wiley.

Kreiner, K. (1976). "Ideology and management in a garbage can situation," in J. G. March and J. P. Olsen, eds., *Ambiguity and Choice in Organizations*, Bergen: Universitetsforlaget.

Lee, S. M. (1972). *Goal Programming for Decision Analysis*. Philadelphia: Auerbach.

Lindblom, C. E. (1959). "The science of muddling through," *Public Administration Review*, 19, 79–88.

   (1965). *The Intelligence of Democracy*. New York: Macmillan.

Long, N. E. (1958). "The local community as an ecology of games," *American Journal of Sociology*, 44, 251–61.

McGuire, C. B. and Radner, R., eds. (1972). *Decision and Organization*. Amsterdam: North-Holland.

March, J. G. (1962). "The business firm as a political coalition," *Journal of Politics*, 24, 662–78.

   (1973). "Model bias in social action," *Review of Educational Research*, 42, 413–29.

   (1977). "Administrative leadership in education." Unpublished manuscript.

   (1978). "American public school administration: a short analysis," *School Review*, 86, 217–50.

March, J. G. and Olsen, J. P., eds. (1976). *Ambiguity and Choice in Organizations*. Bergen: Universitetsforlaget.

March, J. G. and Romelaer, P. (1976). "Position and presence in the drift of decisions," in J. G. March and J. P. Olsen, eds., *Ambiguity and Choice in Organizations*, Bergen: Universitetsforlaget.

March, J. G. and Simon, H. A. (1958). *Organizations*. New York: Wiley.

Marschak, J. and Radner, R. (1972). *Economic Theory of Teams*. New Haven: Yale University Press.

Mayhew, D. R. (1974). *Congress: The Electoral Connection*. New Haven: Yale University Press.

Mill, J. S. (1838). Reprinted in *Mill on Bentham and Coleridge*. London: Chatto and Windus, 1950.

Mueller, D. C. (1976). "Public choice: a survey," *Journal of Economic Literature*, 14, 395–433.

Nelson, R. R. and Winter, S. G. (1973). "Towards an evolutionary theory of economic capabilities," *The American Economic Review*, 63, 440–9.

Newell, A. and Simon, H. A. (1972). *Human Problem Solving*. Englewood Cliffs, N.J.: Prentice-Hall.

Nietzsche, F. (1918). *The Genealogy of Morals*. New York: Boni and Liveright.

Olson, M. (1965). *The Logic of Collective Action*. New York: Schocken.

(1976). "Exchange, integration, and grants," in M. Pfaff, ed., *Essays in Honor of Kenneth Boulding*, Amsterdam: North-Holland.

Pattanaik, P. K. (1973). "Group choice with lexicographic individual orderings," *Behavioral Science*, 18, 118–23.

Pfeffer, J. (1977). "Power and resource allocation in organizations," in B. M. Staw and G. R. Salancik, eds., *New Directions in Organizational Behavior*, Chicago: St Clair.

Pondy, L. R. and Olson, M. L. (1977). 'Organization and performance." Unpublished manuscript.

Porat, A. M. and Haas, J. A. (1969). "Information effects on decision making," *Behavioral Science*, 14, 98–104.

Radner, R. (1975a). "A behavioral model of cost reduction," *The Bell Journal of Economics*, 6 (1), 196–215.

(1975b). "Satisficing," *Journal of Mathematical Economics*, 2, 253–62.

Radner, R. and Rothschild, M. (1975). "On the allocation of effort," *Journal of Economic Theory*, 10, 358–76.

Rapoport, A. (1960). *Fights, Games, and Debates*. Ann Arbor: University of Michigan Press.

Riker, W. and Ordeshook, P. (1974). *An Introduction to Positive Political Theory*. Englewood Cliffs, N.J.: Prentice-Hall.

Rosenberg, H. (1975). *Art on the Edge: Creators and Situations*. New York: Macmillan.

Rothschild, M. and Stiglitz, J. (1976). "Equilibrium in competitive insurance markets: an essay on the economics of imperfect information," *Quarterly Journal of Economics*, 90, 629–49.

Savage, L. J. (1954). *Foundations of Statistics*. New York: Wiley.

Schelling, T. (1971). "On the ecology of micro-motives," *Public Interest*, 25, 59–98.

Schutz, A. (1967). *The Phenomenology of the Social World*. Evanston, Ill.: Northwestern.

Shakespeare, W. (1623). *Hamlet, Prince of Denmark*. Stratford-upon-Avon.

Shefrin, H. M. and Thaler, R. (1977). "An economic theory of self-control." Unpublished manuscript.

Simon, H. A. (1955). "A behavioral model of rational choice," *Quarterly Journal of Economics*, 69, 99–118.

(1956). "Rational choice and the structure of the environment," *Psychological Review*, 63, 129–38.

(1957). *Models of Man*. New York: Wiley.

(1969). *The Science of the Artificial*. Cambridge: MIT Press.

(1973). "The structure of ill-structured problems," *Artificial Intelligence*, 4, 181–201.

Slovic, P., Fischhoff, B., and Lichtenstein, S. (1977). "Behavioral decision theory," *Annual Review of Psychology*, 28, 1–39.

Spence, A. M. (1974). *Market Signalling*. Cambridge: Harvard University Press.

Sproull, L. S., Weiner, S. S., and Wolf, D. B. (1978). *Organizing an Anarchy*. University of Chicago Press.

Steinberg, L. (1972). *Other Criteria: Confrontations with Twentieth Century Art*. New York: Oxford University Press.

Steinbruner, J. D. (1974). *The Cybernetic Theory of Decision*. Princeton University Press.

Stigler, G. J. (1961). "The economics of information," *Journal of Political Economy*, 69, 213–25.

Stigler, G. J. and Becker, G. S. (1977). "*De gustibus non est disputandum*," *The American Economic Review*, 67 (March), 76–90.

Strotz, R. H. (1956). "Myopia and inconsistency in dynamic utility maximization," *Review of Economic Studies*, 23.

Taylor, M. (1975). "The theory of collective choice," in F. I. Greenstein and N. W. Polsby, eds., *Handbook of Political Science*, Vol. 3, Reading, Mass.: Addison-Wesley.

Taylor, R. N. (1975). "Psychological determinants of bounded rationality: implications for decision-making strategies," *Decision Sciences*, 6, 409–29.

Thompson, J. (1967). *Organizations in Action*. New York: McGraw-Hill.

Tullock, G. (1965). *The Politics of Bureaucracy*. Washington, DC: Public Affairs.

Tversky, A. and Kahneman, D. (1974). "Judgment under uncertainty: heuristics and biases," *Science*, 185, 1124–31.

Von Weiszäcker, C. C. (1971). "Notes on endogenous change of taste," *Journal of Economic Theory*, 3, 345–72.

Vroom, V. H. (1964). *Work and Motivation*. New York: Wiley.

Warwick, D. P. (1975). *A Theory of Public Bureaucracy: Politics, Personality, and Organization in the State Department*. Cambridge: Harvard University Press.

Weick, K. E. (1969). *The Social Psychology of Organizing*. Reading, Mass.: Addison-Wesley.

(1976). "Educational organizations as loosely coupled systems," *Administrative Science Quarterly*, 21, 1–18.

Weiner, S. S. (1976). "Participation, deadlines, and choice," in J. G. March and J. P. Olsen, eds., *Ambiguity and Choice in Organizations*, Bergen: Universitetsforlaget.

Wildavsky, A. (1971). *Revolt Against the Masses and Other Essays on Politics and Public Policy*. New York: Basic Books.

Wildavsky, A. and Pressman, H. (1973). *Implementation*. Berkeley: University of California Press.

Williams, B. A. O. (1973). *Problems of the Self*. Cambridge University Press.

Williamson, O. E. (1975). *Markets and Hierarchies*. New York: Free Press.

Wilson, E. O. (1975). *Sociobiology*. Cambridge: Harvard University Press.

Winter, S. G. (1964). "Economic 'natural selection' and the theory of the firm," *Yale Economic Essays*, 4, 225–72.

(1971). "Satisficing, selection, and the innovating remnant," *Quarterly Journal of Economics*, 85, 237–61.

(1975). "Optimization and evolution in the theory of the firm," in R. H. Day and T. Groves, eds., *Adaptive Economic Models*, New York: Academic Press.

3

RATIONALITY AS PROCESS AND AS PRODUCT OF THOUGHT

HERBERT A. SIMON

The opportunity to deliver the Richard T. Ely Lecture, from which this chapter is derived, afforded me some very personal satisfactions. Ely, unbeknownst to him, bore a great responsibility for my economic education, and even for my choice of profession. The example of my uncle, Harold Merkel, who was a student of Commons and Ely at Wisconsin before World War I, taught me that human behavior was a fit subject for scientific study, and directed me to economics and political science instead of high energy physics or molecular biology. Some would refer to this as satisficing, for I had never heard of high energy physics or molecular biology, and hence was spared an agonizing weighing of alternative utiles. I simply picked the first profession that sounded fascinating.

Ely's influence went much further than that. My older brother's copy of his *Outlines of Economics* – the 1930 edition – was on our bookshelves when I prepared for high school debates on tariffs versus free trade, on the Single Tax of Henry George. It provided me with a sufficiently good grounding in principles that I was later able to take Henry Simons' intermediate theory course at the University of Chicago, and the graduate courses of Frank Knight and Henry Schultz without additional preparation.

The Ely textbook, in its generation, held the place of Samuelson (1947) or Bach in ours. If it would not sound as though I were denying any progress in economics over the past half century, I might suggest that Ely's textbook could be substituted for any of our current ones at a substantial reduction in weight, and without students or teacher being more than dimly aware of the replacement. Of course they would not hear from Ely about marginal propensities to do this or that, nor about the late lamented Phillips curve. But monetarists could rejoice in Ely's uncompromising statement of the quantity theory (p. 298, italics), and in his assertion that "the solution of the problem of unemployment depends largely upon indirect measures, such as monetary and banking reform" – Ely does go on to say, however, that "we shall recognize that society must offer a willing and able man an opportunity to work" (p. 528).

58

I have more than personal reasons for directing the reader's attention to Ely's textbook. On page 4, we find a definition of economics that is, I think, wholly characteristic of books contemporary with his. "Economics," he says, "is the science which treats of those social phenomena that are due to the wealth-getting and wealth-using activities of man." Economics, that is to say, concerns itself with a particular subset of man's behaviors – those having to do with the production, exchange, and consumption of goods and services.

Many, perhaps most, economists today would regard that view as too limiting. They would prefer the definition proposed in the *International Encyclopedia of the Social Sciences*: "Economics . . . is the study of the allocation of scarce resources among unlimited and competing uses" (Rees, 1968). If beefsteak is scarce, they would say, so are votes, and the tools of economic analysis can be used as readily to analyze the allocation of the one as of the other. This point of view has launched economics into many excursions and incursions into political science and her other sister social sciences, and has generated a certain amount of hubris in the profession with respect to its broader civilizing mission. I would suppose that the current emphasis upon the relations between economics and the other social sciences is at least partly a reflection of that hubris.

Rationality in economics

The topic of allocating scarce resources can be approached from either its normative or its positive side. Fundamental to the approach from either side are assumptions about the adaptation of means to ends, of actions to goals and situations. Economics, whether normative or positive, has not simply been the study of the allocation of scarce resources, it has been the study of the *rational* allocation of scarce resources.

Moreover, the term "rational" has long had in economics a much more specific meaning than its general dictionary signification of "agreeable to reason; not absurd, preposterous, extravagant, foolish, fanciful, or the like; intelligent, sensible." As is well known, the rational man of economics is a maximizer, who will settle for nothing less than the best. Even his expectations, we have learned in the past few years, are rational (see John Muth, 1961).[1] And his rationality extends as far as the bedroom for, as Gary Becker tells us, "he would read in bed at night only if the value of reading exceeded the value (to him) of the loss in sleep suffered by his wife" (1974, p. 1078).

It is this concept of rationality that is economics' main export commodity in its trade with the other social sciences. It is no novelty in those sciences to propose that people behave rationally – if that term is taken in its broader dictionary sense. Assumptions of rationality are essential components of virtually all the sociological, psychological, political, and anthropological theories with which I am familiar. What economics has to export, then, is not rationality, but a very particular and special form of it – the rationality of the utility maximizer, and a pretty smart one at that. But international flows have to be balanced. If more active intercourse between economics and her sister social sciences is the aim, then we must ask not only what economics will export, but also what she will receive in payment. An economist might well be tempted to murmur the lines of the tentmaker: "I often wonder what the Vintners buy – One half so precious as the stuff they sell."

This chapter will be much concerned with that question and, before I proceed, it may be well to sketch in outline the path I propose to follow in answering it. The argument has three major steps.

First, I would like to expand on the theme that almost all human behavior has a large rational component, but only in terms of the broader everyday sense of rationality, not the economists' more specialized sense of maximization.

Secondly, I should like to show that economics itself has not by any means limited itself to the narrower definition of rationality. Much economic literature (for example, the literature of comparative institutional analysis) uses weaker definitions of rationality extensively; and that literature would not be greatly, if at all, improved by substituting the stronger definition for the weaker one.[2] To the extent that the weaker definition is adequate for purposes of analysis, economics will find that there is indeed much that is importable from the other social sciences.

Thirdly, economics has largely been preoccupied with the *results* of rational choice rather than the *process* of choice. Yet as economic analysis acquires a broader concern with the dynamics of choice under uncertainty, it will become more and more essential to consider choice processes. In the past twenty years, there have been important advances in our understanding of procedural rationality, particularly as a result of research in artificial intelligence and cognitive psychology. The importation of these theories of the processes of choice into economics could provide immense help in deepening our understanding of the dynamics of rationality, and of the influences upon choice of the institutional structure within which it takes place.

We begin, then, by looking at the broader concept of rationality to which I have referred, and its social science applications.

Rationality in the other social sciences: functional analysis

Let me provide some examples how rationality typically enters into social science theories. Consider first so-called "social exchange" theories (see, for example, George Homans, 1961). The central idea here is that, when two or more people interact, each expects to get something from the interaction that is valuable to him, and is thereby motivated to give something up that is valuable to the others. Social exchange, in the form of the "inducements–contributions balance" of Chester I. Barnard (1938) and the author (1947), has played an important role in organization theory, and in even earlier times (see, for example, George Simmel,

1908) was a central ingredient in sociological theories. Much of the theorizing and empirical work on the topic has been concerned with determining what constitutes a significant inducement or contribution in particular classes of exchange situations – that is, with the actual shape and substance of the "utility function." Clearly, the man of social exchange theory is a rational man, even if he is never asked to equate things at the margin.

It is perhaps more surprising to discover how pervasive assumptions of rationality are in psychoanalytic theory – conforming the suspicion that there is indeed method in madness. In his *Five Lectures* Sigmund Freud (1957) has this to say about neurotic illness:

> We see that human beings fall ill when, as a result of external obstacles or of an internal lack of adaptation, the satisfaction of their erotic needs *in reality* is frustrated. We see that they then take flight into *illness* in order that by its help they may find a satisfaction to take the place of what has been frustrated ... We suspect that our patients' resistance to recovery is no simple one, but compounded of several motives. Not only does the patient's ego rebel against giving up the repressions by means of which it has risen above its original disposition, but the sexual instincts are unwilling to renounce their substitutive satisfaction so long as it is uncertain whether reality will offer them anything better.

Almost all explanations of pathological behavior in the psychoanalytic literature take this form: they explain the patient's illness in terms of the functions it performs for him.

The quotation from Freud is illustrative of a kind of functional reasoning that goes far beyond psychoanalysis and is widely used throughout the social sciences, and especially anthropology and sociology. Behaviors are functional if they contribute to certain goals, where these goals may be the pleasure or satisfaction of an individual or the guarantee of food or shelter for the members of a society. Functional analysis in this sense is concerned with explaining how "major social patterns operate to maintain the integration or adaptation of the larger system" (see Frank Cancian, 1968). Institutions are functional if reasonable men might create and maintain them in order to meet social needs or achieve social goals.

It is not necessary or implied that the adaptation of institutions or behavior patterns to goals be conscious or intended. When awareness and intention are present, the function is usually called *manifest*, otherwise it is a *latent* function. The function, whether it be manifest or latent, provides the grounds for the reasonableness or rationality of the institution or behavior pattern. As in economics evolutionary arguments are often adduced to explain the persistence and survival of functional patterns, and to avoid assumptions of deliberate calculation in explaining them.

In practice, it is very rarely that the existence or character of institutions is *deduced* from the functions that must be performed for system survival. In almost all cases it is the other way round; it is empirical observation of the behavior pattern that raises the question of why it persists – what function it performs. Perhaps, in an appropriate axiomatic formulation, it would be possible to *deduce* that every society must have food-gathering institutions. In point of fact, such institutions can be *observed* in every society, and their existence is then rationalized by the argument that obtaining food is a functional requisite for all societies. This kind of argument may demonstrate the sufficiency of a particular pattern for performing an essential function, but cannot demonstrate its necessity – cannot show that there may not be alternative, functionally equivalent, behavior patterns that would satisfy the same need.

The point may be stated more formally. Functional arguments are arguments about the movements of systems toward stable self-maintaining equilibria. But, without further specification, there is no reason to suppose that the attained equilibria that are reached will be global maxima or minima of some function rather than local, relative maxima or minima of some function rather than local, relative maxima or minima. In fact, we know that the conditions that every local maximum of a system be a global maximum are very strong (usually some kind of "convexity" conditions).

Further, when the system is complex and its environment continually changing (that is, in the conditions under which biological and social evolution actually take place), there is no assurance that the system's momentary position will lie anywhere near a point of equilibrium, whether local or global. Hence, all that can be concluded from a functional argument is that certain characteristics (the satisfaction of certain functional requirements in a particular way) are consistent with the survival and further development of the system, not that these same requirements could not be satisfied in some other way. Thus, for example, societies can satisfy their functional needs for food by hunting or fishing activities, by agriculture, or by predatory exploitation of other societies.

Functional analysis in economics

Functional analysis of exactly this kind, though with a different vocabulary, is commonly employed by economists, especially when they seek economic tools to "explain" institutions and behaviors that lie outside the traditional domains of production and distribution. Moreover, it occurs within those domains. As an example, the fact is observed that individuals frequently insure against certain kinds of contingencies. Attitudes are then postulated (for example, risk aversion) for which buying insurance is a functional and reasonable action. If some people are observed to insure, and others not, then this difference in behavior can be explained by a difference between them in risk aversion.

To take a second example, George Stigler and Becker (1977) wish to explain the fact (if it is a fact – their empiricism is very casual) that, as people hear more music, they want to hear still more. They invent a commodity, "music appreciation" (not to be confused with time spent in listening to music), and suggest that listening to music might produce not only immediate enjoyment but also an investment in *capacity* for appreciating music (i.e., in amount of enjoyment produced per listening hour). Once these assumptions are granted, various conclusions can be drawn about the demand for music appreciation. However, only weak conclusions follow about listening time unless additional strong postulates are introduced about the elasticity of demand for appreciation.

A rough "sociological" translation of the Stigler–Becker argument would be that listening to music is functional both in producing pleasure and in enhancing the pleasure of subsequent listening – a typical functional argument. It is quite unclear what is gained by dressing it in the garb of marginalism. We might be willing to grant that people would be inclined to invest more in musical appreciation early in life than later in life (because they would have a longer time in which to amortize the investment) without insisting that costs and returns were being equated at the margin, and without gaining any new insights into the situation from making the latter assumption.

A sense of fairness compels me to take a third example from my own work. In my 1951 paper, I defined the characteristics of an employment contract that distinguish it from an ordinary sales contract, and then showed why reasonable men might prefer the former to the latter as the basis for establishing an employment relation. My argument requires a theorem and fifteen numbered equations, and assumes that both employer and employee maximize their utilities. Actually, the underlying functional argument is very simple. An employee who did not care very much which of several alternative tasks he performed would not require a large inducement to accept the authority of an employer – that is, to permit the employer to make the choice among them. The employer in turn would be willing to provide the necessary inducement in order to acquire the right to postpone his decisions about the employee's agenda, and in this way to postpone some of his decisions whose outcomes are contingent on future uncertain events.[3] The rigorous economic argument, involving the idea of maximizing behavior by employer and employee, is readily translatable into a simple qualitative argument that an employment contrast may be a functional ("reasonable") way of dealing with certain kinds of uncertainty. The argument then explains why employment relations are so widely used in our society.

The translation of these examples of economic reasoning into the language of functional analysis could be paralleled by examples of translation scholarship which run in the opposite direction. Political scientists, for example, long ago observed that under certain circumstances institutions of representative democracy spawned a multiplicity of political parties, while under other circumstances the votes were divided in equilibrium between two major parties. These contrasting equilibria could readily be shown by functional arguments to result from rational voting decisions under different rules of the electoral game, as was observed by Maurice Duverger (1959), in his classic work on political parties, as well as by a number of political scientists who preceded him. In recent years, these same results have been rederived more rigorously by economists and game theorists, employing much stronger assumptions of utility maximization by the voters; it is hard to see that the maximization assumptions have produced any new predictions of behavior.[4]

Summary

Perhaps these examples suffice to show that there is no such gap as is commonly supposed between the view of man espoused by economics and the view found in the other social sciences. The view of man as rational is not peculiar to economics, but is endemic, and even ubiquitous, throughout the social sciences. Economics tends to emphasize a particular form of rationality – maximizing behavior – as its preferred engine of explanation, but the differences are often differences in vocabulary more than in substance. We shall see in a moment that in much economic discussion the notion of maximization is used in a loose sense that is very close to the common-sense notions of rationality used elsewhere in the social sciences.

One conclusion we may draw is that economists might well exercise a certain amount of circumspection in their endeavors to export economic analysis to the other social sciences. They may discover that they are sometimes offering commodities that are already in generous supply, and which can therefore be disposed of only at a ruinously low price. On the other side of the trade, they may find that there is more of interest in the modes and results of inquiry of their fellow social scientists than they have generally been aware.

ON APPLYING THE PRINCIPLE OF RATIONALITY

What is characteristic of the examples of functional analysis cited in the last section, whether they be drawn from economics or from the other social sciences, is that they are not focused on, or even much concerned with, how variables are equated at the margin, or how equilibrium is altered by marginal shifts in conditions (for example, shifts in a supply or demand schedule). Rather, they are focused on qualitative and structural questions, typically on the choice among a small number of discrete institutional alternatives:

Not "how much flood insurance will a man buy?" but "what are the structural conditions that make buying insurance rational or attractive?"

Not "at what levels will wages be fixed?" but "when will work be performed under an employment contract rather than a sales contract?"

If we want a natural science analogy to this kind of theorizing, we can find it in geology. A geologist notices deep scratches in rock; he notices that certain hills of gravel are elongated along a north–south axis, and that the boulders embedded in them are not as smooth as those usually found on beaches. To explain these facts, he evokes a structural, and not at all quantitative, hypothesis: that these phenomena were produced by the process of glaciation.

In the first instance, he does not try to explain the depth of the glacial till, or estimate the weight of the ice that produced it, but simply to identify the basic causative process. He wants to explain the role of glaciation, of erosion, of vulcanization, of sedimentation in producing the land forms that he observes. His explanations, moreover, are after-the-fact, and not predictive.

Toward qualitative analysis

As economics expands beyond its central core of price theory, and its central concern with quantities of commodities and money, we observe it in this same shift from a highly quantitative analysis, in which equilibration at the margin plays a central role, to a much more qualitative institutional analysis, in which discrete structural alternatives are compared.

In these analyses aimed at explaining institutional structure, maximizing assumptions play a much less significant role than they typically do in the analysis of market equilibria. The rational man who sometimes prefers an employment contract to a sales contract need not be a maximizer. Even a satisficer will exhibit such a preference whenever the difference in rewards between the two arrangements is sufficiently large and evident.

For this same reason, such analyses can often be carried out without elaborate mathematical apparatus or marginal calculation. In general, much cruder and simpler arguments will suffice to demonstrate an inequality between two quantities than are required to show the conditions under which these quantities are equated at the margin. Thus, in the recent works of Janos Kornai (1971), Williamson (1975), and John Montias (1976), on economic organization, we find only rather modest and simple applications of mathematical analysis. In the ways in which they involve principles of rationality, the arguments of these authors resemble James March and the author's *Organizations* (1958) more closely than Paul Samuelson's *Foundations* (1947).[5]

What is the predominant form of reasoning that we encounter in these theoretical treatments of social institutions? Do they contain arguments based on maximizing assumptions? Basically, they rest upon a very simple form of causal analysis. Particular institutional structures or practices are seen to entail certain undesirable (for example, costly) or desirable (for example, value-producing) consequences. *Ceteris paribus*, situations and practices will be preferred when important favorable consequences are associated with them, and avoided when important unfavorable consequences are associated with them. A shift in the balance of consequences, or in awareness of them, may motivate a change in institutional arrangements.

Consider the following argument from Montias (1976) typical of this genre of analysis, which relates to the balance in organizations between centralization and decentralization.

> Decentralizing measures are generally aimed at remedying two shortcomings of an "overcentralized" system structure. (1) Superordinates are overburdened with responsibility for the detailed direction and coordination of their subordinates' activities. (2) This "pretty tutelage" deprives subordinates of the opportunity to

65

make decisions that might increase the payoff of the organization of which they are a part.... Why not loosen controls...?... When controls are loosened, unless the incentive system is modified to bring about greater harmony between the goals of supervisors and supervisees, it may induce producers to shift their input and output mix in directions that ... vitiate any benefits that might be repeated by the organization as a whole from the exercise of greater initiative at lower tiers. (p. 215)

Here two costs or disadvantages of centralization (burden on supervisors, restriction of choice-set of subordinates) are set off against a disadvantage of decentralization (goals of subordinates divergent from organization goals).

What can we learn about organization from an argument like this? Certainly little or nothing about the optimal balance point between centralization and decentralization in any particular organization. Rather, we might derive conclusions of these kinds:

1. That increasing awareness of one of the predicted consequences may cause an organization to move in the direction of centralization or decentralization. (For example, an egregious case of "suboptimizing" by a subordinate may cause additional centralized controls to be instituted.)
2. That new technical devices may tilt the balance between centralization and decentralization. For example, invention and adoption of divisionalized profit and loss statements led toward decentralization of many large American business firms in the 1950s, while reduction in information costs through computerization led at a later date to centralization of inventory control decisions in those same firms.

Of course Montias's conclusions could also be derived from a more formal optimization analysis – in fact he presents such an analysis on the two pages following the passage quoted above. But it is not clear that anything new is added by the formalization, since the parameters imputed to the system are largely unmeasured and unmeasurable.

There is something to be said for an Occam's Razor that, eschewing assumptions of optimization, provides an explanation of behavior that is consistent with *either* optimizing or satisficing procedures on the part of the human agents. Parsimony recommends that we prefer the postulate that men are reasonable to the postulate that they are supremely rational when either one of the two assumptions will do our work of inference as well as the other.[6]

Procedural rationality

The kind of qualitative analysis I have been describing has another virtue. In complex situations there is likely to be a considerable gap between the real environment of a decision (the world as God or some other omniscient observer sees it) and the environment as the actors perceive it. The analysis can then address itself either to normative questions – the whole range of consequences that *should* enter into decisions in such situations – or descriptive questions, including the questions of which components of the situation are likely to be taken into account by the actors, and how the actors are likely to represent the situation as a whole.

In the precomputer era, for example, it was very difficult for managers in business organizations to pay attention to all the major variables affected by their decisions. Company treasurers frequently made decisions about working capital with little or no attention to their impact on inventory levels, while production and marketing executives made decisions about inventory without taking into account impacts on liquidity. The introduction of computers changed the ways in which executives were able to reach decisions; they could now view them in terms of a much wider set of interrelated consequences than before. The perception of the environment of a decision is a function of – among other things – the information sources and computational capabilites of the executives who make it.

Learning phenomena are also readily handled within this framework. A number of the changes introduced into planning and control procedures in eastern European countries during the 1960s were instituted when the governments in question learned by experience of some of the dysfunctional consequences of trying to control production by means of crude aggregates of physical quantities. An initial distrust of prices and market mechanisms was gradually and partially overcome after direct experience of the disadvantages of some of the alternative mechanisms. These learning experiences could be paralleled with experiences of American steel companies, for example, that experimented with tonnage incentives for mill department superintendents.

A general proposition that might be asserted about organizations is that the number of considerations that are potentially relevant to the effectiveness of an organization design is so large that only a few of the more salient of these lie within the circle of awareness at any given time, that the membership of this subset changes continually as new situations (produced by external or internal events) arise, and that "learning" in the form of reaction to perceived consequences is the dominant way in which rationality exhibits itself.

In a world where these kinds of adjustments are prominent, a theory of rational behavior must be quite as much concerned with the characteristics of the rational actors – the means they use to cope with uncertainty and cognitive complexity – as with the characteristics of the objective environment in which they make their decisions. In such a world, we must give an account not only of *substantive rationality* – the extent to which appropriate courses of action are chosen – but also *procedural rationality* – the effectiveness, in the light of human cognitive powers and limitations, of the *procedures* used to choose actions. As economics moves out toward situations of increasing cognitive complexity, it becomes increasingly concerned with the ability of actors to cope with the complexity, and hence with the procedural aspects, of rationality. In the remainder of this chapter, I would like to develop this concept of procedural rationality, and its implications for economic analysis.

MIND AS THE SCARCE RESOURCE

Until rather recently, such limited attention as was paid by economists to procedural, as distinct from substantive, rationality was mainly motivated by the problems of uncertainty and expectations. The simple notion of maximizing utility or profit could not be applied to situations where the optimum action depended on uncertain environmental events, or upon the actions of other rational agents (for example, imperfect competition).

The former difficulty was removed to some degree by replacing utility maximization with the maximization of subjective expected utility (SEU) as the criterion of rationality. In spite of its conceptual elegance, however, the SEU solution has some grave defects as either a normative or a descriptive formulation. In general, the optimal solution depends upon all of the moments of the frequency distributions of uncertain events. The exceptions are a small but important class of cases where the utility or profit function is quadratic and all constraints are in the form of equations rather than inequalities.[7] The empirical defect of the SEU formulation is that when it has been subjected to test in the laboratory or the real world, even in relatively simple situations, the behavior of human subjects has generally departed widely from it.

Some of the evidence has been surveyed by Ward Edwards (1968), and more recently by Daniel Kahneman and Amos Tversky (1973). They describe experimental situations in which estimates formed on the basis of initial information are not revised nearly as much by subsequent information as would be required by Bayes's theorem. In other situations, subjects respond largely to the information received most recently, and take inadequate account of prior information.

Behavior that is radically inconsistent with the SEU framework occurs also in naturalistic settings. Howard Kunreuther *et al.* (1978) have recently carried out extensive studies of behavior and attitudes relating to the purchase of flood insurance by persons owning property in low-lying areas. They found that knowledge of the availability of insurance, or rates, and of objective risks was very imperfect, and that the actual decisions whether or not to insure were related much more to personal experience with floods than to any objective facts about the situation – or even to personal subjective beliefs about those facts. In the face of this evidence, it is hard to take SEU seriously as a theory of actual human behavior in the face of uncertainty.[8]

For situations where the rationality of an action depends upon what others (who are also striving to be rational) do, again no consensus has been reached as to what constitutes optimal behavior. This is one of the reasons I have elsewhere called imperfect competition "the permanent and ineradicable scandal of economic theory" (1976b, p. 140). The most imaginative and ambitious attempt to resolve the difficulty was the von Neumann–Morgenstern theory of games, which is embarrassing in the wealth of alternative solutions it offers. While the theory of games reveals the potential richness of behavior when rational individuals are faced with conflict of interest, the capability of reacting to each other's actions (or expected actions), and possibilities for coalition, it has provided no unique and universally accepted criterion of rationality to generalize the SEU criterion and extend it to this broader range of situations.

The so-called "rational expectations" models currently so popular (and due originally to Muth, 1961), pass over these problems rather than solving them. They ignore potential coalitions and attempted mutual outguessing behavior, and correspond to optimal solutions only when the losses are quadratic functions of the errors of estimate.[9] Hence they do not correspond to any classical criterion of rationality, and labelling them with that term, rather than the more neutral "consistent expectations," provides them with a rather unwarranted legitimation.

Finally, it should be remarked that the main motivation in economics for developing theories of uncertainty and mutual expectations has not been to replace substantive criteria of rationality with procedural criteria, but rather to find substantive criteria broad enough to extend the concept of rationality beyond the boundaries of static optimization under certainty. As with classical decision theory, the interest lies not in *how* decisions are made but in *what* decisions are made. (But see, *contra*, such analyses as Richard Cyert and Morris DeGroot, 1977.)

Search and teams

Decision procedures have been treated more explicitly in the small bodies of work that have grown up in economics on the theory of search and on the theory of teams. Both these bodies of theory are specifically concerned with the limits on the ability of the economic actor to discover or compute what behavior is optimal for him. Both aspire not only to *take account* of human bounded rationality, but to *bring it within the compass* of the rational calculus. Let me explain what I mean by that distinction.

Problems of search arise when not all the alternatives of action are presented to the rational actor ab initio, but must be sought through some kind of costly activity. In general, an action will be chosen before the search has revealed all possible alternatives. One example of this kind of problem is the sale of a house, or some other asset, when offers are received sequentially and remain open for only a limited time (see the author, 1955). Another example which has been widely cited is the purchase of an automobile involving travel to dealers' lots (see Stigler, 1961). In both these examples, the question is not how the search is carried out, but how it is decided when to terminate it – that is, the amount of search. The question is answered by postulating a cost that increases with the total amount of search. In an optimizing model, the correct point of termination is found by equating the marginal cost of search with the (expected) marginal improvement in the set of alternatives. In a satisficing model, search terminates when the best offer exceeds an aspiration level that itself adjusts gradually to the value of the offers received so far. In both cases, search becomes just another factor of production, and investment in search is determined by the same marginal principle as investment in any other factor. However cavalierly these theories treat the actual search process, they do recognize explicitly that information gathering is not a free activity, and that unlimited amounts of it are not available.

The theory of teams, as developed by Marschak and Radner (1972), goes a step farther in specifying the procedure of decision. That theory, as is well known, is concerned with the improvement that may be realized in a team's decisions by interchange of information among the team members. But here the theory does not limit itself to determining the aggregate amount of information that should be transmitted, but seeks to calculate what messages should be exchanged, under what conditions, and at what cost. The content of the communication as well as the total amount of information becomes relevant to the theory.

In its attitude toward rationality, the theory of teams is as "classical," however, as is search theory. The bounds on the rationality of the team members are "externalized" and represented as costs of communication, so that they can be folded into the economic calculation along with the costs and benefits of outcomes.

Rational search procedures

To find theories that compare the merits of alternative search procedures, we must look largely outside the domain of economics. A number of such theories have been developed in the past thirty years, mainly by management scientists and researchers in the field of artificial intelligence. An important example is the body of work that has been done on integer programming.

Integer programming problems resemble linear programming problems (to maximize some quantity, subject to constraints in the form of linear equations and inequalities), with the added condition that certain variables can only take whole numbers as their values. The integer constraint makes inapplicable most of the powerful computational methods available for solving linear programming problems, with the result that integer programming problems are far less tractable, computationally, than linear programming problems having comparable numbers of variables.

Solution methods for integer programming problems use various forms of highly selective search – for example branch-and-bound methods that establish successively narrower limits for the value of the optimum, and hence permit a corresponding narrowing of search to promising regions of the space. It becomes a matter of considerable practical and theoretical interest to evaluate the relative computational efficiency of competing search procedures, and also to estimate how the cost of search will grow with the size of the problem posed. Until recently, most evaluation of search algorithms has been empirical: they have been tested on sample problems. Recently, however a body of theory – called theory of computational complexity – has grown up that begins to answer some of these questions in a more systematic way.

I cannot give here an account of the theory of computational complexity, or all of its implications for procedural rationality. A good introduction will be found in Alfred Aho *et al.* (1974). One important set of results that comes out of the theory does require at least brief mention. These results have to do with the way in which the amount of computation required to solve problems of a given class grows with the size of the problems – with the number of variables, say.[10]

In a domain where computational requirements grow rapidly with problem size, we will be able to solve only small problems; in domains where the requirements grow slowly, we will be able to solve much larger problems. The problems that the real world presents to us are generally enormous compared with the problems that we can solve on even our largest computers. Hence, our computational models are always rough approximations to the reality, and we must hope that the approximation will not be too inexact to be useful. We will be particularly concerned that computational costs not increase rapidly with problem size.

It is customary in the theory of computational complexity to regard problems of a given size as "tractable" if computations do not grow faster than at some fixed point of problem size. Such classes of problems are known as "polynomial complex." Problems that grow exponentially in complexity with size are not polynomial complex, since the rate of growth of computation comes to exceed any fixed power of their size.

A large and important class of problems which includes the general integer programming problem, as well as standard scheduling problems, all have been shown to have the same level of complexity – if one is polynomial complex, then all are; if one is not polynomial complex, then none are. These problmes have been labeled "NP-complete." It is conjectured, but not yet proven, that the class of NP-complete problems is not polynomially complex, but probably exponentially complex.

The significance of these findings and conjectures is in showing that computational difficulties, and the need to approximate, are not just a minor annoying feature of our world to be dealt with by manufacturing larger computers or breeding smarter people. Complexity is deep in the nature of things, and discovering tolerable approximation procedures and heuristics that permit huge spaces to be searched very selectively lies at the heart of intelligence, whether human or artificial. A theory of rationality that does not give an account of problem solving in the face of complexity is sadly incomplete. It is worse than incomplete; it can be seriously misleading by providing "solutions" to economic questions that are without operational significance.

One interesting and important direction of research in computational complexity lies in showing how the complexity of problems might be decreased by weakening the requirements for solution – by requiring solutions only to approximate the optimum, or by replacing an optimality criterion by a satisficing criterion. Results are still fragmentary, but it is already known that there are some cases where such modifications reduce exponential or NP-complete problems classes to polynomial-complete classes.

The theory of heuristic search, cultivated in artificial intelligence and information processing psychology, is concerned with devising or identifying search procedures that will permit systems of limited computational capacity to make complex decisions and solve difficult problems. (For a general survey of the theory, see Nils Nilsson, 1971.) When a task environment has patterned structure, so that solutions to a search problem are not scattered randomly throughout it, but are located in ways related to the structure, then an intelligent system capable of detecting the pattern can exploit it in order to search for solutions in a highly selective way.

One form, for example, of selective heuristic search, called best-first search, assigns to each node in the search space an estimate of the distance of that node from a solution. At each stage, the next increment of effort is expended in searching from the node, among those already reached, that has the smallest distance estimate (see, for example, the author and J. B. Kadane, 1975). As another example, when the task is to find a good or best solution, it may be possible to assign upper and lower bounds on the values of the solutions that can be obtained by searching a particular part of the space. If the lower bound on region *A* is lower than the lower bound on some other region, then region *A* does not need to be searched at all.

I will leave the topics of computational complexity and heuristic search with these sketchy remarks. What implications these developments in the theory of procedural rationality will have for economics defined as "the science which treats of the wealth-getting and wealth-using activities of man" remain to be seen. That they are an integral part of economics defined as "the science which treats of the allocation of scarce resources" is obvious. The scarce resource is computational capacity – the mind. The ability of man to solve complex problems, and the magnitude of the resources that have to be allocated to solving them, depend on the efficiency with which this resource, mind, is deployed.

Attention as the scarce resource

Finally, I would like to turn from the rather highly developed approaches to procedural rationality that I have been discussing back to the more qualitative kinds of institutional issues that were considered in the previous section of this chapter. Many of the central issues of our time are questions of how we use limited information and limited computational capacity to deal with enormous problems whose shape we barely grasp.

For many purposes, a modern government can be regarded as a parallel computing device. While one part of its capability for rational problem solving is directed to fire protection, another is directed to paving highways, and another to collecting refuse. For other important purposes, a government, like a human being, is a serial processing system, capable of attending to only one thing at a time. When important new policies must be formulated, public and official attention must be focused on one or a few matters. Other concerns, no matter how pressing, must wait their turn on the agenda. When the agenda becomes crowded, public life begins to appear more and more as a succession of crises. When problems become interrelated, as energy and pollution problems have become, there is the constant danger that attention directed to a single facet of the web will spawn solutions that disregard vital consequences for the other facets. When oil is scarce, we return to coal, but forget that we must then deal with vastly increased quantities of sulfur oxides in our urban air. Or we outlaw nuclear power stations because of radiation hazards, but fail to make alternative provision to meet our energy needs. It is futile to talk of substantive rationality in public affairs without considering what procedural means are available to order issues on the public agenda in a rational way, and to ensure attention to the indirect consequences of actions taken to reach specific goals or solve specific problems.

In a world where information is relatively scarce, and where problems for decision are few and simple, information is almost always a positive good. In a world where attention is a major scarce resource, information may be an expensive luxury, for it may turn our attention from what is important to what is unimportant. We cannot afford to attend to information simply because it is there. I am not aware that there has been any systematic development of a theory of information and communication that treats attention rather than information as the scarce resource.[11] Some of the practical consequences of attention scarcity have already been noticed in business and government, where early designs of so-called "management information systems" flooded executives with trivial data and, until they learned to ignore them, distracted their attention from more important matters. It is probably true of contemporary organizations that an automated information system that does not consume and digest vastly more information than it produces and distributes harms the performance of the organization in which it is incorporated.

The management of attention and tracing indirect consequences of action are two of the basic issues of procedural rationality that confront a modern society. There are others of comparable importance: what decision-making procedure is rational when the basic quantities for making marginal comparisons are simply not known? A few years ago, I served as chairman of a National Academy of Sciences (NAS) committee whose job it was to advise the Congress on the control of automobile emissions (see NAS, Coordinating Committee on Air Quality Studies, 1974). It is easy to formulate an SEU model to conceptualize the problem. There is a production function for automobiles that associates different costs with different levels of emissions. The laws governing the chemistry of the atmosphere determine the concentrations of polluting substances in the air as a function of the levels of emissions. Biomedical science tells us what effects on life and health can be expected from various concentrations of pollutants. All we need do is to attach a price tag to life and health, and we can calculate the optimum level of pollution control.

There is only one hitch – which will be apparent to all of you. None of the relevant parameters of the various "production functions" are known – except, within half an order of magnitude, the cost of reducing the emissions themselves. The physics and chemistry of the atmosphere present a series of unsolved problems – particularly relating to the photochemical reactions affecting the oxides of nitrogen and ozone. Medical science is barely able to detect that there *are* health effects from pollutants, much less measure how large these effects are. The committee's deliberations led immediately to one conclusion – one that congressmen are accustomed to hearing from such committees: We need more research. But, while the research is being done, what provisions should be incorporated in the Clean Air Act of 1977 (or the Acts of 1978 through 2000, for that matter)? For research will not give us clear answers then either. What constitutes procedural rationality in such circumstances?

"Reasonable men" reach "reasonable" conclusions in circumstances where they have no prospect of applying classical models of substantive rationality. We know only imperfectly how they do it. We know even less whether the procedures they use in place of the inapplicable models have any merit – although most of us would choose them in preference to drawing lots. The study of procedural rationality in circumstances where attention is scarce, where problems are immensely complex, and where crucial information is absent presents a host of challenging and fundamental research problems to anyone who is interested in the rational allocation of scarce resources.

CONCLUSION

In histories of human civilization, the invention of writing and the invention of printing are always treated as key events. Perhaps in future histories the invention of electrical communication and the invention of the computer will receive comparable emphasis. What all of these developments have in common, and what makes them so important, is that they represent basic changes in man's equipment for making rational choices – in his computational capabilities. Problems that are impossible to handle with the head alone (multiplying large numbers together, for example) become trivial when they can be written down on paper. Interactions of energy and environment that almost defy conceptualization lend themselves to at least approximate modeling with modern computers.

The advances in man's capacity for procedural rationality are not limited to these obvious examples. The invention of algebra, of analytic geometry, of the calculus were such advances. So was the invention, if we may call it that, of the modern organization, which greatly increased man's capacity for coordinated parallel activity. Changes in the production function for information and decisions are central to any account of changes over the centuries of the human condition.

In the past, economics has largely ignored the processes that rational man uses in reaching his resource allocation decisions. This was possibly an acceptable strategy for explaining rational decision in static, relatively simple problem situations where it might be assumed that additional computational time or power could not change the outcome. The strategy does not work, however, when we are seeking to explain the decision maker's behavior in complex, dynamic circumstances that involve a great deal of uncertainty, and that make severe demands upon his attention.

As economics acquires aspirations to explain behavior under these typical conditions of modern organizational and public life, it will have to devote major energy to building a theory of procedural rationality to complement existing theories of substantive rationality. Some elements of such a theory can be borrowed from the neighboring disciplines of operations research, artificial intelligence, and cognitive psychology; but an enormous job remains to be done to extend this work and to apply it to specifically economic problems.

Jacob Marschak, throughout his long career, had a deep belief in and commitment to the interdependencies and complementarity of the several social sciences. I have shared that belief and commitment, without always agreeing with him in detail as to the precise route for exploiting it. The developments I have been describing strengthen greatly, it seems to me, the rational grounds for both belief and commitment. Whether we accept the more restricted definition of economics that I quoted from Ely's textbook, or the wider definition that is widely accepted today, we have every reason to try to communicate with the other social sciences, both to find out what we have to say that may be of interest to them, and to discover what they can teach us about the nature of procedural rationality.

NOTES

Delivered as the Richard T. Ely Lecture in New York, December 1977. First published in the *Journal of the American Economic Association*, 68 (1978), 1–16.

1 The term is ill-chosen, for rational expectations in the sense of Muth are profit-maximizing expectations only under very special circumstances (see below). Perhaps we would mislead ourselves and others less if we called them by the less alluring phrase, "consistent expectations."

2 For an interesting argument in support of this proposition from a surprising source, see Becker (1962). What Becker calls "irrationality" in his article would be called "bounded rationality" here.

3 Recently, Oliver Williamson has pointed out that I would have to introduce slightly stronger assumptions to justify the employment contract as rational if one of the alternatives to it were what he calls a "contingent claims" contract, but the point of my example is not affected. To exclude the contingent claims contract as a viable alternative, we need merely take account of the large transaction costs it would entail under real world conditions.

4 For an introduction to this literature, see Wiliam H. Riker and Peter C. Ordeshook (1973) and Riker (1962). Anthony Downs' book (1957) belongs to an intermediate genre. While it employs the language of economics, it limits itself to verbal, nonrigorous reasoning which certainly does

not make any essential use of maximizing assumptions (as contrasted with rationality assumptions in the broader sense) and which largely translates into the economic vocabulary generalizations that were already part of the science and folklore of politics. In the next section, other examples of this kind of informal use of rationality principles are examined to analyze institutions and their behavior.

5 A notable exception to this generalization about the economic literature on organizations is the work of Jacob Marschak and Roy Radner (1972) on the theory of teams. These authors chose the strategy of detailed, precise analysis of the implications of maximizing assumptions for the transmission of information in organizations. The price they paid for this rigor was to find themselves limited to the highly simplified situations where solutions could be found for the mathematical problems they posed. We need not, of course, make an either–or choice between these two modes of inquiry. While it may be difficult or impossible to extend the formal analysis of the theory of teams to problems of real world complexity, the rigorous microtheory may illuminate the workings of important component mechanisms in the complex macrosituations. The methodological issues in choosing between analytic tractability and realism are quite parallel to those involved in the choice between laboratory and field methods for gathering empirical information about social phenomena. Neither one by itself marks the exclusive path toward truth.

6 Ockham (or Occam) is usually invoked on behalf of the parsimony of optimizing assumptions, and against the additional *ad hoc* postulates that satisficing models are thought to require in order to guarantee uniqueness of solutions. But that argument only applies when we are trying to deduce unique equilibria, a task quite different from the one most institutional writers set for themselves. However, I have no urge to enlarge on this point. My intent here is not polemical, on behalf of satisficing postulates, but rather to show how large a plot of common ground is shared by optimizing and satisficing analysis. Again, compare Becker (1962).

7 In this case the expected values of the environment variables serve as certainty equivalents, so that SEU maximization requires only replacing the unknown true values by these expected values. See Simon (1956).

8 Kunreuther *et al.* (1978) point out that the theory cannot be "saved" by assuming utility to be radically nonlinear in money. In the flood insurance case, that interpretation of the data would work only if we were willing to assume that money has strongly *increasing* marginal utility, not a very plausible escape route for the theory.

9 That is, only under the conditions where the uncertainty equivalents of note 7 exist. Under other circumstances, a "rational" person would be well advised, if he knew that all others were following the "rational expectations" or "consistent expectations" rule, to recalculate his own optimal behavior on that assumption. Of course if others followed the same course, we would be back in the "outguessing" situation.

10 Most of the theorems in computational complexity have to do with the "worst case," that is, with the maximum amount of computation required to solve *any* problem of the given class. Very few results are available for the expected cost, averaged over all problems of the class.

11 Some unsystematic remarks on the subject will be found in Simon (1976a, chs. 13, 14).

REFERENCES

Aho, Alfred V. *et al.* (1974). *The Design and Analysis of Computer Algorithms*, Reading.

Barnard, Chester I. (1938). *The Functions of the Executive*, Cambridge.

Becker, G. S. (1962). "Irrational behavior and economic theory," *J. Polit. Econ.*, Feb., 70, 1–13.

 (1974). "A theory of social interactions," *J. Polit. Econ.*, Nov./Dec., 82, 1063–93.

Cancian, F. M. (1968). "Functional analysis," in *International Encyclopedia of the Social Sciences*, 6, 29–42.

Cyert, R. M. and DeGroot, M. H. (1977). "Sequential strategies in dual control," *Theory Decn.*, Apr. 8, 173–92.

Downs, Anthony (1957). *An Economic Theory of Democracy*, New York.

Duverger, Maurice (1959). *Political Parties*, rev. ed., New York (*Les Partis Politiques*, Paris, 1951).

Edwards, W. (1968). "Conservation in human information processing," in Benjamin Kleinmuntz, ed., *Formal Representation of Human Thought*, New York.

Ely, Richard T. (1930). *Outlines of Economics*, rev. ed., New York.

Freud, S. (1957). "Five lectures on psychoanalysis" (originally "The origin and development of psychoanalysis" 1910), in *The Complete Psychological Works of Sigmund Freud*, vol. 11, London.

Homans, George. (1961). *Social Behavior: Its Elementary Forms*. New York.

Kahneman, D. and Tversky, A. (1973). "On the psychology of prediction," *Psychol. Rev.*, July, 80, 237–51.

Kornai, Janos (1971). *Anti-Equilibrium*, Amsterdam.

Kunreuther, Howard *et al.* (1978). *Protecting Against High-Risk Hazards:* Public Policy Lessons, New York.

March, James G. and Simon, Herbert A. (1958). *Organizations*, New York.

Marschak, Jacob and Radner, Roy (1972). *Economic Theory of Teams*, New Haven.

Montias, John M. (1976). *The Structure of Economic Systems*, New Haven.

Muth, J. F. (1961). "Rational expectations and the theory of price movements," *Econometrica*, July 19, 315–35.

National Academy of Sciences (NAS), Coordinating Committee on Air Quality Studies (1974). *Air Quality and Automobile Emission Control*, Vol. 1 summary rep., Washington.

Nilsson, Nils (1971). *Problem-Solving Methods in Artificial Intelligence*, New York.

Rees, A. (1968). "Economics," in *International Encyclopedia of the Social Sciences*, 4, 472.

Riker, William H. (1962). *The Theory of Political Coalitions*, New Haven.

Riker, W. H. and Ordeshook, Peter C. (1973). *An Introduction to Positive Political Theory*, New Jersey.

Samuelson, Paul (1947). *Foundations of Economic Analysis*, Cambridge.

Simmel, George (1908). *Soziologie*, Berlin.

Simon, Herbert A. (1951). "A formal theory of the employment relations," *Econometrica*, July, 19, 293–305.

(1955). "A behavioral model of rational choice," *Quart. J. Econ.*, Feb. 69, 99–118.

(1956). "Dynamic programming under uncertainty with a quadratic criterion function," *Econometrica*, Jan. 24, 74–81.

(1976a). *Administrative Behavior*, 3d ed., New York.

(1976b). "From substantive to procedural rationality," in Spiro J. Latsis, ed., *Method and Appraisal in Economics*, Cambridge.

Simon, H. A. and Kadane, J. B. (1975). "Optimal problem-solving search: all-or-none solutions," *Artificial Intel.*, Fall, 6, 235–48.

Stigler, G. J. (1961). "The economics of information," *J. Polit. Econ.*, June, 69, 213–15.

Stigler, G. J. and Becker, G. S. (1977). "De gustibus non est disputandum," *Amer. Econ. Rev.*, Mar. 67, 76–90.

Williamson, Oliver E. (1975). *Markets and Hierarchies*, New York.

4

NORMATIVE THEORIES OF DECISION MAKING UNDER RISK AND UNDER UNCERTAINTY

P. C. FISHBURN

1. INTRODUCTION

Normative decision theory is the study of guidelines for right action. It involves the formulation and defense of principles of comparative evaluation and choice among competing alternatives, proposed as rules that individuals or societies ought to – or perhaps would want to – follow. It deals also with the implications of these principles both on an abstract level and in reference to particular types of decision situations. The general subject is vast since it covers numerous ethical and normative social theories developed during the past few millennia.

The aim of the present chapter is exceedingly narrow in view of the larger perspective of the subject. It is to discuss a comparatively recent episode in the history of normative decision theory that has been heavily influenced by eighteenth-century Enlightenment thought and the subsequent ascendency of rationalism and scientific method in the analysis of human behavior. The principals in this episode are, with few exceptions, twentieth-century mathematicians, economists, and statisticians. The exceptions include Daniel Bernoulli (1738), who proposed a theory to explain why choices of prudent individuals among risky monetary options often violate the principle of expected profit maximization, and the Rev. Thomas Bayes (1763), who helped to pioneer the notion of probability as a theory of rational degrees of belief.

The theory I wish to describe is most succinctly known as expected utility theory. This is actually a family of related theories that divide into two subfamilies differentiated by the phrases (Luce and Raiffa, 1957) "decision making under risk" and "decision making under uncertainty." The first of these pertains to decisions that yield various outcomes with known probabilities: if you choose $2,000 outright over a 50–50 gamble between $0 or $5,000, you have made a decision under "risk." The second applies to the more general case in which outcomes are tied to uncertain events whose probabilities are not known: if you decide to eat a serving of mushrooms of questionable toxicity, you have made a decision under "uncertainty."

The primitive notions of a theory of expected utility are an individual's preference relation $\succ$ (" is preferred to") on a set of risky – or uncertain – decision alternatives. The guidelines or principles of the theory are statements about $\succ$ that are commonly referred to as axioms. The implications of the axioms are further statements about $\succ$ that are deduced from the axioms. As we shall see, some of these show how preferences correspond to a numerical structure that gives rise to an expectation operator that lies behind the name "expected utility."

A main theme of this chapter is that part of the expected utility episode has yet to be written. The reason is that some of the axioms of the standard theories – due to John von Neumann and Oskar Morgenstern (1944) in the case of risk and Frank P. Ramsey (1931) and Leonard J. Savage (1954) in the case of uncertainty – have come under severe criticism as general principles of rational choice. As a consequence, more general theories that retain some of the standard axioms but relax others to accommodate reasonable patterns of preference and choice that conflict with standard theories are being developed. It seems likely that another decade or two will pass before the shifting foundations settle.

My account of foundations adheres to the risk–uncertainty dichotomy. The next four sections focus on the risk category; the final three sections deal with uncertainty. In each part I will first review the standard theory. Examples that challenge the axioms as principles of rational choice will then be given. Finally, we shall look at new directions in the axiomatic foundations.

2. THE THEORY OF VON NEUMANN AND MORGENSTERN

The standard expected utility theory of von Neumann and Morgenstern (1944) was formulated as an adjunct to their theory of games. Others soon recognized it in its own right as an important foundation for decision making under risk. Through the years it has been refined and applied to many areas of economic analysis. A thorough technical account, including extensions and generalizations, is given in Fishburn (1982a).

Abstract versions of von Neumann–Morgenstern expected utility theory, as in the original presentation and elsewhere (Herstein and Milnor, 1953; Fishburn, 1970, 1982a), apply $\succ$ to a set endowed with convexity-like properties. For expository purposes, it will suffice in the present section to work with a convex set P of probability distributions $p, q, \ldots$ defined on a set X of outcomes. Each $p \in P$ can be viewed as a risky alternative that yields outcome $x \in X$ with probability $p(x)$, with the $p(x)$ summing to unity.

Convexity of P means that if $p, q \in P$ and $0 \leqslant \lambda \leqslant 1$, then $\lambda p + (1 - \lambda)q$ is in P. Convexity is defined pointwise so that $(\lambda p + (1 - \lambda)q)(x) = \lambda p(x) + (1 - \lambda)q(x)$ for all $x \in X$. If we begin with a set of distributions that is not convex, it can always be extended to a convex set in an obvious way. For interpretive purposes, the probabilities $\lambda, \lambda_1, \lambda_2, \ldots$ used in such an extension can be thought of as objective probabilities associated with a precisely calibrated random mechanism.

79

The standard theory uses three axioms that formalize notions of order, independence, and continuity. They apply to all $p, q, r \in P$ and all $0 < \lambda < 1$.

AXIOM A1 (order). $\succ$ on P is asymmetric and negatively transitive. That is, $p \succ q \Rightarrow$ not $(q \succ p)$; $p \succ q \Rightarrow (p \succ r$ or $r \succ q)$.

AXIOM A2 (independence). $[p \succ q, \ 0 < \lambda < 1] \Rightarrow \lambda p + (1-\lambda)r \succ \lambda q + (1-\lambda)r$.

AXIOM A3 (continuity). $[p \succ q, q \succ r] \Rightarrow [\alpha p + (1-\alpha)r \succ q$ and $q \succ \beta p + (1-\beta)r$ for some α and β in $(0, 1)]$.

The asymmetry part of axiom A1, $p \succ q \Rightarrow$ not $(q \succ p)$, makes it clear that $\succ$ stands for *strict preference*. It simply says that the individual will not both prefer p to q *and* prefer q to p, or, in the language of normative theory, that it is unreasonable or irrational to hold a definite preference for p over q and a definite preference for q over p at the same time. It leaves open the possibility that neither p nor q is preferred to the other, and in this case we write $p \sim q$ and say that the individual is *indifferent* between p and q:

$$p \sim q \Leftrightarrow \text{neither } p \succ q \text{ nor } q \succ p.$$

An operational definition of the indifference relation $\sim$ is that if $p \succ q$ and the individual must choose one or the other, then we would be quite happy to let anyone else make the choice for him. The union of $\succ$ and $\sim$ is denoted $\succsim$ ("is preferred or indifferent to"), defined by

$$p \succsim q \Leftrightarrow p \succ q \text{ or } p \sim q.$$

Asymmetry implies that, for any distinct $p, q \in P$, exactly one of $p \succ q, q \succ p$ and $p \sim q$ holds, and at least one of $p \succsim q$ and $q \succsim p$ holds. In addition, if $p = q$ then $p \sim q$.

The negative transitivity part of axiom A1, $p \succ q \Rightarrow (p \succ r$ or $r \succ q)$, or, equivalently $[$not $(p \succ r)$ and not $(r \succ q)] \Rightarrow$ not $(p \succ)$, says that if p is (strictly) preferred to q, and if r is any distribution in P, then either p is preferred to r or r is preferred to q (possibly both). In particular, given $p \succ q$, this rules out the combination of $r \succsim p$ *and* $q \succsim r$. It is usually held to be self-evident that any reasonable person who definitely prefers one risky alternative to a second risky alternative will either prefer the first to a third or, failing that, will surely prefer the third to the second.

It is easily proved that, given asymmetry, negative transitivity holds if and only if both $\succ$ and $\sim$ are *transitive*, i.e., for all $p, q, r \in P$,

$$(p \succ q \text{ and } q \succ r) \Rightarrow p \succ r; \quad (p \sim q \text{ and } q \sim r) \Rightarrow p \sim r.$$

Although these might be violated in several ways, the most flagrant violation occurs when preferences form a cyclic pattern, say with $p \succ q$, $q \succ r$ and $r \succ p$. Such a pattern is held to be irrational or foolish since it induces a money pump. If the individual presently has title to q then, since he prefers p to q, he will pay at least a small sum to exchange q for p; then, given p, he will pay something more to exchange it for the preferred r; finally, given r, he will again pay to exchange r for the preferred q. Thus, he begins and ends at q, but is poorer in the process.

Axiom A1 implies that P can be partitioned into indifference classes that are totally ordered in preference. All distributions in one class are indifferent to one another, and all in a "higher" class are preferred to all in a "lower" class. It follows that if Q is any nonempty finite subset of P, then there is at least one $q^* \in Q$ such that $q^* \gtrsim q$ for all $q \in Q$. Hence, every finite Q contains a maximally preferred distribution, thus providing an appealing basis for choice from finite subsets. If $Q = \{p_1, p_2, \ldots, p_n\}$ and axiom A1 is violated by the preference cycle $p_1 \succ p_2 \succ \ldots \succ p_n \succ p_1$, then $\succ$ gives little guidance for a choice from Q. Thus axiom A1 supplies a reasonable criterion of choice based solely on the binary relation $\succ$ that may be inoperative if the axiom fails.

This completes the main arguments for the acceptance of axiom A1 as a principle of sound judgment and choice.

The usual defense of axiom A2 adopts a two-stage argument or a matrix layout for $\lambda p + (1 - \lambda)r$ and $\lambda q + (1 - \lambda)r$, as shown in figure 4.1. Probabilistically, $\lambda p + (1 - \lambda)r$ is tantamount to the choice of p or r with respective probabilities λ and $1 - \lambda$, followed by the choice of $x \in X$ according to the one of p and r selected in the first stage – and similarly for $\lambda q + (1 - \lambda)r$. Since both distributions yield r with probability $1 - \lambda$, it is held that preference between $\lambda p + (1 - \lambda)r$ and $\lambda q + (1 - \lambda)r$ ought to be independent of r and depend entirely on preference between p and q so long as $\lambda > 0$. Thus, if $p \succ q$ and $\lambda > 0$, then $\lambda p + (1 - \lambda)r \succ \lambda q + (1 - \lambda)r$.

The matrix layout in the lower part of figure 4.1 suggests a dominance principle that argues strongly for axiom A2. If $p \succ q$ then the individual is better

Figure 4.1

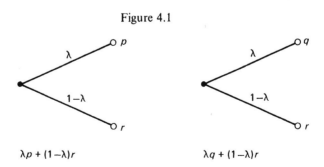

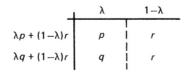

off in the first row of the matrix if the random event with probability λ obtains, and equally well off in either row if the complementary event with probability $1 - \lambda$ obtains. Therefore, common sense dictates that he will be better off with the first row than the second.

Herstein and Milnor (1953) use a slightly different continuity axiom than axiom A3 that enables them to use the following indifference–independence axiom instead of axiom A2:

$$p \sim q \Rightarrow \tfrac{1}{2}p + \tfrac{1}{2}r \sim \tfrac{1}{2}q + \tfrac{1}{2}r.$$

This can be defended by an argument like that given for axiom A2. Neither it nor A2 appears among von Neumann and Morgenstern's own axioms. This is due to their peculiar treatment of indifference as true identity (appendix, second edition of 1947), which subsumes axioms like $p \sim q \Rightarrow \lambda p + (1 - \lambda)r \sim \lambda q + (1 - \lambda)r$ under their identity relation.

Although axiom A3 might be more of a mathematical convenience than a rationality postulate, it too has a cogent rationale. In particular, since the difference between p and $\alpha p + (1 - \alpha)r$ seems negligible if α is nearly 1, it is hard to imagine that $\alpha p + (1 - \alpha)r$ will not be preferred to q for some $0 < \alpha < 1$ whenever p is preferred to q. A symmetric argument with β near 0 supports $q \succ \beta p + (1 - \beta)r$ when $q \succ r$.

Failures of axiom A3 might possibly arise from qualitative differences, as when

$$p = \text{win } \$2$$

$$q = \text{win } \$1$$

$$r = \text{be executed.}$$

The mathematical implications of not adopting axiom A3 or a related continuity postulate have been examined (Hausner, 1954; Chipman, 1960; Fishburn, 1974), but I shall not discuss them here since continuity has not been a major point of contention in recent reexaminations of the foundations.

It should be evident that the axioms under discussion have very little to do with ethical issues that are often addressed by normative theory. They only provide internal consistency and coherence to systems of preferences and say nothing otherwise about what ought to be preferred or chosen. As such, they reflect the strain of scientific rationalism in the present age, but are not in conflict with most systems of ethics. For example, similar axioms of individual preferences have been used within normative theories of fairness and justice in social decision making – a topic I shall comment on briefly in section 5.

Axioms A1 through A3 have several important implications, such as monotonicity ($p \succ q$ and $\beta > \alpha \Leftrightarrow \beta p + (1 - \beta)q \succ \alpha p + (1 - \alpha)q$) and others we shall meet later, but all of these are captured in an elegant mathematical representation for $(P, \succ)$. In particular, axioms A1 through A3 hold for $(P, \succ)$ if and only if there is a real valued function u on P such that, for all $p, q \in P$ and all $0 \leqslant \lambda \leqslant 1$,

$$p \succ q \Leftrightarrow u(p) > u(q),$$

$$u(\lambda p + (1 - \lambda)q) = \lambda u(p) + (1 - \lambda)u(q). \tag{1}$$

Thus, the numerical *utility function* u preserves the preference order $\succ$ and is *linear* in convex combinations as expressed by the equation "the utility of a convex combination equals the convex combination of the utilities of its parts." Moreover, given that u has these properties, so does v on P if, and only if, there are numbers $a > 0$ and b such that, for all $p \in P$,

$$v(p) = au(p) + b.$$

Thus, von Neumann–Morgenstern utilities are unique up to the choice of scale unit and origin.

The notion of expected utility is a direct consequence of the linearity property, equation (1). Suppose P contains every single-outcome distribution, and define u on X from u on P by

$$u(x) = u(p) \text{ when } p(x) = 1.$$

It then follows from equation (1) that if $p(x) > 0$ for at most a finite number of $x \in X$, then

$$u(p) = \sum_X p(x)u(x),$$

i.e., the utility of a risky alternative is the expectation of the utilities of its possible outcomes. If P contains other types of distributions or probability measures, then one or more additional axioms to take care of the technical details (Blackwell and Girshick, 1954; Fishburn, 1970, 1982a) yield the more general integral form

$$u(p) = \int_X u(x) \, dp(x).$$

The von Neumann–Morgenstern theory thus leads to the existence of a utility function u on outcomes that satisfies

$$p \succ q \Leftrightarrow \int u(x) \, dp(x) > \int u(x) \, dq(x)$$

and is supported by an appealing rationale.

3. PROBLEMS IN THE FOUNDATIONS

Criticisms of the axioms, and experiments to test their descriptive plausibility, began to appear in the late 1940s (Preston and Baratta, 1948; Mosteller and Nogee, 1951). In the early 1950s, Allais (1953, 1979a) demonstrated systematic violations of independence, and May (1954) gave sensible reasons why transitivity might fail. For the most part, phenomena like independence violations and distortions of probabilities (Edwards, 1954) were seen as evidence against expected utility as an adequate descriptive theory of actual behavior, but not as evidence against its normative validity. Consequently, alternative descriptive–explanatory models were proposed and tested (Edwards, 1954; Slovic, 1967; Payne, 1973; Libby and Fishburn, 1977; Kahneman and Tversky, 1979) while the status of expected utility as a normative theory remained largely intact.

I believe that the latter situation is now changing, but before looking at new axiomatic proposals I shall briefly cite reasons why transitivity and independence are not inviolable normative principles. Some of these reasons are motivated by empirical evidence and illustrate the potentially fine line between descriptive and normative theory, while others seem more directly normative. I shall begin with the transitivity part of axiom A1, then turn to A2.

Simple examples with monetary outcomes challenge the reasonableness of transitive indifference. For example, a person may be indifferent between $367 and an even-chance gamble for $1,000 or $0, indifferent between the gamble and $368, yet prefer $368 to $367. While this could be attributed to limited discriminatory ability, I see no sense in calling it irrational or nonnormative.

More serious violations of transitivity occur when preferences cycle. The most plausible examples of cyclic preferences arise in multiple criteria situations (May, 1954; Tversky, 1969). To illustrate, suppose a person receives three employment offers with the following characteristics:

	Salary	*Location*	*Work quality*
x:	excellent	satisfactory	good
y:	good	excellent	satisfactory
z:	satisfactory	good	excellent

On the basis of binary comparisons he prefers x to y, y to z, and z to x. In each comparison, he prefers the offer that is better on two of the three criteria and is quite comfortable with the idea of choosing between any two according to his preferences if the third should be withdrawn. Is this irrational?

What about the money pump? The first thing to be said about that is that the money pump concept envisions a dynamic situation with elements of strategy and deception that transcend the basic choice problem. It is a game that a sensible person with cyclic preferences would eschew if he knew what was involved. Thus, I do regard willing participation as a money pump as irrational, or at least naive, but see this as no reason against the admissibility of cyclic preferences in certain situations as reasonable patterns of judgment.

What, then, about the failure of $\succ$ to provide a clear choice when preferences cycle? Obviously, with $x \succ y \succ z \succ x$, there is no transparent way for our person to make a choice from $\{x, y, z\}$ on the basis of his preferences on this set. This does not, however, prevent him from considering his preferences on the set P of probability distribution on $\{x, y, z\}$ – a proposal that is very much in the spirit of decision making under risk. And, if there is a $p^* \in P$ such that $p^* \gtrsim p$ for all $p \in P$, then, from an *ex ante* perspective, he has a maximally preferred choice. The possibility of an axiomatic theory that implies the existence of such a p^* in cyclic-preference situations has in fact been realized, as we shall see in the next two sections.

Several people, including Allais (1953, 1979b), Morrison (1967), MacCrimmon (1968), MacCrimmon and Larsson (1979), and Kahneman and Tversky (1979), have convincingly demonstrated systematic failures of independence in simple monetary settings. The empirical fact is that the nature of r and the size of λ can make a difference in preference between $\lambda p + (1 - \lambda)r$ and $\lambda q + (1 - \lambda)r$, and it is hard to ignore this in assessing the normative adequacy of independence. Moreover, the standard defense of axiom A2 (see figure 4.1) may be based on an illusion created by separating $\lambda p + (1 - \lambda)r$ and $\lambda q + (1 - \lambda)r$ into parts. When the distributions are viewed holistically, important comparative aspects may appear that could be disguised by the two-stage separation argument. A typical example will illustrate the situation.

Let

$$p(\$300) = 1;$$

$$q(\$400) = 0.90, \ q(\$0) = 0.10;$$

$$r(\$0) = 1,$$

and consider $\lambda p + (q - \lambda)r$ versus $\lambda q + (1 - \lambda)r$. When $\lambda = 1$, the choice is between \$300 and a gamble that pays \$400 with probability 0.90 (nothing otherwise). Many people prefer the sure thing and therefore have $p \succ q$.

As λ decreases, both distributions increase the chance of getting \$0, and preferences may switch to $\lambda q + (1 - \lambda)r$ at some point. For example, when $\lambda = 0.10$,

$\lambda p + (1 - \lambda)r$ gives \$300 with probability 0.10 (\$0 otherwise),

$\lambda q + (1 - \lambda)r$ gives \$400 with probability 0.09 (\$0 otherwise),

and now many people with $p \succ q$ will prefer $\lambda q + (1 - \lambda)r$ to $\lambda p + (1 - \lambda)r$ since the latter distribution has only a slightly larger probability of winning a positive amount that is substantially less than what might be won with $\lambda q + (1 - \lambda)r$.

If λ is kept at 0.10 but r is changed from $r(\$0) = 1$ to $r(\$5,000) = 1$, then it seems likely that $\lambda p + (1 - \lambda)r$ will be preferred to $\lambda q + (1 - \lambda)r$.

Here is an example with the Herstein–Milnor axiom

$$p \sim q \Rightarrow \tfrac{1}{2}p + \tfrac{1}{2}r \sim \tfrac{1}{2}q + \tfrac{1}{2}r[\ldots \Rightarrow 2^{-n}p + (1 - 2^{-n})r \sim 2^{-n}q + (1 - 2^{-n})r]$$

that you can try on yourself. Let

$$p(\$1,000,000) = 1;$$

$$q(\$5,000,000) = \gamma, q(\$0) = 1 - \gamma;$$

$$r(\$0) = 1.$$

First, determine a γ at which you are indifferent between p and q. Be quite sure that you would be happy to let anyone else choose from $\{p,q\}$ on your behalf at this value of γ. With γ thus determined, q is fixed. Now compare $2^{-n}p + (1 - 2^{-n})r$ and $2^{-n}q + (1 - 2^{-n})r$ for one or more values of n, say with $n = 3$ or $n = 10$. Are you indifferent between the two, or do you have a preference? If it is the latter, you violate independence.

Violations of independence, or of transitivity, are often attributed to errors in judgment or classified as inconsistencies, but for the most part I feel that this misses the point. The point is that there are certain patterns of preferences, held by reasonable people for good reasons, that simply do not agree with the axioms of expected utility theory and which suggest the need for serious reappraisal of the normative foundations of decision making under risk.

4. NEW DIRECTIONS

Generalizations of the von Neumann–Morgenstern theory can be classified according to whether they focus on monetary outcomes or arbitrary outcomes, and by whether the numerical representation or model for preference between risky alternatives is supported by an explicit set of axioms for $\succ$ on P. A distinction may also be made between generalizations intended primarily as descriptive theories (Kahneman and Tversky, 1979), and those proposed as normative theories (Allais, 1979a, b). However, sometimes this distinction is avoided altogether (Fishburn, 1982b, 1983a), and in other cases both descriptive and normative significance are suggested (Loomes and Sugden, 1982; Bell, 1982; Chew, 1982; Machina, 1982a).

The theories cited here fall into three of the four categories under our initial classification as follows:

money, no axioms: Allais, Bell, Loomes–Sugden, Machina;

money, axioms: Kahneman–Tversky;

arbitrary, axioms: Chew, Fishburn.

Because of the present focus on axiomatic foundations for normative theory in a general setting, I shall restrict my remarks to the final category. Two axiomatizations of $\succ$ on P will be noted. The first, due to Fishburn (1982b), uses neither the transitivity nor independence axioms of von Neumann and Morgenstern, yet renders utility measurable in a well-defined sense. The second, due to Chew and MacCrimmon (1979) and refined by Chew (1982) and Fishburn (1983a), restores the transitivity axiom and obtains a representation that uses two linear functions. All of the theories mentioned above avoid the implications of independence, and all except Loomes and Sugden (1982) and Fishburn (1982b) presume that $\sim$ and $>$ are transitive.

Fishburn (1982b) refers to his theory as the SSB theory because its numerical representation for preference uses a skew-symmetric bilinear (SSB) functional ϕ on $P \times P$. This means that ϕ is a real valued function that, for all $p, q, r \in P$ and all $0 \leqslant \lambda \leqslant 1$, satisfies

$$\phi(p, q) = -\phi(q, p) \quad (skew\text{-}symmetry)$$

and

$$\phi(\lambda p + (1 - \lambda)q, r) = \lambda\phi(p, r) + (1 - \lambda)\phi(q, r).$$

The latter property says that ϕ is linear in its first argument. Since this and skew-symmetry imply linearity in the second argument, ϕ is *bilinear*. I shall return to ϕ shortly.

The SSB theory uses three axioms that apply to all $p, q, r \in P$ and all $0 < \lambda < 1$.

AXIOM B1 (continuity). $[p > q, q > r] \Rightarrow q \sim \alpha p + (1 - \alpha)r$ *for some α in* $(0, 1)$.

AXIOM B2 (convexity). $[p > q, p \gtrsim r] \Rightarrow p > \lambda q + (1 - \lambda)r$; $[q > p, r \gtrsim p] \Rightarrow \lambda q + (1 - \lambda)r > p$; $[p \sim q, p \sim r] \Rightarrow p \sim \lambda q + (1 - \lambda)r$.

AXIOM B3 (symmetry). $[p > q, q > r, p > r, q \sim \frac{1}{2}p + \frac{1}{2}r] \Rightarrow [\lambda p + (1 - \lambda)r \sim \frac{1}{2}p + \frac{1}{2}q \Leftrightarrow \lambda r + (1 - \lambda)p \sim \frac{1}{2}r + \frac{1}{2}q]$.

Axiom B1 is similar to A3. It implies that $>$ is asymmetry, and axioms B1 and B2 together imply that α in B1 is unique.

Axiom B2, which retains some of the flavor of independence, says that if one distribution is preferred to (less preferred than, indifference to) each of two others, then it will be preferred to (less preferred than, indifferent to) any convex combination of those two. In other words, for each $p \in P$, $\{q \in P : p > q\}$, $\{q \in P : q > p\}$, and $\{q \in P : q \sim p\}$ are convex subsets of P. In addition, the first two parts of axiom B2 cover the $>/\sim$ hypotheses of $[p > q, p \sim r]$ and $[q > p, r \sim p]$.

I regard axiom B2 as a reasonable principle for preferences and am not aware of data that question its descriptive validity. However, it may be too strong for a general descriptive theory because of the fine line it presumes between preference and indifference. For example, if $p > q$ and $p \sim r$, then some people may be indifferent between p and $\lambda q + (1 - \lambda)r$ when λ is near to 0.

Axiom B3 is a symmetry condition, or a principle of balance for the indifference relation. It says that if p, q, and r are ordered in preference as $p > q > r$, and if q is midway in preference between p and r in the sense that $q \sim \frac{1}{2}p + \frac{1}{2}r$, then the balanced indifference equation $\lambda p + (1 - \lambda)r \sim \frac{1}{2}p + \frac{1}{2}q$ will be preserved when p and r are interchanged throughout. The conclusion of axiom B3 is a special instance of the more general balance conclusion which says that, given $p > q > r$ and $q \sim \frac{1}{2}p + \frac{1}{2}r$, any indifference equation between convex combinations of distributions in $\{p, q, r\}$ will remain an indifference equation when p and r are interchanged throughout.

As with B2, I regard axiom B3 as an appealing principle of rational judgment and know of no evidence that bears on its descriptive stature. It is hoped that others will consider the matter.

Fishburn (1982b) shows that axioms B1 through B3 hold for $(P, \succ)$ if and only if there is an SSB functional ϕ on $P \times P$ such that, for all $p, q \in P$,

$$p \succ q \Leftrightarrow \phi(p, q) > 0.$$

Thus $\succ$ is the subset of $P \times P$ on which ϕ is positive, and $\sim$ is the subset of $P \times P$ on which ϕ vanishes. Moreover, given ϕ as indicated, an SSB functional ϕ' on $P \times P$ satisfies the representation if, and only if, there exists $a > 0$ such that

$$\phi'(p) = a\phi(p) \quad \text{for all } p \in P.$$

Consequently, SSB utilities are unique up to the choice of scale unit.

If $(P, \succ)$ satisfies the von Neumann–Morgenstern axioms, the axioms B1–B3 also hold, and ϕ for the SSB representation can be separately decomposed as

$$\phi(p, q) = u(p) - u(q),$$

with u a linear utility function. This suggests that, in the more general SSB case, $\phi(p, q)$ can be thought of as a nonseparable measure of preference difference between p and q in the risky context. Loomes and Sugden (1982) use a regret–rejoicing interpretation for ϕ.

As with u, ϕ has an "expected utility" form. Suppose B contains every single-outcome distribution, and define ϕ on $X \times X$ form ϕ on $P \times P$ by

$$\phi(x, y) = \phi(p, q) \quad \text{when } p(x) = q(y) = 1.$$

If $p(x) + q(x) > 0$ for at most a finite number of $x \in X$, then bilinearity yields

$$\phi(p, q) = \sum_{x \in X} \sum_{y \in X} p(x)q(y)\phi(x, y),$$

so that $\phi(p, q)$ is the expected value of $\phi(x, y)$ under the product measure $p \times q$ on $X \times X$. This is generalized to an integral form in Fishburn (1984a).

The second new theory has slightly different axiomatizations in Chew (1982) and Fishburn (1983a). I shall follow the latter for expositional convenience since it adds only one new axiom,

AXIOM B4. $\sim$ on P is transitive,

to B1–B3. Together, axioms B1–B4 imply that $\succ$ too is transitive, hence that axiom A1 holds.

The utility representation for axioms B1–B4 is intermediate to the SSB representation and the linear representation of von Neumann and Morgenstern. Specifically, axioms B1–B4 hold if and only if there are linear functions u and w on P with w nonnegative such that w is strictly positive if P has both maximal and minimal distributions under $\succ$, or if it has neither, and such that, for all $p, q \in P$,

$$p \succ q \Leftrightarrow u(p)w(q) > u(q)w(p).$$

If w is strictly positive, the inequality can be written in the ratio form $u(p)/w(p) > u(q)/w(q)$ and, if the "weighting function" w is constant, then the representation reduces to that of von Neumann and Morgenstern. In addition, if we define ϕ on $P \times P$ by

$$\phi(p, q) = u(p)w(q) - u(q)w(p),$$

then ϕ is an SSB functional that represents $\succ$ in the manner noted above. Thus, the addition of transitivity to the axioms of SSB utility theory implies that $\phi(p, q)$ is separable in p and q according to the preceding equation. Uniqueness conditions for u and w will not be detailed here: see Chew (1982) and Fishburn (1983a).

The "expected utility" form of the (u, w) representation for simple distributions is

$$p \succ q \Leftrightarrow \left[\sum_X p(x)u(x)\right]\left[\sum_X q(x)w(x)\right] > \left[\sum_X q(x)u(x)\right]\left[\sum_X p(x)w(x)\right].$$

Like preceding cases, this can be extended to an integral form by the addition of a few technical axioms.

5. APPLICATIONS

Significant efforts have been made to assess the potential of generalizations of expected utility in areas of economics where the standard theory has proved useful and in areas where its explanatory power has been limited. For example, most of the authors cited in the preceding section show how their generalizations accommodate Allais-type failures of independence, and Chew (1983), Machina (1982a, b), and Loomes and Sugden (1982) examine generalizations of the standard theory of risk attitudes (Pratt, 1964; Arrow, 1965) and the phenomenon of simultaneous gambling and insurance-buying (Friedman and Savage, 1948). In addition, Chew (1983) and Fishburn (1984a) discuss notions of stochastic dominance (Whitmore and Findlay, 1978), and Chew (1983), Machina (1982a), and Fishburn (1984b) consider applications of their generalizations to problems in social choice and social welfare theory.

As would be expected, the more general theories are better able than the standard theory to model certain types of economic behavior, and it appears that they lead to results similar to those obtained from the standard theory in areas where it has been most widely used. Further research will help to clarify the picture.

I shall conclude the present discussion of decision making under risk by noting a consequence of the SSB theory and its application to social choice theory. Let ϕ be an SSB functional on $P \times P$ that represents $\succ$ by $p \succ q \Leftrightarrow \phi(p, q) > 0$, and let Q be a nonempty subset of P with convex hull $H(Q) = \{\sum \lambda_i p_i : p_i \in Q$ and $\lambda_i \geq 0$ with $\sum \lambda_i = 1$, the sum being finite$\}$. It is then an easy consequence of the von Neumann minimax theorem that there is a $p^* \in H(Q)$ such that $p^* \succsim q$ for all

$q \in H(Q)$. Thus, even though the SSB theory allows preference cycles, it implies that the convex hull of every nonempty finite set of distributions contains a distribution that is preferred or indifferent to every other distribution in the hull (Fishburn, 1984a).

An application of this result to voting is suggested in Fishburn (1984b). Suppose a number of people vote in an election among the candidates in a finite set X, and let $\phi(x, y)$ equal the number of voters who reveal a preference for x over y, minus the number who reveal a preference for y over x. By definition, the plurality function ϕ on $X \times X$ is skew-symmetric. Extend ϕ to the set $P \times P$, where P is the set of probability distributions on X, by defining $\phi(p, q)$ as $\sum\sum p(x)q(y)\phi(x, y)$. It follows that ϕ on $P \times P$ is SSB. The result of the preceding paragraph implies that there is a $p^* \in P$ such that

$$\phi(p^*, q) \geqslant 0 \quad \text{for every } q \in P.$$

If such a p^* is used to select the winning candidate, then the election procedure satisfies both the principle of majority choice and Pareto optimality. That is, if candidate x^* has $\phi(x^*, x) > 0$ for every $x \neq x^*$, then $p^*(x^*) = 1$. In addition, if voters order the candidates on their ballots, then $p^*(y) = 0$ if there is another candidate x such that at least one voter prefers x to y and no voter prefers y to x.

6. SUBJECTIVE EXPECTED UTILITY

The standard subjective expected utility model for decision making under uncertainty is composed of a probability measure ρ defined on the subsets (events) of a set S of *states* of the world and a utility function u defined on a set X of decision outcomes such that, for all functions f and g in the set F of functions from S into X,

$$f \succ g \Leftrightarrow \int_S u(f(s)) \, d\rho(s) > \int_S u(g(s)) \, d\rho(s). \tag{2}$$

The states $s \in S$ describe potential realizations of things about which the decision maker is uncertain. They are formulated so that one and only one state will obtain, and, for each event $A \subseteq S$, $\rho(A)$ is the decision maker's personal probability – conceived of as a measure of rational degree of belief – for the proposition that some $s \in A$ will obtain. The outcomes in X are valued by the decision maker in different degrees that are reflected in the utility function u.

A function $f: S \to X$ is a potential *act* that assigns an outcome $f(s) \in X$ to each state $s \in S$. To say that act f is preferred to act g is to say that the person would rather take his chances on the state-dependent array of outcomes provided by f than on those provided by g when he is uncertain about which state will obtain. According to the standard model, f is preferred to g if, and only if, f has greater subjective expected utility than g.

The first complete $(F, \succ)$ axiomatization for this numerical representation of preferences in the face of uncertainty is due to Savage (1954), who drew on earlier ideas of Ramsey (1931), de Finetti (1937), and von Neumann and Morgenstern (1944). Since then, a number of other axiomatizations have been proposed (Fishburn, 1981). Here I shall comment only on Savage's theory and a related approach that has been used as a point of departure for recent generalizations.

Savage uses seven axioms for $(F, \succ)$. The final three axioms are an uncontroversial nontriviality condition, a continuity axiom based on finite partitions of S (which is necessarily a nondenumerable infinite set in his theory), and an appealing dominance principle that is used to obtain the full integral form. The first four axioms embrace his ordering and independence postulates. To state them, we need a few definitions. First, $f = g$ on A if $f(s) = g(s)$ for all $s \in A$, and $f = x$ on A if $f(s) = x$ for all $s \in A$. Second, even A is *null* if $f \sim g$ whenever $f = g$ on the complement $A^c = S \backslash A$ of A. Third, $f \succ g$ *given* A if $f' \succ g'$ whenever $f = f'$ and $g = g'$ on A, and $f' = g'$ on A^c. Finally, $x \succ y$ if $f \succ g$ when $f = x$ and $g = y$ on S. The following apply to all $f, g, f', g \in F$, all $A, B \subseteq S$, and all $x, y, x', y' \in X$.

AXIOM P1. $\succ$ on F is asymmetric and negatively transitive.

AXIOM P2. $[f = f'$ and $g = g'$ on A; $f = g$ and $f' = g'$ on $A^c] \Rightarrow [f \succ g \Leftrightarrow f' \succ g']$.

AXIOM P3. $[A$ is not null; $f = x$ and $g = y$ on $A] \Rightarrow [x \succ y \Leftrightarrow f \succ g$ given $A]$.

AXIOM P4. $[x \succ y, x' \succ y'; f = x$ and $f' = x'$ on A, $f = y$ and $f' = y'$ on A^c; $g = x$ and $g' = x'$ on B, $g = y$ and $g' = y'$ on $B^c] \Rightarrow [f \succ g \Leftrightarrow f' \succ g']$.

Axiom P1 is similar to axiom A1. Axiom P2, which is similar in spirit to the independence axiom A2, says that $\succ$ is independent of states in A^c that have identical outcomes for the two acts. That is, if $f \succ g$ when $f = g$ on A^c, and if f and g are modified on A^c but retain $f = g$ on A^c, then $f \succ g$ after the modification. Together, axioms P1 and P2 imply that the conditional relation $\succ$ *given* A has the ordering properties of axiom P1.

Axiom P3 ties $\succ$ *given* A for nonnull events to preferences between outcomes (or constant acts), thus positing a degree of similarity among conditional orders. Savage refers to the combination of axiom P and P3 as his "sure-thing principle."

The fourth axiom is used to obtain an unambiguous ordering relation $\succ^*$ ("is more probable than") over the events in S when $\succ^*$ is defined by

$$A \succ^* B \text{ if } f \succ g \quad \text{whenever } x \succ y, f = x \text{ on } A, g = x$$

$$\text{on } B, f = y \text{ on } A^c, g = y \text{ on } B^c.$$

Thus, $A \succ^* B$ if the person would rather take his chances on the occurrence of A than B for the preferred outcome x.

Savage's axioms imply that there is a bounded (Fishburn, 1970, chapter 14) real valued function u on X and a probability measure ρ on the subsets of S that satisfy equation (2) for all $f, g \in F$. Moreover, for all $A, B \subseteq S$, ρ satisfies

$$A \succ^* B \Leftrightarrow \rho(A) > \rho(B),$$

$$0 < \lambda < 1 \Rightarrow \rho(C) = \lambda \rho(B) \quad \text{for some } C \subseteq B,$$

so that ρ preserves $\succ^*$ and is continuously divisible. Moreover, ρ is unique, and u is unique up to the choice of scale unit and origin.

Because Savage's axioms imply that S is infinite, others (Anscombe and Aumann, 1963; Pratt, Raiffa, and Schlaifer, 1964; Fishburn, 1967, 1970) have developed theories for finite S that use extraneous scaling properties to construct the set P of probability distributions on X and then apply $\succ$ to the set H of functions from S into P. Each function in H is a *lottery act* that assigns a distribution or lottery in P (rather than a single outcome) to each state. A lottery act corresponds to a Savage act if each assigned distribution has probability 1 for some outcome.

To illustrate further, suppose $S = \{1, \ldots, n\}$ and let

$$H = P^n = \{ p = (p_1, \ldots, p_n) : p_i \in P \text{ for each } i \}.$$

Convex combinations of lottery acts are taken statewise:

$$\lambda p + (1 - \lambda)q = \lambda(p_1, \ldots, p_n) + (1 - \lambda)(q_1, \ldots, q_n)$$
$$= (\lambda p_1 + (1 - \lambda)q_1, \ldots, \lambda p_n + (1 - \lambda)q_n).$$

Because H is convex, axioms A1–A3 can be applied directly to $(H, \succ)$ rather than to $(P, \succ)$. When this is done, it follows that for each state i there is a linear function u_i on P such that, for all $p, q \in H$,

$$p \succ q \Leftrightarrow \sum_{i=1}^{n} u_i(p_i) > \sum_{i=1}^{n} u_i(q_i).$$

If it is assumed also that at least one state is not null and – similar to axiom P3 – that the ordering induced by u_i on P is the same for all nonnull i, then there are unique $\rho_i \geq 0$ with $\sum \rho_i = 1$ and $\rho_i = 0 \Leftrightarrow i$ is null, and linear u on P, unique except for scale unit and origin, such that, for all $p, q \in H$,

$$p \succ q \Leftrightarrow \sum_{i=1}^{n} \rho_i u(p_i) > \sum_{i=1}^{n} \rho_i u(q_i).$$

When $p_i(x_i) = q_i(y_i) = 1$ for all i, this reduces to the finite version of equation (2):

$$(x_1, \ldots, x_n) \succ (y_1, \ldots, y_n) \Leftrightarrow \sum \rho_i u(x_i) > \sum \rho_i u(y_i).$$

Again, because H is convex, the SSB axioms B1–B3 of section 4 can be applied to $(H, \succ)$. I shall comment on this in section 8.

7. MORE PROBLEMS IN THE FOUNDATIONS

Savage's (1954) proof that equation (2) follows from his axioms first obtains ρ on events and then uses ρ to construct probability distributions on X that correspond to acts that map S into finite subsets of X. The natural definition of $\succ$ on these distributions is then shown to satisfy the von Neumann–Morgenstern axioms, and thus leads to equation (2) for such acts. Because of this and the direct use of lottery acts in the finite-states approach, the theories of the preceding section are vulnerable to the criticisms in section 3 of the von Neumann–Morgenstern axioms.

For example, an Allais-type challenge to Savage's independence axiom P2 imagines that S is partitioned into three events, A, B, and C, with $\rho(A), \rho(B)$, and $\rho(C)$ equal respectively to approximately 0.01, 0.09, and 0.90. Outcomes are increments to wealth, and four acts are proposed:

	A	B	C
f:	\$1,000,000	\$1,000,000	\$1,000,000
g:	0	\$5,000,000	\$1,000,000
f':	\$1,000,000	\$1,000,000	0
g':	0	\$5,000,000	0

It is observed that many people have $f \succ g$ and $g' \succ f'$, which contradicts axiom P2 when A used there is taken as $A \cup B$ in the present example.

A different criticism of independence among states that depends on a preference for relative specificity, or against ambiguity, is offered by Ellsberg (1961). Suppose an urn contains 30 red balls and 60 others that are solid black and solid yellow in unknown proportion. One ball is to be chosen at random. Four acts are envisioned:

  f: win \$1,000 if red is chosen (nothing otherwise);
  g: win \$1,000 if black is chosen;
  f': win \$1,000 if red or yellow is chosen;
  g': win \$1,000 if black or yellow is chosen.

Again, many people have $f \succ g$ and $g' \succ f'$. In the first comparison, a third of the 90 balls are known to be red; in the second, two-thirds of the 90 are known to be black or yellow. If $p(r)$, $p(b)$ and $p(y)$ are the respective probabilities for drawing the three colors, then the standard model gives $p(r) > p(b)$ on the basis of $f \succ g$, and $p(b) + p(y) > p(r) + p(y)$, or $p(b) > p(r)$, on the basis of $g' \succ f'$.

A simplified and rearranged version of the preceding example is more explicit in identifying the states according to the unknown composition of the urn. Suppose there are just three balls. One is red and the other two are black and yellow in unknown proportion; i.e., either both are black (bb = state 1), or one is black and the other is yelow (by = state 2), or both are yellow (yy = state 3). Again, one ball is to be drawn at random. The probabilities of winning the \$1,000

93

prize for the four acts in the preceding paragraph are shown as follows for each state:

	1(bb)	2(by)	3(yy)
f:	1/3	1/3	1/3
g:	2/3	1/3	0
f':	1/3	2/3	1
g':	2/3	2/3	2/3

If the decision maker prefers the acts with equal chances for the prize under each state to their variable-chance counterparts, then $f \succ g$ and $g' \succ f'$, and when this is so it violates the standard model of subjective probability since that model has $f \succ g \Rightarrow p(yy) > p(bb)$, whereas $g' \succ f' \Rightarrow p(bb) > p(yy)$.

8. MORE NEW DIRECTIONS

I note here three recent studies (see Fishburn, 1981, for earlier work) that generalize standard theories of subjective expected utility to accommodate violations of independence. All three apply $\succ$ to the n-state set $H = P^n$ of lottery acts discussed in section 6.

The first, by Loomes and Sugden (1982), proposes the representation

$$p \succ q \Leftrightarrow \sum_{i=1}^{n} \rho_i \phi^*(p_i, q_i) > 0,$$

where the ρ_i are state probabilities and ϕ^* is an SSB functional on $P \times P$. Loomes and Sugden do not axiomatize this representation on $P \times P$, but discuss its logic in detail for the monetary-outcomes setting.

The second, by Fishburn (1984c), applies the SSB axioms B1–B3 of section 4 to $(H, \succ)$ to obtain

$$\phi(p, q) = \sum_{i,j} \phi_{ij}(p_i, q_j),$$

where each ϕ_{ij} is bilinear and $\phi_{ij}(p, q) = -\phi_{ji}(q, p)$ for all $i, j \in S$ and all $p, q \in P$. Effects of within-state and between-states consistency axioms are examined. The paper concludes with axioms that are necessary and sufficient for the Loomes–Sugden model, i.e., for

$$\phi(p, q) = \sum_{i=1}^{n} \rho_i \phi^*(p_i, q_i).$$

Three axioms besides B1–B3 are used for this. The first says that $\succ$ on P within state i (a fixed distribution in all other states) is the same for each nonnull i. The second says that some state is not null, and the third is a weak between-states independence axiom.

The preceding work admits nontransitive preferences and accommodates within-state violations of independence. However, its ability to incorporate Ellsberg-type violations of independence is limited (but see Fishburn, 1983b). For example, the preferences in the examples of the preceding section are inconsistent with the Loomes–Sugden model.

The third recent generalization, by Schmeidler (1982), retains more of the von Neumann–Morgenstern utility structure – it reduces to their theory when $S = \{1\}$ – but weakens subjective probability to a nonadditive form that is more consistent with Ellsberg-type violations of independence. Schmeidler uses the von Neumann–Morgenstern ordering and continuity axioms A1 and A3 for $(H, \succ)$ along with a consistency principle like Savage's axiom P3 for similar conditional orders for events. He weakens the independence axiom A2 to apply only to lottery acts p, q, and r that are pairwise comonotonic: p and q are *comonotonic* if, for all $i, j \in S$, not $[p_i \succ p_j \text{ and } q_j \succ q_i]$, where $\succ$ on P is defined in the natural way from preferences between constant lottery acts in H. These four axioms imply the existence of a linear function u on P and a monotonic but not necessarily additive set function ρ^* on events in S such that, for all $p, q \in H$,

$$p \succ q \Leftrightarrow E^*(u, p; \rho^*) > E^*(u, q; \rho^*),$$

where

$$E^*(u, p; \rho^*) = \sum_{j=1}^{m-1} (\alpha_j - \alpha_{j+1})\rho^*\left(\bigcup_{k=1}^{j} A_k\right) + \alpha_m \rho^*(S)$$

when $\{A_1, \ldots, A_m\}$ is a partition of S and $u(p_i) = \alpha_j$ for all $i \in A_j$ with $\alpha_1 > \ldots > \alpha_m$. If axiom A2 holds completely on H, then ρ^* is additive and we get $p \succ q \Leftrightarrow \sum \rho_i^* u(p_i) > \sum \rho_i^* u(q_i)$.

It should be mentioned that Schmeidler allows S to be infinite, so his results are slightly more general than I have suggested and they provide a basis for extending the nonadditive expectation operator E^* to lottery acts with an infinite number of u values.

The recent developments summarized here indicate new directions for normative theories of decision making under uncertainty. I believe that they constitute a nice beginning, but would submit that the greater part of the effort lies ahead.

REFERENCES

Allais, M. (1953). "Le comportement de l'homme rationnale devant le risque- critique des postulats et axiomes de l'école américaine," *Econometrica* 21, 503–46.
(1979a). "The foundations of a positive theory of choice involving risk and a criticism of the postulates and axioms of the American school (1952)," in *Expected Utility Hypotheses and the Allais Paradox*, ed. by M. Allais and O. Hagen. Dordrecht, Holland: Reidel, 27–145.

(1979b). "The so-called Allais paradox and rational decisions under uncertainty," in *Expected Utility Hypothesis Utility and the Allais Paradox*, ed. by M. Allais and O. Hagen. Dordrecht, Holland: Reidel, 437–681.

Anscombe, F. J., and Aumann, R. J. (1963). "A definition of subjective probability," *Annals of Mathematical Statistics* 34, 199–205.

Arrow, K. J. (1965). *Aspects of the Theory of Risk Bearing*. Helsinki: Yrjö Jahssonin Säätiö.

Bayes, T. (1763). "An essay towards solving a problem in the doctrine of chances," *Philosophical Transactions of the Royal Society* 53, 370–418. Reprinted with comments by E. C. Molina in *Facsimiles of Two Papers of Bayes*. Washington, D.C.: The Graduate School, Department of Agriculture, 1940.

Bell, D. E. (1982). "Regret in decision making under uncertainty," *Operations Research* 30, 961–81.

Bernoulli, D. (1738). "Specimen theoriae novae de mensura sortis," *Commentarii Academiae Scientiarum Imperialis Petropolitanae* 5, 175–92. Translated by L. Sommer, *Econometrica* 22 (1954, 23–36.

Blackwell, D., and Girshick, M. A. (1954). *Theory of Games and Statistical Decisions*. New York: Wiley.

Chew, S. H. (1982). "A mixture set axiomatization of weighted utility theory," College of Business and Public Administration Discussion Paper 82-4, University of Arizona.

(1983). "A generalization of the quasilinear mean with applications to the measurement of income inequality and decision theory resolving the Allais paradox," *Econometrica* 51, 1065–92.

Chew, S. H., and MacCrimmon, K. R. (1979). "Alpha–nu choice theory: a generalization of expected utility theory," Faculty of Commerce and Business Administration Working Paper 669, University of British Columbia.

Chipman, J. S. (1960). "The foundations of utility," *Econometrica* 28, 193–224.

de Finetti, B. (1937). "La prévision: ses lois logiques, ses sources subjectives." *Annales de l'Institut Henri Poincaré* 7, 1–68. Translated by H. E. Kyburg in *Studies in Subjective Probability*, ed. by H. E. Kyburg and H. E. Smokler. New York: Wiley, 1964.

Edwards, W. (1954). "The theory of decision making," *Psychological Bulletin* 51, 380–417.

Ellsberg, D. (1961). "Risk, ambiguity, and the Savage axioms," *Quarterly Journal of Economics* 75, 643–69.

Fishburn, P. C. (1967). "Preference-based definitions of subjective probability," *Annals of Mathematical Statistics* 38, 1605–17.

(1970). *Utility Theory for Decision Making*. New York: Wiley.

(1974). "Lexicographic orders, utilities, and decision rules: a survey," *Management Science* 20, 1442–71.

(1981). "Subjective expected utility: a review of normative theories," *Theory and Decision* 13, 139–99.

(1982a). *The Foundations of Expected Utility*. Dordrecht, Holland: Reidel.

(1982b). "Nontransitive measurable utility," *Journal of Mathematical Psychology* 26, 31–67.

(1983a). "Transitive measurable utility," *Journal of Economic Theory* 31, 293–317.

(1983b). "Ellsberg revisited: a new look at comparative probability," *Annals of Statistics* 11, 1047–59.

(1984a). "Dominance in SSB utility theory," *Journal of Economic Theory* 34, 130–48.

(1984b). "Probabilistic social choice based on simple voting comparisons," *Review of Economic Studies* 51, 683–91.

(1984c). "SSB utility theory and decision-making under uncertainty," *Mathematical Social Sciences* 8, 253–85.

Friedman, M., and Savage, L. J. (1948). "The utility analysis of choices involving risk," *Journal of Political Economy* 56, 279–304.

Hausner, M. (1954). "Multidimensional utilities," in *Decision Processes*, ed. by R. M. Thrall, C. H. Coombs, and R. L. Davis. New York: Wiley, 167–80.

Herstein, I. N., and Milnor, J. (1953). "An axiomatic approach to measurable utility," *Econometrica* 21, 291–7.

Kahneman, D., and Tversky, A. (1979). "Prospect theory: an analysis of decision under risk," *Econometrica* 47, 263–91.

Libby, R., and Fishburn, P. C. (1977). "Behavioral models of risk taking in business decisions: a survey and evaluation," *Journal of Accounting Research* 15, 272–92.

Loomes, G., and Sugden, R. (1982). "Regret theory: an alternative theory of rational choice under uncertainty," *Economic Journal* 92, 805–24.

Luce, R. D., and Raiffa, H. (1957). *Games and Decisions*. New York: Wiley.

MacCrimmon, K. R. (1968). "Descriptive and normative implications of the decision-theory postulates," in *Risk and Uncertainty*, ed. by K. Borch and J. Mossin. New York: Macmillan, 3–32.

MacCrimmon, K. R., and Larsson, S. (1979). "Utility theory: axioms versus 'paradoxes'," in *Expected Utility Hypotheses and the Allais Paradox*, ed. by M. Allais and O. Hagen. Dordrecht, Holland: Reidel, 333–409.

Machina, M. J. (1982a). "Expected utility on analysis without the independence axiom," *Econometrica* 50, 277–323.

(1982b). "A stronger characterization of declining risk aversion," *Econometrica* 50, 1069–79.

May, K. O. (1954). "Intransitive, utility, and the aggregation of preference patterns," *Econometrica* 22, 1–13.

Morrison, D. G. (1967). "On the consistency of preferences in Allais' paradox," *Behavioral Science* 12, 373–83.

Mosteller, F., and Nogee, P. (1951). "An experimental measure of utility," *Journal of Political Economy* 59, 371–404.

Payne, J. W. (1973). "Alternative approaches to decision making under risk: moments versus risk dimensions," *Psychological Bulletin* 80, 439–53.

Pratt, J. W. (1964). "Risk aversion in the small and in the large," *Econometrica* 32, 122–36.

Pratt, J. W., Raiffa, H., and Schlaifer, R. (1964). "The foundations of decision under uncertainty: an elementary exposition," *Journal of the American Statistical Association* 59, 353–75.

Preston, M. G., and Baratta, P. (1948). "An experimental study of the auction-value of an uncertain outcome," *American Journal of Psychology* 61, 183–93.

Ramsey, F. P. (1931). "Truth and probability," in *The Foundations of Mathematics and Other Logical Essays*, by F. P. Ramsey. New York: Harcourt, Brace. Reprinted in *Studies in Subjective Probability*, ed. by H. E. Kyburg and H. E. Smokler. New York: Wiley, 1964, 61–92.

Savage, L. J. (1954). *The Foundations of Statistics*. New York: Wiley. Second revised edition, Dover, 1972.

Schmeidler, D. (1982). "Subjective probability without additivity," paper for Tel Aviv University.

Slovic, P. (1967). "The relative influence of probabilities and payoffs upon perceived risk of a gamble," *Psychonomic Science* 9, 223–4.

Tversky, A. (1969). "Intransitivity of preferences," *Psychological Review* 76, 31–48.

von Neumann, J., and Morgenstern, O. (1944). *Theory of Games and Economic Behavior.* Princeton University Press. Second edition, 1947; third edition, 1953.

Whitmore, G. A., and Findlay, M. C. (eds). (1978). *Stochastic Dominance.* Lexington, Massachusetts: D. C. Heath.

5

RISKY CHOICE REVISITED

DAVID E. BELL AND HOWARD RAIFFA

THE PROBLEM

Imagine that you will shortly be asked to *consciously* select one of several urns and from this urn you will then be asked to *randomly* select one ball. For the moment, we assume that each urn contains exactly N balls (say, 1,000), and each ball in the selected urn is equally likely to be chosen. Each ball has a number on it which specifies the incremental monetary return to you for drawing that ball.

Suppose that you have the opportunity to examine the balls and their numbers in all the urns before deciding upon your choice of urn. How would you use that opportunity? A useful answer to this question would have to take some account of the length of time available for your examination. Here we will adopt the view that time is available for any extensive analysis that you would care to make.[1]

We will present three different but related techniques for choosing among urns. In order to decide when and for whom these techniques are appropriate, we shall discuss various behavioral assumptions that underlie each of these techniques. In mathematical parlance, we shall discuss necessary and sufficient behavioral assumptions that justify each of these techniques.

To describe the contents of a given urn A we will use a sequence $(a_1, a_2, \ldots, a_N)$ representing the numbers on the N balls in the urn. Of course, the particular ordering of the sequence is of no consequence since each ball is equally likely to be drawn. Thus an urn with three balls with values 0, 10, and 70 can be listed as: $(0, 10, 70)$, $(0, 70, 10)$, $(10, 0, 70)$, $(10, 70, 0)$, $(70, 0, 10)$, or $(70, 10, 0)$. Instead of talking about "a random drawing from urn A," we shall use the term "lottery A". Occasionally, we shall drop the term "lottery" and just talk about "A". We shall use the notation in Table 5.1. Expressions $A > B$ and $B < A$ are identical in meaning; so are $A \geqslant B$ and $B \leqslant A$, as well as $A \sim B$ and $B \sim A$. We emphasize that $A > B$ means that if you (as decision maker) are required to choose between A and B, then you would prefer A. It does not necessarily imply that either A or B is preferred (by you) to the status quo. Henceforth we shall delete the expression "by you" or "by the decision maker."

Table 5.1

Symbol	Meaning
$A > B$	A is preferred to B
$A \geqslant B$	A is preferred to or indifferent to B
$A < B$	A is less preferred to B
$A \leqslant B$	A is less preferred or indifferent to B
$A \sim B$	A is indifferent to B

We do *not* assume initially that any two lotteries A and B are comparable; that is, we may not be able to say whether $A > B$, $A < B$, or $A \sim B$. However we do assume the

Transitivity principle. If A and B are comparable and $A > B$, if B and C are comparable and $B > C$, then it should be that A and C are comparable and $A > C$. In symbols:

$$[A > B, B > C] \rightarrow [A > C]$$

where the symbol $\rightarrow$ is read "implies." Adopting the same notation, we also require:

$$[A \geqslant B, B > C] \rightarrow [A > C],$$

$$[A > B, B \geqslant C] \rightarrow [A > C],$$

$$[A \sim B, B \sim C] \rightarrow [A \sim C].$$

MONOTONICITY AND STOCHASTIC DOMINANCE

We initiate this presentation by imposing the following

Simple monotonicity principle. If lottery A is modified by adding a positive amount to some ball, keeping all the remaining balls fixed, then the modified lottery is preferred to the original.

It is a simple matter to use the transitivity principle and the simple monotonicity principle to deduce the

Generalized monotonicity principle. Let A be defined by the sequence $(a_1, \ldots, a_N)$. Form urn B by adding a non-negative amount Δ_j to a_j for each $j = 1, \ldots, N$. Then $B \geqslant A$; and if, in addition, at least one $\Delta_j > 0$, then $B > A$.

Note however that this principle does not imply transitivity, so in some cases it may be sufficient to assume generalized monotonicity directly, without committing oneself to transitivity.

Consider two urns $A = (a_1, \ldots, a_N)$ and $B = (b_1, \ldots, b_N)$. If $b_j > a_j$ for all j, then by the generalized monotonicity principle $B > A$. But now if we rearrange the balls in B and relabel them $(b'_1, b'_2, \ldots, b'_N)$, then it will not necessarily be true that $b'_j > a_j$. Still, we want $B > A$. This motivates the following definition.

Definition (stochastic dominance): If $A = (a_1, \ldots, a_N)$ and $B = (b_1, \ldots, b_N)$ are such that $b_j \geqslant a_j$ for all j and $>$ holds for some j, then we shall say that B *stochastically dominates A for these representations.*

It is not difficult to show that B stochastically dominates A for some representation of B and A if and only if B stochastically dominates A when the balls of each urn are ordered from worst to best.[2] Stated slightly differently: if B does not stochastically dominate A when the balls of B and A are ordered from worst to best, then there is no rearrangement of the balls in B and A that will yield stochastic dominance. Hence we can now talk about "B stochastically dominates A" without appending the extraneous phrase "for some representations of B and A."

We now state the

Stochastic dominance principle: If B stochastically dominates A, then $B > A$.

It is now easily seen that the generalized monotonicity principle implies and is implied by (or coimplies) the stochastic dominance principle.

DECREASING MARGINAL VALUE AND CUMULATIVE ADVANTAGE

We initiate this presentation by imposing the following

Principle of decreasing marginal value (DMV). In any (urn) A, the decision maker would prefer to add a positive amount Δ to a lower-valued ball than to a higher-valued ball.

In the sequel we shall often have occasion to manipulate the contents of an urn by changing the values of just two of the balls in the urn and keeping the rest of the balls fixed. If the values of the two balls (to be manipulated) in urn A are x and y, and if we label the remaining $N - 2$ balls by $\underline{z}$, then it will be convenient to represent A by the symbol $[x, y, \underline{z}]$.

The DMV principle, in this new notation, is expressible as:

$$[x + \Delta, y, \underline{z}] > [x, y + \Delta, \underline{z}] \quad \text{if} \quad x > y$$

$$\Delta > 0.$$

The DMV principle is *equivalent* to the

Risk aversion principle. In any urn A if a small positive amount is added to one ball and the same amount subtracted from a higher number ball, then the modified urn A is preferred.

That is,

$$[x + \Delta, y - \Delta, \underline{z}] > [x, y, \underline{z}] \quad \text{if} \quad x < y,$$

$$\Delta > 0,$$

$$x + \Delta < y.$$

The adjective "small" in the statement refers to the restriction that $\Delta < y - x$. These two principles can be seen to be equivalent by replacing y by $y - \Delta$ in the DMV relation and y by $y + \Delta$ in the risk aversion statement.[3]

Definition (*cumulative advantage*): Let $A = (a_1, \ldots, a_N)$ where $a_1 \leqslant a_2, \ldots, \leqslant a_N$; let $B = (b_1, \ldots, b_N)$, where $b_1 \leqslant b_2, \ldots, \leqslant b_N$; and define $\Delta_j = b_j - a_j$. B is said to have a *cumulative advantage* over A if all partial sums

$$\Delta_1, \Delta_1 + \Delta_2, \Delta_1 + \Delta_2 + \Delta_3, \ldots$$

are non-negative.

If lottery B stochastically dominates A, then certainly B has a cumulative advantage over A since $\Delta_j \geqslant 0$ for all j.

Theorem 1:

Assume the transitivity, simple monotonicity, and decreasing marginal value principles hold. If B is distinct from A and if B has a cumulative advantage over A, then $B > A$.[4]

▶ *Proof.* By DMV

$$(b_1, \ldots, b_N) \geqslant (a_1, b_2 + \Delta_1, b_3, \ldots, b_N)$$

$$\geqslant (a_1, a_2, b_3 + \Delta_1 + \Delta_2, b_4, \ldots, b_N)$$

$$\vdots$$

$$\geqslant (a_1, a_2, \ldots, a_{N-1}, a_N + \Delta_1 + \Delta_2 + \ldots + \Delta_N)$$

$$\geqslant (a_1, \ldots, a_N).$$

DMV can be used for all but the last step because the partial sums are non-negative. The last inequality requires simple monotonicity. By transitivity we have $B \geqslant A$. Since B is not identical to A, at least one partial sum is positive and thus $B > A$. ▶

Example

Suppose that you must choose one of the following 3 urns, each containing 4 numbered balls. From the urn of your choice you will select a ball at random and the number will be your prize (penalty) in dollars. Which urn do you choose?

0	1,000		−100	1,800		2,000	1,100
2,700	1,000		1,200	900		200	1,300

Urn A			Urn B			Urn C	

Such a choice is of course an individual decision and personal preferences prevail. To analyze these lotteries in accordance with the principles we have stated, we first write the lotteries as vectors in increasing order:

$$A = (0, 1000, 1000, 2700)$$

$$B = (-100, 900, 1200, 1800)$$

$$C = (200, 1100, 1300, 2000).$$

We see at once that C *stochastically dominates* B since $\Delta_1 = 300$, $\Delta_2 = 200$, $\Delta_3 = 100$, and $\Delta_4 = 200$. However, neither A and C nor A and B are comparable using stochastic dominance.

Comparing A and B, we see that $a_1 - b_1 = \Delta_1 = 100$, $\Delta_2 = 100$, $\Delta_3 = -200$ and $\Delta_4 = 900$. Therefore the partial sums Δ_1, $\Delta_1 + \Delta_2 = 200$, $\Delta_1 + \Delta_2 + \Delta_3 = 0$, and $\Delta_1 + \Delta_2 + \Delta_3 + \Delta_4 = 900$ are each non-negative, and A has a *cumulative advantage* over B and therefore $A > B$ (assuming DMV applied in your preferences).

Comparing A and C, we have $c_1 - a_1 = \Delta_1 = 200$, $\Delta_2 = 100$, $\Delta_3 = 300$, and $\Delta_4 = -700$. C does *not* have a cumulative advantage over A because the partial sum $\Delta_1 + \Delta_2 + \Delta_3 + \Delta_4 = -100$ is negative.

Our principles have led us to conclude that

$$C > B$$

$$A > B$$

but A and C are incomparable.

Therefore we have eliminated B from consideration, but the analysis has not, so far, enabled us to choose between A and C.

We now prove the following important

Corollary to theorem 1: A non-constant lottery is less desirable than the certainty of its average value. (Stated in a slightly different way: given the assumptions of theorem 1, the decision maker always prefers to get the average value of a lottery with certainty than to take his chances with the lottery.)

▶ *Proof.* Let A be the non-constant lottery $(a_1, \ldots, a_N)$ with $a_1 \leqslant a_2 \leqslant \ldots \leqslant a_N$. Let $B = (\bar{a}, \bar{a}, \ldots, \bar{a})$, a lottery with constant entry $\bar{a} = (a_1 + a_2 + \ldots + a_N)/N$. The sequence $\Delta_1, \Delta_2, \ldots, \Delta_N$ ($\Delta_j = \bar{a} - a_j$) is non-negative up to some index k and non-positive thereafter. Therefore the smallest value in the sequence $\Delta_1, \Delta_1 + \Delta_2, \ldots$ is the last, $\Delta_1 + \Delta_2 + \ldots + \Delta_N$, which is zero by definition of $\bar{a}$. Hence B has a cumulative advantage over A and $B > A$. ▶

Note that, although B has a clearly definable value or "worth," namely, $\bar{a}$, we cannot argue that A has a "worth" – only that it is less preferred than B. If each lottery were assumed to have a worth, we would be asserting implicitly that some unidimensional value scales existed for lotteries. If this were so, we could immediately compare any two lotteries merely by a simple comparison of their worths.

The principles we have invoked thus far have been extremely modest, and the conclusions that we have derived from them are also modest.[5] So far, we may only resolve comparisons where one lottery enjoys a cumulative advantage over another. For example, if half the balls in an urn are labeled 100 and the other half 0, then we cannot even say whether this urn is preferred to one with all balls labeled 2. If we want more power out of our assumptions, we will have to put more power into our assumptions.

COMPLETE COMPARABILITY AND UTILITY

We initiate this presentation by imposing the following

Augmentation principle. If urn A is preferred or indifferent to urn B (each having the same number of balls), then after adding an identically-valued ball to each urn, A remains preferred or indifferent to B.

And to be perfectly symmetrical we impose the following

Deletion principle. If urn A is preferred or indifferent to urn B (each having the same number of balls), and if A and B each have a ball with a common value, then if A and B are modified by removing this common-valued ball, A remains preferred or indifferent to B.[6,7,8]

Some people feel uncomfortable with the augmentation principle since adding an identically valued ball to each urn might alter a certainty in one of the urns to an uncertainty. Consider, for example, the following situation. Suppose that a decision maker feels that

$$(3, 3) > (0, 10)$$

because of an intrinsic reluctance to gamble. However, if a 0 ball is added to both urns, the preference may now be

$$(3, 3, 0) < (0, 10, 0)$$

because both urns involve uncertainty, and, of the two, the second is preferred. On a similar basis, we may have

$$(4) < (10)$$

but

$$(4, 4) > (10, 4);$$

however, this would violate the simple monotonicity principle.

At this point we wish to hypothesize that the decision maker, on determining that urn A is preferable to urn B (both urns containing 2 balls), can either establish an amount which, when added to one of the balls in B, would make A and B indifferent, or establish that A is preferable to B no matter how much is added to one particular ball.

We will do this in two stages:

Restricted comparability. For any urns A and B, each containing exactly two balls, either $A > B$, $A < B$, or $A \sim B$.

In other words, the decision maker can make comparisons between any two 50–50 lotteries.

Solvability principle. Let $A, B,$ and C be two-ball lotteries such that $A > C > B$. Suppose that A and B have a common-valued ball. Then there exists a two-ball lottery D of which one ball has the value of the ball common to A and B, such that $C \sim D$.

In more detail, if $A = (x^1, y^1)$, $B = (x^1, y^2)$, and $C = (x, y)$, and if $A > C > B$ then there exists a value y^+ such that

$$(x^1, y^+) \sim (x, y).$$

Observe that, if we adopt the simple monotonicity principle, then the value y^+ must be unique and must lie between y^1 and y^2. It is the solvability principle that underlies the existence of indifference curves.

Theorem 2

If we hypothesize transitivity, simple monotonicity, augmentability–deletability, restricted comparability, and solvability, then we have complete comparability (i.e., for any *two* urns A and B with the same number of balls, $A > B$ or $A < B$ or $A \sim B$).

▶ *Proof.* Suppose $A = (a_1, a_2, a_3)$ and $B = (b_1, b_2, b_3)$. Unless one urn stochastically dominates the other (in which case the preference is clear), there will be a renumbering of A *and* B such that $a_1 > b_1$ and $a_2 < b_2$. Using restricted comparability, suppose that $(a_1, a_2) > (b_1, b_2)$. By simple monotonicity we then have

$$(a_1, b_2) > (a_1, a_2) > (b_1, b_2).$$

By solvability there is a value b^+ where $b_1 < b^+ < a_1$ such that $(a_1, a_2) \sim (b^+, b_2)$. By augmentability we then have $(a_1, a_2, a_3) \sim (b^+, b_2, a_3)$.
Now compare

$$(b^+, b_2, a_3) \quad \text{and} \quad (b_1, b_2, b_3).$$

By deletability we know that this comparison is the same as that of (b^+, a_3) and (b_1, b_3), and by restricted comparability this is possible. Hence B may be compared to (b^+, b_2, a_3), which is indifferent to A. By transitivity we may compare A and B. This proves that all three-balled urns are comparable. Cases with higher numbers of common balls can be proved by induction on the number of balls. ▶

The restriction about A and B having the same number of balls may be lifted if we assume the

Proportion principle. Urns A and B are indifferent if they are proportionally equivalent (i.e., if the proportion of balls having any given value is the same in both A and B).

For example, this principle asserts that $(a) \sim (a, a) \sim (a, a, a)$ and that $(a, b) \sim (a, a, b, b)$.

Theorem 2′

Complete comparability, transitivity, and the proportion principle imply that any two lotteries A and B are comparable.

▶ *Proof.* Let A have N_1 balls and B have N_2 balls. Form urn A' from A by replicating each ball N_2 times; form B' from B by replicating each ball N_1 times. Now urns A' and B' each have N_1 times N_2 balls and by theorem 2 are comparable. By the proportion principle, $A \sim A'$ and $B \sim B'$. Thus by transitivity A and B are comparable. ▶

We may now argue that any urn has a "worth." We will interpret "worth" to mean an object is worth \$$x$ for certain. (A slightly [but significantly, for our purposes] different definition would be the amount the decision maker would *pay* for the object.)

Any urn containing balls all of the same value is evidently worth that value. Now, since all urns are comparable we may compare an arbitrary urn (a, b) with an urn (c, c). If $(a, b) > (c, c)$, we know that the decision maker would rather have (a, b) than receive c; that is, (a, b) is worth more than c. We know that (a, b) is worth less than the maximum of a and b (by simple monotonicity). By comparing (a, b) with urns of the type (c, c) – or just (c), since by theorem 2′ *all* urns are comparable – we will determine a value c^* such that $(a, b) \sim (c^*, c^*)$. We will say that urn (a, b) is *worth* c^*.

We now arrive at an analytical procedure for comparing any two lotteries. It has already been determined in theorem 2 that, if the decision maker can compare all two-ball lotteries, then it is possible to deduce, via the additional principles of behavior, what his preferences "should be" for more complex comparisons. The whole purpose of providing an analytical procedure for comparison of lotteries is not so much that decisions could thereafter be made on behalf of the decision maker, but rather that comparing complex alternatives can be a major cognitive strain and the decision maker may be unsure of his judgments. If he can be sure (i) that the principles we have proposed are reasonable for him and (ii) that we can compare two-ball lotteries, then we can infer appropriate comparisons for him over all other possible pairs of lotteries.[9]

Theorem 3

Assuming restricted comparability, transitivity, solvability, and augmentability, there exists a real-valued function u(.) such that

$$(a_1, a_2) > (b_1, b_2)$$

if and only if

$$u(a_1) + (a_2) \geqslant u(b_1) + u(b_2).$$

(The quantity $\frac{1}{2}u(a_1) + \frac{1}{2}u(a_2)$ is referred to as the [expected] utility of urn $A \equiv (a_1, a_2)$.)

▶ *Proof.*[10] Choose arbitrary levels x_0, x_1 with $x_0 < x_1$. Assign $u(x_0) = 0$, $u(x_1) = 1$. We shall now iteratively define a sequence of values $x_2, x_3, x_4, \ldots$ such that: if $i + j = m + n$, then $(x_i, x_j) \sim (x_m, x_n)$. If there exists a value x^* such that $(x_1, x_1) < (x_0, x^*)$, then by solvability there exists a value x_2 such that $(x_1, x_1) \sim (x_0, x_2)$. Similarly, if $(x_1, x_2) < (x_0, x^*)$, then there exists a value x_3 such that $(x_0, x_3) \sim (x_1, x_2)$. If $(x_0, x_4) \sim (x_1, x_3)$ is the same fashion, then we must argue that $(x_1, x_3) \sim (x_2, x_2)$. Note that $(x_0, x_4, x_0, x_2) \sim (x_1, x_3, x_0, x_2)$ by augmentation; $(x_1, x_3, x_0, x_2) \sim (x_1, x_1, x_2, x_2)$ since $(x_0, x_3) \sim (x_1, x_2)$; and $(x_1, x_1, x_2, x_2) \sim (x_0, x_2, x_2, x_2)$ since $(x_1, x_1) \sim (x_0, x_2)$. By transitivity $(x_0, x_4, x_0, x_0) \sim (x_0, x_2, x_2, x_2)$. By deletion $(x_0, x_4) \sim (x_2, x_2)$. The point is that the way the $\{x_k\}$ are constructed, if $i + j = m + n$, then $(x_i, x_j) \sim (x_m, x_n)$.

Values x_{-k} may be determined by first establishing x_{-1} by $(x_{-1}, x_1) \sim (x_0, x_0)$, then x_{-2} by $(x_0, x_{-2}) \sim (x_{-1}, x_{-1})$, and so on.

The set $\{\ldots x_{-2}, x_{-1}, x_0, x_1, x_2 \ldots\}$ so formed (the set may be finite) is used to define the function $u(.)$. Set $u(x_k) = k$ for all known x_k.

We now have a dilemma about presentation of the proof. At this point we wish to wash our hands and say that with all these points (x_n, n) on the curve u we can smooth through them to define the whole function. We could argue that if x_0 and x_1 are chosen arbitrarily closely (e.g., $x_0 = 0$, $x_1 = 0.000001$), then u is defined for all reasonable cases. We might also utilize the existence of the worth of a lottery by taking the point c, where $x_{x-1} < c < x_k$, such that $(c, c) \sim (x_{k-1}, x_k)$ and defining $u(c) = k - \frac{1}{2}$, and in this manner ultimately discovering the utility of all values. All of these approaches are equivalent and the first is at least the most practical. In case this leaves some doubt as to the veracity of the theorem, we refer the reader to the alternate (elegant!) proof in note 9.

It now remains to show that this definition of u does the job it claims in the theorem. But we have already shown that $i + j = m + n$ implies $(x_i, x_j) \sim (x_m, x_n)$. It is easy to see that $i + j > m + n$ implies $(x_i, x_j) > (x_m, x_n)$, but since $u(x_k) = k$ these statements are just what is claimed. ▶

Theorem 3'

Adding the proportion principle to the conditions of theorem 3 implies that if $A = (a_1, \ldots, a_N)$ and $B = (b_1, \ldots, b_M)$, then A is preferred or indifferent to B if and only if

$$\frac{1}{N} \left[u(a_1) + \ldots + u(a_N) \right] \leqslant \frac{1}{M} \left[u(b_1) + \ldots + u(b_M) \right].$$

▶ *Proof.*[11] This consists of reworking the proofs of theorems 2 and 2' in terms of the utility function. First, assume $M = N = 3$ as before. We know $u(a_1) + u(a_2) = u(b^+) + (b_2)$ and that $A \geqslant B$ if $u(b^+) + u(a_3) \geqslant u(b_1) + u(b_3)$ or if $u(a_1) + u(a_2) + u(a_3) \geqslant u(b_1) + u(b_2) + u(b_3)$. As before, this can be repeated for higher values of N than 3. Using the proportion principles on lotteries A' and B', we know $A' \geqslant B'$ if

$$Mu(a_1) + \ldots + Mu(a_N) \geqslant Nu(b_1) + \ldots + Nu(b_M)$$

which proves the theorem. ▶

NOTES

Previously issued as Harvard Business School Working Paper 80–34. This research was supported in part by the Defense Advanced Research Projects Agency under contract N00014-76-0074.

1 You may think that the problem posed here is rather special. But the general problem of risky choice with monetary rewards can always be transformed into this framework. For example, suppose a choice of investment strategy A will result in a *risk profile* as shown in Figure 5.1. In this figure the probability that strategy A will result in a monetary return of x *or less* is given by the height of the curve at x, which is denoted by $F_A(x)$. The curve F_A is called the *cumulative distribution function* (cdf) of monetary rewards for strategy A. A simple proof of risky choice is to choose between two cdf's F_A and F_B say. Now this problem can be converted into an urn problem

Figure 5.1 Cumulative distribution function of an investment.

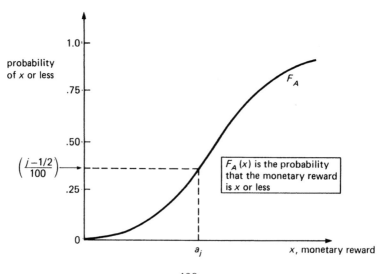

as follows: We concoct the urn to be associated with investment A in such a way that the probability of drawing a ball whose value is x or less is $F_A(x)$ for all x. This can be approximately done as follows using 100 balls – for a better approximation we can choose a larger number of balls. Suppose the balls are originally marked with labels 1 to 100. Let the payoff to be assigned to ball j be the number a_j where

$$F_A(a_j) = \frac{j - 1/2}{100} \quad \text{for} \quad j = 1, \ldots, 100.$$

The urn, so concocted, with balls labelled $a_1, a_2, \ldots, a_{100}$ mirrors the cdf F_A with little probabilistic distortion. Conversely, if we are presented initially with an urn with contents $(a_1, a_2, \ldots, a_N)$, then we can define an associated cdf F_A by letting $F_A(x) \equiv k/N$ if exactly k balls are less than or equal to x.

2 Stochastic dominance can easily be recognized in terms of cdf's. If $B = (b_1, \ldots, b_N)$ stochastically dominates $A = (a_1, \ldots, a_N)$, then from note 1 we can see that for all x, $F_A(x) \geqslant F_B(x)$ (cf. figure 5.2). And conversely, if $F_A(x) \geqslant F_B(x)$, for all x, then the associated urns $A = \{a_j\}$, $B = \{b_j\}$ where

$$F_A(a_j) = F_B(b_j) = \frac{j - 1/2}{N}, \quad \text{for} \quad j = 1, \ldots, N$$

are such that B stochastically dominates A.

Observe, however, that, if the usual associated density functions f_A and f_B are drawn, then stochastic dominance is not graphically obvious.

3 (An aside to those who know utility theory.) If a utility function, u, for money exists – and up to this point we have not assumed that it does – then the principle of decreasing marginal value is equivalent to the concavity of u. In the usual von Neumann–Morgenstern approach to utility, the concavity of u is derived from a behavioral postulate of risk aversion and not directly from a postulate of the decreasing marginal value of money. From a behavioral point of view the DMV principle seems much easier to comprehend than the risk-aversion principle.

4 It is interesting to note that it is not necessary to impose a full set of behavioral assumptions leading to a utility function in order to prove that a cumulative advantage of B over A implies preference of B over A.

5 Although our conclusions thus far are modest we have enough power to prove the following useful result:

(Example of a two-parameter family of lotteries.) Consider a subset of lotteries where each lottery is characterized by a *location* parameter (λ_A for A, λ_B for B, etc.) and a scale parameter (σ_A for A, σ_B for B, etc.). Let

$$a_i = \lambda_A + k_i \sigma_A, \quad i = 1, \ldots, N,$$

and

$$b_i = \lambda_B + k_i \sigma_B, \quad i = 1, \ldots, N.$$

Figure 5.2

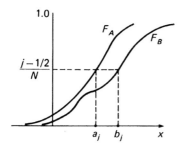

Cumulative distributions

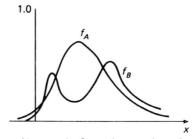

(Areas under f_A and f_B are each one.)

Density functions

109

Notice that the k_i's do not depend on which lottery of the subset is being considered. (One familiar case is the family of normal distributions where the mean is the location parameter and the standard deviation is the scale parameter.) We shall assume the scale parameter is always positive. We assume that the a_i's and b_i's are monotone increasing and this implies that

$$k_1 \leqslant k_2 \leqslant \ldots \leqslant k_N. \tag{1}$$

Now let us investigate when B has a cumulative advantage over A. We have

$$\Delta_i = (\lambda_B - \lambda_A) + k_i(\sigma_B - \sigma_A).$$

We require for each j (from 1 to N) that

$$0 \leqslant \sum_{i=1}^{j} \Delta_i = j(\lambda_B - \lambda_A) + (\sigma_B - \sigma_A)K_j \tag{2}$$

where

$$K_j \equiv \sum_{i=1}^{j} k_i.$$

An important special case is where $\lambda_B > \lambda_A$ and $\sigma_B < \sigma_A$. In this case equation (2) is equivalent to the expression

$$\frac{K_j}{j} \leqslant \frac{\lambda_B - \lambda_A}{\sigma_A - \sigma_B} \quad \text{for} \quad j = 1, \ldots, N$$

and since, because of the ordering of the k_i's (see equation (1)), K_j/j is monotone increasing, it is sufficient to require

$$\frac{K_N}{N} \leqslant \frac{\lambda_B - \lambda_A}{\sigma_A - \sigma_B}. \tag{3}$$

For the normal distribution, as well as other two-parameter symmetric distributions, $K_N = 0$, and hence equation (3) is satisfied; and hence the distribution with larger location and smaller scale parameter has a cumulative advantage; and hence it is preferred.

6 The deletion principle would immediately follow from the augmentation principle if we were only sure that all urns were comparable. If $A \geqslant B$ (each having the same number of balls) and if we delete a common-valued ball from A and B, then by the augmentation principle it is *not* possible that the reduced B is preferred to the reduced A. This, however, only implies preference or indifference of the reduced A over the reduced B if the reduced urns are assumed to be comparable.

7 The augmentation–deletion principle is equivalent to the basic *sure-thing* or *substitution* principle, as we shall now indicate. We will first remind the reader of the following definitions.

The axiom of substitutability (substitution, sure-thing principle). If a lottery is modified by replacing one of its potential consequences by another consequence which the decision maker feels is indifferent to the first, then the decision maker is indifferent between the modified lottery and the original.

An equivalent statement of this axiom is

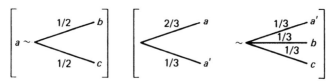

We may write it $\{[a, a] \sim [b, c]\} \rightarrow \{[a, a, a'] \sim [b, c, a']\}$. This sequence clearly demonstrates the equivalence of the augmentation and substitution principles.

8 The augmentation–deletion principle is also equivalent to the *preferential independence* principle. (Some notational preliminaries: let all balls in each urn be given a serial index: $1, 2, \ldots, N$. The value of the i'th ball in an urn will be called the value of the i'th *attribute* of that urn. An urn A can

then be said to have a profile of attribute values $(a_1, a_2, \ldots, a_N)$. Now for notational convenience we shall let X be the first attribute [with typical value x], Y be the second attribute [with typical value y], and Z be the set of remaining attributes [with typical value z].)

Preferential independence. Attributes X and Y are *preferentially independent of attributes* Z if whenever $(x', y', \underline{z}') \geqslant (x^2, y^2, \underline{z}')$ for some value $\underline{z}'$, then $(x', y', \underline{z}) \geqslant (x^2, y^2, \underline{z})$ for all values of $\underline{z}$.

Preferential independence is easily seen to be equivalent to the combined augmentation–deletion principle.

9 If we are now willing to use the full power of multi-attribute value theory (under certainty), then we can get a simple proof of the existence and interpretation of a utility function, u. More precisely we can show that any urn $A = (a_1, a_2, \ldots, a_N)$ can be compared to any other (with any number of balls) via the ranking index

$$\frac{1}{N} \sum_{i=1}^{N} u(a_i)$$

for a suitable function u.

We assume the conditions of theorem 2 and the proportion principle. Since we have complete comparability let $V(a_1, \ldots, a_N)$ be a value function for ordinal preferences. Since every pair of attributes if preferentially independent of the remainder (cf. note 8), V can be expressed as

$$V(a_1, \ldots, a_N) = \sum_{i=1}^{N} v_i(a_i), \quad \text{for} \quad N \geqslant 3$$

(see Keeney and Raiffa; *Decisions with Multiple Objectives* [New York, Wiley, 1976], theorem 3.6 and its corollary). Since the value of an urn is independent of the ordering of the balls we have $v_1 = v_2 = \ldots = v_N$. Call this common value u. We then can rank urns of size N by

$$V(a_1, \ldots, a_N) = \sum_{i=1}^{N} u(a_i).$$

In order to rank urns with unequal numbers of balls all we have to do is divide by N and use the index

$$\frac{1}{N} \sum_{i=1}^{N} u(a_i).$$

This last step follows from the proportionality principle.

If we wish to consider a 2-balled urn (e.g., (a_1, a_2)), then we can merely double the number of balls and we would then have

$$V(a_1, a_2) = V(a_1, a_1, a_2, a_2)$$
$$= \tfrac{1}{4}[u(a_1) + u(a_1) + u(a_2) + u(a_2)]$$
$$= \tfrac{1}{2}[u(a_1) + u(a_2)].$$

Hence the argument holds for $N = 2$ as well as higher N.

10 We wish to prove that we can rank 2-balled lotteries by means of an additive value function without the use of the argument in note 9 which specializes a result for $N \geqslant 3$ down to $N = 2$. In order to use the full power of multi-attribute value theory (under certainty) for two attributes we would have to invoke the corresponding tradeoffs condition (see Keeney and Raiffa, *op. cit.*, theorem 3.2). The *corresponding tradeoffs condition* (CTC) states: If, whenever

$$(x', y') \sim (x' + a, y' - b) \tag{1}$$

$$(x', y^2) \sim (x' + a, y^2 - c) \tag{2}$$

and

$$(x^2, y') \sim (x^2 + d, y' - b), \tag{3}$$

then

$$(x^2, y^2) \sim (x^2 + d, y^2 - c). \tag{4}$$

111

We will show that the substitution principle (see note 7) implies that the CTC holds:

$$[x', y', x^2, y^2] \sim [x' + a, y^2 - c, x^2, y'] \sim [x' + a, y^2 - c, x^2 + d, y' - b] \sim [x', y', y^2 - c, x^2 + d].$$

Hence $[x^2, y^2] \sim [y^2 - c, x^2 + d]$ as required.

The following theorems of ordinal preference can now be invoked:

Theorem. Assumptions of restricted comparability, transitivity and solvability are enough to establish the existence of a value function $V(x_1, x_2)$ over the set of 2-ball lotteries.

Theorem. A value function for preferences over attributes X, Y that satisfy the corresponding tradeoffs condition has an additive representation of

$$V(x, y) = v_1(x) + v_2(y).$$

It is now a simple matter to argue, by interpretation, that $v_1 = v_2$. Calling this common value u, we have

$$V(x, y) = u(x) + u(y)$$

as was to be shown.

11 *Alternate proof*

It will suffice to prove that

$$(a_1, a_2, \ldots, a_N) \sim (\hat{a}, \hat{a}, \ldots, \hat{a})$$

where

$$\frac{1}{N} \sum_{i=1}^{N} u(a_i) = u(\hat{a}).$$

Since an alternate, more rigorous proof is furnished in note 9, we shall prove the above result for $N = 3$. By theorem 2, we have

$$(a_1, a_2, a_3) \sim (a^1, a^1, a_3)$$

where

$$u(a^1) = \tfrac{1}{2} u(a_1) + \tfrac{1}{2} u(a_2).$$

We next have

$$(a^1, a^1, a_3) \sim (a^1, a^2, a^2)$$

where

$$\begin{aligned}
u(a^2) &= \tfrac{1}{2} u(a_1) + \tfrac{1}{2} u(a_3) \\
&= \tfrac{1}{2}[\tfrac{1}{2} u(a_1) + \tfrac{1}{2} u(a_2)] + \tfrac{1}{2} u(a_3) \\
&= \tfrac{1}{4} u(a_1) + \tfrac{1}{4} u(a_2) + \tfrac{1}{2} u(a_3).
\end{aligned}$$

Proceeding in this fashion, we define a sequence of values $a^1, a^2, a^3, \ldots$ where

$$\begin{aligned}
u(a^n) &= \tfrac{1}{2} u(a^{n-1}) + \tfrac{1}{2} u(a^{n-2}), \quad n = 3, 4, \ldots, \\
&= c'_n u(a_1) + c'_n u(a_2) + c''_n u(a_3)
\end{aligned}$$

where

$$c''_n = \tfrac{1}{3}\left[\frac{2^n - 1}{2^n}\right] \quad \text{and} \quad c'_n = \tfrac{1}{2}[1 - c''_n],$$

and

$$(a_1, a_2, a_3) \sim (a^{n-1}, a^{n-1}, a^n).$$

In the limit, $a^n \to \hat{a}$, and by continuity we have

$$(a_1, a_2, a_3) \sim (\hat{a}, \hat{a}, \hat{a})$$

where

$$u(\hat{a}) = \tfrac{1}{3} u(a_1) + \tfrac{1}{3} u(a_2) + \tfrac{1}{3} u(a_3).$$

6

BEHAVIORAL DECISION THEORY: PROCESSES OF JUDGMENT AND CHOICE

HILLEL J. EINHORN AND ROBIN M. HOGARTH

INTRODUCTION

Why are normative theories so prevalent in the study of judgment and choice, yet virtually absent in other branches of science? For example, imagine that atoms and molecules failed to follow the laws supposed to describe their behavior. Few would call such behavior irrational or suboptimal. However, if people violate expected utility axioms or do not revise probabilities in accord with Bayes's theorem, such behavior is considered suboptimal and perhaps irrational. What is the difference, if any, between the two situations? In the latter we implicitly assume that behavior is purposive and goal-directed while this is less (if at all) obvious in the former. (It is problematic how one might treat plant and animal behavior according to a descriptive–normative dichotomy.) Therefore, if one grants that behavior is goal-directed, it seems reasonable to assume that some ways of getting to the goal are better, in the sense of taking less time, making fewer errors, and so on, than others. Indeed, much of decision research concerns evaluating and developing ways for improving behavior, thereby reflecting a strong engineering orientation (Edwards, 1977; Hammond, Mumpower and Smith, 1977; Keeney and Raiffa, 1976). Moreover, comparison of actual behavior with normative models has been important in focusing attention on the discrepancies between them, and this in turn has raised important questions about the causes of such discrepancies.

Central to normative theories are the concepts of rationality and optimality. Recently Simon (1978) has argued for different types of rationality, distinguishing between the narrow economic meaning (i.e., maximizing behavior) and its more general dictionary definition of "being sensible, agreeable to reason, intelligent." Moreover, the broader definition itself rests on the assumption that behavior is functional. That is,

> Behaviors are functional if they contribute to certain goals, where these goals may be the pleasure or satisfaction of an individual or the guarantee of food or shelter for the members of society ... It is not necessary or implied that the adaptation of

113

institutions or behavior patterns of goals be conscious or intended ... As in economics, evolutionary arguments are often adduced to explain the persistence and survival of functional patterns and to avoid assumptions of deliberate calculation in explaining them. (pp. 3–4)

Accordingly, Simon's concept of "bounded rationality," which has provided the conceptual foundation for much behavioral decision research, is itself based on functional and evolutionary arguments. However, although one may agree that evolution is nature's way of doing cost/benefit analysis, it does not follow that all behavior is cost/benefit efficient in some way. We discuss this later with regard to misconceptions of evolution, but note that this view: (a) is unfalisifiable (see Lewontin, 1979, on "imaginative reconstructions"); (b) renders the concept of an "error" vacuous; (c) obviates the distinction between normative and descriptive theories. Thus, while it has been argued that the difference between bounded and economic rationality is one of degree, not kind, we disagree.

The previous review of this field (Slovic, Fischhoff and Lichtenstein, 1977) described a long life of human judgmental biases, deficiencies, and cognitive illusions. In the intervening period this list has both increased in size and influenced other areas of psychology (Bettman, 1979; Mischel, 1979; Nisbett and Ross, 1980). Moreover, in addition to cataloging the types of errors induced by the manner in which people make judgments and choices, concern has now centered on explaining the causes of both the existence and persistence of such errors. This is exemplified by examination of a basic assumption upon which adaptive and functional arguments rest, namely the ability to learn (Einhorn & Hogarth, 1978; Hammond, 1978a; Brehmer, 1980). However, if the ability to learn is seriously deficient, then dysfunctional behavior can not only exist but also persist, thus violating the very notion of functionality. It is therefore essential to delimit the conditions under which this can occur. Indeed, the *general* importance of considering the effects of specific conditions on judgment and choice is emphasized by the following irony: the picture of human judgment and choice that emerges from the literature is characterized by extensive biases and violations of normative models whereas in work on lower animals much choice behavior seems consistent with optimizing principles (e.g., Killeen, 1978; Rachlin and Burkhard, 1978; Staddon and Motheral, 1978). The danger of such pictures is that they are often painted to be interesting rather than complete. In the next section we consider the complexities involved in evaluating discrepancies between optimal models and human responses, and how persistent dysfunctional behavior is consistent with evolutionary concepts.

ARE OPTIMAL DECISIONS REASONABLE?

How are discrepancies between the outputs of optimal models and human responses to be evaluated? First, consider the latter to be generated through a cognitive model of the task and note the different possibilities: (a) both models could inadequately represent the task, but in different ways: (b) the optimal model is a more adequate representation than that of the person – indeed, this is the assumption upon which most decision research is predicated; and (c) the person's model is more appropriate than the optimal model – a hypothesis suggested by March (1978). Furthermore, in the absence of discrepancies, neither model could be appropriate if they misrepresent the environment in similar ways. Therefore, before one compares discrepancies between optimal models and human judgments, it is important to compare each with the environment.

Task vs. optimal model of task

We begin by offering a definition of optimality; namely, decisions or judgments that maximize or minimize some explicit and measurable criterion (e.g. profits, errors time) *conditional on certain environmental assumptions and a specified time horizon.* The importance of this definition is that it stresses the conditional nature of optimality. For example, Simon (1979) points out that, because of the complexity of the environment, one has but two alternatives: either to build optimal models by making simplifying environmental assumptions, or to build heuristic models that maintain greater environmental realism (also see Wimsatt, 1980). Unfortunately, the conditional nature of optimal models has not been appreciated and too few researchers have considered their limitations. For instance, it has been found that people are insufficiently regressive in their predictions (Kahneman and Tversky, 1973). While this is no doubt true in stable situations, extreme predictions are not suboptimal in nonstationary processes. In fact, given a changing process, regressive predictions are suboptimal. The problem is that extreme responses can occur at random or they can signal changes in the underlying process. For example, if you think that Chrysler's recent large losses are being generated by a stable process, you should predict that profits will regress up to their mean level. However, if you take the large losses as indicating a deteriorating quality of management and worsening market conditions, you should be predicting even more extreme losses. Therefore, the optimal prediction is conditional on which hypothesis you hold.

The above is not an isolated case. For example, Lopes (1980) points out that the conclusion that people have erroneous conceptions of randomness (e.g., Slovic, Kunreuther, and White, 1974) rests on the assumption that well-defined criteria of randomness exist. She convincingly demonstrates that this is not the case. (Or consider the work on probability revision within the Bayesian framework (e.g., Slovic and Lichtenstein, 1971).) Much of this work makes assumptions (conditional independence, perfectly reliable data, well-defined sample spaces) that may not characterize the natural environment. Moreover, alternative normative models for making probabilistic inferences have been developed based on assumptions different from those held by Bayesians (Shafer, 1976; Cohen, 1977; also see Schum, 1979, for a discussion of Cohen). In fact, Cohen's model rests on a radically different system that obeys rules quite different from the standard probability calculus. Competing normative models complicate the definition of what is a "bias" in probability judgment and has already led to one debate (Cohen, 1979; Kahneman and Tversky, 1979b). Such debate is useful if for no other reason than that it focuses attention on the conditionality of normative models. To consider human judgment as suboptimal without discussion of the limitations of optimal models is naive. On the other hand, we do not imply that inappropriate optimal models always, or even usually, account for observed discrepancies.

The definition of optimality offered above deals with a single criterion or goal. However, actual judgments and choices typically are based on multiple goals or criteria. When such goals conflict, as when they are negatively correlated (e.g., quantity and quality of merchandise, cf. Coombs and Avrunin, 1977), there can be no optimal solution in the same sense as the single criterion case (Shepard, 1964). That is, the most one can do is to execute the trade-offs or compromises between the goals that reflect one's values. Therefore, the imposition of (subjective) values for resolving conflicts leads to rejecting "objective" optimality and replacing it with the criterion of consistency with one's goals and values. Furthermore, even the single goal situation is transformed into a multiple goal case when judgments and choices are considered over time. For example, consider the single goal of maximizing profit. Conflicts between short-run and longer-run strategies can exist even with a single well-defined criterion. Therefore, unless a time horizon is specified, optimality can also be problematic in what might seem to be simple situations.

Environment vs. problem space

The importance to behavior of the cognitive representation of the task, i.e., "problem space," has been emphasized by Newell and Simon (1972). It is now clear that the process of representation and the factors that affect it are of major importance in judgment and choice. Illustrations of the effects of problem representation on behavior are found in work on estimating probabilities via fault trees (Fischhoff, Slovic and Lichtenstein, 1978); response model effects inducing preference reversals (Grether and Plott, 1979); coding processes in risky choice (Kahneman & Tversky, 1979a); "problem isomorphs" in problem solving (Simon and Hayes, 1976); context effects in choice (Aschenbrenner, 1978; Tversky and Sattath, 1979) and agenda setting (Plott and Levine, 1978); purchasing behavior (Russo, 1977); and causal schemas in probability judgments (Tversky and Kahneman, 1980a).

It is essential to emphasize that the cognitive approach has been concerned primarily with *how* tasks are represented. The issue of *why* tasks are represented in particular ways has not yet been addressed. However, given functional arguments, this is a crucial issue in view of the way minor contextual changes can lead to the violation of the most intuitively appealing normative principles, e.g., transitivity.

The reconciliation of persistent errors and biases with functional arguments

116

has taken two forms. First, it has been claimed that such effects can be overcome by increasing incentives (through higher payoffs and/or punishments). In one sense, this argument is irrefutable since it can always be claimed that the incentive was not high enough. However, direct evidence shows that increased payoffs do not necessarily decrease extreme overconfidence (Fischhoff, Slovic, and Lichtenstein, 1977) or prevent preference reversals (Grether and Plott, 1979). Furthermore, the indirect evidence from clinical judgment studies in naturally occurring settings, where payoffs are presumably high enough to be motivating, continues to indicate low validity and inferiority to statistical models (Dawes, 1979). In addition, claims that people will seek aids/or experts when the stakes are high (Edwards, 1975) are predicated on the assumptions that: (a) people know that they do not know; and (b) they know (or believe) that others do. On the other hand, it is foolish to deny that payoffs, and thus motivation, have no effect on processes of judgment and choice. Indeed, only one needs to recall the fundamental insight of signal detection theory (Green & Swets, 1966), which is that both cognitive and motivational components affect judgment (also see Killeen, 1978).

A second way of reconciling biases with functional arguments involves enlarging the context in which performance is evaluated. This has taken four forms: 1. One view of evolutionary theory (as espoused by the sociobiologists; for example, Wilson, 1978) could lead to the belief that the human system represents the optimal design for a complex environment. Heuristics exist because they serve useful functions and their benefits outweigh their costs. While this view is often espoused, there is surprisingly little evidence to support it. An important exception is the simulation study by Thorngate (1980), where it was shown how heuristics can often pick the best of several alternatives across a range of tasks. However, neither this study nor any other that we are aware of has considered the distribution of tasks in the natural environment in which heuristics would work well or poorly. 2. Hogarth (1980a) has argued that most judgments and choices occur sequentially and that many biases reflect response tendencies which are functional in dynamic environments. Furthermore, the static tasks typically investigated reflect a preoccupation with those relatively simple situations for which optimal models can be constructed. 3. Toda (1962) has claimed that it is coordination of behavior that reflects an organism's efficiency, not individual and thus isolated actions. Furthermore, coordination between functions requires trade-offs and these can be facilitated by limitations (e.g., a limited memory facilitates efficient forgetting of needless detail). 4. Cost/benefit analyses can be expanded to include "the cost of thinking" (Shugan, 1980), which seems compatible with notions of bounded rationality.

While there is much merit in the above arguments, care must be taken since they can easily become tautological; i.e., costs and benefits can be defined *post hoc* in accord with a presumption of optimality. However, can there be actual dysfunctional behavior (rather than seeming dysfunctional behavior) that persists, and, if so, by what mechanism(s)?

Since functional arguments rest on evolutionary theory, it is easy to overlook the fact that nonadaptive behavior can also be compatible with principles of natural selection: 1. Biological evolution is directly related to the amount of variance in the genotype (Lewontin, 1979). For example, the development of wings could be functional for humans on many occasions. However, without an appropriate mutation (the chance of which is miniscule), such evolution cannot take place. While it is evident that physical limitations preclude certain types of behavior regardless of incentives to the contrary, biological limitations can also preclude certain cognitive operations (Russo, 1978). For example, the study of memory indicates limitations on short-term storage and retrieval. Furthermore, Seligman (1970) has explicated biological limitations in the learning process itself. Cognitive limitations can therefore persist and be dysfunctional (relative to given goals) for the same reasons that account for physical limitations. 2. The time-frame of human biological evolution is such that it can be considered constant over many generations. It is thus difficult to determine whether any current trait or mechanism is becoming more or less adaptive, or is a vestige without apparent function (e.g., the human appendix; see also Skinner, 1966). Therefore, without denying general cost/benefit considerations over the very long run, dysfunctional behaviors may persist for extremely long periods by human standards. The demise of the dinosaur, for example, is popularly cited as an example of the effectiveness of natural selection. However, it is easy to forget that dinosaurs existed for about 160 million years. So far, humans are a mere 2.5 million years (Sagan, 1977). 3. Humans adapt the environment to their own needs as well as adapting to the environment. For example, poor eyesight is certainly dysfunctional, yet a major judgment aid, eye glasses, has been invented to deal with this problem. Furthermore, note that this aid actually works against natural selection, i.e., those with poor vision will not be selected against since their survival chances are now equal to those without the need for glasses. In fact, if poor eyesight were correlated with higher reproductive rates, there would be an increase in the aggregate level of this deficiency. 4. The analogy has been drawn between learning and evolution (e.g., Campbell, 1960). However, the attempt to link individual learning with species level survival is problematic (Lewontin, 1979). For example, consider whether response competition within an organism can be viewed as identical to competition between organisms. While the latter can and has been analyzed via game theoretic ideas of zero-sum payoffs and conflicting interests, such an approach seems foreign to individual response competition.

Intuitive responses and optimal models

The above arguments leave us on the horns of a dilemma. Given the complexity of the environment, it is uncertain whether human responses or optimal models are more appropriate. Furthermore, we know of no theory or set of principles that would resolve this issue. Indeed, the optimal–intuitive comparison presents the following paradox: Optimal models have been suggested to overcome intuitive shortcomings. However, in the final analysis the outputs of optimal models are evaluated by judgment, i.e., do we like the outcomes, do we believe the axioms to be reasonable, and should we be coherent?

If the assessment of rationality ultimately rests on judgment, what are its components? To discuss this, imagine being a juror in a trial and having to decide whether someone who has committed a heinous crime acted "rationally." The prosecution argues that the crime was meticulously planned and carried out, thus demonstrating that the person was in complete control of what he/she was doing. Note that this argument defines rationality by the efficiency with which means are used to attain ends. Moreover, this manner of defining rationality is exactly what decision theorists have stressed, that is, given one's goals, what is the best way of attaining them. However, the defense argues that the goal of committing such a crime is itself evidence of irrationality. That is, rationality is to be judged by the goals themselves. Moreover, the argument is made that the deliberative way such despicable goals were reached is itself an indication of irrationality. Finally, the defense argues that when one understands the background of the defendant (the poverty, lack of parental love, etc.) the irrational goals are, in fact, reasonable. This last point emphasizes that goals can only be understood within the person's task representation. Moreover, this argument highlights a crucial problem; namely, to what extent *should* one be responsible for one's task representation (cf. Brown, 1978)?

What are the implications of the above for behavioral decision theory? First, judgments of rationality can be conceptualized as forming a continuum which can be dichotomized by imposing a cutoff when actions must be taken. This idea has been advanced by Lopes (1980) with respect to judging randomness. Moreover, she suggests that the placement of the cutoff can be viewed within a signal-detection framework; i.e., payoffs and costs are reflected by the cutoff point. Secondly, judged rationality is a mixture of the efficiency of means to ends (called "instrumental rationality," Tribe, 1973) and the "goodness" of the goals themselves (cf. Brown, 1978). While the former is familiar to decision theorists, the latter is the concern of moral philosophers, theologians, and the like. However, at a practical level it is of concern to all. In fact, it may well be that the efficacy of decision aids comes from structuring tasks so that the nature of one's goals is clarified (Humphreys and McFadden, 1980). Thirdly, the importance of *behavioral* decision theory lies in the fact that, even if one were willing to accept instrumental rationality as the sole criterion for evaluating decisions, knowledge of how tasks are represented is crucial since people's goals form part of their models of the world. Moreover, their task representation may be of more importance in defining errors than the rules they use within that representation. For example, imagine a paranoid who processes information and acts with remarkable coherence and consistency. Such coherence of beliefs and actions is likely to be far greater than in so-called "normal" people (when does coherence become rigidity?). Thus, the representation of the world as a place where others

119

persecute one is the source of difficulty, and not necessarily the incorrect or inconsistent use of inferential rules or decision strategies.

STRATEGIES AND MECHANISMS OF JUDGMENT AND CHOICE

The inescapable role of intuitive judgment in decision making underscores the importance of descriptive research concerned with how and why processes operate as they do. Moreover, the most important empirical results in the period under review have shown the sensitivity of judgment and choice to seemingly minor changes in tasks. Such results illustrate the importance of context in understanding behavior in the same way that the context of a passage affects the meaning of individual words and phrases. We consider context to refer to *both* the formal structure and the content of a task. On the other hand, normative models gain their generality and power by ignoring content in favor of structure and thus treat problems out of context (cf. Shweder, 1979). However, content gives meaning to tasks and this should not be ignored in trying to predict and evaluate behavior. For example, consider the logical error of denying the antecedent; i.e., "if *A*, then *B*" does not imply "if not-*A*, then not-*B*." However, as discussed by Harris and Monaco (1978), the statement "If you mow the lawn (*A*), I'll give you $5 (*B*)" does imply that if you do not mow the lawn (not-*A*) you will not get the $5 (not-*B*). Or consider a choice between a sure loss of $25 and a gamble with 3:1 odds in favor of losing $100 vs. $0. Compare this with the decision to buy or not buy an insurance policy for a $25 premium to protect you against a .75 chance of losing $100. Although the two situations are structurally identical, it is possible for the same person to prefer the gamble in the first case yet prefer the insurance policy in the second (for experimental results, see Hershey and Schoemaker, 1980a). Such behavior can be explained in several ways: (a) the person may not perceive the tasks as identical since content can hide structure (Einhorn, 1980); and (b) even if the two situations are seen as having identical structure, their differing content could make their meaning quite different. For example, buying insurance may be seen as the purchase of protection (which is good) against the uncertainties of nature, while being forced to choose between two painful alternatives is viewed as a no-win situation.

While context has typically been defined in terms of task variables, it is clear from the above examples that it is also a function of what the person brings to the task in the way of prior experience via learning, and biological limitations on attention, memory, and the like, that affect learning. Therefore, the elements of a psychological theory of decision making must include a concern for task structure, the representation of the task, and the information processing capabilities of the organism.

In order to discuss specific findings in the literature, we artificially decompose processes of judgment and choice into several subprocesses, namely, information acquisition, evaluation, action, and feedback/learning. We are well aware that these subprocesses interact and that their interaction is of great importance in the organization and coordination of decision making. Accordingly, we consider these issues within subsections where appropriate.

The role of acquisition in evaluation

Much work in judgment and choice involves the development and testing of algebraic models that represent strategies for evaluating and combining information (see Slovic and Lichtenstein, 1971). Although work in this tradition continues (e.g., Anderson, 1979), it has been accompanied by increasing dissatisfaction in that processes are treated in a static manner; i.e., judgments and choices are considered to be formed on the basis of information that is given. In contrast, the process of information search and acquisition should also be considered (cf. Elstein, Shulman, and Sprafka, 1978) since evaluation and search strategies are interdependent. In fact, the evaluation strategies proposed in the literature imply various search processes either explicitly (e.g., Tversky and Sattath, 1979) or implicitly (Payne, 1976). Of great importance is the fact that the concern for how information is acquired raises questions about the role of attention and memory in decision making that have received relatively little concern (however, see Hogarth, 1980b; Rothbart, 1980). Furthermore, concern for the dynamics of information search has necessitated the use of different methodologies; e.g., process-tracing approaches such as verbal protocols and eye movements, as well as information display boards (Payne, 1976). However, these methods need not replace more general modeling efforts and may in fact be complementary to them (Payne, Braunstein, and Carroll, 1978; Einhorn, Kleinmuntz, and Kleinmuntz, 1979).

The importance of considering the interdependence of evaluation and acquisition can be seen in considering the issue of whether people lack insight into the relative importance they attach to cues in their judgment policies. The literature contains conflicting evidence and interpretations (Nisbett and Wilson, 1977; Schmitt and Levine, 1977). However, the use of weights in models as reflecting differential cue importance ignores the importance of attention in subjective weight estimates and illustrates our emphasis on understanding persons and tasks. Correspondence between subjective and statistical weights requires that people attend to and evaluate cues and that such cues contain both variance and low intercorrelations. Disagreement between subjective and statistical weights can thus occur for three reasons: (a) people indeed lack insight; (b) people attend to, but cannot use, cues that lack variance (Einhorn *et al.*, 1979); (c) cues to which attention is not paid are correlated with others such that the nonattended cues receive inappropriate statistical weights. Both process-tracing methods and statistical modeling are necessary to untangle these competing interpretations.

Acquisition

Acquisition concerns the processes of information search and storage – both in memory and the external environment. Central to acquisition is the role of attention since this necessarily precedes the use and storage of information. We discuss attention by using an analogy with the perceptual concept of figure–ground noting that, as in perception, the cognitive decomposition of stimuli can be achieved in many ways. Accordingly, different decompositions may lead to different task representations (cf. Kahneman and Tversky, 1979a). Indeed, context can be thought of as the meaning of figure in relation to ground.

In an insightful article, Tversky (1977) analyzed the psychological basis of similarity judgments, and in so doing emphasized the importance of context and selective attention in judgmental processes. He first noted that our knowledge of any particular object "is generally rich in content and complex in form. It includes appearance, function, relation to other objects, and any other property of the object that can be deduced from our general knowledge of the world" (p. 329). Thus, the process of representing an object or alternative by a number of attributes or features depends on prior processes of selective attention and cue achievement. Once features are achieved, the similarity between objects a and b, $s(a, b)$, is defined in terms of feature sets denoted by A and B, respectively. Thus,

$$s(a, b) = \theta f(A \cap B) - \alpha f(A\text{-}B) - \beta f(B\text{-}A) \tag{1}$$

where $A \cap B$ = features that a and b have in common; $A\text{-}B$, $B\text{-}A$ = distinctive features of a and b, respectively; f = salience of features; and θ, α, and β are parameters. Note that equation (1) expresses $s(a, b)$ as a weighted linear function of three variables thereby implying a compensatory combining rule. The importance of equation (1) lies in the concept of salience (f) and the role of the parameters. Tversky first defines salience as the intensity, frequency, familiarity, or more generally the signal-to-noise ratio of the features. Thereafter, the way in which the f scale and the parameters depend on context is discussed. We consider three important effects: asymmetry and focus, similarity vs. differences, diagnosticity and extension.

Asymmetry in similarity judgments refers to the fact that the judged similarity of a to b may not be equal to the similarity of b to a. This can occur when attention is focused on one object as subject and the other as referent. For example, consider the statements, "a man is like a tree" and "a tree is like a man." It is possible to judge that a man is more like a tree than vice versa, thus violating symmetry (and metric representations of similarity). The explanation is that in evaluating $s(a, b)$ vs. $s(b, a)$, $\alpha > \beta$ in 1; i.e., the distinct features of the subject are weighted more heavily than those of the referent. Hence, the focusing of attention results in differential weighting of features such that symmetry is violated.

The similarity/difference effect occurs when $\alpha = \beta$ and $s(a, b) = s(b, a)$. In judging similarity, people attend more to common features, while, in judging difference, they attend more to distinctive features. This leads to the effect in which "a pair of objects with many common and many distinctive features may be perceived as both more similar and more different than another pair of objects with fewer common and fewer distinctive features" (Tversky, 1977, p. 340).

The first effect results from a shift in attention due to focusing on an anchoring point (the subject). The second is caused by a shift in attention induced by different response modes. The third effect, diagnosticity and extension, involves changes in the salience of the features in an object due to the specific object set being considered. For example, consider the feature "four wheels" in American cars. Such a feature is not salient since all American cars have four wheels. However, a European car with three wheels on an American road would be highly salient. Therefore, salience is a joint function of intensity and what Tversky calls diagnosticity, which is related to the variability of a feature in a particular set (cf. Einhorn and McCoach, 1977). An important implication of diagnosticity is that the similarity between objects can be changed by adding to (or subtracting from) the set. For example, consider the similarity between Coca-Cola and Pepsi-Cola. Now add 7-Up to the set and note the increased similarity of the colas.

Although Tversky's paper is of great importance for judgment and choice, it has not been linked to earlier concepts such as representativeness, anchoring and adjusting, or availability. However, the question of context and the figure–ground issues which underlie similarity would seem to be of great importance in understanding these heuristics and their concomitant biases as well as a wide range of phenomena in the literature. To illustrate, we first discuss work on base rates.

Earlier work (reviewed in Slovic *et al.*, 1977) indicated that subjects ignore base rates, and it was postulated that this resulted from use of the representativeness heuristic and/or the apparent salience of concrete or vivid information (Nisbett *et al.*, 1976). However, a base rate can only be defined conditional on some population (or sample space). Whereas many might agree that the base rates defined by experimenters in laboratory tasks make the sample space clear, the definition of the population against which judgments should be normalized in the natural ecology is unclear. Consider an inference concerning whether someone has a particular propensity to heart disease. What is the relevant population to which this person should be compared? The population of people in the same age group? The population of the United States? Of Mexico? There is no generally accepted normative way of defining the appropriate population. Thus, for naturally occurring phenomena it is neither clear whether people do or do not ignore base rates, nor clear whether they should (see also Goldsmith, 1980; Russell, 1948).

Even in the laboratory, base rates are not always ignored. Indeed, Tversky and Kahneman (1980a) have argued that base rates will be used to the extent that they can be causally linked to target events. Their data supported this hypothesis, and Ajzen (1977) independently reached similar results and conclusions. A further implication of causal thinking concerns asymmetries in the use of information; i.e., information that receives a causal interpretation is weighted more heavily in judgment than information that is diagnostic (although probability theory accords equal weight to both). Whether such judgments are biased or not depends on whether one believes that causality should be ignored in a normative theory of inference (as is the case in standard probability theory; see Cohen, 1977, 1979, for a different view).

Bar-Hillel (1980) further explicated the conditions under which base rates are used. She argued that people order information by its perceived degree of relevance to the target event (with high relevant dominating low relevant information). Causality, Bar-Hillel argued, is but one way of inducing relevance (it is sufficient but not necessary). Relevance can also be induced by making target information more specific, which is tantamount to changing the figure–ground relationship between targets and populations. We believe that further elucidation of the role of causality in judgment is needed (Mowrey, Doherty, and Kelley, 1979) and note that the notion of causality, like probability, is conditional on the definition of a background or "causal field" (Mackie, 1965).

Central to the distinction between figure and ground is the concept of cue redundancy. As Garner (1970) has stated, "good patterns have few alternatives," i.e., cue redundancy helps achievement of the object and thus sharpens figure from ground. Tversky (1977) makes the point that for familiar, integral objects there is little contextual ambiguity; however, this is not the case for artificial, separable stimuli. For example, consider the differential effects of acquiring information from intact or decomposed stimuli (the former being more representative of the natural ecology, the latter of experimental tasks). Phelps and Shanteau (1978) have shown that, when expert livestock judges are presented with information in the form of 11 decomposed, orthogonal attributes of sows, they are capable of using all the information in forming their judgment; however, when presented with intact stimuli (photographs), their judgments can be modeled by a few cues. These results illustrate that people can handle more information than previously thought; moreover, they can be interpreted as indicating that cue redundancy in the natural ecology reduces the need for attending to and evaluating large numbers of cues. Redundancy in the natural ecology also implies that cues can indicate the presence of other cues and can thus lead one to expect cue co-occurrences. For example, in a study of dating choice, Shanteau and Nagy (1979) showed that subjects used cues not presented by the experimenters. That is, when choosing between potential dates from photographs, subjects' choices were influenced by the probability that their requests for dates would be accepted even though this cue was not explicitly given.

The importance of redundancy in acquisition has been discussed by Einhorn *et al.* (1979), who note the following benefits: "(a) Information search is limited without large losses in predictive accuracy; (b) attention is highly selective; (c) dimensionality of the information space is reduced, thereby preventing information overload; (d) intersubstitutability of cues is facilitated; and (e) unreliability of cues is alleviated by having multiple measures of the same cue variable" (p. 466). Studies and models that fail to consider cue redundancy in search processes are thus incomplete. For example, consider risky choice in the natural ecology vs. the laboratory (for reviews of risk see Libby and Fishburn, 1977, and Vlek and Stallen, 1980). In the former, probabilities are typically not explicit and must be judged by whatever environmental cues are available. A particularly salient cue is likely to be the size of the payoff itself, especially if people have beliefs about the co-occurrence of uncertainty and reward (e.g., large payoffs occur with small probabilities). Thus, payoff size can be used as a cue to probability (cf. Shanteau and Nagy, 1979). Moreover, the degree of perceived redundancy may also be important in understanding issues of ambiguity in decision making (cf. Yates and Zukowski, 1976). That is, one's uncertainty about a probability estimate (so-called second order probability) may be related to a variety of cues, including payoff size. In fact, Pearson (1897) noted that, although means and variances of distributions are usually treated as independent, in the natural ecology they tend to be correlated and can thus be used as cues to each other. The analogy to means and variances of payoff distributions from gambles seems useful.

The temporal order of information acquisition can also affect salience, both by creating shifts in figure–ground relations and differential demands on attention and memory. Consider, for example, the effects of simultaneous vs. sequential information display. In a study of supermarket shopping, Russo (1977) found that, when unit prices were presented to shoppers in organized lists (ordered by relative size of unit prices, hence simultaneous presentation), purchasing behavior was changed relative to the situation where shoppers either did not have unit price information or such information was simply indicated next to products on the shelves (the latter implying sequential acquisition). An interesting aspect of this study is that it represents a form of decision aiding quite different from those proposed in earlier work. That is, instead of helping people to evaluate information that has already been acquired (e.g., through bootstrapping or multiattribute models), one eases strain on memory and attention by aiding the acquisition process itself. However, that greater understanding of attention and memory processes is necessary for this approach to be successful was underscored in a study by Fischhoff *et al.* (1978) on the use of "fault trees." Fault trees are diagnostic check lists represented in treelike form. The task studied by Fischhoff *et al.* (1978) involved automobile malfunction and had both experts (i.e., automobile mechanics) and novices as subjects. The results indicated that the apparently comprehensive format of the fault tree blinded both expert and novice subjects to the possibility of missing causes of malfunction.

Since information is normally acquired in both intact form and across time (i.e., sequentially), determining the manner and amount of information to be presented in acquisition aids is a subject of great importance. It raises issues of both how external stimuli cue memory and the organization of memory itself (Broadbent, Cooper, and Broadbent, 1978; Estes, 1980). Different ways of organizing information, for example by attributes or by alternatives in a choice situation, could have implications for task representation. In addition, several recent studies of the "availability" heuristic (Tversky and Kahneman, 1973) have further emphasized how ease of recall from memory has important effects on judgment (Kubovy, 1977). Moreover, experimenters should be aware that subjects interpret stimuli rather than respond to them. For example, Tversky and Kahneman (1980a) show that, when information is presented in a manner involving an ambiguous time sequence, intuitive interpretations may reflect a reordering of that information to conform to the time dependence of naturally occurring phenomena.

That the figure–ground relation at a particular point in time affects judgment and choice has been demonstrated in a number of studies. A particularly compelling example is given by Tversky and Kahneman (1980b): It is expected that a certain flu will kill 600 people this year and you are faced with two options: option 1 will save about 200 people; option 2 will save about 600 people with probability of $\frac{1}{3}$ and no people with probability of $\frac{2}{3}$. Now consider a rewording of the alternatives: option 1 will result in about 400 people dying; option 2 gives a $\frac{1}{3}$ probability that none will die and a $\frac{2}{3}$ chance that about 600 people will die. By a simple change in the reference point induced by formulating the same problem in terms of lives lost or saved, cognitive figure and ground are reversed, as were the choices of a majority of subjects. Similar preference reversals can be obtained through the isolation effect where sequential representation of information can isolate and hence highlight the common components of choice alternatives. Aspects seen to be common to alternatives are canceled out and the choice process determined by comparing the distinctive features of the alternatives.

Payne, Laughhunn, and Crum (1979) have linked reference effects to the dynamic concept of aspiration level and further illustrated how this affects the encoding of outcomes as losses or gains relative to a standard (rather than considering the overall wealth position implied by different end states). Sequential effects in choice have also been demonstrated by Levine and Plott (1977) and Plott and Levine (1978) in both field and laboratory studies. The structure of an agenda was shown to affect the outcomes of group choice by sequencing the comparisons of particular subsets of alternatives. Tversky and Sattath (1979) have further considered implications of these effects within individuals when sequential elimination strategies of choice are used. That judgment should be affected in a relative manner by momentary reference points should, however, come as no surprise (cf. Slovic and Fischhoff, 1977). Weber's law predicts just this, and the prevalence of "adjustment and anchoring" strategies in dynamic judgmental tasks is congruent with these findings (Hogarth, 1980a).

Cognitive figure–ground relations vary considerably on the ease with which they can be reversed. On the one hand, the tendency not to seek information that could disconfirm one's hypotheses (Mynatt, Doherty, and Tweney, 1977, 1978) illustrates strong figure–ground relations where confirming evidence is attracted to the figure and possible disconfirming evidence remains in the ground. Consider also the difficulty of reformulating problem spaces in creative efforts where inversion of figure and ground is precisely what is required. On the other hand, situations also arise where figure and ground can invert themselves with minor fluctuations in attention, as in the case of "reversible figures" in perception. Whereas the analogy one could draw between "preference reversals" and "reversible figures" is possibly tenuous, both do emphasize the role of attention. In particular, its fluctuating nature implies that, for certain types of stimulus configurations, task representations can be unstable. Both choice and the application of judgmental rules have often been stated to be inherently inconsistent and hence probabilistic (Brehmer, 1978; Tversky and Sattath, 1979). However, the effects of fluctuating attention in producing such inconsistencies has not been explored.

Lest it be thought that the importance of attention in acquisition is limited to descriptive research, Suppes (1966) has stated: "What I would like to emphasize . . . is the difficulty of expressing in systematic form the mechanisms of attention a rationally operating organism should use" (p. 64). Furthermore, Schneider and Shiffrin (1977) have raised the possibility that attention is not completely under conscious control. Thus the normative problem posed by Suppes takes on added difficulty.

Evaluating/action

Imagine that you are faced with a set of alternatives and have at your disposal the following evaluation strategies: conjunctive, disjunctive, lexicographic, elimination by aspects, additive, additive difference, multiplicative, majority of confirming instances, or random. Furthermore, you could also use combinations of any number of the above. How do you choose? The wide range of strategies one can use in any given situation poses important questions about how one decides to choose (Beach and Mitchell, 1978; Svenson, 1979; Wallsten, 1980). For example, what environmental cues "trigger" particular strategies? What effects the switching of rules? Are strategies organized in some way (e.g., hierarchically), and, if so, according to what principles? Although there has been concern for metastrategies, most notably in Abelson's "script" theory (1976), the need for general principles is acute. This can be illustrated in the following way: each evaluation strategy can be conceptualized as a multidimensional object containing such attributes as speed of execution, demands on memory (e.g., storage and retrieval), computational effort, chance of making errors, and the like. However, each strategy could also be considered as a metastrategy for evaluating itself and others. For example, an elimination by aspects metastrategy would work by eliminating strategies sequentially by distinctive attributes. However, the choice of a metastrategy would imply a still higher level choice process, thereby leading to an infinite regress.

The above emphasizes the need for finding principles underlying choice processes at all levels. One appealing possibility suggested by Christensen-Szalanski (1978, 1980) is that of an overriding cost/benefit analysis, which can induce suboptimal behavior in particular circumstances. However, this raises several issues: 1. The meaning of costs and benefits is necessarily dependent on task representation, and thus context. For example, a tax cut can be viewed as a gain or a reduced loss (Kahneman and Tversky, 1979a; also see Thaler, 1980, for an illuminating discussion of how this affects economic behavior). 2. Cost/benefit "explanations" can always be applied after the fact and thus become tautological (see earlier discussion). 3. The very notion of balancing costs and benefits indicates that conflict is inherent in judgment and choice. For instance, consider our earlier example of the options of insuring against a possible loss versus facing a no-win situation. The former can be conceptualized as an approach–avoidance conflict, the latter as an avoidance–avoidance conflict. In fact, Payne *et al.* (1979) have demonstrated the importance of considering the perceived conflict in choice in the following way: Subjects first made choices between pairs of gambles. A constant amount of money was then added or subtracted from the payoffs such that, for example, an approach–avoidance gamble was changed to an approach–approach situation. With gambles altered in this manner, systematic preference reversals were found. Hence, while the structure of the gambles remained unchanged, the nature of the conflict and the choices did not.

The importance of conflict in choice has been emphasized by Coombs and Avrunin (1977), who considered the joint effects of task structure and the nature of pleasure and pain. They begin by noting the prevalence of single-peaked preference functions (i.e., nonmonotonic functions relating stimulus magnitude to preference) in a wide variety of situations. For example, consider the usual belief that more money is always preferred to less. While this violates single-peakedness, note that great wealth increases the risk of being kidnapped, of social responsibility to spend wisely, of lack of privacy, and so on. Thus, if one also considered these factors, it may be that there is some optimal level beyond which more money is not worth the increased trouble. Hence, there is an approach–avoidance conflict between the "utility for the good" and the "utility for the bad." The nature of this conflict eventuates in a single-peaked function, given the behavioral assumption that "Good things satiate and bad things escalate" (p. 224). Therefore, at some point, the bad becomes greater than the good and overall utility decreases. (In the single object case, it is not central that the bad escalate, only that it satiate at a slower rate than the good.)

The theory becomes more complex when objects are characterized on multiple dimensions. For example, consider a number of alternatives that vary on price and quality and suppose that some are both higher in price and lower in quality than others. Such dominated alternatives would seem to be eliminated quickly from further consideration. Indeed, the second principle in the theory is just this: dominated options are ignored. Hence, the alternatives that remain form a Pareto optimal set. While single-peakedness requires stronger conditions than this, from our perspective the important point is that the remaining set of alternatives highlights the basic conflict: that is, higher quality can only be obtained at a higher cost.

While the role of conflict in choice has received earlier attention (Miller, 1959), its usefulness for elucidating psychological issues in decision making has not been fully exploited (however, see Janis and Mann, 1977). We consider some of these issues by examining the role of conflict in, respectively, judgments of worth or value, deterministic predictions, and probabilistic judgments. Subsequently, conflict in taking action is discussed.

Conflict in judgment

Consider the conflict between subgoals or attributes when one is judging overall value or worth. If dominated alternatives are eliminated, this will result in negative correlations between the attributes of objects in the nondominated set, thereby ensuring that one has to give up something to obtain something else. The resolution of the conflict can take several forms, the most familiar being the use of compensatory strategies (usually of additive form, although multiplicative models have also been used, cf. Anderson, 1979). Psychologically, this approach can be thought of as conflict "confronting" since conflict is faced and resolution achieved through compromise. Of crucial concern in executing one's compromise strategy is the issue of judgmental inconsistency (Hammmond and Summers, 1972). While the origin of such inconsistency is not well understood (cf. Brehmer, 1978), it has often been considered as reflecting environmental uncertainty (Brehmer, 1976). However, inconsistency may exist in the absence of environmental uncertainty., For example, price and quality can each be perfectly correlated with overall worth, yet one could argue that this highlights the conflict and thus contributes to inconsistency. Although the theoretical status of conflict and inconsistency needs further development, it should be noted that methods for aiding people to both recognize and reduce conflict through compensatory compromise have been developed, and several applications are particularly noteworthy (Hammond and Adelman, 1976; Hammond, Mumpower, and Smith, 1977).

Alternatively, conflict in judging overall worth can be resolved by avoiding direct confrontation and compromise. Specifically, noncompensatory strategies allow evaluation to proceed without facing the difficulties (computational and emotional) of making trade-offs. As indicated above, the conditions in both task and person that control strategy selection remain relatively unchartered. However, in addition to the error/effort trade-offs thought to influence such decisions (Russo, 1978), the existence of conflict *per se* and the need to take it into account makes this issue problematic.

The evaluation of information in making predictions from multiple cues raises further questions concerning conflict in judgment. In particular, when a criterion is available for comparison one can consider conflict and uncertainty to arise from several sources: uncertainty in the environment due to equivocal cue–criterion relations; inconsistency in applying one's information combination strategy; and uncertainty regarding the weighting of cues appropriate to their predictiveness. These three aspects and their effects on judgmental accuracy have been considered in great detail within the lens model framework (Hammond *et al.*, 1975). Moreover, the integration of uncertain and contradictory evidence, which is at the heart of prediction, can be seen as an attempt to establish "compensatory balance in the face of comparative chaos in the physical environment" (Brunswik, 1943, p. 257). Brunswik called this process "vicarious functioning," and Einhorn *et al.* (1979) have expanded on this to show that the compensatory process captured in linear models can also be seen in the fine detail of process-tracing models developed from verbal protocols. Furthermore, they argued that linear models represent cognitively complex and sophisticated strategies for information integration. However, the continued predictive superiority of bootstrapping, and even equal-weight linear models, over clinical judgment (Dawes, 1979) attests to the difficulty of establishing the correct compensatory balance (also see Armstrong, 1978a, b, and Dawes, 1977, for further work on the statistical vs. clinical prediction controversy).

The basic issues involved in studying deterministic predictive judgment also underlie interest in probability judgment. That is, both are concerned with the making of inferences from uncertain and conflicting data/evidence. However, the different terminologies used in each approach reflect different historical antecedents; the psychology of inference on the one hand, and a formal theory of evidence (de Finetti, Savage) on the other. Formal approaches are concerned with developing general structures for inferential tasks independent of specific content. However, as noted previously, the psychology of inference is intimately concerned with both content and structure. This distinction is central for understanding the discrepancies between the outputs of formal models and intuitive processes found in recent research. To illustrate, whereas causality has no role in probability theory, it is important in human inference (Tversky and Kahneman, 1980a). Moreover, the existence of causal schemas can lead to the reinforcement of a person's cognitive model after receiving contradictory evidence, rather than its revision. Schum (1980) has demonstrated the enormous statistical intricacies involved in the Bayesian modeling of inferences made from unreliable data. Indeed, one interpretation of this work is that a purely formal approach cannot handle the evaluation of evidence in any relatively complex task (such as a trial). The role of content, however, in simplifying these tasks has not been explored. For example, the use of a heuristic such as representativeness, which depends on content via similarity, takes on added importance in a normative sense (cf. Cohen, 1979). That is, in the face of great complexity, the use of heuristics and content may be necessary to induce structure.

The importance of heuristics in making inferences has long been recognized (Polya, 1941, 1954), and current interest in them seems well justified. However, their present psychological status requires more specification (cf. Olson, 1976). For example, the use of the same heuristic can lead to opposite predictions (for an example concerning "availability," see Einhorn, 1980). In addition, the ease with which heuristics can be brought to mind to explain phenomena can lead to their nonfalsifiability. For example, if representativeness accounts for the nonregressiveness of extreme predictions, can adjustment and anchoring explain predictions that are too regressive?

As in deterministic predictions, there has been much concern with the accuracy of probabilistic judgment. However, measurement of accuracy raises issues of defining criteria and the adequacy of samples. Moreover, in the Bayesian framework subjective probabilities represent statements of personal belief and therefore have no objective referent. Nonetheless, Bayesian researchers have borrowed relative frequency concepts to measure how well probabilistic judgment is calibrated, i.e., the degree to which probability judgments match empirical relative frequencies (Lichtenstein, Fischhoff, and Phillips, 1977) and what variables affect calibration (Lichtenstein and Fischhoff, 1977). Calibration has therefore become the accuracy criterion for probabilistic judgment similar to the achievement index in the lens model. Moreover, the research findings in the two paradigms are also similar; that is, most people are poorly calibrated and even the effectiveness of training is limited for generalizing to other tasks (Lichtenstein and Fischhoff, 1980).

Judgment = choice?

Is judgment synonymous with choice? The normative model treats them as equivalent in that alternative x will be chosen over y if and only if $u(x) > u(y)$; i.e., evaluation is necessary and sufficient for choice. However, from a psychological viewpoint, it may be more accurate to say that while judgment is generally an aid to choice, it is neither necessary nor sufficient for choice. That is, judgments serve to reduce the uncertainty and conflict in choice by processes of deliberative reasoning and evaluation of evidence. Moroever, taking action engenders its own sources of conflict (see below) so that judgment may only take one so far; indeed, at the choice point, judgment can be ignored. The distinction between judgment and choice, which is blurred in the normative model, is exemplified in common language. For example, one can choose in spite of one's better judgment whereas the reverse makes little sense.

The distinction made above should not be construed to mean that judgment and choice are unrelated. In many situations they are inseparable. For example, consider diagnostic and prognostic judgments and the choice of treatment in clinical situations. It seems unthinkable that the choice of treatment could proceed without prior diagnosis and prognosis. More generally, this example illustrates several further points: (a) since judgment is deliberative, there must be sufficient time for its formation; (b) deliberation can itself be affected by the size of payoffs – e.g., people may invest in judgment to insure against accusations of irresponsibility from others and from oneself in the event of poor outcomes (cf. Hogarth, 1980b); (c) when alternatives are ordered on some continuum, a quantitative judgment may be necessary to aid choice, as when choosing a therapy that varies in intensity. These examples point to the importance of considering the conditions under which judgment and choice are similar or different, a crucial question that has barely been posed.

Hillel J. Einhorn and Robin M. Hogarth

Conflict in action

The conflict inherent in taking action, as distinct from conflict in judgment, occurs because action implies greater commitment (cf. Beach and Mitchell, 1978; Janis and Mann, 1977). Such commitment induces conflict in several ways: 1. Whereas the existence of alternatives implies freedom to choose, the act of choice restricts that very freedom. Hence, keeping "one's options open" is in direct conflict with the need to take action. 2. Given a set of nondominated alternatives, Shepard (1964) has stated, "at the moment when a decision is required the fact that each alternative has both advantages and disadvantages poses an impediment to the attainment of the most immediate sub-goal; namely, escape from the unpleasant state of conflict induced by the decision problem itself" (p. 277). Thus, conflict is inherent in choice as an attribute of the choice situation. 3. Unlike judgments, actions are intimately tied to notions of regret and responsibility. For example, consider the decision to have children faced by married career women. An important component in this choice may involve imagining the regret associated with both alternatives later in life. Or imagine the conflict involved in choosing a place to live and work where the responsibility to oneself and the responsibility to one's family do not coincide.

As with the resolution of conflict in judgment, conflict resolution in action can involve either avoidance or confrontation. One important form of avoidance is to not choose. Corbin (1980) has recognized the importance of the "no choice" option noting that it can take three forms: refusal, delay, and inattention. Moreover, she notes that attraction to the status quo has two advantages: it involves less uncertainty, and there may be "less responsibility associated with the effects of 'doing nothing' than with some conscious choice" (Corbin, 1980). Toda (1980a) points out that people often make "meta-decisions" (e.g., to smoke) to avoid the conflict of having to continually decide on each of many future occasions. Thaler and Shiffrin (1980) further point out the importance of developing and enforcing self-imposed rules (rather than allowing oneself discretion) in avoiding conflicts in self-control problems.

Although choice involves considerable conflict, the mode of resolution typically considered in the literature is a confronting, compensatory strategy embodied in the expected utility model. This model is based on the following tenets: 1. The expected utility, $E(U)$, of a gamble whose payoffs are x and y with probabilities p and q $(p + q = 1.0)$, is given by $E(U) = p\,u(x) + q\,u(y)$. Note from the formulation that: (a) the rule says that the evaluation of a gamble is a weighted average of future pleasures and pains, where the weights are probabilities of attaining these outcomes; (b) the evaluation is solely a function of utility and probability, there being no utility or disutility for gambling *per se*; (c) the rule assumes that payoffs are independent of probabilities, i.e., wishful thinking (optimism) or pessimism are not admissible; (d) there is no inconsistency or error in executing the rule. Thus, although the rule specifically deals with the uncertainty of future events, it does not consider the evaluation process itself to be probabilistic (however, see Luce, 1977). Moreover, choice is assumed to follow evaluation by picking the alternative with the highest $E(U)$. 2. The theory assumes that the utility of payoffs is integrated into one's current asset position. Hence, final asset positions determine choice, not gains and/or losses. 3. Although not central to $E(U)$, it is generally assumed that people are risk averse, i.e., utility is marginally decreasing with payoff size.

Whereas the $E(U)$ model has been proposed as a prescriptive theory, much confusion exists in that it has been used extensively to both explain and predict behavior. However, while the descriptive adequacy of $E(U)$ has been challenged repeatedly (Anderson and Shanteau, 1970; Slovic *et al.*, 1977), Kahneman and Tversky's "prospect theory" (1979a) represents a major attempt at an alternative formulation. Since elements of this theory are discussed throughout this review, we only consider the proposed evaluation model. Prospect theory superficially resembles the $E(U)$ model in that the components involve a value function, v; decision weights, $\pi(p)$; and a compensatory combining rule. However, the value function differs from utility in that: 1. It is defined on deviations from a reference point (where $v(0) = 0$) rather than being defined over total assets. Furthermore, the reference point may be either identical to or different from the asset position depending on a number of factors (somewhat akin to Helson's adaptation level). 2. It is concave for gains but convex for losses, inducing "reflection effects" via risk aversion for gains and risk seeking for losses. For example, consider the choice between \$3,000 and a .50 chance at \$6,000 or 0. While many would prefer the sure gain of \$3,000 to the gamble (thus exhibiting risk aversion), if the sign of the payoff is changed, e.g., $-\$3,000$ or a .50 chance at $-\$6,000$ or 0, they might prefer the gamble to the sure loss. Note that the reflection effect contradicts the widely held belief that people generally abhor and seek to avoid uncertainty (Hogarth, 1975; Langer, 1977). 3. It is steeper for losses than gains, i.e., the pain of losing is greater than the pleasure of winning an equal amount.

Although decision weights are not subjective probabilities as such, they reflect the impact of uncertainty on the evaluation of prospects (gambles) and are transformations of probabilities. They have several interesting properties; for example, the sum of complementary decision weights does not sum to one (subcertainty), and small probabilities are overweighted. These properties, when combined with those of the value function in bilinear form induce overweighting of certainty (thus resolving Allais's paradox), violations of the substitution axiom, and avoidance of probabilistic insurance. Karmarkar (1978, 1979) was also able to explain many similar violations of the $E(U)$ model by transforming probabilities into weights (using a single parameter) and then incorporating them in what he called a subjectively weighted utility model.

Although the above models are an important step in analyzing choice behavior, March (1978) has made a penetrating analysis of the deficiencies in conceptualizing tastes/preferences in such models. He points out that people are often unsure about their preferences (see also Fischhoff, Slovic, and Lichtenstein, 1980) and that uncertainty concerning future preferences complicates the modeling of choice. For example, how does one model the knowledge that one's tastes will change over time but in unpredictable ways? Moreover, although instability and ambiguity of preferences are treated as deficiencies to be corrected in normative approaches and as random error in descriptive models, March (1978) points out that "goal ambiguity like limited rationality, is not necessarily a fault in human choice to be corrected but often a form of intelligence to be refined by the technology of choice rather than ignored by it" (p. 598).

The management of conflict induced by unstable preferences over time is also central to self-control (Thaler, 1980). The recognition that one's tastes can change, and that such changes are undesirable, leads to precommitment strategies to prevent the harm that follows such changes. For example, consider saving money in Christmas clubs which pay no interest but which restrict the freedom to withdraw money before Christmas in order to protect one against one's self. Such behavior is difficult to explain without resort to a multiple-self model (Freud, 1960; Sagan, 1977; Toda, 1980b). Conceptualizing decision conflict as the clash between multiple selves is a potentially rich area of investigation and could provide useful conceptual links between phenomena of individual and group behavior. For example, individual irrationality might be seen as similar to the various voting paradoxes found in group decision making (Plott, 1976).

LEARNING/FEEDBACK

The beginning of this review indicated a questioning of the basic assumption upon which functional and adaptive arguments rest, namely, the ability to learn. We now consider this in light of our discussion of heuristic and other rule-based behavior. For example, how are rules tested and maintained (or not) in the face of experience? Under what conditions do we fail to learn about their quality? Are we aware of our own rules?

Hammond (1978a) and Brehmer (1980) have discussed a number of important issues bearing on the ability to learn from experience. The former paper considers six "modes of thought" for learning relations between variables which include: true experiments, quasi-experiments, aided judgment, and unaided intuitive judgment. Moreover, these modes vary on six factors, including the degree to which variables can be manipulated and controlled, feasibility of use, and covertness of the cognitive activity involved in each. Hammond points out that the most powerful modes (involving experimentation) are least feasible and thus not likely to be implemented. Unfortunately, the least powerful modes are most feasible and hence most common. Thus, correct learning will be exceptionally difficult since it will be prey to a wide variety of judgmental biases (Campbell, 1959). The seriousness of this is further emphasized by the seeming lack of awareness of the inadequacy of unaided judgment. Brehmer (1980) has further considered the difficulties inherent in learning from experience by contrasting such learning with laboratory studies (and formal learning through teaching).

The former is far more difficult in that: (a) we do not necessarily know that there *is* something to be learned; or (b) if we do, it is not clear *what* is to be learned; and (c) there is often much ambiguity in judging *whether* we have learned (e.g., what, if anything, did the US learn from the Vietnam war?).

The general difficulties of learning from experience have also been demonstrated in specific areas. For example, Shweder (1977) has analyzed the ability of adults to learn environmental contingencies and points out that: 1. Whereas adults are capable of correlational reasoning, they frequently use cognitive strategies that can result in the genesis and perpetuation of myths, magic, and superstitious behavior. 2. Judgments of contingency are frequently based on likeness and similarity. For example, the treatment of ringworm by fowl excrement in primitive societies is based on the similarity of symptoms to "cure." 3. Contingencies provide the links in structuring experience by implying meaning through context. For example, "the trip was not delayed because the bottle shattered" can be understood when speaking of "launching a ship."

The learning of contingencies between actions and outcomes is obviously central for survival. Moreover, contiguity of actions and outcomes is an important cue for inferring causality (Michotte, 1963) and thus for organizing events into "causal schemas" (Tversky and Kahneman, 1980a). A particularly important type of contingent learning that has received little attention involves the learning and changing of tastes and preferences. For example, consider the unpleasant effect felt by a child after eating a particular vegetable, and the ensuing negative utility so learned; or imagine the changes in the same child's taste for members of the opposite sex as he or she grows older. Concern with the normative model, in which tastes are fixed, has obscured important psychological questions about the nature of tastes/preferences (cf. March, 1978).

The learning of action–outcome connections illustrates an obvious but essential point, that is, learning occurs through outcome feedback (cf. Powers, 1973). Moreover, since multiple actions must be taken over time, judgment is often required to predict which actions will lead to specified outcomes. Thus, feedback from outcomes is used to evaluate both judgments and actions. This assumes that the quality of decisions can be assessed by observing outcomes. Nonetheless, decision theorists have pointed out that outcomes also depend on factors that people cannot control; hence, decisions should be evaluated by the process of deciding. While there is much merit in this argument, the distinction between good/bad decisions and good/bad outcomes is strongly counterintuitive and may reflect several factors: (a) people have a lifetime of experience in learning from outcomes; (b) whereas process evaluation is complex, outcomes are visible, available, and often unambiguous; and (c) evaluation of process is conditional upon an appropriate representation of the task (see above). People cannot ignore outcomes in evaluating decisions.

The role of outcome feedback has been studied extensively within a number of probability learning paradigms. However, Estes (1976a, b) has emphasized the importance of considering what is learned in such tasks. In a series of experiments using simulated public opinion polls, he found that subjects coded outcomes as frequencies rather than probabilities. Indeed, as the history of probability indicates, the notion of probability was late in developing, a key difficulty being the specification of the sample space (such problems persist; see Bar-Hillel and Falk, 1980). Einhorn and Hogarth (1978) note that the transformation of frequency into probability requires paying attention to nonoccurrences of the event of interest as well as the event itself. This added burden on attention and memory may thus favor the coding of outcomes as frequencies rather than probabilities. Moreover, the tendency to ignore nonoccurrences is intimately related to the lack of search for disconfirming evidence (Wason and Johnson-Laird, 1972; Mynatt *et al.*, 1977, 1978). Furthermore, attempts to alter this tendency have been generally unsuccessful, although Tweney *et al.* (1980) have reported some success. Whether or not this tendency can be modified, we note that it is not limited to scientific inference; e.g., how many people seek disconfirming evidence to test their political, religious, and other beliefs by reading newspapers and books opposed to their own views?

The implications of the above for learning from experience were explored by Einhorn and Hogarth (1978). They specifically considered how confidence in judgment is learned and maintained despite low (or even no) judgmental validity. The tasks analyzed are those in which actions are based on an overall evaluative judgment and outcome feedback is subsequently used to assess judgmental accuracy. However, the structure of this task makes learning difficult in that: 1. When judgment is assumed to be valid, outcomes that follow action based on negative judgment cannot typically be observed. For example, how is one to assess the performance of rejected job applicants? 2. Given limited feedback (which can also result from a lack of search for disconfirming evidence), various task variables such as base rates, selection ratios, and the self-fulfilling treatment effects of taking action *per se* can combine to produce reinforcement through positive outcome feedback. Thus, one can receive positive feedback in spite of, rather than because of, one's judgmental ability. A formal model of this process was developed in which outcomes were generated by combining various task variables with the validity of judgment. The results indicated a wide range of conditions where overconfidence in poor judgment can be learned and maintained.

Of great importance to the issue of learning from experience is the role of awareness of the task factors that can influence outcomes. This includes the probabilistic nature of the task itself (cf. Brehmer, 1980), as well as other task variables discussed in multiple-cue probability learning studies (Hammond *et al.*, 1975). Einhorn (1980) has discussed this issue within the concept of outcome-irrelevant learning structures (OILS). This refers to the fact that in certain tasks positive outcome feedback can be irrelevant or even harmful for correcting poor judgment when knowledge of task structure is missing or seriously in error. This concept is obviously similar to the notion of "superstitious" behavior (Skinner, 1948; Staddon and Simmelhag, 1971). However, the concept of OILS raises the issue of what is reinforced (Wickelgren, 1979). For example, consider a consumer who uses a conjunctive rule when purchasing a wide range of products. It could be argued that positive outcomes following purchases reinforce the use of the rule, the specific behaviors, or both. This is a complex issue that would seem to depend on the extent to which people are aware of their own judgmental rules (Hayek, 1962; Nisbett and Wilson, 1977; Smith and Miller, 1978). That is, to what extent are judgmental rules reinforced without awareness, and can inappropriate rules be *un*learned? The importance of this question is that it raises the issue of whether, or to what extent, procedures for correcting judgmental deficiencies can be developed.

It is important to stress that awareness of task structure does not necessarily lead to learning (see Castellan, 1977). Furthermore, it is possible to choose not to learn. For example, consider a waiter in a busy restaurant who believes he can predict those customers most likely to leave generous tips, and the quality of his service reflects this prediction. If the quality of service has a treatment effect on the size of the tip, the outcomes confirm the prediction. With awareness of the task structure, the waiter could perform an experiment to disentangle the treatment effects of quality of service from his predictions; i.e., he could give poor service to some of those judged to leave good tips and good service to some of those judged to leave poor tips. Note that the waiter must be willing to risk the possible loss of income if his judgment is accurate, against learning that his judgment is poor. Therefore, there is conflict between short-run strategies for action that result in reasonably good outcomes vs. long-run strategies for learning that have potential short-run costs. That is, would you be willing to risk the loss of income by doing a real experiment in order to learn? This dilemma is quite frequent, yet it is not clear that awareness of it would lead to the choice to learn.

METHODOLOGICAL CONCERNS

The substantive matters discussed in this review raise various issues regarding the methodology of decision research. We consider some of these by posing the following questions: 1. How can we know whether applications of decision aids improve the quality of decisions? 2. How prevalent are judgmental biases in the natural environment? 3. What methods are most likely to provide insight into decision processes?

The review by Slovic *et al.* (1977) reported a growing number of applications of decision aids in a wide variety of fields and this growth continues (see, e.g., Jungermann, 1980, and references). However, it is appropriate to ask whether such applications work and how one can know this. While care in applying basic principles of experimental design involving consideration of threats to internal and external validity are recognized in some applications (cf. Russo, 1977), many more can be characterized as one-shot case studies where the experimental treatment is the decision aid or procedure. Although painful, it might be remembered that such a design is scientifically useless for assessing treatment efficacy. Moreover, the fact that clients are likely to seek aid from decision analysts (broadly defined) when things are not going well renders evaluation of pretest–posttest designs lacking control groups particularly susceptible to regression effects.

The difficulties in evaluating decision aids have been noted by Fischhoff (1980), who draws an analogy between decision analysis and psychotherapy. He writes that, "like psychotherapy, decision analysis is advocated because the theory is persuasive, because many clients say that it helps them, because many practitioners are extremely talented and because the alternative seems to be to sink back into an abyss (seat-of-the-pants decision making)." Indeed, we note that decision analysis might be called "rational therapy" if that term were not similar to one already in use (see Ellis, 1977, on "rational-emotive therapy"). The importance of Fischhoff's analogy is twofold: it raises basic questions regarding the evaluation of decision aids, and it provides some necessary (if not sufficient) motivation to do something about it.

The issue concerning the prevalence of judgmental biases in the natural environment raises familiar questions of external validity (Brunswik, 1956). Ebbesen and Konečni (1980) have studied several judgment tasks within laboratory and natural settings (e.g., setting of bail, driving a car) and have found major differences in results. In receiving these and other studies they conclude:

> There is considerable evidence to suggest that the external validity of decision making research that relies on laboratory simulations of real-world decision problems is low. Seemingly insignificant features of the decision task and measures cause people to alter their decision strategies. The context in which the decision problem is presented, the salience of alternatives, the number of cues, the concreteness of the information, the order of presentation, the similarity of cue to alternative, the nature of the decomposition, the form of the measures, and so on, seem to affect the decisions that subjects make.

Given the above, the issue of external validity is not liable to be resolved without recourse to theory that attempts to answer how tasks vary between the laboratory and the natural environment and what kinds of effects can be expected from such differences. Howell & Burnett (1978) have taken a first step in this direction by proposing a cognitive taxonomy based on task variables and response demands that affect judgments of uncertainty. However, greater concern with how people's experience influences their judgment is needed. For example, Bar-Hillel (1979) has pointed out that although people ignore sample size in certain laboratory studies, they seem to judge sample accuracy by the ratio of sample size to population. Furthermore, she emphasizes that such a rule can be justified in the natural environment since one typically samples without replacement. For example, "When dining out, one samples, without replacement, some dishes from a menu and generalizes about the restaurant's quality. When shopping in a new store, one samples, without replacement, the price of several items and judges how expensive the store is" (p. 250).

138

Lacking theoretical guidance, one has no recourse but to judge the prevalence of judgmental biases. There are two extreme views. The most optimistic asserts that biases are limited to laboratory situations which are unrepresentative of the natural ecology. However, Slovic *et al.* (1977) point out that in a rapidly changing world it is unclear what the relevant natural ecology will be. Thus, although the laboratory may be an unfamiliar environment, lack of ability to perform well in unfamiliar situations takes on added importance. The pessimistic viewpoint is that people suffer from 'cognitive conceit" (Dawes, 1976); i.e., our limited cognitive capacity is such that it prevents us from being aware of its limited nature. Even in a less pessimistic form, this view is highly disturbing and emphasizes the importance of further research on the factors which foster or impede awareness of the quality of one's judgmental rules.

Both of the above positions presuppose the internal validity of the experimental evidence concerning judgmental biases. However, Hammond (1978b) has criticized much of this research by pointing out the inadequacy of exclusive reliance on between-subjects designs for studying cognition. For example, he notes that many experimental demonstrations of "illusory correlation" rest on the incorrect specification of the sampling unit; i.e., the sampling unit should be defined by the stimuli judged (within each person), not the people doing the judging. Thus, while group data may indicate large effects unless sufficient stimuli are sampled, no single individual can be shown to exhibit the bias (see also Hershey and Schoemaker, 1980b). However, within-subjects designs can also be problematic in that effects due to memory when responding to stimuli across time (e.g., anchoring and carry-over) may distort the phenomenon being studied (Greenwald, 1976). This is particularly important when considering possible biases in judgment made in unique circumstances. Hence, the temporal spacing between administration of stimuli is a crucial variable in within-subjects designs and its effects also need to be studied.

While there is controversy regarding the appropriateness of different experimental designs for studying decision processes, there is more agreement on the need for multimethod approaches (Payne *et al.*, 1978). Such approaches, which can use methods as diverse as statistical modeling and verbal protocols or eye movements, not only provide much needed evidence on convergent validity, but may also be necessary to discriminate between strategies that can result in identical outcomes (Einhorn *et al.*, 1979; Tversky and Sattath, 1979). Furthermore, in addition to positive scientific effects, multimethod approaches may have the salutary effect of convincing researchers that "truth" can be shared.

CONCLUSION

Decision making is a province claimed by many disciplines, e.g., economics, statistics, management science, philosophy, and so on. What then should be the role of psychology? We believe this can be best illustrated by the economic concept of "comparative advantage." For example, how much typing should the

139

only lawyer in a small town perform (Samuelson, 1948)? Even if the lawyer is an excellent typist, it is to both his/her and the town's advantage to concentrate on law, provided that typing is not a rare skill. Similarly, we believe that psychologists can best contribute to decision research by elucidating the basic psychological processes underlying judgment and choice. Indeed, this review has tried to place behavioral decision theory within a broad psychological context, and in doing so we have emphasized the importance of attention, memory, cognitive representation, conflict, learning, and feedback. Moreover, the interdependence and coordination of these processes suggest important challenges for understanding complex decision making. In order to meet these, future research must adopt a broader perspective (cf. Carroll, 1980) by investigating not only the topics discussed here, but also those not usually treated in the decision literature (e.g., creativity, problem solving, concept formation, etc). Indeed, given the ubiquity and importance of judgment and choice, no less a perspective will do.

NOTE

* We wish to thank Jay Russo for his many incisive comments on an earlier draft of this review. We also wish to thank the following people for their suggestions and support: Maya Bar-Hillel, Nick Dopuch, Baruch Fischhoff, Paul Hirsch, Ed Joyce, John Payne, Paul Schoemaker, Rick Shweder, and Paul Slovic. The superb abilities of Charlesetta Nowels in handling the preparation of this chapter are gratefully acknowledged. First published in *Annual Review of Psychology*, 32 (1981), 53–88.

REFERENCES

Abelson, R. P. 1976. Script processing in attitude formation and decision making. In *Cognition and Social Behavior*, ed. J. S. Carroll, J. W. Payne, pp. 33–46. Hillsdale, NJ: Erlbaum. 290 pp.

Ajzen, I. 1977. Intuitive theories of events and the effects of base-rate information on prediction. *J. Pers. Soc. Psychol.* 35:303–14

Anderson, N. H. 1979. Algebraic rules in psychological measurement. *Am. Sci.* 67:555–63

Anderson, N. H., Shanteau, J. C. 1970. Information integration in risky decision making. *J. Exp. Psychol.* 84:441–5

Armstrong, J. S. 1978a. *Long Range Forecasting*. New York: Wiley. 612 pp.

1978b. Forecasting with econometric methods: Folklore versus fact. *J. Bus.* 51:549–64

Aschenbrenner, K. M. 1978. Single-peaked risk preferences and their dependability on the gambles' presentation mode. *J. Exp. Psychol.–Hum. Percept. Perform.* 4:513–20

Bar-Hillel, M. 1979. The role of sample size in sample evaluation. *Organ. Behav. Hum. Perform.* 24:245–57

1980. The base-rate fallacy in probability judgments. *Acta Psychol.*

Bar-Hillel, M., Falk, R. 1980. *Some teasers concerning conditional probabilities*. Presented at 18th Conf. Bayesian Inference and Decision Making. Univ. South. Calif.

Beach, L. R., Mitchell, T. R. 1978. A contingency model for the selection of decision strategies. *Acad. Manage. Rev.* 3:439–49

140

Behavioral decision theory

Bettman, J. R. 1979. *An Information Processing Theory of Consumer Choice.* Reading, Mass: Addison-Wesley. 402 pp.

Brehmer, B. 1976. Note on clinical judgment and the formal characteristics of clinical tasks. *Psychol. Bull.* 83:778–82

1978. Response consistency in probabilistic inference tasks. *Organ. Behav. Hum. Perform.* 22:103–15.

1980. In one word: not from experience. *Acta Psychol.* 45

Broadbent, D. E., Cooper, P. J., Broadbent, M. H. P. 1978. A comparison of hierarchical and matrix retrieval schemes in recall. *J. Exp. Psychol.–Hum. Learn. Mem.* 4:486–97

Brown, H. I. 1978. On being rational. *Am. Philos. Q.* 15:241–8

Brunswik, E. 1943. Organismic achievement and environmental probability. *Psychol. Rev.* 50:255–72

1956. *Perception and the Representative Design of Experiments.* Berkeley: Univ. Calif. Press. 154 pp. 2nd ed.

Campbell, D. T. 1959. Systematic error on the part of human links in communication systems. *Inf. Control* 1:334–69

1960. Blind variation and selective retention in creative thought as in other knowledge processes. *Psychol. Rev.* 67:380–400

Carroll, J. S. 1980. Analyzing decision behavior: the magician's audience. In *Cognitive Processes in Choice and Decision Behavior*, ed. T. S. Wallsten. Hillsdale, NJ: Erlbaum

Castellan, N. J. Jr. 1977. Decision making with multiple probabilistic cues. In *Cognitive Theory*, ed. N. J. Castellan, D. B. Pisoni, G. R. Potts, 2:117–47. Hillsdale, NJ: Erlbaum. 342 pp.

Christensen-Szalanski, J. J. J. 1978. Problem solving strategies: a selection mechanism, some implications, and some data. *Organ. Behav. Hum. Perform.* 22:307–23

1980. A further examination of the selection of problem-solving strategies: The effects of deadlines and analytic aptitudes. *Organ. Behav. Hum. Perform.* 25:107–22

Cohen, L. J. 1977. *The Probable and the Provable.* Oxford: Clarendon. 272 pp.

1979. On the psychology of prediction: whose is the fallacy? *Cognition* 7:385–407

Coombs, C. H., Avrunin, G. S. 1977. Single-peaked functions and the theory of preference. *Psychol. Rev.* 84:216–30

Corbin, R. M. 1980. Decisions that might not get made. See Carroll 1980

Dawes, R. M. 1976. Shallow psychology. See Abelson 1976, pp. 3–11

1977. Case-by-case versus rule-generated procedures for the allocation of scarce resources. In *Human Judgment and Decision Processes in Applied Settings*, ed. M. F. Kaplan, S. Schwartz, pp. 83–94. New York: Academic. 281 pp.

1979. The robust beauty of improper linear models in decision making. *Am. Psychol.* 34:571–82

Ebbesen, E. B., Konečni, V. J. 1980. On the external validity of decision-making research: what do we know about decisions in the real world? See Carroll 1980

Edwards, W. 1975. Comment. *J. Am. Stat. Assoc.* 70:291–3

1977. Use of multiattribute utility measurement for social decision making. In *Conflicting Objectives in Decisions*, ed. D. E. Bell, R. L. Keeney, H. Raiffa, pp. 247–75. New York: Wiley. 442 pp.

Einhorn, H. J. 1980. Learning from experience and suboptimal rules in decision making. See Caroll 1980

Einhorn, H. J., Hogarth, R. M. 1978. Confidence in judgment: persistence of the illusion of validity. *Psychol. Rev.* 85:395–416

Einhorn, H. J., Kleinmuntz, D. N., Kleinmuntz, B. 1979. Linear regression and process-tracing models of judgment. *Psychol. Rev.* 86:465–85

Einhorn, H. J., McCoach, W. P. 1977. A simple multiattribute utility procedure for evaluation. *Behav. Sci.* 22:270–82

Ellis, A. 1977. The basic clinical theory of rational-emotive therapy. In *Handbook of Rational-Emotive Therapy*, ed. A. Ellis, R. Grieger, pp. 3–34. New York: Springer. 433 pp.

Elstein, A. S., Shulman, L. E., Sprafka, S. A. 1978. *Medical Problem Solving: An Analysis of Clinical Reasoning*. Cambridge, Mass: Harvard Univ. Press. 330 pp.

Estes, W. K. 1976a. The cognitive side of probability learning. *Psychol. Rev.* 83:37–64

1976b. Some functions of memory in probability learning and choice behavior. In *The Psychology of Learning and Motivation: Advances in Research and Theory*, ed. G. H. Bower, 10:1–45. New York: Academic. 247 pp.

1980. Is human memory obsolete? *Am. Sci.* 68:62–9

Fischhoff, B. 1980. Decision analysis: clinical art or clinical science? In *Human Decision Making*, Vol. I, ed. L. Sjöberg, T. Tyszka, J. A. Wise. Bodafors, Sweden: Doxa

Fischhoff, B., Slovic, P., Lichtenstein, S. 1977. Knowing with certainty: the appropriateness of extreme confidence. *J. Exp. Psychol.–Hum. Percept. Perform.* 3:552–64

1978. Fault trees: sensitivity of estimated failure probabilities to problem representation. *J. Exp. Psychol.–Hum. Percept. Perform.* 4:330–44

1980. Knowing what you want: measuring labile values. See Carroll 1980

Freud, S. 1960. *The Ego and the Id*. New York: Norton. Originally published 1923. 67 pp.

Garner, W. R. 1970. Good patterns have few alternatives. *Am. Sci.* 58:34–42

Goldsmith, R. W. 1980. Studies of a model for evaluating judicial evidence. *Acta Psychol.* 45

Green, D. M., Swets, J. A. 1966. *Signal Detection Theory and Psychophysics*. New York: Wiley. 455 pp.

Greenwald, A. G. 1976. Within-subjects designs: to use or not to use? *Psychol. Bull.* 83:314–20

Grether, D. M., Plott, C. R. 1979. Economic theory of choice and the preference reversal phenomenon. *Am. Econ. Rev.* 69:623–38

Hammond, K. R. 1978a. Toward increasing competence of thought in public policy formation. In *Judgment and Decision in Public Policy Formation*, ed. K. R. Hammond, pp. 11–32. Denver: Westview. 175 pp.

1978b. *Psychology's Scientific Revolution: Is it in Danger?* Univ. Colo. Inst. Behav. Sci. Cent. Res. Judgment and Policy, Rep. No. 211

Hammond, K. R., Adelman, L. 1976. Science, values and human judgment. *Science* 194:389–96

Hammond, K. R., Mumpower, J. L., Smith, T. H. 1977. Linking environmental models with models of human judgment: a symmetrical decision aid. *IEEE Trans. Syst. Man Cybern.* (SMC)5:358–67

Hammond, K. R., Stewart, T. R., Brehmer, B., Steinmann, D. O. 1975. Social judgment theory. In *Human Judgment and Decision Processes*, ed. M. Kaplan, S. Schwartz, pp. 271–312. New York: Academic. 325 pp.

Hammond, K. R., Summers, D. A. 1972. Cognitive control. *Psychol. Rev.* 79:58–67

Harris, R. J., Monaco, G. E. 1978. Psychology of pragmatic implication: information processing between the lines. *J. Exp. Psychol.* 107:1–22

Behavioral decision theory

Hayek, F. A. 1962. Rules, perception, and intelligibility. *Proc. Br. Acad.* 48:321–44

Hershey, J. C., Schoemaker, P. J. H. 1980a. Risk taking and problem context in the domain of losses: an expected utility analysis. *J. Risk Insur.* 46:111–32

1980b. Prospect theory's reflection hypothesis: a critical examination. *Organ. Behav. Hum. Perform.* 25:395–418

Hogarth, R. M. 1975. Cognitive processes and the assessment of subjective probability distributions. *J. Am. Stat. Assoc.* 70:271–94

1980a. *Beyond static biases: functional and dysfunctional aspects of judgmental heuristics.* Univ. Chicago, Grad. Sch. Bus., Cent. Decis. Res.

1980b. *Judgment and Choice: The Psychology of Decision.* Chichester, England: Wiley

Howell, W. C., Burnett, S. A. 1978. Uncertainty measurement: a cognitive taxonomy. *Organ. Behav. Hum. Perform.* 22:45–68

Humphreys, P., McFadden, W. 1980. Experience with MAUD: aiding decision structuring through reordering versus automating the composition rule. *Acta Psychol.*

Janis, I. L., Mann, L. 1977. *Decision Making: A Psychological Analysis of Conflict, Choice, and Commitment.* New York: Free Press. 488 pp.

Jungermann, H. 1980. "Decisionectics": the art of helping people to make personal decisions. *Acta Physol.* 45

Kahneman, D., Tversky, A. 1973. On the psychology of prediction. *Psychol. Rev.* 80:251–73

1979a. Prospect theory: an analysis of decision under risk. *Econometrica* 47:263–91

1979b. On the interpretation of intuitive probability. A reply to Jonathan Cohen. *Cognition* 7:409–11

Karmarkar, U. S. 1978. Subjectively weighted utility: a descriptive extension of the expected utility model. *Organ. Behav. Hum. Perform.* 21:61–72

1979. Subjectively weighted utility and the Allais paradox. *Organ. Behav. Hum. Perform.* 24:67–72

Keeney, R. L., Raiffa, H. 1976. *Decisions with Multiple Objectives: Preferences and Value Tradeoffs.* New York: Wiley, 569 pp.

Killeen, P. R. 1978. Superstition: a matter of bias, not detectability. *Science* 199:88–90

Kubovy, M. 1977. Response availability and the apparent spontaneity of numerical choices. *J. Exp. Psychol.–Hum. Percept. Perform.* 3:359–64

Langer, E. J. 1977. The psychology of chance. *J. Theory Soc. Behav.* 7:185–207

Levine, M. E., Plott, C. R. 1977. Agenda influence and its implications. *Va. Law Rev.* 63:561–604

Lewontin, R. C. 1979. Sociobiology as an adaptationist program. *Behav. Sci.* 24:5–14

Libby, R., Fishburn, P. C. 1977. Behavioral models of risk-taking in business decisions. *J. Account. Res.* 15:272–92

Lichtenstein, S., Fischhoff, B. 1977. Do those who know more also know more about how much they know? *Organ. Behav. Hum. Perform.* 20:159–83

1980. Training for calibration. *Organ. Behav. Hum. Perform.*

Lichtenstein, S., Fischhoff, B., Phillips, L. D. 1977. Calibration of probabilities: the state of the art. In *Decision Making and Change in Human Affairs*, ed. H. Jungermann, G. de Zeeuw, pp. 275–324. Dordrecht-Holland: Reidel. 527 pp.

Lopes, L. L. 1980. *Doing the impossible: a note on induction and the experience of randomness.* Dep. Psychol., Univ. Wis., Madison

Luce, R. D. 1977. The choice axiom after twenty years. *J. Math. Psychol.* 15: 215–33

Mackie, J. L. 1965. Causes and conditions. *Am. Philos. Q.* 2:245-64

March, J. G. 1978. Bounded rationality, ambiguity, and the engineering of choice. *Bell J. Econ. Manage. Sci.* 9:587-608

Michotte, A. 1963. *The Perception of Causality*. London: Methuen. 425 pp.

Miller, N. E. 1959. Liberalization of basic S-R concepts: extensions to conflict behavior, motivation, and social learning. In *Psychology: A study of a Science*, ed. S. Koch, 2:196-292. New York: McGraw Hill. 706 pp.

Mischel, W. 1979. On the interface of cognition and personality: beyond the person-situation debate. *Am. Psychol.* 34:740-54

Mowrey, J. D., Doherty, M. E., Kelley, S. M. 1979. The influence of negation and task complexity on illusory correlation. *J. Abnorm. Psychol.* 88:334-7

Mynatt, C. R., Doherty, M. E., Tweney, R. D. 1977. Confirmation bias in a simulated research environment: an experimental study of scientific inference. *Q. J. Exp. Psychol.* 29:85-95

1978. Consequences of confirmation and disconfirmation in a simulated research environment. *Q. J. Exp. Psychol.* 30:395-406

Newell, A., Simon, H. A. 1972. *Human Problem Solving*. Englewood Cliffs, NJ: Prentice-Hall. 920 pp.

Nisbett, R. È., Borgida, E., Crandall, R., Reed, H. 1976. Popular induction: information is not necessarily informative. See Abelson 1976, pp. 113-33

Nisbett, R. E., Ross, L. 1980. *Human Inference: Strategies and Shortcomings of Social Judgment*. Englewood Cliffs, NJ: Prentice-Hall. 334 pp.

Nisbett, R. E., Wilson, T. D. 1977. Telling more than we can know: verbal reports on mental processes. *Psychol. Rev.* 84:231-59

Olson, C. L. 1976. Some apparent violations of the representativeness heuristic in human judgment. *J. Exp. Psychol.–Hum. Percept. Perform.* 2:599-608

Payne, J. W. 1976. Task complexity and contingent processing in decision making: an information search and protocol analysis. *Organ. Behav. Hum. Perform.* 16:366-87

Payne, J. W., Braunstein, M. L., Carroll, J. S. 1978. Exploring predecisional behavior: an alternative approach to decision research. *Organ. Behav. Hum. Perform.* 22:17-44

Payne, J. W., Laughhunn, D. J., Crum, R. 1979. *Levels of aspiration and preference reversals in risky choice*. Grad. Sch. Bus., Duke Univ., Durham, NC

Pearson, K. 1897. On the scientific measure of variability. *Nat. Sci.* 11:115-18

Phelps, R. H., Shanteau, J. 1978. Livestock judges: how much infomration can an expert use? *Organ. Behav. Hum. Perform.* 21:209-19

Plott, C. R. 1976. Axiomatic social choice theory: an overview and interpretation. *Am. J. Polit. Sci.* 20:511-96

Plott, C. R., Levine, M. E. 1978. A model of agenda influence on committee decisions. *Am. Econ. Rev.* 68:146-60

Polya, G. 1941. Heuristic reasoning and the theory of probability. *Am. Math. Mon.* 48:450-65

1954. *Patterns of Plausible Inference*, Vol. 2. Princeton, NJ: Princeton Univ. Press. 190 pp.

Powers, W. T. 1973. Feedback: beyond behaviorism. *Science* 179:351-6

Rachlin, H., Burkhard, B. 1978. The temporal triangle: response substitution in instrumental conditioning. *Psychol. Rev.* 85:22-47

Rothbart, M. 1980. Memory processes and social beliefs. In *Cognitive Processes in Stereotyping and Intergroup Perception*, ed. D. Hamilton. Hillsdale, NJ: Erlbaum

Russell, B. 1948. *Human Knowledge: Its Scope and Limits*. New York: Simon & Schuster. 524 pp.

Russo, J. E. 1977. The value of unit price information. *J. Mark. Res.* 14:193–201

1978. Comments on behavioral and economic approaches to studying market behavior. In *The Effect of Information on Consumer and Market Behavior*, ed. A. A. Mitchell, pp. 65–74. Chicago: Am. Mark. Assoc. 112 pp.

Sagan, C. 1977. *The Dragons of Eden*. New York: Random House. 263 pp.

Samuelson, P. A. 1948. *Economics, An Introduction Analysis*. New York: McGraw Hill. 622 pp.

Schmitt, N., Levine, R. L. 1977. Statistical and subjective weights: Some problems and proposals. *Organ. Behav. Hum. Perform.* 20:15–30

Schneider, W., Shiffrin, R. M. 1977. Controlled and automatic human information processing: I. Detection, search, and attention. *Psychol. Rev.* 84:1–66

Schum, D. A. 1979. A review of a case against Blaise Pascal and his heirs. *Univ. Mich. Law Rev.* 77:446–83

1980. Current developments in research on cascaded inference processes. See Carroll 1980

Seligman, M. E. P. 1970. On the generality of the laws of learning. *Psychol. Rev.* 77:406–18

Shafer, G. 1976. *A Mathematical Theory of Evidence*. Princeton, NJ: Princeton Univ. Press. 297 pp.

Shanteau, J., Nagy, G. F. 1979. Probability of acceptance in dating choice. *J. Pers. Soc. Psychol.* 37:522–33

Shepard, R. N. 1964. On subjectively optimum selections among multi-attribute alternatives. In *Human Judgments and Optimality*, ed. M. W. Shelly, G. L. Bryan, pp. 257–81. New York: Wiley. 436 pp.

Shugan, S. M. 1980. The cost of thinking. *J. Consum. Res.* 7

Shweder, R. A. 1977. Likeness and likelihood in everyday thought: magical thinking in judgments about personality. *Curr. Anthropol.* 18:637–58

1979. Rethinking culture and personality theory. Part II: A critical examination of two more classical postulates. *Ethos* 7:279–311

Simon, H. A. 1978. Rationality as process and as product of thought. *Am. Econ. Rev.* 68:1–16

1979. Rational decision making in business organizations. *Am. Econ. Rev.* 69:493–513

Simon, H. A., Hayes, J. R. 1976. The understanding process: problem isomorphs. *Cogn. Psychol.* 8:165–90

Skinner, B. F. 1948. "Superstition" in the pigeon. *J. Exp. Psychol.* 38:168–72

1966. The phylogeny and ontogeny of behavior. *Science* 153: 1205–13

Slovic, P., Fischhoff, B. 1977. On the psychology of experimental surprises. *J. Exp. Psychol.–Hum. Percept. Perform.* 3:544–51

Slovic, P., Fischhoff, B., Lichtenstein, S. 1977. Behavioral decision theory. *Ann. Rev. Psychol.* 28:1–39

Slovic, P., Kunreuther, H., White, G. F. 1974. Decision processes, rationality and adjustment to natural hazards. In *Natural Hazards, Local, National, and Global*, ed. G. F. White, pp. 187–205. New York: Oxford Univ. Press. 288 pp.

Slovic, P., Lichtenstein, S. 1971. Comparison of Bayesian and regression approaches to the study of information processing in judgment. *Organ. Behav. Hum. Perform.* 6:649–744

Smith, E. R., Miller, F. D. 1978. Limits on perception of cognitive processes: a reply to Nisbett and Wilson. *Psychol. Rev.* 85:355–62

Staddon, J. E. R., Motheral, S. 1978. On matching and maximizing in operant choice experiments. *Psychol. Rev.* 85:436–44

Staddon, J. E. R., Simelhag, V. L. 1971. The "superstitious" experiment: a reexamination of its implications for the principles of adaptive behavior. *Psychol. Rev.* 78:3–43

Suppes, P. 1966. Probabilistic inference and the concept of total evidence. In *Aspects of Inductive Logic*, ed. J. Hintikka, P. Suppes, pp. 49–65. Amsterdam: North-Holland. 320 pp.

Svenson, O. 1979. Process descriptions of decision making. *Organ. Behav. Hum. Perform.* 23:86–112

Thaler, R. 1980. Toward a positive theory of consumer choice. *J. Econ. Behav. Organ.*

Thaler, R., Shiffrin, H. M. 1980. *An economic theory of self-control.* Grad. Sch. Bus., Cornell Univ.

Thorngate, W. 1980. Efficient decision heuristics. *Behav. Sci.* 25:219–25

Toda, M. 1962. The design of a fungus-eater: a model of human behavior in an unsophisticated environment. *Behav. Sci.* 7:164–83

1980a. What happens at the moment of decision? Meta decisions, emotions and volitions. In *Human Decision Making*, Vol. 2, ed. L. Sjöberg. T. Tyszka, J. A. Wise. Bodafors, Sweden: Doxa

1980b. Emotion and decision making. *Acta Psychol.* 45

Tribe, L. H. 1973. Technology assessment and the fourth discontinuity: the limits of instrumental rationality. *South. Calif. Law Rev.* 46:617–60

Tversky, A. 1977. Features of similarity. *Psychol. Rev.* 84:327–52

Tversky, A., Kahneman, D. 1973. Availability: a heuristic for judging frequency and probability. *Cogn. Psychol.* 5:207–32

1980a. Causal schemas in judgments under uncertainty. In *Progress in Social Psychology*, ed. M. Fishbein. 1:49–72. Hillsdale, NJ: Erlbaum. 240 pp.

1980b. *The framing of decisions and the rationality of choice.* Dep. Psychol., Stanford. Univ.

Tversky, A., Sattath, S. 1979. Preference trees. *Psychol. Rev.* 86:542–73

Tweney, R. D., Doherty, M. E., Worner, W. J., Pliske, D. B., Mynatt, C. R., Gross, K. A., Arkkelin, D. L. 1980. Strategies of rule discovery in an inference task. *Q. J. Exp. Psychol.* 32:109–23

Vlek, C., Stallen, P. 1980. Rational and personal aspects of risk. *Acta Psychol.*

Wallsten, T. S. 1980. Processes and models to describe choice and inference. See Carroll 1980

Wason, P. C., Johnson-Laird, P. N. 1972. *Psychology of Reasoning. Structure and Content.* London: Batsford. 264 pp.

Wickelgren, W. A. 1979. Chunking and consolidation: a theoretical synthesis of semantic networks, configuring in conditioning, S-R versus cognitive learning, normal forgetting, the amnesic syndrome, and the hippocampal arousal system. *Psychol. Rev.* 86:44–60

Wilson, E. O. 1978. *On Human Nature.* Cambridge, Mass: Harvard Univ. Press. 260 pp.

Wimsatt, W. C. 1980. Reductionistic research strategies and their biases in the units of selection controversy. In *Scientific Discovery*, Vol. 2, ed. T. Nickles. Dordrecht, Holland: Reidel

Yates, J. F., Zukowski, LM. G. 1976. Characterization of ambiguity in decision making. *Behav. Sci.* 21:19–25

7

REPLY TO COMMENTARIES*

HILLEL J. EINHORN AND ROBIN M. HOGARTH

Jacob Bronowski (1978, pp. 78–9) tells the following story about Bertrand Russell, who is reputed once to have said at a dinner party:

> "Oh, it is useless talking about inconsistent things, from an inconsistent proposition you can prove anything you like!" . . . Someone at the dinner table said, "Oh, come on!" He said, "Well, name an inconsistent proposition" and the man said, "Well, what shall we say, 2 = 1." "All right," said Russell, "what do you want me to prove?" The man said, "I want you to prove that you are the pope." "Why," said Russell, "the pope and I are two, but two equals one, therefore the pope and I are one."

Now consider the following from Emerson's essay, "Self-reliance":

> A foolish consistency is the hobgoblin of little minds, adored by little statesmen and philosophers and divines. With consistency a great soul has simply nothing to do. (1883, p. 58)

The above passages reflect the conflict that lies at the heart of current research in behavioral decision theory – namely, the importance of consistency in following rules, axioms, and the like, versus abandoning rules in particular cases when judgments and choices seem to imply a "foolish consistency." The present addendum to our review of behavioral decision theory considers this issue briefly (for more details, see Einhorn and Hogarth, 1981). We begin by examining one example of the recent work on "cognitive illusions" (Tversky and Kahneman, 1981).

Imagine that the following rule was presented to you as a way to be consistent in your choices: If you prefer A to B $(A > B)$, then you should prefer a gamble in which you win A with probability p (and zero with probability $1 - p$) to B with probability p (and zero with probability $1 - p$). Stated formally, if $A > B$, then $(A, p) > (B, p)$. This seems quite sensible since the inclusion of a common probability in both A and B should not change the order of preference. Kahneman and Tversky (1979), however, have shown that, when subjects choose between $A =$ a sure \$3,000 versus $B =$ \$4,000 with $p = 0.8$, most prefer A; but,

147

when asked to choose between $C = \$3,000$ with $p = 0.25$ versus $D = \$4,000$ with $p = 0.20$, most prefer D. Note that $C = (A, 0.25)$ and $D = (B, 0.25)$. Therefore, although the formal rule seems sensible in general, it is violated by many people in specific situations. When people recognize the inconsistency of their choices with a rule they wish to follow, they experience confusion, bewilderment, and conflict. The resolution of the conflict is particularly difficult since there are no higher principles to which one can appeal. To resolve the conflict one must rely on the very intuitions that were not trusted in the first place, otherwise, why have a formal rule? This example clearly illustrates the conflict between the importance of being consistent (Russell, 1948) and the fear that consistency is foolish if it leads to outcomes and results are intuitively unacceptable (Emerson, 1883). Furthermore, although some people change their choices to maintain consistency after extensive discussion, many others do not (Slovic and Tversky, 1974). Therefore, it is not ignorance of the importance of maintaining consistency that explains the adherence to inconsistent choices.

The above example, as well as others in the literature, illustrates the following basic point: choices, inferences, judgments, and the like, are ultimately evaluated by their validity, by which is meant the degree to which they can be justified to oneself and others. The degree of validity or justifiability is itself based on two general factors, neither of which is perfectly related to it. These factors are: (1) the logical deductibility or consistency of statements, hereafter called *truth*; and (2) the accuracy with which the content of particular statements, choices, and so on, matches or predicts what we consider to be reality. Therefore, we posit that

$$\text{validity} = f(\text{truth, accuracy}) \qquad (1)$$

The concept of truth, as defined here, is wholly structural. Thus, a syllogistic conclusion appropriately derived from incorrect (that is, inaccurate) premises is *true* regardless of how inaccurate it is *vis-à-vis* one's world knowledge. Formal systems must have *truth* since, as the Russell story illustrates, the presence of any inconsistency in the system means that anything can be proved (that is, deduced). Accuracy, on the other hand, refers to the degree to which judgments, inferences, etc., match or predict some external criterion or standard. The distinction can perhaps be made clearer by considering the difference between proving theorems (a favorite pastime in formal systems) and proving theories in science. In the former, truth/consistency is paramount; that is, do the results follow from the premises and the set of permissible operations? In the latter, accuracy is crucial; does the theory explain and predict empirical phenomena? Whereas there is no disagreement on the feasibility of proving theorems, philosophers of science have disagreed on whether theories can be proved; for example, recall Popper's views (1959) that theories can only be disproved, never proved. In dealing with specific cases and empirical phenomena, however, cues to accuracy are invariably involved and can conflict with logical truth.

That truth and accuracy can conflict is surprising to many since both are highly related to validity. However, although this does imply that they are themselves highly correlated, the less than perfect relationship means that there will be situations where one is high and the other is low. The earlier example involving choices between gambles is one such case; that is, the cues related to the sure thing in the first set of gambles and the small probability differences in the second set lead to choices that are inconsistent with the rule. Cases of low truth and high accuracy are also possible. For example, the winner of a recent Spanish lottery told a journalist that he picked the winning ticket because it ended in the number 48. His reason involved the fact that he dreamed of the number 7 for seven nights in a row and $7 \times 7 = 48$. As Braine (1978) has pointed out,

> We confuse truth with validity or justifiability. Validity has to do with the quality of the reasons that make a rule suitable as a premise. The pragmatically useful evaluation of an inference rule is almost always a validity judgment ... people ... are not aware that there is a truth judgment that can be made that is not a validity judgment.

The distinction between truth and accuracy in determining validity has several important implications that bear on the appropriateness of various normative standards typically used in decision research. We briefly consider three such implications. (See Einhorn and Hogarth 1981 for more details.)

1. Statements and conclusions drawn from formal systems (for example, probability theory, axiomatic choice theory), while logically consistent (high truth), are nevertheless judged as to their validity. For example, the accuracy of the premises can be judged and, if found wanting, the conclusions are not accepted. At another level, one can tentatively accept conclusions; however, to the extent that people are not aware that the entailments of those premises are not fully known to themselves, they may wait to judge the validity of the conclusions in particular cases. One is reminded of the Socratic dialogues in this regard; that is, by agreeing with a set of seemingly harmless assumptions, Socrates leads his protagonist to absurd conclusions. When engaged in similar discussions, many of us will wait to hear the conclusions before giving full support to the assumptions/axioms, regardless of how reasonable they sound in the abstract. Note that in specific situations the content, and thus the meaning, of information calls forth cues to accuracy that may conflict with truth. Indeed, much work on inference and choice has shown large context effects, including various violations of normative rules. However, normative rules are contentless and thus concerned solely with truth. When truth conflicts with accuracy of content, it is not an easy matter to determine what is the "right" answer. In fact, the determination of what constitutes an error in judgment and choice is the topic of much debate.

This point can be illustrated by considering the results of several psychological experiments which show that people are suboptimal or irrational decision makers. When experimenters adopt normative standards as yardsticks for performance, many forget Savage's (1954) admonition that those models are appropriate for "small worlds" which embody various simplifying assumptions.

Indeed, psychological experiments can be considered "small worlds"; they have not as yet captured the larger world in two important respects. First, subjects rarely receive continuous feedback about their judgments and thus cannot apply habitual, incremental strategies in which feedback can reduce both task complexity and the commitment implied by specific actions. Indeed, understanding decision making as sequences of action–outcome–feedback loops is an important dimension missing from most current research. Second, experimental environments do not contain much redundancy and often serve to demonstrate the skills of experimenters to get subjects to use imperfect single cues in inappropriate ways. That is, subjects are prevented from taking advantage of the redundancies they typically encounter in natural ecologies where they use multiple, intersubstitutable cues and processes (Brunswik, 1952).

2. As pointed out by Einhorn and Hogarth (1981):

> The relationship between truth and validity is not static. For example, consider Bernoulli's initial advocacy of maximizing expected value as a rational strategy of choice (Schoemaker 1980). Such a rule could not account for people refusing to buy the St. Petersburg lottery, which has an infinite expected value, nor the persistent buying of insurance, which has a negative expected value. Faced with these inconsistencies, Bernoulli proposed the concept of utility rather than value. Many years later, von Neumann and Morgenstern (1947) provided the axiom system and proof (logical deduction) that maximizing expected utility follows from acceptance of the axioms. Note that what is now considered by some to be a normative model of rational choice is a consequence of rationalizing behavior that used cues that were thought to be valid (marginally decreasing utility) but not yet incorporated in a formal model.

3. The distinction between truth and accuracy in determining validity bears directly on the inherent limitations of deductive systems for providing guidelines to appropriate behavior in given situations. Such limitations arise because the need to maintain perfect consistency in a formal system necessarily results in narrowing its domain of application. Indeed, this problem has been famous in mathematics ever since Gödel proved his impossibility theorem (see Nagel and Newman, 1958) showing that

> there is an endless number of true arithmetical statements which cannot be formally deduced from any given set of axioms by a closed set of rules of inference.

Thus, incompleteness is an essential component of formal systems. Indeed, such incompleteness may lie at the heart of the uneasiness one may feel at following axioms and rules that lead to conclusions, choices, and inferences that are intuitively unacceptable. However, one should not thereby conclude that logical truth and formal systems are irrelevant in determining validity. Both truth *and* accuracy are important. The challenging task for future research is to improve our normative models by enlarging the context in which they have been used.

Reply to commentaries

This will involve incorporating better descriptions of what people are doing and why they are doing it. If, as Goldman (1978) has put it, "Ought implies can," understanding the psychological and biological limits and capabilities of the organism *ought* to be our first priority.

NOTE

First published in G. R. Ungson and D. N. Braunstein (eds.) (1982). *Decision Making: An Interdisciplinary Enquiry*. Boston, MA: Kent Publishing Co., 53–6.

REFERENCES

Braine, M. D. S. 1978. On the relation between the natural logic of reasoning and standard logic. *Psychological Review*, 85, 1–21.

Bronowski, J. 1978. *The Origins of Knowledge and Imagination*. New Haven: Yale University Press.

Brunswik, E. 1952. *Conceptual Framework of Psychology*. Chicago: University of Chicago Press.

Einhorn, H. J. and Hogarth, R. M. 1981. *Uncertainty and Causality in Practical Inference*. Center for Decision Research, University of Chicago Graduate School of Business, April.

Emerson, R. W. 1883. Self-reliance. In *Emerson's Essays* (First Series). Cambridge, Mass.: Riverside Press.

Goldman, A. 1978. Epistemics: the regulative theory of cognition. *Journal of Philosophy*, 75, 509–23.

Kahneman, D. and Tversky, A. 1979. Prospect theory: an analysis of decision under risk. *Econometrica*, 47, 263–91.

Nagel, E. and Newman, J. R. 1958. *Gödel's Proof*. New York: New York University Press.

Popper, K. R. 1959. *The Logic of Scientific Discovery*. London: Hutchinson.

Russell, B. 1948. *Human Knowledge: Its Scope and Limits*. New York: Simon & Schuster.

Savage, L. J. 1954. *The Foundations of Statistics*. New York: Wiley.

Schoemaker, P. J. H. 1980. *Experiments on Decisions Under Risk: The Expected Utility Hyopothesis*. Boston: Martinus Nijhoff.

Slovic, P. and Tversky, A. 1974. Who accepts Savage's axiom? *Behavioral Science*, 19, 368–73.

Tversky, A. and Kahneman, D. 1981. The framing of decisions and the psychology of choice. *Science*, 211, 453–8.

Von Neumann, J. and Morgenstern, O. 1947. *Theory of Games and Economic Behavior*. Princeton University Press.

8

RESPONSE MODE, FRAMING, AND INFORMATION-PROCESSING EFFECTS IN RISK ASSESSMENT

PAUL SLOVIC, BARUCH FISCHHOFF, AND SARAH LICHTENSTEIN

The chapter on framing by Tversky and Kahneman (1982) demonstrates that normatively inconsequential changes in the formulation of choice problems significantly affect preferences. These effects are noteworthy because they are sizable (sometimes complete reversals of preference), because they violate important tenets of rationality, and because they influence not only behavior but how the consequences of behavior are experienced. These perturbations are traced (in prospect theory; see Kahneman and Tversky, 1979) to the interaction between the manner in which acts, contingencies, and outcomes are framed in decision problems and general propensities for treating values and uncertainty in nonlinear ways.

The present chapter begins by providing additional demonstrations of framing effects. Next, it extends the concept of framing to effects induced by changes of response mode, and it illustrates effects due to the interaction between response mode and information-processing considerations. Two specific response modes are studied in detail: judgments of single objects and choices among two or more options. Judgments are prone to influence by anchoring- and adjustment-processes, which ease the strain of integrating diverse items of information. Choices are prone to context effects that develop as a result of justification processes, through which the deliberations preceding choice are woven into a rationalization of that action. As we shall see, these processes often cause judgments and choices to be inconsistent with one another.

Response mode, framing, and information-processing considerations apply to all decision problems. However, like Tversky and Kahneman, we shall focus primarily on risk-taking decisions ranging from choices among simple gambles to complex decisions about protective actions, such as insurance, vaccination, and the use of seat belts. The studies to be described demonstrate the extreme sensitivity of judgments and decisions to subtle changes in problem format and response mode.

CONCRETENESS AND THE FRAMING OF ACTS

Decision options can often be viewed in a variety of perspectives. For example, Tversky and Kahneman (1982) show that concurrent decision problems are dealt with independently, rather than as an integrated combination. Thus, choosing both a sure gain of $240 and a gamble offering a 75% chance of losing $1,000 and a 25% chance of losing nothing is not viewed as equivalent to its conjunctions: a 25% chance of winning $240 and a 75% chance of losing $760.

By failing to integrate concurrent acts, Tversky and Kahneman's subjects responded to the explicit characteristics of each act and did not perform the simple transformations necessary to effect their merger. Similar behavior has been observed in two experiments that examined the effects of explicit representation of the variance of outcomes of simple gambles. In one experiment, specially constructed gambles manipulated variance without changing the probabilities and payoffs that were explicitly displayed to the subject (Slovic and Lichtenstein, 1968). To illustrate this, consider the upper half of figure 8.1, which shows two bets: a duplex bet and a standard bet, which can be termed *parallel* because both have the same stated probabilities and the same payoffs, namely .6 chance to win $2 and .4 chance to lose $2. Imagine that the bets can be played by spinning pointers on the circular discs shown in figure 8.1 such that one wins or loses the amount indicated by the final position of the pointer. To play a duplex bet, one must spin the pointer on both discs. Thus, one can win and not lose, lose and not win, both win and lose, or neither win nor lose. As a consequence, the duplex bet has much less variance than its parallel standard bet. That is, the standard bet leads either to a gain or a loss of $2; however, by playing the duplex bet, one has a fairly high probability of breaking even. Most subjects perceived duplex bets and their parallel standard bets as equally attractive, which suggests that their judgments were based only upon the explicitly stated probabilities and payoffs. The characteristics of the underlying distribution for the duplex bet did not exert any significant influence.

The second experiment (Payne and Braunstein, 1971) nicely complements the first. This experiment used pairs of duplex gambles with equal underlying distributions but different explicit probability values, as illustrated in the lower half of figure 8.1. Subjects showed strong preferences for one member of such pairs over the other, which further demonstrates the dominance of explicit or surface information.

These two experiments illustrate a form of concrete thinking (Slovic, 1972) whereby decision makers appear to use only the information that is explicitly displayed in the formulation of the problem. Information that has to be inferred from the display or created by some mental transformation tends to be ignored. The tendency for considerations that are out of sight to be out of mind (see also Fischhoff, Slovic, and Lichtenstein, 1978) imposes a serious burden on those entrusted with presentation of risk information.

Figure 8.1 Experimental gambles. Source: Slovic and Lichtenstein (1968); Payne and Braunstein (1971).

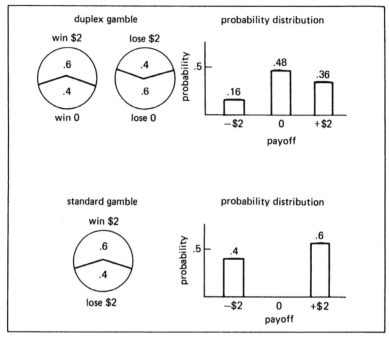

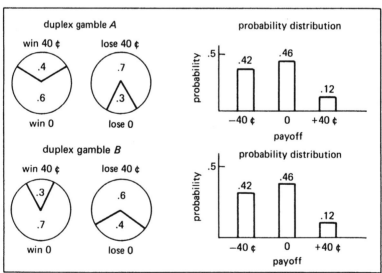

PROTECTIVE ACTION AND THE FRAMING OF CONTINGENCIES

Pseudocertainty

According to prospect theory, outcomes that are merely probable are under-weighted in comparison with outcomes that are obtained with certainty. As a result, any protective action that reduces the probability of harm from, say, .01 to zero will be valued more highly than an action that reduces the probability of the same harm from .02 to .01.

Tversky and Kahneman (1982) note that mental representations of protective actions can easily be manipulated so as to vary the apparent certainty with which they prevent harm. For example, an insurance policy that covers fire but not flood can be presented either as full protection against the specific risk of fire or as a reduction in the overall probability of property loss. Prospect theory predicts that the policy will appear more attractive in the former perspective, labeled *pseudocertainty*, in which it offers unconditional protection against a restricted set of problems.

We have tested this conjecture in the context of one particular kind of protection, vaccination. Two forms of a vaccination questionnaire were created. Form I (probabilistic protection) described a disease that was expected to afflict 20% of the population, and it asked people whether they would volunteer to receive a vaccine that protected half the people who received it. According to form II (pseudocertainty), there were two mutually exclusive and equiprobable strains of the disease, each of which was expected to afflict 10% of the population; vaccination was said to give complete protection against one strain and no protection against the other. The 211 participants in this study were recruited by an advertisement in the University of Oregon student newspapers. Half received form I; the other half received form II. After reading the description, they rated the likelihood that they would get vaccinated in such a situation, using a seven-point scale ranging from 1 ("almost certainly would not get vaccinated") to 7 ("almost certainly would get vaccinated").

Although both forms indicated that vaccination reduced one's overall risk from 20% to 10%, we expected that vaccination would appear more attractive to those who received form II (pseudocertainty) than to those who received form I (probabilistic insurance). The results confirmed this prediction: 57% of those who received form II indicated that they would get vaccinated, compared to 40% for those who received form I.

The pseudocertainty effect highlights the contrast between reduction and elimination of risk. As Tversky and Kahneman have indicated, this distinction is difficult to justify on normative grounds. Moreover, manipulations of certainty would seem to have important implications for the design and description of other forms of protection, such as medical treatments, insurance, and flood- and earthquake-proofing activities.

Seat belts

Research has demonstrated that seat belts are effective in reducing death and injury in automobile accidents and that most people are aware of this fact. However, the percentage of motorists who wear them is small, and numerous and expensive media campaigns have failed to persuade people to "buckle up for safety" (Robertson, 1976).

The reluctance of motorists to wear seat belts is puzzling to many safety officials, in the light of the high personal costs of a serious accident. One clue to motorists' reluctance is the finding of Slovic and others (1977) that perceived probability of loss was a key determinant of protective action in the context of insurance decisions. Extrapolating from insurance to seat belts, Slovic, Fischhoff, and Lichtenstein (1978) argued that resistance to the wearing of seat belts was understandable in the light of the extremely small probability of an accident on a single automobile trip. Because a fatal accident occurs only about once in every 3.5 million person-trips and a disabling injury only once in every 100,000 person-trips, refusing to buckle one's seat belt prior to a single trip is not unreasonable.

The risks of driving can be framed differently, however. During the course of a fifty-year lifetime of driving, the average motorist will take some 40,000 or more trips. The probability that one of these trips will end in a fatality is .01, and the probability of experiencing at least one disabling injury during this period is .33. It is as appropriate to consider these cumulative probabilities of death and disability as it is to consider the odds on a single trip. Slovic, Fischhoff, and Lichtenstein (1978) conducted a pilot study in which subjects were induced to adopt either a lifetime or a trip-by-trip perspective. Subjects in the lifetime condition responded more favorably toward use of seat belts and toward the enactment of laws requiring the wearing of seat belts or the installation of air bags. As a result of exposure to single-trip risk statistics, fewer than 10% of the college students surveyed claimed that their use of seat belts would be changed, but 39% of those exposed to the cumulative probabilities said that they expected their use of seat belts to increase. Whereas 54% of the persons who received single-trip information favored mandatory protection, 78% of those exposed to lifetime probabilities favored such a law. Whether the favorable attitudes toward seat belts engendered by a lengthened time perspective will be maintained and translated into behavior remains to be determined.

INSURANCE DECISIONS AND THE FRAMING OF OUTCOMES

Traditionally, explanations of insurance decisions have been based upon utility theory (Friedman and Savage, 1948), on the assumption that insurance can be conceptualized as a choice between acceptance either of a small probability of a large loss or of a certain small loss (the insurance premium). Recent research casts doubt upon this conceptualization by showing that *certain* losses are more attractive when framed as insurance premiums rather than monetary losses.

We first began thinking about this issue when we noticed that preference data presented in an early paper on prospect theory (Kahneman and Tversky, 1975)

Table 8.1. *Proportions of subjects choosing the certain loss in insurance and preference contexts*

	Probability of loss	
Context	.001	.25
Insurance	37/56	26/40
	66%	65%
Preference	28/72	8/40
	39%	20%

differed from results that we had obtained with similar preferences portrayed as insurance problems (Slovic and others, 1977). Specifically, Kahneman and Tversky presented people with a choice between a certain loss, such as $50, and a probability of losing a larger amount, such as a .25 chance to lose $200. For each pair of options, the expected loss from the gamble was equal to the certain loss from its alternative. Our study had used similar problems in the context of insurance and called the certain loss an insurance premium. Whereas Kahneman and Tversky's subjects preferred the gambles for moderate or high probabilities of loss, ours preferred the insurance.

Intrigued by this discrepancy, we decided to explore the effects of context (insurance versus preference) more systematically. Two situations were studied. In one, people were presented with a choice between accepting a .001 chance of losing $5,000 and a certain loss of $5; in the other, they were asked to choose between accepting a $\frac{1}{4}$ chance of losing $200 and a certain loss of $50. The 208 subjects were paid volunteers who responded to an ad in a university newspaper. Each responded to only one problem situation (.001 or .25 chance of loss), which they initially received in only one context (insurance or preference). The results shown in table 8.1 clearly indicate that the certain loss was more likely to be selected in the insurance as opposed to the preference context.

About one hour after the subjects had made these choices, they were presented again with the same problem, sometimes in the same context, sometimes in the other. When the context remained unchanged, so did choices: only 5% of the subjects changed their responses. However, when the second problem was framed differently, 29% changed their responses. In 85% of the cases when subjects changed their responses, subjects chose the gamble in the preference setting and the insurance premium in the insurance setting. Moreover, people who first saw the problem in the preference context were three times more likely to change as just described than those who saw it first in the insurance context. This suggests that people are more likely to realize that an insurance premium implies a certain loss than they are to realize that a certain loss represents an insurance premium. Varying probabilities and losses in a more systematic way than we did, Schoemaker and Kunreuther (1979) and Hershey and Schoemaker (1980) have obtained similar context effects with a wide variety of problems.

What causes this strong context effect? One explanation is that paying an insurance premium is not psychologically equivalent to choosing a sure loss. The insurance context forces an individual to acknowledge that he or she is at risk. Paying a premium is an instrumental action that provides a benefit: it removes the risk; it buys safety. In contrast, accepting a certain loss is not perceived as saving one from an unattractive gamble. The logic of this interpretation is illustrated by the comments of a subject who chose the gamble in the preference condition and the premium in the insurance condition. When confronted with this inconsistency, the subject refused to change his preference, asserting that paying the premium seemed less aversive than choosing the certain loss. Asked whether he thought the preference and insurance problems were the same, he replied, "Yes, they're the same, but they look different."

A related interpretation is based on prospect theory, according to which one evaluates an option according to the change that it would make in one's position *vis-à-vis* some reference point. The theory asserts also (a) that losses are valued more heavily than gains of the same magnitude; (b) that the individual becomes increasingly less sensitive to a given change in outcome as the stakes get larger (that is, the value function is concave above the reference point and convex below it); (c) that low-probability events tend to be given more weight than high-probability events, although special weight is given to events that are certain.

If the preference context is interpreted as a comparison between a gamble and a certain loss, the reference point is the individual's status quo. The gamble would seem less aversive than the certain loss, both because large losses are somewhat discounted in comparison to small losses (point (b) above) and because consequences that are certain to happen are given special weight (point (c) above).

In the insurance context, however, the reference point is loss of the premium. The choice is then between paying the premium or accepting the gamble. For example, consider paying a $50 premium to avoid a $\frac{1}{4}$ chance of losing $200. Accepting the gamble provides a $\frac{3}{4}$ chance of gaining $50 (not paying the $50 premium and not losing on the gamble) and a $\frac{1}{4}$ chance of losing $150 (losing $200 on the gamble but saving the $50 premium). Because losses loom larger than gains and small probabilities tend to be overestimated, this gamble should be valued negatively; that is, it should seem less attractive than staying at the reference point of the insurance policy.

A third (and much simpler) explanation proposed by Kahneman and Tversky (1979) and by Hershey and Schoemaker (1980) is that the insurance contest may trigger social norms about prudent behavior that are not associated with the preference context. The latter, they claim, may actually stimulate a gambling orientation.

If the interpretations proposed here are validated by further investigations, they would have important implications for insurance decision making and for protective behavior in general. The results suggest that people will be more likely to protect themselves from a probable hazard if they recognize that they are at risk and remain so unless they take protective action. Indeed, data from an extensive survey of people who did and did not insure themselves against flood or earthquake hazards support this notion (Kunreuther and others, 1978).

RESPONSE MODE, FRAMING, AND INFORMATION PROCESSING

The way in which an individual has to respond to the decision problem is an important aspect of framing. Although people are sometimes free to choose their response mode, more often some external source defines the problem either as one of judgment (evaluating individual options) or as one of choice (selecting one from two or more options). Many theories of decision making postulate an equivalence between judgment and choice. Such theories assume that each option X has a value $v(X)$ that determines its attractiveness in both contexts (for example, Luce, 1977). However, the descriptive validity of these theories is now in question. Much recent research has demonstrated that the information-processing strategies used prior to making choices are often quite different from the strategies employed in judging single options. As a result, choices and evaluative judgments of the same options often differ, sometimes dramatically. The conditions under which judgment and choice are similar or different need to be better understood (Einhorn and Hogarth, 1981).

Justification and choice

One conception asserts that much of the deliberation prior to choice consists of finding a concise, coherent set of reasons that justify the selection of one option over the others. For example, Tversky (1972) provided evidence to support an elimination by aspects model of choice. According to this model, options are viewed as sets of aspects; that is, a car has a price, a model, a color, and so forth. At each stage in the choice process, one aspect is selected, with probability proportional to its importance. The options that are not adequate for each selected aspect are eliminated from the set of options considered at the following stage. Tversky argued that elimination by aspects is an appealing process because it is easy both to apply and to justify. It permits a choice to be resolved in a clear-cut fashion, without reliance on relative weights, trade-off functions, or other numerical computations, and eases demands on the decision maker's limited capacity for intuitive calculation.

Another example of justification processes comes from a study of difficult choices (Slovic, 1975). Each of two options was defined by two dimensions differing in importance. To maximize the difficulty of choice, these paired options were designed to have equal value by making the option that was superior on the more important dimension to be so inferior on the lesser dimension that its advantage was canceled. The equating of options was done judgmentally. For example, one set of options involved gift packages with two components, cash

159

Table 8.2 *A typical choice pair*

	Cash	Coupon book worth
Gift package *A*	$10	—
Gift package *B*	$20	$18

Source: Slovic, 1975.

and a coupon book offering miscellaneous products and services. The subject was shown two such gift packages with one component missing (see table 8.2). The subject was asked to supply a value for the missing component large enough to make the two options equally attractive. Many different types of stimuli were used (for example, gift packages, pairs of jobs, routes to work), and the missing component was varied within each pair. Subjects were asked to equate various pairs of options and then to choose among them.

Contrary to the predictions of most choice theories, choices between these equally attractive alternatives were not made randomly. Rather, most subjects consistently selected the option that was superior on the more important dimension. For the example in table 8.2, cash was generally viewed as more important than the coupon book, and, among pairs of equated gift packages, the option that offered more cash was selected 79 % of the time. Apparently, reliance on the more important dimension makes a better justification ("I chose this gift package because it provided more cash") than random selection ("They looked about equally attractive, so I flipped a coin").

Another demonstration of justification in choice comes from a study that presented college students and members of the League of Women Voters with both of the tasks shown in figure 8.2 and table 8.3 (Fischhoff, Slovic, and Lichtenstein, 1980).

In the first task (table 8.3), subjects chose between a high variance and a low variance option involving the loss of life. In the second task, they were asked to evaluate three functions representing the way in which society should evaluate lives in multifatality situations. The instructions for the second task provided elaborate rationales for adopting each of the functional forms over a range between zero and one hundred lives lost in a single accident. Curve 1, the linear form, represents the view that every life lost is equally costly to society. Curve 2, the exponentially increasing function, represents the view that large losses of life are disproportionately serious; for example, that the loss of twenty lives is more than twice as bad as the loss of ten lives. Curve 3 represents a reduced sensitivity to large losses of life; for example, the loss of twenty lives is less than twice as bad as the loss of ten lives. Subjects were asked to study each curve and its rationale and then to indicate the ones with which they agreed most and least.

More than half of all subjects chose option *A* in task 1 (table 8.3) and agreed most with curve 2 in task 2 (figure 8.2). However, option *A* indicates a risk-seeking attitude toward loss of life, whereas curve 2 represents risk aversion.

Table 8.3. *Task 1: emergency response*

A committee in a large metropolitan area met recently to discuss contingency plans in the event of various emergencies. One emergency threat under consideration posed two options, both involving some loss of life. These are described below. Read them and indicate your opinion about the relative merits of each.

Option *A* carries with it a .5 probability of containing the threat with a loss of 5 lives and a .5 probability of losing 95 lives. It is like taking the gamble: .5 lose 5 lives, .5 lose 95 lives.

Option *B* carries with it a .5 probability of containing the threat with a loss of 40 lives and a .5 probability of losing 60 lives. It is like taking the gamble: .5 lose 40 lives, .5 lose 60 lives.

Which option would you select? Option *A* ____ Option *B* ____

Figure 8.2 Task 2: the impact of catastrophic events. Subjects were asked to rank the three proposals in order of preference.

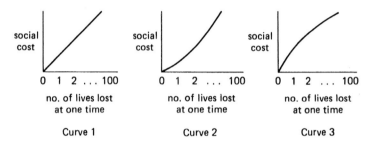

Choice of option *A* would be consistent with curve 3, which was the least favored view. These inconsistent results did not change appreciably when the degree of elaboration in the rationales given for the three curves was changed.

Subjects who were confronted with the inconsistency in their responses refused to change. They claimed to see no connection between the two tasks. Most appeared to be relying on some variant of this justification offered for choosing option *A*: "It would be immoral to allow the loss of forty lives or more when option *A* presents a good chance of coming out of the situation with no loss of life." This perspective was evoked by the structure of the choice problem but not by the task of evaluating the three functional relationships.

Because many theorists have proposed to use such choices as these to infer people's value functions (for example, Johnson and Huber, 1977; Raiffa, 1968), the results presented here may give cause for concern about this practice.

Anchoring and adjustment

Just as choice problems trigger justification processes, single numerical judgments are prone to being influenced by anchoring and adjustment. In this

161

process, a natural starting point is used as a first approximation or anchor for the judgment. This anchor is then adjusted to accommodate the implications of additional information. Often, the adjustment is smaller than it should be, considering the importance of the new information. An example of how anchoring can lead to strong differences between evaluation and choice comes from two experiments (Lichtenstein and Slovic, 1971, 1973), one of which was conducted on the floor of the Four Queens Casino in Las Vegas. Consider the following pair of gambles used in the Las Vegas experiment: bet A: 11/12 chance to win 12 chips, and 1/12 chance to lose 24 chips; bet B: 2/12 chance to win 79 chips, and 10/12 chance to lose 5 chips, where the value of each chip was 25 cents. Notice that bet A had a much better chance of winning and that bet B offered a higher winning payoff. Subjects indicated, in two ways, the attractiveness of each bet in many such pairs. First, they made a simple choice, A or B. Later, they were asked to assume that they owned a ticket to play each bet, and they were to state the lowest price for which they would sell this ticket.

Presumably, both these selling prices and choices were governed by the same underlying factor, the attractiveness of each gamble. Therefore, subjects should have stated higher selling prices for the gambles that they preferred in the choice situation. In fact, subjects often chose one gamble yet stated a higher selling price for the other. For the particular pair of gambles just mentioned, bets A and B were chosen about equally often. However, bet B received a higher selling price about 88 % of the time. Of the subjects who chose bet A, 87 % gave a higher selling price to bet B, thus exhibiting an inconsistent preference pattern. Grether and Plott (1979), two skeptical economists, replicated this study with numerous variations designed to show that the observed inconsistencies were artifactual. They obtained essentially the same results as Lichtenstein and Slovic.

What accounts for this inconsistent pattern of preferences for gambles? Lichtenstein and Slovic concluded that subjects used different cognitive strategies when setting prices and making choices. Subjects often justified the choice of bet A in terms of its good odds, but they set a higher price for B because they anchored on its large winning payoff. For example, people who found a gamble basically attractive used the amount to win as a starting point. They then adjusted the amount to win downward to accommodate the less than perfect chance of winning and the fact that there was some amount to lose as well. Typically, this adjustment was small and, as a result, large winning payoffs caused people to set prices that were inconsistent with their choices.

Another way of looking at these results is in terms of the notion of compatibility. Because a selling price is expressed in terms of monetary units, subjects apparently found it easier to use the monetary aspects of the gamble to produce this type of response. Compatibility made the amount to win an anchor, which caused that aspect to dominate the response. Such bias did not exist with the choices, since each attribute of one gamble could be compared directly with the same attribute of the other. With no reason to use payoffs as a starting point, subjects were free to use other rules to determine (or to justify) their choices.

Compatibility bias

A compatibility hypothesis was tested directly in a study by Slovic and MacPhillamy (1974). They predicted that dimensions common to each option in a choice situation would have greater influence than dimensions that were unique to a particular option. They asked subjects to compare pairs of students and to predict, on the basis of scores on two cue dimensions (tests), which student would get the higher college grade point average. One dimension was common to both students, while the other was unique. For example, student *A* might be described in terms of scores on tests of English skill and quantitative ability, whereas student *B* might be described by scores on tests of English skill and need for achievement.

In this example, the compatibility hypothesis implies that English skill will be weighted particularly heavily, because it is common to both students. The rationale is that a comparison between two students along the same dimension should be cognitively easier than a comparison between the two students along different dimensions. The data strongly confirmed this hypothesis. Dimensions were weighted more heavily when common than when unique. After the experiment, most subjects indicated that they had not wanted to give more weight to the common dimension and that they were unaware of having done so.

There is, of course, no common dimension when students are judged one at a time; hence, one would expect a dimension that was common in choice to be given less weight in a judgment task. Evidence for this was also found. For example, consider student *A*, who scored 470 on English skill and 674 on quantitative ability and whose need-for-achievement score was missing. Twenty-four of 26 subjects gave student *A* a higher rating (that is, judgment) than student *B*, who had scored 566 on English and 474 on need for achievement, but whose quantitative score was missing. However, when choosing between students *A* and *B*, ten subjects who had given a higher rating to student *A* chose *B* but only two reversed in the other direction. Many other such differences between judgment and choice can be found in Slovic and MacPhillamy's (1974) data.

IMPLICATIONS FOR RISK ASSESSMENT

The message of this research is that the amalgamation of different types of information and values in an overall judgment or decision is a difficult cognitive process. Even when all factors are known and made explicit, subtle aspects of problem formulation, acting in combination with our intellectual predispositions and limitations, affect the balance that we strike among them. These effects seem endemic to a wide range of behaviors. Here, we discuss briefly their implications for two important components of risk assessment.

Eliciting labile values

Value judgments indicating the desired trade-offs between important decision outcomes lie at the heart of individual and societal risk assessment. For example, a person considering either surgery or radiation therapy as treatment for lung cancer must balance the enhanced life expectancy that surgery confers against the greater risk of sudden death that it entails (MacNeil, Weichselbaum, and Pauker, 1978). The evaluation that society makes of different energy technologies can be guided, in part, by whether it decides to give particularly great weight to potentially catastrophic accidents. Many observers advocate making such values explicit in order to help individuals and society to make better decisions. Some observers call for direct elicitation of values through surveys, hearings, and the like, whereas others prefer to infer values from the preferences revealed by actual decisions. Both approaches assume that people know their own values and that elicitation methods are unbiased channels that translate subjective feelings into analytically usable expressions.

We doubt these assumptions. First, decision problems with high stakes tend to be unique and unfamiliar. They take us into situations in which we have never thought through the implications of values and beliefs acquired in simpler, more familiar settings. Secondly, due to the strong effects of framing and to information-processing considerations, elicitation procedures become major forces in shaping the expression of values, especially when such values are ill-defined (Fischhoff, Slovic, and Lichtenstein, 1980). In such cases, the method becomes the message. Subtle aspects of how problems are posed, questions are phrased, and responses are elicited can have substantial impact on judgments that supposedly express people's preferences.

One could hope that further research and analysis would identify better ways to ask questions about values. Although some methods distort values and should be avoided, others educate and deepen the respondent's perspectives. If we are interested in what people really feel about a value issue, there may be no substitute for an interactive elicitation procedure, one that employs multiple methods and acknowledges the elicitor's role in helping the respondent to create and enunciate values.

Informing people about risk

One dramatic change in recent years is growing public awareness of the risks encountered in daily experience. Radiation hazards, medicinal side effects, occupational disease, food contaminants, toxic chemicals, and mechanical malfunctions increasingly seem to fill our newspapers and our thoughts. A consequence of this growing awareness has been pressure on designers and regulators of hazardous enterprises to inform people about the risks that they face (Morris, Mazis, and Barofsky, 1980; Slovic, Fischhoff, and Lichtenstein, 1980).

Clearly, better information about risk is crucial to making better personal decisions and to participating more effectively in the political processes whereby societal standards are developed and enforced. Despite good intentions, however, it may be quite difficult to create effective informational programs. Doing an adequate job means finding cogent ways of presenting complex, technical material that is clouded by uncertainty and subject to distortion by the listener's preconceptions – or misconceptions – about the hazard and its consequences. Moreover, as we have seen, people are often at the mercy of the way in which problems are formulated. Those responsible for determining the content and format of information programs thus have considerable ability to manipulate perceptions. Moreover, since these effects are not widely known, people may inadvertently be manipulating their own perceptions by causal decisions they make about how to organize their knowledge.

The stakes in risk problems are high – product viability, jobs, energy costs, willingness of patients to accept treatments, public safety and health, and so forth. Potential conflicts of interest abound. When subtle aspects of how (or what) information is presented make a significant difference in people's responses, one needs to determine the formulation that should be used. Making that decision takes one out of psychology and into the domains of law, ethics, and politics.

NOTES

The authors wish to thank Amos Tversky for comments on an earlier draft of this chapter. The writing was supported by the National Science Foundation under grant PRS79-11934 to Clark University under subcontract to Perceptronics, Inc. All opinions, findings, conclusions, and recommendations expressed in this publication are those of the authors and do not necessarily reflect the views of the National Science Foundation.

First published in R. M. Hogarth (ed.) (1982). *New Directions for Methodology of Social and Behavioral Science: The Framing of Questions and the Consistency of Responses*. San Francisco: Jossey-Bass, 21–36.

REFERENCES

Einhorn, H. J., and Hogarth, R. M. (1981). "Behavioral decision theory: processes of judgment and choice," *Annual Review of Psychology*, 32, 53–88.

Fischhoff, B., Slovic, P., and Lichtenstein, S. (1978). "Fault trees: sensitivity of estimated failure probabilities to problem representation," *Journal of Experimental Psychology: Human Perception and Performance*, 4, 330–44.

(1980). "Knowing what you want: measuring labile values," in T. Wallsten (ed.), *Cognitive Processes in Choice and Decision Behavior*. Hillsdale, N.J.: Erlbaum.

Friedman, M., and Savage, L. J. (1948). "The utility analysis of choices involving risk," *Journal of Political Economy*, 56, 279–304.

Grether, D. M., and Plott, C. R. (1979). "Economic theory of choice and the preference reversal phenomenon," *American Economic Review*, 69, 623–38.

Hershey, J. C., and Schoemaker, P. J. H. (1980). "Risk taking and problem context in the domain of losses: an expected-utility analysis," *The Journal of Risk and Insurance*, 47, 111–32.

Johnson, E. M., and Huber, G. P. (1977). "The technology of utility assessment," *IEEE Transactions on Systems, Man, and Cybernetics*, SMC-7, 311–25.

Paul Slovic, Baruch Fischhoff, and Sarah Lichtenstein

Kahneman, D., and Tversky, A. (1975). "Value theory: an analysis of choices under risk." Paper presented at a conference on public economics, Jerusalem, Israel, June.

(1979). "Prospect theory: an analysis of decisions under risk," *Econometrica*, 47, 262–91.

Kunreuther, H. C., *et al.* (1978). *Disaster Insurance Protection: Public Policy Lessons.* New York: Wiley.

Lichtenstein, S., and Slovic, P. (1971). "Reversals of preference between bids and choices in gambling decisions," *Journal of Experimental Psychology*, 89, 46–55.

(1973). "Response-induced reversals of preference in gambling: an extended replication in Las Vegas," *Journal of Experimental Psychology*, 101, 16–2.

Luce, R. D. (1977). "The choice axiom after twenty years," *Journal of Mathematical Psychology*, 15, 215–33.

MacNeil, B. J., Weichselbaum, R., and Pauker, S. G. (1978). "Fallacy of the five year survival in lung cancer," *New England Journal of Medicine*, 299, 1397–401.

Morris, L., Mazis, M., and Barofsky, I. (eds.) (1980). *Product Labeling and Health Risks.* Banbury Report 6. Cold Spring Harbor, N.Y.: Cold Spring Harbor Laboratory.

Payne, J. W., and Braunstein, M. L. (1971). "Preferences among gambles with equal underlying distributions," *Journal of Experimental Psychology*, 87, 13–18.

Raiffa, H. (1968). *Decision Analysis: Introductory Lectures on Choice Under Uncertainty.* Reading, Mass.: Addison-Wesley.

Robertson, L. S. (1976). "The great seat belt campaign flop," *Journal of Communication*, 26, 41–5.

Schoemaker, P. J. H., and Kunreuther, H. C. (1979). "An experimental study of insurance decisions," *Journal of Risk and Insurance*, 46, 603–18.

Slovic, P. (1972). "From Shakespeare to Simon: speculations – and some evidence – about man's ability to process information," *ORI Research Monograph*, 12, (2).

(1975). "Choice between equally valued alternatives," *Journal of Experimental Psychology: Human Perception and Performance*, 1, 280–7.

Slovic, P., Fischhoff, B., and Lichtenstein, S. (1978). "Accident probabilities and seat belt usage: a psychological perspective," *Accident Analysis and Prevention*, 10, 281–5.

(1980). "Informing people about risk," in L. Morris, M. Mazis, and I. Barofsky (eds.), *Product Labeling and Health Risks.* Banbury Report 6. Cold Spring Harbor, N.Y.: Cold Spring Harbor Laboratory.

Slovic, P., Fischhoff, B., Lichtenstein, S., Corrigan, B., and Combs, B. (1977). "Preference for insuring against probable small losses: implications for the theory and practice of insurance," *Journal of Risk and Insurance*, 44, 237–58.

Slovic, P., and Lichtenstein, S. (1968). "The importance of variance preferences in gambling decisions," *Journal of Experimental Psychology*, 78, 646–54.

Slovic, P., and MacPhillamy, D. J. (1974). "Dimensional commensurability and cue utilization in comparative judgment," *Organizational Behavior and Human Performance*, 11, 172–94.

Tversky, A. (1972). "Elimination by aspects: a theory of choice," *Psychological Review*, 79, 281–99.

Tversky, A., and Kahneman, D. (1982). In R. M. Hogarth (ed.), *New Directions for Methodology of Social and Behavioral Science: The Framing of Questions and the Consistency of Response.* San Francisco: Jossey-Bass.

9

RATIONAL CHOICE AND THE
FRAMING OF DECISIONS

AMOS TVERSKY AND DANIEL KAHNEMAN

The modern theory of decision making under risk emerged from a logical analysis of games of chance rather than from a psychological analysis of risk and value. The theory was conceived as a normative model of an idealized decision maker, not as a description of the behavior of real people. In Schumpeter's words, it "has a much better claim to being called a logic of choice than a psychology of value" (1954, p. 1058).

The use of a normative analysis to predict and explain actual behavior is defended by several arguments. First, people are generally thought to be effective in pursuing their goals, particularly when they have incentives and opportunities to learn from experience. It seems reasonable, then, to describe choice as a maximization process. Secondly, competition favors rational individuals and organizations. Optimal decisions increase the chances of survival in a competitive environment, and a minority of rational individuals can sometimes impose rationality on the whole market. Thirdly, the intuitive appeal of the axioms of rational choice makes it plausible that the theory derived from these axioms should provide an acceptable account of choice behavior.

The thesis of the present article is that, in spite of these *a priori* arguments, the logic of choice does not provide an adequate foundation for a descriptive theory of decision making. We argue that the deviations of actual behavior from the normative model are too widespread to be ignored, too systematic to be dismissed as random error, and too fundamental to be accommodated by relaxing the normative system. We first sketch an analysis of the foundations of the theory of rational choice and then show that the most basic rules of the theory are commonly violated by decision makers. We conclude from these findings that the normative and the descriptive analyses cannot be reconciled. A descriptive model of choice is presented, which accounts for preferences that are anomalous in the normative theory.

A HIERARCHY OF NORMATIVE RULES

The major achievement of the modern theory of decision under risk is the derivation of the expected utility rule from simple principles of rational choice that make no reference to long-run considerations (von Neumann and Morgenstern, 1944). The axiomatic analysis of the foundations of expected utility theory reveals four substantive assumptions – cancellation, transitivity, dominance, and invariance – besides the more technical assumptions of comparability and continuity. The substantive assumptions can be ordered by their normative appeal, from the cancellation condition, which has been challenged by many theorists, to invariance, which has been accepted by all. We briefly discuss these assumptions.

Cancellation. The key qualitative property that gives rise to expected utility theory is the "cancellation" or elimination of any state of the world that yields the same outcome regardless of one's choice. This notion has been captured by different formal properties, such as the substitution axiom of von Neumann and Morgenstern (1944), the extended sure-thing principle of Savage (1954), and the independence condition of Luce and Krantz (1971). Thus, if *A* is preferred to *B*, then the prospect of winning *A* if it rains tomorrow (and nothing otherwise) should be preferred to the prospect of winning *B* if it rains tomorrow because the two prospects yield the same outcome (nothing) if there is no rain tomorrow. Cancellation is necessary to represent preference between prospects as the maximization of expected utility. The main argument for cancellation is that only one state will actually be realized, which makes it reasonable to evaluate the outcomes of options separately for each state. The choice between options should therefore depend only on states in which they yield different outcomes.

Transitivity. A basic assumption in models of both risky and riskless choice is the transitivity of preference. This assumption is necessary and essentially sufficient for the representation of preference by an ordinal utility scale *u* such that *A* is preferred to *B* whenever $u(A) > u(B)$. Thus transitivity is satisfied if it is possible to assign to each option a value that does not depend on the other available options. Transitivity is likely to hold when the options are evaluated separately but not when the consequences of an option depend on the alternative to which it is compared, as implied, for example, by considerations of regret. A common argument for transitivity is that cyclic preferences can support a "money pump," in which the intransitive person is induced to pay for a series of exchanges that returns to the initial option.

Dominance. This is perhaps the most obvious principle of rational choice: if one option is better than another in one state and at least as good in all other states, the dominant option should be chosen. A slightly stronger condition – called stochastic dominance – asserts that, for unidimensional risky prospects, *A* is preferred to *B* if the cumulative distribution of *A* is to the right of the cumulative distribution of *B*. Dominance is both simpler and more compelling than cancellation and transitivity, and it serves as the cornerstone of the normative theory of choice.

Invariance. An essential condition for a theory of choice that claims normative status is the principle of invariance: different representations of the same choice problem should yield the same preference. That is, the preference between options should be independent of their description. Two characterizations that the decision maker, on reflection, would view as alternative descriptions of the same problem should lead to the same choice – even without the benefit of such reflection. This principle of invariance (or extensionality [Arrow, 1982]) is so basic that it is tacitly assumed in the characterization of options rather than explicitly stated as a testable axiom. For example, decision models that describe the objects of choice as random variables all assume that alternative representations of the same random variables should be treated alike. Invariance captures the normative intuition that variations of form that do not affect the actual outcomes should not affect the choice. A related concept, called consequentialism, has been discussed by Hammond (1985).

The four principles underlying expected utility theory can be ordered by their normative appeal. Invariance and dominance seem essential, transitivity could be questioned, and cancellation has been rejected by many authors. Indeed, the ingenious counterexamples of Allais (1953) and Ellsberg (1961) led several theorists to abandon cancellation and the expectation principle in favor of more general representations. Most of these models assume transitivity, dominance, and invariance (e.g., Hansson, 1975; Allais, 1979; Hagen, 1979; Machina, 1982; Quiggin, 1982; Weber, 1982; Chew, 1983; Fishburn, 1983; Schmeidler, 1984; Segal, 1984; Yaari, 1984; Luce and Narens, 1985). Other developments abandon transitivity but maintain invariance and dominance (e.g., Bell, 1982; Fishburn, 1982, 1984; Loomes and Sugden, 1982). These theorists responded to observed violations of cancellation and transitivity by weakening the normative theory in order to retain its status as a descriptive model. However, this strategy cannot be extended to the failures of dominance and invariance that we shall document. Because invariance and dominance are normatively essential and descriptively invalid, a theory of rational decison cannot provide an adequate description of choice behavior.

We next illustrate failures of invariance and dominance and then review a descriptive analysis that traces these failures to the joint effects of the rules that govern the framing of prospects, the evaluation of outcomes, and the weighting of probabilities. Several phenomena of choice that support the present account are described.

FAILURES OF INVARIANCE

In this section we consider two illustrative examples in which the condition of invariance is violated and discuss some of the factors that produce these violations.

The first example comes from a study of preferences between medical treatments (McNeil *et al.*, 1982). Respondents were given statistical information about the outcomes of two treatments of lung cancer. The same statistics were presented to some respondents in terms of mortality rates and to others in terms of survival rates. The respondents then indicated their preferred treatment. The information was presented as follows.[1]

Problem 1 (survival frame)

Surgery: Of 100 people having surgery 90 live through the post-operative period, 68 are alive at the end of the first year, and 34 are alive at the end of five years.

Radiation therapy: Of 100 people having radiation therapy all live through the treatment, 77 are alive at the end of one year, and 22 are alive at the end of five years.

Problem 1 (mortality frame)

Surgery: Of 100 people having surgery 10 die during surgery or the post-operative period, 32 die by the end of the first year, and 66 die by the end of five years.

Radiation therapy: Of 100 people having radiation therapy, none die during treatment, 23 die by the end of one year, and 78 die by the end of five years.

The inconsequential difference in formulation produced a marked effect. The overall percentage of respondents who favored radiation therapy rose from 18% in the survival frame ($N = 247$) to 44% in the mortality frame ($N = 336$). The advantage of radiation therapy over surgery evidently looms larger when stated as a reduction of the risk of immediate death from 10% to 0% rather than as an increase from 90% to 100% in the rate of survival. The framing effect was not smaller for experienced physicians or for statistically sophisticated business students than for a group of clinic patients.

Our next example concerns decisions between conjunctions of risky prospects with monetary outcomes. Each respondent made two choices, one between favorable prospects and one between unfavorable prospects (Tversky and Kahneman, 1981, p. 454). It was assumed that the two selected prospects would be played independently.

Problem 2 ($N = 150$). Imagine that you face the following pair of concurrent decisions. First examine both decisions, then indicate the options you prefer.

Decision (i) Choose between:
A. a sure gain of $240 [84%]
B. 25% chance to gain $1,000 and 75% chance to gain nothing [16%]

Decision (ii) Choose between:
C. a sure loss of $750 [13%]
D. 75% chance to lose $1,000 and 25% chance to lose nothing [87%]

The total number of respondents is denoted by N, and the percentage who chose each option is indicated in brackets. (Unless otherwise specified, the data were obtained from undergraduate students at Stanford University and at the

170

University of British Columbia.) The majority choice in decision (i) is risk averse, while the majority choice in decision (ii) is risk seeking. This is a common pattern: choices involving gains are usually risk averse, and choices involving losses are often risk seeking – except when the probability of winning or losing is small (Fishburn and Kochenberger, 1979; Kahneman and Tversky, 1979; Hershey and Schoemaker, 1980).

Because the subjects considered the two decisions simultaneously, they expressed, in effect, a preference for the portfolio *A* and *D* over the portfolio *B* and *C*. However, the preferred portfolio is actually dominated by the rejected one! The combined options are as follows.

A & D: 25% chance to win $240 and 75% chance to lose $760.
B & C: 25% chance to win $250 and 75% chance to lose $750.

When the options are presented in this aggregated form, the dominant option is invariably chosen. In the format of problem 2, however, 73% of respondents chose the dominated combination *A* and *D*, and only 3% chose *B* and *C*. The contrast between the two formats illustrates a violation of invariance. The findings also support the general point that failures of invariance are likely to produce violations of stochastic dominance and vice versa.

The respondents evidently evaluated decisions (i) and (ii) separately in problem 2, where they exhibited the standard pattern of risk aversion in gains and risk seeking in losses. People who are given these problems are very surprised to learn that the combination of two preferences that they considered quite reasonable led them to select a dominated option. The same pattern of results was also observed in a scaled-down version of problem 2, with real monetary payoff (see Tversky and Kahneman, 1981, p. 458).

As illustrated by the preceding examples, variations in the framing of decision problems produce systematic violations of invariance and dominance that cannot be defended on normative grounds. It is instructive to examine two mechanisms that could ensure the invariance of preferences: canonical representations and the use of expected actuarial value.

Invariance would hold if all formulations of the same prospect were transformed to a standard canonical representation (e.g., a cumulative probability distribution of the same random variable) because the various versions would then all be evaluated in the same manner. In problem 2, for example, invariance and dominance would both be preserved if the outcomes of the two decisions were aggregated prior to evaluation. Similarly, the same choice would be made in both versions of the medical problem if the outcomes were coded in terms of one dominant frame (e.g., rate of survival). The observed failures of invariance indicate that people do not spontaneously aggregate concurrent prospects or transform all outcomes into a common frame.

The failure to construct a canonical representation in decision problems contrasts with other cognitive tasks in which such representations are generated automatically and effortlessly. In particular, our visual experience consists largely of canonical representations: objects do not appear to change in size, shape, brightness, or color when we move around them or when illumination varies. A white circle seen from a sharp angle in dim light appears circular and white, not ellipsoid and grey. Canonical representations are also generated in the process of language comprehension, where listeners quickly recode much of what they hear into an abstract propositional form that no longer discriminates, for example, between the active and the passive voice and often does not distinguish what was actually said from what was implied or presupposed (Clark and Clark, 1977). Unfortunately, the mental machinery that transforms percepts and sentences into standard forms does not automatically apply to the process of choice.

Invariance could be satisfied even in the absence of a canonical representation if the evaluation of prospects were separately linear, or nearly linear, in probability and monetary value. If people ordered risky prospects by their actuarial values, invariance and dominance would always hold. In particular, there would be no difference between the mortality and the survival versions of the medical problem. Because the evaluation of outcomes and probabilities is generally nonlinear, and, because people do not spontaneously construct canonical representations of decisions, invariance commonly fails. Normative models of choice, which assume invariance, therefore cannot provide an adequate descriptive account of choice behavior. In the next section we present a descriptive account of risky choice, called prospect theory, and explore its consequences. Failures of invariance are explained by framing effects that control the representation of options, in conjunction with the nonlinearities of value and belief.

FRAMING AND EVALUATION OF OUTCOMES

Prospect theory distinguishes two phases in the choice process: a phase of framing and editing, followed by a phase of evaluation (Kahneman and Tversky, 1979). The first phase consists of a preliminary analysis of the decision problem, which frames the effective acts, contingencies, and outcomes. Framing is controlled by the manner in which the choice problem is presented as well as by norms, habits, and expectancies of the decision maker. Additional operations that are performed prior to evaluation include cancellation of common components and the elimination of options that are seen to be dominated by others. In the second phase, the framed prospects are evaluated, and the prospect of highest value is selected. The theory distinguishes two ways of choosing between prospects: by detecting that one dominates another or by comparing their values.

For simplicity, we confine the discussion to simple gambles with numerical probabilities and monetary outcomes. Let $(x, p; y, q)$ denote a prospect that yields x with probability p and y with probability q and that preserves the status quo with probability $(1 - p - q)$. According to prospect theory, there are values

$v(\cdot)$, defined on gains and losses, and decision weights $\pi(\cdot)$, defined on stated probabilities, such that the overall value of the prospect equals $\pi(p)v(x) + \pi(q)v(y)$. A slight modification is required if all outcomes of a prospect have the same sign.[2]

The value function

Following Markowitz (1952), outcomes are expressed in prospect theory as positive or negative deviations (gains or losses) from a neutral reference outcome, which is assigned a value of zero. Unlike Markowitz, however, we propose that the value function is commonly S-shaped, concave above the reference point, and convex below it, as illustrated in figure 9.1. Thus the difference in subjective value between a gain of $100 and a gain of $200 is greater than the subjective difference between a gain of $1,100 and a gain of $1,200. The same relation between value differences holds for the corresponding losses. The proposed function expresses the property that the effect of a marginal change decreases with the distance from the reference point in either direction. These hypotheses regarding the typical shape of the value function may not apply to ruinous losses or to circumstances in which particular amounts assume special significance.

A significant property of the value function, called *loss aversion*, is that the response to losses is more extreme than the response to gains. The common reluctance to accept a fair bet on the toss of a coin suggests that the displeasure of losing a sum of money exceeds the pleasure of winning the same amount. Thus the proposed value function is (i) defined on gains and losses, (ii) generally concave for gains and convex for losses, and (iii) steeper for losses than for gains. These properties of the value function have been supported in many studies of risky choice involving monetary outcomes (Fishburn and Kochenberger, 1979; Kahneman and Tversky, 1979; Hershey and Schoemaker, 1980; Payne, Laughhunn, and Crum, 1980) and human lives (Tversky, 1977; Eraker and Sox, 1981; Tversky and Kahneman, 1981; Fischhoff, 1983). Loss aversion may also contribute to the observed discrepancies between the amount of money people are willing to pay for a good and the compensation they demand to give it up (Bishop and Heberlein, 1979; Knetsch and Sinden, 1984). This effect is implied by the value function if the good is valued as a gain in the former context and as a loss in the latter.

Framing outcomes

The framing of outcomes and the contrast between traditional theory and the present analysis are illustrated in the following problems.

Problem 3 ($N = 126$): Assume yourself richer by $300 than you are today. You have to choose between
a sure gain of $100 [72%]
50% chance to gain $200 and 50% to gain nothing [28%]

Problem 4 (*N* = 128): Assume yourself richer by $500 than you are today. You have to choose between

a sure loss of $100 [36%]

50% chance to lose nothing and 50% chance to lose $200 [64%]

As implied by the value function, the majority choice is risk averse in problem 3 and risk seeking in problem 4, although the two problems are essentially identical. In both cases one faces a choice between $400 for sure and an even chance of $500 or $300. Problem 4 is obtained from problem 3 by increasing the initial endowment by $200 and subtracting this amount from both options. This variation has a substantial effect on preferences. Additional questions showed that variations of $200 in initial wealth have little or no effect on choices. Evidently, preferences are quite insensitive to small changes of wealth but highly sensitive to corresponding changes in reference point. These observations show that the effective carriers of values are gains and losses, or changes in wealth, rather than states of wealth as implied by the rational model.

The common pattern of preferences observed in problems 3 and 4 is of special interest because it violates not only expected utility theory but practically all other normatively based models of choice. In particular, these data are inconsistent with the model of regret advanced by Bell (1982) and by Loomes and Sugden (1982) and axiomatized by Fishburn (1982). This follows from the fact that problems 3 and 4 yield identical outcomes and an identical regret structure. Furthermore, regret theory cannot accommodate the combination of risk aversion in problem 3 and risk seeking in problem 4 – even without the corresponding changes in endowment that make the problems extensionally equivalent.

Figure 9.1 A typical value function.

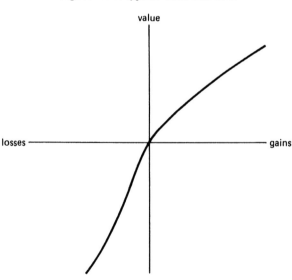

Shifts of reference can be induced by different decompositions of outcomes into risky and riskless components, as in the above problems. The reference point can also be shifted by a mere labeling of outcomes, as illustrated in the following problems (Tversky and Kahneman, 1981, p. 453).

Problem 5 ($N = 152$): Imagine that the US is preparing for the outbreak of an unusual Asian disease, which is expected to kill 600 people. Two alternative programs to combat the disease have been proposed. Assume that the exact scientific estimates of the consequences of the programs are as follows:

If program *A* is adopted, 200 people will be saved. [72%]

If program *B* is adopted, there is 1/3 probability that 600 people will be saved, and 2/3 probability that no people will be saved. [28%]

In problem 5 the outcomes are stated in positive terms (lives saved), and the majority choice is accordingly risk averse. The prospect of certainly saving 200 lives is more attractive than a risky prospect of equal expected value. A second group of respondents was given the same cover story with the following descriptions of the alternative programs.

Problem 6 ($N = 155$):
If program *C* is adopted 400 people will die. [22%]

If program *D* is adopted there is 1/3 probability that nobody will die, and 2/3 probability that 600 people will die. [78%]

In problem 6 the outcomes are stated in negative terms (lives lost), and the majority choice is accordingly risk seeking. The certain death of 400 people is less acceptable than a two-thirds chance that 600 people will die. Problems 5 and 6, however, are essentially identical. They differ only in that the former is framed in terms of the number of lives saved (relative to an expected loss of 600 lives if no action is taken), whereas the latter is framed in terms of the number of lives lost.

On several occasions we presented both versions to the same respondents and discussed with them the inconsistent preferences evoked by the two frames. Many respondents expressed a wish to remain risk averse in the "lives saved" version and risk seeking in the "lives lost" version, although they also expressed a wish for their answers to be consistent. In the persistence of their appeal, framing effects resemble visual illusions more than computational errors.

Discounts and surcharges

Perhaps the most distinctive intellectual contribution of economic analysis is the systematic consideration of alternative opportunities. A basic principle of economic thinking is that opportunity costs and out-of-pocket costs should be treated alike. Preferences should depend only on relevant differences between options, not on how these differences are labeled. This principle runs counter to the psychological tendencies that make preferences susceptible to superficial variations in form. In particular, a difference that favors outcome *A* over outcome *B* can sometimes be framed either as an advantage of *A* or as a disadvantage of *B* by suggesting either *B* or *A* as the neutral reference point. Because of loss aversion, the difference will loom larger when *A* is neutral and *B-A* is evaluated as a loss than when *B* is neutral and *A-B* is evaluated as a gain. The significance of such variations of framing has been noted in several contexts.

Thaler (1980) drew attention to the effect of labeling a difference between two prices as a surcharge or a discount. It is easier to forgo a discount than to accept a surcharge because the same price difference is valued as a gain in the former case and as a loss in the latter. Indeed, the credit-card lobby is said to insist that any price difference between cash and card purchases should be labeled a cash discount rather than a credit surcharge. A similar idea could be invoked to explain why the price response to slack demand often takes the form of discounts or special concessions (Stigler and Kindahl, 1970). Customers may be expected to show less resistance to the eventual cancellation of such temporary arrangements than to outright price increases. Judgments of fairness exhibit the same pattern (Kahneman, Knetsch, and Thaler, 1986a).

Schelling (1981) has described a striking framing effect in a context of tax policy. He points out that the tax table can be constructed by using as a default case either the childless family (as is in fact done) or, say, the modal two-child family. The tax difference between a childless family and a two-child family is naturally framed as an exemption (for the two-child family) in the first frame and as a tax premium (on the childless family) in the second frame. This seemingly innocuous difference has a large effect on judgments of the desired relation between income, family size, and tax. Schelling reported that his students rejected the idea of granting the rich a larger exemption than the poor in the first frame but favored a larger tax premium on the childless rich than on the childless poor in the second frame. Because the exemption and the premium are alternative labels for the same tax differences in the two cases, the judgments violate invariance. Framing the consequences of a public policy in positive or in negative terms can greatly alter its appeal.

The notion of a money illusion is sometimes applied to workers' willingness to accept, in periods of high inflation, increases in nominal wages that do not protect their real income – although they would strenuously resist equivalent wage cuts in the absence of inflation. The essence of the illusion is that, whereas a cut in the nominal wage is always recognized as a loss, a nominal increase that does not preserve real income may be treated as a gain. Another manifestation of the money illusion was observed in a study of the perceived fairness of economic actions (Kahneman, Knetsch, and Thaler, 1986b). Respondents in a telephone interview evaluated the fairness of the action described in the following vignette, which was presented in two versions that differed only in the bracketed clauses.

> A company is making a small profit. It is located in a community experiencing a recession with substantial unemployment [but no inflation/and inflation of 12%].

The company decides to [decrease wages and salaries 7%/increase salaries only 5%] this year.

Although the loss of real income is very similar in the two versions, the proportion of respondents who judged the action of the company "unfair" or "very unfair" was 62% for a nominal reduction but only 22% for a nominal increase.

Bazerman (1983) has documented framing effects in experimental studies of bargaining. He compared the performance of experimental subjects when the outcomes of bargaining were formulated as gains or as losses. Subjects who bargained over the allocation of losses more often failed to reach agreement and more often failed to discover a Pareto-optimal solution. Bazerman attributed these observations to the general propensity toward risk seeking in the domain of losses, which may increase the willingness of both participants to risk the negative consequences of a deadlock.

Loss aversion presents an obstacle to bargaining whenever the participants evaluate their own concessions as losses and the concessions obtained from the other party as gains. In negotiating over missiles, for example, the subjective loss of security associated with dismantling a missile may loom larger than the increment of security produced by a similar action on the adversary's part. If the two parties both assign a two-to-one ratio to the values of the concessions they make and of those they obtain, the resulting four-to-one gap may be difficult to bridge. Agreement will be much easier to achieve by negotiators who trade in "bargaining chips" that are valued equally, regardless of whose hand they are in. In this mode of trading, which may be common in routine purchases, loss aversion tends to disappear (Kahneman and Tversky, 1984).

THE FRAMING AND WEIGHTING OF CHANCE EVENTS

In expected-utility theory, the utility of each possible outcome is weighted by its probability. In prospect theory, the value of an uncertain outcome is multiplied by a decision weight $\pi(p)$, which is a monotonic function of p but is not a probability. The weighting function π has the following properties. First, impossible events are discarded, that is, $\pi(0) = 0$, and the scale is normalized so that $\pi(1) = 1$, but the function is not well behaved near the end points (Kahneman and Tversky, 1979). Secondly, for low probabilities, $\pi(p) > p$, but $\pi(p) + \pi(1 - p) \leqslant 1$ (subcertainty). Thus low probabilities are overweighted, moderate and high probabilities are underweighted, and the latter effect is more pronounced than the former. Thirdly, $\pi(pr)/\pi(p) < \pi(pqr)/\pi(pq)$ for all $0 < p, q, r \leqslant 1$ (subproportionality). That is, for any fixed probability ratio r, the ratio of decision weights is closer to unity when the probabilities are low than when they are high, for example, $\pi(.1)/\pi(.2) > \pi(.4)/\pi(.8)$. A hypothetical weighting function that satisfies these properties is shown in figure 9.2. Its consequences are discussed in the next section.[3]

Nontransparent dominance

The major characteristic of the weighting function is the overweighting of probability differences involving certainty and impossibility, for example, $\pi(1.0) - \pi(.9)$ or $\pi(.1) - \pi(0)$, relative to comparable differences in the middle of the scale, for example, $\pi(.3) - \pi(.2)$. In particular, for small p, π is generally subadditive, for example, $\pi(.01) + \pi(.06) > \pi(.07)$. This property can lead to violations of dominance, as illustrated in the following pair of problems.

Problem 7 ($N = 88$). Consider the following two lotteries, described by the percentage of marbles of different colors in each box and the amount of money you win or lose depending on the color of a randomly drawn marble. Which lottery do you prefer?

Option *A*

90% white	6% red	1% green	1% blue	2% yellow
$0	win $45	win $30	lose $15	lose $15

Option *B*

90% white	6% red	1% green	1% blue	2% yellow
$0	win $45	win $45	lose $10	lose $15

It is easy to see that option *B* dominates option *A*: for every color the outcome of *B* is at least as desirable as the outcome of *A*. Indeed, all respondents chose *B* over *A*. This observation is hardly surprising because the relation of dominance is

Figure 9.2 A typical weighting function.

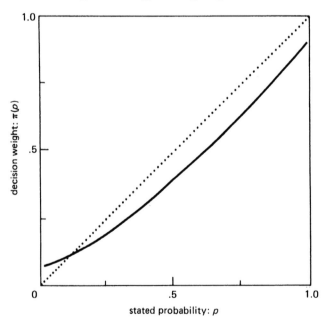

highly transparent, so the dominated prospect is rejected without further processing. The next problem is effectively identical to problem 7, except that colors yielding identical outcomes (red and green in *B* and yellow and blue in *A*) are combined. We have proposed that this operation is commonly performed by the decision maker if no dominated prospect is detected.

Problem 8 (N = 124). Which lottery do you prefer?

Option *C*

90% white	6% red	1% green	3% yellow
$0	win $45	win $30	lose $15

Option *D*

90% white	7% red	1% green	2% yellow
$0	win $45	lose $10	lose $15

The formulation of problem 8 simplifies the options but masks the relation of dominance. Furthermore, it enhances the attractiveness of *C*, which has two positive outcomes and one negative, relative to *D*, which has two negative outcomes and one positive. As an inducement to consider the options carefully, participants were informed that one-tenth of them, selected at random, would actually play the gambles they chose. Although this announcement aroused much excitement, 58% of the participants chose the dominated alternative *C*. In answer to another question the majority of respondents also assigned a higher cash equivalent to *C* than to *D*. These results support the following propositions. (i) Two formulations of the same problem elicit different preferences, in violation of invariance. (ii) The dominance rule is obeyed when its application is transparent. (iii) Dominance is masked by a frame in which the inferior option yields a more favorable outcome in an identified state of the world (e.g., drawing

Figure 9.3 The Müller–Lyer illusion.

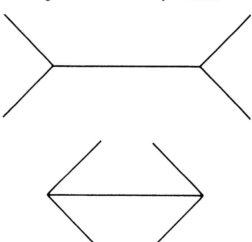

a green marble). (iv) The discrepancy preferences are consistent with the subadditivity of decision weights. The role of transparency may be illuminated by a perceptual example. Figure 9.3 presents the well-known Müller–Lyer illusion: the top line appears longer than the bottom line, although it is in fact shorter. In figure 9.4, the same patterns are embedded in a rectangular frame, which makes it apparent that the protruding bottom line is longer than the top one. This judgment has the nature of an inference, in contrast to the perceptual impression that mediates judgment in figure 9.3. Similarly, the finer partition introduced in problem 7 makes it possible to conclude that option *D* is superior to *C*, without assessing their values. Whether the relation of dominance is detected depends on framing as well as on the sophistication and experience of the decision maker. The dominance relation in problems 8 and 1 could be transparent to a sophisticated decision maker, although it was not transparent to most of our respondents.

Certainty and pseudocertainty

The overweighting of outcomes that are obtained with certainty relative to outcomes that are merely probable gives rise to violations of the expectation rule,

Figure 9.4 A transparent version of the Müller–Lyer illusion.

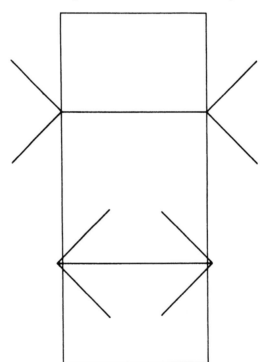

as first noted by Allais (1953). The next series of problems (Tversky and Kahneman, 1981, p. 455) illustrates the phenomenon discovered by Allais and its relation to the weighting of probabilities and to the framing of chance events. Chance events were realized by drawing a single marble from a bag containing a specified number of favorable and unfavorable marbles. To encourage thoughtful answers, one-tenth of the participants, selected at random, were given an opportunity to play the gambles they chose. The same respondents answered problems 9–11, in that order.

Problem 9 (N = 77). Which of the following options do you prefer?
A. a sure gain of $30 [78%]
B. 80% chance to win $45 and 20% chance to win nothing [22%]

Problem 10 (N = 81). Which of the following options do you prefer?
C. 25% chance to win $30 and 75% chance to win nothing [42%]
D. 20% chance to win $45 and 80% chance to win nothing [58%]

Note that problem 10 is obtained from problem 9 by reducing the probabilities of winning by a factor of four. In expected utility theory a preference for *A* over *B* in problem 9 implies a preference for *C* over *D* in problem 10. Contrary to this prediction, the majority preference switched from the lower prize ($30) to the higher one ($45) when the probabilities of winning were substantially reduced. We called this phenomenon the *certainty effect* because the reduction of the probability of winning from certainty to .25 has a greater effect than the corresponding reduction from .8 to .2. In prospect theory, the modal choice in problem 9 implies $v(45)\pi(.80) < v(30)\pi(1.0)$, whereas the modal choice in problem 10 implies $v(45)\pi(.20) > v(30)\pi(.25)$. The observed violation of expected utility theory, then, is implied by the curvature of π (see figure 9.2) if

$$\frac{\pi(.20)}{\pi(.25)} > \frac{v(30)}{v(45)} > \frac{\pi(.80)}{\pi(1.0)}.$$

Allais's problem has attracted the attention of numerous theorists, who attempted to provide a normative rationale for the certainty effect by relaxing the cancellation rule (see, e.g., Allais, 1979; Fishburn, 1982, 1983; Machina, 1982; Quiggin, 1982; Chew, 1983). The following problem illustrates a related phenomenon, called the *pseudocertainty effect*, that cannot be accommodated by relaxing cancellation because it also involves a violation of invariance.

Problem 11 (N = 85): Consider the following two-stage game. In the first stage, there is a 75% chance to end the game without winning anything, and a 25% chance to move into the second stage. If you reach the second stage you have a choice between:

E. a sure win of $30 [74%]
F. 80% chance to win $45 and 20% chance to win nothing [26%]

Your choice must be made before the outcome of the first stage is known.

181

Because there is one chance in four to move into the second stage, prospect *E* offers a .25 probability of winning $30, and prospect *F* offers a .25 × .80 = .20 probability of winning $45. Problem 11 is therefore identical to problem 10 in terms of probabilities and outcomes. However, the preferences in the two problems differ: most subjects made a risk-averse choice in problem 11 but not in problem 10. We call this phenomenon the pseudocertainty effect because an outcome that is actually uncertain is weighted as if it were certain. The framing of problem 11 as a two-stage game encourages respondents to apply cancellation: the event of failing to reach the second stage is discarded prior to evaluation because it yields the same outcomes in both options. In this framing problems 11 and 9 are evaluated alike.

Although problems 10 and 11 are identical in terms of final outcomes and their probabilities, problem 11 has a greater potential for inducing regret. Consider a decision maker who chooses *F* in problem 11, reaches the second stage, but fails to win the prize. This individual knows that the choice of *E* would have yielded a gain of $30. In problem 10, on the other hand, an individual who chooses *D* and fails to win cannot know with certainty what the outcome of the other choice would have been. This difference could suggest an alternative interpretation of the pseudo-certainty effect in terms of regret (e.g., Loomes and Sugden, 1982). However, the certainty and the pseudo-certainty effects were found to be equally strong in a modified version of problems 9–11 in which opportunities for regret were equated across problems. This finding does not imply that considerations of regret play no role in decisions. (For examples, see Kahneman and Tversky, 1982, p. 710.) It merely indicates that Allais's example and the pseudocertainty effect are primarily controlled by the nonlinearity of decision weights and the framing of contingencies rather than by the anticipation of regret.[4]

The certainty and pseudocertainty effects are not restricted to monetary outcomes. The following problem illustrates these phenomena in a medical context. The respondents were 72 physicians attending a meeting of the California Medical Association. Essentially the same pattern of responses was obtained from a larger group ($N = 180$) of college students.

Problem 12 ($N = 72$). In the treatment of tumors there is sometimes a choice between two types of therapies: (i) a radical treatment such as extensive surgery, which involves some risk of imminent death, (ii) a moderate treatment, such as limited surgery or radiation therapy. Each of the following problems describes the possible outcome of two alternative treatments, for three different cases. In considering each case, suppose the patient is a 40-year-old male. Assume that without treatment death is imminent (within a month) and that only one of the treatments can be applied. Please indicate the treatment you would prefer in each case.

Case 1

Treatment *A*: 20% chance of imminent death and 80% chance of normal life, with an expected longevity of 30 years. [35%]

Treatment *B*: certainty of a normal life, with an expected longevity of 18 years. [65%]

Case 2

Treatment *C*: 80% chance of imminent death and 20% chance of normal life, with an expected longevity of 30 years. [68%]

Treatment *D*: 75% chance of imminent death and 25% chance of normal life, with an expected longevity of 18 years. [32%]

Case 3

Consider a new case where there is a 25% chance that the tumor is treatable and a 75% chance that it is not. If the tumor is not treatable, death is imminent. If the tumor is treatable, the outcomes of the treatment are as follows:

Treatment *E*: 20% chance of imminent death and 80% chance of normal life, with an expected longevity of 30 years. [32%]

Treatment *F*: certainty of normal life, with an expected longevity of 18 years. [68%]

The three cases of this problem correspond, respectively, to problems 9–11, and the same pattern of preferences is observed. In case 1, most respondents make a risk-averse choice in favor of certain survival with reduced longevity. In case 2, the moderate treatment no longer ensures survival, and most respondents choose the treatment that offers the higher expected longevity. In particular, 64% of the physicians who chose *B* in case 1 selected *C* in case 2. This is another example of Allais's certainty effect.

The comparison of cases 2 and 3 provides another illustration of pseudocertainty. The cases are identical in terms of the relevant outcomes and their probabilities, but the preferences differ. In particular, 56% of the physicians who chose *C* in case 2 selected *F* in case 3. The conditional framing induces people to disregard the event of the tumor not being treatable because the two treatments are equally ineffective in this case. In this frame, treatment *F* enjoys the advantage of pseudocertainty. It appears to ensure survival, but the assurance is conditional on the treatability of the tumor. In fact, there is only a .25 chance of surviving a month if this option is chosen.

The conjunction of certainty and pseudocertainty effects has significant implications for the relation between normative and descriptive theories of choice. Our results indicate that cancellation is actually obeyed in choices – in those problems that make its application transparent. Specifically, we find that people make the same choices in problems 11 and 9 and in cases 3 and 1 of problem 12. Evidently, people "cancel" an event that yields the same outcomes for all options, in two-stage or nested structures. Note that in these examples cancellation is satisfied in problems that are formally equivalent to those in which it is violated. The empirical validity of cancellation therefore depends on the framing of the problems.

The present concept of framing originated from the analysis of Allais's problems by Savage (1954, pp. 101–4) and Raiffa (1968, pp. 80–6), who reframed these examples in an attempt to make the application of cancellation more compelling. Savage and Raiffa were right: naive respondents indeed obey the cancellation axioms when its application is sufficiently transparent.[5] However, the contrasting preferences in different versions of the same choice (problems 10 and 11 and cases 2 and 3 of problem 12) indicate that people do not follow the same axiom when its application is not transparent. Instead, they apply (nonlinear) decision weights to the probabilities as stated. The status of cancellation is therefore similar to that of dominance: both rules are intuitively compelling as abstract principles of choice, consistently obeyed in transparent problems and frequently violated in nontransparent ones. Attempts to rationalize the preferences in Allais's example by discarding the cancellation axiom face a major difficulty: they do not distinguish transparent formulations in which cancellation is obeyed from nontransparent ones in which it is violated.

DISCUSSION

In the preceding sections we challenged the descriptive validity of the major tenets of expected utility theory and outlined an alternative account of risky choice. In this section we discuss alternative theories and argue against the reconciliation of normative and descriptive analyses. Some objections of economists to our analysis and conclusions are addressed.

Descriptive and normative considerations

Many alternative models of risky choice, designed to explain the observed violations of expected utility theory, have been developed in the last decade. These models divide into the following four classes. (i) Nonlinear functions (e.g., Allais, 1953, 1979; Machina, 1982) are obtained by eliminating the cancellation condition altogether. These models do not have axiomatizations leading to a (cardinal) measurement of utility, but they impose various restrictions (i.e., differentiability) on the utility functions. (ii) The expectations quotient model (axiomatized by Chew and MacCrimmon, 1979; Weber, 1982; Chew, 1983; Fishburn, 1983) replaces cancellation by a weaker substitution axiom and represents the value of a prospect by the ratio of two linear functions. (iii) Bilinear models with nonadditive probabilities (e.g., Kahneman and Tversky, 1979; Quiggin, 1982; Schmeidler, 1984; Segal, 1984; Yaari, 1984; Luce and Narens, 1985) assume various restricted versions of cancellation (or substitution) and construct a bilinear representation in which the utilities of outcomes are weighted by a nonadditive probability measure or by some nonlinear transform of the probability scale. (iv) Nontransitive models represent preferences by a bivariate utility function. Fishburn (1982, 1984) axiomatized such models, while Bell (1982) and Loomes and Sugden (1982) interpreted them in terms of expected regret. For further theoretical developments, see Fishburn (1985).

Table 9.1. *Summary of empirical violations and explanatory models*

Tenet	Empirical Violation	Explanatory model
Cancellation	certainty effect (Allais, 1953, 1979; Kahneman and Tversky, 1979) (problems 9–10, and 12 [cases 1 and 2])	all models
Transitivity	lexicographic semiorder (Tversky, 1969) preference reversals (Slovic and Lichtenstein, 1983)	bivariate models
Dominance	contrasting risk attitudes (problem 2) subadditive decision weights (problem 8)	prospect theory
Invariance	framing effects (problems 1, 3–4, 5–6, 7–8, 10–11, and 12)	prospect theory

The relation between models and data is summarized in table 9.1. The stub column lists the four major tenets of expected utility theory. Column 1 lists the major empirical violations of these tenets and cites a few representative references. Column 2 lists the subset of models discussed above that are consistent with the observed violations.

The conclusions of table 9.1 may be summarized as follows. First, all the above models (as well as some others) are consistent with the violations of cancellation produced by the certainty effect.[6] Therefore, Allais's "paradox" cannot be used to compare or evaluate competing nonexpectation models. Secondly, bivariate (nontransitive) models are needed to explain observed intransitivities. Thirdly, only prospect theory can accommodate the observed violations of (stochastic) dominance and invariance. Although some models (e.g., Loomes and Sugden, 1982; Luce and Narens, 1985) permit some limited failures of invariance, they do not account for the range of framing effects described in this chapter.

Because framing effects and the associated failures of invariance are ubiqitous, no adequate descriptive theory can ignore these phenomena. On the other hand, because invariance (or extensionality) is normatively indispensable, no adequate prescriptive theory should permit its violation. Consequently, the dream of constructing a theory that is acceptable both descriptively and normatively appears unrealizable (see also Tversky and Kahneman, 1983).

Prospect theory differs from the other models mentioned above in being unabashedly descriptive and in making no normative claims. It is designed to explain preferences, whether or not they can be rationalized. Machina (1982, p. 292) claimed that prospect theory is "unacceptable as a descriptive model of behavior toward risk" because it implies violations of stochastic dominance. But, since the violations of dominance predicted by the theory have actually been observed (see problems 2 and 8), Machina's objection appears invalid.

Perhaps the major finding of the present article is that the axioms of rational choice are generally satisfied in transparent situations and often violated in nontransparent ones. For example, when the relation of stochastic dominance is transparent (as in the aggregated version of problem 2 and in problem 7), practically everyone selects the dominant prospect. However, when these problems are framed so that the relation of dominance is no longer transparent (as in the segregated version of problem 2 and in problem 8), most respondents violate dominance, as predicted. These results contradict all theories that imply stochastic dominance as well as others (e.g., Machina, 1982) that predict the same choices in transparent and nontransparent contexts. The same conclusion applies to cancellation, as shown in the discussion of pseudocertainty. It appears that both cancellation and dominance have normative appeal, although neither one is descriptively valid.

The present results and analysis – particularly the role of transparency and the significance of framing – are consistent with the conception of bounded rationality originally presented by Herbert Simon (see, e.g., Simon, 1955, 1978; March, 1978; Nelson and Winter, 1982). Indeed, prospect theory is an attempt to articulate some of the principles of perception and judgment that limit the rationality of choice.

The introduction of psychological considerations (e.g., framing) both enriches and complicates the analysis of choice. Because the framing of decisions depends on the language of presentation, on the context of choice, and on the nature of the display, our treatment of the process is necessarily informal and incomplete. We have identified several common rules of framing, and we have demonstrated their effects on choice, but we have not provided a formal theory of framing. Furthermore, the present analysis does not account for all the observed failures of transitivity and invariance. Although some intransitivities (e.g., Tversky, 1969) can be explained by discarding small differences in the framing phase, and others (e.g., Raiffa, 1968, p. 75) arise from the combination of transparent and nontransparent comparisons, there are examples of cyclic preferences and context effects (see, e.g., Slovic, Fischhoff, and Lichtenstein, 1982; Slovic and Lichtenstein, 1983) that require additional explanatory mechanisms (e.g., multiple reference points and variable weights). An adequate account of choice cannot ignore these effects of framing and context, even if they are normatively distasteful and mathematically intractable.

Bolstering assumptions

The assumption of rationality has a favored position in economics. It is accorded all the methodological privileges of a self-evident truth, a reasonable idealization, a tautology, and a null hypothesis. Each of these interpretations either puts the hypothesis of rational action beyond question or places the burden of proof squarely on any alternative analysis of belief and choice. The advantage of the rational model is compounded because no other theory of judgment and decision can ever match it in scope, power, and simplicity.

Furthermore, the assumption of rationality is protected by a formidable set of defenses in the form of bolstering assumptions that restrict the significance of any observed violation of the model. In particular, it is commonly assumed that substantial violations of the standard model are (i) restricted to insignificant choice problems, (ii) quickly eliminated by learning, or (iii) irrelevant to economics because of the corrective function of market forces. Indeed, incentives sometimes improve the quality of decisions, experienced decision makers often do better than novices, and the forces of arbitrage and competition can nullify some effects of error and illusion. Whether these factors ensure rational choices in any particular situation is an empirical issue, to be settled by observation, not by supposition.

It has frequently been claimed (see, e.g., Smith, 1985) that the observed failures of rational models are attributable to the cost of thinking and will thus be eliminated by proper incentives. Experimental findings provide little support for this view. Studies reported in the economic and psychological literature have shown that errors that are prevalent in responses to hypothetical questions persist even in the presence of significant monetary payoffs. In particular, elementary blunders of probabilistic reasoning (Grether, 1980; Tversky and Kahneman, 1983), major inconsistencies of choice (Grether and Plott, 1979; Slovic and Lichtenstein, 1983), and violations of stochastic dominance in nontransparent problems (see problem 2 above) are hardly reduced by incentives. The evidence that high stakes do not always improve decisions is not restricted to laboratory studies. Significant errors of judgment and choice can be documented in real-world decisions that involve high stakes and serious deliberation. The high rate of failures of small businesses, for example, is not easily reconciled with the assumptions of rational expectations and risk aversion.

Incentives do not operate by magic: they work by focusing attention and by prolonging deliberation. Consequently, they are more likely to prevent errors that arise from insufficient attention and effort than errors that arise from misperception or faulty intuition. The example of visual illusion is instructive. There is no obvious mechanism by which the mere introduction of incentives (without the added opportunity to make measurements) would reduce the illusion observed in figure 9.3, and the illusion vanishes – even in the absence of incentives – when the display is altered in figure 4. The corrective power of incentives depends on the nature of the particular error and cannot be taken for granted.

The assumption of the rationality of decision making is often defended by the argument that people will learn to make correct decisions and sometimes by the evolutionary argument that irrational decision makers will be driven out by rational ones. There is no doubt that learning and selection do take place and tend to improve efficiency. As in the case of incentives, however, no magic is involved. Effective learning takes place only under certain conditions: it requires accurate and immediate feedback about the relation between the situational conditions and the appropriate response. The necessary feedback is often lacking for the decisions made by managers, entrepreneurs, and politicians because (i) outcomes are commonly delayed and not easily attributable to a particular action; (ii) variability in the environment degrades the reliability of the feedback, especially where outcomes of low probability are involved; (iii) there is often no information about what the outcome would have been if another decision had been taken; and (iv) most important decisions are unique and therefore provide little opportunity for learning (see Einhorn and Hogarth, 1978). The conditions for organizational learning are hardly better. Learning surely occurs, for both individuals and organizations, but any claim that a particular error will be eliminated by experience must be supported by demonstrating that the conditions for effective learning are satisfied.

Finally, it is sometimes argued that failures of rationality in individual decision making are inconsequential because of the corrective effects of the market (Knez, Smith, and Williams, 1985). Economic agents are often protected from their own irrational predilections by the forces of competition and by the action of arbitrageurs, but there are situations in which this mechanism fails. Hausch, Ziemba, and Rubenstein (1981) have documented an instructive example: the market for win bets at the racetrack is efficient, but the market for bets on place and show is not. Betters commonly underestimate the probability that the favorite will end up in second or third place, and this effect is sufficiently large to sustain a contrarian betting strategy with a positive expected value. This inefficiency is found in spite of the high incentives, of the unquestioned level of dedication and expertise among participants in racetrack markets, and of obvious opportunities for learning and for arbitrage.

Situations in which errors that are common to many individuals are unlikely to be corrected by the market have been analyzed by Haltiwanger and Waldman (1985) and by Russell and Thaler (1985). Furthermore, Akerlof and Yellen (1985) have presented their near-rationality theory, in which some prevalent errors in responding to economic changes (e.g., inertia or money illusion) will (i) have little effect on the individual (thereby eliminating the possibility of learning), (ii) provide no opportunity for arbitrage, and yet (iii) have large economic effects. The claim that the market can be trusted to correct the effect of individual irrationalities cannot be made without supporting evidence, and the burden of specifying a plausible corrective mechanism should rest on those who make this claim.

The main theme of this article has been that the normative and the descriptive analyses of choice should be viewed as separate enterprises. This conclusion suggests a research agenda. To retain the rational model in its customary descriptive role, the relevant bolstering assumptions must be validated. Where these assumptions fail, it is instructive to trace the implications of the descriptive analysis (e.g., the effects of loss aversion, pseudocertainty, or the money illusion) for public policy, strategic decision making, and macroeconomic phenomena (see Arrow, 1982; Akerlof and Yellen, 1985).

Rational choice and the framing of decisions

NOTES

This work was supported by contract N00014-84-K-0615 from the Office of Naval Research to Stanford University. The present chapter reviews our work on decision making under risk from a new perspective, discussed primarily in the first and last sections. Most of the empirical demonstrations were reported in earlier publications. Problems 3, 4, 7, 8, and 12 were published for the first time in the *Journal of Business*, 59 (1986), S251–78. © 1986 by The University of Chicago. All rights reserved.

1 All problems are presented in the text exactly as they were presented to the participants in the experiments.

2 If $p + q = 1$ and either $x > y > 0$ or $x < y < 0$, the value of a prospect is given by $v(y) + \pi(p)[v(x) - v(y)]$, so that decision weights are not applied to sure outcomes.

3 The extension of the present analysis to prospects with many (nonzero) outcomes involves two additional steps. First, we assume that continuous (or multivalued) distributions are approximated, in the framing phase, by discrete distributions with a relatively small number of outcomes. For example, a uniform distribution on the interval (0, 90) may be represented by the discrete prospect (0, .1; 10, .1; ...; 90, .1). Second, in the multiple-outcome case the weighting function, $\pi_p(p_i)$, must depend on the probability vector p, not only on the component $p_i, i = 1 \ldots, n$. For example, Karmarkar (1978) used the function $\pi_p(p_i) = \pi(p_i)/[\pi(p_1) + \ldots + \pi(p_n)]$. A more elaborate extension that ensures stochastic dominance was proposed by Quiggin (1982). As in the two-outcome case, the weighting function is assumed to satisfy subcertainty, $\pi_p(p_1) + \ldots + \pi_p(p_n) \leqslant 1$, and subproportionality.

4 In the modified version – problems 9'–11' – the probabilities of winning were generated by drawing a number from a bag containing 100 sequentially numbered tickets. In problem 10', the event associated with winning $45 (drawing a number between one and 20) was included in the event associated with winning $30 (drawing a number between one and 25). The sequential setup of problem 11 was replaced by the simultaneous play of two chance devices: the roll of a die (whose outcome determines whether the game is on) and the drawing of a numbered ticket from a bag. The possibility of regret now exists in all three problems, and problems 10' and 11' no longer differ in this respect because a decision maker would always know the outcomes of alternative choices. Consequently, regret theory cannot explain either the certainty effect (9' vs. 10') or the pseudocertainty effect (10' vs. 11') observed in the modified problems.

5 It is noteworthy that the conditional framing used in problems 11 and 12 (case 3) is much more effective in eliminating the common responses to Allais's paradox than the partition framing introduced by Savage (see, e.g., Slovic and Tversky, 1974). This is probably due to the fact that the conditional framing makes it clear that the critical options are identical – after eliminating the state whose outcome does not depend on one's choice (i.e., reaching the second stage in problem 11, an untreatable tumor in problem 12, case 3).

6 Because the present chapter focuses on prospects with known probabilities, we do not discuss the important violations of cancellation due to ambiguity (Ellsberg, 1961).

REFERENCES

Akerlof, G. A., and Yellen, J. 1985. Can small deviations from rationality make significant differences to economic equilibria? *American Economic Review*, 75:708–20.

Allais, M. 1953. Le comportement de l'homme rationnel devant le risque: critique des postulats et axiomes de l'école américaine. *Econometrica* 21:503–46.

1979. The foundations of a positive theory of choice involving risk and a criticism of the postulates and axioms of the American School. In M. Allais and O. Hagen (eds.), *Expected Utility Hypotheses and the Allais Paradox*. Dordrecht: Reidel.

Arrow, K. J. 1982. Risk perception in psychology and economics. *Economic Inquiry* 20:1–9.

Bazerman, M. H. 1983. Negotiator judgment. *American Behavioral Scientist* 27:211–28.

Bell, D. E. 1982. Regret in decision making under uncertainty. *Operations Research* 30:961–81.

Bishop, R.C., and Heberlein, T. A. 1979. Measuring values of extra-market goods: are indirect measures biased? *American Journal of Agricultural Economics* 61:926–30.

Chew, S. H. 1983. A generalization of the quasilinear mean with applications to the measurement of income inequality and decision theory resolving the Allais paradox. *Econometrica* 51:1065–92.

Chew, S. H., and MacCrimmon, K. 1979. Alpha utility theory, lottery composition, and the Allais paradox. Working Paper no. 686. Vancouver: University of British Columbia.

Clark, H. H., and Clark, E. V. 1977. *Psychology and Language.* New York: Harcourt Brace Jovanovich.

Einhorn, H. J., and Hogarth, R. M. 1978. Confidence in judgment: persistence of the illusion of validity. *Psychological Review* 85:395–416.

Ellsberg, D. 1961. Risk, ambiguity, and the Savage axioms. *Quarterly Journal of Economics* 75:643–69.

Eraker, S. E., and Sox, H. C. 1981. Assessment of patients' preferences for therapeutic outcomes. *Medical Decision Making* 1:29–39.

Fischhoff, B. 1983. Predicting frames. *Journal of Experimental Psychology: Learning, Memory and Cognition* 9:103–16.

Fishburn, P. C. 1982. Nontransitive measurable utility. *Journal of Mathematical Psychology* 26:31–67.

1983. Transitive measurable utility. *Journal of Economic Theory* 31:293–317.

1984. SSB utility theory and decision making under uncertainty. *Mathematical Social Sciences* 8:253–85.

1985. Uncertainty aversion and separated effects in decision making under uncertainty. Working paper. Murray Hill, N.J.: AT & T Bell Labs.

Fishburn, P. C., and Kochenberger, G. A. 1979. Two-piece von Neumann–Morgenstern utility functions. *Decision Sciences* 10:503–18.

Grether, D. M. 1980. Bayes rule as a descriptive model: the representativeness heuristic. *Quarterly Journal of Economics* 95:537–57.

Grether, D. M., and Plott, C. R. 1979. Economic theory of choice and the preference reversal phenomenon. *American Economic Review* 69:623–38.

Hagen, O. 1979. Towards a positive theory of preferences under risk. In M. Allais and O. Hagen (eds.), *Expected Utility Hypotheses and the Allais Paradox.* Dordrecht: Reidel.

Haltiwanger, J., and Waldman, M. 1985. Rational expectations and the limits of rationality: an analysis of heterogeneity. *American Economic Review* 75:326–40.

Hammond, P. 1985. Consequential behavior in decision trees and expected utility. Institute for Mathematical Studies in the Social Sciences Working Paper no. 112. Stanford, Calif.: Stanford University.

Hansson, B. 1975. The appropriateness of the expected utility model. *Erkenntnis* 9:175–93.

Hausch, D. B., Ziemba, W. T., and Rubenstein, M. E. 1981. Efficiency of the market for racetrack betting. *Management Science* 27:1435–52.

Hershey, J. C., and Schoemaker, P. J. H. 1980. Risk taking and problem context in the domain of losses: an expected utility analysis. *Journal of Risk and Insurance* 47:111–32.

Kahneman, D., Knetsch, J. L., and Thaler, R. H. 1986a. Fairness and the assumptions of economics. *Journal of Business* 59.

1986. Perceptions of fairness: entitlements in the market. *American Economic Review* 76:728–41.

Kahneman, D., and Tversky, A. 1979. Prospect theory: an analysis of decision under risk. *Econometrica* 47:263–91.

1982. The psychology of preferences. *Scientific American* 246:160–73.

1984. Choices, values, and frames. *American Psychologist* 39:341–50.

Karmarkar, U. S. 1978. Subjectively weighted utility: a descriptive extension of the expected utility model. *Organizational Behavior and Human Performance* 21:61–72.

Knetsch, J. L., and Sinden, J. A. 1984. Willingness to pay and compensation demanded: experimental evidence of an unexpected disparity in measures of values. *Quarterly Journal of Economics* 99:507–21.

Knez, P., Smith, V. L., and Williams, A. W. 1985. Individual rationality, market rationality, and value estimation. *American Economic Review: Papers and Proceedings* 75:397–402.

Loomes, G., and Sugden, R. 1982. Regret theory: an alternative theory of rational choice under uncertainty. *Economic Journal* 92:805–24.

Luce, R. D., and Krantz, D. H. 1971. Conditional expected utility. *Econometrica* 39:253–71.

Luce, R. D., and Narens, L. 1985. Classification of concatenation measurement structures according to scale type. *Journal of Mathematical Psychology* 29:1–72.

Machina, N. J. 1982. "Expected utility" analysis without the independence axiom. *Econometrica* 50:277–323.

McNeil, B. J., Pauker, S. G., Sox, H. C., Jr., and Tversky, A. 1982. On the elicitation of preferences for alternative therapies. *New England Journal of Medicine* 306:1259–62.

March, J. G. 1978. Bounded rationality, ambiguity, and the engineering of choice. *Bell Journal of Economics* 9:587–608.

Markowitz, H. 1952. The utility of wealth. *Journal of Political Economy* 60:151–8.

Nelson, R. R., and Winter, S. G. 1982. *An Evolutionary Theory of Economic Change.* Cambridge, Mass.: Harvard University Press.

Payne, J. W., Laughhunn, D. J., and Crum, R. 1980. Translation of gambles and aspiration level effects in risky choice behavior. *Management Science* 26:1039–60.

Quiggin, J. 1982. A theory of anticipated utility. *Journal of Economic Behavior and Organization* 3:323–43.

Raiffa, H. 1968. *Decision Analysis: Introductory Lectures on Choices under Uncertainty.* Reading, Mass.: Addison-Wesley.

Russell, T., and Thaler, R. 1985. The relevance of quasi-rationality in competitive markets. *American Economic Review* 75:1071–82.

Savage, L. J. 1954. *The Foundations of Statistics.* New York: Wiley.

Schelling, T. C. 1981. Economic reasoning and the ethics of policy. *Public Interest* 63:37–61.

Schmeidler, D. 1984. Subjective probability and expected utility without additivity. Preprint Series no. 84. Minneapolis: University of Minnesota, Institute for Mathematics and Its Applications.

Schumpeter, J. A. 1954. *History of Economic Analysis.* New York: Oxford University Press.

Segal, U. 1984. Nonlinear decision weights with the independence axiom. Working Paper in Economics no. 353. Los Angeles: University of California, Los Angeles.

Simon, H. A. 1955. A behavioral model of rational choice. *Quarterly Journal of Economics* 69:99–118.

    1978. Rationality as process and as product of thought. *American Economic Review: Papers and Proceedings* 68:1–16.

Slovic, P., Fischhoff, B., and Lichtenstein, S. 1982. Response mode, framing, and information processing effects in risk assessment. In R. M. Hogarth (ed.), *New Directions for Methodology of Social and Behavioral Science: Question Framing and Response Consistency.* San Francisco: Jossey-Bass.

Slovic, P., and Lichtenstein, S. 1983. Preference reversals: a broader perspective. *American Economic Review* 73:596–605.

Slovic, P., and Tversky, A. 1974. Who accepts Savage's axiom? *Behavioral Science* 19:368–73.

Smith, V. L. 1985. Experimental economics: reply. *American Economic Review* 75:265–72.

Stigler, G. J., and Kindahl, J. K. 1970. *The Behavior of Industrial Prices.* New York: National Bureau of Economic Research.

Thaler, R. H. 1980. Towards a positive theory of consumer choice. *Journal of Economic Behavior and Organization* 1:39–60.

Tversky, A. 1969. Intransitivity of preferences. *Psychological Review* 76:105–10.

    1977. On the elicitation of preferences: descriptive and prescriptive considerations. In D. E. Bell, R. L. Keeney, and H. Raiffa (eds.), *Conflicting Objectives in Decisions.* New York: Wiley.

Tversky, A., and Kahneman, D. 1981. The framing of decisions and the psychology of choice. *Science* 211:453–8.

    1983. Extensional versus intuitive reasoning: the conjunction fallacy in probability judgment. *Psychological Review* 90:293–315.

von Neumann, J., and Morgenstern, O. 1944. *Theory of Games and Economic Behavior.* Princeton, N.J.: Princeton University Press.

Weber, R. J. 1982. The Allais paradox, Dutch auctions, and alpha-utility theory. Working paper. Evanston, Ill.: Northwestern University.

Yaari, M. E. 1984. Risk aversion without decreasing marginal utility. Report Series in Theoretical Economics. London School of Economics.

10

SAVAGE REVISITED

GLENN SHAFER

1. INTRODUCTION

More than three decades have passed since 1954, when L. J. Savage published *The Foundations of Statistics*. The controversy raised by this book and Savage's subsequent writings is now part of the past. Many statisticians now use Savage's idea of personal probability in their practical and theoretical work, and most of the others have made their peace with the idea in one way or another. Thus the time may be ripe for a reexamination of Savage's argument for subjective expected utility.

Savage's argument begins with a set of postulates for preferences among acts. Savage believed that a rational person's preferences should satisfy these postulates, and he showed that these postulates imply that the preferences agree with a ranking by subjective expected utility. He concluded that it is normative to make choices that maximize subjective expected utility. To do otherwise is to violate a canon of rationality.

In the 1950s and 1960s, Savage's understanding of subjective expected utility played an important role in freeing subjective probability judgment from the strictures of an exaggerated frequent philosophy of probability. Today, however, it no longer plays this progressive role. The need for subjective judgment is now widely understood. Increasingly, the idea that subjective expected utility is uniquely normative plays only a regressive role; it obstructs the development and understanding of alternative tools for subjective judgment of probability and value.

In this chapter, I shall advocate a revision of Savage's understanding. According to this revision, the analysis of a decision problem by subjective expected utility is merely an argument by analogy. It draws an analogy between that decision problem and the problem of a gambler who must decide how to bet in a pure game of chance. Sometimes such arguments are cogent; sometimes they are not. Sometimes other kinds of arguments provide a better basis for choosing among acts. Thus subjective expected utility is just one of several possible tools for constructing a decision.

1.1 Savage's normative interpretation

Savage distinguished between two interpretations for his postulates, an empirical interpretation and a normative interpretation. According to the empirical interpretation, people's preferences among acts generally obey the postulates and hence agree with a ranking by subjective expected utility. According to the normative interpretation, the postulates are a model of rationality. They describe the preferences of an ideal rational person, an imaginary person whose behavior provides a standard or norm for the behavior of real people. The normative interpretation does not assert that the preferences of real people obey the postulates; it asserts only that they should.

Savage was sympathetic to the empirical interpretation; he thought people's preferences usually come close to obeying the postulates (see Friedman and Savage, 1952; Savage, 1954, page 20; Savage, 1971). But his primary emphasis, especially in *Foundations*, was on the normative interpretation.

Savage's distinction between empirical and normative interpretations was immensely influential. He was not quite the first to make such a distinction; Jacob Marschak discussed the "descriptive" and "recommendatory" aspects of expected utility in 1950. But Savage's forceful advocacy of the normative interpretation made the distinction widely appreciated. There was scarcely a hint of the distinction in the three editions of von Neumann and Morgenstern's *Theory of Games and Economic Behavior* (1944, 1947, 1953), yet it is difficult to find a discussion of expected utility written after 1954 that does not acknowledge the importance of the distinction.

The normative interpretation has become steadily more important during the past three decades as psychologists have shown in more and more detail that the empirical interpretation is false. It has also become purer. Our careful look back at Savage's words will show us that he scarcely hid the dependence of his argument on what he took to be empirical facts about people's preferences. But today's Bayesian statisticians often contend that empirical facts are completely irrelevant to the normative interpretation. People should obey Savage's postulates, and what they actually do has no relevance to this imperative (Lindley, 1974).

I shall argue that this is wrong. The normative interpretation cannot be so thoroughly insulated from empirical fact. Savage's argument for the normativeness of his postulates cannot be made without assumptions that have empirical content, and, what we have learned in the past three decades refutes these assumptions just as clearly as it refutes the forthright empirical interpretation of the postulates. The sensible way to respond to what we have learned is to make the normative interpretation explicitly and thoroughly constructive. This means repudiating the claim that subjective expected utility provides a uniquely normative way of constructing decisions. It may also mean abandoning the word *normative* in favor of *constructive* and other less contentious terms.

1.2 The existence and construction of preferences

Just what are the assumptions with empirical content that underlie Savage's argument for the normativeness of subjective expected utility?

There are at least two. First, the assumption that a person always has well-defined preferences in those settings where the postulates are applied. Second, the assumption that a setting can be found that permits a disentanglement of belief and value.

In order to understand the role of the first assumption in Savage's argument, consider his treatment of the idea that preferences should be transitive. Transitivity seems inherent in the idea of preference; I would be using words oddly if I were to say that I prefer f to g, g to h, and h to f. It would be unreasonable, prima facie, for me to insist on using words so oddly. In this sense, transitivity is normative. But Savage went a step further; he declared that it is always normative to have transitive preferences among f, g, and h. This further step is justified if we make the assumption that a person does have preferences among f, g, and h, for then we are merely saying that these preferences, that the person does have, should be transitive. But the further step is not justified if the person does not necessarily already have preferences among f, g, and h. For in this case, we are saying that the person should construct such preferences regardless of how difficult this might be, regardless of how useful it might be, and regardless of what other ways the person might have of spending his or her time.

Psychologists have found that people are usually willing to comply with requests that they choose among options. So how can I claim that the assumption that a person always has preferences is counter to the facts?

Let us reflect on what we need in order to say that an object has a certain property. We need a method or methods of measurement, and we need an empirical invariance in the results of applying these methods. We are entitled to say that a table has a certain length because we have methods of measuring this length and because we get about the same answer from different methods and on different occasions.

In the case of people's preferences, we have methods of measurement. There are questions we can ask. But do we find the requisite empirical invariance? In general, we do not. Trite as this may be, it is the most fundamental result of three decades of empirical investigation. The preferences people express are unstable (Fischhoff, Slovic, and Lichtenstein, 1980). They depend on the questions asked. A person's choice between f and g may depend on whether the conversation includes consideration of h or k (Tversky, 1972). It may also depend on substantively irrelevant aspects of the descriptions of the options, even when these options are treated evenhandedly (Tversky and Kahneman, 1986).

Savage's second assumption with empirical content, the disentanglement of belief and value, is more subtle. The domains of belief and value can be conceptually disentangled for the gambler in a pure game of chance. The gambler has beliefs about the outcome of the game, and he puts values on the different amounts of money he can win from the game. These two domains are initially separate; they are linked only by the gambler's choice of bets. When we analyze a decision problem by subjective expected utility, we are either assuming or deciding on a similar disentanglement. The assumption has empirical content, and the decision may or may not be one that we want to make. I shall argue that the empirical facts do not support the assumption.

The assumption that a person always has well-defined preferences is explicit in Savage's first postulate. We will study this postulate in detail in section 3. The assumption that a person can frame a decision problem so as to disentangle judgments of value from judgments of probability underlies the second, third, and fourth postulates. We will study these postulates in section 4.

1.3 The car radio

Before we plunge into the technicalities of Savage's postulates, let us think about a more general ingredient of his argument: the idea that preferences can be treated as errors. Savage believed that the normative force of his postulates is such that if a person discovers that his or her preferences violate the postulates, he or she will think of the violation as an error and will change some or all of the preferences so as to correct this error. Here is a simple story he used to illustrate this idea of treating a preference as an error to be corrected:

> A man buying a car for $2,134.56 is tempted to order it with a radio installed, which will bring the total price to $2,228.41, feeling that the difference is trifling. But when he reflects that, if he already had the car, he certainly would not spend $93.85 for a radio for it, he realizes that he has made an error.   *Foundations*, page 103

How does the constructive attitude that I am advocating apply to this story?

From the constructive viewpoint, this story is simply an example of the empirical fact that preferences are not invariant with respect to the method of measurements. The man has asked himself in two different ways what value he puts on a car radio, and he has received two different answers. This means that he does not really have a well-defined preference between the car radio and $93.95. His task is to construct such a preference.

Savage's way of resolving the story suggests that the second question the man asks himself is the right one. When he asked himself directly whether the radio is worth $93.85, he finds that it is not, and this tells him that his initial inclination to pay $93.85 more to have the radio in the car was an error.

But it is equally open to the man to decide that he likes the first question best. He may decide that it is in the context of buying a car that he best faces up to the value he is willing to place on the amenities in the car, and the discomfort he would feel in paying $93.85 just for a radio causes him to unreasonably undervalue the amenity provided by the radio when he considers it in isolation. In this case, he might call his feeling that he would not pay $93.85 for the radio the error.

The word error is inappropriate here. It sugests that the man's true preference is well-defined before he deliberates and that he just needs to ask himself the right question in order to find out this true preference; other questions may produce errors. From our constructive viewpoint, we see quite a different picture. The man does not really have a true preference, and he is looking to various arguments (including those provided by the salesman) in an effort to construct one.

These considerations involve, perhaps, only a shallow challenge to Savage's viewpoint. I am merely criticizing his casual use of the word error. So let us move to higher ground and ask what is normative in this man's situation.

There is no obvious response. The man has given inconsistent answers to the two questions, and it is normative for him to resolve this inconsistency. It is normative for him to have a clear preference between the radio and $93.85, so that he can henceforth answer the two questions consistently.

There is a sense in which this is correct. The man has to decide whether to pay extra for the radio or not. But it is important to recognize that this is a contingent necessity. It results not from logic but from the fact that the car is available with the radio installed and the salesman has asked him whether he wants it that way. Were it unavailable, the man might have something better to do than to construct a preference between the radio and $93.85.

In a final attempt to find a role for the word normative in this story, one might suggest that, if the man must decide whether to pay extra for the radio, then it is normative for him to ask both questions and to reflect on the inconsistency of the answers before taking action. It is normative to look at a decision from all points of view, one might argue, precisely because one's true preference is not well-defined. If we recognize the fuzziness of our preferences and ask ourselves about our preferences in many different ways, then we will be likely to make better decisions than if we act on our answer to the first question we ask ourselves.

Even here, however, *normative* is too strong. It is normative, perhaps, to deliberate carefully. But this says very little. It is never possible to look at a decision from all points of view. And whether and in what sense a decision will be improved by consideration of any particular additional way of asking oneself about one's preference may be an open question. Having asked himself whether the radio is worth the extra money, the man may or may not improve his deliberation by asking himself whether he would pay that much for the radio if he already had the car.

Our discussion of Savage's postulates will involve issues similar to those raised by this simple story.

1.4 Outline

In section 2, I review the mathematical formulation of Savage's theory. I also discuss the significance of Savage's representation theory and the ways in which

Savage's perspective on subjective expected utility differed from a constructive perspective.

Then, in sections 3 and 4, I look in detail at Savage's postulates, at the criticisms other authors have made of them, and at their constructive significance. Section 3 is devoted to the first postulate, the requirement that acts be completely ranked in preference. This is the simplest and most important of the postulates. Section 4 is devoted to the second, third, and fourth postulates, which formalize the idea that belief and value can be disentangled in all decision problems as they can be in a gambler's decision problem.

In section 5, I study Savage's problem of small worlds, contrasting his treatment of this problem with a more constructive treatment. A small world consists of the possible states of the world and the possible consequences that a person considers when he or she analyzes a decision problem. States of the world and consequences must necessarily be described at some fixed and therefore limited level of detail; hence the adjective small. A person can always consider a more refined small world, one with more detailed and hence more numerous descriptions of the possibilities. The problem of small worlds is that an analysis using one small world may fail to agree with an analysis using a more refined small world. From the constructive viewpoint, this is merely one aspect of the lack of invariance of preference; the preferences we construct may depend on which questions we ask ourselves, and hence the selection of questions is an essential part of the construction. Since he implicitly assumed the preexistence of well-defined preferences, Savage found the problem of small worlds more mysterious than this. In fact, Savage's treatment of the problem can serve as a demonstration of how far from a constructive perspective he was.

2. SAVAGE'S THEORY

This section reviews the mathematical formulation of Savage's theory. I review what Savage meant by a small world. I state Savage's seven postulates in a form slightly different from the form in which he gave them in *Foundations*. Then I discuss the representation theorem that Savage deduced from these postulates, its significance from Savage's point of view, and its significance from a more constructive point of view.

2.1 Small worlds

Suppose I must choose an act from a set F_0 of possible acts, and suppose the consequences of these acts are uncertain. How might I choose?

Savage suggested that I begin by spelling out the possibilities for those present and future aspects of my situation which will be unaffected by my choice of an act but which, together with this choice, will determine the personal consequences that I want to take into account.

Table 10.1. *Savage's small world*

Act	State Good	Rotten
Break into bowl	six-egg omelet	no omelet and five good eggs destroyed
Break into saucer	six-egg omelet and a saucer to wash	five-egg omelet and a saucer to wash
Throw away	five-egg omelet and one good egg destroyed	five-egg omelet

Let S denote the set of these possibilities. More concretely, suppose S is a set of written descriptions. Each element s of S describes one way the unknowns in my situation might turn out, in enough detail to determine the relevant consequences of each act. Let us also suppose that the elements of S are mutually exclusive and collectively exhaustive. One and only one of these elements describes my situation correctly. We may call each element of S a possible state of the world.

Let C denote the set of the consequences. Again, we may be more concrete by supposing that C is a set of written descriptions; each element c of C describes one way the personal consequences of my choice of an act might turn out. Let us suppose that the elements of C are mutually exclusive and collectively exhaustive; one and only one of these elements describes what will actually happen to me. For each element s in S and each act f in F_0, let $f(s)$ denote the element of C that correctly describes the personal consequences of the act f if s correctly describes my situation. As the notation indicates, each act in F_0 determines a mapping from S to C.

Savage called the pair (S, c) a *small world*.

On pages 13 to 15 of *Foundations*, Savage formulates a small world for a man who must decide whether to break a sixth egg into a bowl of five eggs before making an omelet. This is the only small world that Savage completely spelled out in *Foundations*, and it will serve to illustrate some points that we will encounter later.

The man is considering three possible acts:

$$F_0 = \left\{ \begin{array}{l} \text{break the egg into the bowl} \\ \text{break the egg into a saucer} \\ \text{throw the egg away} \end{array} \right\}.$$

Savage describes the man's situation in terms of a small world (S, C), where S consists of two states of the world, and C consists of six possible consequences. The states of the world simply specify whether the sixth egg is good:

$$S = \left\{ \begin{array}{l} \text{the sixth egg is good} \\ \text{the sixth egg is rotten} \end{array} \right\}.$$

The consequences specify how large an omelet the man gets in the end, whether he destroys one or more good eggs, and whether he has an extra saucer to wash. Table 10.1, taken from page 14 of *Foundations*, spells out how the three acts in F_0 map S to C. The act "break the egg into the bowl," for example, maps "the sixth egg is good" to "six-egg omelet" and maps "the sixth egg is rotten" to "no omelet, and five good eggs destroyed."

Savage used this example to illustrate the idea that a person's choice between the acts in F_0 might depend only on which of the consequences in C may befall him. Indeed it might, but do we have any right to demand this? If the man dislikes throwing eggs away without knowing they are rotten, and if he claims the dislike attaches to the act in itself, not just to the misfortune that results if the eggs are not rotten, do we have reason to fault him? We will return to such questions in section 4.

2.2 The postulates

Savage's postulates can be stated in a number of equivalent ways. The statement given here is strongly influenced by Fishburn (1981, pages 160 and 161). In order to facilitate the later discussion, I give each postulate a title as well as a number, these titles are mine, not Savage's or Fishburn's.

Consider a small world (S, C) for a set F_0 of possible acts. As we have noted, the relation between F_0 and (S, C) can be expressed by saying that each act f in F_0 determines a mapping from S to C: the mapping that maps the state s to the consequence $f(s)$. If we are content not to distinguish between two acts that have the same consequences, then it is convenient for the abstract theory to identify the act f with this mapping from S to C. The set F_0 then becomes simply a set of mappings. Usually, however, F_0 will not include all mappings from S to C.

Let F denote the set of all mappings from S to C. It is convenient to call all the elements of F *acts*; we may call the elements of F_0 *concrete acts*, and we may call the elements of F that are not in F_0 *imaginary acts*.

Savage's first postulate says that his rational person has ranked in preference all the acts in F, concrete and imaginary:

P1. *The existence of a complete ranking.* All the acts in F are ranked in preference, except that the person may be perfectly indifferent between some acts. More precisely: (i) The binary relation $>$ on F is irreflexive and transitive, where "$f > g$" means that the person prefers f to g. (ii) The binary relation $\#$ on F is transitive, where "$f \# g$" means that neither $f > g$ nor $g > f$.

(When we say that $>$ is irreflexive, we mean that $f > g$ and $g > f$ cannot both hold; in particular, $f > f$ cannot hold. When we say that $>$ is transitive, we mean that if $f > g$ and $g > h$, then $f > h$.) The irreflexivity and transitivity of $>$ make precise the idea of a ranking. The transitivity of $\#$ make precise the idea that if neither $f > g$ nor $g > f$, then the person is perfectly indifferent between f

and g. Indeed, since $f \mathrel{\#} f$ for all f and since $f \mathrel{\#} g$ implies $g \mathrel{\#} f$, imposing the further condition that $\#$ be transitive amounts to requiring that $\#$ be an equivalence relation. Thus, the postulate says that F can be divided into equivalence classes, and these equivalence classes can be ranked so that the person prefers acts in equivalence classes higher in the ranking and is indifferent between acts in the same equivalence class.

For each act f in F and each subset A of S, we let f_A denote the restriction of the mapping f to the set A. We call a subset A of S *null* if $f \mathrel{\#} g$ whenever f and g are elements of F such that $f_{A^c} = g_{A^c}$, where A^c denotes the complement of A. This condition says that the person's preferences among acts are not influenced by the consequences they have for states in A; we call A null in this case on the presumption that the person's indifference toward A indicates a conviction that the true state of the world is not in A.

Given a subset A of S and two mappings p and q from A to C, let us write $p > q$ if $f > g$ for every pair f and g of mappings in F such that $f_A = p$, $g_A = q$, and $f_{A^c} = g_{A^c}$.

Given a consequence c in C, let $[c]$ denote the act in F that maps all s in S to c. Let us call such an act a *constant act*.

These definitions and conventions allow us to state Savage's remaining postulates as follows:

P2. *The independence postulate.* If $f > g$ and $f_{A^c} = g_{A^c}$, then $f_A > g_A$.

P3. *Value can be purged of belief.* If A is not null, then $[c]_A > [d]_A$ if and only if $[c] > [d]$.

P4. *Belief can be discovered from preference.* Suppose $[c] > [d]$, f is equal to c on A and d on A^c, and g is equal to c on B and d on B^c. Suppose similarly that $[c'] > [d']$, f' is equal to c' on A and d' on A^c, and g' is equal to c' on B and d' on B^c. Then $f > g$ if and only if $f' > g'$.

P5. *The nontriviality condition.* There exists at least one pair of acts in F, say f and g, such that $f > g$.

P6. *The continuity condition.* If $f > g$, then for every element c of C there is a finite partition of S such that f (or g or both) can be changed to equal c on any single element of the partition without changing the preference.

P7. *The dominance condition.* If $f_A > g_A$, then $f_A > [g(s)]_A$ for some s in A, and $[f(s)]_A > g_A$ for some s in A.

These postulates imply that the person's preferences among acts can be represented by subjective expected utility. That is to say, they imply the existence of a probability measure P on S and a real-valued function U on C such that $f > g$ if and only if $E(U(f)) > E(U(g))$, where the expectations are taken with respect to P.

The last three postulates play a relatively technical role in Savage's theory. The nontriviality condition is not needed to prove the representation theorem; it merely assures that the representation is not trivial. The continuity condition is a simplifying or structural assumption; it implies that U is bounded (Fishburn,

1970, page 206). The dominance condition is not needed for the representation theorem in the case of acts that take only finitely many values in C. I will not discuss these three postulates further in this chapter.

The first four postulates do play significant substantive roles, and I will discuss them in detail, the first postulate in section 3 and the other four in section 4.

2.3 The representation theorem

Whenever we construct probabilities and utilities and use them to construct a preference ranking for acts, the resulting preferences will satisfy the first four of Savage's postulates. These postulates should therefore be of interest to anyone who takes the constructive view that I set forth in section 1. They help us understand the limitations of this particular way of constructing a decision. But why should anyone be interested in Savage's representation theorem, which goes in the opposite direction, from preferences to probabilities and utilities?

The representation theorem would be of interest to the constructive view if preferences between acts were a starting point for construction. If, without first constructing probabilities and utilities, a person could state extensive definite preferences satisfying Savage's postulates, then we could use Savage's representation theorem to find probabilities and utilities that would summarize those preferences. Even if the person could only state extensive definite preferences that nearly satisfy the postulates, we might be able to find probabilities and utilities that nearly summarize those preferences, and the person might gain a clearer self-conception by adjusting his preferences so that they fit these probabilities and utilities exactly and hence, incidentally, satisfying the postulates.

Although Savage did not use the word construction in connection with probability and utility, he did think that preferences are the proper starting point for the investigation of a real person's beliefs and values. He thought, for example, that the most effective way to find out about a person's probability for an event is to ask him to choose between bets on the event (Savage, 1971). He thought that a person could, for the most part, express definite preferences between hypothetical acts, and he thought that these preferences would be in close enough accord with his postulates that they could be used to deduce probabilities and utilities (*Foundations*, page 28).

Was Savage right? Do real people, when they have not deliberately constructed probabilities and utilities for a given problem, always have preferences that are sufficiently definite and detailed, and accord well enough with Savage's postulates, that they determine such probabilities and utilities? This is an empirical question, and the empirical studies I have already cited suffice to establish that it must be answered in the negative.

I conclude that Savage's representation theorem is not a constructive tool. In this chapter I will argue that it is almost always more sensible to construct preferences from judgments of probability and value than to try to work backward from choices between hypothetical acts to judgments of probability and value. Probabilities should be constructed by examining evidence, not by examining one's attitudes toward bets. Utilities are too delicate to be deduced from hypothetical choices; they must be deliberately adopted.

3. THE CONSTRUCTIVE NATURE OF PREFERENCE

In this section, we will study Savage's first postulate, which demands that people rank acts in preference. As I have already argued, this demand depends prima facie on the claim that they do have fairly well-defined preferences between most pairs of acts. If people do have such preferences, then saying they should have a complete preference ranking amounts only to saying that they should straighten out some inconsistencies and fill in some minor hiatuses, and this may be reasonable. But if they do not have all these preferences, then it is hard to see why constructing them would necessarily be the best way for them to spend their time.

In fact, people generally do not have ready-made preferences. When asked to make choices, they look for arguments on which to base these choices. The ways in which the alternatives are described can suggest arguments and therefore influence these choices. This means that people's choices in response to one query may be inconsistent with their choices in response to another query, but this weak kind of inconsistency is inescapable for rational beings who base their choices on arguments.

Before developing these points in greater detail, let us look more closely at the meaning of the first postulate.

3.1 Indecision and indifference

The very meaning of preference seems to involve transitivity: if f is preferred to g and g is preferred to h, then f is preferred to h. It is reasonable, therefore to say that a person who constructs intransitive preferences is being inconsistent. Savage's first postulate demands more, however, than the transitivity of preferences. It also demands transitivity for the binary relation $\#$, which corresponds to lack of preference. Is transitivity involved in the very meaning of lack of preference?

We will be able to understand the significance of transitivity for $\#$ more clearly if we formally distinguish between indecision and indifference. Given a person with a transitive and irreflexive preference relation $>$ on F, let us say that the person is *undecided* between f and g if neither $f > g$ nor $g > f$. And let us say that he is *indifferent* between f and g only if in addition to being undecided between them he is also willing to substitute one for the other in any other preference relation. (More precisely, $f > h$ if and only if $g > h$, and $h > f$ if and only if $h > g$.) With this vocabulary established, the significance of transitivity for $\#$ is easily stated: $\#$ is transitive if and only if the person is indifferent between every pair of acts between which he is undecided.

The demand that a person should be indifferent whenever he is undecided does not seem very reasonable. The person might be undecided between two acts because he feels he lacks the evidence needed for a wise choice, because he feels the choice depends on more fundamental choices or value judgments not yet made, or simply because he feels the choice is one he does not need to make. Indifference says much more.

For the constructive view, indecision is the starting point. Before we start to work constructing preferences, we may be undecided between all pairs of acts. We may not even have thought of all the possible acts. But this does not mean we are indifferent. As we construct preferences, we eliminate some indecision. In the end we may eliminate all indecision; we may, that is to say, rank all acts in a strict order of preference. Or we may, as the postulate suggests, reduce all indecision to indifference, by establishing a ranking of equivalence classes of acts. But Savage has given us no reason why we should feel compelled to carry our elimination of indecision so far. In general, the practical problem will be to choose one act. Why is it normative to go further and rank all acts?

These points were not overlooked by Savage's early critics. The main points were made quite well by Anscombe (1956), Aumann (1962, 1964), and Wolfowitz (1962). Anscombe and Wolfowitz were primarily concerned with statistical problems. Citing the problem of choosing a statistical model, Anscombe made the point that we sometimes cannot even list all the possible choices that are open to use, let alone rank them. Wolfowitz made the point that, in a practical problem of choice, there is a practical need to choose a single act to perform, but no practical need to rank all the other acts. He suggested that the unreasonableness of Savage's demand that a person rank all acts could be illustrated by

> a homely example of the sort which Professor Savage uses frequently and effectively: When a man marries he presumably chooses, from among possible women, that one whom he likes best. Need he necessarily be able also to order the others in order of preference?   Wolfowitz, 1962, page 476

If we were to assume that a man or women, when thinking about marriage, begins with well-defined preferences between every pair of possible spouses, then it would be reasonable to ask that these preferences be transitive. But there are no grounds for this assumption. And there is also no compelling reason for the person to try to construct such a ranking.

The distinction between indecision and indifference is not as clear as it might be in Savage's own discussion of his first postulate, primarily because he expressed the postulate in terms of the relation "is not preferred to." We say that f is not preferred to g, or $f \leqslant g$, if and only if $f > g$ does not hold. Savage imposed two conditions on $\leqslant$: (i) for any pair of acts f and g, at least one of the relations $f \leqslant g$ or $g \leqslant f$ holds, and (ii) $\leqslant$ is transitive. It is obvious that (i) is equivalent to $>$ being irreflexive. It is also true, but not so obvious, that (ii) is equivalent to both $>$ and $\#$ being transitive.

3.2 Where should we put our effort?

In response to Wolfowitz's point, that it is unnecessary to rank alternatives we are not going to choose, some readers will point out that the exercise of constructing such a ranking may help us better understand values that we do have. Indeed it may. But is there any reason to suppose that it will always do so? And is there any reason to suppose that this exercise is always the best way we can use our time?

Instead of trying to rank in order all the men she dislikes, a woman might better spend her time learning more about the man she favors. Or perhaps she should spend her time exploring her possibilities in terms of a more detailed small world, one that relates her possible choice of a husband to other choices.

In my view, we can never say that it is normative for a person to construct a complete preference ranking of the acts in a given small world, because we can never be certain that this is the best way for the person to spend his or her time. It may be better to spend this time looking for further evidence. It may be better to spend it trying to invent other small worlds that provide more convincing frameworks for probability and value judgment. Or it may be time to put an end to deliberation and get on with one's life.

3.3 The empirical claim

Savage acknowledged the possibility of distinguishing between indecision and indifference in the following words:

> There is some temptation to explore the possibilities of analyzing preference among acts as a partial ordering, that is, in effect to replace [the requirement that $f \leqslant g$ or $g \leqslant f$] by the very weak proposition $f \leqslant f$, admitting that some pairs of acts are incomparable. This would seem to give expression to introspective sensations of indecision or vacillation, which we may be reluctant to identify with indifference. My own conjecture is that it would prove a blind alley losing much in power and advancing little, if at all, in realism; but only an enthusiastic exploration could shed real light on the question. *Foundations*, page 21

This admirably undogmatic statement comes at the end of a passage in which Savage explains that it is the normative rather than the empirical interpretation of his postulates that has direct relevance to his argument. Yet comments about realism and introspective sensations of indecision are clearly comments about empirical facts, not about what is merely normative. We may take this passage as a concession that the normative interpretation has empirical content.

My contention that Savage based his normative interpretation on the assumption that his first postulate has substantial empirical validity is supported by his article on the elicitation of probabilities and expectations (Savage, 1971), where he asserts that a real person is approximately like a *Homo economicus*, who does have ready-made preferences among gambles. Moreover, Savage repeatedly said that the way to use his theory is to search for intransitivities and other inconsistencies in one's preferences and then revise these preferences to eliminate the inconsistencies (see, e.g., Savage, 1967, page 309).

3.4 Constant and other imaginary acts

Some scholars who have been sympathetic with Savage's viewpoint and have accepted the idea that a person should have a complete preference ranking for concrete acts have nonetheless balked at the idea that the person should have a complete preference ranking for imaginary acts. They have been especially concerned about constant acts, acts that map all states of nature to a single consequence. Constant acts play a prominent role in the postulates (postulates P3, P4, and P7 all involve constant acts), but in most small worlds they are imaginary. Not only that, they are often hard to imagine. It is often hard, that is to say, to imagine performing an act that would result in the consequence c no matter what. And it seems unlikely that people will have in hand preferences between acts that they have not even imagined performing (see Fishburn, 1970; Luce and Krantz, 1971; Pratt, 1974; Richter, 1975).

Savage never published a response to this concern, but his private response, as reported by Fishburn (1981), had a constructive flavor. He saw no reason why a person could not think about patterns of consequences corresponding to imaginary acts and formulate preferences between such patterns.

I agree with Savage on this point. In order to construct a preference between one pattern of consequences and another, it is not necessary that a person should have available a concrete act that produces this pattern, or even that the person should be able to imagine such an act. It makes as much sense for a woman to try to decide which of two men she would prefer as a husband in the case where neither is willing as it does in the case where both are willing but she prefers to marry neither. And, as long as she is daydreaming, she might as well also compare these men to imaginary constant husbands, husbands whose qualities and contributions to her life are unaffected by her uncertainties about the state of the world.

The scholars who raised the problem of constant acts were identifying an important and valid criticism, however, of the empirical content of Savage's first postulate. While it might be plausible that people have fairly well-defined preferences among the acts available to them, at least in cases where these acts have been present to their imagination for some time, it is less plausible that they have formed such preferences among abstract acts that do not correspond to choices they have thought about.

We will gain some further insight into the problem of imaginary acts when we study the refinement of small worlds in section 5.2.

3.5 The empirical evidence

I contend that Savage's first postulate does not have the degree of empirical validity that it would need in order to be normative. What are the facts? Since 1954 we have accumulated an immense amount of empirical evidence about people's preferences (see, for example, Kahneman, Slovic, and Tversky, 1982; Schoemaker, 1982). Does this evidence show that people always have preferences that are sufficiently definite and extensive that it is reasonable to adjust them so they will satisfy the first postulate perfectly? Or does it show instead that people's preferences are often so fragmentary that they were may be better uses of the time and effort needed to make them satisfy it?

This empirical evidence is itself subject to interpretation, of course. It is easy to find people that are willing to participate in experiments where they are required to make many choices, and at first it seems harmless to say that these choices really are their preferences at the time they are announced. This might lead us to agree that people have very extensive preferences. When we then find that these preferences are intransitive and even flatly inconsistent, we are tempted to conclude that it is indeed normative to fix them up so they will be consistent and transitive. But, as I pointed out in section 1.2, the preferences a person expresses often lack the invariance needed to establish them as properties of the person. When we see the extent to which an experimenter influences choices by the way in which he describes alternatives, we realize that the preferences expressed may be more a property of the experiment than a property of the person expressing them.

Let us look at this issue more closely, considering first the claim that people have inconsistent preferences, and then the claim that they have intransitive preferences.

Inconsistent preferences

Consider the following experiment reported by Tversky and Kahneman (1986).

In the first part of the experiment, participants were asked to choose between two lotteries, *A* and *B*. In both lotteries, one randomly draws a marble from a box and wins or loses a sum of money which depends on the color drawn. The percentages of marbles of the different colors and the corresponding gains and losses are given in table 10.2. All the participants in the experiment chose lottery *B*, presumably because they noticed that it gives a better outcome no matter what ball is drawn.

In the second part of the experiment, participants were asked to choose between lotteries *C* and *D* given in table 10.3. The probability distribution of outcomes is the same for *C* as for *A*, and the same for *D* as for *B*. So from an abstract point of view, the choice between *C* and *D* is the same as the choice between *A* and *B*. We can say that *B* is better than *A* because the probability distribution of outcomes for *B* stochastically dominates that for *A*, and *D* is better than *C* for exactly the same reason. But the stochastic dominance is not so easy to see when one is comparing *C* and *D* as it is when one is comparing *A* and *B*. A majority of the participants in the experiment apparently failed to see it, because they chose *C* over *D*.

As this experiment demonstrates, the preferences people express between two

Table 10.2. *A choice between lotteries*

Lottery	White	Red	Green	Blue	Yellow
A	90% $0	6% win $45	1% win $30	1% lose $15	2% lose $15
B	90% $0	6% win $45	1% win $45	1% lose $10	2% lose $15

Table 10.3. *Another choice between lotteries*

Lottery	White	Red	Green	Yellow
C	90% $0	6% win $45	1% win $30	3% lose $15
D	90% $0	7% win $45	1% lose $10	2% lose $15

probability distributions of gains depend on how the distributions are described. We can express this, if we wish, by saying that people have inconsistent preferences. But it is fairer to say that they do not have any fixed preferences at all. They do not have ready-made answers to the questions asked. Asked to make a choice, they look for arguments. Stochastic dominance is a very convincing argument, if you see it. If you do not see it, then you look for other arguments.

Another remarkable experiment is reported by Tversky and Kahneman (1981). In this experiment, people are told that the United States is preparing for the outbreak of an unusual Asian disease, which is expected to kill 600 people in the absence of any preventive program, and they are asked to choose between two alternative preventative programs. In one case, the possible consequences of the two programs are described as follows:

If program *A* is adopted, 200 people will be saved.
If program *B* is adopted, there is $\frac{1}{3}$ probability that 600 people will be saved, and $\frac{2}{3}$ probability that no people will be saved.

In the other case, they are described as follows:

If program *A* is adopted, 400 people will die.
If program *B* is adopted, there is $\frac{1}{3}$ probability that nobody will die, and $\frac{2}{3}$ probability that 600 people will die.

The two sets of descriptions are equivalent: 200 people being saved is the same as 400 dying. People choose differently, however, depending on which description is used. In the case of the first description, a large majority of people in the experiment chose program *A*, while in the case of the second description a large majority chose program *B*. Apparently the first description encourages people to argue in favor of the program that will at least be sure to save some of the people, while the second description encourages them to argue in favor of the program that may result in no deaths at all. Similar results, indicating risk aversion when problems are framed in terms of gains and risk taking when problems are framed in terms of losses, have been obtained when the gains or losses are modest amounts of money rather than lives.

Again, it is possible to say that people are inconsistent because their choice depends on the description of the problem, and depends in particular on the experimenter's choice of a reference point. But it is more helpful to say that the two ways of describing the public health problem suggest different arguments. This is more helpful because it encourages us to weigh the two arguments against each other and to look for other arguments that might help to choose which program to adopt.

Tversky, Kahneman, and others have used these and other experiments to investigate in detail the kinds of arguments that people do use when they make choices. This work is important and relevant to a constructive theory of decision. Here I am making only the elementary point that it is misleading to summarize these experiments by saying that people are inconsistent.

Intransitive preferences
The study of intransitive preferences goes back at least to Condorcet (1743–1794), who pointed out that a circular pattern of preferences can result from majority voting. Suppose, indeed, that Tom, Dick, and Harry want to decide together among three alternatives A, B, and C. They each rank the alternatives; Tom ranks them ABC (he likes A best and B second best), Dicks ranks them BCA, and Harry ranks them CAB. If they vote on each pair, then A will beat B, B will beat C, and C will beat A.

One might expect similar intransitive sets of preferences to be expressed by a single individual who scores his alternatives on several dimensions and chooses between any pair of alternatives by counting the number of dimensions that favor each element of the pair. Tversky (1969), building on a suggestion by May (1954), devised an experiment in which people do consistently produce such intransitivities.

In fact, Tversky (1969, page 32) demonstrates intransitivities with alternatives that differ on only two dimensions. Tversky considers a situation where we are asked to choose between candidates for a job on the basis of their IQ scores and their experience. Suppose we prefer to choose the more intelligent candidate, but we will choose the more experienced candidate if the difference in their IQ scores is negligible. Let d denote the largest difference in IQ scores we consider negligible, and suppose candidates A, B, and C have the IQ scores and experience shown in table 10.4. Then we will choose A over B, B over C, and C over A.

Transitivity is so essential to the idea of preference that it does seem reasonable to say that we should reconsider our decision rule. Perhaps instead of regarding d

Table 10.4. *A choice among three candidates*

Candidate	IQ	Experience (years)
A	100	3
B	$100 + d$	2
C	$100 + 2d$	1

as a negligible difference in IQ scores we should avoid intransitivities by choosing between candidates on the basis of some weighted average of IQ and experience.

If we take a thoroughly constructive view of preference and decision, however, it is important to ask just how widely the decision rule is to be used – i.e., just when preferences are to be constructed. If we want to choose one or more candidates from a pool of three or more, or if we want to repeatedly choose between pairs of candidates, then we may feel that fairness demands a rule that is transitive, even if somewhat arbitrary. But if we face only a single isolated choice, say a choice between candidate *A* and candidate *B*, then it may be a waste of time to search for a rule that would seem fair in a wider context.

Here, as always, we must weigh arguments. Given two particular candidates for our job, we may be convinced by the argument that the difference in their IQ scores is negligible. And we may not feel that we have enough evidence to construct a convincing argument for a decision rule that uses a particular weighted average of IQ and experience.

"But," the reader may insist, "doesn't it bother you that you are using a rule that produces intransitivities when it is more widely applied?" I must respond that I have enough to worry about as I try to find adequate evidence or good arguments for my particular problem. If I allow myself to be bothered whenever my evidence is inadequate for the solution of a wider problem, then I will always be very bothered. When you call my argument for choosing candidate *B* over candidate *A* a rule and choose other situations in which to apply this rule, you are choosing one out of many possible wider contexts in which my argument might be made. This is not reasonable. There are always many wider contexts in which a particular argument might be made, and it is unreasonable that the argument should be convincing in all of them.

The point I am making here is simple: regarding the difference in IQ as negligible may be about the best we can do. I have made the point at length in order to demonstrate how well it can be made when we insist on talking about evidence, argument, and the construction of preference. Matters become much more confused when we try to make the same point using a vocabulary based on the fiction that we already have preferences and that we are just finding out what they are.

4. THE CONSTRUCTIVE NATURE OF SMALL WORLDS

In the small world of the gambler, value is disentangled from probability and belief. The gambler values the amount of money he wins. He has beliefs about the outcome of the game. The two are initially quite distinct; they become connected only when he chooses a gamble. This means that the first step in constructing an argument based on subjective expected utility is to distinguish sharply the consequences on which we want to place value from the questions of fact about which we have evidence. We must construct sets C and S such that we can put utilities on the consequences in C without regard to our evidence about S, and such that we can put probabilities on the states in S without regard to our feelings about C.

According to the constructive view, we may or may not succeed in distinguishing so sharply between a domain of value and a domain of belief. If we do not succeed, then we will have no subjective expected utility argument. We will have to look for other arguments on which to base our decision. According to Savage's normative view, on the other hand, this disentanglement of value and belief is essential to rational decision.

The assumption that value and belief can be disentangled underlies Savage's second, third, and fourth postulates. In this section I contend that Savage made no real case for this assumption. He simply took it for granted.

The second postulate, the independence postulate, has been the most controversial of Savage's postulates. Both its descriptive and normative status have been put in doubt by well-known examples devised by Allais and Ellsberg. I will review these examples and place myself on the side of those who do not find the postulate compelling.

The third and fourth postulates have not received so much attention. They are sometimes said to be uncontroversial. But, from a constructive viewpoint, they are more important than the independence postulates, because they express more clearly the assumption that one's small world disentangles value from belief. In order to emphasize this point. I will discuss the third and fourth postulates first, before turning to the independence postulate.

4.1 Can value be purged of belief?

The third postulate says that if A is not null, then $[c]_A > [d]_A$ if and only if $[c] > [d]$. Recall that $[c]_A > [d]_A$ means that $f > g$ whenever f and g are acts that agree on A^c but satisfy $f(s) = c$ and $g(s) = d$ for s in A; intuitively, this seems to mean that the person prefers the consequence c to the consequence d when his or her choice is limited to the event or situation A. Thus, the postulate says that if the person prefers c to d in general, then he or she prefers it in every situation A. Specializing to the case where A consists of a single state of the world, say $A = \{s\}$, we can say that the person prefers c to d in every state of the world s. Which state of the world is true is irrelevant to the preference.

This postulate clearly expresses one aspect of the disentanglement of value from belief. It says that the question about which we have beliefs (which element of S is the true state of the world?) is irrelevant to our preferences.

The fact that this postulate may fail to hold is brought out by the following example, which Savage gave on page 25 of *Foundations*:

> Before going on a picnic with friends, a person decides to buy a bathing suit or a tennis racket, not having at the moment enough money for both. If we call possession of the tennis racket and possession of the bathing suit consequences, then we must say that the consequences of his decision will be independent of where the picnic is actually held. If the person prefers the bathing suit, this decision would presumably be reversed, if he learned that the picnic were not going to be held near water.

Apparently the person prefers the bathing suit to the tennis racket only because he considers it probable that the picnic will be held near water. It seems reasonable that he should reverse his preference when he learns that the facts are otherwise. But this reasonable reversal violates the third postulate. Take A to be the event that the picnic is not going to be held near water, c to be possession of the bathing suit, and d to be possession of the tennis racket. The person's preference for the bathing suit over the tennis racket is indicated by the relation $[c] > [d]$. His preference for the tennis racket when he knows that the true state of the small world is in A is indicated by the relation $[d]_A > [c]_A$.

Savage defended the postulate against this apparent counterexample as follows (again page 25 of *Foundations*):

> under the interpretation of "act" and "consequence" I am trying to formulate, this is not the correct analysis of the situation. The possession of the tennis racket and the bathing suit are to be regarded as acts, not consequences. (It would be equivalent and more in accordance with ordinary discourse to say that the coming into possession, or the buying, of them are acts.) The consequences relevant to the decision are such as these: a refreshing swim with friends, sitting on a shadeless beach twiddling a brand new tennis racket while other's friends swim, etc. It seems clear that, if this analysis is carried to its limit, the question at issue [whether $[d]_A > [c]_A$ and $[c] > [d]$ should be allowed] must be answered in the negative.

The suggestion seems to be that we can always resolve the problem by considering more fundamental consequences. By describing the consequences in a more refined way, we can make their valuation independent of which element of S is true.

The difficulty with this suggestion is that the refinement of C may force a refinement of S. This is because the states of the world in S must be detailed enough to determine which element of C will be achieved by each of our concrete acts. Savage suggests that we take C to consist of descriptions such as "refreshing swim with friends" instead of descriptions such as "possession of bathing suit." But if we want each element of S to determine whether the consequence "refreshing swim with friends" is achieved by the purchase of a bathing suit, we may need to refine S so that its elements say not only whether the picnic will be held near water but also whether the temperature is warm enough for a refreshing swim, which friends come, and so on. And now, since S is more refined, we may face anew the problem of making our preferences among the elements of C independent of which element of S is true. Perhaps the swim will be more refreshing with some friends than others. We face a potential infinite regress, and endless sequence of alternative refinements of C and S.

Another way of putting the matter is to say that we have no reason to suppose that for a given set F_0 of concrete acts we will be able to find S and C such that both (1) each state s in S determines which consequence in C will result from each f in F_0, and (2) the value we want to place on each c in C will not depend on which element of S is the true state. These two desiderata push in opposite directions. The first desideratum pushes us to limit the detail in C or increase the detail in S, while the second pushes us to increase the detail in C or limit the detail in S. There is no a priori reason to expect that we can find a compromise that will satisfy both desiderata.

It seems clear, Savage says, that probability and value will finally be disentangled when the "analysis is carried to its limit." This is both lame and vague. In truth, it is not clear what carrying the analysis to its limit would mean, let alone what would happen there. Presumably, carrying the analysis to its limit means looking at ever more refined small worlds, until one arrives at a "grand world," a pair (S, C) so detailed that it takes everything into account. Yet it is hard to make sense of the idea of a grand world.

In section 5, I will examine Savage's own struggle with the idea of a grand world on pages 82–91 of *Foundations*. Let me remark here that one aspect of the problem is the difficulty in sustaining a distinction between consequences and states of the world as we look at the world in more and more detail. Consequences are states of the person, as opposed to states of the world (*Foundations*, page 14). For some problems, at some levels of detail, I can describe states of my person C and states of the world S in such a way that I care about which state in C happens to me but I do not care about which state in S happens to the world. But, when I try to think about very detailed states of the world, states that specify the fate of my own hopes and loved ones, it begins to sound bizarrely hedonistic for me to say that I care not about which of these states happens to the world but only about the consequences for me.

4.2 Can belief be discovered from preference?

The fourth postulate carries the idea underlying the third postulate a step further. If the relation $[c] > [d]$ does mean that the person values c over d without regard to which element of S is true, then, by comparing this absolute preference to the person's other preferences among acts, we can learn about his beliefs about which element of S is true.

Suppose, indeed, that $[c] > [d]$, f is equal to c on A and to d on A^c, and g is equal to c on B and to d on B^c. And suppose that $f > g$. If we assume that value in our small world has been purged of belief – if, that is to say, the preference for c over d is independent of whether the true state of nature is in A and of whether it is in B – then the only available explanation for the preference $f > g$ is that the person considers A more probable than B.

In order for this to work, however, the preference $f > g$ must be unchanged when c and d are replaced by any other pair of consequences c' and d' such that $[c'] > [d']$. As Savage put it, "on which of two events the person will choose to stake a given prize does not depend on the prize itself" (*Foundations*, page 31). The fourth postulate posits that this is the case.

It is easy to create examples, analogous to the example of the tennis racket and bathing suit, in which the fourth postulate does not hold. There is no need to dwell on such examples here. It is worthwhile, though, to reiterate that this postulate derives its force from the assumption that the small world disentangles belief from value. The postulate does not have any normative appeal – it is not even comprehensible – until this assumption is made.

4.3 The independence postulate

Consider an act f and a subset A of the set of states of a small world. Imagine changing the consequences that f would have if the true state of the small world were in A – i.e., imagine changing the values $f(s)$ for s in A. This changes f to a different act, say g. The act g differs from f on A but agrees with f on A^c. The change from f to g may be a change for the worse – i.e., we may have $f > g$. Savage's second postulate, the independence postulate, says that whether it is a change for the worse is independent of the consequences that f has under the other states, those in A^c. In other words, if f' is any act that agrees with f on A, and we change f' in the same way that we changed f, thus obtaining an act g' that agrees with g on A but with f' on A^c, then $f > g$ if and only if $f' > g'$.

Here are some other ways of expressing the independence postulate: (1) *More verbally*, if two acts agree on A^c, then the choice between them should depend only on how they differ on A; it should not depend on how they agree on A^c. (2) *More succinctly*, if $f > g$, $f'_A = f_A$, $g'_A = g_A$, $f_{A^c} = g_{A^c}$, and $f'_{A^c} = g'_{A^c}$, then $f' > g'$. (3) *Yet more succinctly, as in section 3.1, above*, if $f > g$ and $f_{A^c} = g_{A^c}$, then $f_A > g_A$.

In section 4.3.1, I present two examples that have inspired much of the discussion of Savage's independence postulate. One of these was devised by Maurice Allais, the other by Daniel Ellsberg. Both are counterexamples to the empirical validity of the independence postulate, inasmuch as most people (including Savage himself; see *Foundations*, page 103; Allais, 1979, page 533; Ellsberg, 1961, page 656) expresses preferences that violate the postulate when they first encounter the examples.

After reviewing the counterexamples, I discuss a number of arguments that have been offered for the independence postulate and against the counterexamples. In section 4.3.2, I discuss the assertion made by Oskar Morgenstern and others that reasonable people will correct their preferences to conform to the postulate when divergences are pointed out to them. In section 4.3.3, I discuss the "sure thing principle," the intuitive principle on which Savage

Table 10.5. *Allais's example*

	s	t	u
f	$500,000	$500,000	$500,000
g	$0	$2,500,000	$500,000
f'	$500,000	$500,000	$0
g'	$0	$2,500,000	$0

based his case for the independence postulate. In sections 4.3.4 and 4.3.5, I discuss Howard Raiffa's arguments. Finally, in section 4.3.6, I question Paul Samuelson's contrast between commodities and states of a small world. I contend that goals can tie together states of the world just as they tie together commodities.

4.3.1 The counterexamples

The two examples presented here are from Allais (1953) and Ellsberg (1961), respectively. It is generally agreed that Allais's is the more important of the two. Ellsberg's example turns on subtle issues about the knowledge of chances, whereas Allais's, although it is usually presented in a chance setting, does not really depend on the idea of chance. Furthermore, the argument for violating the independence postulate is stronger in Allais's example, because the goal thereby attained is more attractive.

Allais's example
Consider a small world that has three states and has monetary prizes as consequences. The states are s, t, and u, and the prizes are $0, $500,000, and $2,500,000. Consider the acts f, g, f', and g' given in table 10.5. If we set $A = \{s, t\}$, then these acts satisfy $f'_A = f_A$, $g'_A = g_A$, $f_{A^c} = g_{A^c}$, and $f'_{A^c} = g'_{A^c}$. The independence postulate therefore forbids us to prefer f to g and g' to f'.

Suppose, however, that we think the true state of the small world is probably u and almost certainly either t or u. (In the version of the example reported in *Foundations* (pages 101–103), we assign probability .01 to s, probability .10 to t, and probability .89 to u.) In this situation, most people violate the postulate by preferring f to g and g' to f'. When comparing f to g, they reason that they can gain $500,000 for sure by choosing f, and they do not want to risk this very attractive sure thing by gambling for more. But, when comparing f' to g', they realize that they are likley to get nothing at all and, feeling that they have less to lose, they are more willing to gamble for the larger prize.

One way of putting this is to say that there is a strong argument for choosing f over g which is not available when we compare f' and g'. Another way of putting it is to say that the choice between f and g gives us an opportunity to adopt and attain a goal: the acquisition of $500,000.

Table 10.6. *The probability in Allais's example*

	Probability of $2,500,000	Probability of $500,000	Probability of nothing
f	0.00	1.00	0.00
g	0.10	0.89	0.01
f'	0.00	0.11	0.89
g'	0.10	0.00	0.90

Table 10.7. *Ellsberg's example*

	s	t	u
f	$0	$100	$100
g	$100	$0	$100
f'	$0	$100	$0
g'	$100	$0	$0

It is worth emphasizing that the force of the example does not depend on assigning probabilities to s, t, and u. It is quite enough to say that there is strong evidence for u and even stronger evidence against s.

Allais's example is sometimes presented simply in terms of payoffs and probabilities as in table 10.6. When it is presented in this way, we cannot say that the preferences $f > g$ and $g' > f'$ violate the independence postulate, since we are not working in a small world in Savage's sense. It is impossible, however, to assign utilities to the dollar payoffs so that f will exceed g and g' will exceed f' in expected utility.

Readers of Savage's account of the example (*Foundations*, pages 101–103) sometimes gain the impression that Allais originally presented it simply in terms of payoffs and probabilities and that it was Savage who recast it in terms that made the preferences $f > g$ and $g' > f'$ directly contradict the independence postulate. This is not correct, however. In Allais (1953), the example is explicitly presented as a counterexample to the independence postulate (see Allais and Hagen, 1979, pages 88–90 and note 240 on page 586).

Ellsberg's example

Consider another small world with three states, but with a more modest prize: $100. The acts are shown in table 10.7. Here, as in Allais's example, the independence postulate forbids us to prefer f to g and g' to f'. It also forbids us to prefer g to f and f' to g'.

In this case, the forbidden preferences are produced by assuming partial knowledge of objective chances for the state of the small world. Suppose we know that this state is determined by drawing a ball from an urn containing 90 balls. We know that exactly 30 of these balls are labeled s. We know that each of the other 60 is labeled either t or u, but we have no evidence about the proportion.

We know that f offers a $\frac{2}{3}$ chance at the \$100 prize. We do not know exactly what chance g offers; we know only that it is between $\frac{1}{3}$ and 1. When offered a choice between f and g, some people say they are completely indifferent. They reason that since there is no reason to think that there are more balls labeled t than u or more labeled u than t, the subjective probability of getting the prize from g is $\frac{2}{3}$, the same as the probability of getting it from f. But most people are not indifferent. Many prefer f to g, because f offers more security; these are the pessimists. Others, the optimists, prefer g to f because g offers the possibility of a greater chance at the \$100.

Most people also see a difference between g', which offers a $\frac{1}{3}$ chance at the \$100, and f', which offers an unknown chance between 0 and $\frac{2}{3}$. The pessimists, those who choose f over g, choose g' over f'. The optimists, those who chose g over f, choose f' over g'. Both the pessimists and the optimists violate the independence postulate.

The argument for violating the independence postulates is not as strong in this example as in Allais's example, because the goal that can be attained by violating it is not as attractive. In Allais's example, the goal is \$500,000. Here the goal is only a known (in the case of the pessimists) or unknown (in the case of the optimists) chance at a certain amount of money.

4.3.2 Is the postulate absolutely convincing?

Morgenstern (1979, page 180) described the independence postulate as "absolutely convincing"; reasonable people will violate it only if they do not understand it or do not realize how it applies to the problem they are considering. This claim is sometimes buttressed by the observation that both experimental subjects and students in decision theory classes can be convinced to change their preferences to agree with the postulate (MacCrimmon, 1968).

The claim that reasonable people will conform to the independence postulate when they fully understand it can never be conclusively refuted. Any failure to conform can always be attributed to unreasonableness or lack of understanding. Some reasonable people have been convinced that the postulate is not absolutely convincing, however, by the experimental work of Slovic and Tversky (1974). After querying college students about their preferences in the examples of Allais and Ellsberg, these authors explained the independence postulate to those who had violated it, explained the arguments for violating it to those who had obeyed it, and then gave both groups an opportunity to change their preferences. They also studied the effect of this information when it was presented before students were asked to express their preferences. They found that the arguments for violating the postulate were at least as persuasive as the arguments for obeying the postulate.

4.3.3 The sure thing principle

Savage derived the independence postulate from a more intuitive but less precise principle that he called "the sure thing principle." Suppose $A_1, \ldots, A_n$ form a partition of the set S of states of a small world, and suppose f and g are acts. Suppose you are able to compare the consequences of f and g separately for each A_i, in abstraction from their consequences for the other A_j. You are able, that is, to say whether you prefer the pattern of consequences $\{f(s)\}_{s \in A_i}$ to the pattern of consequences $\{g(s)\}_{s \in A_i}$. The sure thing principle says that if you prefer $\{f(s)\}_{s \in A_i}$ to $\{g(s)\}_{s \in A_i}$ for each A_i, then you should prefer f to g.

This principle cannot itself serve as a postulate within Savage's system, because that system talks only about preferences between acts, not about preferences between partial acts such as $\{f(s)\}_{s \in A_i}$ and $\{g(s)\}_{s \in A_i}$. (An act is a mapping from S to C, not a mapping from just part of S to C.) But it seems more immediately understandable and appealing than the independence postulate.

The sure thing principle is appealing because it reflects a familiar strategy for resolving decision problems. When we are trying to decide what to do, we often devise a set $A_1, \ldots, A_n$ of mutually exclusive and jointly exhaustive situations and look for an act that seems to be advantageous or at least satisfactory in all these situations.

We cannot expect that this strategy will always be successful, however. It will not always produce a good argument and, even when it does, this argument may be outweighed by other arguments, as it is in Allais's example.

The strategy suggested by the sure thing principle may fail in several different ways. It may fail because we are unable to construct a convincing argument for any particular act when we consider a given A_i in isolation. It may fail because consideration of the different A_i may produce convincing arguments for different acts. Or, as in Allais's example, it may fail because there is a convincing argument that we will overlook when we consider the different A_i separately.

One reason it is sometimes difficult to construct a convincing argument for a particular act when we consider a given A_i in isolation is that the instructions "suppose you knew that the true state of the small world is in A_i" may not suffice to define a situation for us. (This is also part of the difficulty in turning the principle into a formal postulate.) In examples such as Allais's where objective chances are supplied for each state of the small world, there is an implicit message about how we should define this situation: we should renormalize these chances for the states s in A_i so they add to one. We see this in Savage's own discussion of Allais's example, where he writes of "a 10-to-1 chance to win $2,500,000" (*Foundations*, page 103). But, in problems where probabilities are not given *ex ante*, this solution is not available, and to assume that there are subjective

Table 10.8. *The result of mixing our choices*

	s	t	u
Your strategy	$0 or $500,000	$500,000 or $2,500,000	$0 or $500,000
The opposite	$1 or $500,001	$500,001 or $2,500,001	$1 or $500,001

Note: Each entry represents a 50–50 chance.

probabilities available for renormalization begs one of the questions that Savage's postulates are supposed to resolve.

4.3.4 The mixing argument

The following argument in favor of the independence postulate has been used very effectively by Raiffa (1961, 1968). We may call it the mixing argument.

Suppose f, g, f', and g' satisfy the hypotheses of the independence postulate: $f'_A = f_A$, $g'_A = g_A$, $f_{A^c} = g_{A^c}$, and $f'_{A^c} = g'_{A^c}$. Suppose you violate the postulate by preferring f to g and g' to f'. Imagine I am about to toss a fair coin, and I offer you an opportunity to play the following compound game. If the coin comes up heads, then I will give you a choice between f and g. If the coin comes up tails, I will give you a choice between f' and g'. Since you prefer f to g and g' to f', you can tell me in advance what your choices will be. If the coin comes up heads, you will choose f; if it comes up tails you will choose g'. Let us call this your strategy: f if heads, g' if tails. The opposite strategy, which you apparently find less attractive, is g if heads, f' if tails.

But is there really anything to choose between these two strategies? If we let s denote the true state of nature, then your strategy gives you a 50–50 chance at $f(s)$ or $g'(s)$. The opposite strategy would give you a 50–50 chance at $g(s)$ or $f'(s)$. But, these two 50–50 chances boil down to the same thing, no matter what s is. To see this, recall that (i) if $s \in S$, then $f(s) = f'(s)$ and $g(s) = g'(s)$, and (ii) if $s \in A^c$, then $f(s) = g(s)$ and $f'(s) = g'(s)$.

It is embarrassing enough that your preferences for f over g and g' over f' lead to a preference between two equivalent strategies, but things get worse. If you feel strongly about your preferences for f over g and g' over f', then presumably these preferences will not change when g and f' are both improved slightly. And the argument just given then shows that you prefer one strategy to another which is clearly better.

Just to make this last point as vivid as possible, let us rehearse it using Allais's example. Suppose your preferences for f over g and g' over f' are strong enough for them not to change when we increase all the entries for g and f' in table 10.5 by $1. Table 10.8 gives the results, in this case, of your strategy (f if tails, g' if heads) and the opposite strategy (g if heads, f' if tails). (All the entries in table 10.8 should be interpreted as 50–50 chances; "$0 or $500,000," for example, means a 50% chance at $0 and a 50% chance at $500,000.)

This argument for the independence postulate can be persuasive, but a little thought will convince us that it is simply another way of deriving the postulate from the sure thing principle. The crucial step in the argument is the step where it is concluded from your preferences for f over g and g' over f' that you would prefer the strategy "f if heads, g' if tails" over the strategy "g if heads, f' if tails." This step can only be justified by appeal to the sure thing principle. Attention has shifted to a small world whose two states are heads and tails. Call heads B and tails B^c. The sure thing principle says that, if you prefer the first strategy to the second when B is considered in isolation and also when B^c is considered in isolation, then you will prefer the first strategy to the second overall. But we need not obey this principle. We may refuse to do so on the grounds that our argument for choosing f over g – the fact that f guarantees us \$500,000 – is not available when we must choose one of the strategies in table 10.8.

4.3.5 The imaginary protocol

Another argument for the independence postulate, which has also been used effectively by Raiffa (1968, pages 82 and 83), asks us to imagine a protocol under which we find out about the true state of the small world in steps and do not have to choose between f and g or between f' and g' until after we have found out whether the state is in A.

Let us explain the argument, as Raiffa does, in terms of Allais's example, given in table 10.5, with the states s, t, and u assigned probabilities .01, .10, and .89, respectively. Imagine that the determination of the true state of the small world is made by a two-stage random drawing. First you draw a ball from an urn containing 89 orange balls and 11 white balls. If you draw orange, then u is the true state of the small world. If you draw white, then you make a second drawing from an urn containing 10 red balls and one blue ball. If you draw the blue ball, then s is the true state; if you draw a red ball, then t is the true state.

Suppose you are asked to choose between f and g, but you are not required to do so until after the first drawing. If the first ball is orange, then u is the true state, and you get \$500,000 in either case, so there is really no need to choose. But, if the first ball drawn is white, then you are required to choose between f and g before making the second drawing.

This situation is depicted in figure 10.1 (adapted from Raiffa, 1968, page 82). Notice that, if the first drawing produces an orange ball, then you are awarded \$500,000 with no further ado; no choice or second drawing is required. Similarly, if the first drawing produces a white ball and you choose f, then you are awarded \$500,000 with no further ado; the second drawing is not required.

Figure 10.1 represents the choice between f and g. But, with one simple change, it becomes a representation of the choice between f' and g'. We simply change the underlined \$500,000 to \$0.

The argument for the independence postulate now proceeds in three steps.

Step 1. Under the conditions just described, where you make your choice only if and when a white ball has been drawn, if you choose *f* over *g*, then you should also choose *f'* over *g'*. The situation where you must choose between *f'* and *g'* differs from the situation where you must choose between *f* and *g* only in what you *would have* received had you drawn an orange ball instead of a white ball. And surely you will want to base your choice on your present situation, not on might-have-beens.

Step 2. It should not make any difference if you are required to choose at the outset rather than only if and when you draw a white ball. You can mentally put yourself in the situation where you have just drawn a white ball; you know that in this situation you will prefer *f* to *g* and *f'* to *g'*, and you know that only if you are later in this situation will the choice make any difference. So surely you should prefer *f* to *g* and *f'* to *g'* now.

Step 3. The choice between *f* and *g* or between *f'* and *g'* should only depend on the probability distributions of the consequences of these acts. So the conclusion, that if you prefer *f* to *g* then you should also prefer *f'* to *g'*, must hold whenever the true state of the small world is *s*, *t*, or *u*, with probabilities .01, .10, and .89, respectively, even in the absence of the step by step protocol depicted in figure 10.1.

A different premise is invoked at each step of this argument. In step 1, present choices should not depend on might-have-beens. In step 2, if under the only scenario where a choice makes any difference there is a point at which you would choose in a certain way, that is also the way you should choose now. In step 3, choice should depend only on the overall probability distributions of advantages and disadvantages, not on any protocol for the timing of your knowledge and choices.

I contend that none of these premises are compelling. They would be compelling if we could pretend that preferences are preexistent and well-defined for every situation. But they are not compelling if we recognize that preferences are constructed.

The premise in step 3 is especially objectionable, because it unreasonably limits the way in which preferences may depend on opportunities to adopt

Figure 10.1 The imaginary protocol.

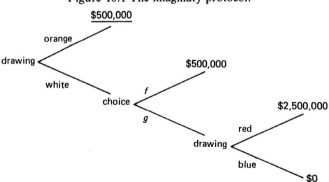

221

feasible goals. Consider the person who prefers g' to f' in the absence of the protocol depicted in figure 10.1, but who would choose the $500,000 were he in the situation where a white ball has just been drawn. If there is no protocol, then he can argue that since he is likley to win nothing he might as well gamble with his slim chances. But if the protocol in figure 10.1 is followed, and if he had just drawn a white ball, then he is in a position where $500,000 is a feasible goal. Why must he ignore this fact? (Even when we are concerned only with probability judgment and not with choice and preference, the presence or absence of a protocol is not irrelevant. See Chafer, 1985.)

The other two premises are also unpersuasive as general and apodictic principles, although they may be persuasive in particular cases. The first premise, which says that might-have-beens should not matter to you, overlooks the fact that your present preferences may be the result of goals that you adopted earlier, when what is now a might-have-been was a real possibility to you. Once we admit that goals and preferences are adopted or constructed, we cannot pretend that history is irrelevant. The second premise is open to the same objection, for it tries to rule out the adoption of any goal that might reverse the preference that you might guess your future self would have were you not to adopt the goal.

In the preceding discussion, I have focused on the version of Allais's example where probabilities are assigned *ex ante* to the possible states of the small world. More difficulties arise if one attempts to extend Raiffa's argument to every day problems, where the state of one's small world is not determined by a chance device. In such problems it may be difficult to construct an imaginary protocol in which the first step leads to knowledge that the true state is or is not in A and no more; "now you know that the true state is in A" may not suffice to define a situation in which we can imagine ourselves.

4.3.6 Goals and commodities

I have repeatedly used the idea of adopting goals to define violations of the independence postulate. My point is that the process of formulating and adopting goals creates a dependence of value on belief, simply because goals are more attractive when they are feasible.

The dependence of the goal formation process on belief is the most fundamental reason for an adherent of the constructive view to reject the sure thing principle. The formation of goals does not usually take place at the level of individual states or restricted sets of states. Typically, we adopt goals that relate to the overall situation we are in. The adoption of goals ties states together, for the attractiveness of a goal depends on its meaningfulness and feasibility in all the states we consider possible, or at least in all the ones we consider probable.

It is interesting, in this connection, to recall the contrasts between small worlds and commodities, drawn sharply by Samuelson (1952). Samuelson, who was at first reluctant to accept Savage's sure thing principle, finally did so because he became convinced that a person cannot make trade-offs between small worlds the way he or she can make trade-offs between commodities.

Suppose we want to rank in preference situations in which we have different amounts of three commodities – flour, apples, and butter. Let (x, y, z) denote the situation where we have x pounds of flour, y apples, and z pounds of butter. Set

$$f = (4, 3, 1), \qquad f' = (4, 3, 0),$$
$$g = (2, 6, 1), \qquad g' = (2, 6, 0).$$

We may very well prefer f to g but g' to f'. If we had a pound of butter, we could make better bread, and so we would rather have more flour and fewer apples; this is a reason to prefer f to g. But if we do not have any butter, then flour is less interesting; we may prefer g' to f'. As this example illustrates, the amount of one commodity we have may influence the trade-offs we make between other commodities. We cannot consider separately our preferences for the commodities in the disjoint sets $A = \{$flour, apples$\}$ and $A^c = \{$butter$\}$, because what we can get in A^c influences our preferences within A. The goal of a loaf of bread ties A and A^c together.

Samuelson's conversion to the sure thing principle was based on the feeling that states of small worlds are not like commodities in this respect. Different states of small worlds are completely separate from one another. What we would have in one state of a small world cannot help us enjoy or use something we would have in another state. So we should be able to think separately about your preferences in disjoint sets of states. What we can get in A^c should not influence our preferences within A.

The constructive view forces us to recognize, however, that our value resides where it is constructed. If we construct goals within the products of our imagination that Savage called states of a small world, then the sure thing principle will hold. But, if we construct goals in our real situation, then these goals may tie the states of the small world together as effectively as the goal of a loaf of bread ties butter and flour together.

5. THE PROBLEM OF SMALL WORLDS

A subjective expected utility analysis of a decision problem using one small world may fail to give the same result as an analysis using a more detailed small world. This is the problem of small worlds. As I pointed out in the introduction, this problem appears from the constructive viewpoint as just one more aspect of the lack of invariance of preference. The preferences we construct depend on the questions we ask ourselves, and hence the selection of questions is an essential part of the construction.

There is much to learn, however, from a closer look at the problem of small worlds. We can learn something about the nature of value from the very fact that we sometimes assign values to consequences at a limited level of description, without considering probabilities for further contingencies that might affect our enjoyment of these consequences.

In this section, I emphasize that the constructive view forces us to take seriously the fact that we work at limited levels of description. When we take the constructive view, we cannot pretend that every utility is really, at a more detailed level of description, an expected utility.

We can also profit from a closer look at the mathematical structure required to make one small world a refinement of another. In this section, I will describe this structure using a notation somewhat different from Savage's own. I will then develop a detailed example of two related small worlds. This is something Savage did not do, and by doing it we gain some insights he may have missed.

I conclude this section with a look at how Savage himself saw the problem of small worlds. For him, the problem was that refinement might change the probabilities that can be deduced from a person's preferences. The fact that Savage construed the problem of small worlds in this way demonstrates just how hopelessly nonconstructive his normative viewpoint was.

5.1 *Are all utilities really expected utilities?*

According to the constructive viewpoint, the method of subjective expected utility involves constructing preferences from separate judgments of value and belief. We distinguish between states of the world, about which we have evidence and for which we can construct probabilities, and consequences, to which we decide to attach values, represented numerically by utilities. The virtue of the method is that it breaks our deliberation into simpler and more manageable parts. We can deal separately with evidence for which state of the world is true and arguments about what we should value.

The idea of refinement threatens this picture. A thing to which we might want to assign a definite value at one level of description seems, at a finer level, to have a value that depends on how various questions of fact turn out. It seems that every utility, on closer examination, is an expected utility.

In the preceding section I point out that a subjective expected utility argument requires a small world (S, C) such that our preferences over C do not depend on which description in S is true. I argued that sometimes we will be unable to make a subjective expected utility argument because we are unable to devise such a small world. Here I am raising a related but different point. I am considering the case where we do make a subjective expected utility argument – the case where we do succeed in devising a small world (S, C) such that we are willing to settle on preferences over C that are independent of which description in S is true – and I am asking whether these preferences might still depend on questions of fact more detailed than those answered by the descriptions in S.

Savage discussed this point as follows on pages 83 and 84 of *Foundations*:

Jones is faced with the decision whether to buy a certain sedan for a thousand dollars, a certain convertible also for a thousand dollars, or to buy neither and continue carless. The simplest analysis, and the one generally assumed, is that Jones is deciding between three definite and sure enjoyments, that of the sedan, the convertible, or the thousand dollars. Chance and uncertainty are considered to have nothing to do with the situation. This simple analysis may well be appropriate in some contexts; however, it is not difficult to recognize that Jones must in fact take account of many uncertain future possibilities in actually making his choice. The relative fragility of the convertible will be compensated only if Jones's hope to arrange a long vacation in a warm and scenic part of the country actually materializes; Jones would not buy a car at all if he thought it likely he would immediately be faced by a financial emergency arising out of the sickness of himself or of some member of his family; he would be glad to put the money into a car, or almost any durable goods, if he feared extensive inflation. This brings out the fact that what are often thought of as consequences (that is, sure experiences of the deciding person) in isolated decision problems typically are in reality highly uncertain. Indeed, in the final analysis, a consequence is an idealization that can perhaps never be well approximated.

When we first consider an example like this one, we are tempted to think that a sufficiently detailed description of Jones's possible future situations would make it possible for him to decouple his utilities from his probabilities. But, as I argued in section 4.1, this sufficiently detailed description is a chimera. No matter how much detail we include in a description of a situation, there always remain uncertainties that can affect the degree to which we will enjoy or value that situation. This is the point of Savage's last sentence.

When we take a constructive view, we can no longer pursue the chimera of the sufficiently detailed description. Instead, we are forced to take seriously the idea that, when a person decides to attach a value or utility to a consequence described at a certain limited level of detail, he or she does this and nothing more.

"I have decided to buy a convertible," Jones tells me, "because my wife and I are taking a vacation to New Mexico this summer, and we really want to enjoy the sun." "You should think this through more carefully, Jones," I respond. "Don't you remember that sunburn you got at Daytona Beach last spring? You never really enjoy these vacations anyway. And, if your wife does like the sun that much, she may not come back to Chicago with you." "You are always dreaming up things to worry about," replies Jones. "I detest this winter weather, and I have set my heart on a tour of the desert in the sun. The trip may be a disaster, but staying home might be a disaster, too. Who knows?"

Jones has decided on a trip to sunny New Mexico in a convertible. He does not want to analyze all the different ways taking the trip might turn out, partly because he does not feel he can construct convincing probabilities for them, but also because these more detailed scenarios are not really the objects of his desire. The trip lies within the bounds of product behavior, and he and his wife have decided they want to go.

A constructive interpretation of subjective expected utility must hold that a utility is not an expected utility in disguise. A utility is a value deliberately attached to a consequence created at a given level of description. The consequence is a product of our imagination. The utility is a product of our will.

We may later analyze the consequence at a finer level of description, and we may then assign it an expected utility rather than just a utility. But any such further analysis is a further act of imagination and will, not something already determined or achieved.

5.2 *Refining small worlds*

In order to study the problem of small worlds as it appears from Savage's normative point of view, we need to understand the technical aspects of refining a small world. Suppose (S, C) and (T, D) are two small worlds. How do we give mathematical form to the idea that (T, D) is a refinement of (S, C)?

Savage answered this question on pages 84–86 of *Foundations*. Unfortunately, he did so in the context of a "tongue in check" (page 83) assumption that (T, D) is actually a "grand world," i.e., an ultimately detailed refinement. This assumption does not affect the technical details of the mathematical structure relating (S, C) and (T, D), but it did, I think, obscure Savage's view. Since he was struggling with the idea of (T, D) being a grand world, he missed the insight he might have gained from a concrete example where (S, C) and (T, D) are both small worlds. (The only example he gave was purely mathematical.) Moreover, he was content to "hobble along" (page 85) with an inadequate notation.

When we examine Savage's account, on pages 84 and 85 of *Foundations*, we see that (S, C) and (T, D) are related in two ways. First, the descriptions in T are more detailed versions of the descriptions in S. Secondly, the consequences in C correspond to acts in (T, D), mapping from T to D. It is easy to establish a mathematical notation for both these aspects of the relation. For each element t of T, let t^* denote the unique element of S that agrees with t but is less detailed. And, for each element c of C, let c^* denote the corresponding act in (T, D).

Why does a consequence in the less refined small world (S, C) correspond to an act in the more refined small world (T, D)? We might think that, just as the descriptions of states of the world in T are merely more detailed versions of the descriptions in S, so the descriptions of the states of the person in D should merely be more detailed versions of the descriptions in C. But Savage felt that pushing to a more defined level of description may mean more than describing the same consequences in more detail. It may mean instead shifting attention to entirely different and more fundamental consequences. We may, for example, shift our attention from monetary income to personal satisfaction. The same level of satisfaction can be achieved with different levels of income, depending on the state of the world. So, if the elements of C are levels of income, and the elements of D are levels of satisfaction, then we do not want to say that each element of D is a more detailed version of some element of C. Instead, we want to say that each element of C determines an element of D when combined with a state of the world in T. This can be expressed mathematically by saying that each element of C corresponds to a mapping from T to D.

Once we have linked (S, C) and (T, D) by specifying t^* for each t in T and c^* for each c in C, we also have a way of relating acts in (S, C) to acts in (T, D). Suppose, indeed, that f is an act in (S, C). Then there is a unique act in (T, D), say f^*, that corresponds to f. The act f^* maps a given element t of T to $(f(t^*))^*(t)$, which is an element of D.

It is interesting and important to note that this mathematical apparatus linking (S, C) and (T, D) goes beyond what we construct when we formulate two small worlds in two different attempts to study the same set of concrete acts. In order to see this clearly, we need a notation that distinguishes between a concrete act and its representation as a mapping within a particular small world. Given a concrete act a, let f_a^S denote the corresponding abstract act in (S, C), and let f_a^T denote the corresponding abstract act in (T, D); f_s^S is a mapping from S to C, and f_a^T is a mapping from T to D.

Suppose we formulate (S, C) and (T, D) in separate attempts to construct a setting for deliberation about a set F_0 of concrete acts. We formulate (S, C) first, find it too crude, and then formulate (T, D) in order to deepen our analysis. This exercise results in four sets of written descriptions, S, T, C, and D, and mappings f_a^S and f_a^T for each concrete act a in F_0. Since S and T consist of written descriptions, the relation between them will be clear; for each t in T, we will be able to pick out t^*, the unique element of S that agrees with t but is less detailed. Moreover, since we have identified the concrete acts in F_0 with acts in (S, C) and (T, D), we have partially determined mappings c^* corresponding to the elements c of C. We may not have fully determined these mappings, however. We must have $(f_a^S) = f_a^T$ for all a in F_0. Equivalently, we must have

$$(f_a^S(t^*))^*(t) = f_a^T(t)$$

for all a in F_0 and all t in T. This determines $c^*(t)$ whenever there is a concrete act a that results in the consequence c if t^* is the true state of the small world (S, C). But there are usually pairs (c, t) for which there is no such concrete act a, and $c^*(t)$ will not be determined for these pairs.

Consider an example. Begin with the small world (S, C) given in table 10.1 in section 2.1. This is the small world that Savage formulated for the omelet maker who must decide whether to crack a sixth egg into a bowl already containing five eggs. Suppose the omelet maker decides to refine (S, C) because he realizes that his guests can distinguish between a Nero Wolfe omelet, i.e., one made with eggs less than 36 hours old, and an ordinary omelet, i.e., one made with eggs that are not so fresh. He refines the states of the world to take the freshness of the eggs into account, and he refines the consequences to take the quality of the omelet into account. Suppose, for simplicity, that the person knows that the five eggs in the bowl are all of similar freshness, and that the sixth egg, if it is good, will not affect whether the omelet meets Nero Wolfe standards. In this case we can use a set T

227

consisting of four states of the world,

$$T = \begin{cases} \text{the sixth egg is good,} \\ \quad \text{and the other five are fresh} \\ \text{the sixth egg is good,} \\ \quad \text{and the other five are stale} \\ \text{the sixth egg is rotten,} \\ \quad \text{and the other five are fresh} \\ \text{the sixth egg is rotten,} \\ \quad \text{and the other five are stale} \end{cases},$$

and a set D consisting of the eleven consequences listed in table 10.9. We are still considering the same concrete acts:

$$F_0 = \begin{cases} \text{break the egg into the bowl} \\ \text{break the egg into a saucer} \\ \text{throw the egg away} \end{cases}.$$

Table 10.9 shows how the three acts map T to D.

When we compare tables 10.1 and 10.9, we see that these tables determine some of the values $c^*(t)$ but not others. Consider, for example, the first of the three consequences in table 10.1, "six-egg omelet." For brevity, let this consequence be denoted by c_1. It is clear that

$$c_1^*(\text{good, fresh}) = \text{six-egg Nero Wolfe omelet,}$$

and

$$c_1^*(\text{good, stale}) = \text{six-egg ordinary omelet.}$$

The six-egg omelet is of Nero Wolfe or ordinary quality depending on whether the five eggs are fresh or stale. But what are $c^*(\text{rotten, fresh})$ and $c_1^*(\text{rotten, stale})$? If, by magic, we get a six-egg omelet even though the sixth egg is rotten, then what is the quality of this six-egg omelet? This question is not answered by tables 10.1 and 10.9. We may be inclined to say that the six-egg omelet will still be a Nero Wolfe omelet if the five eggs are fresh and an ordinary omelet if the five eggs are stale, but this is not a statement of fact. It is merely a natural way to exercise our imagination. We could invent other examples where it is more difficult to settle on a natural way of exercising our imagination.

Savage seems to have overlooked this remarkable extent to which the structure relating small worlds is a product of our imagination, perhaps because he did not study concrete examples. Perhaps this contributed to his reluctance to see any force in the objections to his use of imaginary acts (section 3.4). It seems reasonable to put an imaginary act that always yields a six-egg omelet into our preference ranking if we permit ourselves to think of a six-egg omelet as a simple object of desire. It seems less reasonable if the very meaning of a six-egg omelet depends on deliberate and not yet performed acts of imagination.

Table 10.9. A refinement of Savage's small world

Act	State				
	Good		Rotten		
	Fresh	Stale	Fresh	Stale	
Break into bowl	six-egg Nero Wolfe omelet	six-egg ordinary omelet	no omelet and five good eggs destroyed	no omelet and five good eggs destroyed	
Break into saucer	six-egg Nero Wolfe omelet and a saucer to wash	six-egg ordinary omelet and a saucer to wash	five-egg Nero Wolfe omelet and a saucer to wash	five-egg ordinary omelet and a saucer to wash	
Throw away	five-egg Nero Wolfe omelet and one good egg destroyed	five-egg ordinary omelet and one good egg destroyed	five-egg Nero Wolfe omelet	five-egg ordinary omelet	

Table 10.10. *Probabilities and utilities for* (T, D)

States	Probabilities	Consequences	Utilities
Good, fresh	$\frac{3}{8}$	no omelet	0
Good, stale	$\frac{1}{8}$	five-egg ordinary omelet	8
Rotten, fresh	$\frac{1}{4}$	five-egg Nero Wolfe omelet	16
Rotten, stale	$\frac{1}{4}$	six-egg ordinary omelet	16
		six-egg Nero Wolfe omelet	32

5.3 Savage's problem of small worlds

Consider a small world (S, C) and a refinement (T, D). Suppose a person has preferences over acts in (T, D) that satisfy Savage's postulates and hence determine a probability measure P_T on T and a utility function U_D on D. From these preferences, probabilities, and utilities, how do we find the person's probability measure P_S and utility function U_C for (S, C)? There are two possible methods.

Method 1. Since S amounts to a disjoint partition of T, we can take P_S to be P_T's marginal on that disjoint partition. And we can say that the person's utility for a consequence c in C is his expected utility for the act c^* in (T, D); $U_C(c) = E_T(U_D(c^*))$.

Method 2. Since every act f in (S, C) can be identified with an act f^* in (T, D), the person's preferences over acts in (T, D) determine preferences over acts in (S, C). If these latter preferences satisfy Savage's postulates, then they directly determine a probability measure P_S and a utility function U_C.

For Savage, the problem of small worlds was that these two methods may fail to produce the same answer. Savage showed that, if the preferences over (S, C) do satisfy his postulates, so that method 2 is applicable, then the two methods will give the same utility function on C. But they may give different probability measures on S (*Foundations*, pages 88–90).

I will not reproduce Savage's mathematical reasoning here. But I will illustrate the problem using the example of the omelet. Suppose a person's preferences over the small world (T, D) of table 10.9 satisfy Savage's postulates and yield the probabilities and utilities shown in table 10.10. (In order for Savage's sixth postulate to be satisfied and the probabilities and utilities to be fully determined, we would need to refine T further so that each state specifies the outcome, say, of a sequence of coin tosses. But we need not make such a refinement explicit here.) According to the probabilities in table 10.10, the sixth egg is as likely to be rotten as good, but its being good makes it more likely that the other five are fresh. The utilities indicate that the person is indifferent as to whether or not he washes a saucer or destroys a good egg, but that he prefers a six-egg omelet to a five-egg one and a Nero Wolfe omelet to an ordinary one. (Since the person is indifferent about washing the saucer or destroying a good egg, table 10.10 omits these details in assigning utilities to the consequences in D. It is to be understood, for

Table 10.11. *Probabilities and utilities for* (S, C)

States	Probabilities Method 1	Method 2	Consequences	Utilities
Good	$\frac{1}{2}$	$\frac{7}{13}$	no omelet	0
Rotten	$\frac{1}{2}$	$\frac{6}{13}$	five-egg omelet	13
			six-egg omelet	26

example, that the person assigns utility 8 to both "five-egg ordinary omelet" and "five-egg ordinary omelet and a saucer to wash.")

The probabilities and utilities that table 10.10 gives for (T, D) result in preferences among the acts in the smaller world (S, C) that do satisfy Savage's postulates, and so we can use both method 1 and method 2 to obtain probabilities and utilities for (T, D). The results are shown in table 10.11. Only one set of utilities is given in this table; as we have mentioned, Savage showed that when method 2 is applicable it necessarily gives the same utilities as method 1. (In table 10.11, as in table 10.10, the consequences are described only in the relevant degree of detail.) But the two methods give different probabilities for the sixth egg's being good.

The reader can easily check the numbers given in table 10.11 for method 1. To obtain the probability of the sixth egg being good, add the probabilities $\frac{3}{8}$ and $\frac{1}{8}$ from table 10.10. To obtain the expected utility of a five-egg omelet, calculate

$P_T(\text{fresh})U_D(\text{five-egg Nero Wolfe omelet})$

$+ P_T(\text{stale})U_D(\text{five-egg ordinary omelet})$

$$= (\tfrac{5}{8})(16) + (\tfrac{3}{8})(8) = 13.$$

And so on.

According to method 2, the probability of the sixth egg being good is more than $\frac{1}{2}$. Why? Because an omelet is valued more highly when the eggs are fresh than when they are stale. The distinction between fresh and stale cannot be expressed in (S, C), but since the five eggs are more likely to be fresh when the sixth is good, the preference for fresh over stale shows up as a preference for an act that gives an omelet when the sixth is good over an act that gives an omelet when the sixth is rotten. This gives the impression that the person puts a higher probability on its being good.

How do we get the exact value $\frac{7}{13}$ for $P_S(\text{good})$? One way is to apply formula (7) on page 88 of *Foundations*. A quicker way is to equate $E_S(f)$ and $E_T(f^*)$ for the act f in (S, C), where

$$E_S(U_C(f)) = P_S(\text{good}) \times 13 + P_S(\text{rotten}) \times 0$$

$$= P_S(\text{good}) \times 13.$$

And since

$$f^*(\text{good}, \text{fresh}) = \text{five-egg Nero Wolfe omelet},$$

$$f^*(\text{good}, \text{stale}) = \text{five-egg ordinary omelet},$$

$$f^*(\text{rotten}, \text{fresh}) = \text{no omelet},$$

$$f^*(\text{rotten}, \text{stale}) = \text{no omelet},$$

we have

$$E_T(U_D(f^*)) = P_T(\text{good}, \text{fresh})U_D(\text{five-egg Nero Wolfe omelet})$$

$$+ P_T(\text{good, stale})U_D(\text{five-egg ordinary omelet})$$

$$+ P_T(\text{rotten, fresh})U_D(\text{no omelet}),$$

$$+ P_T(\text{rotten, stale})U_D(\text{no omelet})$$

$$= (\tfrac{3}{8})(16) + (\tfrac{1}{8})(8) + (\tfrac{1}{4})(0) + (\tfrac{1}{4})(0) = 7.$$

Equating the two expected values, we obtain $P_S(\text{good}) = \tfrac{7}{13}$.

The possible divergence between methods 1 and 2 disturbed Savage. He was not disturbed by the possibility that preferences over acts in a small world may fail to satisfy his postulates, for this can be taken as a signal that the small world needs to be refined. But he was disturbed by the possibility that probabilities calculated in a small world that did not satisfy his postulates might change with refinement. If the probabilities are different for two different levels of refinement, then which level is right? How can we tell?

Savage posited the existence of a grand world in order to answer the first of these two questions. Probabilities calculated from a given small world are right if they are the same as the ones calculated from the grand world. Yet even this outrageous fiction left him without an answer to the second question. How can we tell if the probabilities from a given small world are the same as the ones we would get if, counter to fact, we were able to work with a grand world?

Savage called a small world that satisfied his postulates a *pseudomicrocosm*. He called a pseudomicrocosm which would give the same probabilities as the grand world a *real microcosm*. He wrote, "I feel, if I may be allowed to say so, that the possibility of being taken in by a pseudomicrocosm that is not a real microcosm is remote, but the difficulty I find in defining an operationally applicable criterion is, to say the least, ground for caution" (*Foundations*, page 90).

The possibility of being taken in by a pseudomicrocosm that is not a real microcosm is indeed remote. It is remote because one could not possibly have detailed preferences among acts satisfying Savage's postulates unless one deliberately constructed these postulates from probabilities and utilities. Thus Savage's version of the problem of small worlds serves as a demonstration of how far his normative approach was from a sensible, constructive approach to decision.

Savage revisited

NOTE

Research for this chapter was partially supported by Grants MCS-800213 and IST-8405210 from the National Science Foundation. The author benefited from conversation and correspondence with Morris DeGroot, Peter Fishburn, Dennis Lindley, Pamela Townsend, and Amos Tversky. First published in *Statistical Science*, 1 (1986), 463–485.

REFERENCES

Allais, M. (1953). Fondements d'une théorie positive des choix comportant un risque et critique des postulats et axiomes de l'école américaine. *Colloques Internationaux du Centre National de la Recherche Scientifique, Économétrie* 40:257–332. (English translation with the title, "The foundations of a positive theory of choice involving risk and a criticism of the postulates and axioms of the American school," in Allais and Hagen, 27–145, 1979.)

(1979). The so-called Allais paradox and rational decisions under uncertainty. In Allais and Hagen, 437–681, 1979.

Allais, M. and Hagen, O., eds. (1979). *Expected Utility Hypotheses and the Allais Paradox*. Reidel, Dordrecht.

Anscombe, F. J. (1956). Review of *The Foundations of Statistics* by Leonard J. Savage. *J. Amer. Statist. Assoc.* 51:657–9.

Aumann, R. J. (1962). Utility theory without the completeness axiom. *Econometrica* 30:455–62.

(1964). Utility theory without the completeness axiom: a correction. *Econometrica* 32:210–12.

Ellsberg, D. (1961). Risk, ambiguity, and the Savage axioms. *Quart. J. Econom.* 75:643–69.

Fischhoff, B., Slovic, P. and Lichtenstein, S. (1980). Knowing what you want: measuring labile values. In Wallsten, 117–41, 1980.

Fishburn, P. C. (1970). *Utility Theory for Decision Making*. Wiley, New York. Reprinted by Krieger in 1979.

(1981). Subjective expected utility: a review of normative theories. *Theory Decisions* 13:139–99.

Friedman, M. and Savage, J. (1952). The expected utility hypothesis and the measurability of utility. *J. Polit. Econ.* 60:464–74.

Kahneman, D., Slovic, P. and Tversky, A., eds. (1982). *Judgment under Uncertainty: Heuristics and Biases*. Cambridge University Press.

Lindley, D. V. (1974). Discussion of papers by Professor Tversky and Professor Suppes. *J. Roy. Statist. Soc. Ser. B* 36:181–2.

Luce, R. D. and Krantz, D. H. (1971). Conditional expected utility. *Econometrica* 39:253–71.

MacCrimmon, K. R. (1968). Descriptive and normative implications of the decision-theory postulates. In *Risk and Uncertainty* (K. Borch and J. Mossin, eds.) 3–32. Macmillan, New York.

Marschak, J. (1950). Rational behavior, uncertainty prospects, and measurable utility. *Econometrica* 18:111–41.

May, K. O. (1954). Intransitivity, utility, and the aggregation of preference patterns. *Econometrica* 22:1–13.

Morgenstern, O. (1979). Some reflections on utility. In Allais and Hagen, 175–83, 1979.

Pratt, J. W. (1974). Some comments on some axioms for decision making under uncertainty. In *Essays on Economic Behavior Under Uncertainty* (M. Balch, D. McFadden and S. Wu, eds.) 82–92. North-Holland, Amsterdam.

Raiffa, H. (1961). Risk, ambiguity, and the Savage axioms: comment. *Quart. J. Econom.* 75:690–4.

(1968). *Decision Analysis: Introductory Lectures on Choices under Uncertainty.* Addison-Wesley, Reading, Mass.

Richter, M. K. (1975). Rational choice and polynomial measurement models. *J. Math. Pscyh.* 12:99–113.

Samuelson, P. .A (1952). Probability, utility, and the independence axiom. *Econometrica* 20:670–8.

Savage, L. J. (1954). *The Foundations of Statistics.* Wiley, New York. Second edition published by Dover in 1972.

(1967). Difficulties in the theory of personal probability. *Philos. Sci.* 34:305–10.

(1971). Elicitation of personal probabilities and expectations. *J. Amer. Statist. Assoc.* 66:783–801.

Schoemaker, P. J. H. (1982). The expected utility model: its variants, purposes, evidence, and limitations. *J. Econom. Lit.* 20:529–63.

Shafer, G. (1985). Conditional probability. *Internat. Statist. Rev.* 53:261–77.

Slovic, P. and Tversky, A. (1974). Who accepts Savage's axiom? *Behavioral Sci.* 19:368–73.

Tversky, A. (1969). Intransitivity of preferences. *Psycholog. Rev.* 76:31–48.

(1972). Choice by elimination. *J. Math. Psych.* 9:341–67.

Tversky, A. and Kahneman, D. (1981). The framing of decisions and the psychology of choice. *Science* 211:453–8.

(1986). Rational choice and the framing of decisions. *J. Business* 59:S251–78.

von Neumann, J. and Morgenstern, O. (1944, 1947, 1953). *Theory of Games and Economic Behavior.* Princeton University Press.

Wallsten, T. S. (1980). *Cognitive Processes in Choice and Decision Behavior.* Erlbaum, Hillsdale, N.J.

Wolfowitz, J. (1962). Bayesian inference and axioms of consistent decision. *Econometrica* 30:470–9.

III

BELIEFS AND JUDGMENTS ABOUT UNCERTAINTIES

11

LANGUAGES AND DESIGNS FOR PROBABILITY JUDGMENT

GLENN SHAFER AND AMOS TVERSKY

INTRODUCTION

The weighing of evidence may be viewed as a mental experiment in which the human mind is used to assess probability much as a pan balance is used to measure weight. As in the measurement of physical quantities, the design of the experiment affects the quality of the result.

Often one design for a mental experiment is superior to another because the questions it asks can be answered with greater confidence and precision. Suppose we want to estimate, on the basis of evidence readily at hand, the number of eggs produced daily in the US. One design might ask us to guess the number of chickens in the US and the average number of eggs laid by each chicken each day. Another design might ask us to guess the number of people in the US, the average number of eggs eaten by each person, and some inflation factor to cover waste and export. For most of us, the second design is manifestly superior, for we can make a reasonable effort to answer the questions it asks.

As this example illustrates, the confidence and precision with which we can answer a question posed in a mental experiment depends on how our knowledge is organized and stored, first in our mind and secondarily in other sources of information available to us.

The quality of the design of a mental experiment also depends on how effectively the answers to the individual questions it asks can be combined to yield an accurate overall picture or accurate answers to questions of central interest. An analogy with surveying may be helpful. There are usually many different ways of making a land survey – many different angles and lengths we may measure. When we design the survey we consider not only the accuracy and precision with which these individual measurements can be made but also how they can be combined to give an accurate plot of the area surveyed (Lindley, Tversky, and Brown, 1979). Singer (1971) shows how a mental experiment may be designed to give a convincing estimate of the total value of property stolen by heroin addicts in New York City. Other examples of effective designs for mental experiments are given by Raiffa (1974).

237

One way to evaluate competing designs for physical measurement is to apply them to instances where the truth is known. But such empirical evaluation of final results is not always possible in the case of a mental experiment, especially when the experiment is designed to produce only probability judgments. It is true that probability judgments can be interpreted as frequencies. But, as we argue below, this interpretation amounts only to a comparison with a repeatable physical experiment where frequencies are known. How the comparison is made – what kind of repetitions are envisaged – is itself one of the choices we make in designing a mental experiment. There may not be a single set of repetitions to which the design must be referred for empirical validation.

Since empirical validation of a design for probability judgment is problematic, the result of carrying out the mental experiment must be scrutinized in other ways. The result of the whole experiment must be regarded as an argument, which, like all other arguments, is open to criticism and counterarguments.

Understanding and evaluating a design for probability judgment is also complicated by problems of meaning. When we are simply guessing the answer to a question of fact, such as the number of eggs produced daily in the US, the meaning of the question seems to be independent of our design. But, when we undertake to make probability judgments, we find that we need a theory of subjective probability to give meaning to these judgments.

In the first place, we need a numerical scale or at least a qualitative scale (practically certain, very probable, fairly probable, etc.) from which to choose degrees of probability. We also need canonical examples for each degree of probability on this scale – examples where it is agreed what degree of probability is appropriate. Finally, we need a calculus – a set of rules for combining simple judgments to obtain complex ones.

Using a theory of subjective probability means comparing the evidence in a problem with the theory's scale of canonical examples and picking out the canonical example that matches it best. Our design helps us make this comparison. It specifies how to break the problem into smaller problems that can be more easily compared with the scale of canonical examples and how to combine the judgments resulting from these separate comparisons.

Thought of in this way, a theory of subjective probability is very much like a formal language. It has a vocabulary – a scale of degrees of probability. Attached to this vocabulary is a semantics – a scale of canonical examples that shows how the vocabulary is to be interpreted and psychological devices for making the interpretation effective. Elements of the vocabulary are combined according to a syntax – the theory's calculus.

Proponents of different theories of subjective probability have often debated which theory best describes human inductive competence. We believe that none of these theories provide an adequate account of people's intuitive judgments of probability. On the other hand, most of these theories can be learned and used effectively. Consequently, we regard these theories as formal languages for expressing probability judgments rather than as psychological models, however idealized.

The usefulness of one of these formal languages for a specific problem may depend both on the problem and on the skill of the user. There may not be a single probability language that is normative for all people and all problems. A person may find one language better for one problem and another language better for another. Furthermore, individual probability judgments made in one language may not be directly translatable into another.

This article studies the semantics and syntax of two probability languages, the traditional Bayesian language and the language of belief functions, and it uses these languages to analyze several concrete examples. This exercise can be regarded as a first step toward the general study of design for probability judgment. It illustrates the variety of designs that may be feasible for a given problem, and it yields a classification of Bayesian designs that clarifies the role of Bayesian conditioning. Our treatment is incomplete, however, because it does not provide formal criteria or lay out general empirical procedures for evaluating designs. The choice of design is left to the ingenuity of the user.

1. EXAMPLES

With the help of some simple examples we illustrate several designs for probability judgments. We will return to these examples in sections 3 and 4.

1.1 The free-style race

We are watching one of the last men's swim meets of the season at Holsum University. We have followed the Holsum team for several seasons, so we watch with intense interest as Curt Langley, one of Holsum's leading free-stylers, gets off to a fast start in the 1650-yard race. As Curt completes his first 1,000 yards, he is swimming at a much faster pace than we have seen him swim before. His time for the first 1,000 yards is 9 min and 25 s. His best previous times for 1,650 yards have been around 16 min and 25 s, a time that translates into about 9 min and 57 s at 1,000 yards. The only swimmer within striking distance of him is a member of the visiting team named Cowan, whom we know only by name. Cowan is about half a lap (about 12 yards or 7 s) behind Curt.

Will Curt win the race?

The first question we ask ourselves is whether he can keep up his pace. Curt is known to us as a very steady swimmer – one who knows what he is capable of and seldom, if ever, begins at a pace much faster than he can keep up through a race.

It is true that his pace is much faster than we have seen before – much faster than he was swimming only a few weeks ago. It is possible that there has been no real improvement in his capacity to swim – that he has simply started fast and will slow down before the race is over. But our knowledge of Curt's character and situation encourages us to think that he must have trained hard and greatly increased his endurance. This is his senior year, and the championships are near. And he must have been provoked to go all out by Jones, the freshman on the team, who has lately overshadowed him in the long-distance races. We are inclined to think that Curt will keep up his pace.

If Curt does keep up his pace, then it seems very unlikely that Cowan could have enough energy in reserve to catch him. But what if Curt cannot keep up his pace? Here our vision becomes more murky. Has Curt deliberately put his best energy into the first part of the race? Or has he actually misjudged what pace he can keep up? In the first case, it seems likely that he will soon slow down, but not to a disastrously slow pace; it seems to be a toss-up whether Cowan will catch him. On the other hand, if he has misjudged what pace he can keep up, then surely he has not misjudged it by far, and so we would expect him to keep it up almost to the end and, as usually happens in such cases, "collapse" with exhaustion to a very slow pace. There is no telling what would happen then – whether Cowan would be close enough or see the collapse soon enough to take advantage of the situation.

There are many different designs that we might use to assess numerically the probability of Curt's winning. There is even more than one possible Bayesian design. The Bayesian design suggested by our qualitative discussion assesses the probabilities that Curt will keep up the pace, slow down, or collapse and the conditional probabilities that he will win under each of these hypotheses and then combines these probabilities and conditional probabilities to obtain his overall probability of winning. We call this a *total-evidence design* because each probability and conditional probability is based on the total evidence. In section 3 we will formalize and carry out this total-evidence design. We will also carry out a somewhat different Bayesian total-evidence design for the problem. In section 4 we will carry out a belief-function design for the problem.

1.2 The hominids of East Turkana

In the August, 1978, issue of *Scientific American*, Alan Walker and Richard E. T. Leakey discuss the hominid fossils that have recently been discovered in the region east of Lake Turkana in Kenya. These fossils, between a million and two million years of age, show considerable variety, and Walker and Leakey are interested in deciding how many distinct species they represent.

In Walker and Leakey's judgment, the relatively complete cranium specimens discovered in the upper member of the Koobi Fora Formation in East Turkana are of three forms: (I) A "robust" form with large cheek teeth and massive jaws.

These fossils show wide-fanning cheekbones, very large molar and premolar teeth, and smaller incisors and canines. The brain case has an average capacity of about 500 cubic centimeters, and there is often a bony crest running fore and aft across its top, which presumably provided greater area for the attachment of the cheek muscles. Fossils of this form have also been found in South Africa and East Asia, and it is generally agreed that they should all be classified as members of the species *Australopithecus robustus*. (II) A smaller and slenderer (more "gracile") form that lacks the wide-flaring cheekbones of I, but has similar cranial capacity and only slightly less massive molar and premolar teeth. (III) A large-brained (c. 850 cubic cm) and small-jawed form that can be confidently identified with the *Homo erectus* specimens found in Java and northern China.

The placement of the three forms in the geological strata in East Turkana shows that they were contemporaneous with each other. How many distinct species do they represent? Walker and Leakey admit five hypotheses:

1. I, II, and III are all forms of a single, extremely variable species.
2. There are two distinct species: one, *Australopithecus robustus*, has I as its male form and II as its female form; the other, *Homo erectus*, is represented by III.
3. There are two distinct species: one, *Australopithecus robustus*, is represented by I; the other has III, the so-called *Homo erectus* form, as its male form, and II as its female form.
4. There are two distinct species: one is represented by the gracile form II; the other, which is highly variable, consists of I and III.
5. The three forms represent three distinct species.

Here are the items of evidence, or arguments, that Walker and Leakey use in their qualitative assessment of the probabilities of these five hypotheses:

(i)   Hypothesis 1 is supported by general theoretical arguments to the effect that distinct hominid species cannot coexist after one of them has acquired culture.

(ii) Hypotheses 1 and 4 are doubtful because they postulate extremely different adaptations within the same species: the brain seems to overwhelm the chewing apparatus in III, while the opposite is true in I.

(iii) There are difficulties in accepting the degree of sexual dimorphism postulated by hypotheses 2 and 3. Sexual dimorphism exists among living anthropoids, and there is evidence from elsewhere that hints that dental dimorphism of the magnitude postulated by hypothesis 2 might have existed in extinct hominids. The dimorphism postulated by hypothesis 3, which involves females having roughly half the cranial capacity of males, is less plausible.

(iv) Hypotheses 1 and 4 are also impugned by the fact that specimens of type I have not been found in Java and China, where specimens of type III are abundant.

(v)   Hypotheses 1 and 3 are similarly impugned by the absence of specimens of type II in Java and China.

Before specimens of type III were found in the Koobi Fora Formation, Walker and Leakey thought it likely that the I and II specimens constituted a single species. Now on the basis of the total evidence, they consider hypothesis 5 the most probable.

What Bayesian design might we use to analyze this evidence? A total-evidence design may be possible, but it is natural to consider instead a design in which some of the evidence is treated as an "observation" and used to "condition" probabilities based on the rest of the evidence. We might, for example, first construct a probability distribution that includes probabilities for whether specimens of types I and II should occur in Java and China and then condition this distribution on their absence there. It is natural to call this a *conditioning design*. It is not a total-evidence design, because the initial (or "prior") probabilities for whether the specimens occur in Java and China will be based on only part of the evidence.

Later, in section 3, we will work this conditioning design out in detail. In section 4 we will apply a belief-function design to the same problem.

2. TWO PROBABILITY LANGUAGES

In order to make numerical probability judgments, we need a numerical scale. We need, in other words, a scale of canonical examples in which numerical degrees of belief are agreed upon. Where can we find such a scale?

The obvious place to look is in the picture of chance. In this picture, we imagine a game which can be played repeatedly and for which we know the chances. These chances, we imagine, are facts about the world: they are long-run frequencies, they can be thought of as propensities, and they also define fair betting rates – rates at which a bettor would break even in the long run.

There are several ways the picture of chance can be related to practical problems, and this means we can use the picture to construct different kinds of canonical examples and thus different theories or probability languages. In this chapter, we shall consider two such languages: the Bayesian language, and the language of belief functions. The Bayesian language uses a scale of canonical examples in which the truth is generated by chance and our evidence consists of complete knowledge of the chances. The language of belief functions uses a scale of canonical examples in which our evidence consists of a message whose meaning depends on known chances.

We emphasize the Bayesian language because it is familiar to most readers. We study the language of belief functions as well in order to emphasize that our constructive view of probability, while not implying that all probability languages have equal normative claims, leaves open the possibility that no single language has a preemptively normative status.

2.1 *The Bayesian language*

As we see it, a user of the Bayesian probability language makes probability judgments in a particular problem by comparing the problem to a scale of examples in which the truth is generated according to known chances and deciding which of these examples is most like the problem. The probability judgment $P(A) = p$, in this language, is a judgment that the evidence provides support for A comparable to what would be provided by knowledge that the truth is generated by a chance setup that produces a result in A exactly p of the time. This is not to say that one judges the evidence to be just like such knowledge in all respects, nor that the truth is, in fact, generated by chance. It is just that one is measuring the strength of the evidence by comparing it to a scale of chance setups.

The idea that Bayesian probability judgment involves comparisons with examples where the truth is generated by chance is hardly novel. It can be found, for example, in Bertrand (1907) and in Box (1980). Box states that the adoption of given Bayesian probability distribution means that "current belief . . . would be calibrated with adequate approximation by a *physical stimulation* involving random sampling" (p. 385) from the distribution. The Bayesian literature has not, however, adequately addressed the question of how this comparison can be carried out. One reason for this neglect may be the emphasis that twentieth-century Bayesians have put on betting. When "personal probabilities" are defined in terms of a person's preferences among bets, we are tempted to think that the determination of probabilities is a matter of introspection rather than a matter of examining evidence, but see Diaconis and Zabell (1982).

Bayesian semantics

The task of Bayesian semantics is to render the comparison of our evidence to the Bayesian scale of canonical examples effective – to find ways of making the scale of chances and the affinity of our evidence to it vivid enough to our imagination that we can meaningfully locate the evidence on the scale.

By concentrating on different aspects of the rich imagery of games of chance, we can isolate different ways of making the Bayesian scale of chances vivid, and each of these ways can be thought of as a distinct semantics for the Bayesian probability language. Three such semantics come immediately to mind: a frequency semantics, a propensity semantics, and a betting semantics. The *frequency semantics* compares our evidence to the scale of chances by asking how often, in situations like the one at hand, the truth would turn out in various ways. The *propensity semantics* makes the comparison by first interpreting the evidence in terms of a causal model and then asking about the model's propensity to produce various results. The *betting semantics* makes the comparison by assessing our willingness to bet in the light of the evidence: at what odds is our attitude towards a given bet most like our attitude towards a fair bet in a game of chance?

It is traditional, of course, to argue about whether probability should be given a frequency, a propensity, or a betting interpretation. But from our perspective these "interpretations" are merely devices to help us make what may ultimately be an imperfect fit of our evidence to a scale of chances. Which of these devices is most helpful will depend on the particular problem. We do not insist that there exists, prior to our deliberation, some particular frequency or numerical propensity in nature or some betting rate in our mind that should be called the probability of the proposition we are considering.

Which of these three Bayesian semantics tends to be most helpful in fitting our evidence to the scale of chances? We believe that the frequency and propensity semantics are central to the successful use of the Bayesian probability language, and that the betting semantics is less useful. Good Bayesian designs ask us to make probability judgments that can be translated into well-founded judgments about frequencies or about causal structures.

Since we readily think in terms of causal models, the propensity semantics often seems more attractive than the frequency semantics. But this attraction has its danger; the vividness of causal pictures can blind us to doubts about their validity. A simple design based on frequency semantics can sometimes be superior to a more complex design based on propensity semantics. We may, for example, obtain a better idea about how long it will take to complete a complex project by taking an "outside view" based on how long similar projects have taken in the past than by taking an "inside view" that attempts to assess the strength of the forces that could delay the completion of the project (Kahneman and Tversky, 1982).

The betting semantics has a generality that the frequency and propensity semantics lack. We can always ask ourselves about our attitude towards a bet, quite irrespective of the structure of our evidence. But this lack of connection with the evidence is also a weakness of the betting semantics.

In evaluating the betting semantics, one must distinguish logical from psychological and practical considerations. Ramsey (1931), Savage (1954), and their followers have made an important contribution to the logical analysis of subjective probability by showing that it can be derived from coherent preferences between bets. This logical argument, however, does not imply psychological precedence. Introspection suggests that people typically act on the basis of their beliefs, rather than form beliefs on the basis of their acts. The gambler bets on team A rather than on team B because he believes that A is more likley to win. He does not usually infer such a belief from his betting preferences.

It is sometimes argued that the prospect of monetary loss tends to concentrate the mind and thus permits a more honest and acute assessment of the strength of evidence than that obtained by thinking about that evidence directly. There is very little empirical evidence to support this claim. Although incentives can sometimes reduce careless responses, monetary payoffs are neither necessary nor sufficient for careful judgment. In fact, there is evidence showing that people are sometimes willing to incur monetary losses in order to report what they believe (Lieblich and Lieblich, 1969). Personally, we find that questions about betting do not help us think about the evidence; instead they divert our minds to extraneous questions: our attitudes towards the monetary and social consequences of winning or losing a bet, our assessment of the ability and knowledge of our opponent, etc.

Bayesian syntax

It follows from our understanding of the canonical examples of the Bayesian language that this language's syntax is the traditional probability calculus. A proposition that a person knows to be false is assigned probability zero. A proposition that a person knows to be true is assigned probability one. And in general probabilities add: if A and B are incompatible propositions, then $P(A$ *or* $B) = P(A) + P(B)$.

The conditional probability of A given B is, by definition,

$$P(A|B) = \frac{P(A \text{ and } B)}{P(B)}. \tag{1}$$

If $B_1, \ldots, B_n$ are incompatible propositions, one of which must be true, then *the rule of total probability* says that

$$P(A) = \sum_{j=1}^{n} P(B_j)P(A|B_j), \tag{2}$$

and Bayes's theorem says that

$$P(B_i|A) = \frac{P(B_i)P(A|B_i)}{\sum_{j=1}^{n} P(B_j)P(A|B_j)}. \tag{3}$$

As we shall see in section 3, both total-evidence and conditioning designs can use the concept of conditional probability. Total-evidence designs often use equation (2), while conditioning designs use equation (1). Some conditioning designs can be described in terms of equation (3).

2.2 *The language of belief functions*

The language of belief functions uses the calculus of mathematical probability, but in a different way than the Bayesian language does. Whereas the Bayesian language asks, in effect, that we think in terms of a chance model for the facts in which we are interested, the belief-function language asks that we think in terms of a chance model for the reliability and meaning of our evidence.

This can be put more precisely by saying that the belief-function language compares evidence to canonical examples of the following sort. We know a chance experiment has been carried out. We know that the possible outcomes of the experiments are $o_1, \ldots, o_n$ and that the chance of o_i is p_i. We are not told the actual outcome but we receive a message concerning another topic that can be fully interpreted only with knowledge of the actual outcome. For each i there is a proposition A_i, say, such that if we knew the actual outcome was o_i then we would see that the meaning of the message is A_i. We have no other evidence about the truth or falsehood of the A_i and so no reason to change the probabilities p_i.

What degrees of belief are called for in an example of this sort? How strongly should we believe a particular proposition of A?

For each proposition A, set $m(A) = \sum \{ p_i | A_i = A \}$. This number is the total of the chances for outcomes that would show the message to mean A; we can think of it as the total chance that the message means A. Now let $\text{Bel}(A)$ denote the total chance that the message implies A; in symbols, $\text{Bel}(A) = \sum \{ m(B) | B \text{ implies } A \}$. It is natural to call $\text{Bel}(A)$ our degree of belief in A.

We call a function Bel a *belief function* if it is given by the above equation for some choice of $m(A)$. By varying the p_i and the A_i in our story of the uncertain message, we can obtain any such values for the $m(A)$, and so the story provides canonical examples for every belief function.

We call the propositions A for which $m(A) > 0$ the *focal elements* of the belief function Bel. Often the most economical way of specifying a belief function is to specify its focal elements and their "m-values."

Semantics for belief functions

We have based our canonical examples for belief functions on a fairly vague story: We receive a message and we see, somehow, that, if o_i were the true outcome of the random experiment, then the message would mean A_i. One task of semantics for belief functions is to flesh out the story in ways that help us compare real problems to it. Here we shall give three ways of fleshing out the story. The first leads to canonical examples for a small class of belief functions, called *simple support functions*. The second leads to canonical examples for a larger class, the *consonant support functions*. The third leads to canonical examples for arbitrary belief functions.

(i) A sometimes reliable truth machine

Imagine a machine that has two modes of operation. We know that in the first mode it broadcasts truths. But we are completely unable to predict what it will do when it is in the second mode. We also know that the choice of which mode the machine will operate in on a particular occasion is made by chance: there is a chance s that it will operate in the first mode and a chance $1 - s$ that it will operate in the second mode.

It is natural to say of a message broadcast by such a machine on a particular occasion that it has a chance s of meaning what it says and a chance $1 - s$ of meaning nothing at all. So if the machine broadcasts the message that E is true, then we are in the setting of our general story: the two modes of operation for the machine are the two outcomes o_1 and o_2 of a random experiment; their chances are $p_1 = s$ and $p_2 = 1 - s$; if o_1 happened then the message means $A_1 = E$, while if o_2 happened the message means nothing beyond what we already know – i.e., it means $A_2 = \Theta$, where Θ denotes the proposition that asserts the facts we already know. So we obtain a belief function with focal elements E and θ; $m(E) = s$ and $m(\theta) = 1 - s$.

We call such a belief function a *simple support function*. Notice its nonadditivity: the two complementary propositions E and *not E* have degrees of belief $\text{Bel}(E) = s < 1$ and $\text{Bel}(notE) = 0$.

It is natural to use simple support functions in cases where the message of the evidence is clear but where the reliability of this message is in question. The testimony of a witness, for example, may be unambiguous, and yet we may have some doubt about the witness's reliability. We can express this doubt by comparing the witness to a truth machine that is less than certain to operate correctly.

(ii) A two-stage truth machine

Consider a sometimes reliable truth machine that broadcasts two messages in succession and can slip into its untrustworthy mode before either message. It remains in the untrustworthy mode once it has slipped into it. As before, we know nothing about whether or how often it will be truthful when it is in this mode. We know the chances that it will slip into its untrustworthy mode: r_1 is the chance it will be in untrustworthy mode with the initial message, and r_2 is the chance it will slip into untrustworthy mode after the first message, given that it was in trustworthy mode then.

Suppose the messages received are E_1 and E_2, and suppose these messages are consistent with each other. Then there is a chance $(1 - r_1)(1 - r_2)$ that the message "E_1 and E_2" is reliable, a chance $(1 - r_1)r_2$ that the message "E_1" alone is reliable, and a chance r_1 that r_1 that neither of the messages is reliable. If we set

$$p_1 = (1 - r_1)(1 - r_2), \qquad A_1 = E_1 \text{ and } E_2,$$
$$p_2 = (1 - r_1)r_2, \qquad A_2 = E_1,$$
$$p_3 = r_1, \qquad A_3 = \Theta,$$

then we are in the setting of our general story: there is a chance p_i that the message means A_i.

Notice that A_1, A_2, and A_3 are "nested": A_1 implies A_2, and A_2 implies A_3. In general, we call a belief function with nested focal elements a *consonant support function*. It is natural to use consonant support functions in cases where our evidence consists of an argument with several steps; each step leads to a more specific conclusion but involves a new chance of error.

(iii) A randomly coded message

Suppose someone chooses a code at random from a list of codes, uses the chosen code to encode a message, and then sends us the results. We know the list of codes and the chance of each code being chosen – say the list is $o_1, \ldots, o_n$, and the chances of o_i being chosen is p_i. We decode the message using each of the codes and we find that this always produces an intelligible message. Let A_i denote the message we get when we decode using o_i. Then we have the ingredients for a belief function: a message that has the chance p_i of meaning A_i.

Since the randomly coded message is more abstract than the sometimes reliable truth machine, it lends itself less readily to comparison with real evidence. But it provides a readily understandable canonical example for an arbitrary belief function. (For other scales of canonical examples for belief functions, see Krantz and Miyamoto, 1983, and Wierzchón, 1984.)

Syntax for belief functions

Our task, when we assess evidence in the language of belief functions, is to compare that evidence to examples where the meaning of a message depends on chance and to single out from these examples the one that best matches it in weight and significance. How do we do this? In complicated problems we cannot simply look at our evidence holistically and write down the best values for the $m(A)$. The theory of belief functions provides, therefore, a set of rules for constructing complicated belief functions from more elementary judgments. These rules which ultimately derive from the traditional probability calculus, constitute the syntax of the language of belief functions. They include rules for combination, conditioning, extension, conditional embedding, and discounting.

The most important of these rules is Dempster's rule of combination. This is a formal rule for combining a belief function constructed on the basis of one item of evidence with a belief function constructed on the basis of another, intuitively independent item of evidence so as to obtain a belief function representing the total evidence. It permits us to break down the task of judgment by decomposing the evidence.

Dempster's rule is obtained by thinking of the chances that affect the meaning of reliability of the messages provided by different sources of evidence as independent. Consider, for example, two independent witnesses who are compared to sometimes reliable truth machines with reliabilities s_1 and s_2, respectively. If the chances affecting their testimonies are independent, then there is a chance $s_1 s_2$ that both will give truthworthy testimony, and a chance $s_1 + s_2 - s_1 s_2$ that at least one will. If both testify to the truth of A, then we can take $s_1 + s_2 - s_1 s_2$ as our degree of belief in A. If, on the other hand, the first witness testifies for A and the second testifies against A, then we know that not both witnesses are trustworthy, and so we consider the conditional chance that the first witness is trustworthy given that not both are: $s_1(1 - s_2)/(1 - s_1 s_2)$, and we take this as our degrees of belief in A. For further information on the rules for belief functions, see Shafer (1976, 1982b).

3. BAYESIAN DESIGN

We have already distinguished two kinds of Bayesian designs: *total-evidence* designs, in which all one's probability judgments are based on the total evidence, and *conditioning* designs, in which some of the evidence is taken into account by conditioning. In this section we will study these broad categories and consider some other possibilities for Bayesian design.

3.1 Total-evidence designs

There are many kinds of probability judgments a total-evidence design might use, for there are many mathematical conditions that can help determine a probability distribution. We can specify quantities such as probabilities, conditional probabilities, and expectations, and we can impose conditions such as independence, exchangeability, and partial exchangeability. Spetzler and Staël von Holstein (1975), Alpert and Raiffa (1982), and Goldstein (1981) discuss total-evidence designs for the construction of probability distributions for unknown quantities. Here we discuss total-evidence designs for a few simple problems.

Two total-evidence designs for the free-style race

The Bayesian design for the free-style race suggested by our discussion in section 1.1 above is an example of a total-evidence design based on a causal model. This design involves six possibilities:

A_1 = Curt maintains the pace and wins.

A_2 = Curt maintains the pace but loses.

A_3 = Curt soon slows down but still wins.

A_4 = Curt soon slows down and loses.

A_5 = Curt collapses at the end but still wins.

A_6 = Curt collapses at the end and loses.

The person who made the analysis (the story was reconstructed from actual experience) was primarily interested in the proposition

$$A = \{A_1 \text{ or } A_3 \text{ or } A_5\} = \text{Curt wins,}$$

but her insight into the matter was based on her understanding of the causal structure of the swim race. In order to make the probability judgment $P(A)$, she first made the judgments $P(B_i)$ and $P(A|B_i)$, where

$$B_1 = \{A_1 \text{ or } A_2\} = \text{Curt maintains his pace,}$$

$$B_2 = \{A_3 \text{ or } A_4\} = \text{Curt soon slows down,}$$

$$B_3 = \{A_5 \text{ or } A_6\} = \text{Curt collapses near the end,}$$

Table 11.1. *Component judgments for the
first total-evidence design*

$P(B_1) = .8$	$P(A|B_1) = .95$
$P(B_2) = .15$	$P(A|B_2) = .5$
$P(B_3) = .05$	$P(A|B_2) = .7$

and she then calculated $P(A)$ using the rule of total probability – in this case, the formula

$$P(A) = P(B_1)P(A|B_1) + P(B_2)P(A|B_2) + P(B_3)P(A|B_3). \qquad (4)$$

She did this qualitatively at the time, but she offers, in retrospect, the quantitative judgments indicated in table 11.1. These numbers yield $P(A) = .87$ by equation (4).

This example brings out the fact that the value of a design depends on the experience and understanding of the person carrying out the mental experiment. For someone who lacked our analyst's experience in swimming and her familiarity with Curt Langley's record, the design of equation (4) would be worthless. Such a person might find some other Bayesian design useful, or he/she might find all Bayesian designs difficult to apply.

Though it is correct to call the design we have just studied a total-evidence design, there is a sense in which its effectiveness does depend on the fact that it allows us to decompose our evidence. The question of what the next event in a causal sequence is likely to be is often relatively easy to answer precisely because only a small part of our evidence bears on it. When we try to decide whether Curt will still win if he slows down – i.e., when we assess $P(A|B_2)$ – we are able to leave aside our evidence about Curt and focus on how likely Cowan is to maintain his own pace.

Here is another total-evidence design for the free-style race, one which combines the causal model with a more explicit judgment that Cowan's ability is independent of Curt's behavior and ability. We assess probabilities for whether Curt will (a) maintain his pace, (b) slow down, but less than 3%, (c) slow down more than 3%, or (d) collapse. (Whether Curt slows down 3% is significant because this is how much we would have to slow down for Cowan to catch him without speeding up.) We assess probabilities for whether Cowan (a) can speed up significantly, (b) can only maintain his pace, (c) cannot maintain his pace. We judge that these two questions are independent. And, finally, we assess the probability that Curt will win under each of the $4 \times 3 = 12$ hypotheses about what Curt will do and what Cowan can do.

Table 11.2 shows the results of carrying out this design. The numbers in the second column are our probability judgments about Curt, those in the column heads are our probability judgments about Cowan, and those in the third, fourth, and fifth columns are our assessments of the conditional probability that Curt

Table 11.2. *Component judgments for the second total-evidence design*

		Cowan		
		Can speed up significantly .10	Can only maintain pace .70	Cannot maintain pace .20
Curt				
Maintains pace	.85	0.5	1.0	1.0
Slows less than 3%	.03	0.2	1.0	1.0
Slows 3% or more	.07	0.0	0.0	0.5
Collapses	.05	0.2	0.7	0.8

will win. These numbers lead to an overall probability of

$$(.85 \times .10 \times .5) + (.85 \times .70 \times 1.0) + \cdots \approx .88$$

that Curt will win.

Our judgments about Cowan are based on our general knowledge about swimmers in the league. The numbers .10, .70, and .20 reflect our impression that perhaps 20% of these swimmers are forced to slow down in the second half of a 1,650-yard race and that only 10% would have the reserves of energy needed to speed up. We are, in effect, thinking of Cowan as having been chosen at random from this population. We are also judging that Curt's training and strategy are independent of this random choice. Curt's training has probably been influenced mainly by the prospect of the championships. We doubt that Cowan's ability and personality are well enough known to Curt to have caused him to choose a fast start as a strategy in this particular race.

When we compare the design and analysis of table 11.2 with the design we carried out earlier, we see that we have profited from the new design's focus on our evidence about Cowan. We feel that the force and significance of this evidence is now more clearly defined for us. On the other hand, we are less comfortable with the conditional probability judgments in the last three columns of table 11.2; some of these seem to be pure speculation rather than assessments of evidence.

Total-evidence designs based on frequency semantics

In the two designs we have just considered the breakdown into probabilities and conditional probabilities was partly determined by a causal model. In designs that depend more heavily on frequency semantics, this breakdown depends more on the way our knowledge of past instances is organized.

Consider, for example, the problem of deciding what is wrong when an automobile fails to start. If a mechanic were asked to consider the possible causes for this failure, he might first list the major systems that could be at fault (fuel system, ignition system, etc.) and then list more specific possible defects within each system. This would result in a "fault tree" that could be used to construct probabilities. The steps in the tree would not have a causal interpretation, but the tree would correspond, presumably, to the way the mechanic's memory of the frequencies of similar problems is organized. Fischhoff, Slovic, and Lichtenstein (1978) have studied the problem of designing fault trees so as to make them as effective and unbiased as possible.

Here is another simple example based on an anecdote reported by Kahneman and Tversky (1982). An expert undertakes to estimate how long it will take to complete a certain project. He does this by comparing the project to similar past projects. And he organizes his effort to remember relevant information about these past projects into two steps: first he asks how often such projects were completed, and then he asks how long the ones that were completed tended to take. If he focuses on a particular probability judgment – "the probability that our project will be finished within 7 years," say – then he asks first how frequently such projects are completed and then how frequently projects that are completed take less than 7 years.

Why does the expert use this two-step design? Presumably because it facilitates his mental sampling of past instances. It is easier for the expert to thoroughly sample past projects he has been familiar with if he limits himself to asking as he goes only whether they were completed. He can then come back to the completed projects and attack the more difficult task of remembering how long they took.

The emphasis in this example is on personal memory. The lesson of the example applies, however, even when we are aided by written or electronic records. In any case, the excellence of a design depends in part on how the information accessible to us is organized.

3.2 Conditioning designs

Bayesian conditioning designs can be divided into two classes: *observational* designs and *partitioning* designs. In observational designs, the evidence to be taken into account by conditioning is deliberately obtained after probabilities are constructed. In partitioning designs, we begin our process of probability judgment with all our evidence in hand, but we partition this evidence into "old evidence" and "new evidence," assess probabilities on the basis of the old evidence alone, and then conditioning on the new evidence.

It should be stressed that a conditioning design always involves two steps: constructing a probability distribution and conditioning it. The name "conditioning design" focuses our attention on the second step, but the first is more difficult. An essential part of any conditioning design is a subsidiary design specifying how the distribution to be conditioned is to be constructed. This subsidiary design may well be a total-evidence design.

Likelihood-based conditioning designs

Bayesian authors often emphasize the use of Bayes's theorem. Bayes's theorem, we recall, says that if $B_1, \ldots, B_n$ are incompatible propositions, one of which must be true, then

$$P(B_i \mid A) = \frac{P(B_i)P(A \mid B_i)}{\sum\limits_{j=i}^{n} P(B_j)P(A \mid B_j)}. \tag{5}$$

If A represents evidence we want to take into account, and if we are able to make the probability judgments on the right hand side of equation (5) while leaving this evidence out of account, then we can use equation (5) to calculate a probability for B_i given this evidence A.

When we use Bayes's theorem in this simple way, we are carrying out a conditioning design. Leaving aside the "new evidence" A, we use the "old evidence" to make probability judgments $P(B_i)$ and $P(A \mid B_i)$. Making these judgments amounts to constructing a probability distribution. We then condition this distribution on A. Equation (5) is simply a convenient way to calculate the resulting probability of B_i.

This is a particular kind of conditioning design. The subsidiary design that we are using to construct the probability distribution to be conditioned is a total-evidence design that just happens to focus on the probabilities $P(B_i)$ and $P(A \mid B_i)$, where A is the new evidence and the B_i are the propositions whose final probabilities interest us. Since the conditional probabilities $P(A \mid B_i)$ are called "likelihoods," we may call this kind of conditioning design a *likelihood-based* conditioning design.

Both observational and partitioning designs may be likelihood-based. Bayesian theory has traditionally emphasized likelihood-based conditioning designs, and they will also be emphasized in this section. At the end of the section, however, we will give an example of a conditioning design that is not likelihood-based.

A likelihood-based observational design: the search for Scorpion

The successful search for the remains of the submarine *Scorpion*, as reported by Richardson and Stone (1971), provides an excellent sample of a likelihood-based observational design. The search was conducted from June to October, 1968, in an area about 20 miles square located 400 miles southwest of the Azores. The submarine was found on October 28.

Naval experts began their probability calculations by using a causal model to construct a probability distribution for the location of the lost submarine. They developed nine scenarios for the events attending the disaster and assigned probabilities to those scenarios. They then combined these probabilities with conditional probabilities representing uncertainties in the submarine's course, speed, and initial position to produce a probability distribution for its final location on the ocean floor. They did not attempt to construct this probability distribution for the final location in continuous form. Instead, they imposed a grid over the search area with cells about one square mile in size and used their probabilities and conditional probabilities in a Monte Carlo simulation to estimate the probability of *Scorpion* being in each of these approximately 400 cells. They then used these probabilities to plan the search: the cells with the greatest probability of containing *Scorpion* were to be searched first.

Searching a cell meant towing through the cell near the ocean bottom a platform upon which were mounted cameras, magnetometers, and sonars. The naval experts assessed the probability that this equipment would detect *Scorpion* if *Scorpion* were in the cell searched. So when they searched a cell and conditioned on the fact that *Scorpion* was not found there, they were, in effect, using a likelihood-based conditioning to assess new probabilities for its location.

This example is typical of likelihood-based observational designs. The probabilities required by the design were subjective judgments, not known objective probabilities. (The assessed likelihood of detecting *Scorpion* when searching the cell where it was located turned out, for example, to be over-optimistic.) But these judgments were made before the observation on which the experts conditioned was made. In fact, these judgments were the basis of deciding which of several possible observations to make – i.e., which cell to search.

A likelihood-based partitioning design: the hominids of East Turkana

Let us now turn back to Walker and Leakey's discussion of the number of species of hominids in East Turkana one and a half million years ago. They begin, we recall, by taking for granted a classification of the hominids into three types: the "robust" type I, the "gracile" type II, and *Homo erectus*, type III. They were interested in five hypotheses as to how many distinct species these three types represent:

B_1 = one species.

B_2 = two species, one composed of I (male) and II (female).

B_3 = two species, one composed of III (male) and II (female).

B_4 = two species, one composed of I and III.

B_5 = three species.

We summarized the evidence they brought to bear on the problem under five headings:
(i)   A theoretical argument for B_1.
(ii)   Skepticism about such disparate types as I and III being variants of the same species.
(iii) Skepticism about the degree of sexual dimorphism postulated by B_2 and B_3.
(iv)   Absence of type I specimens among the type III specimens in the Far East.
(v)   Absence of type II specimens among the type III specimens in the Far East.
How might we assess this evidence in the Bayesian language?

Partitioning design seems to hold more promise in this problem than total-evidence design. Except for items (i) and possibly (ii), the evidence cannot be interpreted as an understanding of causes that generate the truth, and hence there is little prospect for a total-evidence design using propensity semantics. We also lack the experience with similar problems that would be required for a successful total-evidence design using frequency semantics. And, since it is the diversity of the evidence that complicates probability judgments in the problem, a design that decomposes the evidence seems attractive.

Which of the items of evidence shall we classify as old evidence, and which as new? The obvious move is to classify (i) as old evidence and to treat (ii)–(v), taken together, as our new evidence A. This means we will need to assess probabilities, $P(B_1), \ldots, P(B_5)$ and conditioning probabilities, $P(A|B_1), \ldots, P(A|B_5)$ and calculate $P(B_i|A)$, by equation (5). The apparent complexity of equation (5) is lessened if we divide it by the corresponding expression for B_j, obtaining

$$\frac{P(B_i|A)}{P(B_j|A)} = \frac{P(B_i)}{P(B_j)} \frac{P(A|B_i)}{P(A|B_j)}, \tag{6}$$

or

$$\frac{P(B_i|A)}{P(B_j|A)} = \frac{P(B_i)}{P(B_j)} L(A|B_i:B_j), \tag{7}$$

where $L(A|B_i:B_j) = P(A|B_i)/P(A|B_j)$ is called the *likelihood ratio* favoring B_i over B_j.

Equation (7) represents a real simplification of the design. Since the probabilities, $P(B_1|A), \ldots, P(B_5|A)$ must add to one, they are completely determined by their ratios, $P(B_i|A)/P(B_j|A)$. Therefore, equation (7) tells us that it is not necessary to assess the likelihoods, $P(A|B_i)$ and $P(A|B_j)$. It is sufficient to assess their ratios, $L(A|B_i:B_j)$ (cf. Edwards, Phillips, Hays, and Goodman, 1968).

One further elaboration of this design seems useful. Our new evidence A can be thought of as a conjunction: $A = A_1$ *and* A_2, where A is the event that types I, II, and III should be so disparate (items of evidence (ii) and (iii)) and A_2 is the event that specimens of types I and II should not be found along with the type III specimens in the Far East (items of evidence (iv) and (v)). The two events A_1 and A_2 seem to involve independent uncertainties, and this can be expressed in Bayesian terms by saying that they are independent events conditional on any one of the five hypotheses:

$$P(A|B_i) = P(A_1|B_i)P(A_2|B_i).$$

Substituting this into equation (6), we obtain

$$\frac{P(B_i|A)}{P(B_j|A)} = \frac{P(B_i)}{P(B_j)} \frac{P(A_1|B_i)}{P(A_1|B_j)} \frac{P(A_2|B_i)}{P(A_2|B_j)},$$

or

$$\frac{P(B_i|A)}{P(B_j|A)} = \frac{P(B_i)}{P(B_j)} L(A_1|B_i:B_j)L(A_2|B_i:B_j).$$

Table 11.3. *Component judgments for the likelihood-based partitioning design*

	$P(B_i)$	$L(A_1\|B_i:B_5)$	$L(A_2\|B_i:B_5)$	$P(B_i\|A)$
B_1	.75	.01	.01	.00060
B_2	.05	.50	1.00	.19983
B_3	.05	.05	.01	.00020
B_4	.05	.01	.01	.00004
B_5	.10	1.00	1.00	.79933

We are not, of course, qualified to make the probability judgments called for by this design; it is a design for experts like Walker and Leakey, not a design for laymen. (If we ourselves had to make probability judgments about the validity of Walker and Leakey's opinions, we would need a design that analyzes our own evidence. This consists of their article itself, which provides internal evidence as to the integrity and the cogency of their thought, our knowledge of the standards of *Scientific American*, etc.) It will be instructive, nonetheless, to put ourselves in the shoes of Walker and Leakey and to carry out the design on the basis of the qualitative judgments they make in their article. As we shall see, there are several difficulties.

The first difficulty is in determining the prior probabilities $P(B_i)$ on the basis of the evidence (i) alone. This evidence is an argument for B_1, and so evaluation of it can justify a probability $P(B_1)$, say $P(B_1) = .75$. But how do we divide the remaining .25 among the other B_i? This is a typical problem in Bayesian design. In the absence of relevant evidence, we are forced to depend on symmetries, even though the available symmetries may seem artificial and conflicting. In this case, one symmetry suggests equal division among B_2, B_3, B_4, B_5, while another symmetry suggest equal division between the hypothesis of two species (B_2, B_3, B_4) and the hypothesis of three species (B_5). The $P(B_i)$ given in table 11.3 represent a compromise.

Now consider A_1, the argument that the different types must represent three distinct species because of their diversity. Our design asks us, in effect, to assess how much less likely this diversity would be under the one-species hypothesis and under the various two-species hypotheses. Answers to these questions are given in the column of table 11.3 labeled "$L(A_1\|B_i:B_5)$." These numbers reflect the great implausibility of the intraspecies diversity postulated by B_1 and B_4, the marginal acceptability of the degree of sexual dimorphism postulated by B_2, and the implausibility, especially in the putative ancestor of *Homo sapiens*, of the sexual dimorphism postulated by B_3. Notice how fortunate it is that we are required to assess only the likelihood ratios, $L(A_1\|B_i:B_5) = P(A_1\|B_i)/P(A_1\|B_5)$ and not, say, the absolute likelihood $P(A_1\|B_5)$. We can think about how much less likely the observed disparity among the three groups would be if they represented fewer than three species, but we would be totally at sea if asked to assess the unconditional chance of this degree of disparity among three extinct hominid species.

Finally, consider A_2, the absence of specimens of type I or II among the abundant specimens of type III in the Far East. This absence would seem much less likely if I or II were forms of the same species as III than if they were not, say 100 times less likely. This is the figure used in table 11.3. Notice again that we are spared the well-nigh meaningless task of assessing absolute likelihoods.

As the last column of table 11.3 shows, the total evidence gives a fairly high degree of support to B_5, the hypothesis that there are three distinct species. This is Walker and Leakey's conclusion.

How good an analysis is this? There seem to be two problems with it. First, we lack good grounds for some of the prior probability judgments. Secondly, the interpretation of the likelihoods seems strained. Are we really judging that the observed difference between I and III is 100 times more likely if they are separate species than if they are variants of the same species? Or are we getting this measure of the strength of this argument for separate species in some other way?

We should remark that it is a general feature of likelihood-based partitioning designs that only likelihood ratios need be assessed. In likelihood-based observational designs, on the other hand, we do usually need to assess absolute likelihoods. This is because in an observational design we must be prepared to condition on any of the possible observations. If, for example, the possible observations are A and *not* A, then we need to have in hand both $L(A|B_i:B_j) = \dfrac{P(A|B_j)}{P(A|B_j)}$ and $L(not\ A|B_i:B_j) = \dfrac{P(not\ A|B_i)}{P(not\ A|B_j)}$. Since $P(A|B_i) + P(not\ A|B_i) = P(A|B_j) + P(not\ A|B_j) = 1$, these likelihood ratios fully determine the absolute likeihoods $P(A|B_i)$ and $P(A|B_j)$.

The choice of new evidence

Traditionally, Bayesian statistical theory has been concerned with what we have called likelihood-based observational designs. This is because the theory has been based on the idea of a statistical experiment. It is assumed that one knows in advance an "observation space" – the set of possible outcomes of the experiment – and a "parameter space" – the set of possible answers to certain questions of substantive interest. One assesses in advance both prior probabilities for the parameters and likelihoods for the observations.

Many statistical problems do conform to this picture. The search for *Scorpion*, discussed earlier, is one example. But Bayesian and other statisticians have gradually extended their concerns from the realm of planned experiments, where parameter and observation spaces are clearly defined before observations are made, to the broader field of "data analysis." In data analysis, the examination of data often precedes the framing of hypotheses and "observations." This means that the Bayesian data analyst will often use partitioning designs rather than genuine observational designs.

We believe that Bayesian statistical theory will better meet the needs of statistical practice if it will go beyond observational designs and deal explicitly with partitioning designs. In particular, we need more discussion of principles for the selection of evidence that is to be treated as new evidence. In the example of the hominids, we treated certain arguments as new evidence because we could find better grounds for probability judgment when thinking of the likelihood of their arising than when thinking about them as conditions affecting the likelihood of other events. In other cases, we may single out evidence because its psychological salience can give it excessive weight in total-evidence judgments. By putting such salient evidence in the role of new evidence in a partitioning design, we gain an opportunity to make probability judgments based on the other evidence alone (cf. Spetzler and Staël von Holstein, 1975, p. 346; and Nisbett and Ross, 1980, chapter 3). We need more discussion of such principles, and more examples.

A partitioning design that is not likelihood-based

Here is a problem that suggests a partitioning design that is not likelihood-based. Gracchus is accused of murdering Maevius. Maevius' death brought him a great and sorely needed financial gain, but it appears that Maevius and Gracchus were good friends, and our assessment of Gracchus' character suggests only a slight possibility that the prospect of gain would have been sufficient motive for him to murder Maevius. On the other hand, some evidence has come to light to suggest that beneath the apparent friendship Gracchus actually felt a simmering hatred for Maevius, and Gracchus is known to be capable of violent behavior towards people he feels have wronged him. The means to commit the murder is not at issue: Gracchus or anyone else could have easily committed it. But we think it very unlikely that anyone else had reason to kill Maevius.

Our partitioning design uses the fact of Maevius' murder as the new evidence. We consider the propositions.

H = Gracchus hated Maevius,

GI = Gracchus intended to kill Maevius,

SI = someone else intended to kill Maevius,

GM = Gracchus murdered Maevius,

SM = someone else murdered Maevius,

NM = no one murdered Maevius.

Using the old evidence alone, we make the following probability judgments:

$P(H) = .2, P(GI|H) = .2, P(GI|not\ H) = .01;$

$P(SI) = .001,$ and SI is independent of GI;

$P(GM|GI \text{ and } SI) = .4,\ P(SM|GI \text{ and } SI) = .4,\ P(NM|GI \text{ and } SI) = .2;$

$P(GM|GI \text{ and not } SI) = .8,\ P(NM|GI \text{ and not } SI) = .2;$

$P(SM|SI \text{ and not } GI) = .8,\ P(NM|SI \text{ and not } GI) = .2;$

$P(NM|\text{not } GI \text{ and not } SI) = 1.$

Combining these judgments, we obtain

$$P(GI) = P(GI|H)P(H) + P(GI)|\text{ not } H)P(\text{not } H)$$
$$= (.2)(.2) + (.8)(.01) = .048,$$
$$P(GM) = P(GM|\text{ not } GI)P(\text{not } GI) + P(GM|GI \text{ and } SI)P(GI)P(SI)$$
$$+ P(GM|GI \text{ and not } SI)P(GI)P(\text{not } SI)$$
$$= (0)(.952) + (.4)(.048)(.001) + (.8)(.048)(.999)$$
$$= .03838.$$

Similarly,

$$P(SM) = .00078 \text{ and } P(NM) = .96084.$$

Finally we bring in the new evidence – the fact that Maevius was murdered. We find a probability

$$P(GM|\text{not } NM) = \frac{.03838}{.03838 + .00078} = .98$$

that Gracchus did it.

One interesting aspect of this example is the fact that the "new evidence" – the fact that Maevius was murdered – is actually obtained before much of the other evidence. Only after Maevius' death would we have gathered the evidence against Gracchus.

3.3 Other Bayesian designs

What other Bayesian designs are possible in addition to total-evidence and conditioning designs?

A large class of possible designs is suggested by the following general idea. Suppose one part of our evidence lends itself to a certain design d, while the remainder of our evidence does not fit this design, but seems instead relevant to some of the judgments specified by a different design d'. Then we might first construct a distribution P_0 using d and considering only the first part of the evidence, and then switch to d', using the total evidence to make those judgments for which the second part of the evidence is relevant and obtaining the other judgments from P_0.

An interesting special case occurs when the total evidence is used only to construct probabilities $p_1, \ldots, p_n$ for a set of mutually incompatible and collectively exhaustive propositions $A_1, \ldots, A_n$, and the final distribution P is determined by setting $P(A_i) = p_i$ and $P(B|A_i) = P_o(B|A_i)$ for all B. Since such designs were considered by Jeffrey (1965), we may call them *Jeffrey designs*.

Here is an example of a Jeffrey design. Gracchus is accused of murdering Maevius and the evidence against him is the same as in the preceding example, except that it is not certain that Maevius has been murdered. Perhaps Maevius has disappeared after having been seen walking along a sea cliff. We partition our evidence into two bodies of evidence – the evidence that was used in the probability analysis above, and the other evidence that suggests Maevius may have been murdered. We use the first body of evidence to make the analysis of the preceding section, obtaining the probabilities obtained there: a probability of .03838 that Gracchus murdered Maevius, a probability of .00078 that someone else did, and a probability of .96084 that no one did. We label this probability distribution P_o. Then we use the total evidence to assess directly whether we think Maevius has been murdered or not. Say we assess the probability of Maevius' having been murdered at .95. We then obtain a conditional probability from $P_o:P_o$ (Gracchus did it|Maevius was murdered) $\approx .98$. The final result is a probability of $.95 \times .98 \approx .93$ for the event that Gracchus murdered Maevius. For further examples of Jeffrey designs, see Shafer (1981b) and Diaconis and Zabell (1982).

4. BELIEF-FUNCTION DESIGN

Belief-function design differs from Bayesian design in that it puts more explicit emphasis on the decomposition of evidence. As we have seen, total-evidence designs are basic to the Bayesian language. (Even conditioning and Jeffrey designs must have subsidiary designs for the construction of initial distributions, and these subsidiary designs are usually total-evidence designs.) These total-evidence designs break down the task of judgment by asking us to answer several different questions. It is a contingent matter whether different items of evidence bear on these different questions, though this seems to be the case with the most effective total-evidence designs. The belief-function language, on the other hand, since it directly models the meaning and reliability of evidence, breaks down the task of judgment by considering different items of evidence. It is a contingent matter whether these different items of evidence bear on relatively separate and restricted aspects of the questions that interest us, but again, as we shall see, this seems to be the case with the most effective belief-function designs.

Here we shall explore the possibilities for belief-function design for Curt's swim race and Walker and Leakey's hominids. For further examples of belief-function design, see Shafer (1981a, b, 1982a, b).

4.1 The free-style race

The second of the two Bayesian total-evidence designs that we gave for the free-style race (section 3.1) was based on independent judgments about Curt and Cowan. We gave Curt an 85% chance of maintaining his pace, a 3% chance of slowing less than 3%, a 7% chance of slowing more than 3%, and a 5% chance of collapsing. And we gave Cowan a 10% chance of being able to speed up, a 70% chance of only being able to maintain his pace, and a 20% chance of being unable to maintain his pace. Since we are using the Bayesian language, we compared our evidence to knowledge that the evolution of the race actually was governed by these chances. It is equally convincing, however, to interpret these numbers within the language of belief functions. We compare our knowledge about Curt to a message that has an 85% chance of meaning that he will maintain his pace, etc., and we compare our knowledge about Cowan to a message that has a 70% chance of meaning that he can only maintain his pace, etc.

Formally, we have a belief function Bel_1 that assigns degrees of belief .85, .03, .07, and .05 to the four hypotheses about Curt, and a second-belief function Bel_2 that assigns degrees of belief .10, .70, and .20 to the three hypotheses about Cowan. Judging that our evidence about Curt is independent of our evidence about Cowan, we combine these by Dempster's rule. If no further evidence is added to the analysis, then our resulting degree of belief that Curt will win will be our degree of belief that Curt will maintain his pace or slow less than 3% while Cowan is unable to speed up: $(.85 + .03)(.70 + .20) = .792$. And our degree of belief that Cowan will win will be our degree of belief that Curt will slow 3% or more and Cowan will be able to at least maintain his pace: $(.07)(.10 + .70) = .056$.

These conclusions are weaker than the conclusions of the Bayesian analysis. This is principally due to the fact that we are not claiming to have evidence about what will happen in the cases where our descriptions of Curt's and Cowan's behavior do not determine the outcome of the race. If we did feel we had such evidence, it could be introduced into the belief-function analysis.

We can also relax the additivity of the degrees of belief about Curt and Cowan that go into the belief-function analysis. Suppose, for example, that we feel our evidence about Curt justifies only an 85% degree of belief that he will maintain his pace, but we do not feel we have any positive reason to think he will slow down or collapse. In this case, we can replace the additive degree of belief .85, .03, .07, and .05 with a simple support function that assigns only degree of belief .85 to the proposition that Curt will maintain his pace. If we retain the additive degrees of belief .10, .70, and .20 for Cowan's behavior, this leads to a degree of belief

$$(.85)(.70 + .20) = .765$$

that Curt will win and a degree of belief zero that Cowan will win.

As this example illustrates, a belief-function design can be based on a causal structure like those used in Bayesian total-evidence designs. The belief-function design must, however, go beyond this causal structure to an explicit specification of the evidence that bears on its different parts.

4.2 The hominids of East Turkana

Recall that Walker and Leakey considered five hypothesis:

B_1 = one species.

B_2 = two species, one composed of I (male) and II (female).

B_3 = two species, one composed of III (male) and II (female).

B_4 = two species, one composed of I and III.

B_5 = three species.

In our Bayesian analysis in section 3.2, we partitioned the evidence into three intuitively independent arguments:

1. A theoretical argument for B_1.
2. An argument that the three types are too diverse not to be distinct species. This argument bears most strongly against B_1 and B_4, but also carries considerable weight against B_3 and some weight against B_2.
3. The fact that neither I nor II specimens have been found among the III specimens in the Far East. This provides evidence against hypotheses B_1, B_3, and B_4.

Let us represent each of these arguments by a belief function. Making roughly the same judgments as in the Bayesian analysis, we have

1. Bel_1, with $m_1(B_1) = .75$ and $m_1(\Theta) = .25$,
2. Bel_2, with $m_2(B_5) = .5$, $m_2(B_2 \text{ or } B_5) = .45$, $m_2(B_2 \text{ or } B_3 \text{ or } B_5) = .04$, and $m_2(\Theta) = .01$, and
3. Bel_3, with $m_3(B_2 \text{ or } B_5) = .99$ and $m_3(\Theta) = .01$.

Combining these by Dempster's rule, we obtain a belief function Bel with $m(B_5) = .4998$, $m(B_2 \text{ or } B_5) = .4994$, $m(B_2 \text{ or } B_3 \text{ or } B_5) = .0004$, $m(B_1) = .0003$, and $m(\Theta) = .0001$. This belief function gives fair support to B_5 and overwhelming support to B_2 or B_5: Bel $(B_5) = .4998$ and Bel $(B_2 \text{ or } B_5) = .9992$.

These belief-function results can be compared to the Bayesian results of section 3.2, where we obtained $P(B_5) = .7993$ and $P(B_2 \text{ or } B_5) = .9992$. The different results for B_5 can be attributed to the different treatments of the first item of evidence, the argument against coexistence of hominid species. In the belief-function analysis, we treated this argument simply by giving B_1 a 75% degree of support. In the Bayesian analysis, we had to go farther and divide the remaining 25% among the other four hypotheses. The belief-function analysis, while it reaches basically the same conclusion as the Bayesian argument, can be regarded as a stronger argument, since it is based on slightly more modest assumptions.

5. THE NATURE OF PROBABILITY JUDGMENT

We have suggested that probability judgment is a kind of mental experiment.

Sometimes it is more like a physicist's thought experiment, as when we try to trace the consequences of an imagined situation.

Probability judgment is a process of construction rather than elicitation. People may begin a task of probability judgment with some beliefs already formulated. But the process of judgment, when successful, gives greater content and structure to these beliefs and tends to render initial beliefs obsolete. It is useful, in this respect, to draw an analogy between probability and affective notions such as love and loyalty. A declaration of love is not simply a report on a person's emotions. It is also part of a process whereby an intellectual and emotional commitment is created; so too with probability.

A probability judgment depends not just on the evidence on which it is based, but also on the process of exploring that evidence. The act of designing a probability analysis usually involves reflection about what evidence is available and a sharpening of our definition of that evidence. And the implementation of a design involves many contingencies. The probability judgments we make may depend on just what examples we sampled from our memory or other records, or just what details we happen to focus on as we examine the possibility of various scenarios (Tversky and Kahneman, 1983).

It may be helpful to point out that we do not use the word "evidence" as many philosophers do – to refer to a proposition in a formal language. Instead, we use it in a way that is much closer to ordinary English usage. We refer to "our evidence about Cowan's abilities," to "our memory as to how frequently similar projects are completed," or to "the argument that distinct hominid species cannot coexist." The references are, as it were, ostensive definitions of bodies of evidence. They point to the evidence in question without translating it into statements of fact in some language. This seems appropriate, for in all these cases the evidence involves arguments and claims that would fall short of being accepted as statements of fact.

Evidence, as we use the word, is the raw material from which judgments, both of probability and of fact, are made. Evidence can be distinguished in this respect from information. Information can be thought of as answers to questions already asked, and hence we can speak of the quantity of information, which is measured by the number of these questions that are answered. Evidence, in contrast, refers to a potential for answering questions. We can speak of the weight of evidence as it bears on a particular question, but it does not seem useful to speak of the quantity of evidence.

Though we have directed attention to the notion of mental experimentation, we want also to emphasize that when an individual undertakes to make a probability judgment that individual is not necessarily limited to the resources of memory and imagination. He or she may also use paper, pencils, books, files, and computers. And an individual need not necessarily limit his or her sampling experiments to haphazard search of memory and personal bookshelves. The individual may wish to extend sampling to a large-scale survey, conducted with the aid of randomization techniques.

There is sometimes a tendency to define human probability judgment narrowly – to focus on judgments people make without external aids. But it may not be sensible to try to draw a line between internal and external resources. Psychologists who wish to offer a comprehensible analysis of human judgment should, as Ward Edwards (1975) has argued, take into account the fact that humans are tool-using creatures. Moreover, statisticians and other practical users of probability need to recognize the continuity between apparently subjective judgments and supposedly objective statistical techniques. The concept of design that we have developed in this paper is meant to apply both to probability analyses that use sophisticated technical aids and to those that are made wholly in our heads. We believe that the selection of a good design for a particular question is a researchable problem with both technical and judgmental aspects. The design and analysis of mental experiments for probability judgment therefore represent a challenge to both statisticians and psychologists.

NOTE

This research was supported in part by NSF grant MCS-800213 and 8301282 to the first author and by ONR Grant NR 197-058 to the second author. The chapter benefited from the comments of Jonathan Baron, Morris DeGroot, Persi Diaconis, and David Krantz. First published in *Cognitive Science*, 9 (1985), 309–39.

REFERENCES

Alpert, M., and Raiffa, H. (1982). A progress report on the training of probability assessors. In D. Kahneman, P. Slovic, and A. Tversky (eds.), *Judgment under uncertainty: heuristics and biases*. New York: Cambridge University Press.

Bertrand, J. (1907). *Calcul des probabilitiés* (2nd ed.). Paris: Gauthier-Villars et fils.

Box, G. E. P. (1980). Sampling and Bayes' inference in scientific modelling and robustness. *Journal of the Royal Statistical Society, Series A*, 143, 383–430.

Diaconis, P., and Zabell, S. L. (1982). Updating subjective probability. *Journal of the American Statistical Association*, 77, 822–30.

Edwards, W. (1975). Comment on paper by Hogarth. *Journal of the American Statistical Association*, 70, 291–3.

Edwards, W., Phillips, L. D., Hays, W. L., and Goodman, B. C. (1968). Probabilistic information processing systems: design and evaluation. *IEEE Transactions on Systems Science and Cybernetics*, 4, 248–65.

Fischhoff, B., Slovic, P., and Lichtenstein, S. (1978). Fault trees: sensitivity of estimated failure probabilities to problem representation. *Journal of Experimental Psychology: Human Perception and Performance*, 4, 330–44.

Goldstein, M. (1981). Revising previsions: a geometric interpretation. *Journal of the Royal Statistical Society, Series B*, 43, 105–30.

Jeffrey, R. (1965). *The logic of decision*. New York: McGraw-Hill.

Kahneman, D., and Tversky, A. (1982). Variants of uncertainty. *Cognition*, 11, 143–57.

Krantz, D., and Miyamoto, J. (1983). Priors and likelihood ratios as evidence. *Journal of the American Statistical Association*, 78, 418–23.

Lieblich, I., and Lieblich, A. (1969). Effects of different pay-off matrices on arithmetic estimation tasks: an attempt to produce "rationality." *Perceptual and Motor Skills*, 29, 467–73.

Lindley, D. V., Tversky, A., and Brown, R. V. (1979). On the reconciliation of probability assessments. *Journal of the Royal Statistical Society*, 142, 146–80.

Nisbett, R., and Ross, L. (1980). *Human inference: strategies and shortcomings of social judgment*. Englewood Cliifs, NJ: Prentice Hall.

Raiffa, H. (1974). *Analysis for decision making. An audiographic, self-instructional course*. Chicago: Encyclopedia Britanica Educational Corporation.

Ramsey, F. P. (1931). Truth and probability. In R. G. Braithwaite (ed.), *The foundations of mathematics and other logical essays*. New York: Routledge and Kegan Paul.

Richardson, H. R., and Stone, L. D. (1971). Operations analysis during the underwater search for *Scorpion*. *Naval Research Logistics Quarterly*, 18, 141–57.

Savage, L. J. (1954). *The foundations of statistics*. New York: Wiley.

Shafer, G. (1976). *A mathematical theory of evidence*. Princeton University Press.

(1981a). Constructive probability. *Synthese*, 48, 1–60.

(1981b). Jeffrey's rule of conditioning. *Philosophy of Science*, 48, 337–62.

(1982a). Lindley's paradox. *Journal of the American Statistical Association*. 77, 325–51.

(1982b). Belief functions and parametric models. *Journal of the Royal Statistical Society, Series B*, 44, 322–52.

Singer, M. (1971). The vitality of mythical numbers. *The Public Interest*, 23, 3–9.

Spetzler, C. S., and Staël von Holstein, C. S. (1975). Probability encoding in decision analysis. *Management Science*, 22, 340–58.

Tversky, A., and Kahneman, D. (1983). Extensional vs. intuitive reasoning: the conjunction fallacy in probability judgment. *Psychological Reviews*, 90, 293–315.

Walker, A., and Leakey, R. E. T. (1978). The hominids of East Turkana. *Scientific American*, 238, 54–66.

Wierzchón, S. T. (1984). *An inference rule based on Sugeno measure*. Unpublished paper, Institute of Computer Science, Polish Academy of Sciences, Warsaw, Poland.

12

UPDATING SUBJECTIVE PROBABILITY

PERSI DIACONIS AND SANDY L. ZABELL

1. INTRODUCTION

1.1 Belief revision

The most frequently discussed method of revising a subjective probability distribution P to obtain a new distribution P^*, based on the occurrence of an event E, is Bayes's rule: $P^*(A) = P(AE)/P(E)$. Richard Jeffrey (1965, 1968) has argued persuasively that Bayes's rule is not the only reasonable way to update: use of Bayes's rule presupposes that both $P(E)$ and $P(AE)$ have been previously quantified. In many instances this will clearly not be the case (for example, the event E may not have been anticipated), and it is of interest to consider how one might proceed.

Example. Suppose we are thinking about three trials of a new surgical procedure. Under the usual circumstances a probability assignment is made on the eight possible outcomes $\Omega = \{000, 001, 010, 011, 100, 101, 110, 111\}$, where 1 denotes a successful outcome, 0 not. Suppose a colleague informs us that another hospital had performed this type of operation 100 times, with 80 successful outcomes. This is clearly relevant information and we obviously want to revise our opinion. The information *cannot* be put in terms of the occurrence of an event in the original eight-point space Ω, and the Bayes rule is not *directly* available. Among many possible approaches, four methods of incorporating the information will be discussed: (1) complete reassessment; (2) retrospective conditioning; (3) exchangeability; (4) Jeffrey's Rule.

1. *Complete reassessment.* In the absence of further structure it is always possible to react to the new information by completely reassessing P^*, presumably using the same techniques used to quantify the original distribution P.

2. *Retrospective conditioning.* Some subjectivists have suggested trying to analyze this kind of problem by momentarily disregarding the new information, quantifying a distribution on a space Ω^* rich enough to allow ordinary

266

conditioning to be used, and then using Bayes's rule. For some discussion of this, see de Finetti (1972, ch. 8) and section 2.1. It is worth emphasizing that this type of retrospective conditioning can be an extremely difficult psychological task; see Fischoff (1975), Fischoff and Beyth (1975), Slovic and Fischoff (1977). Nor, in principle, is retrospective conditioning simpler than complete reassessment: since $P^*(A) = P(AE)/P(E)$ in this case, for each A assessment of $P(AE)$ is equivalent to reassessment of $P^*(A)$.

3. *Exchangeability.* The three future trials may be regarded as exchangeable with the 100 trials reported by our colleague. Standard Bayesian computations can then be used. However, given that the operations will have been performed at two, possibly very different, hospitals with possibly very different patient populations, this assumption might very well be judged unsatisfactory.

4. *Jeffrey's rule.* Suppose that the original probability assignment P was *exchangeable.* That is, $P(001) = P(010) = P(100)$ and $P(110) = P(101) = P(011)$. In the situation described, the information provided contains no information about the order of the next three trials and thus we may well require that the new probability distribution remain exchangeable. This is equivalent to considering a partition $\{E_i\}_{i=0}^3$ of Ω, where $E_0 = \{000\}$, $E_1 = \{001, 010, 100\}$, $E_2 = \{110, 101, 011\}$, $E_3 = \{111\}$. Here E_i is the set of outcomes with i ones, and exchangeability implies that for any event A, and any i, $P(A|E_i) = P^*(A|E_i)$. To complete the probability assignment P^*, we need a subjective assessment of $P^*(E_i)$. Then P^* is determined by

$$P^*(A) = \sum P^*(A|E_i)P^*(E_i) = \sum P(A|E_i)P^*(E_i).$$

The rule

$$P^*(A) = \sum P(A|E_i)P^*(E_i) \tag{1.1}$$

is known in the philosophical literature as *Jeffrey's rule of conditioning.* It is valid whenever there is a partition $\{E_i\}$ of the sample space such that

$$P^*(A|E_i) = P(A|E_i) \quad \text{for all } A \text{ and } i. \tag{J}$$

It has the practical advantage of reducing the assessment of P^* to the simpler task of assessing $P^*(E_i)$.

Approaches 2, 3, and 4 are all special routes to the requantification of approach 1; each is valid or useful under different assumptions. For example, retrospective conditioning assumes that one can do a reasonable job of assessing probabilities as if the data had not been observed; exchangeability assumes that future trials are based on the same mechanism as past ones; Jeffrey's rule assumes the availability of a partition and the validity of assumption (J).

In this chapter we study the assumptions and conclusions that attend Jeffrey's rule. Our main contributions are technical: in section 2 we connect Jeffrey's rule with sufficiency; sections 3, 4, and 5 analyze what happens when two or more partitions are considered. In section 3 we discuss commutativity of successive updating. In section 4 we discuss methods for dealing with two partitions simultaneously, giving a necessary and sufficient condition for two probability measures on two algebras to have a common extension. In section 5 we discuss some other motivations for Jeffrey's rule when condition (J) has not been subjectively checked. Jeffrey's rule gives the "closest" measure to P that fixes $P^*(E_i)$, and it is related to the iterated proportional fitting procedure used in the statistical analysis of contingency tables. For ease of exposition, most of this article assumes a countable state space or a countable partition $\{E_i\}_{i=1}^\infty$. In section 6 we describe the mathematical machinery needed to extend the previous results to abstract probability spaces.

1.2 Bibliographical note on probability revision

From the subjectivistic perspective, the conditional probability $P(A|E)$ is the probability we *currently* would attribute to an event A if in addition to our present information we were also to learn E. In the language of betting, it is "the probability that we would regard as fair for a bet on A to be made immediately, but to become operative only if E occurs" (de Finetti, 1972, p. 193; compare Ramsey, 1931, p. 180). In this formulation, the equality $P(A|E) = P(AE)/P(E)$ is not a definition but follows as a theorem derived from the assumption of coherence (de Finetti, 1975, ch. 4).

If we actually *learn* E to be true, it is conventional to adopt as one's new probability

$$P^*(A) = P(A|E). \tag{1.2}$$

Several authors have discussed the limitations on or justifications for this use of the Bayes rule (1.2). Ramsey put the difficulty clearly:

> [The degree of belief in p given q] is not the same as the degree to which [a subject] would believe p, if he believed q for certain; for knowledge of q might for psychological reasons profoundly alter his whole system of beliefs.
>
> (Ramsey, 1931, p. 180; cf. however, p. 192)

For modern discussion of this and related issues, see Hacking (1967), de Finetti (1972, p. 150; 1975, p. 203), Teller (1976), Freedman and Purves (1969). A closely related point is that our "[subjective] probabilities can change in the light of calculations or of pure thought without any change in the *empirical* data" (Good, 1977, p. 140). I. J. Good terms such probabilities "evolving" or "dynamic" and has discussed them in a number of papers (Good, 1950, p. 49; 1968; 1977).

Other reservations about the adequacy of conditionalization as an exclusive model for belief revision center around its assumption about the form in which new information is received. Indeed, Jeffrey's original philosophical motivation for introducing "probability kinematics" was his belief that "It is rarely or never that there is a proposition for which the direct effect of an observation is to change the observer's degree of belief in that proposition to 1" (Jeffrey, 1968, p. 171). Similar criticisms have been raised by Shafer (1979, 1981), whose theory of belief functions is a more radical attempt to deal with the problem. Both hold that conditioning on an event requires the assignment of an initial probability for that event, prior (in principle at least) to its observation, and for many classes of sensory experiences this seems forced, unrealistic, or impossible.

For example, suppose we are about to hear one of two recordings of Shakespeare on the radio, to be read by either Olivier or Gielgud, but are unsure of which, and have a prior with mass $\frac{1}{2}$ on Olivier, $\frac{1}{2}$ on Gielgud. After hearing the recording, one might judge it fairly likely, but by no means certain, to be by Olivier. The change in belief takes place by direct recognition of the voice; all the integration of sensory stimuli has already taken place at a subconscious level. To demand a list of objective vocal features that we condition on in order to affect the change would be a logician's parody of a complex psychological process.

Jeffrey's rule was introduced in Jeffrey (1957) and is further discussed in Jeffrey (1965, ch. 11) and Jeffrey (1968). Isaac Levi (1967; 1970, pp. 147–152) is a vigorous critic of Jeffrey's version of probability kinematics, but has been thoroughly rebutted by Jeffrey (1970, especially pp. 173–179). Jeffrey's idea was partially anticipated by the Oxford astronomer Donkin (1851, p. 356); compare Boole (1854, pp. 251–252), Whitworth (1901, pp. 162–169, 181–182), Keynes (1921, pp. 176–177). An independent proposal of Jeffrey's rule appears in Griffeath and Snell (1974). The last few years have seen a sudden upsurge of interest in Jeffrey conditionalization; papers have appeared by Teller (1976), Field (1978), Garber (1980), Williams (1980), van Fraassen (1980), Armendt (1980), and Shafer (1981).

2. JEFFREY'S RULE OF CONDITIONING

In this section we develop some of the mathematics connected with Jeffrey's rule of conditioning. Formally: Ω is a countable set, P and P^* are probability measures on the subsets of Ω, and $\{E_i\}$ is a partition of Ω.

2.1 Bayesian conditioning

Jeffrey's rule of conditioning is a generalization of ordinary conditioning: given the partition $\{E, E^c\}$, if $P^*(E) = 1$ and $P^*(A) = \sum P(A|E_i)P^*(E_i)$, then $P^*(A) = P(A|E)$. We therefore begin by investigating when one measure P^* can arise from another measure P by conditioning. To be precise, suppose P and P^* are measures on a countable space Ω. We will say that P^* *can be obtained from P by conditioning* if there exists a probability space $(\bar{\Omega}, \mathscr{A}, Q)$, and events $\{E_\omega\}_{\omega \in \Omega}$, $E_\omega \in \mathscr{A}$ (*to be thought of as* "$E_\omega = \omega$ occurred"), such that $Q(E_\omega) = P(\omega)$, and an event $E \in \mathscr{A}$ such that $Q(E) > 0$ and $Q(E_\omega|E) = P^*(\omega)$.

Theorem 2.1. P^* can be obtained from P by conditioning if and only if there exists a constant $B \geqslant 1$ such that

$$P^*(\omega) \leqslant BP(\omega) \quad \text{for all} \quad \omega \in \Omega. \tag{2.1}$$

269

Proof. If P^* can be obtained from P by conditioning, let $(\bar{\Omega}, \bar{\mathscr{A}}, Q)$, $\{E_\omega\}$, E be given. Then for any $\omega \in \Omega$,

$$P^*(\omega) = Q(E_\omega | E) \leqslant \frac{Q(E_\omega)}{Q(E)} = \frac{P(\omega)}{Q(E)}.$$

This gives (2.1) with $B = 1/Q(E)$.

Conversely, suppose (2.1) is satisfied. If $B = 1$, then $P^* = P$ and the theorem is obvious. If $B > 1$, define

$$P^{**}(\omega) = \frac{B}{B-1} P(\omega) - \frac{1}{(B-1)} P^*(\omega).$$

Because of the conditioning, P^{**} is a probability and $P = (1/B)P^* + (1 - 1/B)P^{**}$. This suggests taking $\bar{\Omega} = \Omega\{a, b\}$, $E_\omega = (\omega, a) \cup (\omega, b)$, and $E = \bigcup_\omega (\omega, a)$. Let Q be defined by $Q(\omega, a) = (1/B)P^*(\omega)$ and $Q(\omega, b) = (1 - 1/B)P^{**}(\omega)$.

Condition (2.1) places a restriction on P, P^* when both have countable support (but not when both have finite support and $\mathrm{supp}(P^*) \subseteq \mathrm{supp}(P)$). For example, no geometric distribution can be obtained from a Poisson distribution by conditioning, but any Poisson distribution can be obtained from any geometric distribution. If Ω is uncountable, (2.1) can be replaced by the conditions $P^* \ll P$ and $dP^*/dP \in L_\infty$; compare section 6.

2.2 Jeffrey conditionalization and sufficiency

In the example discussed in section 1, the partition $\{E_i\}$ naturally arose in the course of constructing P^* from P. But one might instead envisage being given another person's $\{P, P^*\}$ and then trying to reconstruct a possible partition $\{E_i\}$ from which the pair $\{P, P^*\}$ could have arisen via Jeffrey conditionalization. Unlike Bayesian conditionalization, this turns out to be always possible.

To apply Jeffrey's rule, it is required to find a partition $\{E_i\}$ such that

$$P(A|E_i) = P^*(A|E_i) \quad \text{for all } A \text{ and } i.$$

This is simply the problem of finding a *sufficient partition* for the two-element family $\mathscr{F} = \{P, P^*\}$; see Blackwell and Girshick (1954, ch. 8). This simple observation makes possible the translation of the ideas of minimal sufficiency and likelihood ratio into the language of Jeffrey's rule.

A partition $\{E_i\}$ is said to be *coarser* than a second $\{\bar{E}_j\}$ if every E_i is a union of sets in $\{\bar{E}_j\}$. For purposes of updating probability, a coarser partition has the advantage that P^* need be specified on fewer sets. A coarsest sufficient partition is said to be *minimal sufficient*. The following (well-known) theorem gives an alternative version of Jeffrey's rule and states that there is always a coarsest partition for which Jeffrey's rule is valid. Some philosophical implications of this fact are discussed by van Fraassen (1980).

Theorem 2.2. Let P, P^* be probability measures with common support on the countable set Ω. If $\{E_i\}$ is a partition of Ω such that $P(E_i) > 0$ and $P(A|E_i) = P^*(A|E_i)$ for all subsets A and elements of the partition E_i, then for each $\omega \in \Omega$,

$$P^*(\omega) = \frac{P^*(E_i)}{P(E_i)} P(\omega), \quad \omega \in E_i. \qquad (2.2)$$

If $R = \{x : P^*(\omega)/P(\omega) = x, \, \omega \in \Omega\}$ and $E_x = \{\omega : P^*(\omega)/P(\omega) = x, \, \omega \in \Omega\}$, then $\{E_x : x \in R\}$ is a minimal sufficient partition for $\{P, P^*\}$.

Proof. The first statement is a version of the Fisher–Neyman factorization theorem; for the second, see Blackwell and Girshick (1954, p. 221).

The following example illustrates the use of the likelihood ratio form of Jeffrey's rule.

Example 2.1. (Whitworth, 1901, pp. 167–168):

Question 138. A, B, C were entered for a race, and their respective chances of winning were estimated at $\frac{2}{11}, \frac{4}{11}, \frac{5}{11}$. But circumstances come to our knowledge in favour of A, which raise his chance to $\frac{1}{2}$; what are now the chances in favour of B and C respectively?

Answer. A could lose in two ways, viz. either by B winning or by C winning, and the respective chances of his losing in these ways were a priori $\frac{4}{11}$ and $\frac{5}{11}$, and the chance of his losing at all was $\frac{9}{11}$. But after our accession of knowledge the chance of his losing at all becomes $\frac{1}{2}$, that is, it becomes diminished in the ratio of $18:11$. Hence the chance of either way in which he might lose is diminished in the same ratio. Therefore the chance of B winning is now

$$\tfrac{4}{11} \times \tfrac{11}{18}, \quad \text{or} \quad \tfrac{4}{18};$$

and of C winning

$$\tfrac{5}{11} \times \tfrac{11}{18}, \quad \text{or} \quad \tfrac{5}{18}.$$

These are therefore the required chances.

3. SUCCESSIVE UPDATING

In the usual applications of subjective probability, information builds up by successive conditioning. In Bayesian conditionalization the order in which new information is incorporated is irrelevant; in Jeffrey conditionalization the situation is more complex.

3.1 The problem

Consider an initial probability P that is Jeffrey-updated to the new probability $P_{\mathscr{E}}$ based on a partition $\mathscr{E} = \{E_i\}_{i=1}^e$ and new probabilities $P_{\mathscr{E}}(E_i) = p_i$, $i = 1, 2, \ldots, e$; clearly $P^*(A|E_i) = P_{\mathscr{E}}(A|E_i) = P(A|E_i)$ holds for our new opinion.

(P^* denotes our new opinion, however it is obtained: by Bayes's theorem, Jeffrey's rule, complete requantification, or whatever. P_δ denotes the specific updated probability measure that results from Jeffrey conditionalization. Here, by assumption, $P^* = P_\delta$. Suppose we then Jeffrey-update on $\mathscr{F} = \{F_j\}_{j=1}^f$ with new probabilities $\{q_j\}$, and indicate this order of updating by $P_{\delta\mathscr{F}}$. To use Jeffrey's rule at the second stage we must, of course, accept the (J) condition, so $P_\delta^*(A|F_j) = P_\delta(A|F_j) = P_{\delta\mathscr{F}}(A|F_j)$. Clearly, the order of updating matters, since the second opinion dominates.

Example 3.1. Suppose $\mathscr{E} = \mathscr{F}$, that is, our belief for each event E_i changes first to p_i and then to q_i. The first revision and second revision differ and we currently believe $P^*(E_i) = q_i$. If the opposite order of revision were employed, we would believe $P^*(E_i) = p_i$ after the second revision.

Example 3.2. Suppose that in a criminal case we are trying to decide which of four defendants, called a, b, c, d, is a thief. We initially think $P(a) = P(b) = P(c) = P(d) = \frac{1}{4}$. Evidence is then introduced to show that the thief was probably left-handed. The evidence does not demonstrate that the thief was definitely left-handed, but it leads us to conclude the P(thief left-handed) $\approx .8$. If a and b are the defendants who are left-handed, then $E_1 = \{a, b\}$, $E_2 = \{c, d\}$ and $P_\delta(E_1) = .8$, $P_\delta(E_2) = .2$. If the *only effect* of the evidence was to alter the probability of left-handedness – in the sense that $P(A|E_i) = P_\delta(A|E_i)$ – then P_δ is obtained from Jeffrey's rule as $P_\delta(a) = .4$, $P_\delta(b) = .4, P_\delta(c) = .1, P_\delta(d) = .1$. Evidence is next presented that it is somewhat likely that the thief was a woman. If the female defendants are a and c, then $F_1 = \{a, c\}$, $F_2 = \{b, d\}$. If $P_{\delta\mathscr{F}}(F_1) = .7$ and Jeffrey-updating is again judged acceptable, then

$$P_{EF}(a) = .56, \quad P_{\delta\mathscr{F}}(b) = .24,$$

$$P_{EF}(c) = .14, \quad P_{\delta\mathscr{F}}(d) = .06.$$

If instead the evidence $(F_1, .7)$, $(F_2, .3)$ is presented first and $(E_1, .8)$, $(E_2, .2)$ is presented second, is $P_{\mathscr{F}\delta}$ equal to $P_{\delta\mathscr{F}}$? Example 3.1 shows that in general the order matters since the currently held opinion governs; in this example the reader may check that the order does not matter. We now investigate why.

3.2 Commutativity

There are two aspects to successive updating: the updating information at each stage,

$$\{E_i, p_i\}_{i=1}^e, \quad \{F_j, q_j\}_{j=1}^f; \tag{3.1}$$

and (J) condition at each stage,

$$P^*(A|E_j) = P(A|E_i) \quad \text{and} \quad P_\delta^*(A|F_j) = P_\delta(A|F_j)$$

272

or, if updating is being considered in the other order,

$$P^*(A|F_j) = P(A|F_j) \quad \text{and} \quad P_{\mathscr{F}}^*(A|E_i) = P_{\mathscr{F}}(A|E_i). \tag{3.2}$$

The (J) condition is an internal or psychological condition that must be checked or accepted at each stage. Mathematics has nothing to offer here.

Mathematics *can* be used to check whether (3.1) is compatible with commutativity. Since Jeffrey updating fixes the probabilities on the partition (i.e., $P_{\mathscr{E}\mathscr{F}}(F_j) = q_j$ and $P_{\mathscr{F}\mathscr{E}}(E_i) = p_i$), commutativity will be possible only if

$$P_{\mathscr{E}\mathscr{F}}(E_i) = p_i \quad \text{and} \quad P_{\mathscr{F}\mathscr{E}}(F_j) = q_j, \tag{3.3}$$

for all i and j. It turns out that this condition is sufficient.

Theorem 3.1. If (3.3) holds, then $P_{\mathscr{E}\mathscr{F}} = P_{\mathscr{F}\mathscr{E}}$.

In other words, when $P_{\mathscr{F}\mathscr{E}}$ and $P_{\mathscr{E}\mathscr{F}}$ both incorporate (3.1), they actually coincide. Theorem 3.1 is an immediate consequence of Csiszár (1975, theorem 3.2) and its proof is omitted. Csiszár's theorem implies that the common measure $P_{\mathscr{E}\mathscr{F}} = P_{\mathscr{F}\mathscr{E}}$ is the *I projection* of the original measure P onto the set of measures that incorporate (3.1). We discuss I projection further in section 5.

3.3 Jeffrey independence

A second approach to the mathematical aspects of commutativity of successive Jeffrey updating uses independence. Two partitions $\mathscr{E} = \{E_i\}, \mathscr{F} = \{F_j\}$ such that $P(E_i) > 0$, $P(F_j) > 0$ for all i and j, are P *independent* if

$$P(E_i|F_j) = P(E_i) \quad \text{and} \quad P(F_j|E_i) = P(F_j) \tag{3.4}$$

for all i, j. Independence says that conditioning on $\mathscr{F}$ does not change the probabilities on $\mathscr{E}$ and vice versa. Analogously,

Definition: $\mathscr{E}$ and $\mathscr{F}$ *are Jeffrey independent* with respect to P, $\{p_i\}$ and $\{q_j\}$ if $P_{\mathscr{E}}(F_j) = P(F_j)$ and $P_{\mathscr{F}}(E_i) = P(E_i)$ holds for all i and j. (Briefly, "J independent with respect to $\{p_i\}$, $\{q_j\}$.") Thus Jeffrey independence says that Jeffrey updating on $\mathscr{E}$ with probabilities p_i does not change the probability on $\mathscr{F}$ and similarly with $\mathscr{E}$ and $\mathscr{F}$ interchanged. The next theorem shows the connection with commutativity.

Theorem 3.2. Let P, $\{E_i, p_i\}$ and $\{F_j, q_j\}$ be given. Then $P_{\mathscr{E}\mathscr{F}} = P_{\mathscr{F}\mathscr{E}}$ if and only if $\mathscr{E}$ and $\mathscr{F}$ are Jeffrey independent with respect to P, $\{p_i\}$, $\{q_j\}$.
Proof. Note that $P_{\mathscr{E}\mathscr{F}}(A) = P_{\mathscr{F}\mathscr{E}}(A)$ for all events A if and only if

$$\sum_{ij} \frac{p_i q_j}{P_{\mathscr{E}}(F_j)P(E_i)} P(AE_iF_j) = \sum_{ij} \frac{p_i q_j}{P_{\mathscr{F}}(E_i)P(F_j)} P(AE_iF_j). \tag{3.5}$$

Choose $A = E_{i_0}F_{j_0}$ to get

$$P_{\mathscr{E}}(F_j)P(E_{i_0}) = P_{\mathscr{F}}(E_{i_0})P(F_{j_0})$$

273

for all pairs i_0, j_0. Keeping i_0 fixed and summing over j_0 yields

$$P(E_{i_0}) = P_{\mathscr{F}}(E_{i_0}); \qquad (3.6a)$$

similarly, fixing j_0 and summing over i_0 yields

$$P_{\mathscr{E}}(F_{j_0}) = P(F_{j_0}). \qquad (3.6b)$$

Thus, $\mathscr{E}$ and $\mathscr{F}$ are Jeffrey independent with respect to P, $\{p_i\}$, $\{q_j\}$. Conversely, if (3.6) holds, then

$$P_{\mathscr{E}}(F_j)P(E_i) = P(F_j)P(E_i) = P_{\mathscr{F}}(E_i)P(F_j).$$

Using this equality shows that (3.5) holds and so $P_{\mathscr{E}\mathscr{F}} = P_{\mathscr{F}\mathscr{E}}$.

Theorem 3.3. Two partitions $\mathscr{E}$ and $\mathscr{F}$ are P independent if and only if $\mathscr{E}$ and $\mathscr{F}$ are Jeffrey independent with respect to *any* update probabilities $\{p_i\}$ and $\{q_j\}$.

Proof. First suppose $\mathscr{E}$ and $\mathscr{F}$ are P independent. Then

$$P_{\mathscr{E}}(F_j) = \sum_i P(F_j|E_i)p_i = \sum_i P(F_j)p_i = P(F_j). \qquad (3.7)$$

To see the converse, suppose $\mathscr{E}$ and $\mathscr{F}$ are not P independent. Then there exist E_{i_0} and F_{j_0} such that $P(F_{j_0}|E_{i_0}) \neq P(F_{j_0})$. Pick p_{i_0} sufficiently close to 1. Then

$$\sum_i P(F_{j_0}|E_i)p_i \neq P(F_{j_0}),$$

hence it follows from (3.7) that $P_{\mathscr{E}}(F_{j_0}) \neq P(F_{j_0})$.

Example 3.3. (J independence $\neq > P$ independence). Suppose $P(E_iF_j)$ is given by the following table

	F_1	F_2	F_3	
E_1	$\frac{1}{4}$	$\frac{1}{8}$	$\frac{1}{8}$	$\frac{1}{2}$
E_2	$\frac{1}{8}$	0	$\frac{1}{8}$	$\frac{1}{4}$
E_3	$\frac{1}{8}$	$\frac{1}{8}$	0	$\frac{1}{4}$
	$\frac{1}{2}$	$\frac{1}{4}$	$\frac{1}{4}$	

Then $\mathscr{E}$ and $\mathscr{F}$ are not P independent, but update probabilities $\mathbf{p}, \mathbf{q}$ exist such that $\mathscr{E}$ and $\mathscr{F}$ are J independent with respect to them (see what follows).

An efficient algorithm for checking J independence, in this and other examples, is the following. Let r_{ij} denote W. E. Johnson's *coefficient of dependence* between E_i and F_j (compare Keynes, 1921, pp. 150–155), that is,

$$r_{ij} = P(E_iF_j)/P(E_i)P(F_j);$$

since $\sum_i r_{ij}p_i = P_{\mathscr{E}}(F_j)/P(F_j)$ and $\sum_j r_{ij}q_j = P_{\mathscr{F}}(E_i)/P(E_i)$, it follows that $\mathscr{E}$ and $\mathscr{F}$ are J independent with respect to $\{p_i\}$, $\{q_j\}$ if and only if

$$\sum_i r_{ij}p_i = 1, \quad \text{all} \quad j; \sum_j r_{ij}q_j = 1, \quad \text{all} \quad i. \qquad (3.8)$$

Let $\mathbf{R} = (r_{ij})$. In Example 3.3

$$\mathbf{R} = \begin{pmatrix} 1 & 1 & 1 \\ 1 & 0 & 2 \\ 1 & 2 & 0 \end{pmatrix}$$

and hence, if

$$\mathbf{p} = \left(p, \frac{1-p}{2}, \frac{1-p}{2} \right), 0 < p < 1,$$

and

$$\mathbf{q} = \left(q, \frac{1-q}{2}, \frac{1-q}{2} \right), 0 < q < 1,$$

then $\mathbf{pR} = \mathbf{1}$, $\mathbf{Rq}^t = \mathbf{1}$; thus $\mathscr{E}$, $\mathscr{F}$ are J independent with respect to $\mathbf{p}$, $\mathbf{q}$.

Remark. It is not hard to show that if at least one of the two partitions $\mathscr{E}$ and $\mathscr{F}$ has only two elements, then J independence for *some* $\mathbf{p}$, $\mathbf{q}$ pair is equivalent to P independence, and hence to J independence for *all* $\mathbf{p}$, $\mathbf{q}$.

Lest the reader think that commutativity always occurs when (3.1) can be incorporated, we conclude this section with an example that has $P_{\mathscr{E}\mathscr{F}}(E_i) = p_i$ (and of course $P_{\mathscr{E}\mathscr{F}}(F_j) = q_j$), but such that $P_{\mathscr{F}\mathscr{E}}(F_j) \neq q_j$.

Example 3.4. Let $\mathscr{E} = \{E, \bar{E}\}$, $\mathscr{F} = \{F, \bar{F}\}$, and define P by

	F	$\bar{F}$	
E	$\frac{1}{8}$	$\frac{1}{4}$	$\frac{3}{8}$
$\bar{E}$	$\frac{3}{8}$	$\frac{1}{4}$	$\frac{5}{8}$
	$\frac{1}{2}$	$\frac{1}{2}$	

Suppose $p_1 = p_2 = \frac{1}{2}$ and $q_1 = \frac{7}{15}$, $q_2 = \frac{8}{15}$. Then a simple computation shows that $P_{\mathscr{E}\mathscr{F}}(E) = \frac{1}{2} = P_{\mathscr{E}\mathscr{F}}(\bar{E})$, but $P_{\mathscr{F}\mathscr{E}}(F) \neq q_1$.

4. COMBINING SEVERAL BODIES OF EVIDENCE

Suppose we undergo a complex of experiences that result in our simultaneously adopting new degrees of belief P^* on two partitions $\mathscr{E} = \{E_i\}$ and $\mathscr{F} = \{F_j\}$, say

$$P^*(E_i) = p_i \quad \text{and} \quad P^*(F_j) = q_j. \tag{4.1}$$

How should we revise our subjective probabilities so as to incorporate these new beliefs? In general, the theory put forth by de Finetti has no neat mathematical answer to this question – you just have to think about things and quantify your opinion as best you can. In this section we discuss two reasonable routes through this quantification procedure. The routes are reasonable in the same sense that exchangeability is a reasonable thing to consider when attempting to quantify probabilities on repeated events – the circumstances that make them subjectively acceptable occur frequently. We first discuss whether measures satisfying (4.1) exist and then if so, how to uniquely select one.

4.1 Coherence of P*

If we are to adopt the degrees of belief P^* in (4.1), they must at least be coherent; that is, P^* must be extendable to a probability measure (which we also denote by P^*). Theorem 4.1 provides a simple necessary and sufficient condition for the existence of such extensions.

Theorem 4.1. Let Ω be a countable set, $\mathscr{E} = \{E_i\}$ and $\mathscr{F} = \{F_j\}$ two partitions of Ω, and P, Q two probability measures on $\mathscr{E}$ and $\mathscr{F}$ respectively. There exists a probability measure P^* on Ω such that (4.1) holds if and only if, whenever disjoint sets A and B are given, with A a union of elements of $\mathscr{E}$, B a union of elements of $\mathscr{F}$,

$$P(A) + Q(B) \leqslant 1. \tag{4.2}$$

Proof. Consider the set $F = \cup\{E_i \times F_j : E_iF_j \neq \phi\}$. This is a closed set in the discrete space $\mathscr{E} \times \mathscr{F}$. Theorem 11 of Strassen (1965) gives a necessary and sufficient condition for the existence of a probability measure P^* on $\mathbf{F}$ with margins P and Q. Strassen's condition is easily seen to be equivalent to (4.2), and P^* may be regarded as the required measure on the partition $\{E_iF_j\}$; within a set of this partition P^* may be defined arbitrarily.

Remark. Condition (4.2) is necessary but not sufficient for theorem 4.1 to hold if Ω is uncountable. See Diaconis and Zabell (1978) and Shortt (1982) for counterexamples and discussion.

4.2 Extending P*

If (4.1) is coherent, it remains to
1. choose a probability P^* on the partition $\{E_iF_j\}$ that agrees wtih (4.1);
2. extend P^* to all of Ω.

If judged valid, the easiest way of accomplishing step 1 is to use *independence*: $P^*(E_iF_j) = P^*(E_i)P^*(F_j) = p_iq_j$; step 2 might then be achieved by Jeffrey updating on $\{E_iF_j\}$.

Richard Jeffrey (1957, ch. 4) has advocated another route from (4.1) to a final probability assignment: successive Jeffrey updating on $\mathscr{E}$ and $\mathscr{F}$. This raises two issues:
1. When does successive updating satisfy (4.1)?
2. When is successive updating reasonable?

Question 1 arises because $P_{\mathscr{E}\mathscr{F}}$ need not equal $P_{\mathscr{F}\mathscr{E}}$. Indeed, example 3.4 provides a situation where (4.1) is coherent (because $P_{\mathscr{E}\mathscr{F}}$ satisfies (4.1)), but

$P_{\mathscr{E}\mathscr{F}} \neq P_{\mathscr{F}\mathscr{E}}$ and $P_{\mathscr{F}\mathscr{E}}$ does not satisfy (4.1). Since matters are simplified when $P_{\mathscr{E}\mathscr{F}} = P_{\mathscr{F}\mathscr{E}}$, we note that the results of section 3 imply that the following three conditions are equivalent:

$$P_{\mathscr{E}\mathscr{F}}(A) = P_{\mathscr{F}\mathscr{E}}(A) \quad \text{for all sets} \quad A. \tag{4.3a}$$

$$P_{\mathscr{E}\mathscr{F}}(E_i) = P_{\mathscr{F}\mathscr{E}}(E_i) \quad \text{and} \quad P_{\mathscr{F}\mathscr{E}}(F_j) = P_{\mathscr{E}\mathscr{F}}(F_j) \quad \text{for all} \quad i \quad \text{and} \quad j. \tag{4.3b}$$

$$P_{\mathscr{F}}(E_i) = P(E_i) \quad \text{and} \quad P_{\mathscr{E}}(F_j) = P(F_j) \quad \text{for all} \quad i \quad \text{and} \quad j. \tag{4.3c}$$

Even when the order does not matter, we still have the responsibility of justifying the resort to successive updating, that is, question 2. One approach to this is via checking the Jeffrey condition at each stage of updating. This is a somewhat unorthodox mental exercise, given that we currently believe (4.1), a condition involving both partitions. If we update first on $\mathscr{E}$, then we must check $P(A|E_i) = P^*(A|E_i)$, which amounts to thinking as if we do not know about $\mathscr{F}$ and are only thinking about $\mathscr{E}$. At the second stage, one then checks $P_{\mathscr{E}}(A|F_j) = P_{\mathscr{E}}^*(A|F_j)$, comparing one's opinion not knowing $\mathscr{F}$ to one's opinion knowing $\mathscr{F}$. Examples such as example 3.4 show that this can be tricky. It is a possible route, however, one more general than the route using independence suggested before.

Remark 1. There is no reason to require $P_{\mathscr{E}\mathscr{F}} = P_{\mathscr{F}\mathscr{E}}$ for successive updating to be useful and valid. If each of the (J) conditions is judged valid in forming $P_{\mathscr{E}\mathscr{F}}$ and if $P_{\mathscr{E}\mathscr{F}}$ satisfies (4.1), then $P_{\mathscr{E}\mathscr{F}}$ is a consistent quantification of current belief.

Remark 2. Condition (4.3) implies that $P_{\mathscr{E}\mathscr{F}}$ and $P_{\mathscr{F}\mathscr{E}}$ cannot both incorporate (4.1) and both be judged acceptable updates (in the sense that the (J) conditions have been checked) without $P_{\mathscr{E}\mathscr{F}} = P_{\mathscr{F}\mathscr{E}}$. This noncommutativity is not a real problem for successive Jeffrey updating.

Remark 3. The approach outlined in this section is an approach to the combination of evidence within the Bayesian framework. See Shafer (1976) for a related, nonadditive approach.

5. MECHANICAL UPDATING

The approach we have taken thus far to justifying Jeffrey's rule is subjective – through checking condition (J). Several authors – Griffeath and Snell (1974), May and Harper (1976), Williams (1980), and van Fraassen (1980) – have pursued a different justification. Given a prior P, partition $\{E_i\}$, and a new measure P^* on $\{E_i\}$, find the "closest" measure to P that agrees with P^* on the partition and take this as defining P^* on the whole space. Since this way of proceeding does not attempt to quantify one's new degrees of belief via introspection, we call this approach *mechanical updating*.

277

5.1 Minimum distance properties

If "close" is defined in any of several common ways, the closest measure is that given by Jeffrey's rule. We illustrate this with three common notions of closeness between measures P and Q on the countable set Ω: (1) The variation distance

$$\|P - Q\| = \sup\{|P(B) - Q(B)| : B \subset \Omega\}$$

$$= \frac{1}{2} \sum_{\omega} |P(\omega) - Q(\omega)|. \tag{5.1}$$

Two measures are close in variation distance if they are uniformly close on all subsets. (2) The Hellinger distance

$$H(P, Q) = \sum_{\omega} (\sqrt{P(\omega)} - \sqrt{Q(\omega)})^2. \tag{5.2}$$

(3) The Kullback–Leibler number of Q with respect to P

$$I(Q, P) = \sum_{\omega} Q(\omega) \log (Q(\omega)/P(\omega)). \tag{5.3}$$

The variation and Hellinger distances are actual metrics on the space of probability distributions, the Kullback–Leibler number is not, being asymmetric in its arguments. Kailath (1967) and Csiszár (1977) are good surveys, with bibliographies, of the properties of (5.1), (5.2), and (5.3).

Theorem 5.1. Let Ω be a countable set, P a probability on Ω, and $\{E_i\}$ a partition of Ω. Suppose $P^*(E_i) \geq 0$ are given numbers such that $\sum P^*(E_i) = 1$. Let Q be a probability on Ω such that $Q(E_i) = = P^*(E_i)$. Then

$$\|Q - P\| \geq \sum |P(E_i) - P^*(E_i)|, \tag{5.4}$$

$$H(Q, P) \geq \sum (\sqrt{P(E_i)} - \sqrt{P^*(E_i)})^2, \tag{5.5}$$

$$I(Q, P) \geq \sum P^*(E_i) \log (P^*(E_i)/P(E_i)). \tag{5.6}$$

In (5.5) and (5.6) equality holds if and only if $Q(A) = \sum P(A|E_i)P^*(E_i)$.

Remarks. (a) Although the probability measure given by Jeffrey's rule minimizes the variation distance, it does not do so uniquely; see May (1976). (b) In Theorem 5.1, the minimum distance between P and Q is the distance between P and Q viewed as measures on the partition $\{E_i\}$. (c) A result like Theorem 5.1 holds for several other notions of distance; see section 6, where a generalization of theorem 5.1 is given (theorem 6.1).

5.2 I projections and the IPFP

Mechanical updating allows the possibility of updating on collections of sets more general than partitions. Suppose we want to adopt new degrees of belief

$P^*(E_i) = p_i$, $1 \leqslant i \leqslant n$, where $\mathscr{E} = \{E_1, E_2, \ldots, E_n\}$ is not necessarily a partition of Ω. This situation is closely related to Jeffrey's proposal of updating simultaneously on several partitions, mentioned in section 4, inasmuch as updating simultaneously on partitions $\mathscr{E}_1, \mathscr{E}_2, \ldots, \mathscr{E}_k$ is the same as updating on $\mathscr{E} = \bigcup_{i=1}^{k} \mathscr{E}_i$. Conversely, updating on $\mathscr{E} = \{E_1, \ldots, E_n\}$ can be viewed as updating simultaneously on the partitions $\mathscr{E}_1 = \{E_1, E_1{}^c\}$, $\mathscr{E}_2 = \{E_2, E_2{}^c\}, \ldots$, $\mathscr{E}_n = \{E_n, E_n{}^c\}$. In general, the set $C = \{Q : Q(E_i) = p_i$ for all $i\}$ is a convex set of probability measures on Ω that can be empty, contain a single element, or contain many elements. In the first case P^* is incoherent, in the second P^* is uniquely determined. When the third case holds, we can use the Kullback–Leibler number as a notion of "distance" to pick a unique member of C closest to P.

Theorem 5.2. Let $S(P, \infty) = \{Q : I(Q, P) < \infty\}$. If $S(P, \infty) \cap C \neq \phi$, then there exists a unique element $Q_J \in C$ such that $I(Q_J, P) = \inf\{I(Q, P) : Q \in C\}$.

Proof. This is an immediate consequence of Csiszár (1975, theorem 2.1), C being convex and closed with respect to the variation distance.

In Csiszár's terminology, Q_J is the *I projection of P onto C*. (The term is meant to suggest the projection of a vector in $\mathbf{R}^n$ onto a subspace.) The I projection is closely related to a technique widely used in the statistical analysis of contingency tables.

A standard method of adjusting an $r \times c$ contingency table so that it has the desired marginal totals is the iterated proportional fitting procedure (IPFP). In this, one first adjusts the table to have specified row sums, say (by dividing the numbers of a given row by the appropriate factor), next adjusts the new table to have the correct column sums, and then continues iteratively. It follows from Csiszár (1975, theorem 3.2) that this procedure converges to the I projection of the initial table onto the set of tables with the specified row and column sums (provided, of course, this set is nonempty). That is, the IPFP finds the "closest" table to the original table with the prescribed margins. This is essentially the same as finding the closest measure to an initial probability with prescribed values on two partitions.

The IPFP can be used to compute Q_J of theorem 5.2 by treating the problem as an n-dimensional contingency table with given margins $P^*(E_i)$, $1 - P^*(E_1), \ldots$.

5.3 Comparing different metrics

Theorem 5.1 suggests that Jeffrey's rule is an uncontroversial form of mechanical updating in the sense that it agrees with virtually every minimum-distance rule. As noted earlier, in the case of two or more partitions, the I projection or maximum-entropy solution can be viewed as a limiting form of successive Jeffrey updating. This is perhaps of some interest inasmuch as mechanical updating via the other minimum-distance methods need not, in general, yield the same answer as the I projection.

Example 5.1. (*I* projection $\neq$ minimum variation distance.) Consider passing from an initial table

$$\mathbf{P}^0 = \begin{array}{|c|c|} \hline \frac{1}{4} & \frac{1}{4} \\ \hline \frac{1}{4} & \frac{1}{4} \\ \hline \end{array} \quad \text{to} \quad \mathbf{P} = \begin{array}{c} \begin{array}{cc} \frac{1}{3} & \frac{2}{3} \end{array} \\ \begin{array}{c} \frac{1}{3} \\ \frac{2}{3} \end{array} \begin{array}{|c|c|} \hline p_1 & p_2 \\ \hline p_3 & p_4 \\ \hline \end{array} \end{array},$$

a new table with the specified margins, which is otherwise as "close" to the original table as possible, according to some notion of closeness.

1. The independent table $\mathbf{P}^I$ given by $p_1 = \frac{1}{9}$, $p_3 = p_3 = \frac{2}{9}$, $p_4 = \frac{4}{9}$ minimizes $I(\mathbf{P}, \mathbf{P}^0)$, since $\mathbf{P}^0$ is independent and I projections preserve the association factor of a 2×2 table (see, e.g., Mosteller, 1968, p. 3). The variation distance for this table is

$$\|\mathbf{P}^I - \mathbf{P}^0\| = \frac{1}{2} \sum_{i=1}^{4} |p_i - \frac{1}{4}|$$

$$= \frac{1}{2}|\frac{1}{9} - \frac{1}{4}| + |\frac{2}{9} - \frac{1}{4}| + \frac{1}{2}|\frac{4}{9} - \frac{1}{4}|$$

$$= \frac{7}{36}.$$

2. To find the table $\mathbf{P}^V$ with minimum variation distance from $\mathbf{P}^0$, subject to the margin constraints, note that, given p_1, one has $p_2 = p_3 = \frac{1}{3} - p_1$ and $p_4 = p_1 + \frac{1}{3}$. Hence

$$\|\mathbf{P} - \mathbf{P}^0\| = \frac{1}{2} \sum |p_i - \frac{1}{4}|$$

$$= \frac{1}{2}\{|\frac{1}{4} - p_1| + 2|\frac{1}{12} - p_1| + |-\frac{1}{12} - p_1|\}$$

which is minimized by $p_1 = \frac{1}{12}$, the median of $\{-\frac{1}{12}, \frac{1}{12}, \frac{1}{12}, \frac{1}{4}\}$. Hence $\mathbf{P}^V = (\frac{1}{12}, \frac{1}{4}, \frac{1}{4}, \frac{5}{12})$ and $\|\mathbf{P}^V - \mathbf{P}^0\| = \frac{1}{6}$.

There has been considerable interest recently in maximum entropy methods, especially in the philosophical literature (Rosenkrantz, 1977; Williams, 1980; van Fraassen, 1980). Example 5.1 suggests that any claims to the effect that maximum-entropy revision is the only correct route to probability revision should be viewed with considerable caution because of its strong dependence on the measure of closeness being used.

6. ABSTRACT PROBABILITY KINEMATICS

In this section we briefly discuss the generalization of Jeffrey's rule of conditioning from the countable setting to general spaces.

Consider a probability space $(\Omega, \mathscr{A}, P)$, thought of as describing our current subjective beliefs about the σ algebra of events $\mathscr{A}$. Let P^* be a new probability measure on $\mathscr{A}$ and $\mathscr{A}_0 \subseteq \mathscr{A}$ a sub-σ-algebra of $\mathscr{A}$. Let C be an $\mathscr{A}_0$-measurable set such that $P(C) = 0$ and $\bar{P} \ll \bar{P}^*$ on $\Omega - C$, where $\bar{P}, \bar{P}^*$ are the restrictions of P, P^* to $\mathcal{A}_0$. The appropriate version of Jeffrey's condition (J) is

$$\mathcal{A}_0 \quad \text{is sufficient for} \quad \{P, P^*\}. \tag{J'}$$

When condition (J') holds, Jeffrey's rule of conditioning becomes:

$$P^*(A) = \int_{\Omega - C} P(A|\mathcal{A}_0)P^*(d\omega) + P^*(A \cap C), \tag{6.1}$$

where $P(A|\mathcal{A}_0)$ is the conditional probability of A given $\mathcal{A}_0$. If $P^* \ll P$, we can take $C = \phi$.

Much of the mathematical machinery for dealing with Jeffrey conditionalization in this generality has been developed (for a different purpose) by Csiszár (1967). His Lemma 2.2 translates into a likelihood-ratio version of Jeffrey's rule (compare (2.2)): Let λ be a σ-finite measure that dominates P, P^*. Let $\bar{\lambda}, \bar{P}, \bar{P}^*$ be the restrictions to $\mathcal{A}_0$. Assume $\bar{\lambda}$ is σ finite. Let $\bar{p}(x), \bar{p}^*(x)$ be the densities of P, P^* with respect to $\bar{\lambda}$, and p^* the density of P^* with respect to λ. If condition (J') holds, then

$$p^*(x) = \bar{p}^*(x)/\bar{p}(x) \quad \text{if} \quad \bar{p}(x' = 0$$

$$= p^*(x) \qquad \text{if} \quad \bar{p}(x) = 0. \tag{6.2}$$

Identity (6.2) is a version of the Fisher–Neyman factorization theorem (see Halmos and Savage, 1949).

Csiszár's results allow us to give a single theorem that includes theorem 5.1, showing that the closest measure to P that agrees with P^* on $\mathcal{A}_0$ is the measure given by (6.1). Csiszár introduced the notion of f divergence, where f is a convex function defined on the interval $(0, \infty)$. If μ_1 and μ_2 are two measures on $(\Omega, \mathcal{A})$, the f divergence of μ_1 and μ_2 is

$$I_f(\mu_1, \mu_2) = \int p_2(x)f\left(\frac{p_1(x)}{p_2(x)}\right)\lambda(dx),$$

where $\mu_i \ll \lambda$ and $p_i = d\mu_i/d\lambda$, $i = 1, 2$. Taking $f(u) = u \log u$ gives the Kullback–Leibler number, $f(u) = (u^{1/2} - 1)^2$ the Hellinger distance, $f(u) = |u - 1|/2$ the variation distance. Csiszár shows that several other notions of distance are also f divergences for an appropriate f.

Theorem 6.1. Let C be the set of probability measures on $(\Omega, \mathcal{A})$ that agree with P^* on $\mathcal{A}_0$, and let f be a convex function on $(0, \infty)$. Then under condition (J')

$$I_f(P^*, P) = I_f(\bar{P}^*, \bar{P}) = \inf\{I_f(Q, P): Q \in C\}. \tag{6.3}$$

If f is strictly convex, then P^* is the unique probability measure on $\mathcal{A}$ that minimizes the right side of (6.3).

Proof. The first equality follows from the sufficiency of $\mathcal{A}_0$ for $\{P, P^*\}$, the second from Csiszár's (1967, sec. 3) version of the minimum information discrimination theorem of Kullback and Leibler: $I_f(Q, P) \geqslant I_f(\bar{Q}, \bar{P})$. Since $I_f(\bar{Q}, \bar{P}) = I_f(\bar{P}^*, \bar{P})$, (6.3) follows. If f is strictly convex, then $I_f(\cdot, P)$ is also, and the theorem follows.

NOTE

The authors are grateful to I. J. Good, Richard C. Jeffrey, David Freedman, Paul Meier, Jim Pitman, Sherry May, and Amos Tversky for helpful comments and suggestions. First published in the *Journal of the American Statistical Association*, 77 (1982), 822–30.

REFERENCES

Armendt, B. (1980), "Is there a Dutch book argument for probability kinematics?" *Philosophy of Science* 47, 583–8.

Blackwell, D., and Girschick, M. A. (1954), *Theory of Games and Statistical Decisions*, New York: John Wiley.

Boole, G. (1854), *An Investigation of the Laws of Thought on Which Are Founded the Mathematical Theories of Logic and Probabilities*, London: Macmillan.

Csiszár, I. (1967), "Information type measures of difference of probability distributions and indirect observations," *Studia Scientiarum Mathematicarum Hungarica*, 2, 299–318.

(1975), "I-divergence geometry of probability distributions of minimization problems," *Annals of Probability*, 3, 146–58.

(1977), "Information measures: a critical survey," *Transaction of the Seventh Prague Conference*, (Prague, 1974), Prague: Academia, 73–86.

De Finetti, B. (1972), *Probability, Induction and Statistics*, New York: John Wiley.

(1975), *Theory of Probability* (vol. 2), New York: John Wiley.

Diaconis, P., and Zabell, S. (1978), "Updating subjective probability," Technical Report No. 136, Stanford University, Dept. of Statistics.

Donkin, W. F. (1851), "On certain questions relating to the theory of probabilities," *The Philosophical Magazine*, Ser. 4, 1, 353–68.

Field, H. (1978), "A note on Jeffrey conditionalization," *Philosophy of Science*, 45, 361–7.

Fischoff, B. (1975), "Hindsight ≠ foresight: the effect of outcome knowledge on judgement under uncertainty," *Journal of Experimental Psychology: Human Perception and Performance*, 1, 288–99.

Fischhoff, B., and Beyth, R. (1975), "I knew it would happen – remembered probabilities of once future things," *Organizational Behavior and Human Performance*, 13, 1–16.

Freedman, D., and Purves, R. (1969), "Bayes method for bookies," *Annals of Mathematical Statistics*, 40, 1177–86.

Garber, D. (1980), "Discussion: Field and Jeffrey conditionalization," *Philosophy of Science*, 47, 142–5.

Good, I. J. (1950), *Probability and the Weighting of Evidence*, New York: Hafner.

(1968), "Corroboration, explanation, evolving probability, simplicity, and a sharpened razor," *British Journal for the Philosophy of Science*, 19, 123–43.

(1977), "Dynamic probability, computer chess, and the measurement of knowledge," in *Machine Intelligence 8*, ed. E. W. Elcock and D. Mitchie, New York: Ellis Horwood Ltd. and John Wylie, 139–50.

Griffeath, D., and Snell, L. J. (1974), "Optimal stopping in the stock market," *Annals of Probability*, 2, 1–13.

Hacking, I. (1967), "Slightly more realistic personal probability," *Philosophy of Science*, 34, 311–25.

Halmos, P., and Savage, L. J. (1949), "Application of the Randon–Nikodym theorem to the theory of sufficient statistics," *Annals of Mathematical Statistics*, 20, 225–41.

Jeffrey, R. (1957), "Contributions to the theory of inductive probability," Ph.D. thesis, Princeton University, Dept. of Philosophy.

(1965), *The Logic of Decision*, New York: McGraw-Hill.

(1968), "Probable knowledge," in *The Problem of Inductive Logic*, ed. I. Lakatos, 166–80, Amsterdam: North-Holland.

(1970), "Dracula meets wolfman: acceptance vs. partial belief," *Induction, Acceptance, and Rational Belief*, ed. M. Swain, 157–85, Dordrecht: D. Reidel.

Kailath, T. (1967), "The divergence and Bhattacharya distance measures in signal detection," *IEEE Transactions on Communications Technology*, 15, 52–60.

Keynes, J. M. (1921), *A Treatise on Probability*, London: Macmillan.

Levi, I. (1967), "Probability kinematics," *Philosophy of Science*, 18, 197–209.

(1970), "Probability and evidence," in *Induction, Acceptance, and Rational Belief*, ed. M. Swain, 134–56, Dordrecht: D. Reidel.

May, S. (1976), "Probability kinematics: a constrained optimization problem," *Journal of Philosophical Logic*, 5, 395–8.

May, S., and Harper, W. (1976), "Toward an optimization procedure for applying minimum change principles in probability kinematics," in *Foundations of Probability Theory, Statistical Inference, and Statistical Theories of Science* (vol. 1), eds. W. L. Harper and C. A. Hooker, 137–66, Dordrecht: D. Reidel.

Mosteller, F. (1968), "Association and estimation in contingency tables," *Journal of the American Statistical Association*, 63, 1–28.

Ramsey, F. P. (1931), "Truth and probability," in *The Foundations of Mathematics and Other Logical Essays*, ed. R. G. Braithwaite, 156–198, London: Routledge and Kegan Paul: reprinted (1964) in *Studies in Subjective Probability*, eds. H. E. Kyburg, Jr., and H. E. Smokler, 61–92, New York: John Wiley.

Rosenkrantz, R. D. (1977), *Inference, Method, and Decision*, Dordrecht: D. Reidel.

Shafer, G. (1976), *A Mathematical Theory of Evidence*, Princeton University Press.

(1979), "Two theories of probability," in *PSA 1978*, vol. 2, East Lansing, Michigan: Philosophy of Science Association.

(1981), "Jeffrey's rule of conditioning," *Philosophy of Science*, 48, 337–62.

Shortt, R. (1982), "Distributions with given margins," Ph.D. dissertation, Massachusetts Institute of Technology, Dept. of Mathematics.

Slovic, P., and Fischoff, B. (1977), "On the psychology of experimental surprises," *Journal of Experimental Psychology: Human Perception and Performance*, 3, 544–51.

Strassen, V. (1965), "The existence of probability measures with given marginals," *Annals of Mathematical Statistics*, 36, 423–39.

Teller, P. (1976), "Conditionalization, observation, and change of preference," in *Foundations of Probability Theory, Statistical Inference, and Statistical Theories of Science* (vol. 1), eds. W. L. Harper and C. A. Hooker, 205–53, Dordrecht: D. Reidel.

van Fraassen, Bas. C. (1980), "Rational belief and probability kinematics," *Philosophy of Science* 47, 165–87.

Whitworth, W. A. (1901), *Choice and Chance* (5th ed.), Cambridge: Deighton Bell.

Williams, P. M. (1980), "Bayesian conditionalization and the principle of minimum informatiom," *British Journal for the Philosophy of Science*, 31, 131–44.

13

PROBABILITY, EVIDENCE, AND JUDGMENT

A. P. DEMPSTER

INTRODUCTION

The technical feasibility of Bayesian statistics is rapidly improving as research and development activity exploits opportunities created by the computing revolution. This chapter offers an analysis and critique of Bayesian statistics, not from an internal aspect of flourishing technical development, but rather from an external aspect of the real world analyses and problem-solving tasks which the technology is designed to aid. I wish to raise for discussion the question: are the current norms and prescriptions of Bayesian statistics adequate to the tasks?

From an external standpoint, the central function of Bayesian statistics is the provision of probabilities to quantify prospective uncertainties given a current state of knowledge. The uncertainties refer to questions of fact about natural and social phenomena and about the effect of human decisions on these phenomena. The external motivation can be purely scientific, but in statistical practice there are usually decision- or policy-analytic components.

How broadly should Bayesian statistics be defined? I believe that the statistics profession has been hindered by the orthodoxy of academic mathematical statistics over the past 50 years which has largely removed evaluation of prospective uncertainties from the domain of statistical science. Thus, although statistics is the dominant source of useful probabilistic technologies, statisticians are often perceived as narrowly focused, and new professions such as 'decision analysis" or "risk analysis" are created to fill the void. The Bayesian movement should avoid a similar trap. Bayesian statistics should therefore experiment with a variety of paradigms. In particular, I hope that Bayesian statistics can assimilate extended technologies such as the diagnosis/robustness methods of Box (1980) and the belief function techniques of Shafer (1976, 1981, 1982, 1983). The ultimate standard should be professional consensus based on *post hoc* assessments of effectiveness for problem-solving.

A recurrent theme in the field of probability assessment is the question of balance between judgment and evidence. *Evidence* means knowledge either in the form of specific facts (e.g., statistical data) or arguments from theories or hypotheses which represent and structure broad areas of generally accepted facts. *Judgment* consists of commitments of belief in the relevance of evidence to the problem at hand. One caricature of Bayesian statistics maintains that the likelihood function of the data is based on objective evidence while the prior distribution requires only judgment. In fact, both evidence and judgment are involved in both parts of the formal structure, as they are in every probability assessment. Likelihood functions often rest on frequency-based sampling models, or similar applied probabilistic chance models, but the end use of Bayesian inference depends critically on *judgments*, first of the quality of the past evidence supporting parametric model assumptions, and second of the relevance of assumed exchangeability among sampled and unsampled units for elementary events. Likewise, perceptive consumers of Bayesian statistics always evaluate the evidential bases of prior distributions as well as the judgmental bases, and one can scarcely doubt that the practical impact of a formal Bayesian analysis is and should be sensitive to the consumer's assessment of quality of *evidence* underlying the prior distribution.

My purpose is to explore various themes related to *probability, evidence*, and *judgment* from the standpoint of professional practice and problem-solving. If Bayesian statistics can dispassionately recognize its weaknesses as well as its strengths, then perhaps it can grow and assimilate related technologies. These technologies may not conform strictly to the normative axioms of SEU (subjective expected utility) but they may be friendly amendments in the sense of addressing a common goal of improved assessment of uncertainty.

THE CONSTRUCTIVE/PRESCRIPTIVE ATTITUDE

Two important innovators have been stressing a similar fundamental attitude to the wide sense Bayesian enterprise.

Glenn Shafer's original writing on belief functions stressed that probability requires evidence (Shafer, 1976), but more recently he has been emphasizing, in Shafer (1981, 1982, 1983), that probabilities are *constructed* from evidence. Now Shafer and Tversky (1983) refer to an active thought experiment which explicitly compares the current evidence with a scale of canonical examples. Shafer (1982) differentiates constructive probability from the frequentist, necessary, or personalist types described by Savage (1954), since these familiar types appear to assume that probabilities exist before they are constructed. Similarly, he queries the content of elicitation methods of obtaining personal probabilities:

> What meaning and what persuasiveness do the answers have once it is admitted that there really are no predetermined probabilities in the back of our minds?
> (Shafer, 1983)

Howard Raiffa has been developing a similar theme, proposing that we need a concept of *prescriptive* approaches to decision analysis to put alongside the more

285

widely recognized normative and descriptive approaches. It is important to pay attention to how people actually think and behave in the real world (descriptive analysis), and it is important to propose and argue for specific general rules which formal assessments ought to obey (normative analysis), but there is much in the way professionals actually implement formal analyses (prescriptive analysis) which is not captured by the terms descriptive and normative, as these terms are currently used. In remarks prepared to open the 1983 decision making conference he and his colleagues wrote:

> In limited domains the SEU model may be used as a prescriptive tool in order to guide behavior, but this conscious effort involves a reflective thought process that is far more complex than the bare bones of the SEU model seems to indicate. Real people, in real situations, don't naturally act coherently, and one usually cannot discover via revealed behavior their latent probability distributions and utility functions. Rather, the way the SEU model is put to prescriptive use turns the model upside down. We don't start by assuming that the decision maker can, in an unaided fashion, compare any two alternatives but rather we test whether he can compare a few simple hypothetical consequences. Already in this limited domain he might exhibit intransitivities among the few consequences that he is willing initially to compare, but he then must be willing to reflect upon these inconsistencies and modify his preferences so that they line up transitively. In an iterative fashion he must be willing, in a particular instance, to act quite unnaturally: to deliberately police his choices of hypothetical simple situations, one by one, in order to conform to the desideratum of consistency. Gradually, if he is successful, a probability distribution over states and a utility function over consequences will emerge. These will literally have to be constructed bit by bit, and it is pure myth that latently these probabilities and utilities existed deep down and that the analyst merely has to cut away the fat in order to display the pre-existing structure. Next a leap of faith is required: the decision maker must be willing to use his probability and utility functions that he has laboriously constructed to calculate SEUs that will guide his selection of real-world alternatives.

(Bell, Raiffa, and Tversky, in this volume)

In correspondence quoted by Raiffa, Shafer pointed out that philosophers have often used the terms normative and prescriptive interchangeably, so that prescriptive may have too much the connotation of what one ought to do on high authority with "no alternative to be considered," but Shafer did write that prescriptive suggests actively helping real people, as when a doctor prescribes. Raiffa agreed that "constructive captures an essence of what we mean by prescriptive" but worried that constructive "may seem to some to be too systematic, too linear in conception, too structured." Raiffa indicated that no uniqueness conception is implied by prescriptive. Some may wish to approach construction "holistically (with perhaps a checklist of concerns)" while others may wish "to think in a decompose–recompose manner using the SEU framework." And, "there is a whole myriad of other frameworks."

With this legislative history in place, I believe that we have witnessed the emergence of a useful technical concept which can be labeled interchangeably by the terms constructive or prescriptive. The following remarks are intended to support this emergence and to suggest additional attitudes which may help to round out the concept.

I perceive a very basic distinction between constructive or prescriptive analysis and current approaches to descriptive studies of actual human probabilistic reasoning or decision making. The implicit assumption of the latter is that the formal structures of prescriptive analysis are somehow embedded in the human psyche. It is as though one attempted to observe and understand the activity of a human cycling along a road, while regarding the bicycle simply as part of the human being, instead of viewing the bicycle as a deliberately constructed tool designed for a purpose. A formal probability or decision model, like a bicycle, exists abstractly apart from any user. Such tools evolve in large and small ways. Their intended purposes and modes of use must be learned. And the learning process results in many types and degrees of skill among users. Descriptive analyses which ignore and hence aggregate over technological complements of human behavior may confuse and miss essential aspects of probability assessments.

An important task is to describe and systematize the procedures which probability assessors or decision analysts use in prescriptive practice to match the analogs of bicycles to real needs. In the long paragraph quoted above, Raiffa refers to an iterative process whereby a decision analyst might approach a self-consistent SEU model, but Raiffa makes no explicit reference to how evidence or judgment enter the process. As noted above, Shafer (1981, 1982, 1983) and Shafer and Tversky (1983) emphasize judgmental comparison of evidence with a scale of canonical examples in a consciously designed thought experiment. In thinking about probability, I see a critical distinction between the *meaning* of a numerical probability, and the *source* of a numerical probability, and I see the catalog of canonical examples as primarily an aid to communicating *meaning* – because many more of us are comfortable with odds quoted in familiar games of chance than we are with odds quoted in less controlled circumstances. The idea of a designed thought experiment is an attractive way to label the source mechanism, but still the set of hooks from human judgmental capabilities to external evidence is left undefined and unanalyzed. I believe that major opportunities exist for clarification and progress here, inviting both proposals for how one ought to relate evidence to uncertainty judgments, and examples and characterizations of how well-reputed and highly trained professionals actually do it. In effect, normative and descriptive attitudes need to be directed at the constructive/prescriptive problem.

Raiffa's distinction between normative and prescriptive was neatly captured by Jevons (1877), specifically in relation to the theory of probability:

> Nothing is more requisite than to distinguish carefully between the truth of a theory and the truthful application of the theory to actual circumstances.

It appears to me that the twentieth century emphasis on axioms governing uncertainty and choice have left the normative theory pretty much in the form it had 100 years ago. Even the recent Dempster–Shafer extension to belief functions has roots 200 to 300 years ago in the work of Bernoulli and Lambert (Shafer, 1978). Such early giants of probability theory made their major gains while operating in a prescriptive mode on problems of physical and social anaysis. We should follow that lead.

WHO IS THE MODELER/ANALYST/DECISION MAKER?

The standard normative Bayesian theory postulates a single actor who is assumed to possess a well-defined formalization of the factual structure of observables, choices, and outcomes, of probabilistic uncertainty, and of numerical utilities. The idealized person was called 'you' by Good (1950), suggesting that the reader is being instructed on how to carry out his or her own analysis. Constructive/prescriptive analysis by professionals should, however, reflect the fact that in most situations several or many actors are involved. If the standard theory is to be applied, then the real world identification of the actor needs to be explained and justified. Alternatively, and perhaps preferably, the theory should be broadened to define roles for several actors.

Sometimes the actors may be individuals, or social groups represented by institutions whose utilities range from partially congruent to directly opposed. This line of thought leads to consideration of multiattribute utilities or to game theory. My concern is more with probability assessment, and with the situation of a Bayesian statistician functioning along with substantive experts in the service of a client whose goals are accepted as well-defined and legitimate.

One simple scenario involves only the statistician and client. Much of the bias of professional statisticians against Bayesian statistics stems from the belief that statisticians should not invoke technology whose evidential basis is missing or too soft to be communicated to the client. I agree with the bias, but not with the solution of replacing Bayesian analysis by something entirely different which succeeds only in hiding the problem. A preferable solution is to work to bring out and harden the evidentiary and judgmental bases of prior distributions and likelihoods, in a form which can be successfully communicated to the client. An alternative is to back off to a theory such as belief function theory which is weaker in the sense of making fewer demands for evidence and correspondingly providing more limited assessments of uncertainty. I suspect that both strategies have their place, depending on the problem.

The following anecdote illustrates my point that the client–consultant relationship may require Bayesians to pay more attention to the evidentiary basis of probability assessments. About a year ago I wrote to a set of colleagues asking them to rank a list of potential candidates for a position. Most responses included evidence in the form of thumbnail sketches of strengths and weaknesses. One prominent Bayesian gave a ranking, and even a numerical score to each candidate. But the evidence was missing, except in the case of one candidate unknown to the reviewer, who was given a score of 4 out of 10 with the explanation that in the reviewer's judgment we would not have put a less qualified candidate on our list while the reviewer would surely have been familiar with a more qualified candidate. I felt cheated, but it was my own fault for not specifically requesting the evidence. We all need to acquire the habit. Then the need for serious study of the mental processes relating evidence to probability will appear both natural and obvious.

A second scenario involves not only the client and statistician, but also multiple experts. For example, on a medical question there may be evidence from epidemiological studies, from population surveys, from animal studies, from clinical trials, and from clinical practice. What technologies, if any, should be invoked to combine different sources of evidence?

In principle, it is more desirable to pool the evidence and construct one probability assessment than it is to construct separate assessments and then combine, because the joint modeling effort almost certainly requires difficult judgments of independence or partial dependence which only make sense at the disaggregated level of empirical evidence. Indeed, the major challenge may be to construct a small world of factual knowledge which incorporates all the formal evidence. Log linear models should prove useful tools here, due to their flexible range of dependence parameters.

In a different direction, it should be mentioned that a central feature of belief function theory is a means for combining multiple sources of information which are judged independent. Extensions to partial dependence models are needed.

Whatever the normative limitations adopted, and whatever the range of models contemplated, Bayesian statistics needs formal prescriptive devices for combining multiple sources of evidence.

HARD AND SOFT PROBABILITIES

Consumers of probability assessments are familiar with the notion that some numerical probabilities are harder, or more certain, and others are softer, or more uncertain. This hard–soft dimension is rather vague, in the sense that no well-established single technology for quantification exists. The standard normative Bayesian theory recognizes only probability, not shades of probability, but there is a back-door prescriptive approach through sensitivity analysis which varies the formal assumptions and examines the corresponding variation of the resulting probability assessments. Extensions of Bayesian theory, such as belief function theory, or other theories of upper and lower probability, have an explicit technical mechanism for representing the hard–soft dimension, but these tools have not been widely tested in practice.

The canonical example of a hard probability is one derived from *evidence*, consisting of a relative frequency with a large denominator, and *judgment*, to the effect that the specific prospective application is not recognizable as selected on the basis of an observable characteristic associated with different evidence possessing acceptable hardness. Softening may come about for many reasons: the denominator may be small (sample size problems); the survey may not be of good quality, or may only be a vaguely recalled recollection of experience (data problems); or there may be several data sources of varying degrees of size and quality which are judged relevant to the event. The last is illustrated by John Venn's (1888) hypothetical question concerning which life tables apply to a consumptive Englishman living in Madeira.

All the factors of the preceding paragraph appear in generalized form in the context of more complex statistical designs and more complex sampling and stochastic models. Design type and quality are critical to prescriptive acceptability of Bayesian inferences. Bias is a fundamental statistical concept apart from any technical probability-based definitions of the term. Bias enters a design through weaknesses in protocols which specify measurement techniques and unit selection techniques, and through weakness in the execution of protocols. Finally, even flawlessly designed and executed protocols may yield results whose application to prospective new circumstances is based on the sense that the new circumstances are judged sufficiently different that the effects of the differences must be quantitatively assessed.

Formal analysis of quantitative evidence depends on assumptions whose degrees of hardness must be communicated to the statistician's client in a convincing fashion. Assumptions are of many kinds. Parametric statistical models are often justified from informal hearsay or recalled empirical evidence which may deserve discounting. Similarly, scientific causal models range from well-established to highly speculative. Attempts to justify very small probabilities are generally based on trees of empirical evidence glued together with independence assumptions, or on other extrapolations beyond the reach of direct sampling experience. Any formal model depends on an implicit small world hypothesis that many obvious variables can be ignored. Assumptions which depend on forecasts, especially forecasts of human or social activities, may often be judged soft.

Sensitivity analysis of Bayesian inference may be expensive due to repeated attempts at model-construction, the computation of posterior probabilities and expectations under many Bayesian scenarios, and finally interpretation of the resulting variation in computed posterior probabilities and expectations. The technology is well worth pursuing, since without it Bayesian methodology has no way to convey the hard–soft dimension, and may therefore be judged unacceptable by clients. The awkwardness is that the Bayesian paradigm does not *per se* recognize the end result of a judgment-based range of posterior assessments.

By contrast, belief function theory has explicit mechanisms both for introducing softness into a source of evidence and for representing final softness. The mechanism for introducing softness is called *discounting*, and is defined and illustrated in many places by Shafer (e.g., 1976, 1982). Softness in final uncertainty is achieved by replacing a single numerical probability by a pair of

290

numbers called probability (a lower probability, or a kind of irreducible belief) and plausibility (or upper probability, or one minus the degree of irreducible belief in the complement). The theory needs much more prescriptive development and testing before its costs and benefits can be assessed.

THE EFFECTIVES OF UNUSUAL EVENTS

Major changes of perceptions of uncertainty often come in the form of events recognized as surprising or unexpected. Improbable events always happen, but some are singled out as surprising because of their potential or actual effects on human concerns, whether unexpected cures caused by an experimental drug, or unexpected disasters created by a nuclear generating plant failure. Laplace (1820) attempted to explain the phenemenon in terms of some outcomes being *extraordinary*, and some not, whence the occurrence of extraordinary events with small probability merit special attention. I tend to regard such interpretations as a valid use of subjective probability, as in ordinary significance testing. Bayesians tend to reject such retrospective or postdictive (Dempster, 1964) interpretations of probability, and attempt to incorporate the changes in probability assessment associated with unusual events within the normative Bayesian mechanism.

The essential point, however, is that the occurrence of unusual events often prompts a reexamination of the prescriptive foundations of an analysis. New variables are often introduced, or models are changed so that old variables treated as relatively unimportant are more influential in probability assessments. Old sources of evidence are examined more carefully, and new evidence may be sought. It seems to be implausible that such changes could all be characterized as an application of Bayes's theorem.

In any case, the relevant question is whether or not analyses constructed after an unusual event is recognized are biased. Is there an overreaction to the event? In pure science, one can protect against such bias by requiring that whole investigations be replicated, and make no pronouncements until the results are in. Applications to operational questions often are not permitted such replications, and decisions about effectiveness or risk must be made in real time.

My own view is that reconstructions prompted by unusual observations are important and necessary, and that all the mechanisms of prescriptive analysis may be employed and not just Bayesian rules, but that debiasing should be attempted by including in the model allowances for a wide range of extraordinary events which might have but did not occur, in addition to those which did occur.

ACKNOWLEDGMENTS

The issues and formulations of this chapter were influenced by the discussion at two conferences which I attended in the summer of 1983: (1) Conference on Decision Making: Descriptive, Normative, and Prescriptive Interactions, 75th Anniversary Colloquium Series, Harvard Business School, June 16–18, 1983, organized by David E. Bell, Howard Raiffa, and Amos Tversky, (2) Workshop on Dealing with Uncertainty in Risk Analysis, Arthur D. Little, Inc., August 4, 5, 1983, organized by Joseph Fiksel, Louis A. Cox, Jr., and Helen D. Ohja.

REFERENCES

Box, G. E. P. (1980). Sampling and Bayes' inference in scientific modelling and robustness. *J. Roy. Statist. Soc. A* 143, 383–404 (with discussion).

Dempster, A. P. (1964). On the difficulties inherent in Fisher's fuducial argument. *J. Amer. Statist. Assoc.* 59, 56–66.

Good, I. J. (1950). *Probability and the Weighing of Evidence.* London: Griffin.

Jevons, W. S. (1877). *The Principles of Science: A Treatise on Logic and Scientific Method* (second edition). New York: Macmillan. (New York: Dover, 1958.)

Laplace, P. S. (1820). *Essai philosophique sur les probabilités.* (English translation: *A Philosophical Essay on Probabilities.* New York: Dover, 1951.)

Savage, L. J. (1954). *The Foundations of Statistics.* New York: Wiley.

Shafer, G. (1976). *A Mathematical Theory of Evidence.* Princeton: University Press.

— (1978). Non-additive probabilities in the work of Bernoulli and Lambert. *Arch. History Exact Sciences,* 19, 309–70.

— (1981). Constructive probability. *Synthese* 48, 1–60.

— (1982). Belief functions and parametric models. *J. Roy. Statist. Soc. B,* 44, 322–52 (with discussion).

— (1983). Constructive decision theory. *Tech. Rep.* Harvard Business School.

Shafer, G. and Tversky, A. (1983). Weighing evidence: the design and comparison of probability thought experiments. Research paper. *Tech. Rep.* Harvard Business School.

Venn, J. (1888). *The Logic of Chance* (third edition). New York: Macmillan.

DISCUSSION

H. RUBIN (*Purdue University*)

It seems to me that Professor Dempster is trying to justify what people have been doing through ignorance of probability and statistics.

In combining evidence, as in any other situation, we must get the *client's* whole picture. The *client,* and not the *statistician,* must make the assumptions. The statistician may point out that certain assumptions are unimportant, and has the obligation to warn the client of consequences of his assumptions of which he is unaware. Asking stupid questions can only get stupid answers. I find it difficult to envision a situation where I would ask for a ranking, although I might ask for evaluations.

Probability is *not* relative frequency, and I personally have needed "harder" probabilities than can be obtained from any sample size which I can envision as physically possible. The probabilistic assumptions made in model specification are frequently "harder" than any sample will permit, and rightly so.

Professor Dempster seems clearly unhappy with many of the things a rational Bayesian approach forces him to accept, and consequently is searching for a way for mathematical results to help him out. Having been brought up in a more anti-Bayesian framework, I am also unhappy about the situation; however, if the truth disagrees with my philosophy, I must change my philosophy. Since mathematics is true (unless it is inconsistent, in which case there is so much to change that we must investigate everything anew, including the bases for Professor Dempster's arguments), we must accept the mathematics. We may look for robustness arguments to enable us to deal with difficult situations, but we must avoid selectively accepting those theorems which we like and rejecting those we do not like as a basis for behavior.

T. SEIDENFELD (*Washington University, St. Louis*)

Each of our speakers, one for roughly thirty years (Good, 1952) and the other for roughly sixteen (Dempster, 1967), has expressed sympathy for a liberalization of strict Bayesian theory. Their common motive, I believe, is to find a defensible representation for what, loosely put, is a state of ignorance. I allude to the view that a belief state may correspond to a set (or interval) of probability functions (or values). The roots of this intervalism differ, I suspect, for our two speakers.

My understanding in this, For Professor Good the indeterminacy arises because we introspect imperfectly and this, too, is rational. So I guess we must see our own opinions (and values?) through uncertain eyes. For Professor Dempster, I think the problem arises when trying to make sense of that old enigma, fiducial inference, where we would like to express the "ignorance" we profess about the unknown parameter. Thus, the intervalism is used to represent uncertainty, not due to introspective opacity, but uncertainty that is present when the *statistical* evidence fails to determine a precise "prior." On this approach it is incompletely described by the intervalism. Thus, for example, we read Shafer (in his reconstruction of Dempster's position, 1982, p. 350), trying to avoid identifying his belief functions with Good's lower probabilities. However, the question I address to Professor Dempster does not depend upon how the probability intervals arise or where the numbers come from.

In allowing a liberalization of the strict Bayesian theory for belief, there is a concomitant liberalization of decision theory. The change in postulates for decisions forces a separation from the "revealed preference" theory that is the occasional partner to strict Bayesianism. Let me illustrate.

For convenience, let us suppose that a belief-state is represented by a convex set of probability functions, D. The simplest form of dominance between acts is realized by the following decision rule, expressed in the language of choice functions.

293

Let X be a set of feasible options and $C(X)$ the choice set of "winners" from X. For each probability $d \in D$, denote expectation under d by $E_d[\cdot]$.

Rule 1: $x \in C(X)$ just in case there is no option $y \in X$ which, for each $d \in D$, satisfies

$$E_d[y] > E_d[x].$$

Rule 1 is a binary choice rule. It identifies the "winners" as those feasible options which, in a pairwise choice over X, are expectations *un*dominated with respect to the set D.

Our concerns with dominance take us beyond binary comparisons. Consider a decision problem with these three feasible options:

x yields an outcome worth 1 utile if E occurs, 0 utilies otherwise.

y yields an outcome worth 0 utiles if E occurs, 1 utile otherwise.

z is the "constant act" worth 0.4 utiles.

The choice problem is graphed in figure 13.1. Act z fails to maximize expected utility over each probability $d \in D$. However, rule 1 – binary comparisons – does not detect this.

Savage (1954, pp. 123–124) notes this phenomenon with his example of choice over a set of "priors." Of course, Savage is thinking of the (convex) set of priors corresponding to a group decision. There is the familiar duality between

Figure 13.1

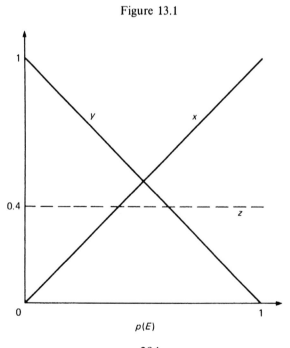

$p(E)$

individual and group choice. For instance, the well known theorem of Blackwell and Girshick (1954, p. 118) yields Arrow's impossibility result by this duality – reinterpret the states as the individuals' preference profiles.

In an early paper, Good (1952, p. 114) offered a stricter requirement for admissibility than rule 1. Recently, I. Levi (1980, p. 96) (also 1974) has focused attention on it.

Rule 2: $x \in C(X)$ just in case there is some $d \in D$ which, for all $y \in X$, satisfies

$$E_d[x] \geq E_d[y].$$

If we use rule 2 (or even rule 1) for choice we do poorly in the economists' game of revealed preference. Not even rule 1 supports independence of irrelevant alternatives (IIA). Let us adopt A. K. Sen's taxonomy for choice functions (1977)[1] (using the duality of individual and social choice problems). Understand IIA to be the conjunction of Sen's properties α and β (hence, now Arrow's principle I).

Property α: (consistency over "contractions") If $S \subset T$ are feasible sets and $x \in C(T)$ then $x \in C(S)$, provided that $x \in S$.
Property β: (consistency over "expansions") If $S \subset T$ are feasible sets with $x \in C(S)$ and $y \in C(S)$, then $x \in C(T)$ if $y \in C(T)$.

Given a choice function $C(\cdot)$, define the (weak preference) relation R_C over elements x, y of a feasible set X by:

$$x R_C y \text{ if and only if for some } S \subset X, x \in C(S) \text{ and } y \in S.$$

Given a (complete and reflexive) relation R over pairs of feasible options, define the choice function generated by R:

$$\hat{C}(X, R) = \{x : x \in X \text{ and for all } y \in X, x R y\}.$$

Last, call a choice function *normal* if its weak-preference relation R_C regenerates itself through $\hat{C}$, i.e., if

$$C(X) = \hat{C}(X, R_C).$$

Sen shows (1977), p. 65) that a choice function is normal and generates an ordering if and only if it satisfies α and β.

That rule 2 violates property β is evident from the simple example (above). Using $X = \{x, y, z\}$ from figure 13.1, we see that $C(\{x, z\}) = \{x, z\}$ and similarly $C(\{y, z\}) = \{y, z\}$. But $C(\{x, y, z\}) = \{x, y\}$. For rule 1, consider the augmented feasible set $X' = \{w, x, y, z\}$ with w the mixed act: x with probability .5 and y with probability .5. Then $C(X) = X$ while $C(X') = \{w, x, y\}$.

Clearly, both rule 1 and rule 2 satisfy property α. But only rule 1 satisfies

Property γ: For each class M of feasible sets, if $x \in C(X)$ for each $X \in M$, then $x \in C(\cup M)$.

To see rule 2 lacks γ, repeat the example used to show it fails β. That rule 1 satisfies γ is straightforward. Hence, by Sen's proposition 8 (1977, p. 64) – a choice function is normal if it satisfies α and γ – rule 1 is, whereas rule 2 is not normal.

Last, though not normal, rule 2 is "path independent," i.e. it has the property that $C(X \cup Y) = C(C(X) \cup C(Y))$. This follows from Sen's proposition 19 (1977, p. 69) – a choice function is path independent iff it satisfies α and

Property ε: If $X \subset Y$, then $C(Y)$ is not a proper subset of $C(X)$. Clearly, rule 2 has property ε.

Non-normality of rule 2 (despite its path independence) gives up all pretense to "revealed preference." It is not only that indifference is intransitive (recall both rules fail β while satisfying α), but with rule 2 the choice function cannot be recovered from examination of choices over feasible sets containing fixed pairs of options.

Rule 2 strikes me as the correct liberalization of the strict Bayesian policy to maximize expected utility. Thus, I find myself committed to abandoning the doctrine of "revealed preference." A philosphical platitude is germane. One person's *modus ponens* is another's *modus tollens*. Which way does logic's arrow point for our speaker?

Aside: Levi notes that, in effect, rule 2 can be weakened to rule 2 by having preferences go indeterminate over monotonic transformations of a given utility. This wipes out the difference between "second best" and "second worst" (see Levi, 1980, pp. 176–177) without abandoning rule 2. That is, rule 1 can be seen as the upshot of using rule 2 with ordinal (not cardinal) utility.

REPLY TO THE DISCUSSION

Professor Rubin's brief opening paragraphs apparently refer to my remarks on the sources of numerical probabilities for use in a specific practical situation. His final paragraph comments on my acceptance, or lack thereof, of "a rational Bayesian framework." I will take these in reverse order.

Like him, I was brought up in a more or less anti-Bayesian environment, but I do not believe that any current unhappiness I might have with Bayes overlaps with his unhappiness. That is, I think that the arguments made 20 to 30 years ago by Savage and others, criticizing Wald's decision analysis from a Bayesian standpoint, were sufficiently compelling to dispel nagging doubts, and I am content with the mathematical precision, elegance, and coherence of Bayesian theory. My problem is that I am attracted also by the mathematical precision, elegance, and coherence of the Shafer–Dempster theory. He is wrong in suggesting that I seek salvation in "mathematical results." Since my paper contains no mathematics, I might have expected the opposite criticism. Mathematics *per se* is neutral on the issue of selecting a theory for practical use. In fact, neither mathematical truth nor philosophical truth, however finely honed these concepts may be in abstract modern academic discourse, seem to me to come close to resolving the choice of a theory. The only way forward that I see is to proceed case by case to build a catalog of examples where instances of one theory or another have been constructed and appear to meet a modicum of scientific acceptance after careful critical analyses.

I agree with Herman that probability is *not* relative frequency. In many situations which command scientific approval, however, a relative frequency is agreed to be the source of a usable numerical probability. It is evident that formal Bayesian analyses require hard probabilities in the sense of mathematically precise specifications, and I agree that such precision is not attainable in fact, and perhaps not even in principle, from empirical frequencies. In a specific application, therefore, scientific evaluation requires bringing forth and assessing evidence which might be judged exchangeable with a canonical source such as a game of chance or a long run frequency. He wishes to put the responsibility for such judgments on his clients, which is desirable for clients sufficiently educated about the requirements for effective and acceptable use of methodology and techniques. I think it likely that better results will more often be obtained by a statistician and client working as a team.

Professor Seidenfeld suggests a distinction between Jack Good's lower probabilities and those of Dempster or Shafer, namely, that the former are drawn from imperfect introspection while the latter are intended to be based on evidence of one sort or another. This may very well be the case. More generally, Jack has good reason to be proud of many of his imperfect introspections whether or not they lead to lower probabilities. I believe, however, that Shafer and I make another distinction in our writing, namely that the mathematics of belief functions is more circumscribed than that of lower probabilities in a way which permits widespread use of the so-called Dempster rule of combination.

Professor Seidenfeld also asks me a question about rule 1 vs. rule 2 in relation to liberalizing Bayes. My response is that I would not formulate the question as he does. The Bayesian decision analyst's process is straightforward, to compute posterior expected utility for contemplated choices and select a maximizer. Using lower probabilities or belief functions, the extension is to compute lower posterior expected utilities and use them as guides which are unfortunately less decisive than precise numerical expectations. Interest focuses not on the definition and study of rules, since the problem is perceived as misformulated or nonsolvable in such terms. Instead, effort should be directed at formulating prescriptive methodology for constructing acceptable probabilities and utilities in specific real world circumstances.

To illustrate, consider his simple framing of a decision problem with choices, x, y, and z. *Suppose D is specified to be* $\{d: .3 < d < .7\}$. Then rule 1 says that x, y, *and z are all admissible since none is dominated across the interval.* Rule 2 eliminates z from consideration since none is dominated across the interval. Rule 2 eliminates z from consideration because there is no $d \in D$ for which z is preferred to both x and y. The lower expectations E_* for x, y, and z are respectively .3, .3, and .4. These should be interpreted as the amount of posterior expected utility the user can count on, given his weak state of knowledge. The technology has not solved the problem of choice but at least it appears that rule 2 receives little support.

NOTES

First published in J. M. Bernardo, M. H. DeGroot, D. V. Lindley, and A. F. M. Smith (eds.) (1985). *Bayesian Statistics 2.* New York: Elsevier Science Publishers B.V. (North-Holland), 119–31.

1 I thank I. Levi for bringing this important article to my attention.

REFERENCES IN THE DISCUSSION

Blackwell, D. and Girshick, M. A. (1954). *Theory of Games and Statistical Decisions.* New York: Wiley.

Dempster, A. P. (1967). Upper and lower probabilities induced by multivalued mapping. *Ann. Math. Statist.*, 38, 325–39.

Good, I. J. (1952). Rational decisions. *J. Roy. Statist. Soc. B*, 14, 107–14.

Levi, I. (1974). Indeterminate probabilities. *J. Phil.*, 71, 391–418.

(1980). *The Enterprise of Knowledge.* Cambridge: The MIT Press.

Savage, L. J. (1954). *Foundations of Statistics.* New York: Wiley.

Sen, A. K. (1977). Social choice theory: a re-examination. *Econometrica*, 45, 53–89.

Shafer, G. (1982). Lindley's paradox. *Amer. Statist. Assoc.*, 77, 325–51 (with discussion).

14

THE EFFECTS OF STATISTICAL TRAINING ON THINKING ABOUT EVERYDAY PROBLEMS

GEOFFREY T. FONG, DAVID H. KRANTZ, AND RICHARD E. NISBETT

Do people solve inferential problems in everyday life by using abstract inferential rules or do they use only rules specific to the problem domain? The view that people possess abstract inferential rules and use them to solve even the most mundane problems can be traced back to Aristotle. In modern psychology, this view is associated with the theories of Piaget and Simon. They hold that, over the course of cognitive development, people acquire general and abstract rules and schemas for solving problems. For example, people acquire rules that correspond to the laws of formal logic and the formal rules of probability theory. Problems are solved by decomposing their features and relations into elements that are coded in such a way that they can make contact with these abstract rules.

This formalist view has been buffeted by findings showing that people violate the laws of formal logic and the rules of statistics. People make serious logical errors when reasoning about arbitrary symbols and relations (for a review, see Evans, 1982). The best known line of research is that initiated by Wason (1966) on his selection task. In that task, subjects are told that they will be shown cards having a letter on the front and a number on the back. They are then presented with cards having an A, a B, a 4, and a 7 and asked which they would have to turn over in order to verify the rule, "If a card has an A on one side, then it has a 4 on the other." This research showed that people do not reason in accordance with the simple laws of conditional logic, which would require turning over the A and the 7. Subsequent work showed that people do reason in accordance with the conditional for certain concrete and familiar problems. For example, when people are given envelopes and asked to verify the rule, "If the letter is sealed, then it has a 50-lire stamp on it," they have no trouble with the problem (Johnson-Laird, Legrenzi, and Sonino-Legrenzi, 1972). Many investigators have concluded from results of the latter sort that people do not use abstract rules of logic when solving concrete probelms. Instead, people use only domain-specific rules (e.g., D'Andrade, 1982; Golding, 1981; Griggs and Cox, 1982; Johnson-Laird et al., 1972; Manktelow and Evans, 1979; Reich and Ruth, 1982). If people solve a problem correctly, it is because they are sufficiently familiar with the content domain to have induced a rule that allows them to solve problems in that domain.

Research on inductive reasoning has followed a similar history. Kahneman and Tversky (e.g., 1971, 1973; Tversky and Kahneman, 1974) demonstrated that people fall prey to a multitude of failures to employ statistical rules when reasoning about everyday life problems. In particular, people often fail to reason in accordance with the law of large numbers, the regression principle, or the base rate principle. (For reviews see Einhorn and Hogarth, 1981; Hogarth, 1980; Kahneman, Slovic, and Tversky, 1982; Nisbett and Ross, 1980).

We and our colleagues, however, have shown that people do use statistical concepts in solving particular kinds of problems in particular domains (Jepson, Krantz, and Nisbett, 1983; Nisbett, Krantz, Jepson, and Fong, 1982; Nisbett, Kranzt, Jepson, and Kunda, 1983). For example, Jepson *et al.* (1983) presented subjects with a variety of problems drawn from three very broad domains. All of the problems dealt with events that are variable and, as such, can be analyzed in terms of statistical concepts such as sample size. One domain examined by Jepson *et al.* consisted of problems for which the random nature of the sample is obvious. In one problem, for example, the protagonist has to judge characteristics of a lottery. As expected, the great majority of the answers for these "probabilistic" problems were statistical answers, that is, they incorporated intuitive notions of the law of large numbers or the regression principle in their answer. At the other extreme, a different group of problems dealt with subjective judgments about the properties of some object or person. In one of these problems, for example, the protagonist has to decide which of two college courses he should take, either on the basis of one visit to each class or on the basis of the evaluations of students who took the courses the previous term. Statistical responses were relatively rare for these "subjective" problems, constituting only about a quarter of the total. In between these extremes, there were a number of problems that, while not containing broad hints as to the random nature of the events in question, dealt with events that are of a sufficiently objective nature that it is relatively easy to recognize that they are characterized by a degree of random variation. These problems dealt primarily with athletic events and academic achievements. For these "objective" problems, slightly more than half of the answers were statistical in nature.

Nisbett *et al.* (1983) interpreted these and similar results as reflecting the fact that people possess intuitive but abstract versions of statistical rules. They called these intuitive rules "statistical heuristics," and argued that people call on such heuristics to the degree that (a) problem features are readily coded in terms of statistical rules, that is, when the sample space and sampling process are clear, and when the events can be coded in common units (as is the case for athletic events and academic achievements, for example); (b) the presence of chance factors or random variation is signaled by the nature of the events or by other cues in the problem; and (c) the culture recognizes the events in question as being associated with random variation (for example, gambling games) and thus prescribes that an adequate explanation of such events should make reference to statistical principles.

This account presumes that statistical heuristics are abstract. It explains people's frequent failures to use abstract rules as being the result of difficulty in coding problem elements in terms that trigger the rules or as the result of the presence of competing heuristics. But the evidence to date does not rule out the view that statistical heuristics are not abstract at all, but rather are local, domain-bound rules that happen to overlap with formal statistical rules. These rules are better developed in some domains than in others, and it is for this reason that people are much more likely to give statistical answers for some problems than for others.

If statistical heuristics are abstract, then it should be possible to improve people's statistical reasoning about everyday events by formal instruction in the rule system, without reference to any domain of everyday events. Such abstract instructional methods should help people apply the rules over a broad range of problem content. On the other hand, if such formal instruction fails to help people to solve concrete problems, despite the fact that people can be shown to have learned a substantive amount about the formal properties of the rules, this would be discouraging to the formal view. It would also be discouraging to the formal view if it were to turn out that abstract instruction affects only people's solution of probabilistic problems, where the relevance of statistical rules is obvious, and where competing rules have relatively little strength.

In order to test the view that formal training *per se* results in an increase in people's use of statistical principles across a variety of domains, we trained subjects, in brief but intensive laboratory sessions, on the concepts associated with the law of large numbers. We then presented them with a number of problems in each of three broad domains, dealing, respectively, with events generally construed as probabilistic, with objectively measurable events, and with events that are measurable only by subjective judgments.

We also tested the formal view in another way. Some subjects were not given formal instruction, but instead were shown how to apply the law of large numbers for three concrete example problems, all of which dealt with objectively measurable events. If subjects are capable of inducing generalized rules of some degree of abstraction from such training, then they might be expected to reason more statistically about problems in the other domains as well, even though they have not been presented with examples in those domains. Whereas the empirical view suggests that statistical training will be domain specific, with training in one domain failing to generalize to other domains, the formalist view predicts that statistical training in one domain should generalize readily to other domains.

All of the problems presented to subjects concerned everyday life events and were of a type that, in previous work, we have found at least some subjects answer in a statistical fashion. All questions were open-ended, and we coded the written answers according to a system that distinguished among varying degrees of statistical thinking. This procedure provided us with a great deal of information about how people reason about events in everyday life and allowed us to determine whether training can enhance not only the likelihood of employing statistical concepts, but also the likelihood that those concepts will be employed properly.

EXPERIMENT 1

Testing method

Subjects' intuitive use of statistical reasoning was tested by examining their answers to 15 problems to which the law of large numbers could be applied and 3 for which the law of large numbers was not relevant. In this section we describe the instructions that introduced the test problem, the design of the 18 problems, and the system of coding the open-ended answers. The actual text of the problems is given in appendix A in this chapter.

Instructions

The instructions for the control subjects read as follows:

> We are interested in studying how people go about explaining and predicting events under conditions of very limited information about the events. It seems to us to be important to study how people explain and predict under these conditions because they occur very frequently in the real world. Indeed, we often have to make important decisions based on such explanations and predictions, either because there is too little time to get additional information or because it is simply unavailable.
>
> On the pages that follow, there are a number of problems that we would like you to consider. As you will see, they represent a wide range of real-life situations. We would like you to think carefully about each problem, and then write down answers that are sensible to you.

For groups that received training, the first paragraph of the above instructions was presented as part of the introduction to the training materials. After the training, the test booklet was introduced by the second paragraph, which ended with the sentence, "In many of the problems, you may find that the Law of Large Numbers is helpful."

Problem types and problem structure

The 18 problems were divided into three major types as follows:

Type 1. Probabilistic. In these six problems, subjects had to draw conclusions about the characteristics of a population from sample data generated in a way that clearly incorporated random variation. Randomness was made clear in various ways: by the explicitly stated variation in sample outcomes (for example, the number of perfect welds out of 900 made by a welding machine ranged from 680 to 740), by including in the problem a random generating device (for example, shaking a jar of pennies before drawing out a sample), or by simple stating that a sample was "random."

Type 2. Objective. In these six problems, subjects had to draw conclusions about characteristics of a population on the basis of "objective" sample data but with no explicit cue about randomness of the data. One problem, for example, asked subjects to decide which of two makes of car was more likely to be free of troublesome repairs, on the basis of various facts about the repair records. Other problems dealt with the outcomes of athletic events and with academic accomplishments.

Type 3. Subjective. In these six problems, subjects had to draw conclusions about subjective characteristics of a population from "subjective" sample data. In one problem, for example, a high school senior had to choose between two colleges. The underlying subjective characteristic in this problem was liking for the two schools and the data consisted of his own and his friends' reactions to the schools.

In order to systematize the kinds of problems we presented to subjects across the three domains, we selected six different underlying problem structures and for each structure we wrote one problem of each of the above three types. The structures varied in type of samples drawn, type of decision required, and type of competing information.

Structure 1 problems required subjects to draw conclusions about a population from a single small sample. Structure 2 problems pitted a small sample against a large sample. Structure 3 problems required subjects to explain why an outcome selected because of its extreme deviation was not maintained in a subsequent sample (i.e., regression). Structure 4 problems were similar to those in structure 2, except that the large sample was drawn from a population that was related to, although not identical to, the target population. Structure 5 problems pitted a large sample against a plausible theory that was not founded on data. Structure 6 (false alarm) problems involved conclusions drawn from a sample that was large, but also highly biased. As such, criticism or arguments in these problems should be based on the sample *bias*, but not on sample size. We included these problems to determine whether subjects who received training on the law of large numbers would then proceed to invoke it indiscriminately, or if they would apply it only to the problems of structures 1–5, for which it was genuinely relevant.

In short, the 18 test problems followed a 3 × 6 design, with problem type crossed with problem structure. The order of the 18 test problems was randomized for each subject, with the constraint that no two problems with the same structure appeared successively.

Coding system

To study the use of statistical reasoning, a simple 3-point coding system was developed for the 15 problems for which the law of large numbers was applicable (structures 1–5). To illustrate this coding system, we present examples of responses to the "slot machine problem," the probabilistic version of structure 2 (small sample vs. large sample). The protagonist of the story, Keith, was in a Nevada gas station where he played two slot machines for a couple of minutes each day. He lost money on the left slot machine and won money on the right slot machine. Keith's result, however, ran counter to the judgment of an old man sitting in the gas station, who said to Keith, "The one on the left gives you about an even chance of winning, but the one on the right is fixed so that you'll lose much more often than you'll win. Take it from me – I've played them for years." Keith's conclusion after playing the slot machines was that the old man was wrong about the chances of winning on the two slot machines. Subjects were asked to comment on Keith's conclusion. Every response to the test problems was classified into one of three categories:

1 = an entirely deterministic response, that is, one in which the subject made no use of statistical concepts. In responses of this type, there was no mention of sample size, randomness, or variance. The following was coded as a deterministic response to the slot machine problem: "Keith's reasoning was poor, provided the information given by the man was accurate. The man, however, may have been deceiving Keith."

2 = a poor statistical response. Responses given this score contained some mention of statistical concepts, but were incomplete or incorrect. These responses contained one or more of the following characteristics: (1) the subject used both deterministic and statistical reasoning, but the deterministic reasoning was judged by the coder to have been preferred by the subject; (2) the subject used incorrect statistical reasoning, such as the gambler's fallacy; (3) the subject mentioned luck or chance or the law of large numbers but was not explicit about how the statistical concept was relevant. The following is an example of a poor statistical response to the slot machine problem:

> I think that Keith's conclusion is wrong because the old man had better luck on the left one, so he thought it was better. Keith had better luck on the right one so he thought it was better. I don't think you could have a better chance on either one.

3 = a good statistical response. Responses given this score made correct use of statistical concept. Some form of the law of large numbers was used, and the sample elements were correctly identified. If the subject used both deterministic and statistical reasoning, the statistical reasoning was judged by the coder to have been preferred by the subject. In general, the subject was judged to have clearly demonstrated how the law of large numbers could be applied to the problem. The following was coded as a good statistical response to the slot machine problem:

> Keith's conclusion is weak. He is wrong in making the assumptions against the old man. Keith is judging the machines on only a handful of trials and not with the sample number the old man has developed over the years. Therefore, Keith's margin of error is much more great than the old man's.

The coding system thus distinguished each response on the basis of whether or not a statistical concept had been used and, within the class of statistical responses, whether or not it was a "good" statistical response, that is, one that showed a correct use of the law of large numbers.

Such coding obviously runs into borderline cases. A coding guidebook was created which documented the principal types of borderline cases and the recommended treatment of them, for each problem. Reliability was tested by having four coders code a sample of 20 test booklets (300 law of large numbers problems). There was exact agreement among all four coders on 86% of these responses. Having achieved a high level of reliability, the primary coder (who had been one of the four coders), coded all of the responses, blind to conditions. His coding comprised the data we present here and in experiment 2.

The coding of the three structure 6 (false alarm) problems is described in a separate section below.

Training procedures

All training procedures began with an introductory paragraph about decisions with limited information (quoted in full above as the first paragraph in the testing instructions for the control subjects).[1] Next followed a paragraph introducing the law of large numbers. This always began as follows:

> Experts who study human inference have found that principles of probability are helpful in explaining and predicting a great many events, especially under conditions of limited information. One such principle of probability that is particularly helpful is called the *Law of Large Numbers*.

Rule training condition

Subjects read a four-page description of the concept of sampling and the law of large numbers. This description introduced the important concepts associated with the law of large numbers and illustrated them by using the classic problem of estimating the true proportion of blue and red gumballs in an urn from a sample of the urn. Thus, the gumballs in the urn constituted the *population*, the proportion of blue and red gumballs in the urn formed the *population distribution* (in the example, the population distribution of gumballs was set at 70% blue and 30% red), and a selection of gumballs from the urn constituted a *sample*.

The concept of sampling was then presented by explaining that since it is often impractical or impossible to examine the entire population to determine the population distribution ("Imagine counting a million gumballs!"), it is necessary to rely instead on samples to *estimate* the population distribution. *Sample distributions*, subjects were told, vary in their closeness to the population distribution, and the only factor determining the closeness of a *random* sample to the population is *sample size*. Finally, the law of large numbers was presented in the following way:

> As the size of a random increases, the sample distribution is more likely to get closer and closer to the population distribution. In other words, the larger the sample, the better it is as an estimate of the population.

When subjects had finished reading this description, the experimeter performed a live demonstration of the law of large numbers, using a large glass urn filled with blue and red gumballs. In order to maximize subjects' understanding of the concepts they had just read, the demonstration was designed to adhere closely to the description. Each of the concepts introduced in the description was illustrated in the demonstration. For example, the population distribution of the urn was 70 % blue and 30 % red, just as it had been in the description.

After reintroducing all of the concepts, the experimeter drew four samples of size 1, then four of size 4, and finally four of size 25. (The gumballs were returned to the urn after each sample.) The experimenter summarized each sample on a blackboard, keeping track of the deviation between each sample and the population. Subjects were told that the average deviation of a sample from the population would decrease as the sample size increased, in accordance with the law of large numbers. Thus, for example, samples of size 25 would, on the average, deviate less from the population than would samples of size 4 or 1. (By good luck, these expected results were obtained in all the training sessions.)

Examples training condition

Subjects in the examples training condition read a packet of three example problems with an answer following each problem that provided an analysis of it in terms of the law of large numbers. The three example problems were drawn from structure 1 (generalizing from a small sample), structure 3 (regression), and structure 5 (large sample vs. theory without supporting data), and were presented in that order. The three examples were all drawn from the domain of objective problems. After the paragraph that introduced the law of large numbers, there followed a single sentence describing one example of the principle (a public opinion poll based on a large sample is more likely to be accurate than one based on a small sample). The example problems were then introduced in the following way:

> The basic principles involved in the law of large numbers apply whenever you make a generalization or an inference from observing a sample of objects, actions, or behaviors. To give you an idea of how broad the law of large numbers is, we have, in this packet, presented three situations in which the law of large numbers applies. Each situation is analyzed in terms of the law of large numbers.

For each example in turn, subjects read the problem and were asked to consider it for a few moments before turning the page to read the law of large numbers answer. The answers to the example problems were constructed so that subjects could learn how the law of large numbers might be applied to a variety of real-life situations. The format of the answers was constant across training domain and structure and included the following characteristics:

1. A statement about the goal of the problem.
2. Identification of the sample or samples and their distributions in the problem.
3. Explanation of how the law of large numbers could be applied to the problem. This identified the population distribution(s) and explained the relationship between the sample(s) and the population(s).
4. The conclusion that could be drawn from the application of the law of large numbers.

The three example problems are presented in appendix B in this chapter.

Full training condition

Subjects received rule training, followed by examples training, except that the first sentence of the passage introducing the examples was replaced by the following sentence: "One reason that the law of large numbers is important to learn is that it applies *not only* to urns and gumballs."

Demand condition

Subjects received only the one-sentence definition of the law of large numbers that introduced the examples training, along with the brief example. We included this condition in order to assess whether training effects might be due to experimenter demand or to simply making statistical rules salient to subjects. If performance of the demand group turned out not to be higher than that of the control group, these alternative explanations would be ruled out.

In addition, there was a *control* condition, which received no training before answering the test problems.

In summary, there were five conditions in experiment 1, as shown in figure 14.1. They were defined by crossing the presence or absence of rule training with

Figure 14.1 Design of experiment 1.

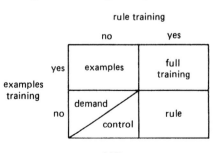

presence or absence of examples training. Note that the bottom-left cell of figure 14.1, where neither type of training was given, contains both the control and the demand conditions.

Subjects and procedure

The 347 subjects were adults (229) and high school students (118) from various New Jersey suburban communities. They were paid to participate in the experiment. The adult subjects varied widely in age and education, but almost all were females who were not employed fulltime outside the home. Most of them had participated previously in psychology experiments at Bell Laboratories. Because adults and high school students showed the same pattern of results, their responses were combined in the analyses we present.

Subjects were scheduled in groups of 4–6, with the same training condition presented to the entire group. Training condition was randomly determined. Subjects were told the general nature of the experiments, given the appropriate training, and then given the 18-problem test booklet. They were given 80 min to complete the problems.

Results

Overview of data analysis

Recall that subjects' responses were coded using a 3-point system: a code of "1" was given for responses that contained no mention of statistical concepts such as variability or sample size, whereas a "2" or '3" was given for responses that incorporated statistical notions. Within the class of statistical responses, a "2" was given for "poor" statistical responses, and a "3" was given for "good" statistical responses.

We analyzed the data in terms of two dichotomies. The first one asks whether the response was deterministic (code = 1) or statistical, regardless of quality (code = 2 or 3). We refer to analyses based on this dichotomy as analyses of *frequency* of statistical responses. The second dichotomy (code = 2) or good (code = 3). We refer to analyses based on this dichotomy as analyses of *quality*. The quality dichotomy is conditional: it is defined only for statistical responses and is undefined (missing) for deterministic responses.

These two analyses allowed us to separate the questions of whether training increased the incidence of any kind of statistical reasoning from whether it increased the *proper* use of statistical principles. If we found that training led to an increase in frequency but a decrease in quality, this would lead to the pessimistic conclusion that training merely serves to make statistical concepts salient to subjects without conveying any real sense about how such concepts should be used properly. On the other hand, if training was found to increase *both* frequency and quality, then this would support the optimistic notion that

Table 14.1. *Frequency and quality of statistical answers in experiment 1*

Condition	n	Frequency		Quality	
		Overall proportion	Log-linear effect	Overall proportion	Log-linear effect
Control	68	.421	−0.515	.542	−0.501
Demand	73	.440	−0.420	.577	−0.316
Rule	69	.557	0.188	.666	0.165
Examples	69	.535	0.074	.659	0.181
Full training	68	.643	0.673	.708	0.461

training not only makes salient the usefulness of statistical principles in analyzing inferential problems, but also improves the ability to use those principles correctly.

Because our basic variables were dichotomous, we used a log-linear modeling approach (e.g., Bishop, Fienberg, and Holland, 1975), in which we modeled frequency and quality as a function of (1) training differences, (2) individual differences within training groups, (3) problem differences, and (4) problem × training interaction. This approach closely parallels a three-factor ANOVA model, in which training is a between-subjects variable and problems are crossed with subjects (i.e., problems are treated as repeated measures).

Effect of training on frequency of statistical reasoning

Column 3 of table 14.1 shows the overall frequency of statistical responses for each of the five experimental groups.[2] It is clear that training increased the frequency of statistical responses, as predicted. Specifically, there resulted a three-level ordering of the conditions. At the lowest level, subjects who received no training (the control and demand conditions) were least likely to employ statistical principles in their answers (42 and 44%, respectively, across all 15 problems). At the middle level, subjects who received only rule training or only examples training were more likely to reason statistically (56 and 54%, respectively). And at the highest level, subjects in the full training condition (those who received both rule and examples training) were most likely to use statistical reasoning in their answers (64%).

The statistical reliability of these proportions cannot be directly assessed from the binomial, since they involve repeated measures over subjects. An alternative strategy would be to employ an analysis of variance on subject means. Such an approach, although quite feasible, would ignore problems as a source of variance, and thus would be inappropriate for our purposes.

Instead, we assessed the reliability of group differences by log-linear analysis. The log-linear effects of training groups, subjects within groups, and problems were all large and highly reliable; the training group × problem interaction was small and only marginally significant.

Geoffrey T. Fong, David H. Krantz, and Richard E. Nisbett

The simplest way to assess the effects of training is given by the effect sizes for an additive log-linear model based only on training group and problems as factors.[3] These effects are shown in table 14.1, column 4. The standard error or each pairwise difference was 0.19, which we obtained from jackknifing.[4] Hence, the difference between the control and the demand conditions and between the rule and examples conditions were not statistically reliable, whereas all of the other pairwise differences were highly reliable ($p < .01$). Thus *both* formal training and training by "guided induction" over examples were effective in increasing the use of statistical heuristics. In addition, training effects were not due to mere experimenter demand or mere salience of statistical rules, since the demand condition was significantly lower than any of the training conditions. In fact, there was no evidence that the demand instructions had any effect whatsoever, compared to controls.

Effect of training on quality of statistical reasoning

But does training have a beneficial effect on people's ability to use statistical principles *approximately*? The rightmost columns in table 14.1 show the overall quality proportions and corresponding effects.[5] The jackknifed estimate of the standard error of the differences in quality between any two conditions was 0.18.

The effect of training on the quality of statistical responses was strikingly similar to the effects of training on frequency, though somewhat smaller in magnitude. As degree of training increased, the ability to utilize statistical concepts properly increased. This resulted in a similar three-level ordering of the conditions. However, the log-linear analysis indicated that the differences between the full training condition and the rule and examples conditions were significant only at the .10 level.

The effects of training on frequency and quality can be seen clearly in figure 14.2, where the five conditions in experiment 1 are represented by the filled points. (The open points are from experiment 2, which are added to demonstrate the stability of training effects across experiments and across different subject populations.) Each training group is represented by one point, with the log-linear frequency effect on the abscissa, and log-linear quality effect on the ordinate. The standard errors of differences for frequency and for quality are shown by a horizontal and vertical bar, respectively.

The diagonal line in figure 14.2 is the least-squares regression line for the five conditions in experiment 1. It is clear that there is a very stable relationship between the training effect on frequency and on quality, $r(3) = .98$, $p < .005$. The slope of the line is 0.80, which corresponds to the finding that the effect of training on quality was slightly less than the effect on frequency. (Equal effects would be indicated by a slope of 1.00.) This slope is an interesting way to characterize the nature of training procedures. One can imagine procedures that would lead to a much lower slope (for example, emphasizing the identification of chance processes without much concern for explaining the principles underlying them),

310

or a much higher slope (for example, emphasizing the principles of mathematical statistics, with advice to use great caution in applying such principles broadly).

To summarize, training on the law of large numbers increased the likelihood that people will employ statistical concepts in analyzing everyday inferential problems. Moreover, there appears to be a three-level ordering such that either rule or examples training alone improves performance and that training on both has an additional effect. Training also serves to increase the proper application of statistical concepts in the same way, although this effect is somewhat weaker.

The effect of problem type on the use of statistical principles

Collapsing across training condition, subjects were most likely to employ statistical reasoning for probabilistic problems (75%), less likely to do so for objective problems (48%), and least likely for subjective problems (33%).[6] This result is consistent with the findings of Nisbett *et al.* (1983) that the use of statistical reasoning is associated with features of the inferential problem that relate to the clarity of the sampling elements and sample space, the salience of the presence of chance factors, and the cultural prescriptions concerning whether causal explanations should include statistical concepts.

Analysis of the quality proportions for the three problems types showed a quite different pattern. There was no significant differences. (The overall proportions for probabilistic, objective, and subjective problems were .63, .53, and .55, respectively.) This suggests that the source of the differences among problem types in statistical reasoning is in the likelihood that a person will notice the

Figure 14.2 Effects of training on frequency and quality of statistical answers in experiment 1 and experiment 2. Closed points (●) = experiment 1; open points (○) = experiment 2; P = probabilistic examples training; O = objective examples training; S = subjective examples training; C = control.

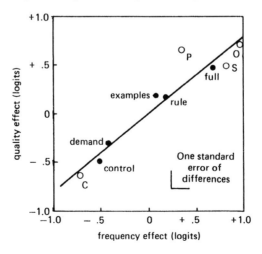

relevance of statistical principles to begin with. Given that a person has done so, the three problem types do not differ significantly in whether the person will be able to generate a *good* statistical response.

Thus, frequency of statistical answers was strongly associated with problem type while quality was only weakly associated with problem type. This result is consistent with the notion that people solve problems by use of abstract rules rather than by use of domain-dependent rules: different domains differ with respect to the likelihood that people will recognize the relevance of statistical rules, but, once the relevance is recognized, the same abstract rules are applied across domains with approximately the same degree of success.

Relationship between training and problem type

Are the effects of statistical training limited to the more obvious probabilistic problems, or do they extend to the objective and subjective problems? Figure 14.3 presents the frequency of probabilistic answers by training condition and problem type. The profiles are nearly parallel, which suggests that there is no interaction between training and problem type.

The log-linear analysis verifies this: although the interaction between training condition and the 15 problems was significant ($\chi^2(56) = 80$, $p < .05$), the pattern of residuals from the additive model indicates very clearly that the source of the interaction was due to variation of problems *within* problem type and not at all to systematic differences *between* problem types. Thus, training increased statistical reasoning for subjective events just as it did for objective and probabilistic events.

Figure 14.3 Frequency of statistical answers as a function of condition and problem type in experiment 1.

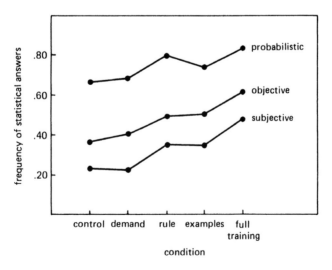

Figure 14.4 presents the quality of probabilistic answers by training condition and problem type. Note that the three profiles are much closer to each other than are the profiles in figure 14.3: this reflects the fact that frequency was strongly related to problem type, whereas quality was unrelated. We used the same analytic approach to test whether the effect of training on quality of statistical reasoning interacted with problem type. The training × problem interaction was not significant, $\chi^2(54) = 60$, $p > .20$. Thus, as with frequency, training effects on quality did not interact with problem type.

These results are consistent with a strong version of the formalist view. Formal rule training improves statistical reasoning and enhances the quality of such reasoning for all kinds of events, not just for probabilistic problems for which there are few plausible alternative kinds of solutions. This finding suggests that operations directly on the abstract rules themselves may be sufficient to produce change in subjects' analysis of essentially the full range of problems they might confront.

These results support the formalist view in a second way. The examples training consisted of example problems only in the domain of objective events. The empirical view predicts domain specificity of training: examples training should lead to greater use of the law of large numbers for the objective test problems but should have less effect for probabilistic and subjective problems. The formalist view, in contrast, predicts domain independence of training. In this view, examples training, insofar as it makes contact with people's relatively abstract rule system of statistical principles, should generalize to other domains as well.

Figure 14.4 Quality of statistical answers as a function of condition and problem type in experiment 1.

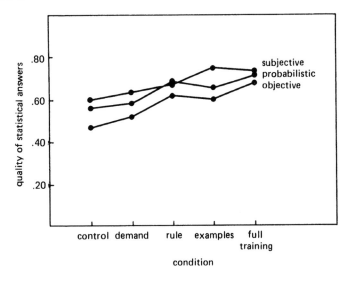

As shown in figures 14.3 and 14.4, the results are much more consistent with the formalist view. Training on objective example problems improved performance on both probabilistic and subjective problems essentially as much as it improved performance on the objective problems. There was no residual advantage for problems in the domain on which training took place.

False alarms

Since subjects can only learn so much in a 25-min training session, and since a little learning is a dangerous thing, we should be concerned that our training session may be dangerous in some way. One danger is false alarms, that is, the use of the law of large numbers in situations where it is inappropriate. For example, subjects might claim that the sample size is too small even for problems in which the sample size is quite large. It should be clear that the overuse of the law of large numbers as well as the failure to use it can lead to erroneous conclusions. We explored the possibility that our training may have promoted the indiscriminate use of the law of large numbers by including false-alarm problems in our test package.

There were seven problems for which false-alarm data could be examined. In the three structure 5 (large sample vs. theory without supporting data) problems, the conclusion based on a large sample was contradicted by an opposing argument that was plausible but which was unsupported by data. An answer was given a false-alarm code if it stated that the sample was too small to combat the argument. The three structure 6 (false alarm) problems involved conclusions drawn from large but biased samples. A false-alarm code was given if a subject accepted the criticism that the sample size was too small. And the objective version of structure 1 (which we will refer to as O1) asked subjects to comment on two conclusions – one based on a large sample (part a) and one based on a very small sample (part b). Part a was used to assess subjects' tendency to false alarm; part b was used to assess the subjects' ability to use the law of large numbers correctly. Of the seven false-alarm problems, three of them (O5, S5, and S6) elicited virtually no false alarms (less than 2%). For a fourth problem (P6), the false-alarm rate was about 10%, with the false alarms distributed approximately equally among the five conditions. The results for these four problems suggest that trained subjects do indeed increase their use of the law of large numbers in a discriminating fashion.

For the other three problems, the false-alarm rates were only somewhat higher for the three trained groups (about 16%) than for the two untrained groups (about 10%). And it is interesting that the specific pattern of false alarms across the three trained groups varied depending on whether subjects had received examples training. In P5 (the probabilistic version of structure 5), for instance, subjects exposed to examples training (the examples and full training conditions) were less likely to false alarm than those exposed to rule training only. This is probably because the examples training package included a structure 5 problem.

These subjects had thus been alerted to the possibility that large samples were indeed "large enough" to make confident conclusions and were therefore less likely to false alarm on P5. In contrast, subjects receiving only rule training were not given any information about when a sample was large enough. It is not surprising, then, that these subjects were more likely to false alarm to this problem.

There is also evidence from problem O1 that the tendency to false alarm was negatively related to the proper use of the law of large numbers. For this problem, there was a strong negative relationship between false alarms to part a and the quality of statistical responses to part b. Of the subjects who false alarmed on part a, none gave a good statistical answer to part b, that is, quality was equal to .00. In contrast, for those subjects who had not false alarmed, quality was equal to .16. This analysis suggests that a little learning can be somewhat dangerous, but that subjects who absorb the training more thoroughly are able to use it in a discriminating fashion.

In summary, our 25 min training session did *not* lead to widespread overuse of the large of large numbers.[7] Instead, subjects were surprisingly sophisticated in avoiding the improper use of the law of large numbers, sometimes citing intuitive versions of statistical concepts such as power and confidence intervals in their answers. Moreover, subjects who did false alarm were also likely to use the law of large numbers correctly when it was appropriate.

EXPERIMENT 2

The results of experiment 1 indicate very clearly that people can be taught to reason more statistically about everyday inferential problems. They can be taught through example problems showing how statistical principles can be applied, and they can also be taught through illustrating the formal aspects of the law of large numbers. These results are consistent with the formalist view that people possess abstract inferential rules and that these can be improved both by guided induction through examples and by direct manipulation.

One of the important results in experiment 1 was the absence of an interaction between training and problem type. Examples training had an equal effect in enhancing statistical reasoning across all three problem types. Thus, training on objective problems increased the use of statistical thinking no more for objective events than for subjective events, such as choosing a college or explaining a person's compassionateness, or for probabilistic events, such as those involving lotteries or slot machines. That training effects were entirely domain independent is quite remarkable when contrasted with the strong domain specificity of subjects' spontaneous *use* of statistical reasoning. Subjects were much more likely to use statistical principles for probabilistic problems than for objective problems and much more likely to use them for objective problems than for subjective problems.

Geoffrey T. Fong, David H. Krantz, and Richard E. Nisbett

Experiment 2 was designed to explore more fully whether training effects might vary as a function of the training domain. In experiment 1, all subjects who received examples training were given example problems only in the objective domain. In experiment 2, subjects were taught how to apply the law of large numbers in one of the three problem domains: probabilistic, objective, or subjective. All subjects were then tested on all three problem domains. This design makes it possible to see whether there are domain-specific effects of training. The empirical view suggests that subjects would be expected to show more improvements for problems in the domain in which they were trained than for other problems. The formal view, on the other hand, predicts that there will be no such interaction between training domain and testing domain.

Method

Subjects

The subjects were 166 undergraduates at the University of Michigan who were enrolled in introductory psychology classes. They participated in the two-hour experiment in small groups.

Design and procedure

Subjects were randomly assigned to one of four conditions. The *control* condition was identical to that in experiment 1. In the other three conditions, subjects were given training identical to the full training condition in experiment 1, except that the type of example problems varied. Subjects in the *probabilistic training* condition read three probabilitistic example problems and were shown how each could be analyzed by the application of the law of large numbers. Subjects in the *objective training* condition were given in the same three objective example problems that were used in experiment 1. And subjects in the *subjective training* condition were given three subjective example problems. The probabilistic and subjective examples matched the objective examples in structure: they were drawn from structures 1, 3, and 5.

All subjects then answered the same set of 18 test problems (15 law of large numbers problems and 3 false-alarm problems) used in experiment 1.

The subjects' responses to the open-ended questions were coded by two raters under the same coding system used in experiment 1. The reliability of the coding was high – there were exact matches by the two coders on 88 % of the responses.

Results

The data analytic procedures we used in experiment 1 were employed here. From the 3-point coding system, we derived frequency and quality dichotomies and then used log-linear models to estimate the effects of training, test problem, and training × test problem interaction. The jackknifed estimate of the standard error of the difference between any two conditions for frequency and quality were 0.20 and 0.18 on the log-linear scale, respectively. These standard errors correspond very closely to those found in experiment 1.

Effect of training

As in experiment 1, training significantly enhanced the frequency of statistical responses. Subjects in the control conditions were least likely to use statistical concepts for the 15 test problems (53 % of responses were statistical). The three training groups were significantly more likely than controls to give statistical answers (72, 81, and 79 % for the probabilistic, objective, and subjective training groups, respectively. All comparisons with the control condition were significant at the .001 level). In addition, subjects trained on probabilistic examples were less likely than subjects trained on objective or subjective examples to reason statistically ($p < .01$ and .05, respectively): the objective and subjective example conditions did not differ from each other.

Training also increased the quality of statistical answers. The quality proportions were .47 for the control group and .70, .70, and .66 for the probabilistic, objective, and subjective groups, respectively. Once again training significantly enhanced the quality of statistical responses (all comparisons with the control condition were significant at the .001 level). But, in contrast to the frequency data, no training domain was more effective than any other in enhancing the quality of statistical answers.

The relationship between the training effects on frequency and on quality was very consistent with experiment 1, as can be seen by looking back to figure 14.2, where the open points represent the frequency and quality effects of the three training conditions and the control condition for experiment 2.

Effect of problem type

The strong effect of problem type found in experiment 1 was replicated here. Collapsing across conditions, subjects were most likely to reason statistically for probabilistic problems (91 %), less likely to do so for objective problems (68 %), and least likely for subjective problems (56 %).[8]

As in experiment 1, the quality of statistical answers varied only slightly across the three problem types. The quality proportions were .69, .65, and .60 for the probabilistic, objective, and subjective problems, respectively. These differences were not statistically significant.

Relationships between training domain and test domain

The primary goal of this experiment was to examine the relationship between training domain and test domain. Figure 14.5 and 14.6 present the frequency and quality of statistical answers as a function of training domain and test domain. If training effects were domain specific, we should find that frequency and quality for problems in a given domain will be highest for those subjects who were trained on that domain. These domain-specificity data points are represented as larger data points in the two figures. Figures 14.5 and 14.6 make it clear that this was not the case: the domain-specific data points are not consistently higher than the other data points. For example, subjects who were trained on problems in the probabilistic domain were actually *less* likely to think statistically on the probabilistic test problems than were subjects trained on objective or subjective

Figure 14.5 Frequency of statistical answers as a function of condition and problem type in experiment 2.

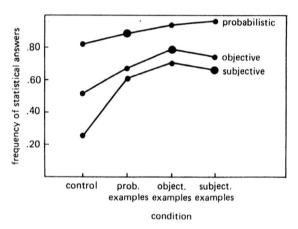

Figure 14.6 Quality of statistical answers as a function of condition and problem type in experiment 2.

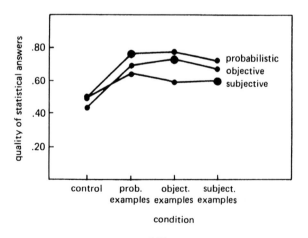

318

problems. In short, training significantly increased statistical reasoning: the domain of training had no differential effect.

The log-linear analysis confirms the absence of domain specificity of training. There was no significant interaction between training domain and test domain, either for frequency, $\chi^2(42) = 55$, $p = .10$, or for quality, $\chi^2(42) = 49$, $p > .15$.

Finally, the false-alarm rates for experiment 2 were generally higher than they were for experiment 1 for the control group as well as for the trained groups. The difference may be due to the fact that the subjects in experiment 2 were college students, but this is only speculation.

Discussion

The results of experiments 1 and 2 show that instruction in statistics can have a marked effect on the way people reason about a broad range of everyday problems. Such training affects not only their reasoning about transparently probabilistic events such as lotteries, but also their reasoning about events that most people analyze using only deterministic rules.

Both formal training, restricted to descriptions of the formal aspects of the law of large numbers, and "guided induction," that is, teaching the rule by means of examples, were effective in improving both the frequency and the quality of statistical reasoning. The former finding suggests that the more abstract aspects of academic training in statistics may, by themselves, be sufficient to produce significant improvements in the way people reason. We test this hypothesis in experiments 3 and 4. The latter finding indicates that the use of examples adds greatly to people's ability to use their abstract rule systems.

The two types of training were approximately additive on the log-linear scale, that is, examples training plus rule training added as much improvement, both in frequency and quality, as would be expected from the sum of the effects of each type of training in isolation. It is important to note that, in the present experiments at least, the effect of examples training does not appear to be in the form of rules about how to "map" the law of large numbers onto the content of particular domains. This is because there was no domain specificity of training effects. In general, subjects taught examples in one domain learned no more about how to solve problems in that domain than they did about how to solve problems in other domains. There are two hypotheses that may account for this domain independence of examples training. What subjects learn from examples training may be an abstracted version of the law of large numbers. Alternatively, or perhaps in addition, they may learn an abstracted version of how to apply the principle to problems in general.

The domain independence of training effects we found should not be presumed to be highly general, however. Every teacher knows that students sometimes apply a rule beautifully in a domain in which they have been taught the rule and yet fail to apply it in another domain in which it is just as applicable. Two aspects of the present work probably contributed to the domain independence of statistical training that we found. First, the domains we used were very broad, constituting three haphazard samples of problems, one sample united only by the fact that some obvious randomizing device was present, another consisting of problems where a protagonist had to make a judgment about some objectively measurable aspect of a person or object, and another consisting of problems where a protagonist had to make a judgment about some subjective aspect of a person or object. Had we studied substantially narrower domains – the domain of sports, for example, or the domain of judgments about personality traits – and had we taught subjects specific tools for coding events in those domains and for thinking about their variability, we might well have found some domain specificity of training effects.

A second factor that almost surely contributed to the lack of domain specificity of training effects was the fact that testing immediately followed training. Thus subjects could be expected to have their newly improved statistical rules in "active memory" at the time they were asked to solve the new problems. This fact could be expected to reduce domain-specificity effects to a minimum.

It may have occurred to the reader to suspect that the temporal relation between testing and training might not only reduce domain-specificity effects of training but might be essential in order to produce any effects of training at all. In fact, it could be argued that all our "training" did was to increase the salience of subjects' statistical heuristics and did not teach them anything new at all. As we have known since Socrates' demonstration with the slave boy, it is always hard to prove whether we have taught someone something they did not know before or whether we have merely reminded them of something they already knew.

We have two main lines of defense, however, against the suggestion that our training effects in experiments 1 and 2 were due simply to making the law of large numbers more salient to subjects. First, *reminding* subjects about the law of large numbers and encouraging them to use it had no effect either on the frequency or on the quality of their answers. This is shown clearly by the fact that subjects in the demand condition were no higher than subjects in the control condition on either measure. Secondly, our training manipulations improved not only the frequency of statistical answers, which would be expected on the basis of a mere increase in salience, but the *quality* of answers, which would not be expected on the basis of a mere increase in salience.

The most effective response to the artifactual possibility of salience, however, would be to separate the time and context of training from the time and context of testing. We did this in two different experiments. In experiment 3, we examined the effect of differing amounts of formal course training in statistics on subjects' tendencies to give statistical answers to problems. In experiment 4, we examined the effect of course training in statistics, and we also disguised the context of testing as an opinion survey. In addition to helping rule out the salience and testing context alternatives, these experiments speak to practical questions about the effects of statistical training in formal courses on everyday inferential problems.

EXPERIMENT 3

In experiment 3 we examined the effect of varying amounts of formal course training on the way people reasoned about two different versions of a problem from everyday life. The two versions were very similar, except that one had a powerful probabilistic cue. The study thus allows a comparison of the effects of training on both the likelihood of using statistical reasoning and the quality of statistical reasoning for both a problem for which statistical reasoning is relatively common and a problem for which it is relatively rare.

Subjects and method

Four groups of subjects participated. These groups were chosen for their background, or lack of background, in formal statistical training. The *no statistics* group were 42 college undergraduates who were attending a lecture on attitudes; none had taken college level statistics. The *statistics* group were 56 students attending the same lecture who had taken an introductory statistics course. The *graduate* group were 72 graduate students in psychology, who were attending the first session of a course on statistical methods; all had taken at least one statistics course, and many had taken more than one. And the *tech* group were 33 technical staff members at a research laboratory who were attending a colloquium on probabilistic reasoning. Nearly all were Ph.D. level scientists who had taken many statistics courses.

Subjects were presented with a problem about restaurant quality. There were two versions. In the *no randomness cue* version, a traveling businesswoman often returns to restaurants where she had an excellent meal on her first visit. However, she is usually disappointed because subsequent meals are rarely as good as the first. Subjects were asked to explain, in writing, why this happened.

The *randomness cue* version included a random mechanism for selection from the menu. In this version, the protagonist was a businessman in Japan who did not know how to read the language. When eating at a restaurant, he selected a meal by blindly dropping a pencil on the totally unreadable menu and ordering the dish closest to it. As in the other version, he is usually disappointed with his subsequent meals at restaurants he originally thought were superb. Why is this?

Answers were classified as "statistical" if they suggested that meal quality on any single visit might not be a reliable indicator of the restaurant's overall quality (e.g., "Very few restaurants have only excellent meals; odds are she was just lucky the first time"). "Nonstatistical" answers assumed that the initial good experience was a reliable indicator that the restaurant was truly outstanding, and attributed the later disappointment to a definite cause such as a permanent or temporary change in the restaurant (e.g., "Maybe the chef quit") or a change in the protagonist's expectation or mood (e.g., "Maybe her expectations were so high on the basis of her first visit that subsequent meals could never match them"). Explanations that were statistical were coded as to whether they merely referred vaguely to chance factors ("poor statistical") or whether they also articulated the notion that a single visit may be regarded as a small sample, and hence as unreliable ("good statistical"). Thus, the coding system was essentially the same as the one used in experiments 1 and 2.

Results

Figure 14.7 shows the frequency and quality of answers as a function of training and type of problem. The left side of figure 14.7 demonstrates clearly that the frequency of statistical answers increased dramatically with level of statistical training, $\chi^2(6) = 35.5$, $p < .001$. Almost none of the college students without statistical training gave a statistical answer to the version without the randomness cue, whereas 80% of Ph.D. level scientists did so.

Inclusion of the randomness cue markedly increased the frequency of statistical answers, $\chi^2(4) = 27.1$, $p < .001$. For the untrained college students, for example, the presence of the randomness cue increased frequency from 5 to 50%. The randomness cue thus apparently encourages the subject to code restaurant experiences as units that can be sampled from a population.

The right side of the figure indicates that degree of statistical training was also associated with *quality* of statistical answers, $\chi^2(3) = 12.3$, $p < .001$. Only 10% of the statistical answers by untrained college students were rated as good, whereas almost 80% of the statistical answers by Ph.D. level scientists were rated as good.

Although the presence of the randomness cue was very important in determining whether subjects would think statistically at all, it did not affect the *quality* of statistical answers for subjects at any level of training. This duplicates the findings of experiments 1 and 2, showing that problem difficulty does not affect the quality of answers, given that the answers are statistical. Apparently cues about randomness can trigger the use of statistical rules, but they do not

Figure 14.7 Frequency and quality of statistical answers as a function of group and problem version in experiment 3. Closed points (●) represents responses to the randomness cue version. Open points (○) represent responses to the no randomness cue version.

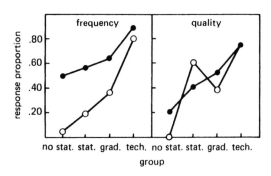

necessarily produce good statistical answers. Such cues can only trigger rules at whatever level of sophistication the subject happens to possess them. This correlational study thus buttresses our assertion that, whatever plausibility the salience alternative has for the frequency results, it has very little plausibility for the quality results.

Discussion

These data indicate that, when one examines people who represent a broad range of statistical expertise, one can find very marked differences in the tendency to approach certain kinds of problems statistically. The data also indicate that, even when statistical approaches are preferred by untutored subjects, as for the version of the problem having the randomness cue, the quality of answers given by such subjects will be markedly inferior to that which more expert subjects can give.

But, while suggestive, the data do not show to precisely what degree formal rule training *per se* is effective. First, statistical training was undoubtedly confounded with intellectual ability, and perhaps even with experiences in superb restaurants. Second, more extensive training in statistics is normally associated with more extensive training in content disciplines that teach the use of statistical and methodological rules in at least an informal way, across a variety of domains. Thus statistical training is also confounded with other types of potentially relevant training.

In experiment 4, we removed these sources of confounding and also provided a testing context that would not be expected to cue subjects into using statistical rules. We conducted experiment 4 in order to examine the effects of formal statistical training in a setting completely outside of the context of training. Students enrolled in an introductory statistics course were contacted at home and were asked to participate in a telephone survey on "students' opinions on sports." Some of the questions could be analyzed with reference to statistical concepts such as the law of large numbers and the regression principle. None of the students was aware that the survey was related to the statistics class they were enrolled in. If training has an effect in this situation, this would provide very strong evidence for the formal view that statistical heuristics are represented at a highly abstract level and that statistical training provides inferential tools that are quite domain and context independent.

EXPERIMENT 4

Subjects

The subjects were 193 randomly selected males at the University of Michigan who were enrolled in an introductory statistics course. The course had a total enrollment of over 600 students.

Geoffrey T. Fong, David H. Krantz, and Richard E. Nisbett

Method

We obtained the class list from the instructor and randomly selected half of the males to be contacted during the first week of the semester, and the other half to be contacted during the last week of the semester.

The protocol we used was designed to convince subjects that we were conducting a genuine opinion survey. The interviewer introduced herself in the following way:

> I am calling from the Research Center for Group Dynamics at the University of Michigan. We're conducting a campus survey about students' opinions on sports. Some of the questions in this survey ask for opinions on current events in professional and collegiate sports: other questions ask for general opinions about sports. The whole survey takes only about 10 to 15 min. Would you have time now to answer our questions?

After asking for some demographic information[9] the interviewer went on to the questions. To enhance the idea that this was a legitimate opinion survey, the first two questions indeed asked subjects to give their real opinions about certain sports controversies (e.g., what colleges should do about recruiting violations). Respondents were quite unaware that the survey was really designed to test their statistical knowledge – none voiced any suspicion.

Following the filler items, subjects were asked a series of questions that could be answered with reference to statistical concepts. This was the first such question:

> In general, the major league baseball player who wins Rookie of the Year does not perform as well in his second year. This is clear in major league baseball in the past 10 years. In the American League, eight Rookies of the Year have done worse in their second year; only two have done better. In the National League, the Rookie of the Year has done worse the second year 9 times out of 10. Why do you suppose the Rookie of the Year tends not to do as well his second year?

Responses to this regression question were tape-recorded and coded for the presence of statistical reasoning and for whether a statistical response was a good one. A typical nonstatistical response for this question would be, "The Rookie of the Year doesn't do as well because he's resting on his laurels; he's not trying as hard in his second year." A good statistical response would be, "A player's performance varies from year to year. Sometimes you have good years and sometimes you have bad years. The player who won the Rookie-of-the-Year award had an exceptional year. He probably did better than average in his second year, but not as well as he did when he was a rookie."

Results and discussion

Results indicated that training in a standard statistics course had a significant effect in enhancing the use of statistical explanations for this question. For those contacted at the beginning of the term, 16 % gave statistical answers. For those contacted at the end of the term, over twice as many (37 %) gave answers that utilized statistical thinking. This increase in frequency was significant, $z = 3.23$, $p < .005$. In addition, the statistics course also enhanced the quality of statistical responses, from .12 to .38, though this was only marginally significant, $z = 1.77$, $p < .10$.

Similar results were obtained on another problem, which asked subjects to explain why the top batting average after 2 weeks of the season is around .450, when such a high average has never been obtained over an entire season. Frequency increased from .50 to .70, $z = 2.87$, $p < .01$, and quality increased from .24 to .50, $z = 2.74$, $p < .01$.

The statistics course did not have any effect on two other problems that we included in the sports survey. One problem asked whether a more talented squash player should choose a five-point or a one-point tie breaker. The other asked subjects to critique a large sample study about whether marriage has an adverse effect on a professional athlete's performance. We have no explanation for why a statistics course failed to enhance statistical reasoning for these two problems.

This study indicates clearly that statistical training can enhance the use of statistical rules in reasoning about everyday life and can do so completely outside the context of training.

GENERAL DISCUSSION

The experiments presented here demonstrate that statistical training serves to enhance the use of statistical principles in reasoning. The effects of training are impressive in their generality across method, context, type of subject, and even domain. Statistical training conferred benefits whether the training consisted of several statistics courses, a single semester-long course, or even a 25-min training session. Training effects occurred not only when the testing context was identical to the training context, but also when the testing context was completely different from the training context in time and situation. Training enhanced statistical thinking not only for college students enrolled in introductory psychology, but also for high school students and adults. Training enhanced both the frequency and quality of statistical thinking not only for events commonly associated with uncertainty and probability, but also, to the same extent, for events rarely associated with such concepts.

A qualification that must be placed on the present results is that the effects at least of relatively brief training sessions may be limited to problems for which some untrained subjects are able to give a statistical answer. Many previous demonstrations of people's difficulty with statistical principles are based on problems to which no subjects, or almost no subjects, apply statistical reasoning (e.g., Hamill, Wilson, and Nisbett, 1980; Kahneman and Tversky, 1973; Tversky and Kahneman, 1983). Quite deliberately, we avoided such difficult problems in the present investigations. Even for the subjective problems in experiments 1 and

2, the average rate of statistical answers for untrained subjects was slightly in excess of 20%.

It is indeed striking that statistical training enhanced statistical thinking for subjective judgments, such as those made about the social world. Social judgments, such as attributions of success or failure, or judgments of a person's traits based on a first impression, are those that, by their very nature, have a critical impact on our lives. At the same time, social judgments are those for which unexplained variation plays a major role.

But, because social events are difficult to code, and because the sample space for such events is typically difficult to define, social judgments are also those that are least likely to be made with reference to statistical considerations. This is shown by the domain-specificity effects found in the experiments presented here and by Jepson *et al.* (1983) on the use of statistical thinking for probabilistic, objective, and subjective events. It is a disturbing state of affairs that the domain where statistical thinking is most necessary on an everyday basis is the one where it is least likely.

Our training studies, however, suggest that people are able to understand and accept the applicability of statistical principles for social events as well as for nonsocial events. The lack of an interaction between training and problem domain indicates that statistical training enhances statistical thinking for social events just as much as it does for nonsocial events. This domain independence of statistical training makes us optimistic that people can indeed be taught to understand the role of uncertainty and sample size in making social judgments.

More generally, the studies reported here make an important point concerning pedagogy in statistics. In the early 1800s, Laplace wrote, " the theory of probabilities is at bottom nothing but common sense reduced to calculus." It seems to us that courses in statistics and probability theory today concentrate almost entirely on the calculus, while often ignoring its common-sense roots. Experiments 3 and 4 clearly demonstrate how classroom training in statistics can potentially have a significant effect on how people make judgments. If introductory statistics courses were to incorporate examples of how statistical principles such as the law of large numbers can be applied to judgments in everyday life, we have no doubt that such courses would have a more far-reaching effect on the extent to which people think statistically about the world.

These studies suggest very strongly that people make use of abstract inferential rules in the form of statistical heuristics. We also know this because training on the purely formal aspects of the law of large numbers improves statistical thinking over a broad range of content, and because showing subjects how to use the rule in a given content domain generalizes completely to quite different content domains. We are aware of no more convincing evidence, in fact, for the existence of abstract rules of reasoning than the present work.

What is the origin of abstract inferential rules about the law of large numbers? Why do people develop such high-level representations of the law of large numbers? We suspect the answer comes, in large measure, from the ubiquity of the principle. The basic notion that large samples are more reliable than small samples underlies concept formation and generalization. It can be argued that, during cognitive development, the child learns, through repeated exposure to the law of large numbers across many domains, a highly abstract representation of the principle.

The experiments presented here demonstrate the dual usefulness of inferential training studies. Such studies are important for pragmatic reasons because they provide information about how everyday reasoning might be improved. It is heartening to discover that a 25-min session on the law of large numbers can serve to significantly enhance people's use of statistical thinking, and that a formal course in introductory statistics can lead to a greater appreciation of variability in judgments, even those made outside the context of the classroom or laboratory. In addition, such studies are important for theoretical reasons not only because of what they tell us about how inferential rules are utilized, but also about how they are represented and how they can be modified.

APPENDIX A

The eighteen test problems used in experiments 1 and 2

Probabilistic – structure 1

At Stanbrook University, the Housing Office determines which of the 10,000 students enrolled will be allowed to live on campus the following year. At Stanbrook, the dormitory facilities are excellent, so there is always great demand for on-campus housing. Unfortunately, there are only enough on-campus spaces for 5,000 students. The Housing Office determines who will get to live on campus by having a Housing Draw every year; every student picks a number out of a box over a three-day period, these numbers ranging from 1 to 10,000. If the number is 5,000 or under, the student gets to live on campus. If the number is over 5,000, the student will not be able to live on campus.

On the first day of the draw, Joe talks to five people who have picked a number. Of these, four people got low numbers. Because of this, Joe suspects that the numbers in the box were not properly mixed, and that the early numbers are more favorable. He rushes over to the Housing Draw and picks a number. He gets a low number. He later talks to four people who drew their numbers on the second or third day of the draw. Three got high numbers. Joe says to himself, "I'm glad that I picked when I did, because it looks like I was right that the numbers were not properly mixed."

What do you think of Joe's reasoning? Explain.

Probabilistic – structure 2

For his vacation, Keith decided to drive from his home in Michigan to California to visit some of his relatives and friends. Shortly after crossing the border into

Nevada, Keith pulled into a gas station and went inside to buy a state map. There, in a corner of the gas station, were two slot machines. Keith had heard about slot machines before, but had never actually seen one. He went over to the slot machines and looked at them, trying to figure out how they worked. An old man who was sitting close to the machines spoke to Keith. "There ain't no winning system for slot machines. It's all luck. You just put in a coin, pull the lever, and hope that you'll win. But let me tell you this: some machines are easier to lose on than others. That's because the owners can change the mechanism of the slots so that some of them will be more likely to make you lose. See those two slot machines there? The one on the left gives you about an even chance of winning, but the one on the right is fixed so that you'll lose much more often than you'll win. Take it from me – I've played them for years." The old man then got up and walked out of the gas station.

Keith was by now very intrigued by the two slot machines, so he played the machine on the left for a couple of minutes. He lost almost twice as often as he won. "Humph," Keith said to himself. "The man said that there was an even chance of winning at that machine on the left. He's obviously wrong." Keith then tried the machine on the right for a couple of minutes and ended up winning more often than he lost. Keith concluded that the man was wrong about the chances of winning on the two slot machines. He concluded that the opposite was true – that the slot machine on the right was more favorable to the player than the machine on the left.

> Comment on Keith's conclusion and his reasoning. Do you agree? Explain your answer.

Probabilistic – structure 3

Bert H. has a job checking the results of an X-ray scanner of pipeline welds in a pipe factory. Overall, the X-ray scanner shows that the welding machine makes a perfect weld about 80% of the time. Of 900 welds each day, usually about 680 to 740 welds are perfect. Bert has noticed that on some days, all of the first 10 welds were perfect. However, Bert has also noticed that on such days, the overall number of perfect welds is usually not much better for the day as a whole than on days when the first 10 welds show some imperfections.

> Why do you suppose the number of perfect welds is usually not much better on days where the first batch of welds was perfect than on other days?

Probabilistic – structure 4

Joanna has a large collection of pennies with dates in the 1970s. Donny admires her collection and decides to start his own collection of pennies, but decides to collect only 1976 pennies because he wants to commemorate the Bicentennial. Looking through his pockets, he discovers he has only a dime. Examining it carefully, he finds that it is a 1971 dime, with a "D" (Denver) mint mark. Donny thinks it would be fun to collect 1976 pennies with the same initial as his name and asks Joanna what proportion of the 1976 pennies in her collection have a "D" mint mark on them. She doesn't know, but they decide to find out. They take the huge jar of her pennies out. Since the jar has thousands of pennies in it, Donny shakes the jar and then reaches into it and picks out a handful from the middle of the jar. Donny finds all the 1976 pennies that he scooped out (four of them) and finds that two of them have "D" mint marks. Because of this, he estimates that around 50 % of all Joanna's 1976 pennies have the "D" mint mark. But Joanna looks through the other 36 pennies they have scooped out (dated 1970–1975 and 1977–1979) and discovers that only 2 of them have the "D" mint mark. She argues that only 4 of 40 pennies altogether have the "D" mark, and estimates that around 10 % of the 1976 pennies in her collection are "D" pennies.

Comment on the validity of Joanna's and Donny's reasoning. Whose conclusion about the 1976 pennies in Joanna's collection is more likely to be correct? Explain.

Probabilistic – structure 5

An auditor for the Internal Revenue Service wants to study the nature of arithmetic errors on income tax returns. She selects 4,000 Social Security numbers by using random digits generated by an "Electronic Mastermind" calculator. For each selected social security number she checks the 1978 Federal Income Tax return thoroughly for arithmetic errors. She finds errors on a large percentage of the tax returns, often 2 to 6 errors on a single tax return. Tabulating the effect of each error separately, she finds that there are virtually the same number of errors in favor of the taxpayer as in favor of the government. Her boss objects vigorously to her assertions, saying that it is fairly obvious that people will notice and correct errors in favor of the government, but will "overlook" errors in their own favor. Even if her figures are correct, he says, looking at a lot more returns will bear out this point.

Comment on the auditor's reasoning and her boss's contrary stand.

Probabilistic – structure 6

A brewery buys nearly all of its reusable glass bottles from a local glass manufacturer. One summer, however, the local company is unable to deliver enough bottles, and the brewery orders a shipment from a large glass manufacturer that distributes its products nationwide. On the first day that these new bottles are used, however, the bottle-filling machinery has to be stopped four times because of jamming, and, as a result, production for the day is unusually low. (Ordinarily the brewery does not experience more than one jamming stoppage per day and frequently there are none at all.) The foreman is worried about the new bottles. He decides to test the new bottles produced by the national manufacturer carefully. He randomly selects 300 cases of these new bottles and instructs the bottle-filler operators to record carefully each jamming incident. Meanwhile, company mechanics carefully lubricate and check adjustments on the bottle-filling machinery. When they are finished, the bottle-filling machinery is running more smoothly than it has for years. During the next 2 days, the 300 cases of new bottles are fed to the machine. There are only two jamming incidents, one each day. The foreman concludes that there is in fact little or no real disadvantage of the new bottles with respect to jamming of the bottle-filling machinery.

> Comment on the foreman's reasoning. Is it basically sound? Can his procedure be criticized?

Objective – structure 1

A talent scout for a professional basketball team attends two college games with the intention of observing carefully the talent and skill of a particular player. The player looks generally excellent. He repeatedly makes plays worthy of the best professional players. However, in one of the games, with his team behind by 2 points, the player is fouled while shooting and has the opportunity to tie the game by making both free throws. The player misses both free throws and then tries too hard for the rebound from the second one, committing a foul in the process. The other team then makes two free throws, for a 4-point lead, and goes on to win by 2 points.

The scout reports that the player in question "has excellent skills, and should be recruited. He has a tendency to misplay under extreme pressure, but this will probably disappear with more experience and better coaching."

> Comment on the thinking embodied in the scout's opinion that the player (a) "has excellent skills" and that the player has (b) "a tendency to misplay under extreme pressure." Does the thinking behind either conclusion have any weaknesses?

Objective – structure 2

The Caldwells had long ago decided that when it was time to replace their car they would get what they called "one of those solid, safety-conscious, built-to-last Swedish cars" – either a Volvo or a Saab. As luck would have it, their old car gave up the ghost on the last day of the closeout sale for the model year both for the Volvo and for the Saab. The model year was changing for both cars and the dollar had recently dropped substantially against European currencies; therefore, if they waited to buy either a Volvo or a Saab, it would cost them substantially more – about $1,200. They quickly got out their *Consumer Reports* where they found that the consensus of the experts was that both cars were very sound mechanically, although the Volvo was felt to be slightly superior on some dimensions. They also found that the readers of *Consumer Reports* who owned a Volvo reported having somewhat fewer mechanical problems than owners of

Saabs. They were about to go and strike a bargain with the Volvo dealer when Mr Caldwell remembered that they had two friends who owned a Saab and one who owned a Volvo. Mr Caldwell called up the friends. Both Saab owners reported having had a few mechanical problems but nothing major. The Volvo owner exploded when asked how he liked his car. "First that fancy fuel injection computer thing went out: $250 bucks. Next I started having trouble with the rear end. Had to replace it. Then the transmission and the clutch. I finally sold it after 3 years for junk."

> Given that the Caldwells are going to buy either a Volvo or a Saab today, in order to save $1,200, which do you think they should buy? Why?

Objective – structure 3

Howard was a teacher in a junior high school in a community known for truancy and delinquency problems among its youth. Howard says of his experiences: "Usually, in a class of 35 or so kids, 2 or 3 will pull some pretty bad stunts in the first week – they'll skip a day of class, get into a scuffle with another kid, or some such thing. When that kind of thing happens, I play it down and try to avoid calling the classes' attention to it. Usually, these kids turn out to be no worse than the others. By the end of the term you'll find they haven't pulled any more stunts than the others have." Howard reasons as follows: "Some of these kids are headed toward a delinquent pattern of behavior. When they find out nobody is very impressed, they tend to settle down.

> Comment on Howard's reasoning:
> (a) Do you agree that it is likely that the students who pull a "pretty bad stunt in the first week" are "headed toward a delinquent pattern of behavior"?
> (b) Do you agree that it is likely that the students who initially pull a "pretty bad stunt" turn out to be no worse than the others because they find no one is impressed with their behavior?

Objective – structure 4

The psychology department of the University of Michigan keeps records on the performance of all its graduate students and relates this performance score to all kinds of background information about the students. Recently there was a debate on the admissions committee about whether to admit a particular student from Horace Maynard College. The student's scores on the GRE and his GPA were marginal – that is, almost all students actually admitted to the department have scores as high or higher, while most rejected students have lower scores. The students letters of recommendation were quite good, but none of the writers of the letters was personally known to any of the Michigan faculty.

One member of the admissions committee argued against admission, pointing out that department records show that students who graduate from small, nonselective colleges like Maynard perform at a level substantially below the median of all Michigan graduate students. This argument was countered by a committee member who noted that 2 years ago Michigan had admitted a student from Maynard who was now among the three highest ranked students in the department.

> Comment on the arguments put forward by these two committee members. What are their strengths and weaknesses?

Objective – structure 5

The superintendent of schools was urging the school hard to make an expensive curriculum shift to a "back-to-basics" stress on fundamental learning skills and away from the electives and intensive immersion in specialized arts and social studies topics that had recently characterized the secondary schools in the district. He cited a study of 120 school systems that had recently begun to emphasize the basics and 120 school systems that had a curriculum similar to the district's current one. The "back-to-basics" school systems, he said, were producing students who scored half-a-year ahead of the students in the other systems on objective tests of reading, mathematics, and science. Of the 120 "back-to-basics" school systems, 85 had shown improved skills for students in the system vs. only 40 with improved skills in the 120 systems which had not changed. One of the school board members took the floor to argue against the change. In her opinion, she said, there was no compelling reason to attribute the improved student skills in the "back-to-basics" systems to the specific curriculum change, for two reasons: (1) school systems that make curriculum changes probably have more energetic, adventurous administrators and faculty and thus the students would learn more in those school systems no matter what the curriculum was; (2) *any* change in curriculum could be expected to produce improvement in student performance because of increased faculty interest and commitment.

> Comment on the reasoning of both the superintendent and the board member. On the basis of the evidence and arguments offered, do you think it is likely that the "back-to-basics" curriculum is intrinsically superior to the district's current curriculum?

Objective – structure 6

An economist was arguing in favor of a guaranteed minimum income for everyone. He cited a recent study of several hundred people in the United States with inherited wealth. Nearly 92% of those people, he said, worked at some job that provided earned income sufficient to provide at least a middle-class life style. The study showed, he said, that contrary to popular opinion, people will work in preference to being idle. Thus a guaranteed income policy would result in little or no increase in the number of people unwilling to work.

Comment on the economist's reasoning. Is it basically sound? Does it have weaknesses?

Subjective – structure 1

Gerald M. had a 3-year-old son, Timmy. He told a friend: "You know, I've never been much for sports, and I think Timmy will turn out the same. A couple of weeks ago, an older neighbor boy was tossing a ball to him, and he could catch it and throw it all right, but he just didn't seem interested in it. Then the other day, some kids his age were kicking a little soccer ball around. Timmy could do it as well as the others, but he lost interest very quickly and started playing with some toy cars while the other kids went on kicking the ball around for another 20 or 30 min."

Do you agree with Gerald's reasoning that Timmy is likely not to care much for sports? Why or why not?

Subjective – structure 2

David L. was a senior in high school on the East Coast who was planning to go to college. He had compiled an excellent record in high school and had been admitted to his two top choices: a small liberal arts college and an Ivy League university. The two schools were about equal in prestige and were equally costly. Both were located in attractive East Coast cities, about equally distant from his home town. David had several older friends who were attending the liberal arts college and several who were attending the Ivy League university. They were all excellent students like himself and had interests that were similar to his. His friends at the liberal arts college all reported that they liked the place very much and that they found it very stimulating. The friends at the Ivy League university reported that they had many complaints on both personal and social grounds and on educational grounds. David initially thought that he would go to the liberal arts college. However, he decided to visit both schools himself for a day. He did not like what he saw at the private liberal arts college: several people whom he met seemed cold and unpleasant; a professor he met with briefly seemed abrupt and uninterested in him; and he did not like the "feel" of the campus. He did like what he saw at the Ivy League university: several of the people he met seemed like vital, enthusiastic, pleasant people; he met with two different professors who took a personal interest in him; and he came away with a very pleasant feeling about the campus.

Which school should David L. choose, and why? Try to analyze the arguments on both sides, and explain which side is stronger.

Subjective – structure 3

Janice is head nurse in a home for the aged. She says the following of her experiences: "There is a big turnover of the nursing staff here, and each year we hire 15–20 new nurses. Some of these people show themselves up to be unusually warm and compassionate in the first few days. One might stay on past quitting time with a patient who's having a difficult night. Another might be obviously shaken by the distress of a patient who had just lost a spouse. I find though that, over the long haul, these women turn out to be not much more concerned and caring than the others. What happens to them, I think, is that they can't remain open and vulnerable without paying a heavy emotional price. They usually continue to be considerate and effective but they build up a shell."

> Comment on Janice's reasoning. Do you think it is likely that she correctly identifies the nurses who are unusually warm and compassionate? Do you agree it is likely that most of the ones who are unusually warm at first later build up a shell to protect themselves emotionally?

Subjective – structure 4

The director of a Broadway production of Shakespeare's *As You Like It* had just finished auditions for the female lead in the show. Two of the candidates gave readings for the part he liked a great deal. Another was an actress whom the director had worked with before in three Shakespeare comedies. The director thought she had been superb in each. Unfortunately, of her three readings for the lead in this play, one had been fairly good, but two had been quite flat. This third actress had to know immediately whether she was going to be chosen for the part. If not, she would take a minor role in a movie that would keep her on the West Coast for the next 6 months.

> What should the director do – hire the third actress or hire one of the two whose readings he liked better? Why?

Subjective – structure 5

Two New Yorkers were discussing restaurants, Jane said to Ellen, "You know, most people seem to be crazy about Chinese food, but I'm not. I've been to about 20 different Chinese restaurants, across the whole price range, and everything from bland Cantonese to spicy Szechuan and I'm really not very fond of any of it." "Oh," said Ellen, "don't jump to conclusions. I'll bet you've usually gone with a crowd of people, right?" "Yes," admitted Jane, "that's true. I usually go with half a dozen people or more from work." "Well, that may be it," said Ellen. "People go to Chinese restaurants with a crowd of people they hardly know. I know you, you're often tense and a little shy, and you're not likely to be able to relax and savor the food under those circumstances. Try going to a Chinese restaurant with just one good friend. I'll bet you'll like the food."

Comment on Ellen's reasoning. Do you think there is a good chance that if Jane went to a Chinese restaurant with one friend, she'd like the food? Why or why not?

Subjective – structure 6

Martha was talking to a fellow passenger on an airplane. The fellow passenger was on his way to Hawaii for a month's vacation. "I don't like vacations myself," Martha said. "I've always worked. I put myself through college and law school and now I have a full-time legal practice. Frequently, of course, I've had slow periods when I wasn't working at all, but I never liked those times. For example, there would usually be a week or two between the end of school and the beginning of a summer job and another week or two of enforced idleness at the end of the summer. And there were many occasions when I was getting started in my career when I had no real work to do for fairly long periods. But I never enjoyed the leisure. I know there are some people who talk about using vacations to "recharge" themselves. But I suspect many of these people don't really enjoy their work or don't have a very high energy level. I do have a lot of energy, and I do enjoy my work, and I guess that's why I don't really like vacations."

Analyze Martha's reasoning. Do you think she has good evidence for feeling she doesn't like vacations?

APPENDIX B

The long objective example problems used in experiment 1, also used in the objective examples training condition of experiment 2

Example 1 (structure 1)

A major New York law firm had a history of hiring only graduates of large, prestigious law schools. One of the senior partners decided to try hiring some graduates of smaller, less prestigious law schools. Two such people were hired. Their grades and general record were similar to those of people from the prestigious schools hired by the firm. Although their manners and "style" were not as polished and sophisticated as those of the predominantly Ivy League junior members of the firm, their objective performance was excellent. At the end of 3 years, both of them were well above average in the number of cases won and in the volume of law business handled. The senior partner, who had hired them argued to colleagues in the firm that "This experience indicates that graduates of less prestigious schools are at least as ambitious and talented as graduates of the major law schools. The chief difference between the two types of graduates is in their social class background, not in their legal ability, which is what counts."

Comment on the thinking that went into this senior partner's conclusion. Is the argument basically sound? Does it have weaknesses? (Disregard your own initial opinion, if you had one, about graduates of nonprestigious law schools, and concentrate on the thinking that the senior partner used.)

Please consider this problem for a few moments. After you have considered the problem and analyzed it for a minute or two, turn the page for our analysis.

The senior partner is trying to draw a conclusion about a certain population. We can think of the members of this *population* as newly graduated lawyers, from nonprestigious law schools, who otherwise meet the law firm's hiring standards. If we divide the members of this population into *two categories*, "excellent" and "mediocre or worse," we can think of the *population distribution* as the percentage in each category. The senior partner has concluded that the percentage in the "excellent" category is very high, or anyway just as high as in another population involving graduates of prestigious law schools. This conclusion was based on observing a *sample* of *size = 2*, in which the *sample distribution* was 100% "excellent," 0% "mediocre or worse."

Apart from any other considerations, however, the *sample distribution* for size 2 is apt to be quite different from the *population distribution*: the latter could be only 60 or 50% or even perhaps as low as 40% "excellent" and a 2–0 sample split would not be so unusual; just as one would not be at all amazed to draw two out of two red gumballs from an urn with only 40% reds. So the senior partner's attitude is quite unwarranted: a larger sample is needed.

Example 2 (structure 3)

Susan is the artistic director for a ballet company. One of her jobs is auditioning and selecting new members of the company. She says the following of her experience: "Every year we have 10–20 young people on a 1-year contract on the basis of their performance at the audition. Usually we're extremely excited about the potential of 2 or 3 of these young people – a young woman who does a brilliant series of turns or a young man who does several leaps that make you hold your breath. Unfortunately, most of these young people turn out to be only somewhat better than the rest. I believe many of these extraordinarily talented young people are frightened of success. They get into the company and see the tremendous effort and anxiety involved in becoming a star, and they get cold feet. They'd rather lead a less demanding life as an ordinary member of the corps de ballet."

Comment on Susan's reasoning. Why do you suppose that Susan usually has to revise downward her opinion of dancers that she initially thought were brilliant?

Please consider this problem for a few moments. After you have considered the problem and analyzed it for a minute or two, turn the page for our analysis.

We can analyze this problem using the law of large numbers by thinking of each ballet dancer as possessing a *population* of ballet movements. Susan is interested in excellence, so we can divide the members of each population into two categories:

336

"brilliant movements"and "nonbrilliant, or other, movements." We can think of the *population distribution* as the percentage or proportion in each category. For many dancers, the population distribution is actually 0% brilliant and 100% other: these dancers simply lack the talent to perform a brilliant movement. For many other dancers, there is a small or moderate percentage of "brilliant movement" gumballs in their urn. A true ballet star would therefore have a population distribution with a greater percentage of "brilliant" movements than an ordinary member of the corps de ballet.

By conducting auditions, Susan is observing *samples* of each dancer's population distribution. An audition, however, is a very small sample of a dancer's movements. We know from the law of large numbers that small samples are very unreliable estimates of the population. When a dancer performs some brilliant moves during an audition, it is often because the dancer has happened to draw a couple of the "lucky gumballs" that day: it does not prove that the population distribution for that dancer consists of a large percentage of "brilliant movements." It is reasonable to think that there are really very few dancers that have population distributions with a large percentage of brilliant movements; and so, when Susan sees a dancer performing brilliantly at audition, the chances are it is just a lucky draw from a dancer who is capable of performing some, but not necessarily a great number of, "brilliant movements." Therefore, when Susan hires such dancers and evaluates them after seeing a much larger sample of their movements, it is not surprising that she finds that many of these dancers that were brilliant at audition turn out to be only somewhat better than the rest.

Example 3 (structure 5)

Kevin, a graduate student in sociology, decided to do a research project on "factors affecting performance of major league baseball players" in which he gathered a great amount of demographic data on birthplace, education, marital status, etc., to see if any demographic factors were related to the performance of major league baseball players (e.g., batting average, pitching victories). Kevin was unable to use data for all the major league teams because information for some of the players was unavailable, but he was able to obtain data for some 200 players in the major leagues.

One finding that interested Kevin concerned the 110 married players. About 68% of these players improved their performance after getting married, while the remainder had equal or poorer performance. He concluded that marriage is beneficial to a baseball player's performance. At a social hour sponsored by the Office of the Commissioner of Major League Baseball, he happened to mention his finding to a staff member of the office. The staff member listened to Kevin's results and then said, "Your study is interesting but I don't believe it. I'm sure that baseball performance is worse after a marriage because the ball player suddenly has to take on enormous responsibilities: taking care of his spouse and children. Plus the factor of being stressed by having to be on the road so much of the time and therefore away from the family. The player will no longer be able to devote as much time to baseball as before he was married. Because of this he will lose that competitive quality that is necessary for good performance in baseball."

What do you think of the staff member's argument? Is it a sound one or not? Explain your reasoning.

Please consider this problem for a few moments. After you have considered the problem and analyzed it for a minute or two, turn the page for our analysis.

Kevin is trying to find out how performance in major league baseball is affected by being married. To do this, he obtained data for 200 players in the major leagues and discovered that out of the 110 that had gotten married, 68% had improved performance after the wedding (and 32% had equal or poorer performance). According to the law of large numbers, which states that the larger the sample, the better it is in estimating the population, there is substantial evidence that marriage is beneficial to a baseball player's performance. Recall that in the gumball demonstration, samples of size 25 were very good estimates of the population: these samples did not differ much from population. Extending the argument, samples of size 100 are extremely accurate estimates of the population. Thus, it can be concluded that, in general, marriage is beneficial to a baseball player's performance.

What about the staff member's theory that baseball performance is worse after a marriage because the ball player assumes enormous responsibilities and will no longer be able to devote as much time to baseball as before? Although this argument may have some intuitive appeal, it should be discounted because it is not supported by any data and is, in fact, contradicted by Kevin's large sample of 110 players.

NOTES

This research was supported by NSF Grants SES82-18846 and SES85-07342, and ONR Grant 442PT/85-2281 to Richard Nisbett. Geoffrey T. Fong was supported by a CIC-Lilly Foundation Minority Graduate Fellowship and a Rackham Fellowship at the University of Michigan. Experiment 1 was conducted while David Krantz was at AT & T Bell Laboratories, whose support is gratefully acknowledged. We thank Michael Smith, Bonnie Thompson, Alison Frank, Roseann O'Rourke, and Kathy Wandersee for their assistance and Edward Rothman for his help on experiment 4. We thank Reid Hastie, Darrin Lehman, Ziva Kunda, and Saul Sternberg for their comments on previous drafts of this chapter. And, finally, we thank Drake's Candy Store in Ann Arbor, Michigan, for supplying the gumballs used in experiments 1 and 2.

First published in *Cognitive Psychology*, 18 (1986), 253–92. Copyright © 1986 by Academic Press, Inc. All rights of reproduction in any form reserved.

1 All training materials can be obtained from the authors.
2 Each of the frequency means represents the proportion of problems for which subjects in that condition utilized some kind of statistical concept. Thus, the frequency mean of .42 for the control condition is based on 1,007 responses (68 subjects × 15 problems each, minus 13 unanswered problems).
3 The additive log-linear model can be expressed as: $\log p_{ijk} - \log(1 - p_{ijk}) = \mu + \alpha_i + \beta_j + \varepsilon_{ijk}$, where p_{ijk} is the probability of a statistical response by the kth subject in the jth training group for the ith problem. The parameters were estimated by maximizing the likelihood of the 15 × 347 (problem ×

subject) matrix of zeros and ones, subject to the identifying constraints that the sum of the problem effects, $\sum \alpha_i$, and the sum of the training group effects, $\sum \beta_j$, are zero. The estimation was accomplished by the Loglin function of the statistical package S (a product of AT&T Bell Laboratories). The Loglin function uses an algorithm developed by Haberman (1972). The entries in table 14.1, column 4, are the estimated values of β_j. The fit was barely improved by including the problem × training interaction parameters, γ_{ij}, to the model. The fit was considerably improved by including subject parameters, δ_{jk}, to the model, but this created difficulties in identifying β_j, because a few of the subject parameter estimates were $+\infty$ or $-\infty$, corresponding to 15 out of 15 or 0 out of 15 statistical answers. Therefore, we stuck with the simple additive model when we tested for differences among training conditions. The β_js from the above model are good descriptive statistics for assessing the effects of training condition, and their sampling properties can be estimated by jackknifing (see note 4).

4 Jackknifing was performed with 10 subsamples, each formed by randomly dropping 10% of the subjects. The estimated standard error of the pairwise differences (that is, differences between any two β_js) varied only slightly from one pair of groups to another.

5 The quality data were analyzed using the same models as for the frequency data (see note 3). The corresponding parameter estimates, β_j, are shown in the rightmost column of table 14.1. The 15×347 data matrix of zeros and ones for quality had nearly half missing data, since quality was defined only for statistical answers. The nonlinearity of the log-linear model leads to some minor differences between the quality proportions and their corresponding log-linear effects. For example, note that although the rule proportion is greater than the examples proportion, the rule log-linear effect is actually less than the examples log-linear effect.

6 The predicted ordering of the three problem types with respect to frequency of statistical answers (probabilistic > objective > subjective) resulted for each of the five problem structures for which the law of large numbers was relevant (structures 1–5). The probability of this occurring by chance is extremely low, $p = (1/6)^5 < .001$.

7 Complete details of the false-alarm analyses for experiments 1 and 2 can be obtained from the authors.

8 Although the pattern of these proportions is similar to that in experiment 1, their magnitude is substantially greater. One reason is that whereas the five conditions in experiment 1 varied considerably in the degree of training, three of the four conditions in experiment 2 were essentially full training conditions (all were given rule training). When averaging across conditions, the proportions for experiment 2 will reflect this more extensive training.

9 In order to ensure that subjects had enough knowledge of sports to be able to understand the survey questions, they were asked to rate their knowledge about sports. Those who rated themselves as having little or no knowledge of sports were not used in this experiment.

REFERENCES

Bishop, Y. M. M., Fienberg, S. E., and Holland, P. W. (1975). *Discrete multivariate analysis: theory and practice*. Cambridge, MA: MIT Press.

D'Andrade, R. (1982, April). *Reason versus logic*. Paper presented at the Symposium on the Ecology of Cognition: Biological, Cultural, and Historical Perspectives, Greensboro, North Carolina.

Einhorn, H. J., and Hogarth, R. M. (1981). Behavioral decision theory: processes of judgment and choice. *Annual Review of Psychology*, 32, 53–88.

Evans, J. St. B. T. (1982). *The psychology of deductive reasoning*. London: Routledge & Kegal Paul.

Golding, E. (1981). *The effect of past experience on problem solving*. Paper presented at the Annual Conference of the British Psychological Society, Surrey University.

Griggs, R. A., and Cox, J. R. (1982). The elusive thematic-materials effect in Wason's selection task. *British Journal of Psychology*, 73, 407—20.

Geoffrey T. Fong, David H. Krantz, and Richard E. Nisbett

Haberman, S. J. (1972). Log-linear fit for contingency tables – algorithm AS51. *Applied Statistics*, 21, 218–25.

Hamill, R., Wilson, T. D., and Nisbett, R. E. (1980). Insensitivity to sample bias: generalizing from atypical cases. *Journal of Personality and Social Psychology*, 39, 578–89.

Hogarth, R. M. (1980). *Judgment and choice: the psychology of decision*. New York: Wiley.

Jepson, C., Krantz, D. H., and Nisbett, R. E. (1983). Inductive reasoning: competence or skill? *Behavioral Sciences*, 6, 494–501.

Johnson-Laird, P. N., Legrenzi, P., and Sonino-Legrenzi, M. (1972). Reasoning and a sense of reality. *British Journal of Psychology*, 63, 395–400.

Kahneman, D., Slovic, P., and Tversky, A. (eds.). (1982). *Judgment under uncertainty: heuristics and biases*. New York: Cambridge University Press.

Kahneman, D., and Tversky, A. (1971). Subjective probability: a judgment of representativeness. *Cognitive Psychology*, 3, 430–54.

(1973). On the psychology of prediction. *Psychlogical Review*, 80, 237–51.

Manktelow, K. I., and Evans, J. St. B. T. (1979). Facilitation of reasoning by realism: effect or non-effect? *British Journal of Psychology*, 70, 477–88.

Nisbett, R. E., Krantz, D. H., Jepson, C., and Fong, G. T. (1982). Improving inductive inference. In D. Kahneman, P. Slovic, and A. Tversky (eds.), *Judgment under uncertainty: heuristics and biases*. New York: Cambridge University Press.

Nisbett, R. E., Krantz, D. H., Jepson, C., and Kunda, Z. (1983). The use of statistical heuristics in everyday inductive reasoning. *Psychological Review*, 90, 339–63.

Nisbett, R. E., and Ross, L. (1980). *Human inference: strategies and shortcomings of social judgment*. Englewood Cliifs, NJ: Prentice-Hall.

Reich, S. S., and Ruth, P. (1982). Wason's selection task: verification, falsification and matching. *British Journal of Psychology*, 73, 395–405.

Tversky, A., and Kahneman, D. (1974). Judgment under uncertainty: heuristics and biases. *Science (Washington, D.C.)*, 185, 1124–31.

(1983). Extensional versus intuitive reasoning: the conjunction fallacy in probability judgment. *Psychological Review*, 90, 293–315.

Wason, P. C. (1966). Reasoning. In B. M. Foss (ed.), *New horizons in psychology I*. Harmondsworth, England: Penguin.

IV

VALUES AND UTILITIES

15

THE MIND AS A CONSUMING ORGAN

T. C. SCHELLING

Lassie died one night. Millions of viewers, not all of them children, grieved. At least, they shed tears. Except for the youngest, the mourners knew that Lassie did not really exist. Whatever that means. Perhaps with their left hemisphere they could articulate that they had been watching a trained dog and that *that* dog was still alive, healthy, and rich; meanwhile in their right hemispheres, or some such place (if these phenomena have a place), the real Lassie had died.

Did they enjoy the episode?

We know they would not have enjoyed the death of the dog that played Lassie. Did the adults and older children wish that Lassie had not died? Do the dry-eyed parents of a moist-eyed teenager wish their child had not watched? If he had not watched, what would have been his grief at breakfast, reading the news that Lassie was dead? And would he regret missing the final episode?

What about declaring that Lassie did not die and showing an alternative episode, one that was filmed after Lassie's death was screened, and explaining that, Lassie being only fictional, the screen writers thought it best, in view of the widespread grief (evidenced by some people's wanting to know where to send flowers) to rewrite the story?

I do not think it works. But maybe a substitute screen writer could be blamed for an unauthentic episode. Lassie's true creator having been hospitalized but, now having recovered, swearing that the real Lassie had not been going to die and that the dying episode was a counterfeit.

But there are rules that must not be violated. An important one is no feedback from the audience. You cannot show two episodes and let each viewer choose, nor poll the audience to determine whether Lassie dies.

Nor can the viewers simply imagine themselves a different episode in which Lassie is spared. The problem is not the lack of imagination, but discipline and authenticity. Fantasy is too self-indulgent. George Ainslie's work illuminates the issue.[1] Daydreams escalate. Before I can spend the $10,000 that my poker partner bet because he thought that I was bluffing, I revise the figure to $100,000; then I put it in gold at $40 dollars an ounce, spend a couple of years hiking home

343

from a plane crash in Northern Canada, phone my broker to sell and hit the $800 dollar market, and start plotting to invest my two million in something equally good... By then I realize that it is all counterfeit if I can make it up so easily.

There is no suspense, no surprise, no danger. Likewise there is no emergency in which Lassie can risk her life with which I can quicken my pulse as long as I know that I write the ending.

Engrossing fiction, whatever else it is, is disciplined fantasy. If you know your authors you can even choose, as people choose their opponent's skill in a chess machine, the risk of tragedy. Killing a character in whom the reader has made an investment puts the lives of the remaining characters in credible jeopardy, and some authors acquire a reputation for poignant endings.

There is something here akin to self-deception. Jon Elster's work on self-deception is persuasive.[2] His interest is rational cognitive self-deception, reasoning one's way into a belief one knew to be false, inducing the belief through practice, or permanently removing something from memory together with the memory of the decision to remove it. There are other phenomena that could be called self-deception that are less permanent and less cognitive. Riding a safe roller-coaster can give some people the same exhilaration as a genuinely risky trip. Their eyes and semicircular canals rupture the communication channels. I do not know who I thought was being stabbed in the shower in *Psycho*, but after the movie my wife and I, who had arrived at the theater in separate cars, left one car behind and drove home together. I have not been able to determine whether it is the scare that I enjoy or the relief that comes after. Richard Solomon has discussed an "opponent process" that might generate net utility from the infliction of pain or fright; his parachutists enjoyed a high that lasted twenty-four hours after the jump.[3] I wonder whether someone thrown from an airplane, saved by a parachute that he did not know he had, would be exhilarated by the experience. In skydiving and in horror movies the sensation of risk is controlled; self-deception is partial; the glands that secrete euphoriant stimuli are encouraged to be deceived, but not the control centers that make us sick.

A puzzle occurs to me. I have never been instructed in how to produce good daydreams. It could be that I do not have the talent to create fiction, for myself or for anybody else, and I rely on novelists to provide fully articulated fantasies with which I can identify in a participatory way. But possibly I simply do not know the rules of construction. Like a sculptor who finds challenge in the stone itself, artistic fantasy may require the challenge of self-imposed restraint. Perhaps I could be taught strategies of self-discipline to prevent that runaway inflation to which my favorite daydreams are so susceptible. There may be ways to introduce genuine surprise, perhaps by some random drawing from a library in my mind. The problem suggested by Elster's comments on self-induced beliefs, and on sneaking up on one's own insomnia, is that in the act of reining in one's daydreams to give them greater authenticity one may not be able to hold reins and forget one's holding them.

It does not detract, as far as I can tell, from the suspense and credibility of the fiction I read that I chose the book, i.e. chose an author I knew, or knew something about the book by hearsay. (Douglas Hofstadter, in *Gödel, Escher, Bach*, pointed out that by unconsciously estimating the pages remaining we spoil some of the terminal surprise of a novel, just as by checking our watch during an adventure film we can tell whether we are on another false summit or have reached the climax.)

I doubt whether these puzzles can be resolved by just thinking about them. The rules of argument for certain philosophical problems require idealizing a person as a reasoning machine, one that not only can think logically but cannot think not logically, that has no hallucinations and no chemical or electrical means of putting things into memory or taking them out. Whether that kind of person can do something that would be called "fooling himself," and what the limits are on what he may fool himself about, is an intriguing question.[4] But it is not the only question, because that is not the only kind of person worth studying. What makes dreams, daydreams, books, and films captivating, credible, and irresistible, with or without music or stimulants, requires more than reflection. Though we can often simulate by reasoning what can be done by reasoning, spellbinding requires other modes of study.

Maybe real dreams are more promising. Some work of Kilton Stewart indicated that people in the Malay peninsula have developed techniques for taming their dreams, reshaping dreams in progress.[5] Apparently they do not make up their dreams in advance, but assume enough command to keep the dreams from getting out of hand. I cannot claim even to understand what that means, but I also do not understand the particular control that I had when that nice girl was being stabbed in the shower.

Lassie represents only one of the ways that, as consumers, we live in our minds. She was fiction and her medium was television; Rin Tin Tin was radio and movies. But novels, plays, puppets, and stories, impromptu or composed, new or familiar, are of the species. They are primarily for enjoyment. And they usually, but not always, capture the mind.

By capture I mean to engage it, to hold it, to occupy or to preoccupy it so that one's thoughts are not elsewhere; to give the reader or viewer or listener a stake in the outcome; to make him identify in some fashion with characters in the story, if only by caring what happens. The engagement has dynamics; it progresses. Interruption is disagreeable, though a person can sometimes go on "hold" while the man in the projection room changes the reel.

The characteristic that interests me is the engrossment – not merely the surrender of attention but the participation, the sense of being in the story or part of it, caring, and wanting to know. (There is some fiction that does not have that quality; irony and humor require a more conscious attention, and some plots are constructed to be admired rather than absorbed into. Some surprise turns of plot are intended to jolt the reader out of the story and into a relation with the author;

and some science fiction is more like turning the leaves of a mail-order catalogue than participating in a story.)

There is also non-fiction that works like fiction. For many of us it is impossible to watch sports on television just to admire the performance. Not only do we end up caring how the game comes out, we are incapable of watching the game symmetrically. It is more fun to be engaged. And that Lassie phenomenon occurs: I cannot change the side I am on, especially not to be on the winning side, because changing sides discredits the notion that I have a side, just as I cannot mentally bring Lassie back to life without denying that Lassie is mortal and I care what happens to her.

It is this suspense and concern that qualifies certain live events to be considered as impromptu fiction. Snippets of football, like an eighty yard punt return, can be good entertainment for a few minutes, but I have never known a TV channel to replay old games regularly; and people who look forward to a delayed broadcast do all they can to avoid overhearing the outcome in advance.

What puzzles me is how to relate these observations to a theory of what people are up to. Take the rational consumer in economic theory: what is he consuming?

What do I consume when I purchase *The Wizard of Oz*? Physically I buy a book, or a reel of videotape. But that is a raw material; I "consume" two hours of entertainment. But should I say that, like Dorothy, I consumed a trip to Oz? Or, to phrase it awkwardly, that I procured Dorothy's trip to Oz, in which I participated? I do not mean a sight-seeing trip – television can always show me places that I cannot afford to visit – but the adventure, with the risk and poignancy and excitement and surprise.

A way to try to make sense of the question is to ask what the substitutes are. If you lower the price of air travel I may travel less by bus, but if I see *Around the World In Eighty Days* am I less likely to travel? Can I do without a dog if I have Lassie? Do I need as much romance, repartee, or fresh air and sunshine if I get plenty of it from nine until midnight on a screen in my living-room? I am not sure what I should be expected to consume less of once I have seen two killings in *Psycho*. And since some consumer goods whet appetites, the notion of substitutes may not be the correct one.

There is no question but that part of what I get from a two hour movie or two hours in a book is "two hours' worth" of something. I get two hours of timeout, of escape, of absent-mindedness. Escape from what? Certainly from boredom. Escaping boredom is escaping the tedium of consciousness, of one's own company, of being here and now and one's self, not someplace else or somebody else.

And there is escaping things the knowledge of which makes one unhappy. If "truth" is what we know and are aware of, in the most engrossing fiction we escape truth. Whatever else it is, drama is forgetfulness. We can forget and forget that we are forgetting. It is temporary mind control. If memories are pain, fiction is anesthesia.

The mind as a consuming organ

But is it more than that? Is it more than timeout? Do we consume the contents of the story, or just the time? And what implication does this kind of consuming have for what we are doing with our minds the rest of the time?

There is a funny correspondence between the mind and the home computer. For years, of course, the mind has been likened to a calculating machine, and much "artificial intelligence" is an indirect way of studying the human mind. Texts in cognitive science treat perception, recall and recognition, and reasoning with the same schemata as are used in analyzing electronic machines and their software, with the same flow charts and terminology. But I have in mind what families bought last Christmas.

These are the machines you use to calculate the payback period of a new furnace or the answer to a child's geometry problem and, when you have done that, to shoot down enemy missiles or go spelunking in a cave full of reptiles. The computer is a tool *and a plaything, and that* is what makes it like the mind.

An important difference is that to switch a computer from tool to toy or toy to tool you usually have to insert a cartridge or disc, but the mind is able to go from work mode to fantasy like a computer that, halfway through an income-tax program, finds oil on your property.

But fantasy and fiction are not all that I have in mind. Aside from those two related forms of make-believe, most of the things that affect my welfare happen in my mind. I can say this, I suppose, because I am part of that minority of the human race that is comfortable most of the time, trained from childhood to be reflective and socially sensitive, and most of the day not required to be busily alert at tasks that entirely absorb one's attention. The things that make me happy or unhappy, at any level of consciousness that I can observe, are the things I believe and am aware of.

I like to be liked, I like to be admired. I like not to be guilty of cowardice; I like to believe that I shall live long and healthily and that my children will too, that I have done work I can be proud of and that others appreciate, that my life will be rich with challenge but I shall meet the challenges and have many accomplishments. That the talk I gave yesterday was a good one, and what I am writing today will be read and appreciated.

If I were hungry or cold or itched all over my body or had to work physically to exhaustion, those would be the conditions that determined my welfare. But I think I have stated the situation correctly for myself and for most of the people that I know.

An unavoidable question is whether I could be happier if only I could believe things more favorable, more complimentary, more in line with my hopes and wishes, than what I believe to be true. That might be done by coming to believe things that are contrary to what I know, such as that my health or my reputation is better than it is, my financial prospects better than they are or my children's prospects, and that I have performed ably and bravely on those occasions when I did not. Or it might be accomplished by improving the mix of my beliefs by

347

dropping out – forgetting – some of the things that cause me guilt, grief, remorse, and anxiety.

Whether I would be happier, whether my welfare should be deemed greater, with those improved beliefs is one of the questions; another is whether, if I had the choice, I would elect a change in my beliefs. Set aside for the moment the question whether there is any way I could do that. The question whether I could choose to revise the contents of my mental library, so that even in my most rational thinking I would come to more positive conclusions, is independent of whether or not we know the technology by which it might be done. (I admit that whether I would choose it might depend on the technology.)[6]

A third question is whether you would encourage me to manipulate my own beliefs in the interests of my own happiness, or permit me to if you had anything to say about it. Maybe for that question we have to be more explicit about technologies. There are animals that reportedly self-administer pure pleasure through electrodes in their brains, to the point of endangering their survival by not stopping to eat or drink. The nature of that euphoria we may never know until we try it; and whether it sounds like music, feels like a rocking chair, tastes like chocolate, reads like a novel, or is merely a pleasant absence of sensation may determine our attitudes. Currently it is considered all right to do it with stereo headphones but not electrodes.

Of course, if we ever can select our favorite beliefs off some menu we shall have to be practical about it. I might want to forget I had cancer but not to forget showing up for treatment. I must avoid beliefs that collide with each other or with reality in such a way that I have to confront my own confusion and recognize my beliefs as unreliable, coming to doubt the beliefs I selected off the menu. Just as lawyers advise us to stick close to the truth because the truth is consistent and easier to remember, self-deceivers will be wise to pick sparingly from that menu.

A little later I shall invite you to think about that menu, about what you would like to find on a menu of beliefs and disbeliefs, of ways to insert things into memory and to remove things, to manipulate awareness and the ease or difficulty of recall, and in other ways to affect what is resident in your mind. But first let me recall some of the methods already available, that work well or ill according to who uses them and what for. Most of them we do not think of as mind control, although several fit that description. They would not be described as *belief* control, but that may be because we speak about beliefs as if they were little entities in the mind. That notion misses some relevant dimensions. We forget things all the time, in the sense that we do not *currently* have them in mind, are unaware of them. We can be using knowledge that is not in mind, aware of conclusions that derive from things we are momentarily unaware of. We do not usually call this forgetting; but when it is important to get things out of mind, and we make an effort at forgetting, doing things and thinking things that are incompatible with the awareness of what it is we are trying to forget, what we are doing deserves to be called "forgetting" even though it is temporary. People do say they went to a movie to forget tomorrow's examination.

The language of belief is confusing here. I have observed in myself, so often that it no longer surprises me, that if I give a performance before some audience I am jollier at dinner, and eat more, if I am pleased with my performance. Disagreeable feedback spoils the evening. At my age the statistical record of my performance ought to reflect so many observations of good, poor, and mediocre performance that one more experience at either tail of the distribution could hardly affect a rational self-assessment. I try to remind myself of that on those occasions when feedback depresses me; but my welfare function apparently is not constructed that way. It feels to me as if I am taking the audience reaction as evidence, and what makes me feel good or bad is the belief that my *average* career performance is high or low and will continue so in the future. I think it is plain bad reasoning. I am making a rudimentary statistical error, attaching weights that are distorted by vividness or recency and "forgetting" the bulk of my experience. I mention this as evidence that there are kinds and degrees of forgetting even despite our knowing better.

Before we compose that menu of mental self-controls and self-stimuli that we might wish we could choose from, an inventory of techniques already available is useful. I offer a suggestive list. I exclude things that require a large investment in time, effort, or therapeutic care, like education, psychoanalysis, and hermitage, and those that entail irreversible surgery, like castration and lobotomy, and also those that cope with diagnosed pathologies and are based on prescription drugs or dietary supplements that require the attention of a physician. I am rather thinking of tranquilizers, caffeine, and sleeping pills.

First is sleep itself. Sleep is somewhat addictive: giving it up each morning is for many people one of the hardest things they do. Sleep can be escape from awareness of what is fearsome or hideous. Sleep with dreams can be enjoyable, but not reliably for most of us. Meditation and other modes of relaxation apparently offer escape from anxiety and mental torment for some people. Maybe the more generic term "unconsciousness" will include the state of apparent sleep that goes with blood alcohol and other anesthesia.

Different from sleep itself are things that bring on sleep. These can be sleeping pills, white noise, rocking, alcohol, or breathing exercises. Sleep is an equilibrium state after we get there; getting there requires controlling stimuli. The distinction between sleep as a state and getting to sleep as a transition is sharp even though some techniques for arriving at sleep, like relaxation, are also substitutes for sleep, and some of the things that induce sleep, like alcohol, help to sustain sleep.

Then we have tranquilizers – pills or alcohol – that are intended not only to relieve distress but to remove inhibitions, shyness, anxiety, specific phobias, and fear in general, so that one can perform and remain calm despite stimuli that might otherwise be disabling.

We have things that help us to remain alert. Caffeine in coffee and in tablet form prevents dozing and sleep, as do some prescription drugs. Unexpected stimuli, including noise and even pain, can help, and sometimes aerobic exercise. A useful distinction here is between staying awake and enhancing awareness.

There are techniques to enhance mental concentration. These may take the form of suppressing stimuli and intrusive signals. Insulation against noise is an example. Even fatigue sometimes helps concentration.

Sensory deprivation is a technique, the purposes and results of which I am not sure of. Generally it includes earplugs, masks over the eyes, avoidance of tactile sensation of stimulation of skin, and deliberate relaxation, as well as tanks of warm water. Classical and operant conditioning can affect what one likes, dislikes, fears, enjoys, remembers, or forgets.

Sensory enhancement is a possibility. Marijuana is sometimes reported to make colors more brilliant, music more profound, dance more sublime.

Drive enhancement of various kinds is apparently available to increase gustatory or sexual appetite. Aside from deliberate starvation there are visual and olfactory stimuli, conditioning, imaginative self-stimulation, and the ubiquitous alcohol.

Hypnosis has been successful in effecting permanent change in desires, in the effectiveness of stimuli, in the treatment of addictions and phobias, and in what one forgets or is reminded of.

Subliminal stimulation can apparently have some effect, whether in stimulating, reminding, or providing information. Subliminal visual stimulation in connection with television never became the menace that some feared, but the technology remains a possibility. Cassettes are advertised that offer subliminal help.

Finally I would mention electrical and chemical control of memory and other mental processes. We should consider the possibility, which I believe not absolutely ruled out by current theories of information storage in the brain, that memories could be extinguished permanently by electrical stimulation or surgery. In science fiction this would be done by having the patient recall vividly the memory to be extinguished, in order that the memory itself or its location could be targeted, the exciting of the memory being the process that offers the target. If the act of recall produces merely a xerox and not the original, there is nothing accomplished; but there are enough ways to erase something erroneously in the memory of even good computers to suggest that deliberate memory extinction may not be forever beyond reach.

I leave to an endnote an extreme therapy that differentiates the reasoning mind from the reactive one.[7]

Now to consider that menu of believings, forgettings, awarenesses, remindings, and other modes of mind control that we might be tempted to administer to ourselves if they were reliably available at moderate cost without side effects. We need to put a boundary on what we should let ourselves wish for. Would it not be delightful if we could change our taste in foods, and enjoy turnips as much as we enjoy smoked oysters? Think of the money we would save, to say nothing of calories and cholesterol. Instant wit, efficient memorization, bravery, poise, optimism, and immunity to disagreeable noises would look good in a Christmas stocking. The capacity to like, even love, one's work, colleagues, neighbors, spouse, and neighborhood would make rose-colored glasses a bargain. In contemplating the self-paternal self-deception that might interest us if only it were available, we shall get nowhere (or rather we shall get infinitely far too fast) if we let our wishes escalate the way our daydreams sometimes do.

A modest place to begin is phobias. We could wish for either of two things about phobias – that we did not have them, or that we did. The usual definition of a phobia is a disabling or severely discomforting fear, persistent, illogical, and serving no prudential purpose. The more famous of them have Greek names. Most people who react with repugnance to enclosure, open space, rodents, reptiles, insects, viscera, blood, audiences, precipices, needles, and the dark suffer directly from the sensation when it cannot be avoided and suffer the costs of avoidance when it can be. Phobias appear to be based upon memories of real or imagined scenes and events or associations of real or imagined scenes or events. There are therapies like conditioning, hypnosis, relaxation and stimulus control that can weaken or extinguish the phobia, and there must be corresponding ways to enhance or aggravate them. Whether, for some phobias or most of them, there is something that could be "forgotten" that would extinguish the phobia I do not know. But for at least some phobias some of the time it can help to forget the phobia itself. Just as closing one's eyes can sometimes eliminate a stimulus that produces vertigo or a reaction to blood or even darkness, forgetting a phobia can sometimes reduce one's awareness of the presence of the conditions that trigger the phobia. There are people who are suddenly stricken when reminded that they are in circumstances – enclosures, high places – to which their normal reaction is phobic. Thus a modest minimum that might be achieved through specific forgetfulness would be occasional neutralization of a phobia by merely forgetting it. (An analogy: forgetting one's insomnia makes it easier to get to sleep.)

Acquiring a phobia can be useful. Some of the therapies offered to people who smoke attempt to produce a mental association of cigarettes with dirty lungs, lip cancer, and foul breath. If these are presented as realistic consequences of smoking and the smoker is expected to reflect on them and to decide never to smoke again, and then never to smoke again, there is no need to characterize the aversion as a phobia; but if the patient is unable to respond reasonably to the danger itself, through lack of self-control or absent-mindedness, raising the fear in order of magnitude and putting the enhanced fear itself beyond reason permits the resulting fear to be both unreasonable and useful. (The dangers of such techniques are demonstrated by extreme cases of anorexia. Cigarettes have the advantage that one need not smoke in moderation but can quit, and the contrived horror is avoided by not smoking at all.)

The idea of deliberately cultivating latent disagreeable thoughts suggest an important distinction. Some of the things we would like to believe and forget are beliefs and memories that directly affect our internal welfare, our state of hope and happiness, regret, anxiety, guilt, fear, compassion, or pride. If I am going to

351

smoke anyway, believing that cigarettes cannot hurt me improves my welfare. That cigarettes are dangerous is a belief that, if available for adoption, I should adopt only if I thought I would act on it and quit the habit that worries me.

But the instrumental beliefs and the "consumable" beliefs cannot always be distinguished. There is evidence that people who believe themselves to be exceptionally at risk – people who after a severe cardiac episode are flatly told by their physicians that continued smoking will likely kill them – not only have a higher success rate in quitting than people who are merely advised to cut down or quit, but suffer less in quitting than the people who succeed on the more ambivalent advice. (I believe the difference is between the mental activity of the person who believes himself *to have quit* and that of the person who thinks of himself as *trying to quit*. For the latter there is suspense and the need to decide over and over on the occasions that invite one to smoke.)

What might our menu offer for daydreams? One possibility would be a mechanism to keep my mind from wandering. Often when I try to pay attention to a speaker I hear something that sends my mind on a detour. Paradoxically, the more stimulating what I listen to, the more I miss because of so many opportunities for my wayward mind to pursue a thought and, in doing so, to miss the next one.

The same thing happens when I think to myself. I am supposed to be working on a problem and I wake up to discover that for some unmeasured period my mind has been playing, not working.

Mind-wandering is not about beliefs but about mental behavior. But there is also make-believe. Children seem better at it than adults. That may be because children can do it together. I spend some time in pure reverie – what my dictionary calls "dreamy imaginings, especially of agreeable things" – in which I am the protagonist, but I do not usually admit it and would be mortified to recapitulate my daydream for somebody else, and have not done it as a duet since childhood. Along one dimension the quality has certainly deteriorated, that of believing in the plot. I may be able to imagine vividly an audience that I hold spellbound, but the feeling that I am really doing it is a weak one. Children who make-believe out loud together seem to enjoy a higher quality of involvement. That may be partly because they are unabashed about it. Should we wish that the menu contain something to make our daydreams more real? I do not mean make the plot more realistic, just make the imagined experiences feel more like real experiences.

I can think of two different kinds of daydreams to which this notion of enhancement might apply. One is pure entertainment unrelated to the activity one is engaged in or the environment in which one finds oneself. I do it sitting on a bus or on an airplane. The other one is – I am a little shy to admit – investing something that I am doing with a make-believe interpretation. People who run for exercise sometimes pretend to themselves that they are in a race or on some heroic errand. There is not much else to do while running; so any mental recreation is at low opportunity cost. A little anesthesia is welcome. Any arduous task ought to become a little less burdensome if one could dress it up with some make-believe. I refuse to answer whether I would order some instant make-believe if it were available on the market; I would certainly order it only if it came in a plain wrapper. Trying to improve the quality of our daydreams sounds shamefully childish; the childishness of our actual daydreams is, fortunately, known only to ourselves.

So we come to the final item under "daydreams" on our menu, the daydream suppressant. If daydreams are a childish waste of time, a bad habit, might we like to be rid of the habit? Are daydreams merely low-grade entertainment, as involuntary as preoccupation with something on a TV screen that the management will not turn off? If we cannot improve our daydreams, would we like them turned off? Whether we would like it may depend on what it is we are going to do instead. If we daydream to escape thinking about what we are supposed to be thinking about, eliminating the daydreams may just make us find some other escape. Until I know what the other escape is, I am not sure whether I would rather stick with my daydreams. If it means I will get my work done more expeditiously, I should welcome it. If I am facing a long bus ride and the alternative to daydreaming is studying the upholstery on the seat in front of me, or looking for the letters of the alphabet in the billboards we pass, it may be better to improve the quality of the dreams than to reduce the quantity.

The human mind is something of an embarrassment to certain disciplines, notably economics, decision theory, and others that have found the model of the rational consumer to be a powerfully productive one. The rational consumer is depicted as having a mind that can store and process information, that can calculate or at least make orderly successive comparisons, and that can vicariously image, imagine, anticipate, feel, and taste, and can simulate emotion in order to compare and choose. To decide whether to risk being caught in bad weather on an off-season mountaineering expedition, whether to face immediate embarrassment or to get a reputation for running away, whether to have another child, whether to change to a pleasanter occupation at reduced earnings, whether to go without wine to save money for a stereo system, or even just whether to choose a restaurant meal over the telephone, the mind has to be capable of somehow sampling the pleasures and discomforts, the joys and horrors on the basis both of remembered experience and description and creative extrapolation.

Just how one decides whether he is in the mood for broiled salmon or roast duck is not the concern of the decision sciences, at least not unless the way it is done turns out to conflict in some fashion with the rest of the model of rational choice. It sometimes seems to me – to me as a consumer and not as an economist – that I choose dinners from menus a little the way I used to choose movies from "coming attractions": I mentally consume a morsel of broiled salmon, register the quality of the taste but erase the taste itself, do the same for the roast duck, and let the two sensations feed into an analog computer that signals my choice.

But I cannot be sure; if I watch myself and find that that is what seems to happen, it may be the result of the watching.

Now we probably believe, if we bother to think about it, that ultimately the roast duck that I order is enjoyed in my brain. But not in my *mind*. We can say that I consume the roast duck, or we can say that I consume tastes and smells that I produce with roast duck; we could say that I consume chemical and electrical activity in the brain that is triggered by the sensory nerves of taste and smell, but unless our interest is the brain that does not add anything. Still, there is mental activity; looking at the roast duck is not eating it, but it is part of the activity, and the visual aesthetics of the meal seem "mental" in a way that appeasement of appetite does not. Anticipating the roast duck, contemplating the first bite, has a "mental" quality.

If a gourmet host dawdled thirty minutes choosing the grandest meal of his career, looking at the raw meat shown him by the chef, discussing wine with the wine steward, watching it brought to the table and tastefully served; smiled at the friends assembled around him, delicately sampled the wine and nodded his approval, and watched the first course served impeccably onto everybody's plate and died instantly of a heart attack, we would be tempted to say that the last half-hour of his life was perhaps the best half-hour of his life. More than that, we might say it was the most enjoyable meal of his life, one of the best he had ever "consumed."

If instead he did not die but proceeded to the more conventional enjoyment and two days later described this superb meal in mouth-watering detail to a few of his gourmet friends, we might be tempted to judge that he enjoyed the meal as much in the telling as in the eating, much as a person who barely wins a bitterly fought tournament enjoys the winning more in reflecting back on it than on the hot afternoon on which he nearly lost it.

These observations bring me to the notion of the mind as a *consuming organ*. We consume with our mouths and noses and ears and eyes and proprioceptors and skin and fingertips and with the nerves that react to external stimuli and internal hormones; we consume relief from pain and fatigue, itching and thirst. But we also consume by thinking. We consume past events that we can bring up from memory, future events that we can believe will happen, contemporary circumstances not physically present like the respect of our colleagues and the affection of our neighbors and the health of our children; and we can even tease ourselves into believing and consuming thoughts that are intended only to please. We consume good news and bad news.

We even – and this makes it a little like traditional economics – spend resources to discover the truth about things that happened in the past. People wish to know that children dead for many years died without too much pain or died proudly. It gets very compounded. If an estranged child makes a painful and urgent journey to arrive at a parent's bedside in time to become reconciled just before the parent dies, all that the parent gets is an hour's love and relief before leaving this world. Whatever the worth of a single hour of ecstasy, compared with vicariously enjoying Dorothy's trip to Oz, it is entirely a mental consuming. The days away from work and the airfare the child spent to be at the dying parent's bedside is a consumer expenditure, a gift to the parent. If the parent dies too soon and never knows that the child is on the way, the investment is largely wasted. If the trip succeeds, the child may consider it the most worthwhile expenditure of his consuming career. One hour's mental consumption.

Furthermore, others will want to know, and will care, whether the child made it to the bedside. There are some who care enough to make large expenditures to hasten the child's arrival or to prolong the parent's life long enough for the reconciliation to take place.

And, finally, the whole story can be fiction. We can be gripped with suspense and caring as we wonder whether an entire lifetime is going somehow to be vindicated by an ecstatic discovery that, after barely an hour, will be extinguished by death.

So we have at least two distinct roles for our minds to play, that of the information processing and reasoning machine by which we choose what to consume out of the array of things that our resources can be exchanged for, and that of the pleasure machine or consuming organ, the generator of direct consumer satisfaction. Actually, like a television set that can frighten small children or bring grief in the form of bad news, the mind can directly generate horror as well as ecstasy, irritation as well as comfort, fear and grief as well as enjoyable memories, reflections, and prospects. But that is partly because of still another characteristic of the mind, namely, it does not always behave nicely.

Just as it may fail us when we need to remember, or panic when we need all our faculties, the mind can remember things that cause grief, with flashbacks that spoil our appetite, by remembering ugly things it insists on associating with beauty, or humming interminably a tune we would like to get out of our minds. It is like a complex piece of machinery that has a mind of its own and is not disposed to be our obedient servant. Or possibly we must have not learned how to get the right service out of our minds. In our culture we stress the importance of the mind as an auxiliary instrument, the information storage and retrieval and articulating mechanism that performs intellectual tasks like communicating and reasoning, and we do not emphasize learning to make our minds produce the thoughts and memories and exploratory previews that bring joy and comfort, and to screen out or expunge the other kind.

The mind evolved as an organ of many uses and many capabilities, an imperfect organ, an organ whose imperfections along some dimensions are compensated for or adapted to by the mind's development along others. The dimensions that we associate with analytical thought and speech, even the orderly filing system of our memory, are fairly recent in human evolution;[8] they may not have achieved the autonomy that is assumed in some decision theories and philosophies. Consider the question whether a person can be said to have values and to know his values, and to make choices in accordance with those known values. When it is time to make a decision, that is, when, beset by certain stimuli that call for a response, the rational individual is supposed to be able to illuminate and scrutinize his preference map in order not only to calculate how to achieve a particular outcome but to remind himself which outcomes he prefers. His brain may not only selectively transmit information but also selectively illuminate his preference map. We know that people are incapable of keeping their eyes from focusing on potato chips, sexy pictures, or animated cartoons; we know that both externally administered and internally secreted chemicals can suppress or anesthetize certain activities; we have little empirical basis for believing (and much for not believing) that the mind will neutrally and indiscriminately process information and scrutinize memory to permit a person to make a choice unaffected by momentary stimuli, whether related to food, sex, affection, esthetic pleasure, or attractive violence. The unconscious accommodation of one's beliefs to achieve a reduction in "cognitive dissonance" is often treated as a defective or undesirable process, one to be on guard against. Maybe it is to be welcomed like the reduction of other annoying dissonances. At least, the mind is *trying* to help!

This is all apart from the fact that the mind is a wanderer, a source of fantasy, and an easy captive for puzzles, mysteries, and daydreams.

As far as I know, it is all the same mind. Marvelous it is that the mind does all these things. Awkward it is that it seems to be the same mind from which we expect both the richest sensations and the most austere analyses.

There is an interesting question of perspective. Like the question, do creatures reproduce themselves by way of genes, or do genes reproduce themselves by way of creatures; do I navigate my way through life with the help of my mind, or does my mind navigate its way through life by the help of me? I am not sure who is in charge.

NOTES

1 "Beyond microeconomics: conflict among interests in a multiple self as a determinant of value," xerox, January, 1982, pp. 18–23.

2 Jon Elster, *Ulysses and the Sirens* (Cambridge University Press, 1979), chapter 2, especially pp. 47–65, or alternatively "Ulysses and the sirens: a theory of imperfect rationality," *Social Science Information*, 41 (1977), 475–588.

3 R. L. Solomon and J. D. Corbit, "An opponent-process theory of motivation," *Psychological Review*, 81 (1974), 119–45.

4 There is a probability, P, that I have a disease that will kill me suddenly during the next few years, and a reliable test for whether or not I have the disease. Do I want the test? (If I am compulsive about the test do I regret my physician told me of it?) Scoring the anticipation of death at zero and of confident good health at 1, in utility notation the issue seems to be whether $(1 - P)U(1)$ is greater or less than $U(1 - P)$. I doubt whether the two values are equal even for people who consider them logically obliged to be equal.

5 Cited in Robert E. Ornstein, *The Psychology of Consciousness*, 2nd edn (New York: Harcourt Brace Jovanovich, 1977), pp. 142–3.

6 In *Cognitive Therapy and Its Disorders* (New York: New American Library, 1976), Aaron T. Beck, M.D., describes a system of psychotherapy that can improve the quality of a patient's beliefs by substituting more favorable correct beliefs for depressing wrong beliefs. Substituting still more favorable incorrect beliefs would require a different procedure.

7 I love somebody whose face is hideously disfigured in an accident. I know that it will be difficult to love her forever if I continuously see her as ugly as she is going to be. I was in the same accident; I am in the same hospital; I have not seen her yet, I have only heard about her facial disfigurement. My doctor visits and asks if there is anything I would like.

I ask to be blinded.

This is not self-deception in the Elster sense. Not only do I know that she is ugly; every day my blindness will remind me that she must be too ugly to love if I see her. It keeps me, however, from reacting to visual stimuli that I would not be able to accommodate.

There is something here like reaction to a mask. Might the doctor propose that, though there is nothing plastic surgery can do to restore the looks of the person I love, she can wear a mask?

How does this relate to cosmetics? If I know that somebody looks prettier than she would if her face were clean of cosmetics, and if I prefer her looks with cosmetics, is it that the cosmetics make me think she is more beautiful, or do I just react to a sight that includes the cosmetics as well as the face?

Maybe the term "self-delusion" can be used for these processes, saving "self-deception" for the more purely intellectual.

8 More recent than the *Iliad*, if we can believe the fascinating argument of Julian Jaynes, *The Origin of Consciousness in the Breakdown of the Bicameral Mind* (Boston: Houghton Mifflin Company, 1982).

357

16

DISAPPOINTMENT IN DECISION MAKING UNDER UNCERTAINTY

DAVID E. BELL

Your boss tells you that he is delighted with your performance over the past year and is giving you a $5,000 bonus. Are you pleased? If you were not expecting a bonus, you will be delighted. If you were expecting a $10,000 bonus, you will be disappointed. The satisfaction you feel with the bonus you are given will depend on your prior expectations. The higher your expectations, the greater will be your disappointment. People who are particularly averse to disappointment may learn to adopt a pessimistic view about the future.

If you accept a 50–50 gamble between $0 and $2,000, there is a 50% chance that you will be disappointed when the lottery is resolved. You may prefer to swap the lottery ticket for a sure $950 not so much because of arguments about decreasing marginal value, but because doing so removes the possibility of disappointment. Of course, someone who feels that the "thrill of victory" is worth the possible "agony of defeat" may take the opposite choice.

Disappointment, then, is a psychological reaction to an outcome that does not match up to expectations. The greater the disparity, the greater the disappointment. We will use the word elation to describe the euphoria associated with an outcome that exceeds expectations. Decision makers who anticipate these feelings may take them into account when comparing uncertain alternatives. The purposes of this chapter are (i) to model disappointment and to investigate the behavioral implications for a decision maker who is prepared to make economic trade-offs to reduce disappointment, and (ii) to compare these implications with known behavioral violations of expected utility maximization when only the amounts of economic payoffs are taken into account.

This chapter is a continuation of my research into the components of risk aversion. The economic explanation of risk aversion, that each additional dollar is worth slightly less due to satiation (decreasing marginal value), is surely a significant factor, but perhaps not the only one. Imagine two individuals with equal wealth and identical tastes for consumables. One is timid, nervous, and full of self-doubt; the other is outgoing, self-confident, and with a sense of purpose. We might suppose that the latter will be less risk averse than the former. Indeed, his relative risk attitude, in the sense of Dyer and Sarin (1982), may even be risk prone.

In earlier work (Bell, 1982, 1983; also Loomes and Sugden, 1982), I have explored the implications of regret as a factor in risk attitude. Regret is a psychological reaction to making a wrong decision, where wrong is determined on the basis of actual outcomes rather than on the information available at the time of the decision. Just as disappointment is caused by comparing an outcome with prior expectations, so regret is caused by comparing an outcome with the payoff one could have had by making a different choice. For example, if you are given a 50–50 lottery between $0 and $10 and lose, you will suffer disappointment. Had you *selected* the same lottery over an alternative of $4 for sure and lost, you would have suffered both disappointment and regret. For one to suffer only regret and not disappointment, the outcome of a chosen lottery would have to be exactly equal to one's expectations, but less than one could have obtained (*ex post*) from an alternative lottery.

There are many other "reference effect" phenomena. A bonus of $5,000 may exceed one's expectations, but still lead to dissatisfaction if you learn that your colleague got a bonus of $10,000. Perhaps the most influential reference point is the status quo of the decision maker. It has been widely observed that a decision maker will make significant economic trade-offs to remove the possibility of a net loss on a transaction.

Building a utility model that incorporates all of these effects may well be desirable not only to provide a better description of behavior, but also, to the extent that a decision maker is prepared to trade off dollars explicitly to gain a state of psychological satisfaction, for prescriptive purposes.

In this chapter, to avoid unnecessary complication, we will consider only the effect of disappointment (and elation) on decision making under uncertainty. We will assume throughout that the decision maker has constant marginal value for money and never suffers from regret, from envy, or from a tendency to overweigh losses. The models that follow are perfectly adaptable to the case of nonconstant marginal value for money, by making an appropriate transformation of the attribute scale. A future paper will explore the implications of a model that incorporates decreasing marginal value and a variety of reference effects.

In section 1 we examine systematic violations of the substitution principle of utility theory and show that a simple model incorporating disappointment offers an explanation for them. In section 2 we present assumptions about the way disappointment and elation affect a decision maker's preference for outcomes and derive a preference model that will be used throughout the remainder of the chapter. Section 3 shows how one might assess the components of the model in an interview with a decision maker. We show how a reasonable attitude with respect to disappointment can lead to risk prone behavior.

In section 4 we consider how disappointment might lead to a preference by the decision maker for different methods of resolving a lottery. Perhaps the decision maker would prefer a 25 % chance at $1,000 to be resolved by two sequential flips of a coin rather than by drawing a diamond from a deck of cards. In this section we show how violations of the substitution principle, in the context of a single dollar attribute, might be caused by such preferences. We also consider how news should be broken to people. An analysis of disappointment is compatible with the empirically learned behavior that bad news should be broken gently. Finally, we examine the implications of these matters for the relative desirability of different auction procedures.

1. A SIMPLE MODEL OF DISAPPOINTMENT

The substitution principle is key to the derivation of expected utility theory. Though some regard it as virtually a self-evident requirement for consistency, in much the same way that the transitivity principle seems so compelling, others attack it as the weak link that allows behavioral contradictions in practice. The principle asserts (see Keeney, 1982, for example) that any preference ordering of two alternatives with uncertain consequences will not be affected either by substituting for any one consequence an equally desirable consequence (which may itself be a lottery) or by deleting a consequence common to both alternatives. This principle is usually the one relied upon to demonstrate inconsistency in preference orderings.

We will use an example of Kahneman and Tversky (1979) to illustrate both the compelling nature of the substitution principle and why disappointment provides an explanation for some observed violations of it. (See also the discussion by Machina, 1981, pp. 172–3.) Kahneman and Tversky report that a prize of $3,000 for sure is preferred by a majority of respondents over an 80% chance at $4,000 (and a 20% chance at nothing), whereas a majority prefer a 20% chance at $4,000 over a 25% chance at $3,000. The following logic, relating to three decision situations illustrated in figure 16.1, asserts that such behavior is undesirable.

Diagram *A* in figure 16.1 shows the first of the two decision problems, diagram *B* shows the second. Diagram *C* illustrates a third situation in which a preliminary drawing determines whether there is anything to play for; with probability 0.25 the decision maker obtains the right to make a decision identical to that in diagram *A*.

Figure 16.1 The substitution principle implies that either the upper branches or the lower branches should be selected at all decision forks.

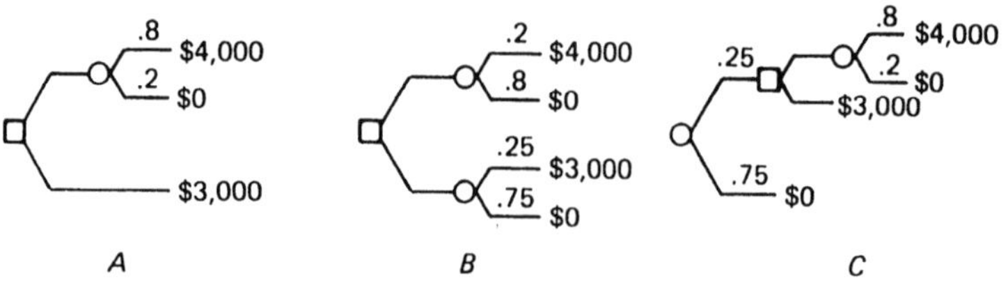

360

Disappointment in decision making

The argument underlying the substitution principle is that it seems impossible to find an economic rationale for taking a different decision in diagram C from that taken in diagram A. Certainly the financial implications are identical in the two cases. Now we argue that the decision in diagram B should be the same as that in diagram C. Suppose we know that the decision maker will choose the $3,000 alternative in diagram C. Then there is no loss to the decision maker in announcing this choice at the outset. The only difference between situations C and B is whether the uncertainty is resolved in two stages or one. Since there are no economic implications to such a distinction, there should be no difference in the decision.

It is a common observation that people will agree with the step-by-step logic of the above argument, but nonetheless feel uncomfortable with the conclusion. The hypothesis of this paper is that psychological feelings of disappointment are ignored in the rational economic analysis, but play a role in the informal evaluation of alternatives by decision makers.

Consider the disappointment you would feel in situation A if you chose to gamble and got nothing. You would have had high expectations – an 80% chance of $4,000 – suddenly dashed. If this prospect alarms you, the $3,000 prize for sure may look very attractive by comparison. In situation B, however, I would not anticipate great disparity between the disappointment that I would feel at losing either of the two lotteries. In neither case do I have much chance of winning, so losing is almost to be expected, and the news of my loss reduces my expected asset value by only $750 or $800 compared to $3,200 in situation A.

This observation highlights where the logic behind the substitution principle breaks down. It is not a matter of indifference to me how a lottery is resolved. In situation B, I may prefer to go with the $4,000 gamble on the grounds that it has a higher expected value and the disappointment implications are similar for each alternative. However, in situation C, if the first stage is successful, my expectations rise dramatically and I become afraid of losing what I have gained.

A simple model will demonstrate that the above explanation is coherent. If someone owns an unresolved lottery having a probability p of yielding x and a probability $(1 - p)$ of yielding y his psychological expectation may be supposed to be reflected by the quantity $px + (1 - p)y$. (We will denote such a gamble by (x, p, y) where x is at least as preferred as y and p is the probability of winning.) If y occurs, the decision maker's disappointment might be in direct proportion to the difference between what he expected and what he got:

$$\text{Disappointment} = d(px + (1 - p)y - y) = dp(x - y) \tag{1}$$

where $d \geqslant 0$ is a constant reflecting the degree to which a unit of disappointment affects the decision maker. If x occurs, there will be a sense of elation which we may suppose is proportional to the difference between what the decision maker expected and what he got:

$$\text{Elation} = e(x - px - (1 - p)y) = e(1 - p)(x - y) \tag{2}$$

361

where $e \geqslant 0$ is a constant reflecting the degree to which a unit of elation affects the decision maker. Equations 1 and 2 are identical except that elation and disappointment have been defined as positive quantities and the constants e and d, reflecting trade-offs for the decision maker between dollars and psychological well-being, have been permitted to differ. To this point, we have implicitly assumed that the decision maker's multiattribute preference over dollars and disappointment (elation) is linear and additive:

Total utility = economic payoff + psychological satisfaction

where psychological satisfaction is positive for elation and negative for disappointment.

Two special cases are worth highlighting. If $p = 0$, i.e., there is no chance to win, then losing is to be expected and by (1) the level of disappointment is zero, appropriately enough. Similarly, if $p = 1$, the elation, by (2), is zero. If $d = e$, i.e., if disappointment and elation are equally compelling, then they cancel out when taking expectations:

$$p(\text{elation}) + (1 - p)(-\text{disappointment}) =$$

$$p[e(1 - p)(x - y)] + (1 - p)[-dp(x - y)] = 0.$$

Note that, although in this case disappointment and elation have no influence on *decisions*, they still do affect the desirability of individual outcomes.

But suppose one effect is more powerful than the other? If a decision maker suffers greatly when disappointed, but is relatively less influenced by elation $(d > e)$, then the gamble (x, p, y) will have a certainty equivalent of

$$px + (1 - p)y + (e - d)p(1 - p)(x - y). \tag{3}$$

Figure 16.2(A) graphs the certainty equivalents of $(1, p, 0)$ gambles as a function of p. Notice that, even though we have assumed constant marginal value for

Figure 16.2(A) Dollar certainty equivalents for $(1, p, 0)$ lotteries. (B) Utility function for money implied by (A).

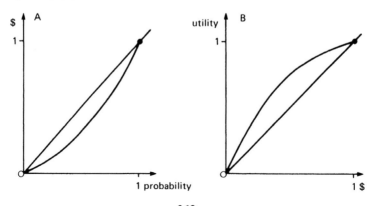

Table 16.1. *Certainty equivalent using the simple disappointment model for selecting lotteries*

Lottery	Certainty equivalent
(3,000, 1, 0)	3,000
(4,000, 0.8, 0)	$3{,}200 + 640(e - d)$
(3,000, 0.25, 0)	$750 + 563(e - d)$
(4,000, 0.2, 0)	$800 + 640(e - d)$

money, a relative aversion to disappointment over elation will cause risk averse behavior by the decision maker. The certainty equivalents graphed in figure 16.2(A) are entirely consistent with an explanation that says the decision maker has decreasing marginal value for dollars and is an expected utility maximizer using the utility function $u(x)$ over dollars defined implicitly by the equation

$$u(p + (e - d)p(1 - p)) = p$$

or, explicitly, if we let $k = d - e$, by

$$u(x) = (k - 1 + \sqrt{(1 - k)^2 + 4kx})/2k. \tag{4}$$

This function is graphed in figure 16.2(B). It has three properties often desirable in a utility function (Keeney and Raiffa, 1976, p. 166); it is increasing (if $e - d > -1$), it is concave (if $d > e$), and it exhibits decreasing risk aversion.

However, the decision maker does not obey the substitution principle using economic payoffs alone. Table 16.1 gives the certainty equivalents, using (3), for the four alternatives used in figure 16.1. To reflect the empirically observed rank orders requires only that

$$3{,}000 > 3{,}200 + 640(e - d)$$

and

$$800 + 640(e - d) > 750 + 563(e - d)$$

or

$$-0.65 < e - d < -0.31.$$

Kahneman and Tversky have characterized a class of substitution principle violations referred to as the *common ratio effect* as follows:

For $x > y > 0$ and $1 \geqslant p > 0$, $1 > q$, $r > 0$, if $(x, q, 0) \sim (y, p, 0)$ then $(x, qr, 0) > (y, pr, 0)$.

This behavioral rule is predicted by the simple formulations of this section if and only if $d > e$. For if $(x, q, 0) \sim (y, p, 0)$, then

$$qx + (e - d)q(1 - q)x = py + (e - d)p(1 - p)y. \tag{5}$$

363

In order for $(x, qr, 0) > (y, pr, 0)$, we require

$$qrx + (e - d)qr(1 - qr)x > pry + (e - d)pr(1 - pr)y. \qquad (6)$$

Multiply (5) by r^2 and subtract from (6) to give the requirement that

$$qxr(1 - r)(1 + e - d) > pyr(1 - r)(1 + e - d)$$

which will be true if $qx > py$. From (5), this inequality will be true if $1 + (e - d)(1 - q) < 1 + (e - d)(1 - p)$ and, in particular, if $(e - d)(p - q) < 0$. Since $x > y$ and $e - d > -1$, we know that $(x, p, 0) > (y, p, 0)$ which implies $p > q$. Hence, the result is true as long as $e < d$.

Using equation (3), we might interpret the quantity $(d - e)p(1 - p)(x - y)$ as a measure of the risk involved in the gamble. It is, after all, the reduction in the certainty equivalent caused by the presence of uncertainty. This measure is very similar to the variance measure of risk, common in financial applications, namely $\lambda p(1 - p)(x - y)^2$ for some constant λ. Note that the term in $(x - y)$ is linear in (3), but squared in the variance formula. Stone (1973) gives a three parameter family that generalizes most of the well-studied risk measures. In the special case of (x, p, y), this family is $p|c - x|^\alpha \delta + (1 - p)|c - y|^\alpha$ where c, α and δ are three parameters, δ being 0 or 1. This family has the common property that all deviations from a reference point "c" are considered bad, contributing positively to the risk measure. By contrast, the measure $(d - e)p(1 - p)(x - y)$ was derived in a way that permits "good deviations" and is not a member of Stone's family.

The variance is a natural measure of risk if one is trying to reflect the effects of decreasing marginal value, because of the approximate relationship (Pratt, 1964):

$$Eu(x) \simeq u(0) + E(x)u'(0) + \tfrac{1}{2}E(x - E(x))^2 u''(0)$$

where primes represent differentiation. Our simplifying assumption that the marginal value of money is constant removes this natural advantage of the variance. Although much empirical work has been done to identify simple statistics that explain hypothetical choices made by businessmen (Wehrung *et al.*, 1978, and MacCrimmon and Wehrung, 1983) no analysis has been done, to my knowledge, on (3), perhaps because it has no obvious analog for continuous distributions. Although this chapter studies only two outcome gambles, it is possible to deduce a generalization of (3) from the assumptions in section 2, namely, that the certainty equivalent of a distribution with mean μ and variance σ^2 is $\mu - k\sigma$ where k depends not only on the decision maker, but also on the particular characteristics of the distributions. Two distributions that are related by a simple change of scale (see assumptions 6 and 7) will have the same k value, so that, for example, all normal distributions will have the same k value. Note that (x, p, y) and (x', p, y') are related by a simple scale change, but that (x, p, y) and (x, q, y) are not. Formula (3) fits the format $\mu - k\sigma$ when $k = (d - e)\sqrt{p(1 - p)}$.

The joy of winning

The simple representations (1), (2), and (3) were introduced to illustrate that the idea of disappointment can be modeled and applied systematically to decision situations. Since the disappointment a decision maker feels at an outcome is likely to be sensitive to context, no simple model will be an accurate representation in all circumstances. The formation of expectations may vary from person to person. While a mathematician may expect the probabilistic average, an optimist may expect more, a pessimist less. In multiple outcome gambles one's expectations may be the mode. A decision analyst may feel it appropriate to expect the certainty equivalent, an exercise (fortunately convergent) in cyclical reasoning, which may explain why decision analysts take so long to make decisions.

The gambles in figure 16.3 may demonstrate that the simple model is not sufficiently rich. All four lotteries have an expected value of $1,000 so that, according to (1), the disappointment on receiving $0 should be the same in all four of them. Many people might feel that the disappointment would be greatest in the fourth case where the chance of losing was so remote, despite the fact that less was lost. The important question for our model is whether or not the level of disappointment is the same in all four cases.

Consider a 50–50 lottery between $0 and $2,000 and also a lottery with a normal distribution having mean $1,000 and standard deviation of $10. Compare your reaction to receiving $0 in each case. The disappointment may be greater in the second case than in the first. In the first lottery, the zero outcome had a 50% chance of occurring and bordered on being "expected." In the second lottery, an outcome as low as $0 was virtually impossible and a feeling of great dismay would be understandable. Even if the example is not so extreme, say a standard deviation of $1,000, the outcome $0 is still worse than about 84% of the distribution. It may be disappointing to do so badly.

This discussion suggests that disappointment may be related not only to a level of prior expectations, but also in a direct way to the likelihood with which the outcome occurred. Even if you were not expecting to win much, it is discouraging to lose, especially when the odds were against it. On the other hand, it is plain fun to win things. It is exciting to win at party games even if the skill required is none

Figure 16.3 Test of simple disappointment model: is the level of disappointment the same at all $0 outcomes?

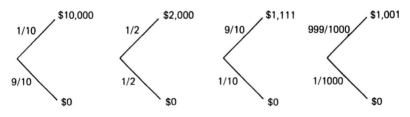

and the prize paltry. There is a thrill to be had from being dealt an unusually good bridge hand quite apart from any significance it may have to the course of the game. Figure 16.4 shows gambles that have been constructed with the same top prize of $10,000 and expected values equal to $9,000. According to (2), the elation should be the same on winning each of them. Many people might feel that the elation goes up with the odds against winning. (When looking at the lotteries, do not forget to adjust your expectations to allow for owning the lottery, *before* considering the elation on winning.)

2. BASIC ASSUMPTIONS

Despite the above complications about how expectations are formed and whether elation and disappointment depend directly upon the probabilities involved, there is a way to model these concepts that avoids the necessity of being explicit on these matters and permits a straightforward assessment task on the part of the decision maker. The assumptions needed for this model are covered in this section.

Let $L_0(x, p, y)$ represent the state of owning an unresolved lottery (x, p, y). Let $L_1(x, p, y)$ represent the outcome in which $L_0(x, p, y)$ results in x. Let $L_2(x, p, y)$ represent the outcome in which $L_0(x, p, y)$ results in y. (Recall that we always assume $x \geqslant y$.)

Assumption 1 (simple orderings). *For $i = 0, 1, 2$, the decision maker can make preference comparisons of the form*

$$L_i(x_1, p_1, y_1) >, \quad \sim \quad or \quad < L_i(x_2, p_2, y_2).$$

These orderings are transitive.

Of course, a fair degree of introspection is required to say whether winning the top prize from the lottery $(100, \frac{1}{10}, 0)$ is better or worse than winning the top prize from $(110, \frac{1}{2}, 0)$. Although this talent is required in principle, it will not be called upon in assessment procedures.

Assumption 2 (sure-thing indifference). *For $i = 0$ and 1, $L_i(x, p, x) \sim L_i(x, 1, y)$ and for $i = 0$ and 2, $L_i(y, p, y) \sim L_i(x, 0, y)$.*

Figure 16.4 Test of simple elation model: is the level of elation the same at all $10,000 outcomes?

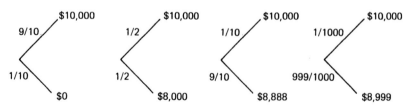

The decision maker is presumed not to be affected by the presence of impossible consequences.

Assumption 3 (monotonicity in the probability of winning). *If $p > q$, then*

$$L_0(x, p, y) > L_0(x, q, y)$$

and

$$L_i(x, p, y) < L_i(x, q, y) \quad for \quad i = 1, 2.$$

Note that these two conditions are compatible because $L_1(x, p, y)$ is more likely than $L_1(x, q, y)$. It is conceivable that someone may actually prefer $(1, \frac{1}{3}, 0)$ over $(1, \frac{1}{4}, 0)$ because of the greater excitement on winning, but we are content to exclude such people from our theory.

Assumption 4 (monotonicity in value of prizes). *If $x' > x$, then*

$$L_i(x', p, y) > L_i(x, p, y) \quad for \quad i = 0, 1$$

and

$$L_2(x', p, y) < L_2(x, p, y).$$

If $y < y'$, then

$$L_i(x, p, y) < L_i(x, p, y') \quad for \quad i = 0, 2$$

and

$$L_1(x, p, y) > L_1(x, p, y').$$

Assumption 4 implies that $(x, p, x) > (x, p, y) > (y, p, y)$ so that it is reasonable to suppose that there exists a value c_0 with $(c_0, p, c_0) \sim (x, p, y)$. As long as the effects of disappointment/elation are not infinitely great, it is also appropriate to posit certainty equivalents for the winning and losing outcomes.

Assumption 5 (solvability). *For all x, p, and y, and $i = 0, 1, 2$ there exists a c_i depending on x, p and y such that*

$$L_i(c_i, p, c_i) \sim L_i(x, p, y).$$

The functions $c_i(x, p, y)$ are the cash certainty equivalents of the situations $L_i(x, p, y)$. The quantity $c_0(x, p, y)$ is simply the traditional concept of a certainty equivalent.

Although we do not seek to model prior expectations explicitly, it seems reasonable to suppose that our prior expectations for the gamble $(x + k, p, y + k)$ will be exactly an amount k higher than those for (x, p, y). Similarly, my expectations for $(2x, p, 2y)$ would be twice those for (x, p, y). (Our assumption of a constant marginal value for money is important here. More generally, we would say that the *value* of the prizes must double in order for expectations to double.) In short, while not explicitly modeling the formulation of expectations, we will assume, at least implicitly, that they are linear in the payoffs.

Assumption 6 (constant marginal value for payoffs). *For all x, p, y, a, and b ($b > 0$), and $i = 1, 2$*

$$c_i(a + bx, p, a + by) = a + b \cdot c_i(x, p, y).$$

This assumption is based on a presumption that expectations are linear in the payoffs and that, for a given p, disappointment and elation are proportional to the difference between outcome and expectations.

Assumption 7 (risk neutrality in the absence of disappointment). *For all x, p, and y,*

$$c_0(x, p, y) = pc_1(x, p, y) + (1 - p)c_2(x, p, y).$$

The underlying presumption is that the decision maker would be risk neutral if it were not for the effects of disappointment and elation. Once again, this presumption derives from our assumption of constant marginal value for money. Since $c_1(x, p, y)$ and $c_2(x, p, y)$ are the cash equivalents for the outcomes, the assumption follows.

Theorem 1. *Assumptions 1, 2, 5, 6, and 7 imply that for $i = 0$, 1, and 2, the situations $L_i(x, p, y)$ have certainty equivalents of $y + (x - y)\pi_i(p)$ for some functions π_i.*

Proof. Assumptions 1 and 5 allow us to establish the functions $c_i(x, p, y)$ used in assumptions 6 and 7. Assumption 6 implies that $c_i(x, p, y) = y + c_i(x - y, p, 0) = y + (x - y)c_i(1, p, 0)$ for $i = 1, 2$. Assumption 2 is merely assumption 6 in the special case $b = 0$, or $x = y$. Assumption 7 shows that assumption 6 also applies in the case $i = 0$. Let $\pi_i(p) = c_i(1, p, 0)$.

For the remainder of the chapter we will adopt a more mnemonic notation in place of the π_i's. We will replace π_0 simply by π. This choice highlights the similarity between our result and that used by Kahneman and Tversky (p. 276, equation 2) in their prospect theory. Had we chosen to retain the possibility of a nonconstant marginal value for money by use of a nonlinear value function $v(x)$, our assumptions would have led to the model

$$v(y) + \pi(p)(v(x) - v(y)). \tag{7}$$

One major distinction between our model and that of prospect theory is that we make no distinction between positive and negative payoffs; that is, we do not take account of the status quo as a reference point. For example, prospect theory evaluates the gamble (x, p, y) if $0 > x > y$ as $v(x) + \pi(p)[v(y) - v(x)]$ whereas the disappointment formula continues to evaluate this gamble as in (7). It is worth repeating that reference points such as status quo, a foregone outcome (regret), and an assumption of nonconstant marginal value are excluded from our current analysis, only because their presence would complicate both the analysis and our understanding of the effect disappointment has on decision making not because these factors are unimportant.

Despite these differences with prospect theory, the notation $\pi(p)$ is worth adopting because of the common interpretations of π as a behavioral subjective probability, since the decision maker acts in accordance with simple expected values once this transformation of probability is made. (This terminology for π applied to the traditional utility model would call $u(x)$ a behavioral subjective value.)

Instead of using $y + (x - y)\pi_1(p)$ as the certainty equivalent of the winning situation, we will use $x + (x - y)w(p)$. The function $w(p)$ may be thought of more directly as the value of the elation that comes with winning in the lottery $(1, p, 0)$. Similarly, in place of $y + (x - y)\pi_2(p)$ as the certainty equivalent of the losing outcome we will use $y - (x - y)l(1 - p)$. The function $l(p)$ may be thought of as the (positively valued) psychological cost of losing in the gamble $(1, 1 - p, 0)$. With this notation, $w(p)$ and $l(p)$ are each related to an outcome that occurs with probability p.

To summarize, we have

$$c_0(x, p, y) = y + (x - y)\pi(p) \tag{8}$$

$$c_1(x, p, y) = x + (x - y)w(p)$$

and

$$c_2(x, p, y) = y - (x - y)l(1 - p).$$

The following properties of the functions π, w, and l are deducible from the assumptions:

(i) $\pi(0) = w(1) = l(1) = 1 - \pi(1) = 0$ (assumption 2) $\tag{9}$

(ii) π is increasing, w and l are decreasing functions of p (assumption 3) $\tag{10}$

(iii) $\pi(p) = p + pw(p) - (1 - p)l(1 - p)$ (assumption 7). $\tag{11}$

This model is very flexible for our purposes. The simple model used in section 1 is a special case, where

$$w(p) = (1 - p)e, \quad l(p) = (1 - p)d,$$
$$\pi(p) = p[1 + (e - d)(1 - p)]. \tag{12}$$

Even if we presume that the certainty equivalent of the gamble is also the prior expectation, we obtain a model in the same class. That is, suppose we have

$$c_2(x, p, y) = y + [y - c_0(x, p, y)]d$$

and

$$c_1(x, p, y) = x + [x - c_0(x, p, y)]e$$

as parallels to (1) and (2), then using assumption 7 and solving these equations for c_0, we may deduce that

$$c_0(x, p, y) = y + (x - y)\pi(p)$$

where

$$\pi(p) = p(1 + e)/[1 + ep + d(1 - p)].$$

We also can show that $w(p) = (1 - \pi(p))e$ and $l(p) = d\pi(1 - p)$.

3. ASSESSMENT PROCEDURES

If we are interested only in the effects of disappointment on decision making, then only the function π need be assessed, which may be done by the obvious mechanism of asking directly for certainty equivalents for the gambles $(1, p, 0)$. However, it would be important, in any prescriptive analysis that incorporates disappointment, for the assessment procedure to require explicit trade-offs between psychology and economy. Assessment of the functions ω and l requires the decision maker to compare outcomes (and the psychological consequences that go with them) instead of alternatives. Such procedures are open to question on the grounds that decision maker responses are not testable in any satisfactory manner and because it is easy to imagine situations where discrepancies occur. (For example, you may choose to work late rather than go home, but you wish that the option of working late were unavailable. This example was inspired by Schelling, 1983.)

The following assessment procedure is presented to show the kinds of inputs that are required. Such an assessment procedure need not be routine.

A straightforward assessment procedure for $w(p)$ begins by asking the decision maker to identify an amount $\$k_1(p)$ such that winning \$1 from $(1, p, 0)$ is just as satisfying as winning \$1 from $(1, \frac{1}{2}, k_1(p))$. (Note that the upper and lower prizes are flexible, they could be \$1,000 and 0, for example.) From this answer, we obtain indifferences of the form

$$c_1(1, \tfrac{1}{2}, k_1(p)) = c_1(1, p, 0). \tag{13}$$

Since (13) is equivalent to the equation

$$1 + (1 - k_1(p))w(\tfrac{1}{2}) = 1 + w(p) \tag{14}$$

we have, by varying p, assessed $w(p)$ up to the constant $w(\frac{1}{2})$. Similarly, if $k_2(p)$ is the dollar amount such that

$$c_2(k_2(p), (\tfrac{1}{2}), 0) = c_2(1, p, 0),$$

then

$$-k_2(p)l(\tfrac{1}{2}) = -l(1 - p)$$

or

$$l(p) = l(\tfrac{1}{2})k_2(1 - p). \tag{15}$$

Note that so far we have not asked any questions that explicitly trade off psychological effects against dollars. The essence of these trade-offs is contained in the constants $w(\frac{1}{2})$ and $l(\frac{1}{2})$.

Though these parameters could be obtained by direct questioning, it seems reasonable to think of recovering them implicitly via direct assessment of $c_0(1, p, 0)$. Using equations (11), (14), and (15), we may deduce a relation between π, k_1, and k_2:

$$\pi(p) = p[1 + (1 - k_1)w(\tfrac{1}{2})] - (1 - p)l(\tfrac{1}{2})k_2.$$

Hence, any two direct assessments $\pi(p_1)$, $\pi(p_2)$ will serve to define $w(\frac{1}{2})$ and $l(\frac{1}{2})$.

Risk prone behavior

Studies of utility commonly make hypotheses about properties of the utility function that should hold for "most people." These studies generally assume that people are risk averse in monetary gambles and that the extent of their risk aversion (Pratt, 1964) decreases as they become wealthier (Raiffa, 1968, p. 91).

Such generalizations in the case of preferences for disappointment are less well-founded, but the following one, which may be reasonable, not only suggests that risk aversion may increase with p, but also permits the possibility of risk proneness for small values of p. The assumption is based on the generic examples used in figures 16.3 and 16.4. The gamble $(1/p, p, 0)$ has an expected value of 1 for all p. The assumption is that the disappointment, on receiving 0 from this gamble, increases with p. The gamble $(1, p, -p/(1 - p))$ has an expected value of 0 for all p. The assumption is that the elation, on receiving 1 from this gamble, decreases with p.

Assumption 8. *For* $1 > p > q > 0$,

$$c_2(1/p, p, 0) < c_2(1/q, q, 0)$$

and

$$c_1(1, p, -p/(1 - p)) < c_1(1, q, -q/(1 - q)).$$

Theorem 2. *Assumption 8 implies that there exists a probability p^*, which might be zero or one, with the property that the decision maker is risk averse whenever $1 > p > p^*$, risk neutral for $p = p^*$, and risk prone for $0 < p < p^*$.*

Proof. Assumption 8 can be rewritten as

$$-l(1 - p)/p < -l(1 - q)/q$$

and

$$1 + w(p)/(1 - p) < 1 + w(q)/(1 - q)$$

so that $w(p)/(1 - p)$ and $l(p)/(1 - p)$ are decreasing functions of p. The decision maker is risk averse so long as $\pi(p) < p$, which is true if $pw(p) < (1-p)l(1-p)$ or $w(p)/(1-p) < l(1-p)/p$. We know that $w(p)/(1-p) - l(1-p)/p$ is decreasing in p so that either $\pi(p) - p$ has a constant sign for all p or there exists a critical value p^* as required.

If we assume for a moment that w and l are differentiable functions, we may establish a necessary and sufficient condition for $p^* > 0$, that is, that the decision maker is ever risk prone. For small p, $\pi(p) - p = pw(p) - (1-p)l(1-p) = pw(0) - (1-p)l(1) + pl'(1)$. Since $l(1) = 0$, the condition to be satisfied for risk proneness is $w(0) + l'(1) > 0$. In the simple formulation $w(p) = (1-p)e$, $l(p) = (1-p)d$ we have $w(0) = e$, $l'(1) = -d$, so that this inequality becomes $e > d$. In this case, the decision maker is either risk prone or always risk averse. Figure 16.2(A) was drawn assuming $e < d$.

Supporting the underdog

Frequently, one is watching a sports event involving two teams, without any intrinsic reason for supporting either. While I know of no formal study to support these conclusions, two observations seem to be widely acknowledged. The first is that spectating is more fun if you choose a team to support and the second is that uncommitted people tend to support the underdog, the team thought less likely to win. Why is this? Certainly, I prefer the team I am supporting to have a high probability of winning (attendance increases dramatically when the home team looks likely to win), yet when faced with a free choice I choose to support the team with the lesser chance.

Suppose the spectator believes that the underdog has a probability p of winning, where $p < \frac{1}{2}$. Since there is no intrinsic reason for supporting either team, the only payoff to the spectator is psychological. If the team he supports wins he is elated; if it loses he is disappointed. The expected psychological benefits from supporting the favorite and underdog are modeled as if something was at stake, but no economic value is assigned:

Favorite: $(1-p)w(1-p) - pl(p)$

Underdog: $pw(p) - (1-p)l(1-p)$.

Supporting the underdog makes sense if $p[w(p) + l(p)] > (1-p)[w(1-p) + l(1-p)]$ or

$$w(p)/(1-p) + l(p)/(1-p) > \omega(1-p)/p + l(1-p)/p.$$

Since $w(p)/(1-p)$ and $l(p)/(1-p)$ are decreasing functions, this equation will hold if and only if $p < \frac{1}{2}$.

Supporting *somebody* is a good idea if $pw(p) - (1-p)l(1-p) > 0$ or $\pi(p) - p > 0$. A spectator will get the most enjoyment out of watching a game where the underdog has a probability of winning that maximizes the quantity

$\pi(p) - p$. If $\pi(\frac{1}{2}) < \frac{1}{2}$, this analysis suggests that in a close contest it might be wiser not to support anyone, and that this position is always true for those who dislike any form of gambling.

Political contests are another example where there is evidence of support from uncommitted people to the underdog. According to our model, if an undecided voter goes to vote, he or she should vote for the underdog.

Risk prone behavior and supporting the underdog are, by our model, one and the same phenomenon. Supporting a cause with little chance of success offers only the possibility of elation and eliminates the possibility of sizable disappointment. It is a case of minimizing the downside risk.

An example: reacting to the odds

As a simple example of nonlinear w and l functions, let us suppose that instead of being proportional to the *probability* of winning (losing), elation (disappointment) is proportional to the *odds* against the event occurring. Winning one dollar at odds of 10 to 1 is presumed to be twice as elating as winning one dollar at odds of 5 to 1. We assume $w(p) = (1 - p)e/p$ and $l(p) = (1 - p)d/p$ where e and d are constants, not necessarily equal to those in (3). There is some question as to the appropriateness of this illustration as $p \to 0$ since it implies infinite disappointment for rare bad events (nuclear power?), so we must use caution on results for extreme probabilities. However, with this model we have

$$c_2(1/p, p, 0) = -l(1 - p)/p = -d/(1 - p)$$

which decreases with p, agreeing with assumption 8. Also, $c_1(1, p, -p/(1 - p)) = 1 + e/p$ which decreases with p, also in accordance with assumption 8. The function π has an especially simple form, namely

$$\pi(p) = p + pw(p) - (1 - p)l(1 - p) = p + (1 - p)e - pd$$

or

$$\pi(p) = e + (1 - e - d)p \qquad 0 < p < 1. \tag{16}$$

Figure 16.5 (A) A function $\pi(p)$ deduced from a disappointment model. (B) The function $\pi(p)$ derived from experimental data by Kahneman and Tversky (1979).

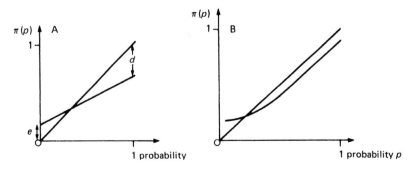

373

To satisfy assumption 3, we require $e + d < 1$. Figure 16.5 shows a graph of this straight line next to the π function of Kahneman and Tversky (their figure 4). Both graphs are discontinuous at 0 and 1.

This odds model induces the common ratio effect in behavior discussed in section 1. It also causes risk prone behavior for small p as long as $e > 0$. The underdog will always be supported in preference to the favorite.

The empirical results of Preston and Baratta (1948) suggest that the breakeven point p^* where $\pi(p^*) = p^*$ occurs around $p^* = \frac{1}{4}$. This result implies that $d = 3e$. On an absolute level, their results suggest a value for e of around 0.1.

4. SENSITIVITY TO METHOD OF UNCERTAINTY RESOLUTION

In section 2 we developed a model that captures the idea that people's reaction to decision outcomes is a function not only of the absolute value of their payoff, but also to the change in their expectations and to the likelihood of such outcomes. So far we have looked at the implications of disappointment for decision making in standard situations including violations of the substitution principle and risk proneness.

Now we extend our analysis of the implications of disappointment for a class of decision situations that has received little empirical study and almost no normative analysis, the possible preference of the decision maker for different methods for resolving what are otherwise identical situations.

The logical argument underlying the substitution principle *fails* if we agree that the method of resolution may matter. While the economic implications may not change, the psychological implications might.

For example, the Irish Sweepstakes is run as a two-stage lottery. In the first stage, 20 or so tickets are drawn at random to match one for one the horses running in the Irish Derby. At the second stage, you win the lottery if you draw a horse at the first stage and if your horse wins the race. Since the prize money is significant, the disappointment from winning a horse, but not the race, would be substantial. The disappointment would be greatest had you drawn the favorite. Many first stage winners are offered sizable amounts for their tickets. The threat of losing may make such an offer very attractive. (There are competing arguments however. The severe regret that would accompany having sold what proved to be the winning ticket might be intolerable. Also, as one such first stage winner put it, "My luck has been with me so far, why should I sell now?" The analysis here confines itself to the effects of disappointment.)

The general question is, when faced with a $(1, pq, 0)$ lottery, would you rather have it resolved in two stages, the first being $((1, q, 0), p, 0)$ and the second (if necessary) being $(1, q, 0)$, rather than all at once? Even though a substitution principle will not hold when disappointment is an issue if preference is modeled on assets alone (see figure 16.1), a substitution principle *should* hold if assets and disappointment are assumed to be a complete description of the decision maker's concerns.

Assumption 9 (backward substitution). *If c_0 is the certainty equivalent of a lottery (x, p, y), then in a two-stage lottery in which (x, p, y) is a possible prize of the first stage, a prize of c_0 for sure may be substituted for (x, p, y) without affecting the certainty equivalent of the entire two-stage gamble. In particular, the decision maker is just as satisfied to win c_0 as to win (x, p, y).*

Theorem 3. *The certainty equivalent of a two-stage gamble $((1, q, 0), p, 0)$ is $\pi(p)\pi(q)$.*

Proof. By assumption 9, we are indifferent between $((1, q, 0), p, 0)$ and $(\pi(q), p, 0)$. But this is equivalent to a sure-thing of $\pi(p)\pi(q)$.

In general, we have

$$c_0((x, q, y), p, (w, r, z)) = c_0(y + (x - y)\pi(q), p, z + (w - z)\pi(r))$$

$$= z + (w - z)\pi(r)$$

$$+ \pi(p)[y - z + (x - y)\pi(q) - (w - z)\pi(r)]$$

$$= z + (y - z)\pi(p) + (w - z)\pi(r)$$

$$+ (x - y)\pi(p)\pi(q) - (w - z)\pi(r)\pi(p). \tag{17}$$

Theorem 4. *The certainty equivalent of two independent gambles to be resolved sequentially is equal to the sum of their individual certainty equivalents. In particular, the decision maker is indifferent to the order of their resolution.*

Proof. Suppose the lotteries are (x, p, y) and (w, q, z). One possible order of resolution is

$$((x + w, p, y + w), q, (x + z, p, y + z)),$$

the other is

$$((w + x, q, z + x), p, (w + y, q, z + y)).$$

Using (17), we see that the first of these lotteries has a certainty equivalent of

$$y + z + (w - z)\pi(q) + (x - y)\pi(p) + (x - y)\pi(p)\pi(q) - (x - y)\pi(p)\pi(q)$$

or

$$y + z + (w - z)\pi(q) + (x - y)\pi(p).$$

This quantity equals the sum of the separate certainty equivalents. Hence, the order of resolution is of no consequence.

Theorem 3 is counter-intuitive for me since it implies, for example, that I should be indifferent between $((1,000, 1/80, 0), 4/5, 0)$ and $((1,000, 4/5, 0), 1/80, 0)$. Yet I much prefer the first lottery on the grounds that the only way to be seriously disappointed is if I take the second lottery and then win the first stage but lose the second. The theorem prompts me to notice that this dire consequence has only 1 chance in 400 of occurring and that other endpoints should carry more weight in my decision.

Backward induction does not tell us how best to resolve a given lottery. Which is better, $(1, 1/18, 0)$, $((1, 1/6, 0), 1/3, 0)$, or $((1, 1/9, 0), 1/2, 0)$? If we assume that the excitement of winning intensifies rapidly as the odds against winning increase, then we might conclude that the most preferred resolution procedure is that in which the odds against winning on a single resolution are greatest. Note that this procedure does not contradict assumption 3 because we are comparing only lotteries with equal overall chance of winning. Hence, $(1, 1/18, 0)$ is the best choice because our elation is $e(1/18)$ if we win. The lottery $((1, 1/6, 0), 1/3, 0)$ is least preferred because neither stage is particularly exciting, relative to $e(1/18)$ and $e(1/9)$.

Assumption 10 (maximize the maximum elation). *If* $p_1 q_1 = p_2 q_2$ *and* $p_1 < p_2 < q_2$, *then*

$$((1, p_1, 0), q_1, 0) > ((1, p_2, 0), q_2, 0).$$

The odds model (16) satisfies this assumption. For

$$(e + (1 - e - d)p_1)(e + (1 - e - d)q_1) > (e + (1 - e - d)p_2)(e + (1 - e - d)q_2)$$

is equivalent to $p_1 + q_1 > p_2 + q_2$ when $p_1 q_1 = p_2 q_2$ and $e + d < 1$. Also, if $p_1 q_1 = p_2 q_2$, then $(p_1 + q_1)^2 > (p_2 + q_2)^2$ if and only if $(p_1 - q_1)^2 > (p_2 - q_2)^2$, which will hold when $p_1 < p_2 < q_2$.

The assumption implies, for example, that contestants in the Irish Sweepstake lottery should prefer fewer horses to be running since the thrill of drawing a horse on the first round will more than offset the increase in disappointment on the second round should that horse not win.

Assumption 10 has an interesting association with the common ratio effect.

Theorem 5. *The common ratio effect and assumption* 10 *have equivalent implications for the function* π.

Proof. The common ratio effect, as noted earlier, says that if $(x, p, 0) \sim (y, q, 0)$ where $x > y$, then, if $0 < r < 1$, we have $(x, pr, 0) > (y, qr, 0)$. That is, if $x\pi(p) = y\pi(q)$, then $x\pi(pr) > y\pi(qr)$, from which we deduce that $\pi(pr)\pi(q) > \pi(qr)\pi(p)$ when $p < q$. Assumption 10 is equivalent, by theorem 3, to $\pi(p_1)\pi(q_1) > \pi(p_2)\pi(q_2)$ when $p_1 q_1 = p_2 q_2$ and $|p_1 - q_1| > |p_2 - q_2| > 0$. Set $p_1 = pr$, $q_1 = q$, $p_2 = p$. If $p < q$, then $|pr - q| > |qr - p|$. Hence, the common ratio effect and assumption 10 have equivalent implications for the shape of the function π.

The common ratio effect answers the original question posed in this section: since $\pi(pq) > \pi(p)\pi(q)$ the decision maker prefers the uncertainty resolved all at once rather than in stages. Note that assumption 10 and the common ratio effect apply to only one form of two-stage gambles involving two outcomes. Quite different algebra is required to study gambles such as $(1, p, (1, q, 0))$.

Ellsberg's paradox

Two urns filled with colored balls are before you. One has equal numbers of red and black balls, the other contains an unknown proportion of red and black balls. You choose an urn and a color. Then you draw a ball from your chosen urn. If the ball is the color you selected, you win a prize. Ellsberg (1961), who constructed this scenario, noted that people strongly preferred to draw from the first urn despite the fact that an economic analysis suggests no reason to prefer one over the other.

Suppose, should you choose the second urn, that after you have chosen a color but before you have picked a ball, you are told the true proportion of red and black balls. For simplicity, let us suppose that the probability of drawing a red ball is known in advance to be either r (which is $> \frac{1}{2}$) or $1 - r$, with equal likelihood.

Your choice, then, is between $(1, \frac{1}{2}, 0)$ or $((1, r, 0), \frac{1}{2}, (1, 1 - r, 0))$. The first urn will be preferred if

$$\pi(\tfrac{1}{2}) > \pi(1 - r) + \pi(\tfrac{1}{2})(\pi(r) - \pi(1 - r)). \tag{18}$$

This inequality is approximately equivalent to

$$0 > (2r - 1)(1 - 2\pi(\tfrac{1}{2}))\pi'(\tfrac{1}{2})$$

as long as r is sufficiently close to $\frac{1}{2}$ where π' is the derivative of π. In this case, the first urn will be preferred as long as $\pi(\frac{1}{2}) < \frac{1}{2}$, that is, if $w(\frac{1}{2}) < l(\frac{1}{2})$, a condition we expect if disappointment has a greater effect than elation.

The linear model (12) (or (3)) satisfies (18) exactly. The odds model (16) satisfies it exactly if $e < d$. Presentation of Ellsberg type choices usually do not discuss the precise mechanics of the resolution, and we do not know what participants assume about these mechanics. Though the interpretation given here may not be common, it serves to underscore the fact that the manner of resolution of lotteries, which has always been assumed to be irrelevant (since they are usually hypothetical anyway), is a potentially important element of the problem description.

Breaking good/bad news

So far our discussion has studied two-stage lotteries whose method of resolution is determined before the resolution takes place. The opposite order is possible if someone other than the decision maker already knows the outcome and can select the method of resolution in the decision maker's best interest.

For example, suppose that you have the job of telling someone that a close friend/relative has been killed in a car crash. How do you go about it? A normal reaction is to break the news in stages. ("I have some bad news. There's been a terrible accident. I'm afraid . . . .") The interpretation is that you are gradually lowering the recipient's expectations so that the truth does not come all at once. Your mechanic knows this method too. ("It was a bigger job than we thought. We had to rebuild the engine. And replace the chassis . . . .")

Breaking good news seems rather different. Suppose that you noticed your brother had inadvertently neglected to check the status of his Irish Sweepstakes ticket, and you found that not only had he drawn a horse but that the horse had won, how would you tell him the news?

It is arguable whether the method of breaking news is chosen more for the benefit of the teller than the tellee, but an analysis of the disappointment implications suggests that it will usually, but not always, be the case that bad news should be broken gently and good news all at once. Before our analysis begins one more assumption is required. So far, we have no explicit model of the net psychological effect of two sequential resolutions. How do you feel after winning one bet, but losing another? The following assumption was implicit in assumption 9. It says that psychological effects accumulate additively.

Assumption 11 (additive psychological effects). *If the decision maker is indifferent between $\pi(q) + c$ and winning $\pi(q)$ in the lottery $(\pi(q), p, y)$, then the decision maker is also indifferent between winning the lottery $(1 + c, q, c)$ and getting the prize of 1 in the lottery $((1, q, 0), p, y)$. A similar condition is assumed when the second stage lottery is lost, and when the first stage lottery is lost.*

We know that $c_1(\pi(q), p, y) = \pi(q) + (\pi(q) - y)w(p)$. Also, $c_1(1 + c, q, c) = 1 + c + w(q)$. Hence, winning a prize of 1 from $((1, q, 0), p, y)$ is, by assumption 11, worth $1 + (\pi(q) - y)w(p) + w(q)$. The second two terms are just the elation values at each round.

Now consider the problem of breaking good news. In figure 16.6(A), suppose that we know the lottery resulted in 1. Should we tell the owner of the gamble the

Figure 16.6 (A) One way to break good news. (B) One way to break bad news.

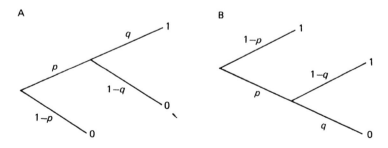

net result giving him an elation value of $w(pq)$, or should we tell him step by step, just as the gamble was resolved, giving him an elation of $\pi(q)w(p) + w(q)$?

Good news should be broken abruptly if and only if

$$w(pq) \geqslant \pi(q)w(p) + w(q). \tag{19}$$

Examination of figure 16.6(B) shows that bad news should be broken gently if and only if

$$l(pq) \geqslant (1 - \pi(1 - q))l(p) + l(q). \tag{20}$$

For a general function f, the constraint $f(pq) \geqslant qf(p) + f(q)$ is satisfied if and only if $f(x)/(1 - x)$ is decreasing in x. Assumption 8 tells us that $w(x)/(1 - x)$ and $l(x)/(1 - x)$ are decreasing in x so that (19) and (20) would hold if $\pi(x) = x$. Inequality (19) will hold if $\pi(q) \leqslant q$, and inequality (20) will hold if $\pi(1 - q) \geqslant 1 - q$. Both of these conditions will be valid if q is sufficiently large, in particular, if it exceeds $1 - p^*$ (see theorem 2). However, it only takes $w(p)$ and $l(p)$ to be slightly convex to overcome the nonlinearity of π in (19), (20). For example, (19) and (20) hold in the odds model (16).

Auctions

An item, worth $\$V$ to you, is for sale by auction. How much should you bid? Your strategy depends upon the precise mechanics of the auction. In an English auction, people make bids of increasing size until someone has bid an amount that no one cares to exceed. The highest bidder pays his bid price and collects the object. Your strategy should be to bid $\$1$ higher than the current bid until such a time as (i) you win the object or (ii) you withdraw from the bidding because to continue would require a bid of $\$V$ or more. (See Engelbrecht-Wiggans, 1980, for a detailed survey of auctions and bidding.)

In a Dutch auction, the seller starts the proceedings by offering the object for sale at some high price and gradually reduces the price until someone signals that he is prepared to pay that price.

In a sealed-bid auction, each bidder writes down a bid and seals it in an envelope. All envelopes are opened simultaneously and the highest bidder pays his bid price and gets the object.

Finally, a philatelist's auction is similar to a sealed bid auction except that the highest bidder, who still gets the object, pays only the bid price of the second highest bidder. It is possible to show that your optimal bid is $\$V$ in a philatelist's auction. Hence, the only information you need in order to bid optimally in either an English or philatelist's auction is the value to you of the auctioned item. If everyone bids optimally, both systems will result in the item being sold to the person who values it the most, at a price equal to the value assigned to it by the person who values it second most.

The Dutch and sealed bid auctions are also equivalent to each other with respect to informational needs, strategy, and outcome. One should estimate the probability of winning with any given bid B, call this function $p(B)$, and bid the amount that maximizes the quantity $(V - B)p(B)$ which represents the expected value from bidding $\$B$. Assuming $p(B)$ is differentiable and increasing in B, the optimal bid B^* is the solution to the equation

$$B = V - p(B)/p'(B). \tag{21}$$

However, if we account for disappointment, the optimal strategy in a sealed bid auction is to bid B to maximize

$$(V - B)\pi(p(B)).$$

The optimal bid (call this B^o to differentiate it from B^*, the solution to (21)) is now given by solving the equation

$$B = V - \pi(p(B))/p'(B)\pi'(p(B)). \tag{22}$$

Even though these equations are implicit in B, it is clear that the optimal bid has been reduced because of disappointment if the right-hand side of (22) is less than that of (21), that is, if the optimal bid B^* from (21) satisfies

$$\pi'(p(B^*)) < \pi(p(B^*))/p(B^*).$$

This equation will always be satisfied by the odds model and will be satisfied by the linear model if $(d - e)p(B^*) < \frac{1}{2}$. In the presence of disappointment, low probability/high payoff gambles become relatively more attractive so that the optimal bid is reduced.

Equation (22) would also give the correct strategy for a Dutch auction, except for one key distinction. A sealed bid auction is resolved instantaneously (in one stage), but a Dutch auction is resolved in multiple stages as the price is gradually lowered. For example, suppose the asking price has been reduced to $V^*(> B^o)$. Your expectations of successfully bidding for the object have increased because you have new information that no one was prepared to bid more than V^*. Your probability of winning with a bid of $B(\leqslant V^*)$ is now $p(B)/p(V^*)$, where we assume $p(V^*) < 1$. Now your optimal bid has changed to the solution of

$$B = V - \frac{\pi(p(B)/p(V^*))p(V^*)}{p'(B)\pi'(p(B)/p(V^*))}. \tag{23}$$

(Of course, if all the other bidders suffer from disappointment, their bids will be affected too, thus changing $p(B)$. We will ignore this phenomenon.)

What bid will you actually make? Only when V^*, the asking price, is equal to B^{**}, the solution of (23), will you actually make a bid. Hence, the price at which you will take the object (if the bid price ever becomes that low) is found by solving the following equation for B:

$$B = V - \pi(1)p(B)/p'(B)\pi'(1) = V - (1/\pi'(1)) \cdot (p(B)/p'(B)). \tag{24}$$

A comparison of (21) and (24) shows that the effect of disappointment is to increase what you are prepared to pay in a Dutch auction if $\pi'(1) > 1$. It is clear that as the asking price drops close to the price you were originally prepared to pay, the potential for disappointment increases and causes you to raise your bid to eliminate the possibility of losing. This response is well understood by expert negotiators. As you (the naive negotiator we will suppose) finally realize that a settlement is close, your expectations rise. At this point your opponent (an expert negotiator) suddenly backs off from the agreement. Your distress at the impending disappointment causes you to make concessions you would not otherwise have made.

Apart from financial implications, which auction method is preferred from a psychological point of view? The sealed bid and philatelist's auctions break both good and bad news suddenly. The Dutch auction breaks bad news suddenly – someone else bids and you are out – but breaks good news slowly; as the asking price descends you gradually realize you are going to win.

The English auction breaks bad news slowly. As the asking price goes up, you slowly get the message that are you not going to win. If you do win, this news comes to you somewhat slowly as other bidders drop out, but the probability of winning was likely to be no better than half at the end since at least one other person must have been bidding. Clearly, the English auction is kinder on the psyche than the other three. Even better might be a blind English auction in which only the auctioneer is aware of who is making the bids. This procedure would leave you in doubt right up to the end about the number of people left in the bidding and therefore, presumably, make the victory more sweet.

5. SUMMARY AND CONCLUSIONS

For many decisions it is apparent that any quantitative analysis must account for the various conflicting objectives of the decision maker. Psychological satisfaction, as opposed to satisfaction derived from consumption, is an appropriate objective that should be included in any decision analysis if the decision maker regards it as a criterion for decision. It can be argued that doing so lowers short-term financial efficiency, but taking weekday vacations in the mountains also does so. Indeed the benefits may be similar, alleviation of stress may have the intangible payoff of improving the general efficiency of the decision maker.

In particular, a consumer may wish to spend some of those dollars in avoiding disappointment, an aspect of risk aversion that does not seem to be reflected by a utility function over dollar assets alone. This chapter does not suggest that people ought to make financial trade-offs to avoid disappointment, nor does it assert (though I believe it to be true) that people do so. As is the case with normative analyses, it merely indicates the behavior that is the logical result of such an objective. Although the implications of this analysis are, in a number of ways, consistent with behavior observed in laboratory experiments, it would be surprising to hear that subjects become sufficiently involved with their hypothetical choices to make psychological effects primary motivators of their selections. It may be that the psychological impacts of a decision are generated by the same thought process used in making a decision, namely that the value of an outcome is judged relative to various reference points such as status quo, foregone assets, and prior expectations.

Disappointment, and related concepts such as regret, have important implications for the study of decision making under uncertainty. Although the axioms of von Neumann and Morgenstern are the cornerstones of decision analysis, they cannot be expected to hold if preference has not been calculated over all attributes of interest to the decision maker. While it has taken a study of descriptive behavior to force recognition of the importance of psychological impacts to the decision maker, it is not our intent to revise the normative theory continually until it matches empirical evidence. Such an approach would make decision analysis useful as a predictive tool but of less value as a prescriptive tool.

We observed that decision makers often agree with the logic of decision analysis but feel uncomfortable at an intuitive level with its implications. Far from encouraging departure from traditional economic analysis, this chapter may convince decision makers that what is currently omitted from expected utility analysis *deserves* to be omitted and that a formal analysis may be exactly what is needed to prevent a decision maker's intuition from forcing economically inefficient decisions.

NOTES

First published in *Operations Research*, 33 (1985), 1–27. © 1985 Operations Research Society of America.

REFERENCES

Bell, D. E. (1982). "Regret in decision making under uncertainty," *Opns. Res.* 30, 961–81.
—— (1983). "Risk premiums for decision regret," *Mgmt. Sci.* 29, 1156–66.
Dyer, J. S., and Sarin, R. K. (1982). "Relative risk aversion," *Mgmt. Sci.* 28, 875–86.
Ellsberg, D. (1961). "Risk, ambiguity, and the Savage axioms," *Quart. J. Econ.* 75, 643–69.
Engelbrecht-Wiggans, R. (1980). "Auctions and bidding models: a survey," *Mgmt. Sci.* 26, 119–42.
Kahneman, D., and Tversky, A. (1979). "Prospect theory: an analysis of decision under risk," *Econometrica* 47, 263–91.
Keeney, R. L. (1982). "Decision analysis – an overview," *Opns. Res.* 30, 803–38.
Keeney, R. L., and Raiffa, H. (1976). *Decisions with Multiple Objectives.* John Wiley & Sons, New York.
Loomes, G., and Sugden, R. (1982). "Regret theory: an alternative theory of rational choice under uncertainty," *Econ. J.* 92, 805–24.
MacCrimmon, K. R., and Wehrung, D. A. (1986). *Taking Risks.* The Free Press, New York.

Machina, M. J. (1981). "'Rational' decision making versus 'rational' decision modeling," *J. Math. Psychol.* 24, 163–75.

Pratt, J. W. (1964). "Risk aversion in the small and in the large," *Econometrica* 32, 122–36.

Preston, M. G., and Baratta, P. (1948). "An experimental study of the auction-value of an uncertain outcome," *Am. J. Psychol.* 61, 183–93.

Raiffa, H. (1968). *Decision Analysis.* Addison-Wesley, Reading, Mass.

Schelling, T. (1983). "The mind as a consuming organ." John F. Kennedy School of Government, Harvard University, Cambridge, Mass. (chapter 15).

Stone, B. K. (1973). "A general class of three-parameter risk measures," *J. Finance* 28, 675–85.

Wehrung, D. A., Bassler, J. F., MacCrimmon, K. R., and Stanburg, W. T. (1978). "Multiple criteria dominance models: an empirical study of investment preferences." In *Multiple Criteria Problem Solving*, pp. 494–508, S. Zionts (ed.). Springer-Verlag, New York.

17

MARGINAL VALUE AND INTRINSIC RISK AVERSION

DAVID E. BELL AND HOWARD RAIFFA

INTRODUCTION

We examine the connection between, and distinction between, decreasing marginal value (whatever that may mean) and risk aversion (from Pratt, 1964). When a decision maker (DM henceforth) declares indifference between $1,500 for certain and a 50–50 lottery with payoffs $0 and $5,000, the DM may have two concerns: (1) a feeling that going from $0 to $2,500 is "worth far more" than going from $2,500 to $5,000, and (2) being "nervous" about the uncertainty in the gamble. We will call the first concern "strength of preference" and the second concern "intrinsic risk aversion." How much of the $1,000 difference between the arithmetical average of the gamble payoffs and the certainty equivalent is due to each of these concerns? Apart from a natural curiosity about such things we have other motivations:

(a) Many utility-assessment procedures currently rely heavily on answers to questions about gambles (e.g., Keeney and Raiffa, 1976); but decision makers are often uncomfortable with making choices among risky alternatives. Can alternative procedures that do not rely heavily on gambling questions be used justifiably?

(b) Many value-assessment procedures rely exclusively on strength-of-preference protocols (e.g., by comparing increments of gain or loss) and never confront subjects with risky choices. But some of these studies are then used to guide risky-choice options. How bad is this nonjustifiable procedure?

(c) We wish to explore the possibility of talking about a particular person's "risk-aversion parameter" without having this contaminated with his or her preferences for incremental changes – again, whatever that may mean.

Dyer and Sarin (1979a,b) have explored some of these topics. They take strength of preference (they refer to this as measurable value) as a primitive notion and derive decompositions of multiattribute strength of preference functions by considering the effects of various independence assumptions between attributes.

Here we concentrate specifically on attempting to explain strength of preference for a single attribute. Our conclusions are consistent with their results.

1. VALUE FUNCTIONS, STRENGTH-OF-PREFERENCE FUNCTIONS, AND UTILITY FUNCTIONS

Consider a single attribute like money or time and assume that DM has a well-structured ordinal preference over this attribute.

Definition 1: A *value* function, $v(.)$, reflects (ordinal) preferences if and only if

$$b \succsim c \Rightarrow v(b) \geq v(c) \qquad (1)$$

where $\succsim$ is read: "preferred or indifferent to".

If v is a value function so is $\sqrt{v}$, $\log v$, or any strictly monotonic increasing function of v. Ordinal comparison reflects the notion that the DM would "rather have" b than c.

Subjects are quite often willing to make a different kind of preference judgement such as: It is more important to me to go from a to b than to go from c to d. Or, symbolically, we will write

$$[a \to b] \succ [c \to d]. \qquad (2)$$

If v is a value function we can *not* use it to talk meaningfully about these value differences. The reason is that the relation

$$v(b) - v(a) > v(d) - v(c)$$

is not necessarily invariant for all strictly monotonic transformations of v. For the time being, we will not try to interpret such statements about increments but treat them as primitives. We shall assume that the DM can consistently assess preferences for incremental changes; furthermore, without the embellishments of an axiomatic presentation, we shall assume that there is a function S that assigns a real number to any increment $[a \to b]$. Thus $S[a \to b]$ will be interpreted as the DM's preference value for the increment $[a \to b]$.

We assume

$$\{[a \to b] \succsim [c \to d]\} \Rightarrow \{S[a \to b] \geq S[c \to d]\} \qquad (3a)$$

$$S[a \to a] = 0, \quad \text{for all } a, \qquad (3b)$$

$$S[a \to b] = -S[b \to a] \qquad (3c)$$

and

$$S[a \to b] + S[b \to c] = S[a \to c]. \qquad (3d)$$

Definition 2. We will say that $s(.)$ is a strength-of-preference function if and only if

$$\{[a \to b] \succsim [c \to d]\} \Rightarrow \{[s(b) - s(a)] > [s(d) - s(c)]\}. \tag{4}$$

Note that if S were given, we could define s by arbitrarily setting $s(a) = 0$ for some a and then defining $s(b) \equiv S[a \to b]$. A strength-of-preference function is unique up to positive linear transformations.

By assumption (3d) if $[a \to b]$ is preferred to $[a \to c]$, then $[d \to b]$ is preferred to $[d \to c]$ for all choices of d. Hence it is reasonable to assume that in this case the DM would "rather have" b than c. Therefore $s(.)$ is also an ordinal value function.

Our aim in this paper is to related strength-of-preference functions to utility functions and in order to do this we shall first hafe to introduce some notation for gambles. Discrete gambles will suffice for our purposes. Consider a gamble which will result in one of the outcomes $x_1, \ldots, x_i, \ldots, x_m$ with probabilities $p_1, \ldots, p_i, \ldots, p_m$ respectively. In this case, we shall talk about a gamble with uncertain outcome $\tilde{x}$ (a random variable) where the tilde above $\tilde{x}$ implies that there is a well-specified probability mass function for x. We assume that the DM has a well-structured set of preferences for gambles that satisfy the usual von Neumann–Morgenstern axioms (see von Neumann and Morgenstern, 1944, or Bell and Raiffa, 1979) and that the DM behaves as if he were maximizing expected utility. More precisely, we assume the existence of $u(.)$ function such that an index of relative desirability of $\tilde{x}$ is

$$Eu(\tilde{x}) \equiv \sum_i p_i u(x_i) \tag{5}$$

where the expectation operation E is taken with respect to the probability mass function of $\tilde{x}$.

Definition 3. A *utility* function u reflects preferences for gambles if and only if a preference for gamble $\tilde{x}'$ over $\tilde{x}''$ means that $\tilde{x}'$ has a higher expected utility than $\tilde{x}''$; symbolically,

$$\tilde{x}' \succsim \tilde{x}'' \Leftrightarrow Eu(\tilde{x}') \geqslant Eu(\tilde{x}'')$$

where $Eu(\tilde{x}')$ and $Eu(\tilde{x}'')$ are defined as in (5).

A utility function $u(.)$ is meaningful up to positive linear transformations. It is well known, of course, that a utility function is a bona-fide value function but not the converse.

The remainder of the chapter will attempt to relate these three concepts of preference. The next section discusses two interpretations of the concept of strength of preference, the first in relation to choices over gambles, the second in relation to ordinal comparisons.

There is a dilemma however. Statements by the DM about ordinal comparisons or about choices among gambles may, in principle at least, be checked by actually offering real choices. This possibility may not be available for statements concerning preference for increments. Therefore, it is inevitable that some people will have strength-of-preference functions that are not compatible with either of our interpretations and may not wish to conform to them.

In section 3 we treat strength of preferences as a primitive concept and, with only a modest amount of additional structure, relate strength-of-preference functions with utility functions in a way that is compatible with our earlier interpretations.

Our concluding section summarizes why we feel our arguments about strength-of-preference are compelling and show how these would affect, and enhance, preference assessment protocols for the future.

2. INTERPRETING STRENGTH OF PREFERENCE

2.1 *Preferences for increments: a gambling interpretation*

Imagine a decision maker who has a coherent set of preferences for lotteries involving incremental monetary payoffs – coherent in the sense that his basic preferences can be captured by a utility function $u(.)$. Utility is not a primitive but a derivative concept. What is primitive is that for the given DM one lottery is preferred or indifferent to another lottery. Utilities may be introduced as a derivative notion whenever the set of preferences satisfies certain desiderata.

Now let us consider the question of whether going from a to b is "worth more" than going from c to d. The difficulty is that we cannot receive an increment of a to b unless we happen to be at a. Therefore the question may be meaningless (in non-primitive terms) if a is not the same as c – which would reduce the problem to an ordinal comparison of b and d.

But suppose that we start out with a 50–50 lottery between a and b, let us denote this by $\langle a, b \rangle$, and ask whether adding $\Delta(>0)$ to a is more valuable than adding Δ to b. It seems possible to argue that if

$$\langle a + \Delta, b \rangle \succ \langle a, b + \Delta \rangle$$

then

$$[a \to a + \Delta] \succ [b \to b + \Delta].$$

One might feel confident in feeling this way not because of any gambling interpretation, but just because adding Δ to x is more important the lower the value of x is.

Therefore the statement $[a \to b] \succ [c \to d]$ could be interpreted, by analogy with the argument above, to mean that $\langle b, c \rangle \succ \langle a, d \rangle$. If a utility function exists this statement is equivalent to

$$\frac{u(b) + u(c)}{2} > \frac{u(a) + u(d)}{2}$$

387

or to

$$u(b) - u(a) > u(d) - u(c). \tag{6}$$

These inequalities are clearly invariant with respect to positive linear transformations and from definition 2, $u(.)$ is a strength-of-preference function.

Interpretation 1: The increment from a to b is preferred to the increment from c to d if the 50–50 gamble between b and c is preferred to that between a and d. Using notation, we have

$$\langle b, c \rangle \succ \langle a, d \rangle \Leftrightarrow [a \to b] \succ [c \to d]. \tag{7}$$

Operationally, it does not make sense to ascertain the validity of the left-hand side of (7) in order to conclude the validity of the right-hand side of (7). The other way around, however, may make some sense.

For example, suppose that c is the certainty equivalent of $\langle a, b \rangle$. Presumably the particular choice of c involves two cognitive considerations for the DM:
(i) the "intrinsic worths" of a, c, and b – admittedly this is vague – and
(ii) the DM's attitude towards risk.

The von Neumann theory of utility chooses not do dissect and identify these two components. There is no need to do so for the purpose of the the theory. But still if

$$c \sim \langle a, b \rangle \tag{8}$$

we could now conclude from interpretation 1 that

$$[a \to c] \sim [c \to b], \tag{9}$$

i.e., going from a to c is equally valuable to going from c to b.

A number of economics textbooks explain why $c \neq (a + b)/2$ by saying that the increase in satisfaction gained from $(a + b)/2$ to b is not as great as gained from a to $(a + b)/2$. This implies that they believe $s(\cdot)$ is identical to $u(\cdot)$. (As an example see McGuigan and Moyer, 1975.)

While (8) is operationally more meaningful than (9), some subjects might think that a query based on (9) is, cognitively speaking, more basic than a query based on (8); they also might think (9) while responding to (8). The danger, of course, is that a direct response to a query based on (9) might abstract out risk attitudes, and it would then be inappropriate to equate (9) and (8) and base a utility function on such responses.

The following experiment would be interesting: with naive subjects, ask preference for increment type questions (without specifying the equivalence of (9) and (8)) and test how appropriate these responses are for gambling choices.

2.2 Preferences for increments: a conjoint interpretation

A natural way to compare a to b versus c to d is by considering how much one is prepared to "pay" of some other attribute (dollars or hours of labor) for the increment (see Suppes and Winet, 1954, for example). The problem with this approach is that dollars, for example, may have a different marginal value in the two increments. Therefore we seek an attribute that has constant marginal value – whatever that means.

Instead of thinking solely of a single attribute X, let us now introduce a second attribute Y and suppose for the moment[1] that these are the only two attributes that are ever of concern to the DM. Assume that our DM has a completely ordered preference relation $(\succsim)$ on ordered pairs (x, y) – ordinal preference under certainty – and suppose these preferences satisfy all the necessary requirements to admit an additive value representation, viz.:

$$V(x, y) = v^*(x) + w^*(y).\tag{10}$$

In this case the set of iso-preference curves is considerably constrained. (See figure 17.1A. In the figure and in what follows it is helpful to distinguish the function v^* from the functional value v. In other words: v^* sends an x-value into a transformed v-value. Similarly with w^* and w.) If we now transform (x, y) points into (v, w) points by defining

$$v = v^*(x) \quad \text{and} \quad w = w^*(y),\tag{11}$$

where v^* and w^* are defined in (10), then the transformed iso-preference curves in the (v, w)-plane are parallel straight lines. The transformations v^* and w^* straighten out the indifference curves in the (x, y)-plane in a way that is not related to risky disincentives. Now the attribute v has constant marginal value – as measured in units of w – and w has constant marginal value – as measured in units of v. This effectively removes the problem of measuring the marginal value of one attribute in terms of another which itself has variable marginal value.

The functions v^* and w^* in (10) are not unique – each is determined up to a positive linear transformation where the multiplicative constants are linked together. The incremental value $v^*(x_2) - v^*(x_1)$ is not meaningful by itself but what is invariant is the comparison of $[v^*(x_4) - v^*(x_3)]$ versus $[v^*(x_2) - v^*(x_1)]$.

Figure 17.1

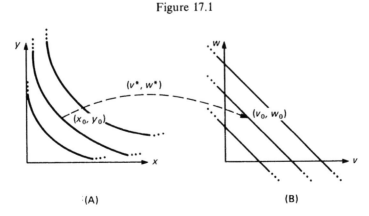

(A)   (B)

We can interpret this more directly by suppressing $v*$ in the following way: Suppose we start with (x_1, y_0) and ask how much of the second component the DM would be willing to give up to go from x_1 to x_2. Suppose the answer is Δ' where Δ' depends on x_1, x_2, and y_0. We have

$$(x_1, y_0) \sim (x_2, y_0 - \Delta').$$

Now we ask: Starting with (x_3, y_0) – the same y_0 – how much would you just be willing to give up in the y-component to go from x_3 to x_4 in the x-component? Suppose the answer is Δ'' where Δ'' depends on x_3, x_4, and y_0. We would then have

$$(x_3, y_0) \sim (x_4, y_0 - \Delta'').$$

We could then argue that if Δ' were greater than Δ'', then going from x_1 to x_2 could be considered more valuable than going from x_3 to x_4; symbolically:

$$\{\Delta' > \Delta''\} \Rightarrow [x_1 \rightarrow x_2] \succ [x_3 \rightarrow x_4]. \tag{12}$$

Intuitively this is saying that if, starting at y_0, the DM is willing to give up more of the y-component in going from x_1 to x_2 than going from x_3 to x_4, then $[x_1 \rightarrow x_2]$ is preferred to $[x_3 \rightarrow x_4]$. It is important to observe that given an additive structure the argument that leads to (12) *does not depend on the choice of* y_0.

Interpretation 2: If X and Y have an additive representation, i.e., $V(x, y) = v*(x) + w*(y)$, then the increment from x_1 to x_2 is preferred to the increment from x_3 to x_4 – symbolically

$$[x_1 \rightarrow x_2] \succ [x_3 \rightarrow x_4] \quad \text{if} \quad v*(x_2) - v*(x_1) > v*(x_4) - v*(x_3).$$

To motivate further the strength-of-preference interpretation, suppose that we introduce three attributes, X, Y, and Z, and assume an additive representation:

$$V(x, y, z) = v_1(x) + v_2(y) + v_3(z).$$

If x_2 is the mid-value point on x_1 and x_3, by interpretation 2, this means that

$$v_1(x_2) - v_1(x_1) = v_1(x_3) - v_1(x_2).$$

Suppose that y_0, y_1, z_0 and z_1 are values such that

$$v_1(x_2) - v_1(x_1) = v_2(y_1) - v_2(y_0) = v_3(z_1) - v_3(z_0)$$

then we can say that

$$[x_1 \rightarrow x_2] \sim [y_0 \rightarrow y_1] \sim [z_0 \rightarrow z_1].$$

Since $[x_1 \rightarrow x_3]$ is indifferent to $[y_0 \rightarrow y_1]$ *and* $[z_0 \rightarrow z_1]$ (more correctly stated $[(x_1, y_0, z_0) \rightarrow (x_3, y_0, z_0)] \sim [(x_1, y_0, z_0) \rightarrow (x_0, y_1, z_1)])$ this suggests more concretely that the increment $[x_1 \rightarrow x_3]$ is "worth twice" the increment $[x_1 \rightarrow x_2]$. This statement is reflected by the value differences.

We have been most careful in the above arguments to maintain that the value function was additive over *all* the attributes that the decision maker might consider. The reason for this is that if X and Y are only additive conditionally on other attributes being held constant at particular values then the strength-of-preference interpretation of $v^*(x)$ might not be invariant. For example, if $V(x, y, z) = v_3(z)(v_1(x) + v_2(y))$, the strength-of-preference measure is $v_1(x)$ if X is measured against Y but log v_1 if measured against Z. This problem does not arise if the multiattribute value function is completely additive. We defer discussion of less restrictive conditions on the choice of a suitable Y to an appendix.

In this section we have given two possible interpretations of strength of preference. In a study of the value of recreational facilities, Sinden (1974) compared these two interpretations and found them to have different implications.

3. FROM STRENGTH OF PREFERENCE TO UTILITY

In this section, we attempt to identify a relation between strength-of-preference functions and utility functions. We will do this in two ways: first of all by interpreting strength of preference via section 2 and then by treating strength of preference as a primitive. We will show that both viewpoints lead to the same conclusion!

3.1 Strength of preference: using the derivative concept

If we use interpretation 1, there is nothing to discuss since in that case the strength-of-preference function is identical to the utility function. But can we conclude in general that if $[x_1 \rightarrow x_2] \sim [x_2 \rightarrow x_3]$ then $x_2 \sim \langle x_1, x_3 \rangle$? The answer, of course, in general, is *negative*.

Let us consider attributes X and Y chosen in accordance with interpretation 2, namely that

$$V(x, y) = v^*(x) + w^*(y),$$

and let us also assume that X is utility independent[2] of Y. Suppose we consider a lottery, as in figure 17.2, which, with probability p_i, results in outcome (x_i, y_0) for $i = 1, \ldots, n$. For simplicity, we write v_i for $v^*(x_i)$.

Figure 17.2

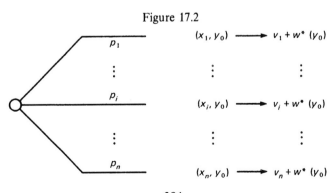

A suitable utility function which assigns $u(x_i, y_0)$ to (x_i, y_0) may, for example, be very concave because the concavity reflects both the DM's strength of preferences for the x_i's and the DM's intrinsic risk aversion.

The utility function $u(.,.)$ now induces a new utility function $u*(.)$ of one argument, where we define

$$u*[v_i + w*(y_0)] \equiv u(x_i, y_0). \tag{13}$$

The function $u*(.)$ may now exhibit far less local risk aversion at $v_i + w*(y_0)$ than $u(., y_0)$ exhibits at x_i, because the transformation sending x_i into v_i eliminates one source of the concavity of u, namely the strength of preferences for the x_i's.

Suppose the certainty equivalent of the lottery in figure 17.2 is $(\hat{x}, y_0)$, i.e.,

$$u(\hat{x}, y_0) = \sum p_i u(x_i, y_0).$$

Notice that, since X is utility independent of Y, then the value $w*(y_0)$ in (13) does not affect the certainty equivalent so that $u*$ would have to exhibit constant risk aversion (i.e., to be linear or negative exponential).

Thus, for example, suppose x_1, x_2, and x_3 are transformed via $v*$ into v_1, v_2, and v_3. If we now assume that the DM is indifferent between x_2 and a p-chance at x_3 and a $(1 - p)$ chance at x_1, where $p \neq 1/2$, then in terms of the v_i's this would mean that

$$u*(v) = -e^{-cv},$$

where the risk aversion parameter, c, is determined from the equation

$$-e^{-cv_2} = -p e^{-cv_3} - (1 - p) e^{-cv_1}.$$

Illustration: Suppose that the DM believes that, in dollars, $[0 \rightarrow 30K] \sim [30K \rightarrow 100K]$, that is $30K is the intrinsic mid-value point between $0 and $100K. Converting dollars into a strength-of-preference scale we can let $v*(0) = 0, v*(30K) = 1$, and $v*(100K) = 2$. But now suppose the DM also says that $30K outright is preferred to a 50–50 gamble between $0 and $100K. Then, even in the strength of preference scale, risk aversion is exhibited. Suppose that the DM says $30K is indifferent to a .6 chance at $100K and a .4 chance of $0. Then we would have

$$e^{-c} = .6 e^{-2c} + .4 e^{-0c}$$

for which $c \simeq .4$. Therefore a suitable utility function for the v-space is $u*(v) = -e^{-.4v}$.

It is not not difficiult to see that if additivity holds and if X is utility independent of Y then we also get that Y is utility independent of X and, much more excitingly, in the transformed w-space, where $w = w*(y)$, the induced utility function for w-values (holding x's constant) is also negative exponential (or linear) *with the same* risk aversion parameter c. This says that if we transform the

x and y scales by squeezing out preferences for increments – a certainty notion – we are left in the transformed spaces with a problem of pure risk aversion and the structures in the v and w spaces are negative exponential with the same risk parameters. This risk parameter can then be thought of as a basic psychological (personality) trait of the individual.

Empirically, it would now be desirable to try the following types of experiments. Start with money. Transform money into a strength-of-preference scale (using certainty trade-offs) and then explore whether the subject has constant risk aversion (or approximately so) in the transformed scale. Then go to some other frequently used numeraire, like time (or remaining life years). Transform this scale into a strength-of-preference scale; next normalize the units of measurements of the transformed monetary scale and time scale by a conjoint trade-off; and then investigate (a) whether the subject has constant risk aversion in the transformed time scale, and (b) whether the subject's constant risk aversion parameters for the transformed monetary and transformed time scales are the same – of course, all this within reasonable experimental error. How exciting it would be if each subject would exhibit roughly the same risk aversion parameter for time as well as for money!

In closing this subsection, let us observe that if we are solely interested in the X-attribute, we can ask strength-of-preference questions directly on x's without *explicitly* bringing the second attribute, Y, into the picture. The Y-attribute gets into the act solely as a hypothetical construct that helps us to rationalize why an assumption of constant risk aversion is reasonable for the transformed X-attribute.

3.2 Strength of preference: using the primitive concept

Our only assumption about preferences for increments is, for the moment, that the DM can give consistent answers in accordance with the structure imposed by equations (3).

Suppose that consequences A, B, C, and D are such that

$$[A \to B] \sim [B \to C] \sim [C \to D].$$

Without any loss of generality we can therefore introduce a strength-of-preference function that assigns

$$s^*(A) = 0, \quad s^*(B) = 1, \quad s^*(C) = 2, \quad s^*(D) = 3.$$

Suppose further that the DM feels that B is indifferent to a p-chance at A and a complementary chance at C, viz.:

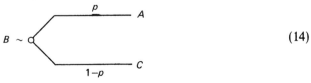

(14)

This indifference relation in (14) can also be interpreted as follows: If the DM were in state B, he would be indifferent between remaining in B or taking a p-chance of going from B to A and a complementary chance of going from B to C, viz.:

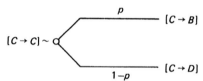

$$(15)$$

Now substituting

$[C \to C]$ for $[B \to B]$,   (from (3b)),

$[C \to B]$ for $[B \to A]$,   (from (3d) and (3c)),

$[C \to D]$ for $[B \to C]$,   from (3d),

the indifference relation (15) becomes

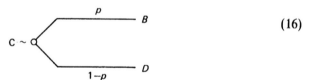

which can be reexpressed as

$$(16)$$

Finally, reexpressing (14) and (16) in terms of s-values (remembering the s-values of A, B, C, and D are respectively 0, 1, 2, and 3) we get

This implies that if $u^*(.)$ is a utility function on s-values, then $u^*(.)$ must be linear or negative exponential, i.e.,

$$u^*(s) = s \quad \text{or} \quad u^*(s) = -e^{-cs},$$

for some risk aversion parameter c.

Note that this is the same conclusion reached via interpretation 2. Interpretation 1, which was more restrictive, led to just the linear case, $u^*(s) = s$.

Of course we have used an additional assumption, that of substitutability of preference increments for lotteries (after (15)). This, to us, is not unrealistic. Our

394

assumption that strength of preference is a primitive notion means that in comparing $[a \rightarrow b]$ with $[c \rightarrow d]$ the DM has some sensation in mind associated with these exchanges. By assumning that the DM obeys the von Neumann–Morgenstern axioms for lotteries (since we assume a utility function exists) it seems only a small leap to extend the substitutability argument to other rewards such as increments.

4. SUMMARY AND CONCLUSIONS

Strength of preference is a well-known, well-studied (e.g., Ellsberg, 1954) notion and our reasoning cannot be said to be "correct" unless empirical studies suggest close agreement to observed responses or unless many people who wish to behave rationally feel these arguments to be compelling.

We have suggested that strength of preference for a given attribute can be measured in a derivative fashion in terms of trade-offs with some other attribute that does not interact with the one being measured. This led to a utility function showing constant risk aversion in terms of the strength of preference measure.

We have shown that, regardless of how strength of preference is defined – treating it as a primitive concept – if a utility function exists (and if the substitution principle can be extended to increments) it should also, logically, show constant risk aversion with respect to strength of preference. From this we are led to the following conclusions:

(i)   that strength of preference for increments is a tangible (if somewhat elusive) concept that can, in some circumstances, be defined explicitly;

(ii) that constant risk aversion *relative to strength-of-preference values* is an appealing idea; and

(iii) that an *intrinsic risk-aversion* parameter (defined in terms of the utility function on the transformed strength-of-preference scale) can be meaningfully introduced for an (idealized) "coherent" subject, where this parameter is independent of the particular underlying attribute over which the gamble is expressed – provided, of course, the various strength-of-preference scales are appropriately normalized.

NOTES

First issued in 1979 as Harvard Business School Working Paper 79-65.

1 This assumption is elaborated in the appendix at the end of the chapter.

2 The appendix uses the condition X utility independent of Y as an additional restriction on the choice Y for the purpose of interpretation 2.

REFERENCES

Bell, D. E., and Raiffa, H. (1979). "Risky choice revisited." Harvard Business School Working Paper 80-34. (Chapter 5 in this volume.)

Dyer, J. S., and Sarin, R. (1979a). "Measurable multiattribute value functions," *Operations Research*, 27, 810–22.

(1979b) "Group preference aggregation rules." *Management Science*, 25, 822–32.

Ellsberg, D. (1954). "Classic and current notions of measurable utility," *Economic Journal*, 64, 528–56.

Keeney, R. L., and Raiffa, H. (1976). *Decisions with Multiple Objectives.* Wiley, New York.

Pratt, J. W. (1964). "Risk aversion in the small and in the large," *Econometrica*, 32, 122–6.

McGuigan, J. R., and Moyer, R. C. (1975). *Managerial Economics.* The Dryden Press, Chicago, Illinois.

Sinden, J. A. (1974). "A utility approach to the valuation of recreational and aesthetic experiences," *American Journal of Agricultural Economics*, 56, 61–72.

Suppes, P., and Winet, M. (1954). "An axiomatization of utility based on the notion of utility differences," *Management Science*, 1, 259–70.

Von Neumann, J., and Morgenstern, O. (1944). *The Theory of Games and Economic Behavior.* Princeton University Press, New Jersey.

APPENDIX

We have attempted to relate the strength-of-preference function $s(.)$ to ordinal value by conjoint trade-offs (section 2.2) and to utility by the arguments of sections 3.1 and 3.2. These three subsections are mutually consistent if there exist only two attributes of interest to the decision maker, X and Y, and if X is utility independent of Y.

An example that illustrates that other potential attributes cannot be ignored involves three attributes X, Y, and Z and where

$$u(x, y, z) = u_1(x) + u_2(y) + u_3(z) + k_1 u_1(x) u_2(y) + k_2 u_2(y) u_3(z).$$

With Z fixed, X and Y are conditionally additive and utility independent. Our interpretations of strength of preference lead to $s(x) = \log(1 + k_3 u_1(x))$ (where k_3 is a constant that depends on the particular value of Z). With Y fixed, X and Z are conditionally additive and utility independent. From this we deduce $s(x) = u_1(x)$. Such a contradiction is evidently unsatisfying.

Therefore, we must make more stringent requirements of an attribute Y against which to measure the strength of reference for X. The attribute Y must be value additive with respect to all attributes of interest to the decision maker. In addition it must be utility independent of all these attributes. We find this latter restriction unfortunate since it requires us to include some consideration of choices under risk in measuring strength of preferences. But, since we wish to relate strength of preference to utility, perhaps this is inevitable.

With this new requirement our theory is internally consistent. If Y_1 and Y_2 are two attributes that satisfy the conditions and if Z represents all other attributes (including X) then we have Z and Y_2 preferentially independent of Y_1; Z and Y_1

preferentially independent of Y_2, from which we deduce (Keeney and Raiffa, 1976, p. 105) that

$$v(z, y_1, y_2) = v_0(z) + v_1(y_1) + v_2(y_2).$$

This additive ordinal structure means that Y_1 and Y_2 yield the same strength of preference function for Z (and X).

To summarize, we are not saying that people do arrive at preferences for increments to conjoint trade-offs, nor are we suggesting that they should (though we find it compelling). We show only that via sections 2.2 and 3.2 and this appendix our interpretations of strength of preference are internally consistent and, we hope, individually appealing.

18

KNOWING WHAT YOU WANT: MEASURING
LABILE VALUES

BARUCH FISCHHOFF, PAUL SLOVIC, AND SARAH LICHTENSTEIN

An article of faith among students of value, choice, and attitude judgments is that people have reasonably well-defined opinions regarding the desirability of various events. Although these opinions may not be intuitively formulated in numerical (or even verbal) form, careful questioning can elicit judgments representing people's underlying values. From this stance, elicitation procedures are neutral tools, bias-free channels that translate subjective feelings into scientifically usable expressions. They impose no views on respondents beyond focusing attention on those value issues of interest to the investigator.

What happens, however, in cases where people do not know, or have difficulty appraising, what they want? Under such circumstances, elicitation procedures may become major forces in shaping the values expressed, or apparently expressed, in the judgments they require. They can induce random error (by confusing the respondent), systematic error (by hinting at what the "correct" response is), or unduly extreme judgments (by suggesting clarity and coherence of opinion that are not warranted). In such cases, the method becomes the message. If elicited values are used as guides for future behavior, they may lead to decisions not in the decision maker's best interest, to action when caution is desirable (or the opposite), or to the obfuscation of poorly formulated views needing careful development and clarification.

The topic of this chapter is the confrontation between those who hold (possibly inchoate) values and those who elicit values. By "values," we mean evaluative judgments regarding the relative or absolute worth or desirability of possible events. Such events may be general (being honest) or specific (winning a particular lottery). Their consequences (or outcomes) may have one or many salient attributes and may be certainties or possibilities. Such a broad definition captures just about any task ever included under the topics of value, choice, or preference, as well as many that would fit comfortably under attitudes, opinions, and decision making. Our discussion is limited to situations in which people are reporting their values as honestly as possible; the further complication of measuring values in the face of strategic behavior is not considered.

The recurrent theme of this chapter is that subtle aspects of how problems are posed, questions are phrased, and responses are elicited can have substantial impact on judgments that supposedly express people's true values. Furthermore, such lability in expressed preferences is unavoidable: questions must be posed in some manner and that manner may have a large effect on the responses elicited. Pursuit of the issues raised here can at best alert elicitor and respondents to such impacts, making these effects deliberate rather than covert.

One might hope that such analysis would identify the "right" way to ask about values. To foreshadow our conclusions, we believe that the quest for a right way is, at times, ill-founded. Although there are some obvious pitfalls to avoid, instability is often inherent in our values. Rather than trying to circumvent such lability, we should try to exploit the insight it provides into the nature of values, and their formation, change, and application.

WHEN AND HOW PEOPLE MIGHT NOT KNOW WHAT THEY WANT

People are most likely to have clear preferences regarding issues that are familiar, simple, and directly experienced. Each of these properties is associated with opportunities for trial-and-error learning, particularly such learning as may be summarized in readily applicable rules or homilies.[1] Those rules provide stereotypic, readily justifiable responses to future questions of values. When adopted by individuals, they may be seen as habits; when adopted by groups, they constitute traditions.

The acceptability and perceived validity of such adages as "honesty is the best policy" and "cleanliness is next to godliness" is to some extent appropriate. As guides to living, they have been subjected to some empirical testing (being clean either has or has not brought satisfaction to oneself, one's neighbors, one's ancestors). They are often derived and formulated to be coherent with a wider body of beliefs and values. And they are readily applicable, both because of their simplicity and because the individual has had practice in working through their implications for various situations. Such facility should help to guarantee that people will give similar answers (regarding, say, the importance of cleanliness), expressing the same underlying views, regardless of how the question is posed.

The power of these rules of thumb comes from their development and application to the settings found in a simple and unchanging society with repetitive problems.[2] Their viability becomes quite suspect in a world where the issues are unfamiliar and complex, the old intuitions impotent, the old rules untested and perhaps untestable.

Today we are asked to take responsibility for choosing a mate, a job, a family size, for guiding social policy, and for adopting or rejecting new technologies. Each of these issues confronts us with greater freedom of choice and more lasting consequences than ever before. They take us into situations for which we have never thought through the implications of the values and beliefs acquired in simpler settings. We may be unfamiliar with the terms in which issues are

Table 18.1. *Psychological states associated with not knowing what you want*

Having no opinion
Not realizing it
Realizing it
Living without one
Trying to form one
Having an incoherent opinion
Not realizing it
Realizing it
Living with incoherence
Trying to form a coherent opinion
Having a coherent opinion
Accessing it properly
Accessing only a part of it
Accessing something else

formulated (e.g., social discount rates, miniscule probabilities, or megadeaths). We may have contradictory values (e.g., a desire to avoid catastrophic losses and a realization that we are not more moved by a plane crash with 500 fatalities than by one with 300). We may occupy different roles in life (parents, workers, children) that produce clear-cut, but inconsistent values. We may vacillate between incompatible, but strongly held, positions (e.g., freedom of speech is inviolate, but should be denied to authoritarian movements). We may not even know how to begin thinking about some issues (e.g., the appropriate trade-off between the opportunity to dye one's hair and a vague, minute increase in the probability of cancer 20 years from now). Our views may undergo predictable changes over time (say, as the hour of decision approaches) and we may not know which view should form the basis of our decision. We may see things differently in theory than in the flesh. We may lack the mental capacity to think through the issues reliably and therefore come up with different conclusions each time we consider an issue.

One possible partition of the psychological states that might accompany not knowing what we want appears in table 18.1. Perhaps the most dangerous condition is the first, having no opinion and not realizing it. In that state, we may respond with the first thing that comes to mind once a question is asked. As a defense against uncertainty, we may then commit ourselves to maintaining that first expression and to mustering support for it, suppressing other views and uncertainties. We may then be stuck with stereotypic or associative responses reflecting immediate stimulus configurations rather than serious contemplation. Perhaps the most painful state is to acknowledge having incoherent or conflicting values requiring further analysis.

The states described in table 18.1 are determined in part by the actual state of our values and in part by how we assess them in a particular situation. The critical elements of that assessment would seem to be: (1) our need for closure, itself a function of the importance of the issue at hand, the need to act, and the audience for our judgments; (2) the depth of the analysis, determined by the thoroughness of the elicitation procedure and our general familiarity with the issue at hand; and (3) our awareness of the problems raised in this chapter – that is, the possibility of not knowing what we want and the power of the elicitor to tell (or hint) to us what our values are.

PSYCHOPHYSICS OF VALUE

Finding that judgments are influenced by unintended aspects of experimental procedure and that those influences are worthy of study is an oft-told tale in the history of psychology. Indeed, McGuire (1969b) describes much of that history as the process by which one scientist's artifact becomes another's main effect. Central to this process is the recognition that the effective stimulus cannot be presumed, but must be discovered (Boring, 1969). A selective survey of this history appears in table 18.2.[3]

Although no attempt has been made at more elaborate categorization of these variables, perhaps the critical factor for experimental design has been whether an effect leads to random or systematic variations in the observed judgments. Recognition of systematic effects is, of course, most productive, leading to the identification of basic psychological principles (e.g., the psychological refractory period uncovered by varying speed of stimulus presentation) or theories (e.g., range–frequency theory derived from effects caused by varying the range and homogeneity of presented stimuli) or design principles (e.g., counterbalanced for situations in which order effects have been observed). The discovery of variables producing random error typically allows little response other than estimation of the size of the effect and the sample size needed to obtain desired statistical power. Although at times noise-reduction techniques may be available (e.g., testing in the morning or providing payment for accuracy), they are usually undertaken with some trepidation for fear of turning a large random error into a smaller systematic one and creating a task very unrepresentative of its real-world analog.

We cite these effects for several reasons. One is because many of them seem to be as endemic to judgments of value as they are to the judgmental context in which they were originally observed. Parducci (1974), for example, has found that judged satisfaction with one's state in life may depend highly on the range of states considered. Turner and Krauss (1978) present evidence suggesting that order of questions presentation in surveys may have marked effects on people's evaluation of the state of the nation and its institutions. Lichtenstein and Slovic (1973) found that the judged attractiveness of casino gambles is greatly affected by stimulus–response compatibility. The second reason the effects are cited is to set the stage for the following discussion of effects more specific to the judgment of values. Like the phenomena in table 18.2, these effects may be considered as

Table 18.2. *From artifact to main effect*

Lability in judgment due to	Led to
Organism	
Inattention, laziness, fatigue, habituation, learning, maturation, physiological limitations, natural rhythms, experience with related tasks	Repeated measures Professional subjects Stochastic response models Psychophysiology Proactive and retroactive inhibition research
Stimulus presentation	
Homogeneity of alternatives, similarity of successive alternatives (especially first and second), speed of presentation, amount of information, range of alternatives, place in range of first alternative, distance from threshold, order of presentation, areal extent, ascending or descending series	Classic psychophysical methods The new psychophysics Attention research Range–frequency theory Order-effects research Regression effects Anticipation
Response mode	
Stimulus–response compatibility, naturalness of response, set, number of categories, halo effects, anchoring, very small numbers, response category labeling, use of end points	Ergonomics research Set research Attitude measurement Assessment techniques Contrasts of between- and within-subject design Response-bias research Use of blank trials
"Irrelevant" context effects	
Perceptual defenses, experimenter cues, social pressures, presuppositions, implicit payoffs, social desirability, confusing instructions, response norms, response priming, stereotypic responses, second-guessing	New look in perception Verbal conditioning Experimenter demand Signal-detection theory Social pressure-comparison, and facilitation research

today's artifacts on the way to becoming tomorrow's independent variables. The third reason is to forswear any pretense of trying to create a scientific revolution. The pattern we are following is a hoary and respected one in the history of psychology: collecting and sorting a variety of documented and suspected sources of lability in a particular form of judgment. By bringing together such a diverse collection of effects, we hope to: (1) facilitate an appreciation of the extent to which people's apparent values are determined by the elicitor; (2) provide a tentative organization of effects and the contexts in which they may arise; and (3) explicate the implications of these results for various areas in basic and applied psychology.

OVERVIEW

If, as Rokeach (1973), claims, people have relatively few basic values, producing an answer to a specific value question is largely an exercise in inference. We must

Table 18.3. *Ways that an elicitor may affect*
a respondent's judgments of value

Defining the issue
  Is there is a problem?
  What options and consequences are relevant?
  How should options and consequences be labeled?
  How should values be measured?
  Should the problem be decomposed?
Controlling the respondent's perspectives
  Altering the salience of perspectives
  Altering the importance of perspectives
  Choosing the time of inquiry
Changing confidence in expressed values
  Misattributing the source
  Changing the apparent degree of coherence
Changing the respondent
  Destroying existing perspectives
  Creating perspectives
  Deepening perspectives

decide which of our values are relevant to that situation, how they are to be interpreted, and what weight each is to be given. This inferential process is determined in part by how the question is defined and in part by which perspectives we invoke in solving the inferential problem it poses. Once we have reached a summary judgment, we must decide how strongly we believe in it and in the perspective upon which it is based.

As outlined in table 18.3, the following three sections describe how an elicitor can affect the expression or formulation of values by controlling the definition of problems, the recruitment and integration of perspectives, and the confidence placed in the result of the inferential process. That control may be overt or covert, deliberate or inadvertent, reversible or irreversible. A fourth section is devoted to the topic of irreversible effects whereby the respondent is actually changed by the elicitation process, through having existing perspectives destroyed or new ones created.

The notion of an external elicitor is used mainly as a syntactical device to avoid unclear antecedents. Questions of value must be posed in some way. If an external elicitor does not pose them for us, then we must pose them for ourselves (if only by accepting some "natural" formulation offered by our environment). Indeed, the power of the effects described here may be magnified when we pose problems to ourselves, unless we direct at our own questions the same critical eye that we turn to someone else asking us about our values.

DEFINING THE ISSUE
Is there a problem?

Before a question of value can be posed, someone must decide that there is something to question. In this fundamental way, the elicitor impinges on the respondent's values. By asking about the desirability of premarital sex, interracial dating, daily prayer, freedom of expression, or the fall of capitalism, the elicitor may legitimize events that were previously viewed as unacceptable or cast doubts on events that were previously unquestioned. Opinion polls help set our national agenda by the questions they do and do not ask. Advertising helps set our personal agendas by the questions it induces us to ask ourselves (two-door or four-door?) and those it takes for granted (more is better).

What options and consequences are relevant?

Once a question has been broached, its scope must be specified. Bounds must be placed on the options and consequences to be considered. The lore of survey research is replete with evidence regarding the subtle ways in which these bounds can be controlled by the elicitor's demeanor and the implicit assumptions and presumptions in the phrasing of questions (Payne, 1952). There are, it seems, many ways to communicate to a respondent: (1) whether the set of possible options is restricted to the named, the feasible, the popular, or the legal: (2) whether new options may be created; and (3) whether the question may be rejected out of hand. The set of relevant consequences may also be shaped to include or exclude intangible consequences (those without readily available dollar equivalents), ethical (versus efficiency) issues, social (versus personal) impacts, secondary and tertiary consequences, means (versus ends), and the well-being of nature (versus that of humans). Control may be inadvertent as well as deliberate. For example, what may seem to the elicitor to be irrelevant and dominated alternatives, sensibly deleted for the sake of simplicity, may provide important contextual information for the respondent.

A tempting solution for the elicitor would be to specify the problem as little as possible, leaving respondents to define the option and consequence sets as they see fit. Unfortunately, this approach increases the probability that the elicitor and respondents will be talking about different things without solving the problem of inadvertent control. Indeed, one might even argue that impassive elicitation is the most manipulative of all. For it means that the entire questioning experience is conducted under the influence of the unanalyzed predispositions and presumptions of the elicitor without even a courtesy warning to the respondent (Rosenthal and Rosnow, 1969): "Here are my prejudices, let's try to be wary of them." There is no reason to believe that people will be spontaneously aware of what has been left out but not brought to their attention (Fischhoff, 1977a; Fischhoff, Slovic, and Lichtenstein, 1978; Lovins, 1977; Nisbett and Wilson, 1977; Tribe, Schelling, and Voss, 1976).

How should options and consequences be labeled?

The elicitor's influence on the definition of options and consequences does not end with their enumeration. Once the concepts have been evoked, they must be given labels. As B. A. Marks (1977) suggests, in a world with few hard evaluative standards, such symbolic interpretations may be very important. Although the factors of abortion remain constant, individuals may vacillate in their attitude as they attach and detach the label of "murder." The value of a dollar may change greatly if it is called "discretionary funds," "public funds," or "widows' and orphans' funds."

Political scientists have been accused of ideologically biasing their research by describing acts, options, and outcomes with terms drawn from neoclassical economics with its particular (mostly conservative) political bias (Ashcraft, 1977). More generally, Karl Mannheim (1936) observed that "the political theorist's ... most general mode of thought including even his categories is bound up with general political and social undercurrents ... extend[ing] even into the realm of logic itself" (p. 117). Presumably, political scientists' choice of language imposes that perspective on respondents to their surveys and readers of their texts.

Although not new, these issues are still troublesome. Furthermore, they cannot be avoided, for some meaning must be given to events, and the meaning generated by the respondent may be even less appropriate than that imposed by the elicitor (Poulton, 1977). When the respondent sees the validity of contradictory symbolic meanings (e.g., abortion both is and is not murder), conflict in meaning cannot be resolved. In such cases, the only recourse is to step back, somehow, and decide on exogenous grounds just what this elicitation session is all about. If necessary, that longer look should come sooner rather than later. Often, changes in perspective are irreversible (Fischhoff, 1977b). The psychological impact of an offered interpretation may not be rescindable (try to forget that "this is what I, your mother, want you to do, but decide for yourself" or that "this is your childhood sweetheart's favorite restaurant").

How should values be measured?

After the problem has been structured, the units of measurement must be chosen. It is not difficult to construct options whose relative desirability is changed when the evaluative criterion undergoes any of the following shifts: (1) from profit to regret; (2) from maximizing to satisficing; (3) from the fair price to the price I would pay; (4) from final asset position to changes in asset position; (5) from the price I would pay to avoid a malady to the price I would have to be paid to accept it; (6) from lives saved to lives lost; and (7) from the ratio of benefits to costs to the differences between benefits and costs.[4] As before, choice of units may be specified by the elicitor or left to that nether region created by the "neutral" stance of nonspecification.

Moreover, the size of the unit chosen may affect the responses. Unless some help is provided to the respondent (say, through the use of anchors or logarithmic scales), it may be very difficult to express values that range over several orders of magnitude for a given set of stimuli because people find it hard to use either very small or very large numbers (Poulton, 1968).

Baruch Fischhoff, Paul Slovic, and Sarah Lichtenstein
Should the problem be decomposed?

Many (or most) interesting questions of value are subtle, complex, and multifaceted, with intricate interrelations and consequences. The elicitor must choose between presenting the event to be evaluated as a whole or offering some kind of decomposition. Offering an unanalyzed whole incurs the risk that the respondent will fixate on a single aspect of the problem or treat all aspects superficially, so as to minimize cognitive strain.

Unfortunately, the act of decomposition has consequences besides clarification. One charge leveled against divide-and-conquer strategies is that they destroy the intuitions of the respondent (Dreyfus and Dreyfus, n.d.). Drawing on the work of Gestalt psychologists and Polanyi (e.g., 1962), these critics argue that people think most naturally and adequately by analogy with past experiences and that all such thought (regarding issues of fact or value) is context dependent. Therefore, any attempt to evaluate separately the attributes of a particular event or designate the importance of attributes in the abstract is likely to produce spurious results. In addition to destroying the respondent's natural understanding, decompositon procedures may impose a response mode that does not allow people to articulate their understanding of (holistic) value issues.[5]

Furthermore, decompositions are not unique; different cuts may lead to different judgments of the same issue. Sequential evaluations of alternatives has been found to produce different preferences than simultaneous evaluation (Tversky, 1969). Plott and Levine (1978) have shown that the order in which attributes are considered is a crucial variable in determining preference orderings. Some theories of choice (Aschenbrenner, 1978) predict shifts in the attractiveness of simple gambles as a function of their decomposition. Kahneman and Tversky (1979) demonstrated a variety of reversals in preference depending on whether prospects were considered as a whole or decomposed into two stages. The effective element here was isolating (in the first stage) one suboutcome that was known for certain. Certain losses and gains are weighted more heavily than uncertain outcomes in determining overall attractiveness.

Finally, as Tribe (1972) has argued, decomposition itself typically carries a message. It stresses ends over means. It proclaims the superiority of the elicitor's overall perspective (and the overall social importance of analysis and its purveyors; Gouldner, 1976). It conveys a message of analyzability or solvability where that may be inappropriate.

CONTROLLING THE RESPONDENT'S PERSPECTIVE

Altering the salience of perspectives

People solve problems, including the determination of their own values, with what comes to mind. The more detailed, exacting, and creative their inferential process is, the more likely they are to think of all they know about a question.

The briefer that process becomes, the more they will be controlled by the relative accessibility of various considerations. Accessibility may be related to importance, but it is also related to degree of associative priming, the order in which questions are posed, imaginability, concreteness, and other factors only loosely related to importance.

One way in which the elicitor may unintentionally prime particular considerations is seen in Turner and Krauss's (1978) observation that people's confidence in national institutions was substantially higher in a National Opinion Research Center poll than in a Harris poll taken at the same time when the latter prefaced the confidence questions with six items relating to "political alientation." Another is Fischhoff, Slovic, Lichtenstein, Read, and Combs's (1978) finding that people judged the risks associated with various technologies to be more acceptable following a judgment task concerning the benefits of those technologies than following a task dwelling on their risks. According to Wildavsky (1966), the very act of asking people for their own personal values may suppress the availability of social values. Indeed, one could speculate that, in general, when conflicting values are relevant to a particular issue, the priming or evocation of one will tend to suppress the accessibility of its counterpart.

Expressed values sometimes reflect the direct applications of established rules. Consistency with past preferences is one such rule; cautiousness is another. Whether or not a rule is evoked will depend on situational cues. As an example of a rule that needed to be evoked before it was used, we have found that most people will prefer a gamble with a .25 chance to lose $200 (and a .75 chance to lose nothing) to a *sure loss* of $50. However, when that sure loss is called an *insurance premium*, people will reverse their preferences and forego the $50. For these people, insurance was an acceptable but initially inaccessible rule; without a specific prompt, the sure loss was not seen as a premium.

Altering the importance of perspectives

Once an ensemble of relevant values has been elicited, some order must be placed on them. This order or weighting may also fall under elicitor control. Such control is, in fact, what experimental demand characteristics are all about: unintentionally telling the subject how to think, what to look at, and what is expected. The unintended impacts of elicitor expectancies show the power of inadvertent influence (Rosenthal, 1969). Although Rosenthal minimizes the importance of operant conditioning in such influence, it is not hard to imagine the impact of an incredulous "hmm" or a querulous "half as important?" on the behavior of a confused or uncertain respondent. Nor is it hard to imagine how the demeanor of the elicitor might encourage or discourage the weight given to intangible or non-western values. Canavan-Gumpert (1977) has shown how reward and criticism can shift people's attention between the costs and benefits involved with a particular event.

One unavoidable decision made by the elicitor that may have great influence on the values that emerge is choice of response mode. Lichtenstein and Slovic (1971, 1973; see also Grether and Plott, 1979, and Lindman, 1971) showed that people use different cognitive processes when evaluating the worth of gambles via a comparative mode ("Which would you rather play?") than they use when judging each gamble separately ("How much is playing each worth to you?") The different processes triggered by the change in response mode lead people to rather awkward reversals of preference ("I prefer *A*, but attach a higher value to *B*.") One possible explanation of such reversals, based on related work by Tversky (1972) and Slovic (1975), is that people make choices by searching for rules or concepts that provide a good justification, that minimizes the lingering doubts, and that can be defended no matter what outcome occurs (example: "Quality is more important than quantity.") Different response modes increase the importance of different rules. In the gambles example, *A* offered a higher probability of winning whereas *B* promised a greater payoff. Here, the preference mode may have emphasized that "the stakes don't matter if you're not going to win anyway," whereas the bidding mode focused attention on the payoff.

Another effect peculiar to choice behavior was found by Slovic and MacPhillamy (1974), who observed that dimensions common to each alternative had greater influence on choices than did dimensions that were unique to a particular alternative. Interrogation of the respondents after the study indicated that most did not intend to give more weight to the common dimension and were unaware that they had done so.

Choosing the time of inquiry

People's values change over time, sometimes systematically, sometimes not. The point in time at which the elicitor chooses to impinge on the respondent will determine in part what the respondent says. Some changes are secular and relatively irreversible. A society and its members may become more or less predisposed to consider environmental values (Harblin, 1977) or equity issues or the rights of women as time goes on. The age distribution in that society as a whole may be shifting, leading to a greater preponderance of young or old people with their characteristic perspectives. By waiting or by hastening, an elicitor has some power to create a different picture of people's expressed values.

Other changes over time, with varying degrees of predictability, are maturation, satiation, cumulative deprivation, increasing risk aversion as one approaches an event, mood changes with time of day, day of the week, or season of the year. Consider people who regularly take stock of the world late at night and whose existential decisions are colored by their depleted body state. Is that value to be trusted or should one rely on the way they value their lives at high noon on a bright spring day? Should an elicitor rely on an auto worker's opinion of the intrinsic satisfaction of assembly-line work on the bus Monday morning or while on holiday and refreshed? In a multiple-play experiment on insurance-buying behavior (Slovic, Fischhoff, Lichtenstein, Corrigan, and Combs, 1977), we found that participants who were generally risk seeking shifted to risk aversion on the final round (just before cashing out). Which attitude should we say characterized them? Or might not both of these perspectives be part of the individual's value system?

Any gap in time between judgment of an event and its occurrence may introduce an element of random or systematic variation in people's judgment. Hypothetical judgments of what an event would be like may not capture how it will look in the flesh. The contrast between the limited funds budgeted for rescue operations and disaster relief and the almost unlimited resources made available for a particular rescue is one product of this failure of anticipation, as is our greater readiness to pay for the protection of known rather than statistical lives (Fried, 1969). We know relatively little about people's ability to anticipate the impact that specified future contingencies will have on their perceptions and values – nor which perspectives, the anticipated or the actual, is a better guide to action (or true preferences). The scanty evidence we have suggests that sometimes, at least, it is better to go with one's anticipations if derived in a relatively thoughtful setting (Fischhoff, Slovic, and Lichtenstien, 1979).

CHANGING CONFIDENCE IN EXPRESSED VALUES

The power of values comes from their roles as guides to actions, as embodiments of ourselves, and as expressions of our relation to the world (Rokeach, 1973). It may matter greatly what we think their source to be, how strongly we believe in them, and how coherent they seem. Attitudes towards values may, however, be as labile as the values themselves.

Misattributing the source

Much of the history of social psychology involves attempts to get people to misattribute the source of their values, by counterattitudinal role playing, by explosure to undirected (overheard) conversations, by conformity pressure, or by inducing social comparison processes. These manipulations lead people to adopt as their own, without critical analysis, attitudes that originated with others (McGuire, 1969a). Cognitive psychology offers some new wrinkles in this misattribution process, showing the ease with which presuppositions are absorbed as facts (Loftus, Miller, and Burns, 1978), inferences are confused with direct observations (Harris and Monaco, 1978), mere repetition improves the believability of statements (Hasher, Goldstein, and Toppino, 1977), and people egocentrically assume that others share their views (Ross, Greene, and House, 1977).

Changing the apparent degree of coherence

People will act and press others to act on values in which they believe most deeply. Depth of belief is a function of source, as mentioned, and of the degree of which such values appear to be in conflict. A superficial analysis may create an illusion of confidence in values simply because conflicting values are not considered. Incoherence in beliefs is typically apparent only when the elicitor adopts or encourages different perspectives. It is easy to avoid taking that extra step, particularly when the respondent is interested in keeping things simple.

Such collusion towards simplicity is encouraged by one implicit message of many elicitation procedures: "This topic is knowable, analyzable; after one session, we will both know your values." It is magnified by the aura of precision and professionalism fostered by elaborate, numerical response modes. That aura manifests the can-do, technological-fix, mastery-of-the-world attitude that characterizes our society (Tribe et al., 1976). Ellul (1969) has argued that one way to control people's minds is to lead them to believe that they can have an opinion on anything and everything. Those opinions will necessarily be superficial, guaranteeing that people will have elaborated, thoughtful positions on nothing. When we ask or answer questions of value, a useful antidote to overconfidence might be to recall the effort invested by Rawls (1971) and his colleagues to produce a reasonably coherent position on just one difficult value issue, social justice.

It is, of course, natural to feel that we are the ranking experts, the final arbiters of our own values. Yet, in order to know how good our best assessment of those values is, we must recognize the extent to which they are under the control of factors that we (as scientists as well as individuals) understand rather poorly.

CHANGING THE RESPONDENT

In most of the effects previously cited, the elicitor neither creates nor destroys values, but merely affects the ways in which they are accessed, organized, and evaluated. Some effects, however, suggest ways in which the respondent may be irreversibly changed by the questioning procedure, perhaps for the better, perhaps for the worse. These fall into three categories: the elicitor may destroy an existing perspective on a value issue, create a perspective where none existed before, or deepen the respondent's understanding of the issue at hand or of value questions in general.

Destroying existing perspectives

As mentioned, one charge leveled against those who break complex questions of value into more manageable component questions is that their divide-and-conquer strategy destroys the intuitions of their respondent. A generalization of this position might be that any elicitation procedure deviating from the normal way in which judgments are made may erode the respondent's "feel" for the issue at hand. The failure of formal decision-making procedures to attract the loyalty of corporate decision makers has repeatedly been attributed to these individual's refusal to trade the comforts of their intuitions for the promises of the formal methods (Harrison, 1977).

Other aspects of an elicitation mode may destroy parts of our "natural" perspective on issues (Barnes, 1976). For example, the dyadic nature of the elicitation procedure, with an elicitor who is reluctant to influence the response, may deprive the respondent of the opportunity to invoke social comparison processes (Upshaw, 1974). Discussion with others may be a natural part of the way in which many people formulate their judgments. It may also be an effective procedure, perhaps by recruiting additional information and externalizing alternative perspectives that are too difficult to carry in one's head simultaneously. In these examples, the elicitation procedure may be seen as destroying respondents' natural perspectives by depriving them of tools upon which they are accustomed to rely (Edwards, 1975).

Creating perspectives

An insidious possibility when posing unfamiliar questions to individuals with poorly formulated opinions is covertly creating a perspective where none existed. One possible process for accomplishing this feat is for the respondent to satisfy the elicitor's hunger for a recordable response by saying whatever comes to mind. Once emitted, this associative response may assume a life of its own. The respondent may subsequently conclude (Bem, 1972), "If that's what I said, then that must be what I meant." As shown in studies of counterattitudinal role playing (McGuire, 1969a), such positions can show a tenacity that is independent of their source or validity (Ross, 1977). The fact that such spontaneous responses are provided in a formal setting with a relatively esteemed listener may heighten such commitment effects, leading to newly invented but firmly held values. The very fact that one is out of one's depths in such situations makes it quite difficult to get a critical view on this new perspective.

Elicitation may induce people to think about issues they wish to avoid and would have ignored had they not been "bullied" by the elicitor. In some cases, the elicitor cannot be faulted for forcing people to take their heads out of the sand and face the issues implicit in the decisions they must make in any case. The use of decision analysis in medical contexts will create many such situations as physicians and patients are forced to provide explicit values for pain and death (Bunker, Barnes, and Mosteller, 1977). In other cases, the elicitor may be asking respondents to abrogate their own rights by telling, say, how much they would have to be compensated for a particular degradation to their environment without offering the response option (Brookshire, Ives, and Schulze, 1976): "a clean environment is non-negotiable." In the extreme, the elicitor may be guilty of "anaesthetizing moral feeling" by inducing the respondent to think about the unthinkable (Tribe, 1972). The mere act of thinking about some issues in "cold, rational" terms may lead to the legitimation of alternatives that should be dismissed outright.

Deepening perspectives

Although the preceding discussion has emphasized unsavory aspects of the impact of the elicitor on the respondent, there are obviously situations in which the only valid elicitation procedure is a reactive one. Consider a national poll of values on issues relevant to nuclear waste disposal, the results of which will be used to guide policy makers. An individual who has no elaborated beliefs may not be responding in his or her best interests by giving the value the question seems to hint at. On the other hand, providing no response effectively constitutes disenfranchisement. An elicitor might reasonably be expected to help in translating the respondent's basic predispositions into codable judgments whose implications and assumptions are well understood. Surely, an elicitor does small service to a respondent with incoherent values by asking questions that tap only a part of those values, particularly if that part might be abandoned (or endorsed more heartily) upon further contemplation?

How might the elicitor deepen the respondent's perspective without unduly manipulating it? One reasonably safe way may be to help the respondent work through the logical implications of various points of view. We presented college students and members of the League of Women Voters with the two tasks shown in figure 18.1. The first asked them to choose between a high-variance and a low-variance option involving the loss of life. The second asked them to choose one of three functions as representing the way in which society should evaluate lives in multifatality situations. Its instructions (omitted in figure 18.1) provided elaborate rationales for adopting each of the three function forms. The predominant response pattern, chosen by over half of all subjects, was option A in the civil defense question and curve 2 in the second task.[6] The former indicates a risk-seeking attitude towards the loss of life. The latter indicates a risk-averse attitude. Confronting subjects with this inconsistency allowed them the opportunity to reflect on its source and on their true values.

Many social decisions require people to determine desirable rates for growth or for discounting future costs and benefits. Wagenaar and Sagaria (1975) have shown that people have very poor intuitions on the cumulative impact of those rates when they are compounded over a period of years: "Neither special instructions about the nature of exponential growth nor daily experience with growth processes enhanced the extrapolations" (p. 416). When issues with compounded rates arise, the elicitor should work through the details of the extrapolations, leaving nothing to the imagination.

A more difficult intervention is to educate respondents about the assumptions upon which their beliefs are contingent. Tougher still is trying to communicate factual information the respondent may not have known or taken into consideration. Kunreuther, Ginsberg, Miller, Sagi, Slovic, Borkan, and Katz

(1978) found that residents of hazard-prone areas typically underestimate the likely property damage from floods and overestimate that to be expected from earthquakes. Although there are obvious problems with presenting damage information without unfairly influencing subsequent judgments, it would seem to be a valid input to helping someone evaluate the national flood insurance

Figure 18.1 Two tasks that elicited inconsistency in values towards catastrophic loss of life.

Task 1: Civil defense

A civil defense committee in a large metropolitan area met recently to discuss contingency plans in the event of various emergencies. One emergency under discussion was the following: "A train carrying a very toxic chemical derails and the storage tanks begin to leak. The threat of explosion and lethal discharge of poisonous gas is imminent."

Two possible actions were considered by the committee. These are described below. Read them and indicate your opinion about the relative merits of each.

Option A: carries with it a .5 probability of containing the threat without any loss of life and a .5 probability of losing 100 lives. It is like taking the gamble:

  .5 lose 0 lives

  .5 lose 100 lives

Option B: would produce a certain loss of 50 lives

  lose 50 lives

Which option do you prefer

—————— Option A

—————— Option B

Task 2: The impact of catastrophic events

(Two pages of instructions explaining the meaning of the curves preceded the following:)

Please rank the three proposals in order of preference.

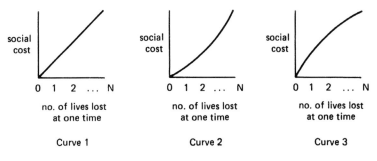

Table 18.4. *Ways one may deal with incoherence*

Nonresolution
Ignore incoherence
Deny incoherence
Live with incoherence
Empirical resolution
Collect evidence (see what you like)
Defer to others
Like whatever you get
Analytical resolution
Creative new alternatives
Recognize metaproblem
Analyze values more deeply, creating or uncovering coherence

program. Likewise, just telling people in vivid details what they may experience in a new job can increase their probability of success and satisfaction (Mitchell and Beach, 1977).

IMPLICATIONS FOR RESPONDENTS

How do we manage to get by with so much incoherence in our beliefs? Why are we not paralyzed with indecision (to the extent that we are aware of that incoherence) or punished by the consequences of acting on conflicting views?

Paralysis seems averted by the nonintuitive nature of the effects described here and the fact that the world seldom asks us more than one question on a given topic. If we are confronted with inconsistency, it is relatively easy to define our way out of contradictions with specious arguments like "that's different," "things have changed," or "it all depends." There is always some extraneous factor that can be invoked to explain a difference. According to Rokeach (1973), people experience discomfort at inconsistency in their values only when it hints at incompetence or immortality. For better or worse, we are usually spared that experience. Table 18.4 lists some ways one might deal with incoherence.

An intriguing option is just living with incoherence. In the experiment described in figure 18.1, half of the subjects had inconsistent preferences. Of those, half decided to deny the incoherence; most of these offered no argument at all, although some tried to demonstrate an underlying coherence by a deeper analysis of their own preferences (typically, by specifying domains in which risk seeking and risk aversion were appropriate). A more satisfying solution is to think one's way through to coherence. Such analytic resolution might involve devising new, conflict-free options or recognizing that the problem at hand is misstated.

We may escape punishment for acting on incoherent values because: (1) day-to-day life affords us much opportunity for hands-on experience that obviates the need for analytic judgment; (2) we are proficient at convincing ourselves that we like what we get (sour grapes, dissonance reduction); and (3) we cannot easily evaluate the outcomes of our decisions (Einhorn and Hogarth, 1978; Fischhoff, 1980). Unbeknownst to ourselves, we may be stumbling all the time, tripped up by our own inconsistent values. The chaos reigning in our society's attempts to regulate various technological hazards suggests a lot of counterproductive effort (Kates, 1977; Lowrance, 1976).

IMPLICATIONS FOR ELICITORS

The purveyors of formal methods of decision making constitute one group of elicitors. Decision analysts (and economists and operations researchers) not only elicit values, but take the numbers they receive seriously in determining decisions that are (purportedly) in the respondents' best interests. The possibility of instability in values is typically treated by sensitivity analysis. The analyst recalculates the decision model while allowing one value at a time to vary over its range. If the final recommendation is insensitive to changes in each value variable, then the instability is considered to be inconsequential.

Although we have only the rudiments of a theory describing the effect of instability on decisions (Fischer, 1976; Fischhoff, 1980), some preliminary results suggest that the expected value of continuous decisions (e.g., invest X dollars) is relatively insensitive to shifts in individual values. Thus, one dose of one of the psychophysical effects described in table 18.2 might not have too much impact. Unfortunately, little is known about how multiple errors compound within an anaysis, nor what is the effect of correlated errors. The use of one perspective throughout an analysis (the usual practice) may produce many shifts of response in the same direction. For example, one might persistently deflate the apparent importance of environmental values or reduce the discriminability of values of all sorts.

Whatever the promise of sensitivity analysis, in some contexts it completely misses the point. Many of the effects described here reflect the introduction of distorted perspectives or newly created, possibly foreign, values into a decision-making process. Blanket invocation of sensitivity analysis will not excuse the imposition of an elicitor's perspective on the respondent. When shifts in perspective lead to reversals of preference, sensitivity analysis avoids the real issues of which perspective is, in fact, appropriate. Furthermore, the long-range goal of involving people in decision making should be, in part at least, the creation of an informed electorate (or management). The goal will not be served by a procedure that uncritically accepts people's misinformed ideas about their own values.

The resolution of this problem would seem to take one outside the narrow confines of formal decision-making methods. One needs metadecisions on questions such as: Which of several possible inconsistent values is to be accepted? How much education and involvement is needed before people can be treated as though they are expressing their own values?[7] When choosing questions, should axiomatic acceptability be abandoned for the sake of intuitive appeal and ease of

415

response? When parties disagree on an issue, is it fair to adopt a procedure that imposes one perspective so strongly that people are impelled to agree (perhaps with a value that none of them likes)?

A decision analysis that explicitly faced such issues would be much messier than those one usually finds today. However, it would be somewhat better protected from the possibility of the whole enterprise collapsing under the cumulative weight of the issues of value liability that it otherwise ignores or finesses. That "new" decision analysis would probably include an explicit acknowledgment of the artful use of a variety of questions and the gentle development of respondent's opinions, both of which characterize the actual practice of the "old" decision analysis in the hands of its best practitioners.

All elicitors, be they decision analysts or students of judgment, decision making, choice, or attitudes, must decide at some point whether or not they have adequately captured their respondents' values. The usual criteria are reliability and internal consistency (e.g., transitivity). However, where the task is poorly understood because of complexity or unfamiliarity (e.g., preferences for shades of gray), consistency of response within a given experimental mode may tell us little beyond the power of that mode to impose a particular perspective or generate a consistent, coping heuristic.

Insight into people's values may come rather from posing diverse questions in the hope of eliciting inconsistent responses. If situation-specific clues play a large role in determining what people express as their values, it is the variance in judgment between situations that reveals what those cues may be. Therefore, one would want to start the study of values with methodological pluralism (Royce, 1974) or even Dadaism (Feyerabend, 1975) designed to elicit the broadest range of variation in expressed values. With a large set of possible determinants of value in hand, one can then try to establish their salience, potency, and prevalence. This approach has the admirable property of (potentially) turning past morasses into silk purses, for any set of inconsistent results becomes a possible source of systematic variance. Inconsistency in values is treated as a success rather than a failure of measurement, for it indicates contexts defined sharply enough to produce a difference. Indeed, this was the approach adopted by Poulton (1968) in producing his six models for the "new psychophysics."

CONCLUSION

Expressed values seem to be highly labile. Subtle changes in elicitation mode can have marked effects on what people express as their preferences. Some of these effects are reversible, others not; some deepen the respondent's perspective, others do not; some are induced deliberately, others are not; some are specific to questions of value, others affect judgments of all kinds; some are well documented, others are mere speculation. Confronting these effects is unavoidable if we are to elicit values at all.

To the extent that these effects are real and powerful, they have different implications for different groups of elicitors.

If one is interested in how people express their values in the real world, one question may be enough. That world often asks only one question (e.g., in a ballot measure). A careful analysis of how an issue is posed may allow one to identify that question and accurately predict responses.

If one is interested in how people create, revise, and express their opinions, the contrast between different procedures may be a source of insight.

If one is interested in what people really feel about a value issue, there may be no substitute for an interactive, dialectical elicitation procedure, one that acknowledges the elicitor's role in helping the respondent to create and enunciate values. That help would include a conceptual analysis of the problem and of the personal, social, and ethical value issues to which the respondent might wish to relate.

The most satisfying way to interact with our respondents and help them make value judgments in their own best interests is to provide them with new analytical tools. Such tools would change respondents by deepening their perspective. In the extreme, they could include relevant instruction in philosophy, economics, sociology, anthropology, and so on, as well as training in decision-making methodology.[8] More modestly, one could convey an understanding of the basic models for values (compensatory, disjunctive, etc.), of useful heuristics (and their limitations), of commonly accepted rules of rationality and their rationales, of common pitfalls, and of new concepts encountered in a particular problem. Perhaps the simplest and most effective message of all might be the theme of this chapter: Consider more than one perspective.

NOTES

This research was supported by the Advanced Research Projects Agency of the Department of Defense and was monitored by the Office of Naval Research under Contract *N00014-79-C-0029* (*ARPA Order No. 3668*) to Perceptronics, Inc. First published in T. Wallsten (ed.) (1980). *Cognitive Processes in Choice and Decision Behavior*. Hillsdale, NJ: Erlbaum, 117–41.

1 These are, incidently, conditions quite similar to those cited by Nisbett and Bellows (1977) as necessary for valid introspection.

2 However, one should not tout folk or personal wisdom too highly. Even in those settings, people comfortably hold contradictory adages ("Nothing ventured, nothing gained" and "Fools rush in where angels fear to tread"). The testing procedures for validating such wisdom leaves much to be desired. People may not realize when experience provides a test for their well-worn rules and may not remember their experiences properly when they do consider validity. They may forget a rule's failures and remember its successes, or vice versa. Finally, the translation of subjective feelings to observable judgments has an unavoidable error component due to inattention, distraction, laziness, and mistakes. Such error can introduce enough slippage into the opinion evaluation and formulation process to make clarity somewhat difficult.

3 No attempt will be made to document this incomplete list drawn from various parts of the lore of psychology. Useful references include Carterette and Friedman (1974), Galanter (1974), Helson (1964), Kling and Riggs (1971), L. E. Marks (1974), Parducci (1974), Posner (1973), Poulton (1968), Rosenthal and Rosnow (1969), Upshaw (1974), and Woodworth and Schlosberg (1954).

417

4 Kahneman and Tversky (1979) provide the most extensive and insightful discussion of the power of shifts in point of reference, the principle underlying many of these effects.

5 If true, this criticism would attribute the greatest validity to elicitation procedures that leave options in their most natural form. For example, Hammond's social judgment theory approach (Hammond and Adelman, 1976), in which complete options are judged, should be preferred to the Keeney and Raiffa (1976) procedure, in which whole options are evaluated but only two attributes are varied at a time. That procedure, in turn, should be preferred to Edwards' (Gardiner and Edwards, 1975) SMART method that forces total decomposition. Ironically, Dreyfus and Dreyfus (n.d.) chose Hammond and Adelman (1976) as a case in point for the flaws of decomposition.

6 These results were not changed appreciably either by changing the degree of elaboration in the rationale given for three curves, nor by describing civil defense option B as an action option that reduced the number of casualties (to a small, but definite, number). The civil defense question was posed in nine ways, varying the variance, expectation, and probability of loss with option A (with B always a sure loss of A's expectation). Option B was never chosen by more than 10% of subjects except in the one case where A specified a .99 chance of losing no lives and a .01 chance of losing 100 lives, whereas B specified the certainty of losing one life.

7 Perhaps the only way to ensure meaningful citizen participation in public policy issues is to impanel a representative group of citizens, such as a jury, to follow an issue through the various stages of debate, deliberation, and clarification.

8 Rozeboom (1977) has argued that the elicitors themselves should have more of such training.

REFERENCES

Aschenbrenner, K. M. (1978). Singlepeaked risk preferences and their dependability on the gambles' presentation mode. *Journal of Experimental Psychology: Human Perception and Performance*, 4, 513–20.

Ashcraft, R. (1977). Economic metaphors, behaviorism, and political theory: some observations on the ideological uses of language. *The Western Political Quarterly*, 30, 313–28.

Barnes, S. B. (1976). Natural rationality: a neglected concept in the social sciences. *Philosophy of the Social Sciences*, 6, 115–26.

Bem, D. J. (1972). Self-perception theory. In L. Berkowitz (ed.), *Advances in Experimental Social Psychology*. New York: Academic Press.

Boring, E. G. (1969). Perspective: artifact and control. In R. Rosenthal and R. L. Rosnow (eds.), *Artifacts in Behavioral Research*. New York: Academic Press.

Brookshire, D. S., Ives, B. C., and Schulze, W. D. (1976). The valuation of aesthetic preferences. *Journal of Environmental Economics and Management*, 3, 325–46.

Bunker, J. P., Barnes, B. A., and Mosteller, F. (1977). *Costs, Risks and Benefits of Surgery*. New York: Oxford University Press.

Canavan-Gumpert, D. (1977). Generating reward and cost orientation through praise and criticism. *Journal of Personality and Social Psychology*, 35, 501–13.

Carterette, E. C., and Friedman, M. P. (1974). *Handbook of Perception* (vol. 2). New York: Academic Press.

Dreyfus, H., and Dreyfus, S. (n.d.). Uses and abuses of multiattribute and multiaspect models of decision making. Unpublished manuscript, University of California, Berkeley.

Edwards, W. (1975). Comment. *Journal of American Statistical Association*, 70, 291–3.

Einhorn, H., and Hogarth, R. (1978). Confidence in judgment: persistence of the illusion of validity. *Psychological Review*, 85, 395–416.

Ellul, J. (1969). *Propaganda*. New York: Knopf.

Feyerabend, P. (1975). *Against Method*. New York: Humanities Press.

Fischer, G. W. (1976). Multidimensional utility models for risky and riskless choice. *Organizational Behavior and Human Performance*, 17, 127–46.

Fischhoff, B. (1977a). Cost–benefit analysis and the art of motorcycle maintenance. *Policy Sciences*, 8, 177–202.

   (1977b). Perceived informativeness of facts. *Journal of Experimental Psychology: Human Perception and Performance*, 3, 349–58.

   (1980). Clinical decision analysis. *Operations Research*, 28, 28–43.

Fischhoff, B., Slovic, P., and Lichtenstein, S. (1978). Fault trees: sensitivity of estimated failure probabilities to problem representation. *Journal of Experimental Psychology: Human Perception and Performance*, 4, 342–55.

   (1979). Subjective sensitivity analysis. *Organizational Behavior and Human Performance*, 23, 339–59.

Fischhoff, B., Slovic, P., Lichtenstein, S., Read, S., and Combs, B. (1978). How safe is safe enough? A psychometric study of attitudes towards technological risks and benefits. *Policy Sciences*, 8, 127–52.

Fried, C. (1969). The value of human life. *Harvard Law Review*, 82, 1415–37.

Galanter, E. (1974). Psychological decision mechanisms and perception. In E. C. Carterette and M. P. Friedman (eds), *Handbook of Perception* (Vol. 2). New York: Academic Press.

Gardiner, P. C., and Edwards, W. (1975). Public values: multiattribute–utility measurement for social decision making. In M. F. Kaplan and S. Schwartz (eds.), *Human Judgment and Decision Processes*. New York: Academic Press.

Gouldner, A. (1976). *The Dialectic of Ideology and Technology: The Origins, Grammar and Future of Ideology*. New York: Seabury Press.

Grether, D. M., and Plott, C. R. (1979). Economic theory of choice and the preference reversal phenomenon. *American Economic Review*, 69, 623–38.

Hammond, K. R., and Adelman, L. (1976). Science, values and human judgment. *Science*, 194, 389–96.

Harblin, T. D. (1977). Mine or garden? Values and the environment – probable sources of change. *Zygon*, 12, 134–50.

Harris, R. J., and Monaco, R. E. (1978). Psychology of pragmatic implications: information processing between the lines. *Journal of Experimental Psychology: General*, 107, 1–22.

Harrison, F. L. (1977). Decision making in conditions of extreme uncertainty. *Journal of Management Studies*, 14, 169–78.

Hasher, L., Goldstein, D., and Toppino, T. (1977). Frequency and the conference of referential validity. *Journal of Verbal Learning and Verbal Behavior*, 16, 107–10.

Helson, H. (1964). *Adaptatin Level Theory*. New York: Harper & Row.

Kahneman, D., and Tversky, A. (1979). Prospect theory. *American Economic Review*, 47, 263–91.

Kates, R. W. (1977). *Managing Technological Hazard*. Boulder: University of Colorado, Institute of Behavioral Science.

Keeney, R. L., and Raiffa, H. (1976). *Decisions with Multiple Objectives*. New York: Wiley.

Kling, J., and Riggs, L. (1971). *Woodworth and Schlosberg's Experimental Psychology*. New York: Holt, Rinehart & Winston.

Kunreuther, H. L., Ginsberg, R., Miller, L., Sagi, P., Slovic, P., Borkan, B., and Katz, N. (1978). *Disaster Insurance Protection: Public Policy Lessons*. New York: Wiley.

Baruch Fischhoff, Paul Slovic, and Sarah Lichtenstein

Lichtenstein, S., and Slovic, P. (1971). Reversals of preference between bids and choices in gambling decisions. *Journal of Experimental Psychology*, 89, 46–55.

——— (1973). Response-induced reversals of preference in gambling: an extended replication in Las Vegas. *Journal of Experimental Psychology*, 101, 16–20.

Lindman, H. R. (1971). Inconsistent preferences among gambles. *Journal of Experimental Psychology*, 89, 390–7.

Loftus, E., Miller, D. O., and Burns, H. J. (1978). Semantic integration of verbal information into visual memory. *Journal of Experimental Psychology: Human Learning and Memory*, 4, 19–31.

Lovins, A. B. (1977). Cost–risk–benefit assessments in energy policy. *The George Washington Law Review*, 45, 911–43.

Lowrance, W. W. (1976). *Of Acceptable Risk*. Los Altos, Calif.: William Kaufman.

McGuire, W. J. (1969a). The nature of attitudes and attitude change. In G. Lindzey and E. Aronson (eds.), *The Handbook of Social Psychology*. Reading, Mass.: Addison-Wesley.

——— (1969b). Suspiciousness of experimenter's intent. In R. Rosenthal and R. L. Rosnow (eds.), *Artifact in Behavioral Research*. New York: Academic Press.

Mannheim, K. (1936). *Ideology and Utopia*. New York: Harcourt.

Marks, B. A. (1977). Decision under uncertainty: the narrative sense. *Administration and Society*, 9, 379–94.

Marks, L. E. (1974). *Sensory processes: The New Psychophysics*. New York: Academic Press.

Mitchell, T. R., and Beach, L. R. (1977). Expectancy theory, decision theory, and occupational preferences and choice. In M. Kaplan and S. Schwartz (eds.), *Human Judgment and Decision Processes in Applied Settings*. New York: Academic Press.

Nisbett, R. E., and Bellows, N. (1977). Verbal reports about causal influences on social judgments: private access vs. public theories. *Journal of Personality and Social Psychology*, 35, 613–24.

Nisbett, R. E., and Wilson, T. D. (1973). Telling more than we can know. *Psychological Review*, 84, 231–59.

Parducci, A. (1974). Contextual effects: a range-frequency analysis. In E. C. Carterette and M. P. Friedman (eds.), *Handbook of Perception* (vol. 2). New York: Academic Press.

Payne, S. L. (1952). *The Art of Asking Questions*. Princeton University Press.

Plott, C. R., and Levine, M. E. (1978). A model of agenda influence on committee decisions. *American Economic Review*, 68, 146–60.

Polanyi, M. (1962). *Personal Knowledge*. London: Routledge & Kegal Paul.

Posner, M. (1973). *Cognition: An Introduction*. Glenview, Ill.: Scott, Foresman.

Poulton, E. C. (1968). The new psychophysics: six models for magnitude estimation. *Psychological Bulletin*, 69, 1–19.

——— (1977). Quantitative subjective assessments are almost always biased, sometimes completely misleading. *British Journal of Psychology*, 68, 409–25.

Rawls, J. (1971). *A Theory of Justice*. Cambridge: Harvard University Press.

Rokeach, M. (1973). *The Nature of Human Values*. New York: Free Press.

Rosenthal, R. (1969). Interpersonal expectations: effects of the experimenter's hypothesis. In R. Rosenthal and R. L. Rosnow (eds.), *Artifact in Behavioral Research*. New York: Academic Press.

Rosenthal, R., and Rosnow, R. L. (1969). *Artifact in Behavioral Research.* New York: Academic Press.

Ross, L. (1977). The intuitive psychologist and his shortcomings. In L. Berkowitz (ed.), *Advances in Social Psychology.* New York: Academic Press.

Ross, L., Greene, D., and House, P. (1977). The "false consensus effect": an egocentric bias in social perception and attribution processes. *Journal of Experimental Social Psychology,* 13, 279–301.

Royce, J. R. (1974). Cognition and knowledge: psychological epistemology. In E. C. Carterette and M. P. Friedman (eds.), *Handbook of Perception: Historical and Philosophical Origins of Perception.* New York: Academic Press.

Rozeboom, W. W. (1977). Metathink. *Canadian Pschological Review,* 18, 197–203.

Slovic, P. (1975). Choice between equally-valued alternatives. *Journal of Experimental Psychology: Human Perception and Performance,* 1, 280–7.

Slovic, P., Fischhoff, B., Lichtenstein, S., Corrigan, B., and Combs, B. (1977). Preference for insuring against probable small losses: implications for the theory and practice of insurance. *Journal of Risk and Insurance,* 44, 237–58.

Slovic, P., and MacPhillamy, D. J. (1974). Dimensional commensurability and cue utilization in comparative judgment. *Organizational Behavior and Human Performance,* 11, 172–94.

Tribe, L. H. (1972). Policy science: analysis or ideology? *Philosophy and Public Affairs,* 2, 66–110.

Tribe, L. H., Schelling, C. S., and Voss, J. (1976). *When Values Conflict: Essays on Environmental Analysis, Discourse and Decisions.* Cambridge, Mass.: Ballinger.

Turner, C. F., and Krauss, E. (1978). Fallible indicators of the subjective state of the nation. *American Psychologist,* 33, 456–70.

Tversky, A. (1969). Intransitivity of preferences. *Psychological Review,* 76, 31–48.

(1972). Elimination by aspects: a theory of choice. *Psychological Review,* 79, 281–99.

Upshaw, H. (1974). Personality and social effects in judgment. In E. C. Carterette and M. P. Friedman (eds.), *Handbook of Perception* (vol. 2). New York: Academic Press.

Wagenaar, W. A., and Sagaria, S. D. (1975). Misperception of exponential growth. *Perception and Psychophysics,* 18, 416–22.

Wildavsky, A. (1966). The political economy of efficiency: cost–benefit analysis, systems analysis and program budgeting. *Public Administration Review,* 26, 292–308.

Woodworth, R. S., and Schlosberg, H. (1954). *Experimental Psychology.* New York: Henry Holt.

421

19

SOURCES OF BIAS IN ASSESSMENT
PROCEDURES FOR UTILITY FUNCTIONS

JOHN C. HERSHEY, HOWARD C. KUNREUTHER AND
PAUL J. H. SCHOEMAKER

INTRODUCTION

The standard model of choice utilized by decision scientists in analyzing problems is expected utility (EU) theory [41]. This model is presumed to be descriptive of people's basic preferences, while having normative implications for more complex problems. Recently, however, there has been an extensive literature which suggests that even basic choice is more complicated than utility theory suggests (see [6] for a review). In view of this, this chapter presents a framework for systematically investigating biases stemming from various information processing limitations. We define bias, for this purpose, as a violation of the EU axioms. The experimental data presented in this study, together with a large body of existing evidence, lead us to the conclusion that traditional EU theory may have to be modified if it is to serve as a descriptive and normative model of choice under uncertainty.

Our analysis was, in part, motivated by a recent article of Fishburn and Kochenberger [8] who analyzed 30 empirical utility functions published in earlier literature [35], [12], [9], [10], [3]. These plotted utility functions were defined on net present values, returns on investments, or simply net monetary gain or loss. Some studies used business contexts, some personal and others both. Fishburn and Kochenberger (F–K) divided each graph into a below- and above-target segment, and fitted linear, power, and exponential functions separately to each subset of data. Of the 30 graphs they examined, 28 were characterized by F–K as having concave (risk-averse) and/or convex (risk-seeking) segments, broken down as follows:

	Concave above	Convex above	Total
Convex below	13	5	18
Concave below	3	7	10
	16	12	28

The remaining two were linear.

In terms of percentages, 64% of the below-target functions were convex and 57% of the above-target functions were concave. The predominant composite shape, they concluded, was convex–concave (46%) followed by concave–convex (25%).

We question the pooling of utility functions, as was done for instance in the F–K study, when the utility functions are obtained via different elicitation procedures. Specifically, we shall present evidence that the shape of the utility function is influenced by and possibly distorted because of (1) response mode biases, (2) biases induced by probability and outcome levels, (3) aspiration level effects, (4) inertia effects, and (5) context effects. The present chapter thus raises a set of methodological issues that have significant implications for both descriptive and prescriptive analyses of choice under uncertainty.

ELICITATION METHODS

To begin our analysis, we assume that von Neumann–Morgenstern (NM) utility functions [41] are constructed via standard reference lotteries where the client provides indifference judgments between a sure option and a two-outcome lottery. In conducting the elicitation interview, the decision analyst will thus present the client with the following choice:

$$S \text{ versus} \begin{cases} p & G \\ 1-p & L \end{cases}$$

where S is the sure amount, p is the probability of winning G (for gain), and L (for loss) the lower outcome of the lottery. Of course, $0 < p < 1$ and $L < S < G$. Note that L and G refer to relative rather than absolute amounts; hence they are not constrained signwise. Of these four variables, three will have been set by the decision analyst, whereas the fourth is varied to obtain an indifference judgment such that $U(S) = pU(G) + (1 - p)U(L)$. Hence, there exist essentially four different methods for constructing NM utility functions, namely:

1. The certainty equivalence (CE) method, where the client states an indifference level for S for given values of p, G, and L.

2. The probability equivalence (PE) method, where an indifference level for p is elicited, for given values of G, L, and S.

3. The gain equivalence (GE) method, where the probabilistic outcome G is elicited, and p, L, and S are fixed.

4. The loss equivalence (LE) method, where the probabilistic outcome L is elicited, while p, G, and S are held constant.

Hence, one important choice the decision analyst must make is which of these four response modes to use. The most common ones are the CE and PE methods. As we will show, however, these two methods may produce significant differences in the shapes of the resulting utility functions. This, of course, is counter to EU theory.

Another important decision involves the dimensions of the lottery. Specifically, what probability and outcome levels should one use in eliciting risk preferences? If the shape of the utility function depends on the endpoints associated with G and L magnitudes, and/or the values of p utilized, we must be aware of this in designing a set of reference lotteries. Again, in theory the choice of levels is arbitrary. Due to the substitution and other axioms of utility theory, an NM utility function constructed with 50–50 reference lotteries should assume the same shape as one obtained with, for example, 30–70 lotteries. As we will see, however, this may not be the case due to probability distortions.

A third decision to be made by the analyst concerns the domain of outcomes to be used. Three lottery types may be distinguished, namely pure loss lotteries ($L < G \leqslant 0$), mixed lotteries ($L < 0$ and $G > 0$), and pure gain lotteries ($G > L \geqslant 0$). Of course, within the EU model it is arbitrary which approach is used, as the same functional shape (within positive linear transformations) should occur. Hence, an NM function constructed on $[-\$1,000, \$1,000]$ using mixed lotteries should be identical to one using pure lotteries within the positive and negative subintervals of this range. In practice, however, the functions may well differ (as we will show), due to aspiration level and possibly other factors.

A fourth decision to be made is how to present the choice to the decision maker; will it be one where the client must assume risk or one where risk is transferred away? For instance, the decision analyst might ask for how much (at a minimum) the client would sell a given lottery (i.e., transfer risk). Alternatively, it might be asked whether the client would exchange a sure gift for that lottery (i.e., assume the risk), which may be quite different psychologically from a transfer of risk, due to inertia effects.

Finally, the decision analyst must choose a decision context for the reference lotteries used. This aspect of the elicitation procedure is important as different wordings, scripts, or scenarios may lead to different stated risk preferences. If the underlying choices are structurally the same, such contextual differences should be without effects. However, since different contexts often emphasize different aspects [1], people may process information differently, thereby inducing inconsistent responses.

In figure 19.1 we diagram the five types of choices the analyst must make (either implicitly or explicitly). In the remainder of the paper we will demonstrate that each of these five choices may indeed influence the utility function in

Figure 19.1 Choices for selecting an elicitation procedure.

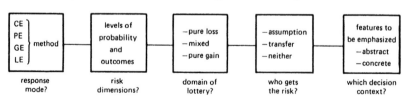

424

nonnormative ways. As such we view this paper as a first step in the development of a much needed methodology for utility encoding. Compared to probability encoding [34], the utility side has largely been ignored in decision analysis although it similarly suffers from serious, systematic biases.

RESPONSE MODE BIAS

In table 19.1 we have summarized which methods were used in each of the five studies examined by Fishburn and Kochenberger [8], together with their findings. Interestingly, for those studies [35], [12], [3] using the certainty equivalence method, 16 of the 17 below-target shapes were convex and 13 of the 17 above-target shapes were concave, whereas for those studies [9], [10] using the probability equivalence method, 9 of the 11 below-target shapes were concave and 8 of the 11 above-target shapes convex. (Note that none of these studies employed the GE or LE methods.) Hence, there appears to be a strong interaction between the response mode used and the predominant shapes obtained by F–K as shown in the following cross-classification derived from table 19.1.

| | Response mode | |
Composite shape	Certainty equivalence	Probability equivalence
Convex below– concave above	12	1
Concave below– convex above	0	7

The conclusion by F–K, that the predominant composite shape is convex–concave may thus be artifactual, reflecting instead the higher incidence of the certainty equivalence method in the studies examined. Indeed, differences in response mode account for almost all of the variance among the two most predominant shapes.[1]

Experiment 1

To examine this response mode bias more systematically, we conducted an experiment with 64 Wharton students taking an undergraduate course in decision sciences. All students were familiar with NM utility theory, both from lectures and reading Swalm [35]. The subjects were randomly assigned to one of two groups. The first group was given ten questions using the certainty equivalence (CE) method; the other group received the *same* questions using the

425

Table 19.1. *Measurement methodologies and composite shapes for the utility functions examined by F–K*

Source	Sure amount	Probability level	Gain and loss outcome	Composite shape (above and below)				
				Concave convex	Convex convex	Concave concave	Convex concave	
Swalm [35]	elicited	constant (at 0.5)	variable	10	2	1	0	
Halter and Dean [12]	elicited	variable (0.1, 0.2, ..., 0.9)	constant (−$50,000, +$100,000)	2	0	0	0	
Grayson [9]	constant (at $0)	elicited	variable	1	1	2	4	
Green [10]	constant (at $0)	elicited	variable	0	0	0	3	
Barnes and Reinmuth [3]	elicited	constant (at 0.5)	variable	0	2	0	0	
All studies combined				13	5	3	7	

Table 19.2. *Risk-taking patterns under* CE *and* PE *methods (exp.* 1)

Question	Sure loss	Gamble p	L	Certainty equivalence method (N = 32)			Probability equivalence method (N = 32)			Chi-square
				Risk averse	Indifferent	Risk seeking	Risk averse	Indifferent	Risk seeking	
1	$ 100	0.5	$ 200	6%	28%	66%	32%	23%	45%	6.97*
2	900	0.9	1,000	9	13	78	44	13	44	10.22**
3	100	0.05	2,000	19	13	69	41	13	47	3.90
4	10	0.5	20	0	13	88	6	38	56	8.17*
5	100	0.1	1,000	16	28	56	32	13	55	3.60
6	90	0.9	100	3	16	82	35	29	35	15.55**
7	1,900	0.95	2,000	19	31	50	47	25	28	6.04*
8	10	0.05	200	34	22	44	31	13	56	1.37
9	10	0.1	100	22	28	50	38	22	41	1.88
10	190	0.95	200	3	31	66	38	22	41	11.72**

Note: Asterisks denote significant interaction at the 0.05(*) or 0.01(**) level. Percentages may not total 100% due to rounding.

probability equivalence (PE) method. The exact wordings for these two groups were as follows (for question 1):

CE group: You face a situation where you have a 50% chance of losing $200. Would you be willing to pay $100 to avoid this situation?

YES   NO   INDIFFERENT

PE group: You can pay $100 to avoid a situation where you may lose $200. Would you pay if there were a 50% chance of losing?

YES   NO   INDIFFERENT

After making their binary choice, subjects in the CE group were asked to adjust the sure loss of $100 so as to effect indifference, whereas subjects in the PE group adjusted the 0.5 probability. Hence, for each question, a two-step procedure was followed as is common in actual applications. Although the same binary choice was initially made under each method, subjects functioned all along in either a certainty equivalence mode or a probability equivalence one. Indeed, a key difference between these two response modes is whether one adjusts and "negotiates" with concrete dollar amounts or with more abstract probability "points" whose actual costs or benefits depend on how the corresponding uncertainty is resolved.

All ten questions involved pure losses, as shown in table 19.2 (see the columns on the left). The middle columns list the percentages of subjects who were risk averse, indifferent, or risk seeking under the CE and PE methods. (Note that it would be inappropriate to conduct parametric tests on the risk premiums between the two methods.) In the last column, chi-squares (and their significance levels) are listed to indicate whether the response mode used affected the distribution of preferences (i.e., for each question, a 2×3 contingency table was constructed).

For six of the ten questions, the subjects' preferences (measured simply by type of risk-taking attitude) were influenced by the elicitation method used. As shown in table 19.2 the impact of different elicitation methods on preferences appears strongest for gambles where there is a relatively high probability of losing and weakest when it is relatively low.

It is telling as well to examine how much risk-taking occurred across all ten questions for subjects in each of the two groups. In the CE group 29 of the 32 subjects gave risk seeking responses for a majority of the questions, as compared with only 16 in the PE group. This difference is statistically significant ($p < 0.01$), and in the same direction as in tables 19.1 and 19.2, i.e., the CE methods leads to more risk seeking than the PE method.[2]

In a recent experiment by Wehrung *et al.* [42] similar response mode biases were observed. They examined around 90 executives using both the certainty equivalence and gain equivalence (GE) methods. Although these two methods generally yielded significant differences (within the same person), Wehrung *et al.* did not find a systematic bias toward risk aversion for a given method (as we did). One reason could be that both of their methods entailed payoff (as opposed to probability) adjustments. Another might be that Wehrung *et al.*'s GE questions used rate of return responses, whereas their CE questions focused on after-tax net profit. Such a contextual difference, as we will see later, may be a confounding factor.

RISK DIMENSIONS

Let us now turn to the role of probability and payoff levels. A large body of experimental literature (see Schoemaker [30] for a review) suggests that people have difficulty combining information from different dimensions, including the multiplication of probabilities and dollar amounts. Such information processing limitations are, for instance, evident from the descriptive and predictive power of various types of non-compensatory choice models (e.g., disjunctive and lexicographic models). One recent example is the preference tree model by Tversky and Sattath [38], which describes choice as a covert hierarchical elimination process. A similar approach is taken in Bettman's [4] information processing theory of consumer choice.

In general it seems that people often focus on one dimension at a time, for example, probabilities or outcomes [29]. Under such a model one would not expect the type of utility curves proposed by F–K. Indeed, Laughhunn *et al.* [20] found, in a study of 224 managers, a strong tendency toward risk seeking in the loss domain except for very large losses. When the possibility of bankruptcy was introduced, the managers actually became risk averse, in spite of the low probability of bankruptcy. Not always, however, will the focus shift this way. For instance, Kunreuther [19] showed that consumers may ignore low probability events with catastrophic losses if the probability falls below a certain threshold.

Such single dimension focus and shifting of attention as a function of the levels of the dimensions is not compatible with the below-target risk-seeking hypothesis advanced by F–K. For instance, a recent study by Hershey and Schoemaker [13] showed that the utility function over losses cannot be characterized as being either purely convex or purely concave. This study of basic risk-taking attitudes toward losses involved 18 questions, where the choice for each was between a sure loss S and a probabilistic loss L with a probability p of occurring. To account partially for their results within the EU model, Hershey and Schoemaker proposed a Markowitz [23] type utility function which is risk averse for small losses and risk seeking for large ones. Even this utility function, however, did not fully explain the empirical data, and hence it was further proposed that people distort probabilities in the manner suggested in prospect theory [16] (i.e., overweighting of low probabilities and underweighting of high ones). These conclusions, however, only concern the loss side. To similarly examine the gain side, particularly the risk-aversion hypothesis, we present the following data.

Experiment 2

As part of the Hershey–Schoemaker experiment reported in [13], data were collected as well as on the gain side (although not reported). The subjects were 82 Wharton MBA students taking an introductory quantitative methods course. These students were presented with the 18 binary choices shown in table 19.3. Note that all are actuarially fair. Preferences are shown on the right.

The first six questions provide evidence of considerable risk seeking on the gainside, particularly for small amounts. Analyses of within-subject preferences, for instance, showed that 57% of the subjects were willing to gamble for a majority of the questions, with only 23% preferring the sure amount for a majority of the questions. (The remaining subjects had exactly three risk-averse and three risk-seeking responses.) In total, 34% were willing to gamble for all six questions, while only 10% chose the sure amount for all six questions. The percentage differences in both of these percentage comparisons are statistically significant at the 0.01 level.

In the next set of seven questions, the potential gain G was fixed at $10,000 while the probability of winning was varied from 0.001 to 0.999. For these questions, risk aversion increases as the sure amount (S) increases. Within-subject analysis revealed that 83% chose the safe alternative for a majority of the seven questions.

For questions fourteen through eighteen, the probability of gain was fixed at 0.01 while the potential gain increased from $100 to $1,000,000. Only 16% were risk averse for question fourteen, but this preference increased steadily to the point where 81% were risk averse for question eighteen. Within-subject analysis indicated that 85% of those who preferred the risky alternative for question fourteen had switched preferences by question eighteen.

429

Table 19.3. *How risk averse are subjects for gains?*
(*exp.* 2)

Question	Gamble p	Gamble G	Sure amount S	Percent risk averse $(N = 82)$
1	0.001	$ 10,000	$ 10	47.6%
2	0.005	2,000	10	41.5
3	0.01	1,000	10	39.0
4	0.05	200	10	25.6
5	0.10	100	10	23.2
6	0.20	50	10	31.7
7	0.001	10,000	10	50.0
8	0.01	10,000	100	54.9
9	0.10	10,000	1,000	69.5
10	0.50	10,000	5,000	74.4
11	0.90	10,000	9,000	78.0
12	0.99	10,000	9,900	70.7
13	0.999	10,000	9,990	74.4
14	0.01	100	1	15.9
15	0.01	1,000	10	35.4
16	0.01	10,000	100	59.8
17	0.01	100,000	1,000	69.5
18	0.01	1,000,000	10,000	80.5

Taken together, these results indicate considerable risk seeking for gains, particularly for small amounts and low probabilities. The empirical findings could be explained by (1) a convex portion in the utility curve for gains, (2) an overweighting of low probabilities, or (3) a combination of the two. Some recent pilot experiments, however, make explanation (1) unlikely. For instance, the vast majority of the subjects tested preferred $160 for sure over a 0.8 chance at $200 (which is contrary to the convex utility curve explanation). This leaves explanations (2) and (3) which both include probability distortions.

The nature of this bias makes it particularly difficult to speak of *the* utility function for an individual. For example, if the function is elicited with 50–50 lotteries, it may be shaped differently from when it is based on 70–30 lotteries. Empirical evidence for such probability dependency of the utility curve was offered by Van Dam [39] and Karmarkar [17], who found systematic relationships between the degree of risk aversion and the type of odds used in the preference lotteries. Officer and Halter [25] encountered similar difficulties when using indifference probabilities for the construction of $U(x)$. It merits further research to learn to what extent probabilities biases reflect differential dimension focus and/or probability thresholds. Risk-taking attitudes, however, cannot be generally characterized as purely risk seeking for losses and risk averse for gains, even though this may be a fair statement within certain probability and outcome ranges.[3]

DOMAIN OF LOTTERIES

When eliciting preferences to derive NM utility functions, the decision scientist can use pure loss lotteries ($L < G \leqslant 0$), mixed lotteries ($L < 0$ and $G > 0$), and/or pure gain lotteries ($G > L \geqslant 0$). Earlier studies, however, suggest that mixed lotteries induce a much greater degree of risk aversion than do choices under a pure loss situation. For example, Williams [43] found that translations of pure loss outcomes into a mixture of losses and gains (by adding a fixed amount to all outcomes) produced a dramatic shift from risk seeking to risk aversion.

Payne *et al.* [26], [27] found this same result for three outcome lotteries. They further showed that additional translations into pure gain lotteries induced yet greater risk aversion. One suggested explanation for this "domain bias" centers on the role of aspiration levels. Such target or reference points are formally incorporated in Fishburn's α-t model [7] and prospect theory [16]. These recent models are supported by Payne *et al.*'s [26] finding that preference reversals within pairs of mixed lotteries are most pronounced when the translations are such that one lottery has only positive outcomes or only negative outcomes, while the other has mixed ones.

Interestingly, the effect of the lottery domain is discernible as well from the five studies examined by F–K. The Grayson [9], Green [10] and Halter–Dean [12] studies employed mixed lotteries (i.e., losses combined with gains), the majority of which were assessed relative to the status quo.[4] The other two studies [3], [35], on the other hand, used predominantly pure gain and pure loss lotteries. The following simple cross-classification of the F–K data shows the importance of this difference.

Gamble used	Loss side		Gain side		Total number of curves
	Convex	Concave	Convex	Concave	
Pure	14	1	4	11	15
Mixed	4	9	8	5	13
	($\chi_1^2 = 11.8$; $p < 0.001$)		($\chi_1^2 = 3.5$; $p < 0.07$)		

On the loss side, the pure gamble methods yielded 14 out of 15 risk-seeking curves, compared with only 4 out of 13 when mixed gambles were used. On the gain side, however, the effect was reversed, i.e., the pure lottery method yielded greater risk aversion (11 out of 15) than the mixed gamble studies (5 out of 13). As shown below the cross-classifications, these differences are both statistically significant under a chi-square test, being somewhat weaker on the gain side.[5]

Unfortunately, the above results are confounded with a response-mode effect, since, except for the Halter and Dean study, those experiments using the CE method employed pure lotteries whereas those using the PE method utilized mixed lotteries. In the following experiment, we therefore examine translations

431

Table 19.4. The effect of domain shifts (exp. 3)

| Question | Pure loss questions (N = 7) | | | Mixed gambles questions (N = 35) | | | Chi-square for translation effect | Within-subject results (N = 26) | | |
| | Averse | Neutral | Seeking | Averse | Neutral | Seeking | | Number of subjects being more risk averse with | | Statistical significance of Difference |
								Mixed Q	Loss Q	
1	11%	21%	67%	53%	26%	21%	25.63**	14	2	0.002
2	23	32	45	77	14	9	29.61**	17	1	0.000
3	24	20	56	74	14	11	26.42**	17	3	0.001
4	6	21	73	26	34	40	14.06**	14	3	0.006
5	17	27	56	71	20	9	33.58**	19	2	0.000
6	18	24	58	46	14	40	8.90*	10	5	0.15
7	21	28	51	60	20	20	16.49**	13	2	0.004
8	39	24	37	66	29	6	12.05**	8	4	0.19
9	27	28	45	71	26	3	24.74**	11	5	0.11
10	15	32	52	40	26	34	7.94*	11	4	0.06

Note: Asterisks denote significant association at the 0.05(*) or 0.01(**) level in the corresponding 2 × 3 chi-square tables. Within-subject significance levels were derived from a one-tailed binomial test. See table 19.2 for the levels of the pure loss questions.

from pure loss lotteries to mixed lotteries while holding the response mode constant.

Experiment 3

The experiment was conducted with 26 undergraduate Wharton students who were generally unfamiliar with NM utility theory. Each subject received two consecutive questionnaires separated by one week. One of these questionnaires contained only pure loss choices, identical to those shown earlier in table 19.2. The questions asked for certainty equivalence judgments, using a context of risk transfer. In the other questionnaire the same ten gambles were used except that all had been translated into mixed gambles. The amounts added were such that each mixed gamble had an expected value of exactly zero. The order of the two questionnaires was randomized. No order effects were found. An additional 45 subjects answered only the loss questionnaire and not the mixed one, whereas nine other subjects answered only the mixed questionnaire.

Table 19.4 demonstrates, using a chi-square analysis of across-subject results, that positive translations from pure to mixed lotteries significantly increased the percentage of risk-averse responses for all ten questions. The last three columns of table 19.4 provide *within-subject* findings for those 26 subjects who completed both questionnaires. For most questions subjects exhibited significantly ($p < 0.05$) more risk aversion for mixed lotteries than pure loss ones.

These findings confirm that translations of lottery domains lead to the predicted shifts in preference, *when holding the response mode constant.* Such preference shifts are inconsistent with a utility function that is uniformly concave, although they may be partly consistent with a utility function which is convex for losses and concave for gains.[6] It merits further research whether the measured shape *within* the loss (or gain) domain itself is influenced by the sub-domain chosen. If so, this would of course be inconsistent with NM utility theory.

TRANSFER VS. ASSUMPTION OF RISK

An important choice the decision scientist must make is whether to place the client in a position of transferring risk or assuming risk (or neither). With pure loss lotteries, for example, under the CE method, the client is typically asked to specify a sure payment such that he or she would be indifferent between retaining the pure lottery and transferring it. The indifference premium for purchasing insurance protection is a natural example of this. On the other hand, with mixed lotteries, when using the CE response mode, the client is typically asked to specify a sure receipt or purchase price that constitutes the indifference point between obtaining the mixed lottery and maintaining the status quo. A natural example is the reservation price for entering into a speculative venture (e.g., oil drilling). These two types of questions differ not only as to the domain of the lotteries employed, but also in the sense that one question involves a transfer of risk while the other involves assumption of risk. This latter difference may lead to an "inertia" (or "status quo") bias.

The inertia bias concerns a tendency of people to prefer their current wealth position unless presented with clearly superior alternatives (after including transactions costs). It may thus be much easier to convince a person to retain a given risk (when already part of the psychological status quo) than to assume that risk. A convincing example of this is offered by Thaler [36], who compared the prices people would pay to protect against a low probability lethal illness vs. the compensation they would require to expose themselves voluntarily (e.g., for medical research) to this illness. Typically, the mean responses differ by a factor of ten or more, ruling out income effects or transactions costs as a likely explanation. Williams [43] was one of the first to propose the inertia hypothesis for gambles. Since his experiments only showed that subjects were more willing to retain pure risks than assume speculative risks, he proposed that future experiments control for the separate effects of inertia and lottery domain. In the following experiment we examine the effect of transfer vs. assumption of risk for otherwise identical mixed lotteries.

Experiment 4

The subjects for this experiment were similar to those of experiment 3. The mixed lottery questionnaire in that experiment, which was given to 35 students, contained 10 questions with the following wording (the example refers to the first question).

> You can chose to be in a situation where there is a 50% chance of winning $100 and a 50% chance of losing $100. Would you choose to be in this situation if it did not cost you anything?

YES   NO   INDIFFERENT

In table 19.4 we showed the subjects' risk preferences for this and the other nine questions to demonstrate the effect of translating a gamble through the origin. To test for a possible inertia bias, 33 other subjects were presented with the same questions worded as follows:

> You are in a situation where you have a 50% chance of winning $100 and a 50% chance of losing $100. Would you be willing to transfer this risk to another person at no cost to you?

YES   NO   INDIFFERENT

Since this question is identical in underlying structure to the earlier one, EU theory would not predict a significant difference in the percentages of risk-averse, indifferent, and risk-seeking responses.[7]

In table 19.5, we compare subjects' responses between these two types of wording, i.e., transfer vs. assumption of risk. For reference, the left side of table 19.5 shows the specific mixed lottery corresponding to each question. The middle

Table 19.5. *Transfer vs. assumptions of risk (exp. 4)*

Question	Probabilistic loss L	P(L)	Probabilistic gain G	P(G)	Assumption of risk (N = 35) Risk averse	Indifferent	Risk seeking	Transfer of risk (N = 33) Risk averse	Indifferent	Risk seeking	Chi-square
1	$100	0.5	$100	0.5	53%	26%	21%	48%	42%	9%	2.80
2		0.9	900	0.1	77	14	9	55	24	21	4.04
3	1,900	0.05	100	0.95	74	14	11	52	27	21	3.79
4	10	0.5	10	0.5	26	34	40	33	39	27	1.27
5	900	0.1	100	0.9	71	20	9	39	33	27	7.63*
6	10	0.9	90	0.1	46	14	40	48	24	27	1.27
7	100	0.95	1,900	0.05	60	20	20	64	15	21	0.27
8	190	0.05	10	0.95	66	29	6	42	27	30	7.54*
9	90	0.1	10	0.9	71	26	3	30	36	33	15.17**
10	10	0.95	190	0.05	40	26	34	36	30	33	0.19

Note: Asterisks denote significant interaction at the 0.05(*) or 0.01(**) level.

columns indicate the percentages who were risk averse, indifferent, and risk seeking under each wording. The final column contains the chi-square values and significance levels. The results show that there is a significant inertia bias, in the expected direction, for three of the 10 questions.[8]

The inertia effect is strongest for lotteries offering a large probability of a small gain and a small probability of a large loss. One explanation is that such gambles are likely candidates for threshold and certainty effects (regarding the probability dimension), making them more of a sure option (as coded psychologically) than the other lotteries. This explanation, of course, assumes that the inertia effect will be stronger for relatively certain options than for very iffy alternatives. This conjecture, however, would need independent verification.

CONTEXT EFFECTS

The above inertia effect is a special type of context effect. In general we shall define context effects as influences on preferences that are without normative basis. As shown, the way information is presented to individuals regarding choices under uncertainty affects their final choice. Further evidence supporting this point comes from a number of studies that are summarized in Tversky and Kahneman [37]. Their principal point is that there are predictable shifts in preference when the same problem is framed in different ways. In particular, they claim that choices involving gains are often risk seeking. The framing of problems, of course, may influence whether a given outcome is viewed as a gain or a loss.

We are especially interested in the effect of context when decision situations are presented in abstract versus more concrete formulations. For instance, consider the following two alternative ways of phrasing the same choice:

Insurance formulation
    Situation *A*:   You stand a 1 out of 100 chance of losing $1,000.
    Situation *B*:   You can buy insurance for $10 to protect you from this loss.

Gamble formulation
    Situation *A*:   You stand a 1 out of 100 chance of losing $1,000.
    Situation *B*:   You will lose $10 with certainty.

According to EU theory both formulations involve a choice between $[0.01U(W_0 - 1000) + 0.99U(W_0)]$ and $U(W_0 - 10)$, where W_0 represents the current wealth level. Hershey and Schoemaker [13] found that under the insurance formulation, 81% of the subjects preferred situation *B*, compared with 56% under the gamble formulation. Apparently individuals focus on protective aspects when the situation is presented in an insurance context so that this is perceived as a gain. In the gamble formulation, however, people are more likely to perceive the $10 as a loss.

Similar results had earlier been obtained by Schoemaker and Kunreuther [31] with respect to the presentation of information on deductibles in insurance policies. It was found that subjects had a stronger preference for low deductibles when they were presented in an insurance formulation than in a pure gamble formulation. Individuals appear to view a lower deductible as valuable protection against a commensurate portion of the potential loss, but do not look at it this way when the option is presented as a statistical lottery. Apparently, context focuses attention on different aspects of the problem.

A related explanation of the preference for low deductibles is provided by Thaler [36] who suggests that it is due to regret considerations. Individuals prefer not to have to think about expenditures when they incur an accident or, for instance, are in a hospital. Selecting the lowest deductible minimizes regret in confronting this problem. In this context, it is intriguing to speculate why many individuals who take the lowest deductible often choose not to collect on their policy after suffering a loss. If they are concerned that their insurance premium will increase if they make a claim, then it is not clear why the low deductible policy would have been chosen in the first place. However, if different considerations are attended to at different phases of the decision process, this behavior becomes understandable.

In an earlier experiment [13], Hershey and Schoemaker established such shifts in perspective using a between-subject design. In the following experiment we test the insurance context effect on a within-subject basis.

Experiment 5

We conducted a two-question experiment with 217 Wharton undergraduate students (mostly sophomores) taking an introductory management course. The

Table 19.6. *Within-subject analysis of insurance context effect*

Insurance formulation	Gamble formulation			
	Prefer sure alternative	Indifferent	Prefer risky alternative	Total
Prefer sure alternative	47%	2%	13%	62%
Indifferent	2	2	7	11
Prefer risky alternative	2	1	24	27
Total	51%	5%	44%	100%

Note: Each entry denotes the percentage of subjects stating the designated preference combination ($N = 217$).

choice involved a 0.001 chance of losing $5,000 versus a sure loss of $5. Each subject received this question in both an insurance and a pure gamble format. To avoid carry-over effects, the questions were interspersed with several others, and counterbalanced. No order effect was observed.

The within-subject results, shown in table 19.6, confirm that individuals tend to be more risk averse under the insurance formulation than under the gamble formulation ($p < 0.01$, sign test). Of the 217 pairs of within-subject responses, 22% shifted toward risk seeking under the gamble formulation (relative to the insurance formulation), with only 5% shifting preference in the opposite direction. These findings are consistent with prospect theory's reference shift prediction [16, p. 287], as well as evoking process and societal norm explanations offered in [13].

The central point emerging from all of these results is that people do *not* hold preferences free of context. Whereas expected utility theory focuses on the decision's structure, individuals are quite sensitive to the decision's context (Abelson [1], Vlek and Stallen [40], and Einhorn and Hogarth [6]). Indeed, without context, the choice is not likely to be very meaningful. Additional illustrations of the importance of decision framing and context are presented in [37].

DISCUSSION

In this chapter we have raised several methodological and empirical questions regarding the uniqueness of Von Neumann–Morgenstern utility functions. The starting point for this analysis was several recent behavioral studies on decisions under risk whose implications for normative theory needed to be examined.

We showed experimentally that considerable indeterminacy exists as to the nature of people's risk-taking attitudes. The low convergence of risk-taking measures across tasks and situations [32] lends general support for this contention. For instance, Neter and Williams [24] found little correspondence between insurance choices predicted from expected utility calculations (after having derived utility functions for their subjects) and the actual choices made by

437

the subjects in the concrete decision situations. In a related vein, Dyckman and Salomon [5] showed that utility functions obtained using random device analogs (e.g., colored chips in a box) were rather different (more risk averse) from those based on simulations of actual decision situations.

In the context of constructing utility functions, we examined five related factors (see figure 19.1) that may influence the shape of the resulting utility curve. Empirical evidence was provided for each bias, from existing literature as well as from our experiments. Moreover, it is important to note that the tests we conducted are quite conservative. In experiments 1, 3, 4, and 5 the focus is on the percent of risk-averse, risk-neutral, and risk-seeking responses between an experimental and control group. Hence, we only measure influences that are strong enough to induce a shift from one risk category to another. However, biases within risk categories may occur as well in terms of the degrees of risk aversion (or seeking), which would never surface when just looking at categorical responses. A much stronger test would thus be to compare risk premiums parametrically. This, however, would require specific knowledge as to each subject's utility function. For example, for a given choice a CE risk premium (expressed in dollars) can only be compared with a PE risk premium (expressed in probability points) for consistency once a specific utility function is available. Given the conservativeness of the tests we conducted, the results attest yet more convincingly to the pervasiveness of the biases examined.

In a general sense, all five factors studied should be viewed as context effects, since each is counter to EU theory. Although we examined the factors in isolation, they are likely to interact, either strengthening or counteracting each other. A fuller understanding of their joint workings will be attempted in future work, for instance through factorial designs.

In addition to the five factors examined in this article, others may affect the assessment of utility functions as well. We will briefly mention three. First, the exact variable used to operationalize gains and losses may matter. For instance, utility functions defined on dollar returns versus percentage returns or investment may differ in ways counter to their functional relationship. Secondly, the choice of endpoints in the domain variable may bias the ensuing function. Thus, a utility function defined on $50,000 to $150,000 may differ by more than a linear transformation from its corresponding portion in a function defined on, for example, $0 to $500,000 (see [18]). Finally, whether or not chaining is used may affect the resulting function, for example because response errors are propagated differently. An examination of these and other factors, both in isolation and in terms of their interactions, constitutes an important area for further research.

Generally speaking, context effects are not new. Well-known examples include Bar-Hillel's conjunctive and disjunctive probability biases [2], Ronen's sequence bias in compound events [28], Slovic and Lichtenstein's response mode effects [33], the so-called preference reversal phenomenon [11], [21], [22], or deductible effects [31]. In this paper, however, we have attempted to relate contextual biases to the specific problem of constructing utility curves and drawing generalizations of people's risk-taking attitudes. Both, we feel, are plagued with serious indeterminacy problems which require beter descriptive theories for their resolution.

The context boundedness of utility functions thus is the major point of this chapter. As shown in [5], [11], [13], [15], [16], [22], [28], [33], [37], and our experiments, the way in which a problem is formulated, including its script, presentation, and response mode, affects people's preferences in nonnormative ways. Such context dependencies raise serious questions as to the construct validity of the NM utility function. The confounding effects of the measurement process and problem context in particular suggest that in practical applications it is well-advised to seek convergent validation of risk-taking measures. For instance, problems might be presented in various forms to check for consistency. The client could then be asked to reconcile any incompatibilities. This chapter has identified five different areas for such coherency checks. One general strategy for minimizing the biases is to express all choices in terms of final wealth positions. The full implications of our findings, however, need to be further examined in future research. At present, this chapter mainly serves to demonstrate the need for a more systematic approach to utility encoding, as well as the development of criteria to evaluate the quality of utility assessments.

NOTES

Helpful comments on an earlier draft were received from Robin Hogarth, Amos Tversky, Detlof von Winterfeldt, and two anonymous referees. The authors of this chapter are listed in alphabetical order. First published in *Management Science*, 28 (1982), 936–54.

1 Since the studies differed in other ways as well, such as the exact attribute variable used and the larger decision context, other factors may also have played a role. For instance, the Barnes and Reinmuth [3] study principally used CE's, although it began with a PE question. Another important difference is the use of chaining, i.e., using the client's earlier responses for subsequent reference lotteries. For example, this was done in studies [3] and [35], but not in [9] or [12].

2 This response mode bias was recently replicated by Hershey and Schoemaker [15] using a within-subject design. The response mode effect was again statistically significant, and in the hypothesized direction.

3 If utility functions are indeed predominantly as F–K propose, then systematic asymmetries between gain and loss lotteries would be expected. The evidence for such a reflection hypothesis, however, is rather weak [14].

4 In the Halter and Dean [12] study, however, both options occasionally had negative expected values, which may explain their higher incidence of risk-seeking curves relative to the other mixed lottery studies (see table 19.1).

5 In examining the shapes of the published utility functions, we accepted the F–K classifications. Of course, some of the 28 functions might have been classified differently if certain outliers had been eliminated or if the sum of squared horizontal rather than vertical deviations had been minimized. The strong statistical significance of our analyses, however, suggests robustness of our basic conclusions to such adjustments.

6 Recent findings of Payne *et al.* [27], however, do not support such a convex–concave utility function as underlying various observed translation effects.

7 As with experiments 1 and 3, the dollar risk premiums derived from the two types of wording need not necessarily be the same, from an EU perspective, making parametric tests of the responses inappropriate.

439

8 It should be noted that this inertia bias may have played a role in experiment 3 as well, where the pure loss questions involved a transfer of risk and the mixed lotteries an assumption of risk. To control for this confounding, we compared the pure loss risk preferences of table 19.4 with the second set of preferences ($N = 33$) of table 19.5, as both involved a transfer of risk. The associated chi-squares were significant ($p < 0.05$) for 8 of the 10 questions, establishing the existence of a significant unconfounded translation effect.

REFERENCES

1. Abelson, R. P. (1976). "Script processing in attitude formation and decision making," *Cognition and Social Behavior*, edited by J. S. Carroll and J. W. Payne. Lawrence Erlbaum Associates, Hillsdale, N.J., 33–45.

2. Bar-Hillel, M. (1973). "On the subjective probability of compound events," *Organizational Behavior and Human Performance*, 9, 396–406.

3. Barnes, J. D., and Reinmuth, J. E. (1976). "Comparing imputed and actual utility functions in a competitive bidding setting," *Decision Sci.*, 7, 801–12.

4. Bettman, J. (1979). *An Information Processing Theory of Consumer Choice*, Addison-Wesley, Reading, Mass.

5. Dyckman, T. R., and Salomon, R. (1972). "Empirical utility functions and random devices: an experiment," *Decision Sci.*, 3, 1–13.

6. Einhorn, H. J., and Hogarth, R. M. (1981), "Behavioral decision theory: processes of judgment and choice," *Ann. Rev. Psychology*, 32, 53–88.

7. Fishburn, P. C. (1977). "Mean-risk analysis with risk associated with below target return," *Amer. Econom. Rev.*, 67, 116–26.

8. Fishburn, P. C., and Kochenberger, G. A. (1979). "Two-piece Von Neumann–Morgenstern utility functions," *Decision Sci.*, 10, 503–18.

9. Grayson, C. J. (1960). *Decisions Under Uncertainty: Drilling Decisions by Oil and Gas Operators*, Graduate School of Business, Harvard University, Cambridge, Mass.

10. Green, P. E. (1963). "Risk attitudes and chemical investment decisions," *Chemical Engineering Progress*, 59, 35–40.

11. Grether, D. M., and Plott, C. R. (1979). "Economic theory of choice and the preference reversal phenomenon," *Amer. Econom. Rev.*, 69, 623–38.

12. Halter, A. N., and Dean, G. W. (1971). *Decisions Under Uncertainty*, South-Western Publishing, Cincinnati, Ohio.

13. Hershey, J. C., and Schoemaker, P. J. H. (1980). "Risk taking and problem context in the domain of losses: an expected utility analysis," *J. Risk Insurance*, 47, 111–32.

14. (1980). "Prospect theory's reflection hypothesis: a critical examination," *Organizational Behavior and Human Performance*, 25, 395–418.

15. (1982). "Adjustment bias in indifference judgments between gambles and sure amounts," Working Paper, Decision Sciences Department, The Wharton School, University of Pennsylvania. Subsequently published as "Probability versus certainty equivalence methods in utility measurement: are they equivalent?" *Management Science*, 31 (1985), 1213–31.

16. Kahneman, D., and Tversky, A. (1979). "Prospect theory: an analysis of decision under risk," *Econometrica*, 47, 263–91.

17. Karmarkar, U. S. (1978). "Subjectively weighted utility: a descriptive extension of the expected utility model," *Organizational Behavior and Human Performance*, 21, 61–72.

18. Krzysztofowicz, R., and Duckstein, L. (1980). "Assessment errors in multiattribute utility functions," *Organizational Behavior and Human Performance*, 26, 326–48.

19. Kunreuther, H. C. (1980). "The economics of protection against low probability events," Working Paper 81-3, International Institute for Applied Systems Analysis, Laxenberg, Austria. Subsequently published in *Decision Making: An Interdisciplinary Inquiry*, ed. by G. Ungson and D. Braunstein. Boston, Mass.: Kent Pub. Co., 1982, 195–215.

20. Laughhunn, D. J., Payne, J. W., and Crum, R. (1980). "Managerial risk preferences for below-target returns," *Management Sci.*, 26, 1238–49.

21. Lichtenstein, S., and Slovic, P. (1973). "Response-induced reversals of preference in gambling: an extended replication in Las Vegas," *J. Experimental Psychology*, 101, 16–20.

22. Lindman, H. R. (1971). "Inconsistent preferences among gambles," *J. Experimental Psychology*, 89, 390–7.

23. Markowitz, H. (1952). "The utility of wealth," *J. Political Economy*, 60, 151–8.

24. Neter, J., and Williams, C. A., Jr. (1971). "Acceptability of three normative methods in insurance decision making," *Journal Risk Insurance*, 38, 385–408.

25. Officer, R. R., and Halter, A. N. (1968). "Utility analysis in a practical setting," *Amer. J. Agricultural Econom.*, 50, 257–77.

26. Payne, J. W., Laughhunn, D. J., and Crum, R. (1980). "Translation of gambles and aspiration level effects in risky choice behavior," *Management Sci.*, 26, 1039–60.

27. (1981). "Further tests of aspiration level effects in risky choice behavior," *Management Sci.*, 27, 953–8.

28. Ronen, J. (1973). "Effects of some probability displays on choices," *Organizational Behavior and Human Performance*, 9, 1–15.

29. Schoemaker, P. J. H. (1979). "The role of statistical knowledge in gambling decisions: moment vs. risk dimension approaches," *Organizational Behavior and Human Performance*, 24, 1–17.

30. (1980). *Experiments on Decisions Under Risk: The Expected Utility Hypothesis*, Martinus Nijhoff, Boston, Mass.

31. Schoemaker, P. J. H., and Kunreuther, H. (1979). "An experimental study of insurance decisions," *J. Risk Insurance*, 46, 603–18.

32. Slovic, P. (1972). "Information processing, situation specificity, and the generality of risk-taking behavior," *J. Personality Social Psychology*, 22, 128–34.

33. Slovic, P., and Lichtenstein, S. (1968). "The relative importance of probabilities and payoffs in risk taking," *J. Experimental Psychology*, 78, 1–18.

34. Spetzler, C. S., and Von Holstein, C. A. (1975). "Probability encoding in decision analysis," *Management Sci.*, 22, 340–58.

35. Swalm, R. D. (1966). "Utility theory – insights into risk taking," *Harvard Business Rev.*, 47, 123–36.

36. Thaler, R. (1980). "Toward a positive theory of consumer choice," *J. Econom. Behavior and Organization*, 1, 39–60.

37. Tversky, A., and Kahneman, D. (1981). "The framing of decisions and the psychology of choice," *Sci.*, 211, 453–8.

38. Tversky, A., and Sattath, S. (1979). "Preference trees," *Psychological Rev.*, 86, 542–73.

39. Van Dam, C. (1973). *Beslissen in Onzekerheid*, H. E. Stenfert Kroese, B. V., Leiden, The Netherlands.

40. Vlek, C., and Stallen, P. J. (1980). "Rational and personal apsects of risk," *Acta Psychologica*, 45, 273–300.
41. Von Neumann, J., and Morgenstern, O. (1947). *Theory of Games and Economic Behavior*, 2nd edn., Princeton Univ. Press, Princeton, N.J.
42. Wehrung, D. A., MacCrimmon, K. R., and Brothers, K. M. (1980). "Utility measures: comparisons of domains, stability, and equivalence procedures," Working Paper 603, University of British Columbia. Subsequently published as "Utility assessment: domains, stability, and equivalence procedures," *Infor*, 22 (1984), 98–115.
43. Williams, C. A. (1966). "Attitudes toward speculative risks as an indicator of attitudes toward pure risks," *J. Risk Insurance*, 33, 577–86.

20

SIMPLICITY IN DECISION ANALYSIS:
AN EXAMPLE AND A DISCUSSION

WARD EDWARDS, DETLOF VON WINTERFELDT, AND DAVID L. MOODY

The ideas in this chapter grow out of a simple view of what the function of decision-analytic tools is: to help a decision maker with a set of problems. (This chapter uses the label "decision maker" to refer either to an individual or to a coherent group.)

The thrust of this view is easier to understand if we add a list of other things that could have been said. Decision-analytic tools are *not* intended primarily for any of the following purposes:

1. Capturing intuitive preferences.
2. Modeling future preferences.
3. Modeling environmental processes.
4. Embodying axiomatic or methodological rigor, or conforming to axiomatic structures.

Decision analysts often defend and try to implement these four goals, for the excellent reason that attainment of each of them often helps. But they derive their merit from the primary goal of helping decision makers with problems, not the other way around.

Unfortunately, each of these subgoals can lead to results that hinder, rather than facilitate, attainment of the main goal. Capturing intuitive preferences in detail can lead to complicated, hard-to-understand, hard-to-communicate elicitation methods and models. Often the decision-analytic procedures form future preferences, or even help invent options about which to have preferences, rather than modeling preferences. Modeling of environmental processes is very useful for many technological problems, but its appearance of objectivity can create or nurture myths. The most obvious examples arise in contexts in which money is important; elaborate modeling can easily contribute to the myth that maximization of some quantity preceded by a dollar sign is *the* goal that the organization exists to implement. Axiomatic and methodological rigor and embodiment of axiomatic structures ensure logical consistency – a useful property for relations among beliefs, values, and actions to have.

Perhaps the most important thing wrong with all four of the numbered

443

subgoals is that they can interfere with a fifth: to make procedures that help the decison maker as simple as the problem permits. Simplicity helps in many ways. It helps a nontechnician (or even a technician) to understand what is going on. It makes analyses briefer and easier to perform. It makes judgments easier to make. Above all it helps the decision maker to use and communicate about the tools that have been developed and their results, and thus promotes adoption and use.

Decision analysts have been developing and using tools that serve such purposes for the last 15 years and more. Many words could be written about what they are, how they work, how they relate to the tools other decision analysts use, what the experimental evidence bearing on their validity is, what their mathematical properties are, etc. Too many. Von Winterfeldt and Edwards have put them in a book. Its title is *Decison Analysis and Behavioral Decision Theory* and it was published by Cambridge University Press in early 1984.

Wanting to present the tools, the ideas behind them, and their relation to the field, we faced a dilemma. We could have tried to compress a book into a fairly short chapter. Instead we chose to do something else. This chapter is a summary of a case study. Many, though not all, of the tools for simplification are embodied in it. After we present it, we shall try to identify and justify various simplifying ideas.

PRIORITIZING RESEARCH PROJECTS FOR THE CONSTRUCTION ENGINEERING RESEARCH LABORATORY

Problem

The Construction Engineering Research Laboratory (CERL) is a part of the US Army Corps of Engineers. Its research produces products and systems in response to construction related Army needs and requirements. Environmental problems, energy systems, and information technologies have received most attention in the past few years. Examples of CERL product/systems (as they call their projects) include systems for energy conservation in Army installations, techniques for noise reduction at training facilities, and computer-aided engineering and architectural design systems. About 65% of all work is done in-house, the rest on contract.

As usual, the total amount of money requested to implement all the ideas proposed each year exceeds the funds available. Of approximately 200 proposals each year, only about 100 are funded. Consequently the management of CERL has the yearly task of selecting attractive new research projects, deciding on the desirability of continuing old ones, and selecting funding levels for all projects to be funded, rejecting other projects. This problem is complicated by the diversity of CERL's product/systems and by the fact that several divisions within CERL in effect compete for research funds.

The management of CERL sought to develop more rational procedures for selecting funding levels for product/systems. They wanted a formal prioritization system for research proposals and projects. After several unsuccessful attempts at developing such a system (which included cost–benefit approaches and attempts to assess return on investment for selected product/systems), management decided to try out multiattribute utility as a technique for evaluating and prioritizing projects. What follows is a description of the procedures used. The output was called a "Multiattribute Aid for Prioritization (MAP)."

Structuring

The procedure we used, called SMART, is well described by the literature (see, e.g., Edwards, 1977; Edwards and Newman, 1982). It includes four steps.

The first step is to elicit a value structure called a value tree. Strictly speaking, the higher-level nodes in a value tree are not needed, since only the utilities of the twigs (bottom or right most nodes) are elicited. But, like many other users of multiattribute utility, we prefer a tree structure as a way of eliciting values because it makes clear how lower-level values relate to and define higher-level ones. We will mention some other advantages of value tree structures later.

The second step is to obtain weights for each twig of the value tree from the relevant stakeholder or stakeholder group. (A more elaborate and more recent version of the procedure takes into account the possibility of many conflicting stakeholder groups with partly conflicting interests – but that issue is not relevant to this example.)

The third step is to obtain what the literature might call single-dimension value measures or even single-dimension utility measures; we prefer to call them location measures, since we see little point in distinguishing between values and utilities. (We will say more about this heresy later.) Location measures are on a 100-point scale; they may be objective measures, subjective value transformations on objective measures, direct ratings, or the outputs of calculations.

The fourth formal step is to aggregate or subaggregate. A crucial fifth step is sensitivity analysis – typically a judgmental and computational procedure that consists of varying parameters and even structures. The goal, and frequent consequence, is simply increased insight into the problem. The sixth step, external to SMART as it is external to every decision-analytic procedure, is to decide.

Formally, each possible research program is a collection or portfolio of interacting projects. Evaluating each such portfolio as a unit, considering interactions, values that apply to the collection rather than to its members separately, contributions of one project to another, total resource constraints, and the like, would be ideal, and very difficult. If, as in CERL's case, the number of projects funded at any one time is over 100, the number of elements of such a portfolio is very large, and the number of options of elements of such a portfolio is very large, and the number of options to be evaluated is many times that. Virtually anyone, confronted with this kind of evaluation problem, begins the simplification process by treating each project as noninteractive with the others. But even that is not enough to control the combinatorial explosion. In principle, each possible funding level of a given project is an option. The normal simplification is to pick one funding level, perhaps last year's for a continuing project or the proposed level for a new one, and evaluate the project only at that level.

As Baker and Freeland (1975) make clear, this form of informal treatment of portfolio issues is normal for evaluation of research projects. Keefer (1978) and Sarin, Sicherman, and Nair (1978) discuss the issue. Until very recently, the only explicit attempt to treat portfolio issues in a multiattribute utility context was by Golabi, Kirkwood, and Sicherman (1981). They were asked to aid the US Department of Energy in selecting a portfolio of solar photovoltaic application experiments from responses to a Program Research and Development Announcement. Technical value of each proposed experiment was measured by means of a multiattribute utility procedure. Since each procedure came with a budget attached, it was not necessary to consider the fact that different budgets define different projects. One obvious programmatic constraint was on total cost. A second and trickier constraint was that the client wanted the program to be diverse in a number of different ways; e.g., geographical location, type of application, and degree of public utility cooperation. The solution was to treat the technical quality of each portfolio as the sum of the technical qualities of the experiments included in it. Concern with diversity was treated by defining categories for each dimension of diversity, and requiring that at least a prespecified fraction of proposals fall into each category. The net result was 41 linear constraints. The final solution consisted of maximizing aggregate technical quality of the portfolio subject to budget and diversity constraints – an integer linear programming problem, solved iteratively.

Vari and Vecsenyi (1983) had hoped to treat the portfolio problem explicitly in their application of multiattribute utility methods to evaluation of research proposals, but found that their clients preferred an informal treatment. Keeney (1987), in an examination of a nuclear waste disposal facility siting evaluation, exhibits how difficult explicit treatment of portfolio issues can be, especially if sequencing is important.

Such complexities were not required for CERL's problem. CERL wanted to evaluate the technical quality of each proposed research activity. A single funding level for each project was assumed, and portfolio issues were treated informally.

The first and most important element of the task was to develop a value tree capturing the values of CERL scientists, managers, and others relevant to product/system priorities. Von Winterfeldt and Edwards spent four days at CERL interviewing all key CERL scientists and managers in depth. Of particular interest was the issue of divisional specificity of value dimensions. CERL has four main divisions: Facility Planning and Design; Construction Management and Technology; Energy and Energy Conservation; and Environmental Quality.

Table 20.1. *CERL value tree, MOD 1*

A.	CERL-wide issues
	AA. Relevance to CERL mission
	AB. Conformity to guidance from STOG, QCR, MAD, and similar sources
	AC. Contribution to strategy
	ACA. Conformity to a well developed and accepted strategy
	ACB. Contribution to or initiation of a developing or new strategy
	AD. Degree of uniqueness
	AE. Contribution to CERL program diversification
B.	Division-specific issues
	BA. Prior effort in this product/system needs to be carried to completion
	BB. Appropriate use of available people and/or equipment resources
C.	Proponents, users, champions
	CA. Type of external support
	CAA. Rank
	CAB. Organizational location
	CB. "Loudness" of external support
	CC. Importance of the problem addressed by the product system
D.	Anticipated degree of success
	DA. Anticipated degree of technical success
	DB. Timeliness
	DBA. Likelihood of completion on schedule
	DBB. Duration of anticipated need for product/system after completion
	DC. Ease of technology transfer
	DCA. Anticipated life-cycle cost of product/system to user(s)
	DCB. Availability of user resources needed for successful transfer
E.	Direct cost to CERL
F.	Anticipated cost savings to user(s)

The energy and environment divisions are budgeted separately, but Facility Planning and Design and Construction Management and Technology essentially compete for the same budget. These four divisions together shared a total budget of over $7 million in fiscal year 1981. In addition, several smaller sets of activities do not fit the divisional boundaries. These include basic research, combat engineering, and mobilization. An early decision was to apply the prioritization system only to the major division. Management wanted to develop a prioritization system that cut across budgetary boundaries. This offered an interesting challenge. Would it be possible to abstract from divisional values and find value dimensions that would apply to all programmatic activities? As we mentioned earlier, the product/systems CERL develops are extremely diverse. If proposals in the environmental division were evaluated using contribution to environmental quality as a criterion, that criterion might be quite inapplicable to new information technologies. Fortunately, we realized very early in our interviews that divisional objectives are in fact quite similar. They have to do with user requirements, the extent of Army need for the product/system and of Army perception of that need, and ability to transfer CERL's output to its intended users. We suspect that such abstract values necessarily develop in a laboratory that produces a very broad spectrum of products and services.

Table 20.2. *CERL value tree, MOD 4*

A.	Mission-oriented issues
AA.	Relevance to Army Mission Areas
AB.	Conformity to validated requirements
AC.	Well defined problem and solution fits into (mission-related) activities
AD.	Opportunity for technological breakthrough
B.	Resources and effort issues
BA.	Future effort required for completion of product/system
BB.	Appropriate use of resources
C.	Characteristics of champion and/or champions
CA.	Position of champion
CB.	Emphasis of external support
D.	Anticipated degree of success
DA.	Anticipated degree of technical success
DB.	Timeliness
DC.	Duration of anticipation usage for product/system after completion
DD.	Ease of technology transfer
E.	Direct remaining R&D cost to CERL
F.	Anticipated benefits to users
FA.	Tangible benefits
FB.	Other benefits

The interviews were relatively informal, but focused on eliciting values structures. We asked questions like "What is a high priority product/system?"; we probed intradivisional values, e.g., the need for staff continuity; and we suggested some values of our own, e.g., the value of enhancing professional stature. The result was the Value Tree MOD 1 shown in table 20.1. A copy of this value tree was circulated to all division heads and to top-level management for comment. Subsequently Edwards visited CERL again to explore in detail their responses to the proposed tree. The numerous changes that resulted were supposed to put the tree in final form. That final form turned out to be not quite final, and another visit was necessary to make additional modifications and to establish consensus. The final tree is shown in table 20.2. It differs from the initial tree in wording, and is much simpler. It has only two levels and is more precise about the mission-oriented values.

Weighting

The next step was to obtain weights. As is often the case, the weights needed to be available before the location measures were. In this instance, the reason was in part that the managers wanted their prioritization system to be designed before setting out to make the judgments needed to use it, and in part because they wanted to use the same system, including the same weights, from year to year. Those familiar with the literature on weighting will recognize that this fact by itself rules out, whenever it applies, a very large collection of weight elicitation

Table 20.3. *An example of SMART weight elicitation*

Values	Columns			Normalized weights
	1	2	3	
A	75	50	17	.52
B	45	30	10	.31
C	15	10		.10
D	10			.7
Sums	145			1.00

techniques. We would try to avoid most of these techniques anyhow, because they are complex.

SMART depends for weight elicitation on ratio judgments of importance. The values compared with one another are each set of nodes in the value tree that depends directly from a single higher node. For example, in table 20.2 nodes *A* through *F* would be compared with one another, nodes *AA* through *AD* would be compared with one another, and so on. Final weights for the twigs are obtained by multiplying the normalized weight of each twig by the normalized weight of each node from which that twig depends. Thus, in this example, the final weight of *AA* is the normalized weight of *AA* times the normalized weight of *A*. If node *AAA* existed, its final weight would be that product times the normalized weight of *AAA*. This procedure reduces judgmental labor by exploiting the tree structure.

The first judgmental step in weighting is for the respondent to array the values to be compared with one another in rank order of importance.

Thus, in table 20.3, *A* is the most and *D* is the least important value of that set of four. Then the bottom node (*D* in the table) is taken as standard and given an arbitrary weight of 10. Use of 10 rather than 1 permits respondents to assess ratios of less than 2:1 without recourse to decimal points. The respondent then judged, in a ratio sense, the importance of each more important value relative to the lowest one – a very easy judgment. Ties are permitted.

Consistency checking is equally easy. The respondent moves over to the next column, in which *C* is the bottom node. This amounts to pretending that value *D* does not exist or has a weight of 0. Then the respondent makes the same judgments above, using *C* ratio than *D* as standard. Judgments in column 2 leading to ratios that do not correspond to the ratios in column 1 are inevitable. The elicitor draws the respondent's attention to such inconsistencies, and invites changes in any or all judgments until a consistent pattern is reached.

Respondents soon learn to recognize inconsistent patterns, since the arithmetic required to do so is obvious. Some simply make their responses consistent; others object to the redundancy of the judgments. For such objectors, the natural solution is to reduce the number of columns required. It is a good idea to require that at least the first two columns is filled out, in order to ensure that the respondent checks for consistency in at least an arithmetical sense.

After consistency is obtained, the next step is to transform the weights in column 1 onto a 0-to-1 scale by normalizing them. The normalized weights permit one more consistency check. If the respondent is dissatisfied with a statement like "Value *A* gets 52% of the weight," another set of judgments is needed.

The final step is to obtain final weights by multiplying through the tree, as described above. This permits one last consistency check. The respondent is asked to scrutinize the result and to determine whether it reports how he or she really feels. If not, the available remedies are either direct reassessment of final weights (maintaining the requirement that they sum to 1) or else reassessment of parts or all of the ratio structures leading to them. Most respondents are content with the original structure of final weights. On the rare occasions when they are not, they more often change the final weights than rejudge ratio structures. Of course this kind of check is not available or relevant if the value structure used for assessing weights is a list rather than a tree structure.

"Importance" is a natural but intellectually slippery concept. Respondents seem to have absolutely no difficulty in assessing it, so long as the decision context is clearly specified. But the concept is intelligible only if one knows the range of each variable. A weight is simply a transformation of a scale, and that scale is meaningful only if its end points are clearly defined.

How can people make such judgments with such assurance? If purely subjective direct judgments of location are appropriate, the task is relatively easy. Someone, preferably the same person who assesses weights, must define the meaning of 0 and 100 on each scale. For variables having a natural physical scale, the problem is somewhat harder. Once again, the task is to assess the 0 and 100 points, but these may not be known in advance. We believe, though we cannot directly prove, that respondents believe natural maxima and minima on such dimensions are inherent in the problem, and so use these in making their assessments. If this were not the case, we doubt that they could make such judgments so easily.

This sketchy discussion of the relation between ranges and weights comes nowhere near doing justice to the intricacy of the topic. For a far fuller treatment, see Edwards and Newman (1982); for one that covers the topic in detail, see von Winterfeldt and Edwards (1986). Pages 285–286 review methods for incorporating issues of ranges into the original SMART procedure (Edwards, 1977) in detail; these procedures, which consist essentially of emphasizing natural ranges of dimensions during weight elicitation, were used in the CERL elicitation. Pages 286–287 present an alternative approach, in the psychophysical spirit of SMART, called swing weighting – a preferred procedure not available to us in 1982.

We consulted with the division chiefs in CERL about how weights should be obtained. They understood that weights were expressions of priorities among

Table 20.4. *CERL weights for the value tree* (*1982*)

Node code		Normalized weight	Twig weight
A.	Mission oriented values .39		
	AA.	.50	.1950
	AB.	.13	.0507
	AC.	.06	.0234
	AD.	.31	.1209
B.	Resources and effort .05 issues		
	BA.	.50	.0250
	BB.	.50	.0250
C.	Characteristics of .18 champion(s)		
	CA.	.67	.1206
	CB.	.33	.0594
D.	Anticipated degree of .12 technical success		
	DA.	.15	.0180
	DB.	.46	.0552
	DC.	.08	.0096
	DD.	.31	.0372
E.	Direct remaining .02 cost to CERL		
F.	Anticipated benefits .24 to user(s)		
	FA.	.67	.1608
	FB.	.33	.0792

values, and, since they felt that making such judgments was a top management responsibility, they were quite content to accept a procedure in which weight judgments would be made by the Chief Scientist and the Commanding Officer, the two top managers of CERL.

Edwards spent an uninterrupted afternoon with these two managers, away from phones and other distractions. Weight elicitation began with a rational careful explanation of what weights were, emphasizing the notion of trade-offs, the fact that ranges are weights, and the counterintuitive nature of range changes. Then each manager, working independently, judged weights. Finally they compared normalized weights, and revised until they had an agreed and consistent additive weight structure with agreed triangular consistency checks. The whole process took about $3\frac{1}{2}$ hours. Table 20.4 shows the result. Values related to need (mission-oriented values) and use (anticipated benefits) received highest weights. The weight for direct cost was relatively low. CERL is a very stable and secure organization; neither its own funding nor that of elements within it is subject to much year-to-year fluctuation.

Table 20.5. *Examples of scoring instructions for rating product/systems*

AA. Relevance to Army Mission Areas
100 – P/S directly supports five sub-mission areas
90 – P/S directly supports four sub-mission areas
75 – P/S directly supports three sub-mission areas
60 – P/S directly supports two sub-mission areas
50 – P/S directly supports one sub-mission area
0 – P/S supports *no* sub-mission area

Sub-mission areas: Base/facility development
Installation support activities
Energy conservation and alternate sources
Environmental quality
Military engineering

FA. Tangible benefits to users
100 – P/S provide for reduction in work efforts and/or improvement in productivity plus reduction in equipment, training, materials, and operating costs
80 – P/S provides reduction in work effort and/or improvement in productivity plus reduction in equipment and materials
60 – P/S provides reduction in work effort and/or improvement in productivity
40 – P/S provides reduction in work effort and/or improvement in productivity *but* higher costs for materials and equipment
0 – P/S provides no tangible benefits

Judging location measures

Once value structure and weights were firmly established, each division chief established a small committee on which he sat to rate that division's product/systems on each branch of the tree. The analysts and the program officer managers working together had prepared detailed worksheets for scoring the product/systems on each twig; each worksheet included a careful definition of the scores. Table 20.5 presents two examples. These definitions had an interesting history. Initially, the program office managers wanted much more objective definitions, preferably using either more objectively measurable values or proxy variables for the subjective values or both. Attempts to develop such objective definitions were vigorously rejected by top managers and division leads alike; they wanted values that expressed what they really cared about, subjective or not, but they also wanted guidelines for judgment. Those two preferences are common in secure organizations. Most managers acknowledge that evaluations are and should be subjective; they want guidance about how to make a complex subjective task simpler and more orderly, not less subjective.

Independently of these ratings by the division chiefs, Moody and the other program office manager rated the 97 product/systems that were evaluated on all attributes. Arrangements for disagreements to be resolved by top management were made; they were unnecessary. Disagreements were easily resolved in the discussions between division chiefs and program office managers.

Results

The overall value of each product/system could now simply be computed using the additive model and the weights provided by top management. Top management and each division leader discussed the results and made decisions about support and funding levels or exclusion of that division's existing and proposed product/systems. Surprisingly little disagreement occurred; all participants felt that MAP substantially facilitated these tough decisions.

Tables 20.6 and 20.7 are copies of two of the actual reports that MAP generated in its 1982 application, on which decisions were based. Table 20.6 presents actual scores and overall ratings for a single product/system, and table 20.7 presents both overall ratings and subaggregations of scores for the entire research program of CERL's Facility Systems Division. The subaggregated evaluations of various top-level dimensions in table 20.7 are obviously more informative and more useful than are the overall ratings, but do not overwhelm the top decision makers with more information than they can use. Table 20.6, on the other hand, is a report card on an individual project, useful both to the researcher in charge of it and to the manager of the division within which the project falls. More complex organizations have more complex evaluation problems, requiring many more intermediate levels of aggregation. The most complex instance we have heard of has 10 management levels and uses a value tree having well over 1,000 nodes.

Uniquely, so far as we know, this application of multiattribute utility measured a large number of objects of evaluation. A look at some of the statistics that describe the twig ratings of the 97 product/systems is instructive. Table 20.8 shows the means, standard deviations, and ratings of these ranges, together with the twig weights. The most obvious finding was that all mean ratings are greater than 50 except on twig BA. Ratings on the attributes related to anticipated degree of success are particularly high. This is to be expected; informal processes eliminate obviously unattractive product/systems before they reach formal evaluation. The next finding is that the attribute intercorrelations are generally low (see table 20.9). No dramatic halo effects occurred. The five high attribute intercorrelations (in boxes in table 20.9) have obvious explanations. For example, a highly placed champion (CA) is in a position to create validated requirements (AB).

The third finding (see table 20.8) was that the entire range for most attributes was used. The serious exceptions are AA, BB, and DB. Such instances raise several questions. Were the ranges and end-point definitions initially plausible? In at least the case of DB, definition of the zero point apparently was not. Do the weight judgments reflect the ranges actually stated, even though they were not realized? We think so, encouraged by some informal *ex post facto* trade-off judgments that the decision makers performed. Should all of the plausible range be used for each twig? Clearly not. In instances like this in which the entire evaluation scheme, including weights, must be in place before evaluations are

453

Table 20.6. *CERL research program priority system: detailed product/system report, Facility Systems Division, December 29, 1982*

SPEC: AT41   Product/system code: S13
Title: Systematic Evaluation of Architectural Criteria (SEARCH)

A. Mission oriented issues (.39)	73	B. Resources and effort (.05)	87	C. Proponents/users/champions (.18)	65
AA. Relevance (.50)	60	BA. Completion effort (.50)	75	CA. Position of champion (.67)	75
AB. Validated requirements (.13)	100	BB. Resource use (.50)	100	CB. Emphasis of support (.33)	45
AC. Problem definition (.06)	90				
AD. Technological opportunity (.31)	80				
D. Anticipated success (.12)	90	E. Remaining CERL (cost) (.02)	75	F. Anticipated benefits (.24)	66
DA. Chance of success (.15)	90			FA. Tangible benefits (.67)	60
DB. Timeliness (.46)	100			FB. Intangible benefits (.33)	80
DC. Duration of usage (.08)	100				
DD. Technology transfer (.31)	75				

Overall rating 73

Table 20.7. *CERL research program priority system: summary report, Facility Systems Division, September 8, 1982*

Code	Product/system title	Priority system ratings						Overall rating
		Mission	Resources	Champions	Success	Cost	Benefits	
S1	Installation level housing operation management system (HOMES)	70	88	95	95	50	87	82
S22	Constructibility review	74	88	78	100	75	83	81
S2	OCE/MACOM level HOMES	70	88	95	95	75	75	80
S40	Expedient facility catalog	80	75	60	100	75	73	77
S37	Programmable calculator technology for engineer units	63	88	95	95	100	62	74
S25	Microprocessor applications to the military construction process	70	75	95	65	75	68	74
S14	Concept computer-aided engineering and architecture design system (CAEDS)	71	82	60	90	50	80	74
S10	Engineer modeling study	71	45	78	93	25	77	74
S13	Systematic evaluation of architectural criteria (SEARCH)	73	87	65	90	75	66	73
S32	Training range criteria	77	87	55	79	75	70	72
S39	Microprocessors for DEHs	71	87	45	96	75	70	70
S53	Master planning strategy	66	100	25	100	100	100	69
S5	Military construction planning and design strategy in the 1990s	58	62	72	81	75	70	67

Table 20.8. *CERL twig weights and various descriptors*

Twig	Weight	Mean	Standard deviation	Range Min	Max
AA	.1950	61	11.0	50	90
AB	.0507	69	26.5	0	100
AC	.0234	71	20.1	0	100
AD	.1209	71	20.7	0	100
BA	.0250	45	27.0	0	100
BB	.0250	89	11.1	50	100
CA	.1206	59	29.1	0	100
CB	.0594	53	27.6	0	100
DA	.0180	80	15.7	25	100
DB	.0552	94	6.5	70	100
DC	.0096	87	16.7	20	100
DD	.0372	73	22.4	0	100
E	.0200	63	21.0	25	100
FA	.1608	68	15.2	20	100
FB	.0792	64	20.0	0	100

done, even 97 product/systems may not be enough to span the full range of 15 variables, especially since they are subject to informal preselection. Far smaller numbers of options characterize most applications; one would expect few if any ranges to be fully covered. So long as the weights are appropriately related to the ranges, that fact makes no difference to order or spacing of the output values. Procedures based on plausible ranges seem attractive even for contexts in which the single-dimension values for all options are known before the weights are assessed. If procedures based on trade-offs or gambles are to be used for weight elicitation, they can equally well be based on the option locations on scales defined by plausible rather than actual ranges. If an analyst finds such procedures harder to use with end-points other than 0 and 100, that finding should raise questions about the meaning of intermediate numbers obtained from questions in which the end-points are 0 to 100. If the trade-off judgments or gambles are expressed in physical units, the issue should not arise, since only by accident (or approximation) will the arbitrary definitions of 0 and 100 coincide with convenient round values of the physical variables.

Both top managers and division chiefs in CERL have liked MAP very well. It has been used, completely unchanged, every year since 1982, including 1987. It has thus generated a set of data unique, not only in applications of multiattribute utility measurement, but in applications of numerical methods of evaluation in general: the twig-by-twig scores of a consistently applied evaluation scheme, known in detail to those affected by it, as applied to many hundreds of product/system proposals over a five-year period. After five years of use, top managers have come to recognize need for revision at least of weights. One of us (Edwards) plans to use the revision (to occur in 1988) as an occasion for research into the organizational consequences of institutionalizing an explicit numerical

Table 20.9. *Interattribute correlation matrix*

	AA	AB	AC	AD	BA	BB	CA	CB	DA	DB	DC	DD	E	FA	FB
AA	1.00														
AB	0.03	1.00													
AC	-0.05	0.25	1.00												
AD	-0.03	0.15	0.28	1.00											
BA	-0.16	-0.16	0.05	-0.09	1.00										
BB	-0.10	0.07	0.05	0.02	0.26	1.00									
CA	0.07	0.69	0.32	0.06	-0.11	0.04	1.00								
CB	-0.01	0.54	0.31	0.08	-0.11	-0.06	0.69	1.00							
DA	-0.04	0.01	-0.28	-0.23	0.23	0.29	0.02	-0.06	1.00						
DB	0.00	-0.36	0.03	-0.11	0.24	-0.10	-0.34	-0.32	0.21	1.00					
DC	-0.09	0.26	0.22	-0.14	-0.11	-0.02	0.28	0.22	0.18	-0.25	1.00				
DD	-0.22	0.32	0.55	0.21	0.06	0.09	0.14	0.28	0.30	-0.05	0.29	1.00			
E	-0.24	-0.29	-0.01	-0.16	0.79	0.27	-0.29	-0.27	0.12	0.28	-0.19	0.00	1.00		
FA	-0.04	-0.15	0.20	0.30	0.20	0.02	0.00	-0.07	0.03	0.08	0.05	-0.02	0.14	1.00	
FB	0.20	0.28	0.14	0.37	-0.14	0.03	0.27	0.13	-0.08	-0.09	0.23	-0.03	-0.23	0.10	1.00

evaluation scheme. Preliminary data analyses suggest the following tentative conclusions. MAP has become a program design tool and a monitoring guide. New internal proposals exploit the MAP format and deal with the value issues specified in MAP. In adapting to MAP, proposal writers consider both the desirability of scoring well and the ease of manipulating the environment into which a product/system is to fit in trying to achieve a high score.

A final note. MAP contributed to decision making about the allocation of roughly $10,000,000 in 1982 alone. It cost less than $30,000, plus a lot of CERL staff time, to develop and use once. This undercut the normal cost of such an effort considerably; but a normal price for this job should not be greater than $75,000, in 1982 currency. CERL actually spent an identifiable .3% of the amount to be allocated in order to buy a tool to help think about the allocation. Either that figure or the .75% normal cost is extremely cheap. A frequently encountered rule of thumb asserts that, for any given expenditure, one should add 10% to be spent in thinking about how to spend the original amount properly. Our experience suggests that assistance in such thought processes seldom costs anything like 10% – and typically saves much more than that.

FOUR THEMES FOR SIMPLIFICATION

The preceding example included comments on various simplifying ideas. It also embodies four key ideas about how to simplify that seem important enough, and perhaps controversial enough, to deserve a section all their own.

Keeping the analyst's eye on the ball

This chapter began with the assertion that the only function of decision analysis is to help the decision maker with his or her problems. Any other goals the analyst may have should derive from that one. The example illustrates the power of that assertion. The analysts responded to the organizational problem as the key people from the organization saw it.

Preexisting conceptual baggage imported by the analysts consisted of exactly four ideas. One was that a difference exists between values and their importance, and these should be separately assessed. Earlier work avoided even that complication by assessing aggregate utilities directly; see Miller, Kaplan, and Edwards (1967, 1969). The additional complexity of disaggregating utility is well worth the extra effort, at least in most instances. A second preexisting idea was that decomposition of aggregate values into attributes should be done using a tree structure. The third preexisting idea was that the concept of a weighted average is necessary and sufficient to put the elements of the problem back into output form, ready for the decision maker to use. The fourth preexisting idea, not displayed here, was that extensive sensitivity analysis is wise and helpful.

This list leaves out capturing of preferences, modeling of preferences or of environmental processes, conformity to axioms or methodological precepts. Any or all of these can be useful, but should be demanded only if they are. In this example, none were.

The treatment of money in the example seems particularly relevant. It is about allocating money. Yet it does not use explicit dollar measures at all. The example ensued after several attempts at cost–benefit analysis had not satisfied the decision makers; of course we cannot know what a different analyst might have done or produced.

Pruning radically

Decision analysis is almost completely concerned with instrumental acts producing instrumental values. A dollar, as an intrinsic object, has no value at all. A million of them would be a major nuisance. Even in medical decision making, such values as avoidance of invalidism are obviously instrumental.

The consequences of an instrumental act derive whatever value they may have from later acts and consequences to which they may lead. Every meaningful decision tree extends at least to death, and normally beyond. Such trees are unmanageably bushy; all analysts agree that they must be pruned. While such devices as five-year time horizons help, analysts normally allow the problem itself to dictate where to prune. The analyst's modeling preferences and value for simplicity, and the client's trade-off between simplicity and completeness, also help to control the choice.

The point is that any choice of a place to prune is arbitrary. Since "consequence" is the name we use for the node at which the pruning occurs, it follows that every consequence is in effect a summary of an unimaginable chain of acts and events that, if modeled, would appear further to the right in the decision tree.

Utilities are the numbers we use to express the merits of consequences, and are therefore as arbitrary as consequences themselves. In particular, since every consequence summarizes an enormous chain of chance events and their outcomes, utilities must summarize the probabilities of those outcomes. This makes the familiar decision-analytic distinction between utility and probability almost completely arbitrary.

That fact is liberating to the would-be simplifier. Three of its effects showed in the example. It used probabilities as dimensions of a multiattribute utility structure. It exhibited pruning in its most heroic form: by treating probabilities as utilities, it avoided any need for decision tree construction and the associated calculations. And the distinction between value and utility did not appear.

The first two simplifications need no further comment. The third does. If you are given the choice between $450 for sure and a 50–50 gamble for $1,000 or nothing, you may take the sure thing. (You also may not – but, if you do not, you probably do not teach decision analysis for a living either.) The phenomenon assumed to underlie this and similar observations is called risk aversion. Recent findings (e.g., Kahneman and Tversky, 1979) show that the opposite often occurs if the amounts are negative instead of positive. (The first findings of risk seeking for losses that we know of appeared in Edwards, 1953, 1954a, b, too early to be of use.)

Bell and Raiffa (1979; see also Bell, 1981, 1982) have pointed out (as Edwards did in 1962) that, though traditionally utility functions are defined over total wealth, in fact winning is inherently different from losing – a fact obscured by the traditional definition. People might be expected to behave quite differently in situations in which they might lose than they do in situations in which they can only win. Such data were originally observed by Edwards (1953, 1954a, 1954b), and define one focus of Kahneman and Tversky's Prospect Theory (1979). Formally, the central argument of Bell's line of thought might be put as follows. Although someone with a concave utility function may be risk averse the fact that he or she is risk averse does not imply that any utility function is concave; something else may be going on. Many other values may be relevant: dislike of losing, desire to outdo others, concern about ruin or change of life style, and so on. Which value or values bear on the decision problem will, of course, depend on what the problem is.

If utilities are evaluative summaries of enormously complicated futures composed of consummatory values, instrumental values, and probabilities, then the distinction between value and utility may not make sense. *All* decisions are risky. The identification of a decision as riskless means only that the analyst, in interaction with the client, has pruned the decision tree at its root. That is why the example neither needs nor uses the value–utility distinction.

Von Winterfeldt and Edwards (1976) discuss this issue at length on pp. 211–215. A quote sums up the discussion:

> In our opinion, the distinction between value and utility is spurious because (1) there are no sure things, and therefore values that are attached to presumably "riskless" outcomes are in fact attached to gambles; (2) risk aversion can frequently be explained by marginally decreasing value functions and/or by regret attributes of a value function; (3) repetitive choices tend to eliminate risk aversion, and an argument can be made that all choices in life are repetitive; (4) error and method variance within value and utility measurement procedures overshadow to a great extent the subtle distinctions that one may extract from the theoretical differences. (p. 213)

These points are all elaborated in the further treatment of the topic on the pages cited above.

Using strengths of preferences

Many decision analysts like elicitation methods based on preferences among bets. These, at a minimum, require the intellectual combination of three numbers to produce a fourth (e.g., the two outcomes of a bet and an intermediate value for sure to produce a probability). They depend for their meaning on a model, maximization of expected utility, the descriptive validity of which has been controversial among psychologists at least since 1948.

It seems far simpler to ask the respondent directly. If the probability of an event is needed, one can ask for it. If one wants to know whether value A is twice as important as B, one can ask, making sure that the respondent understands what "important" means. If one wants to know the shape of a single-dimensional utility function over some objective value-relevant measure, one can either identify end points and draw a straight line or, sometimes, ask the respondent to draw a function.

Probably the most controversial and most useful version of this simple idea is that of assessing strength of preference directly. This applies to both single-dimensional utilities and weights. The respondents at CERL judged single-dimensional utilities directly, reaching consensus by discussion.

Such procedures have a long and honorable tradition in the discipline called psychophysics. (For reviews, see Baird and Noma, 1978, and Stevens, 1975.) It is probably fair to say that most assessments of the loudness of noises, the brightness of lights, the intensity of colors, and other sensory questions to which psychophysicists have devoted study with applied goals in mind are now routinely assessed by means of such judgments. The evidence strongly argues that such assessments are reliable and usefull. Are utilities somehow different from sones, gusts, and other direct assessments of sensory intensities?

Exploiting flatness of decision-theoretical maxima

The truism that decision-theoretical maxima are flat is well known in a wide variety of contexts. Discussions of it, along with references to other papers that make the same kinds of arguments, are the topic of von Winterfeldt and Edwards (1973) and Edwards and von Winterfeldt (1982). See also chapter 11 of von Winterfeldt and Edwards (1986).

Decision analysts can use this fact to simplify their procedures in a variety of ways. Probably most important is the use of additive models. The closeness of the approximation of additive models to nonadditive ones is another truism. Combine that closeness with the fact that, if two utilities or expected utilities are close to one another, you can lose very little by receiving either one, and you soon find yourself wondering why nonadditive models get used. A good reason, of course, is that occasionally preferences may interact in such a way that an additive model is clearly wrong. The extreme example is one in which the direction of preference over attribute A changes depending on the value of attribute B. No familiar nonadditive model incorporates that kind of interaction; it is usually a sign of poor problem structuring. A less extreme but equally valid example is illustrated by the relationship between reliability and perfofmance, and similar obviously multiplicative quantities. Chinnis *et al.* (1975) found, in a military example of that kind, that their respondents were uncomfortable with an additive relationship, even though it made little numerical difference, because they did not want (in their example) a piece of equipment to get a positive score for performance if the reliability was 0, or vice versa.

Another way in which analysts can exploit flatness is by using it to simplify elicitation procedures. Any strictly monotonic function with continuous derivatives is excellently approximated by an appropriate straight line – and the two points that define the line are far easier to elicit than the function itself. A similar comment applies to any function with an interior maximum, except that one must elicit three points rather than two.

The simplifications that result from flat maxima bring us full circle to the point with which this section of the chapter began. If the goal is to help the decision maker with a problem, and no more, then any approximate procedure good enough to help the decision maker make a wise decision (not necessarily the wisest one, but one that differs in expected utility from the wisest one by only a few percentage points) is good enough. This point is widely recognized by decision analysts; it is the real meaning of the frequent and valid comment that by far the most important thing decision analysts do is to help structure the problem. Structure is much more important than the details of the decision rule applied to the problem once structured. Therefore, why not use the simplest procedures that embody the basic ideas about partitioning the problem and recombining the partitioned elements? The result is of course approximate – but so are all decision-analytic procedures, especially those used for eliciting numbers.

OTHER FORMS OF SIMPLICITY: BEHN AND VAUPEL

No discussion of simple ways to help decision makers with their problems could possibly omit an admiring mention of *Quick Analysis for Busy Decision Makers*, by Robert D. Behn and James W. Vaupel (1982). It is by far the simplest and best-written presentation available of how to develop and use decision trees. No one interested in simplifying decision analysis can afford not to read it. Behn and Vaupel aspire to be even simpler than we do, and almost certainly succeed.

After that heartfelt praise, we feel a responsibility to a strange fact. The content of this paper has literally no overlap with the content of that book. Why?

Clearly a major difference is that Behn and Vaupel deal with problems of a kind very different from the one presented here. The key issue with which they are concerned is uncertainty; that is why their book is about decision trees. They prefer to treat uncertainty explicitly, and have developed very simple ways of structuring decision trees to do so.

A second major difference is that every one of Behn and Vaupel's examples is a decision problem with prespecified options. In the problems we most often encounter, options are either ill-specified or not specified at all, and the focus is on evaluation as a tool to provide inputs for the decision maker to consider, rather than on calculations that aim to specify what he or she should do.

A third difference is that Behn and Vaupel almost completely avoid elicitation methods that depend on strength-of-preference judgments. They consider such judgments to be harder to make and less accurate than judgments that, via maximization of expected utility, use respondents as null instruments for reporting difference or no difference between two options. Given that restriction, their elicitation methods are indeed the simplest available. For example, they assess multiattribute utilities by using an additive model and trading off to the most important continuous dimension. SMART is an additive model. We think highly of trading off to the most important dimension whenever the options are prespecified. Whether or not strength-of-preference judgments are feasible and accurate is a watershed issue that differentiates approaches to decision analysis from one another. In the 1986 book, von Winterfeldt and Edwards review the formal and empirical issues at length. Three points seem worth repeating here. (1) An axiomatic structure for strength-of-preference judgments already exists (see Dyer and Sarin, 1979). (2) Strength-of-preference judgments are easy and intuitive. (3) Experimental and real-world evidence shows that utility measures produced by strength-of-preference judgments are reasonably close to utility measures based on indifference judgments about gambles. Evidence also shows that direct numerical judgments of probabilities or odds are easier to make than any other form of such judgments, and at least as well calibrated.

We suspect that Behn and Vaupel might be as much in sympathy with this chapter as we are with the content of their book.

NOTE

The case study on which this chapter was based was funded by the US Army Construction Engineering Research Laboratory under Contract DACA 88-82M 0228.

REFERENCES

Baird, J. C., and Noma, E. (1978). *Fundamentals of Scaling and Psychophysics.* New York: Wiley.

Baker, N., and Freeland, J. (1975). "Recent advances in R&D benefit measures and project selection methods," *Management Science* 21, 1164–75.

Behn, R. D., and Vaupel, J. W. (1982). *Quick Analysis for Busy Decision Makers.* New York: Basic Books.

Bell, D. E. (1981). "Components of risk aversion," *Proceedings of the Ninth IFORS Conference,* ed. J. P. Brans. Amsterdam: North Holland, 235–42.

(1982). "Regret in decision making under uncertainty," *Operations Research* 30, 961–81.

Bell, D. E., and Raiffa, H. (1979). *Marginal value and intrinsic risk aversion.* Harvard Business School, Cambridge, MA (chapter 17).

Dyer, J. S. and Sarin, R. K. (1979). "Measurable multiattributable value functions," *Operations Research,* 27, 810–22.

Ward Edwards, Detlof von Winterfeldt, and David L. Moody

Edwards, W. (1953). "Probability preferences in gambling," *American Journal of Psychology* 66, 349–64.

(1954a). "Probability preferences among bets with differing expected values," *American Journal of Psychology* 67, 56–67.

(1954b). "The reliability of probability preferences," *American Journal of Psychology* 67, 68–95.

(1962). "Subjective probabilities inferred from decisions," *Psychological Review* 69, 109–35. Reprinted in Luce, R. D., Bush, R. R., and Galanter, E. (eds.), *Readings in Mathematical Psychology*, II. New York: Wiley, 1965.

(1977). "How to use multiattribute utility measurement for social decision making," *IEEE Transactions on Systems, Man, and Cybernetics SMC-7*, 326–40. A slightly modified version of this paper appears as: "Use of multiattribute utility measurement for social decision making," in *Conflicting Objectives in Decisions*, ed. by Bell, D. E., Keeney, R., and Raiffa, H. New York: Wiley, 1977.

Edwards, W., and Newman, J. R. (1982). *Multiattribute Evaluation*. Beverley Hills: Sage Publications.

Edwards, W., and von Winterfeldt, D. (1982). "Costs and payoffs in perceptual research," *Psychological Bulletin* 91, 609–22.

Golabi, K., Kirkwood, C. W., and Sicherman, A. (1981). "Selecting a portfolio of solar energy projects using multiattribute preference theory," *Management Science* 27, 174–89.

Kahneman, D., and Tversky, A. (1979). "Prospect theory: an analysis of decisions under risk," *Econometrica* 47, 263–91.

Keefer, D. L. (1978). "Allocation planning for R&D with uncertainty and multiple objectives," *IEEE Transactions on Engineering Management EM-25*, 8–14.

Keeney, R. L. (1987). "An analysis of the portfolio of sites to characterize for selecting a nuclear repository," *Risk Analysis*, 7, 195–218.

Miller, L. W., Kaplan, R. J., and Edwards, W. (1967). "JUDGE: a value-judgment-based tactical command system," *Organizational Behavior and Human Performance* 2, 239–74.

(1969). "JUDGE: a laboratory evaluation," *Organizational Behavior and Human Performance* 4, 97–111.

Sarin, R., Sicherman, A., and Nair, K. (1978). "Evaluating proposals using decision analysis," *IEEE Transactions on Systems, Man, and Computers SMC-8*, 128–31.

Stevens, S. S. (1975). *Psychophysics: Introduction to its Perceptual, Neural, and Social Prospects*. New York: Wiley.

Vari, A., and Vecsenyi, J. (1983). "Decision analysis of industrial R&D problems: pitfalls and lessons," in *Analyzing and Aiding Decision Processes*, ed. by Humphreys, P., Svenson, O., and Vari, A. Budapest: Hungarian Academy of Sciences, 183–95.

von Winterfeldt, D., and Edwards, W. (1973). "Flat maxima in linear optimization models," University of Michigan, Engineering Psychology Laboratory Report No. 011313-4-T, November.

(1986). *Decision Analysis and Behavioral Research*. New York: Cambridge University Press.

21

VALUE-FOCUSED THINKING AND THE STUDY OF VALUES

RALPH L. KEENEY

This chapter concerns the proper role of values and the formation of values in decision-making processes. Such values, as used in this chapter, refer to preferences for states or things. We suggest that values should play a more central role in formalizing decision-making processes than is currently the case. By using value-focused thinking, a style of thinking that concentrates more and earlier on values, it may be reasonable to expect more appealing decision problems than those that currently face us. In other words, value-focused thinking should lead to better alternatives than those generated by existing "conventional" procedures.

There are four topics in this chapter. The first concerns identification of the proper role for values in the decision-making environment. The next discusses structuring and quantifying values to state unambiguously what the decision maker, decision makers or individuals concerned about the problem wish to achieve. The third indicates some approaches to facilitate the creation of alternatives based on stated values. The fourth suggests that the study of values has sufficient breadth and depth as well as sufficient potential rewards for researchers and students to be a legitimate discipline for serious study.

1. IDENTIFYING DECISION OPPORTUNITIES

Much of the focus of decision making is on the choice among alternatives. Indeed, it is common to characterize a decision problem by the alternatives available. Often it seems as if the alternatives present themselves with little background investigation and the decision problem begins when at least two alternatives have appeared. Descriptively, I think this represents many decision situations. Prescriptively, it should be possible to do much better.

What reason is there for ever being interested in a decision problem? Why should one ever make the effort to *choose* an alternative rather than simply to let occur whatever would? The answer is values. Somebody (the decision maker or decision makers or concerned party) feels that the implications of the alternatives are or might be different enough in terms of their values to warrant attention. This desire to achieve more in terms of values is the motivation for any interest in any decision problem. The implication is that the primitive notion for a decision problem should be values and not alternatives.

If, in fact, we begin with values, we might not even think of situations as decision problems, but rather as decision opportunities. Periodically, we might examine achievement in terms of our values and ask, can we do better? The thinking process might suggest creative alternatives that result in increased achievement of our values. This should be a better allocation of our time than spending most of it choosing among readily apparent alternatives in decision problems.

Thinking about values is constraint-free thinking. It is thinking about what you wish to achieve or what you wish to have. It is not that all of this thinking need be self-centered, because what you want might be for others or for society. Thinking of alternatives that might be particularly desirable is also constraint-free thinking. However, selecting among alternatives is constrained thinking. Even though some of the choices may be difficult, constrained thinking is easier than constraint-free thinking because the former significantly limits the range of concern. But the payoffs of constraint-free thinking may be greater. In any case, it seems that the decision processes that we have analyzed with decision analysis and systematic approaches to aid decision making have focused more on the constrained decision problem than on the constraint-free decision opportunity.

There are several ways to represent values. For a specific decision opportunity or decision problem, we might characterize values formally using a von Neumann–Morgenstern utility function or a measurable value function (see for example Keeney and Raiffa, 1976, or Dyer and Sarin, 1979). Either of these would formalize the overall objective in the decision environment, which consists of the decision opportunity and the resulting decision problem. It is interesting to note that, with a utility function, one need not be concerned about constraints. Whereas there might be a cost preference in a problem with a constrained formulation, the utility function could handle this simply by assigning lower utilities to higher costs. This could be done so that alternatives which might be eliminated (perhaps inappropriately) with constrained approaches would, in fact, turn out to be very undesirable if, in fact, that elimination seemed appropriate.

In a decision environment, it may be reasonable to begin by structuring objectives and quantifying the utility function or value function to represent the values of the decision maker or concerned party. This would formalize the foundation for value-focused thinking. As indicated by the arrows in figure 21.1, value-focused thinking should influence development of alternatives in examining decision opportunities, appraisal of alternatives in analyzing decision problems, identification of useful information for either, interpersonal interaction in circumstances such as bargaining and negotiation, and communication.

466

Value-focused thinking

Some of the elements of value-focused thinking and the formalization of that process are clearly emphasized in decision analysis as it is practiced. Specifically, decision analysis used to analyze decision problems and suggest which alternatives are better under specified conditions and to determine the value of sample information. To some degree, it provides insight about useful information and the language for the communication process. For guiding interpersonal interaction in decision problems and for creating alternatives, current practice of decision analysis has not been particularly helpful. Thinking about values first should provide more guidance about what decision analysis to conduct and even about what to consider as objectives or alternatives in that problem. The latter are key elements of the decision opportunity. Regarding communication, a focus on values, which of course may be multiattribute in nature, addresses the ends of the process. It results in the consideration of alternatives as a means to those ends, rather than as the focus of the decision problem.

Figure 21.1 Overview of value-focused thinking. An arrow should be read as "influences."

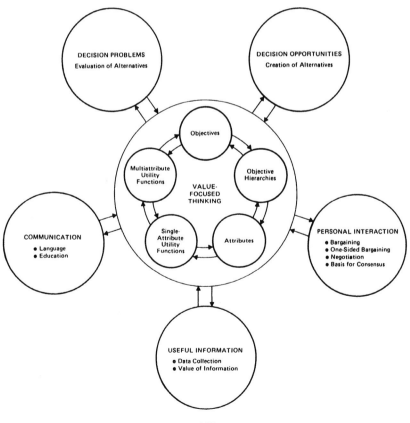

The rest of the chapter is organized as follows. The next three sections will concentrate on the formalization of value-focused thinking. Section 2 discusses the elements of systematized thinking about values. Section 3 examines interrelated hierarchies of objectives, and section 4 discusses the quantification of values. Section 5 examines the creation of alternatives with the decision opportunity and the role that communication and personal interaction have in that creative process. Section 6 summarizes the motivation for a discipline to study values and suggests several general questions that would be addressed by such a discipline. Section 7 is a summary.

2. ELEMENTS OF SYSTEMATIZED THINKING ABOUT VALUES

It is possible to categorize systematized thinking about values into five elements. These are identifying the objectives, structuring the objectives into a hierarchy, specifying or creating attributes to measure the degree to which each objective is achieved, quantifying values (e.g., strength of preference, utility) for different levels of each attribute with a single-attribute value function or utility function, and combining the single-attribute functions into a multiattribute value or utility function. In operationalizing each of these elements, it is necessary to make specific value judgments. Each value judgment gives one piece of information about the overall values of concern. We build an overall picture of values using several "overlapping" value judgments and consistency among them.

Before discussing each of the elements, we should note that the values of interest need not represent those of a decision maker. They may represent those of an individual or organization planning to examine decision opportunities. Also, in operationalizing these elements, the individual or group expressing the values need not be the same as the individual or group facing the decision opportunity or decision problem. Although it might be useful if the individuals controlling any eventual decisions are involved, this is not essential for meaningful or important analysis. For example, an analyst might structure a crucial problem facing the United States government, postulate particular value structures and utility functions, create alternatives, analyze the problem and identify insights, and publish and communicate those insights. If the decision makers for such a problem, whoever they may be, happen to read or otherwise be informed of those insights, such an analysis might be one of the most important done.

For notation, let O_i, $i = 1, \ldots, n$, represent the n lower-level objectives in the objectives hierarchy. Then define X_i as an attribute for measuring O_i. The notation x_i will represent a specific level of X_i so a consequence x of interest can be designated $x = (x_1, \ldots, x_n)$. The discussion in this and following sections will focus on utility functions, although the same reasoning is appropriate for any formal representation of values (e.g., strength of preference value function). Thus, let u_i be a utility function over attribute X_i and let u be the utility function over the set of attributes. Now we can discuss each of the elements in detail.

Objectives

An objective is a statement of something that is desired to be achieved. It typically indicates an object and a direction of preference. Examples are "maximize profit" or "minimize environmental damage." With an objective like "maximize profit," we know that more profit is preferred to less profit, but we do not have a complete specification of the relative desirability of different levels of profit. This concern is addressed when we assess the utility function as discussed below.

In many cases, people state an objective such as "reach the profit goal of $50 million." Such a statement, which I often refer to as a goal rather than as an objective, does not indicate the relative preference of all levels of profit. Specifically, in this case, any profit less than $50 million is equally undesirable, since it does not meet the goal; and any profit above $50 million is implied to be equally desirable, since it does meet the goal. In analysis, one might try to maximize the probability of achieving that goal. The shortcoming, of course, is that the implied value structure is likely not appropriate. Most people would say that profits of $100 million are preferred to $51 million by a large amount and that profits of $49 million are preferred to a loss of $10 million by a large amount. On the other hand, profits of $51 million are probably not that much more important than profits of $49 million. An analysis which maximizes the probability of reaching the goal does not take such preferences into account. Goals seem particularly relevant for motivating individuals or organizations, but they are not as useful for creating or appraising alternatives.

Another type of statement that often occurs when specifying objectives is that individuals being interviewed state preferences for alternatives as their objectives. For instance, a company may suggest that their objective is to open up operations in a new area of the country. What they mean is that their intention is to open up operations and that they feel this will help achieve whatever their objectives really are. By pursuing the reasoning of why they wish to open up operations in another section of the country, the true objectives may be identified.

Once objectives have been articulated, the result will be a list indicating several aspects to be achieved by some decision or by the actions of an organization. When structuring values to create decision opportunities rather than to evaluate previously identified alternatives, the range of objectives should be far-reaching. Stated in another way, one cannot tailor the objectives to the alternatives being considered if one of the purposes of structuring values is to suggest alternatives that might be particularly desirable.

Objectives hierarchy

Once a list of objectives is created, it is necessary to structure these in a reasonable manner. An objectives hierarchy, also called a value tree, has been utilized by almost anyone who has attempted to systematically structure the components of value in cases where multiple components exist. At the higher levels of the hierarchy, general statements of values exist, which are made more specific in the lower levels of the hierarchy. For example, for a higher-level objective like "minimize environmental damage," lower-level objectives may be "minimize the fish killed" and "minimize the loss of virgin timber." The lower-level objectives, which are placed under a higher-level objective in a hierarchy, define more specifically what is meant by that higher-level objective. At times, these lower-level objectives break the higher-level objective into parts and in other instances the lower-level objectives are means to the end specified by the higher-level objective. The next section examines in detail the relationships between different hierarchies of objectives.

Attributes

For each of the lowest-level objectives in a hierarchy, an attribute is needed to indicate the degree to which that objective is achieved. This attribute further specifies the meaning of the objective and the value judgments associated with it. For instance, for the objective "minimize fatalities," one possible attribute is the number of fatalities, a second possible attribute is the number of years of life lost, and a third possible attribute is the number of quality-adjusted life years lost (see Raiffa *et al.*, 1978). With fatalities, the death of a healthy 60-year-old and a permanently ill 20-year-old would count the same. However, using years of life lost, the death of a healthy 60-year-old could result in the loss of 20 years whereas the permanently ill 20-year-old may result in the loss of 30 years (assuming their expected lifetimes were 80 and 50 respectively). Using quality-adjusted life years, the same 60-year-old may have 15 quality-adjusted life years remaining because of potential sickness in later years, and the permanently ill 20-year-old may have 10 quality-adjusted life years remaining. Thus, the 60-year-old would be considered a more significant fatality using quality-adjusted life years. This is not to suggest that any of these is correct, but to indicate that important value judgments are necessarily made in the selection of any attributes.

For many problems, there are no readily available attributes for some objectives. Such objectives include pain in medical problems, the corporate image or decision difficulty or flexibility in corporate problems, the self-esteem or prestige in personal problems, or national pride and psychological well-being in national problems. In these cases, it is appropriate to create an attribute to measure the degree to which the associated objective is achieved. Basically, one must define at least two different levels of achievement to describe the possible consequences of concern with respect to the objective being measured. Examples of this process are discussed in Keeney (1981a).

470

Single-attribute utility functions

The next element in systematizing thinking about values is to determine a utility function for the single attributes. This is important for evaluating alternatives, but also for identifying new objectives that might lead to the creation of new alternatives. Specifically, if a single-attribute utility function is not linear, it is at least partly proxy for an objective other than that being directly measured. If one is risk averse, for instance, there is either another objective not included in the hierarchy or a potential double counting of effects.

As an example, I once found that an executive in charge of finance at a major utility was very risk averse with respect to the cost of a proposed large power plant. When pursuing the reasons for this degree of risk aversion, it was clear that the cause was not only the cost to the customer, which was meant to be addressed by the cost objective, but also the difficulty of obtaining the necessary funds in the bond market to finance the project. In fact, regarding possible increased charges to customers, the executive was almost linear in his utility function. The risk aversion was essentially all induced by his concerns with financing difficulties. In other circumstances, S-shaped utility functions are often the result of additional objectives in the problem rather than irrationality on the part of the individual being assessed. Some of the recent work by Bell (1982, 1985) on decision regret and decision disappointment is shedding some light on this issue.

Multiattribute utility functions

In combining the single-attribute utility functions into a multiattribute utility function, there is almost always an attempt to utilize independence assumptions (see Fishburn, 1970, Keeney and Raiffa, 1976, Farquhar, 1977, and Dyer and Sarin, 1979, for examples). Several points are noteworthy in this process. First, as discussed in Keeney (1981b), any violation of independence suggests that additional objectives, and thus attributes, are appropriate for the decision problem. In the extreme form of the argument, if the objectives address fundamental concerns rather than proxy concerns related to those fundamental concerns, the utility function should be additive. A violation of additivity, of course, indicates that there is some synergy between at least two of the attributes. That synergy indicates, perhaps, another objective.

In a simple example, suppose we have a problem with two objectives to maximize the well-being of individual 1 and to maximize the well-being of individual 2. If these are measured by attributes X_1 and X_2, then there are several arguments to suggest that additive independence might not hold. However, utility independence may be appropriate (see Keeney and Raiffa, 1976). In this case, the utility function over the two attributes would be

$$u(x_1, x_2) = k_1 u_1(x_1) + k_2 u_2(x_2) + k_3 u_3(x_1) u_2(x_2), \qquad (1)$$

where k_1, k_2, and k_3 are positive constants. This is clearly nonadditive over the two attributes X_1 and X_2, but it is additive if one considers three terms. Thus, one might consider the term $u_1(x_1)u_2(x_2)$ to be a measure of equity corresponding to a third objective of "maximize equity between the two individuals." If the utility independence assumptions were appropriate for the two attributes, then clearly the additive independence assumptions would need to be appropriate for these three attributes.

Violations of utility independence or preferential independence also indicate the presence of additional objectives in the decision problem. It is worthwhile to point out that it may not be desirable to determine an attribute and assess an associated utility function over each objective determined by such violations. In assessing utility functions, either single-attribute or multiattribute, it may be useful only to clarify the objectives. This might help in creating new alternatives, even though it may not be worth the effort to formalize further. Because of this, it is difficult to identify whether there is double counting in a particular decision problem. For instance, suppose in a decision problem on national ambient air quality standards that two attributes were parts per million of air pollution and number of resulting fatalities. Clearly, one of the reasons for being interested in air pollution is the effect that air pollution has on mortality. However, air pollution may be of interest for other reasons such as degradation to the environment. If that is the case and if the weight on the utility function for air pollution corresponds to the appropriate weight for the environmental concerns only, then there is no double counting. If the weight on air pollution also includes concerns for mortality, then double counting is occurring. It may also be the case that an attribute such as number of fatalities is meant to account for the impacts on morbidity as well as for fatalities. In this case, there is the implicit assumption that the degree of morbidity is directly related to the number of fatalities. In such a case, the weight on the fatalities attribute *per se* should be greater than if it simply accounted for mortality effects only. In order to appraise potential double counting and eliminate it, it is necessary to understand which objectives are meant to be measured by each of the attributes.

3. INTERRELATED HIERARCHIES OF OBJECTIVES

There is no unique objectives hierarchy for a particular decision problem or decision opportunity, or for guiding one's life. However, an appropriate objectives hierarchy for guiding all decisions would be an objectives hierarchy for quality of life for individuals or the collective quality of life for society. If one could adequately structure this "fundamental objectives hierarchy" and quantify achievement of the various objectives with a utility function, this utility function should provide guidance for all decision making. There is significant literature that might help characterize a reasonable set of fundamental objectives to deal with the quality of life. It should then be possible to assess a utility function over these attributes. Operationally, it may be difficult to use explictly in an analysis, but it should be useful for defining what is to be done in any analysis.

The set of attributes for the fundamental objectives hierarchy should, almost by definition, be combined with an additive utility function that is linear in each of the component attributes. The reasoning, as discussed in Keeney (1981b), is relatively straightforward. The fundamental attribute with the utility approach is utility itself, and of course preferences over utility levels must be linear. If the utility function is not additive, it is an indication that another objective, with an associated attribute, has not been explicitly articulated as discussed in section 2. Once the necessary new objectives and attributes are identified, the resulting utility function over fundamental attributes should be additive. Finally, the component utility over each of the attributes is the measure of what is fundamentally relevant with respect to that individual attribute. Thus, by definition, if the attributes are fundamental, utility must be linear in the component utility functions of the additive utility function.

With a specific decision opportunity or decision problem, we would rarely expect analysis to proceed with the fundamental objectives hierarchy. Rather, a hierarchy over very different objectives might be expected. This objectives hierarchy should relate, however, to the fundamental objectives hierarchy. Although, in practice, we would usually not quantify the relationship between the fundamental objectives hierarchy and an operational hierarchy for each specific case, it is worthwhile to discuss the relationship explicitly.

Suppose we have specified a set of fundamental attributes $X_i, i = 1, \ldots, n$, for a decision problem. Then, we would like to determine $u(x)$ for all x, and, for each alternative A_j, the probability distribution $p_j(x)$ that describes the possible consequences of that alternative. Next, the expected utility of each alternative A_j is calculated using u and p_j. However, even though we might determine u, it would probably be very difficult to determine the p_j.

For our objectives hierarchy for a specific decision opportunity or decision problem, let us suppose there are a set of attributes $Y_k, k = 1, \ldots, m$. To quantify values, we assess a utility function $u'(y)$ over the Y attributes. In providing the value judgments necessary to specify u', one should consider both the relationship between the various levels of x associated with each particular level of y and the preferences for the various levels of x as quantified by $u(x)$. The first relationship could be quantified by the probability distribution $p'(x/y)$, which indicates the probabilities of various x levels given that the level of Y is y. The utility function $u'(y)$ could then be derived from

$$u'(y) = \int u(x)p'(x/y), \qquad (2)$$

where $\int$ represents summation or integration, which is appropriate. In actuality, because either the X attributes are not articulated explicitly or the p' cannot be measured, one often directly assesses the utility function u'.

In conducting this process, we have used what are often referred to as proxy attributes; that is, the Y attributes are proxy for the fundamental X attributes. In assessing the utility function $u'(y)$, one must, of course, intuitively integrate fact with value as indicated by equation (2), where the facts are quantified by the p' and the values by the u.

An interesting observation about the assessment process is that many implicit value judgments must be made. In most cases, we might expect that the Y attributes would only relate to a subset of the X attributes. Thus, in assessing a utility function u', one is probably not even thinking about the X attributes that are not related to the Y attributes of concern. This is *de facto* assuming that the set of Y attributes are utility independent, using terminology from Keeney and Raiffa (1976), from the unrelated X attributes.

In reality, there would be chains of interrelated objectives hierarchies. Some of these would be more closely tied to the fundamental objective hierarchy than others. A decision that is faced by any analyst in the presence of a decision opportunity or a decision problem is, of course, to structure an objectives hierarchy for that problem. There is some flexibility about the degree of closeness between this specific hierarchy and the fundamental objectives. Let us suppose two such hierarchies have been identified as candidates for a particular situation. If attributes for each of these hierarchies are identified, then there should be some relationship between their attributes corresponding to that indicated in equation (2). This circumstance presents an important opportunity to develop a sound representative of preferences. If you assess a utility function over one set of the attributes and the probabilistic relationship tying the two sets of attributes together, the utility function over the second set of attributes can be derived. This should then be compared with the directly assessed utility function over the second set of attributes. No doubt, inconsistencies would result. Identification of these inconsistencies, however, is one purpose of such an elaborate procedure. Not only does this provide a mechanism to identify and eliminate the inconsistencies but, more importantly, it also provides strong motivation for individuals involved to think more deeply about the values in the problem being addressed. Since values should drive such situations, systematic thought on values is likely well spent.

A simple example that indicates that fruitfulness of structuring related objectives hierarchies concerns public fatality risks (see Keeney, 1980). For a class of N people at risk, one objectives hierarchy defines consequences as $p = (p_1, \ldots, p_N)$ where p_i is the probability individual $I_i, i = 1, \ldots, N$, is a fatality in the time period of concern. A second objective hierarchy simply uses the single-attribute consequence f representing the number of fatalities. By investigating a value assumption that quantifies equity among the p-consequences, it is proven that the induced utility function over f-consequences must be risk prone. By using an assumption to minimize expected fatalities, the implied value trade-offs among the p_i terms must be linear and the induced utility function over f-consequences must be risk neutral (i.e., linear). In this example, the probabilistic relationships between p-consequences and f-consequences are not difficult to specify because the p-consequences completely specify those relationships.

However, using equation (2), the concepts would be similar for more complex situations.

The hierarchy of objectives hierarchies provides motivation for a concern about generic objectives hierarchies. Basically, the fundamental objectives hierarchy for an individual or for an organization should remain extremely stable over time. Preferences over the fundamental attributes should also be extremely stable. When one identifies preferences that are not very stable over time, it is an indication that these preferences are over proxy attributes or even over alternatives. Technically, what might have changed to cause these apparent intertemporal differences in values is not a change in fundamental values at all. Rather it is a change in the knowledge pertaining to the relationship between the fundamental attributes and the proxy attributes. Technically, it is a change in p', in equation (2), rather than a change in u, that leads to a change in u'.

There are particularly interesting possibilities in the utilization of generic utility functions for decisions faced by organizations, including governments. First, I suspect that there is potentially more agreement over utility functions for fundamental attributes than there is over proxy attributes. The reasoning is that the disagreement could only occur about values if it were over fundamental attributes, whereas the disagreements could also be over the relationship between fundamental attributes and proxy attributes if we are talking about preferences over proxy attributes.

Secondly, there are often numerous decision problems faced by organizations that could utilize aspects of the same proxy objectives hierarchy. Thus, it may be worth the effort to formalize the relationship between the proxy attributes and the fundamental attributes in an attempt to derive an appropriate utility function over the proxy attributes. This utility function would then be utilized in decision making involving those attributes. A simple illustration is the following.

There are numerous decision problems concerning the regulation of carbon monoxide emissions, or in fact other air pollutants. One of the fundamental objectives of concern in such decision problems is the possible loss of life. As a nation, we might determine that a reasonable utility function over the number of lives lost is linear. However, in examining the problems involving carbon monoxide, it may be reasonable to use the parts per million of carbon monoxide in ambient air quality as a proxy attribute for loss of life. To derive a utility function over the proxy attribute, we need to determine the relationship between ambient carbon monoxide levels and fatalities. A select committee of experts with various viewpoints might be convened to determine a probability distribution for potential fatalities given any specific level of carbon monoxide. Various analyses would be conducted to support the committee. Any disagreements that occur between various experts should be pursued in depth in an attempt to reach the "best judgment" relationship. It may be practical to spend significant funds for this effort because this relationship would be utilized in a large number of decision problems.

A similar idea may be useful on parts of the relationship between proxy attributes and the fundamental attributes. For instance, with radioactivity emissions, it may be useful to have an official dose–response relationship relating the possibilities of health effects or death to doses. In specific problems, one would need to relate the various decision alternatives to the amount of dose different individuals would receive. Periodically, it would be necessary to update, or at least reaffirm, the relationships utilized between proxy and fundamental objectives. However, by concentrating our collective efforts, it should be possible to reinvent the wheel less often and redirect the effort saved to design a significantly better wheel.

4. QUANTIFYING VALUES

This section discusses some of the techniques that I have found useful in quantifying values appropriate for a decision problem or a decision opportunity. This quantification involves carrying out the steps discussed in section 2 from specifying objectives and identifying an objectives hierarchy to assessing a multiattribute utility function. In interpreting these tricks of the trade, so to speak, it is essential to keep in mind that the major purpose of building the value model is to structure and understand the decision environment. Part of this is addressed by quantifying a utility function and evaluating alternatives in terms of expected utility. However, as indicated in figure 21.1, there are other key aspects in understanding and contributing in a decision situation. This includes effective use of time in both modeling and collecting data, the creation of potentially desirable alternatives, and communicating the essence of the problem to relevant parties. I feel that if a state-of-the-art quantification of values is conducted, the contribution made will be worth the effort involved for most decision situations, and the resulting utility function will likely not be the weakest part of an overall analysis.

Perhaps a bit of personal philosophy is relevant before proceeding. Because I am interested in a prescriptive representation of the values, I am not overly concerned about biasing the individuals expressing the values. If I make suggestions that cause them to think deeper about their probelm and reach what they consider to be a better understanding, that "biasing" would be a part of what I would attempt to do. On the other hand, if they sincerely believe that a particular representation of values is appropriate, for me to force them to change would be an inappropriate biasing. Clearly there is a continuum ranging from appropriate to inappropriate, and at some stage the distinction between them is indeed fine. However, in actuality I feel that the likelihood of not biasing is essentially nil. By an involvement in the problem, there will be some bias.

Making the assessee comfortable

It is important in any attempt to determine a value structure to make the individuals who are expressing the values feel comfortable. There are many different general techniques that help. In some cases, it is important to make the assessee feel that he/she is the key individual in this joint process you are going through or at least not make him/her feel that he/she is insignificant. In numerous assessments with professionals, I have stated initially that, without their judgments based on their experience, no structuring of values could be done. This is very important when one is dealing with a decision maker, such as a medical doctor, who may feel that some of the power to make a decision might be lost by being explicit about values. In a similar vein, it is often useful to point out that what you are attempting to do is a complement to, rather than a substitute for, what they have traditionally done.

Another essential ingredient to make the individuals comfortable is to assure them that they will be the first to see any written material on the assessment and that they will have the right to make any alterations before others see it. If one of the results of structuring values is a utility function, this does make explicit potentially sensitive value judgments. A device which often helps in this regard is to preserve flexibility for the assessee. One can do this by providing different parameters for a utility function or by stating that some of the value judgments were based on the author's, rather than the assessee's, judgment. For example, even if the value trade-off between potential cost and potential lives lost is important to a problem, the assessee may not wish his or her value judgment to be explicitly documented on this trade-off. He/she may, however, clearly indicate that the value trade-off is in the range of $2 to $5 million per statistical life lost. Rather than state this, the author may just indicate something to the effect that "For this type of problem, a reasonable range in the value trade-off between life lost and dollars is from $1 million to $10 million per life lost." The report may then conduct a sensitivity analysis over this range, which, of course, would be appropriate to do in any case.

A final comment about making the individual feel comfortable involves an attempt to find some similar background or interests between the assessor and the assessee. This could range all the way from where one grew up or went to school, to which football teams look good in the college ranks this year, to yesterday evening's terrific dinner. On one occasion where I had hoped to assess the utility function over the costs of a major project from the executive in charge of finance at the firm, the project manager within the firm informed me that I could have no more than five minutes. I took the five minutes (that being better than none). Fortunately, when meeting the executive, I noticed he wore an MIT ring and I mentioned that I had taught there. The upshot is that he canceled two successive appointments and I had two pleasurable hours that included both a general discussion about MIT and time for a very reasonable assessment of an appropriate utility function for the financial costs of the project to the firm.

It is interesting to note that the process of quantifying values seems much simpler with individuals higher up in an organization. The "real decision makers" seem to like structuring their values more than middle-level individuals. One explanation is that these executives know very well that they are always making decisions involving such values and feel partially relieved that there are some formal techniques that may assist them. A second possibility is that middle-level individuals have not thought about the values as much and must also try to put themselves into the position of another individual, namely their management, when proceeding with structuring values.

Providing insight quickly

A key element of the assessment procedure that might significantly increase the likelihood of obtaining a reasonable value structure is to make an insightful contribution early in the interaction process. Some of these insights are fairly generic in nature. For instance, suppose the assessment of a single-attribute utility function indicates it to be nonlinear. As we have stated, this suggests that the attribute is proxy to some degree. If the utility function is quite distinct from linear, pursuing the reasoning for the nonlinearity may be enlightening. One example, referred to in section 2, concerned the case where a utility executive had a very risk averse utility function for the cost of a proposed power plant. The reasoning indicated that the related objective concerned the difficulties of financing the project in the capital makers in addition to the eventual cost consequences to customers of the plant. Bringing this to the attention of the executive increased his interest in and willingness to contribute to the assessment exercise.

A second example concerns a preliminary analysis with the Environmental Protection Agency to structure a decision framework for examining possible carbon monoxide ambient air quality standards. Discussion indicated that the key health effect thought to be related to carbon monoxide exposure was heart attacks. However, essentially all of the data on the impacts of carbon monoxide pertained to angina attacks and other health effects deemed to be less significant. Using judgments obtained in a few minutes, it became apparent that some individuals felt that the heart attack rate would be in the neighborhood of 5 % of the angina attack rate and also that one heart attack was a thousand times more important than one angina attack. Roughly speaking, this suggested that heart attacks were fifty times more important than angina attacks for any proposed policy decision. Hence it seemed appropriate to attempt to relate carbon monoxide exposure to heart attack rates utilizing the best professional judgment available. There would naturally be uncertainties about such a relationship, as there would be if much laboratory data existed, but not to address the relationship was tantamount to skipping the problem.

Assessing the utility function

One of the most useful devices for quantifying values is simply to ask "why" questions. You, the assessor, and the assessee are jointly trying to build a model of his/her value structure. He/she presumably has values somewhere in his/her mind, even if not on a conscious level, and you have a generic framework to represent values. The essence is for you to assist the assessee in articulating verbally or graphically his/her values so you can mathematically represent them. Communication is essential. You would like to get to the point where you almost know what the assessee will respond about any value question. It is crucial in this endeavor to ask many questions about the assessee's thinking and expressions. Why is *A* preferred to *B*? Why is attribute *X* important at all? Why isn't an attribute *Y* included? Isn't the inclusion of separate attributes for water pollution and spawning grounds disrupted a double counting? Why aren't preferences for costs linear? What are you thinking about when you are trying to decide whether consequence *A* is preferred to *B*? And the responses to each of these can be followed up by another "why" question. The process facilitates both communication and understanding if done in a meaningful and professional manner.

In assessing a utility function, one attempts to identify pairs of consequences that are indifferent. A particularly useful procedure is a convergence technique that begins with two consequences that are easily differentiated in terms of value and proceeds to compare pairs of consequences that are successively more difficult to differentiate in terms of value. This procedure, first of all, allows the assessees to start thinking in terms of the type of questions being asked and makes them feel more comfortable since they can answer the first questions easily and in a manner that they definitely feel is consistent with their value judgments. Secondly, once the questions in this convergence procedure get difficult, we have essentially identifed a range over which sensitivity analysis seems appropriate. It is also often the case that within this range, the specific point of indifference between a pair of consequences is not important for creating or evaluating alternatives. If it is important, this too is nice to know. Finally, as a practical matter, if it appears that the assessee finds it equally difficult to express a preference for consequence *A* over consequence *B* and a preference for consequence *B* over consequence *A'* where *A* and *A'* are reasonably similar, then it probably is reasonable to assume that a consequence roughly half way between *A* and *A'* is indifferent to *B*.

Another device that is sometimes useful in assessing utility functions over a single attribute is to have consequences represented with a corresponding level of a second attribute to minimize potential impacts of framing (see Tversky and Kahneman, 1981). One example concerned assessment of potential increases in electricity rates. The prime measure was the cost of the average residential customer's monthly bill in dollars. Another attribute, which had a one-to-one relationship with the first, is the percent change relative to the current average residential customer's bill. By placing the corresponding levels of these two attributes side-by-side, the assessment over one attribute can be done with a fuller knowledge of the implications of the different levels of that attribute. Knowing that an average residential customer's bill might be $40 monthly and that this is a 25% increase might be a fuller description of the consequences than simply knowing that the average monthly bill would be either $40 or a 25% increase over the current circumstance. However, once the utility function over the attribute is complete, only one of the attributes needs to be used to evaluate alternatives.

Identifying value dependencies

One of the key elements in the assessment process is to identify any dependencies between attributes. This is done by checking for the possibility of independence assumptions such as utility independence and additive independence. Many details about these procedures are discussed in Keeney and Raiffa (1976). However, other checks for dependence occur more informally earlier in the assessment process. The first is in structuring the objectives hierarchy and identifying attributes. Here, we simply pursue reasoning about why various objectives or attributes are important.

It is sometimes the case that one attribute in a problem is important only for its relationships to other attributes which are also in the problem. A particularly striking case of this occurred when structuring values to appraise water resource plans for the Tisza river basin of Hungary (see Keeney and Wood, 1977). One of the initial twelve objectives related to the ability of Hungary to control its own water resources and the discussion indicated that this particular objective was very important. When we pursued the reasoning for this objective, responses indicated that control was important to (among other things) reduce the likelihood of floods and the resulting impact of floods. But, in fact, flood consequences were included in the problem under other objectives. Another reason for the control objective was to have the ability to improve the agricultural and industrial output of Hungary as they related to water resources. But, again, objectives pertaining to these concerns were also in the hierarchy. We eventually determined that almost all of the more fundamental consequences related to the objective of control were also included in the objectives hierarchy. Only a concern related to the prestige of national control over such a significant factor as water resources was not accounted for elsewhere. The objective of control remained, but its relative importance in the assessment of the utility function was much lower. It had been relegated to be a proxy for prestige alone and the interdependencies with the other attributes were, therefore, eliminated.

There are some generic types of dependencies that have been identified often enough to recognize them readily. One has to do with impacts where both the absolute amount and the percent of the impact are significant. There are many environmental examples; one concerns the potential loss of salmon in rivers as a result of construction activity at power plants (see Keeney and Robilliard, 1977). The loss of 2,000 salmon in a river with an annual run of 1 million is much less important than the loss of 2,000 salmon in a river with a run of 4,000 salmon. Thus, absolute losses are not enough to capture the situation. However, the loss of 10% in a river with a run of a million salmon is much more significant than the loss of 10% in a river with 4,000 salmon. There is, however, a complex interrelationship between the values over impacts characterized by the percent loss and the absolute number loss. A change in attributes in this case to the percent loss and the number of salmon in the river provided a means to obtain a reasonable utility function over the original attributes. Another generic dependency can be indicated by considering the evaluation of the impacts of different types of physical trauma. If the intent is to scale trauma because of its relationship to mortality and morbidity, there are very strong dependencies among attributes (see Fryback and Keeney, 1983). If one has suffered extremely severe burns, the likelihood of being a fatality is so high that the simultaneous suffering of a severe blow on the head does not matter much. If the burns had not occurred, the blow itself could be extremely significant. The generic situation has different proxy attributes, each only important because of the causal relationship to the same fundamental objective.

Involving the decision makers

Even though the data describing the possible impacts of the alternatives may be provided by various individuals with different professional backgrounds, it is usually preferable that the executives provide the value judgments for a decision situation. One device that I have found useful to involve these "real decision makers" is to do a first-cut analysis using a representative utility function provided by individuals lower in the organization. Then the entire analysis can be presented, in the same manner as a final presentation would be given, to the executives. This should provide some insights about the problem they face, but it also seems to motivate them to ask numerous "what if" questions, one of which is, "What would happen if you utilized my values?" The first-cut analysis has other important implications. It indicates what it is that you are attempting to do and why you are doing it. This serves an important purpose in making the executives feel comfortable. The first-cut analysis also indicates which objectives and attributes seem most relevant to the decision problem. The assessment of the utility functions for the executives can focus on those objectives. Also, we have found that executives sometimes modify the attributes utilized to measure a few of the objectives.

State-of-the-knowledge utility assessments

I view a state-of-the-knowledge utility assessment to consist of the following. At least two objectives hierarchies for a specific decision opportunity or decision problem would be specified. Utility functions over each would be assessed using procedures illustrated in the references in this chapter. Time and effort would be spent to relate the different levels of attributes in one objective hierarchy to those levels in the other objectives hierarchy. Technically, we would determine the p' term for each of the values of y in equation (2). The resulting inconsistencies would be pursued in depth and various aspects of the process would be repeated until consistency was achieved. With all the value judgments and professional judgments that would necessarily be a part of determining u, u', and p', one could likely severely restrict the forms of each of these by simply bounding specific parameters in each. In visual terms, if we bounded each of the utility functions from below and above, using judgments that the assessee was very comfortable with, and if we similarly bounded the p', and if we ensured consistency, then any consistent utility function with either objectives hierarchy should be logically sound for any purposes of the problem.

The conclusion of this section will simply state some observations about the assessment of utility functions. First, it is very useful to have a computer program to quantify the utility function given the value judgments expressed. Sicherman (1982) developed such a program which takes the pairs of indifferent consequences and provides the parameters in a utility function of a specified form. For multiple attributes, that form which uses multiplicative and additive utility functions is determined from the independence assumptions verified during the assessment process. Numerous functional forms are available for single-attribute utility functions. Secondly, I have found no relationship between the mathematical skills of the assessee and his/her ability to provide consistent value judgments. I also believe that there is no relationship between mathematical skills and the ability to adequately represent values appropriate for the probelm being addressed. The distinction between the two preceding comments is that consistency is not identical to adequacy. What is relevant in the assessment process is that the assessee is willing to think hard about his/her values and put effort forth to communicate clearly. Needless to say, the assessor can facilitate this process greatly.

5. CREATING ALTERNATIVES USING VALUES

This section suggests how to create alternatives using structured values. A number of specific techniques for generating alternatives are discussed, as well as some advantages of creating alternatives using values.

In order to contrast with the value-focused approach, let us briefly outline the decision analysis procedure focused on alternatives. Once the alternatives are identified, a set of objectives and the utility function to evaluate the alternatives are determined. The range of the utility function is chosen to be broad enough to include the possible consequences of various alternatives. The expected utility of each alternative is calculated, and the one with the highest expected utility is proposed as the best alternative if, of course, the assumptions in the analysis are reasonable. Often in decision problems, there is an alternative, such as the status quo or an obvious choice, about which there is relatively less uncertainty concerning the consequences. If no better alternatives are found, this alternative will probably do. The entire analysis uses this alternative as an anchor and more or less tries to find alternatives that are incrementally better. The anchor plays a role similar to that in the assessment of probabilities (see Tversky and Kahneman, 1974) but the implications are potentially far worse. One's thought processes about what alternatives are possible or reasonable are anchored, and so creativity in developing alternatives is not promoted. Even dimensions of thought, characterized by the attributes, are anchored by those attributes chosen to be sufficient for the existing alternatives. The significant implication is that the alternatives often might not be as good as could be the case.

Focusing thinking on particularly desirable alternatives

The value-focused approach begins with the value structure and utility function. As before, let us suppose we have assessed a utility function u over attributes X_i, $i = 1, \ldots, n$ where the levels x_i of each attribute go from a least desirable level of x_i^0 to a most desirable level of x_i^*. The x_i^* needs to be set high, meaning a bit above what might be achieved with alternatives that seem particularly desirable on that attribute. The most desirable consequence would then, of course, be $x^* = (x_1^*, \ldots, x_n^*)$, and we will assign a utility to this consequence of u^*. This best consequence is what we wish to use as an anchor in value-focused thinking. Our general approach is to slowly lower aspirations from an expected utility of u^* thinking very hard about how to create a realistic alternative reaching the utility at each lower level. Once we have identified alternatives with those higher utilities, they should be carefully evaluated and a "best" alternative chosen. In simple terms, we begin with the hypothetical best and degrade the minimum amount possible rather than, as with an approach focused on the alternatives, begin with a minimally acceptable alternative and hopefully increase to better utilities. Below are some suggestions for operationalizing this concept.

A key element is to define a reasonable u^*. This can be done by examining the value structure attribute by attribute. With each attribute X_i, we identify a realistic alternative which could maximize desirable achievement along that attribute. We also assume that any uncertainty about X_i for that alternative is resolved in a favorable manner. The resulting implication would provide level x_i^*. For instance, if one objective is to maximize profits measured by the attribute of millions of dollars of profit, we think of alternatives that maximize profits. We also assume that uncertainty about potential profits for that alternative are favorably resolved. The level of profit associated with such a situation might define the maximum level of profits, which becomes one of the elements of the consequence x^*. By proceeding with each of the attributes in this manner, we not only define x^*, but also promote creative thinking about realistic alternatives. There is the presumption there that alternatives that maximize one dimension may be poor on other dimensions, although this need not be the case. Some of the alternatives identified as maximizing the achievement of one objective might be legitimate contenders for the overall best alternatives. The process can be repeated, for instance, by considering two attributes at a time and trying to find good alternatives assuming they are the only objectives that exist for the problem.

Another approach to generate creative alternatives is to examine readily apparent alternatives to identify what aspects of the consequences seem particularly desirable. We determine whether there are generic features leading to that desirability that could be kept in sets of alternatives. Then we attempt to identify alternatives that maintain the good features of the readily apparent alternatives and make significant improvements on the worse features. For instance, some of the desirable consequences of readily apparent alternatives may be high profits. In examining features of alternatives that lead to those high profits, we may find that many involve opening up a new market for a product. By keeping the feature of new market opened and varying other aspects of the alternatives, we may create a better option.

One-sided bargaining

One common situation occurs when another individual, or perhaps several individuals or an organization, needs to be convinced or give authorization in order for you to proceed with an alternative that is desirable to you. It is very helpful in such cases to examine the problem from the point of view of the other person or persons. From their point of view, the alternatives in the problem are the status quo or the alternative you are suggesting, and, of course, they may have a different objective hierarchy than yours. From your perspective, the alternatives include the status quo and anything you can think of. The generic problem is one that I refer to as one-sided bargaining. You 'bargain' for their side and make sure that they improve their lot so that they give their authorization, and you also bargain for yourself. This situation may be viewed as one of removing constraints.

An interesting factor about one-sided bargaining is that it seems relatively easy to do in many individual professional problems. As a trivial example, but one which many professionals have faced, consider the situation where you are asking your boss for the authorization to attend a conference or a meeting. You want to go to the meeting, but you have been told that, because it costs $2,000 and funds are tight now you cannot go. In a business situation, I have simply figured out easy ways to make an additional $3,000 for the firm which could pay for the trip. You need only bill a few extra days of consulting time to pay for this. In an academic situation, I have simply gone to individuals with grant money and suggested that I would write a decent paper and publish it and give sponsorship to their grant if they wanted to fund my travel to the conference and provide secretarial support on the paper. In both situations it seemed that the alternative generated was better for all concerned. The interplay between the descriptive and prescriptive aspects of decision analysis is interesting here, since you are essentially using your description of their values as a basis for your bargaining their position prescriptively. You are also trying to trade off overall impacts on them versus overall impacts on you in a way that is prescriptively reasonable to you, but which will be viewed as descriptively fair and responsible by them.

Clarifying individual preferences for group action

Another common set of decision problems where the creation of alternatives is important concerns some group decision problems. The ideas can easily be illustrated assuming that two people are involved and must agree upon an alternative. One key element in the thought process is to require each individual to create alternatives separately. The alternatives are exchanged and each individual evaluates all the alternatives based upon their own values. Finally, the preferences of the individuals for the alternatives are combined. This general ideal of obtaining individual preference from the best source, namely that individual, and then combining the values is important. Let us illustrate with a simple example where two individuals selected a restaurant for dinner and both were displeased by its quality. Afterwards, discussion indicated that individual 1 thought that it would be a good restaurant because he thought individual 2 would like it and individual 2 thought it would be a good restaurant because she thought individual 1 would like it. With a new state of knowledge, it was clear that even before dinner, both preferred another restaurant to the chosen one.

By attacking the problem using the individual objectives hierarchies first, we also get a broader range of alternatives to be considered in the problem. Once the values are combined in any fashion, there are some constraints put on the process and the thinking about alternatives in the process. Many of the ideas in the one-sided bargaining problem about keeping the good features of alternatives and eliminating the bad could also be used in the group problem where one keeps the features that are good to one individual and attempts to incorporate the features that are good to the other individual in creating the alternative. Some of these ideas are elaborated in bargaining and negotiation contexts in Raiffa (1982).

Coordinated alternatives

Another generic idea that has a much higher likelihood of being induced by value-focused thinking is the identification of distinct alternatives to achieve different parts of what one hopes to achieve. If one begins with a reasonably complete value structure and utility function to represent it, whether the achievement is produced by several alternatives chosen in some coordinated fashion or by one distinct alternative is unimportant. Had the focus initially been on alternatives, there would probably have been an attempt to achieve all of the objectives by a single alternative.

As an illustration, consider a situation faced by a friend of mine who indicated that he was interested both in spending more leisure time pursuing nonprofessional activities in a nice climate and in minimizing the costs of this leisure. The problem was framed as whether to purchase a condominium in a sunny location with many recreational and leisure time activities available. In discussing options, it became clear that one objective was to minimize any hassle that might, for instance, occur from managing such property. If one owned a recreational condominium and did not lease it when it was vacant, costs would be very high although the hassle factor would be low. Owning and leasing when vacant would be less costly, but hassles could be significant. Not owning and renting such a condominium for a few months out of each year would be very expensive. And, of course, not going to such a condominium would be inexpensive with little hassle, but would forgo the desired recreational advantages. In this case, a class of reasonable alternatives seemed apparent. They involved renting a condominium for the time desired, but consulting perhaps 10% of the days while staying at such a condominium. The minimal consulting involvement would bring the effective cost of renting down to a very reasonable level, and it would avoid any hassles of ownership. It would also provide flexibility to try different resorts with a minimum of difficulty. Furthermore, the small amount of consulting involvement could very likely be developed in a manner that would be enjoyable and interesting. The point is simple, two distinct alternatives, namely consulting a little and renting condominiums, chosen in a coordinated fashion were preferable to any single alternative intended to achieve all of the objectives.

Advantages of value-focused thinking for creating alternatives

There are a number of advantages which are associated with value-focused thinking that are worth mentioning. First, value-focused thinking promotes identification of process alternatives better than thinking focused on the alternatives. Perhaps it is the case that some of the important objectives deal with the process, such as an objective that the process be fair. Thinking of potential process alternatives does not seem to hamper thinking of direct alternatives, however.

There is also some experience that suggests structuring the value function initially indicates where to focus in studying a particular decision problem. In a case a few years ago, we were concerned with alternatives to deal with the possible theft and misuse of plutonium. One of the attributes in the first structured objectives hierarchy of the problem was the number of grams of plutonium that might be stolen. For the possible ranges of the attributes, the scaling factor for the amount stolen was much greater than the scaling factors for all of the other attributes together. This suggested that aggregating that much of the entire decision problem into the utility assessment over the attribute of the amount of plutonium stolen seemed inappropriate. More modeling should be focused on that attribute and alternatives should be created that had a differential impact on it.

Often, you are not in a position to develop alternatives directly, but there are actions that you can take to improve the chances that better alternatives are created. In such a situation, value-focused thinking may not only be more helpful than thinking focused on alternatives, but the latter may almost be irrelevant. Let me illustrate with a simple personal example. It became clear to me when first interviewing for employment with a BS degree in engineering that, in dealing with others, it was worthwhile to focus on dimensions over which they had some control. Like many graduates, I was idealistic and wanted a job which provided an interesting professional challenge, had enjoyable colleagues, was terrific in all other ways, and gave me enough money to scrape by on. It seemed as if it was greedy to even state that the salary mattered much. When asking the question "How important is salary?", which I now do not think is even reasonably posed, I would state that it was not too important. Well, I got a number of job offers interviewing this way, but I also figured out that at the BS level, the employers really did not have a lot of control over the quality of the people who were working with or the professional challenge in the problems being addressed. Indeed, it seemed as if the only attribute they did control was salary. I "upgraded" my terminology. To the question, "Is salary important?", I responded that it was very important, but I hastily added that many other aspects of the problem were also very important. I still got job offers, but the increase in salary relative to before was not insignificant.

This example relates to a key attribute that is often left out of many personal decision processes. Including the attribute might promote thinking of more alternatives and selecting alternatives "less conservatively." The attribute has to do with the information that is learned from the chosen alternative that may be relevant to other problems one will face in life. There are many games of life that one is playing and the issue is not whether one plays, but whether one plays well or poorly where well and poorly must be defined by the individual "player." For better or worse, bargaining with potential employers and actual employers is a process that one might face several times in life. To practice early might lend important insights for important problems later. Similar circumstances relate to one's decisions with investments and tax strategy. If you have any funds, you are in the investment game, and, whether you pay taxes or simply did not file, you are in the tax game. In examining alternatives concerning either, inclusion of the attribute to account for what is learned that may be relevant to additional decision problems in the future may promote creative thinking about alternatives.

A final advantage to value-focused thinking was alluded to earlier in this chapter. Namely, in problems with more than one individual involved, there is perhaps a greater opportunity to develop a consensus or at least an agreement on a combined alternative by focusing first on values. There is a reasonable amount of evidence (see, for example, Gardiner and Edwards, 1975) that suggests that antagonists do not differ as much in their fundamental values as they do in their selection of alternatives. This would be reasonable since the latter includes both values and judgments about possible consequences. Furthermore, I believe it to be the case that most antagonists would be more in agreement concerning the relative values of fundamental objectives than about proxy objectives for the same reason. To the degree that this presumption is correct, building up a basis for joint decision making on foundations which are reasonably similar, that is values, may be useful in creating a consensus or a constructive compromise. To the extent that fundamental differences in values are identified, it should be possible to utilize these for the benefit of all parties concerned by creating alternatives for which the differential impacts most desired by each of the parties can accrue to them in exchange for some of the less desired impacts being transferred to others.

6. A DISCIPLINE TO STUDY VALUES

The intent of this section is straightforward. It suggests that there is sufficient substantial material about values that could be beneficially studied in an integrated fashion. I believe that a discipline to study values, which might be referred to as "valuology", would offer ample intellectual reward for scholars and students and potentially important contributions to individuals, organizations, and society. The basis for the latter claim is simple. There are millions of decision problems faced every day. Values should be the driving force behind choice in decision problems and even the identification of such problems. To better understand everything about values and their appropriate role in our lives could make a useful contribution to better decision making and perhaps a better quality of life.

But why have a discipline to study values! Certainly values are studied in ethics, in law, in the sciences, in the arts, and in management. The psychologists focus on descriptive aspects of values, the economists concentrate on normative aspects, decision analysts are concerned with prescriptive aspects, and philosophers are concerned with moral aspects of values. The answer is that, although values are ubiquitously important in virtually every aspect of human behavior, there is no integrated approach to the study of values. A discipline to study values could provide such an integrated approach and the benefits could be much greater than with the status quo decentralized approach.

Rather than hypothesize about the contributions that might be expected from a systematic and integrated study of values, we will indicate some of the topics that would be of concern to a discipline devoted to the study of values. The following is suggestive:

Procedures for systematically identifying values

It would be useful to have better procedures to identify objectives in a problem and structure them into a hierarchy. It may be that hierarchies are not particularly useful for certain types of problems and identifying such types would be useful. Better methods to identify attributes to capture the true meaning of an associated objective would be helpful. In this regard, more experience in developing and communicating with constructed indices could be useful.

Quantification of values

By quantifying values, we mean assessing utility functions or value functions. Better procedures, integrated more closely with computer support to provide instantaneous feedback, could improve the process. This would be particularly useful when we have two or more related objectives hierarchies and utilize utility functions or value functions for each and check them for consistency as discussed in section 3.

Personal use of values

The potential opened up by focusing on decision opportunities rather than decision problems is, perhaps, greatest with personal decisions. As soon as a level of disappointment or dissatisfaction begins to settle in with an individual, it can be identified as a warning signal to start thinking of decision opportunities and creating better alternatives. Often, in such situations, readily available alternatives do not come to mind. But what can be brought into consciousness are the grounds for the dissatisfaction and objectives which could "remedy" the situation. At its extreme, this would contribute to developing an entirely different approach to thinking about one's personal problems and opportunities in life. It is the development of value-focused thinking to guide one's personal life actions.

Group and societal value structures

Since the individual mind is the thinking unit and there is no collective mind, how might one responsibly structure values for a group or society? One possibility is the straightforward answer of structuring values for individuals, or representatives of an organization or society, and combining these in some fashion. This is what has been done to date in situations where values for an organization have been structured, but questions remain about whether this is the best way to proceed. Perhaps it would be more reasonable to involve interplay between the different value structurings. The relevance of communication is crucial here because different individuals may mean different things by the same words or the same things by different words. There is also the potential for significant interplay between descriptive and prescriptive value structures. For instance, if the government is contemplating selection of different alternatives, it may wish to do what it feels is best prescriptively for the public but also to do that which it feels would be best accepted descriptively by the public. This points to the crucial role of public education regarding value issues in general and the specifics in any situation.

Deep value probing

For almost all decision opportunities and decision problems, it would not be reasonable to utilize directly the fundamental set of objectives. To some degree, proxy objectives will almost always be utilized. A key issue in many situations is what are the fundamental objectives lurking behind those proxy objectives which can more readily be identified. Some research along this line is currently being conducted by Bell (1982, 1985) on the role of regret and disappointment for individuals. Research on the corresponding concerns and deeply held fundamental values in corporate and governmental problems would be fascinating.

Public involvement

For many complex decision problems, the technical, scientific, or economic issues may be of the nature that excludes the possibility of reasonable participation by most members of the public. The contributions of a layman to an increased understanding of the implications of too much carbon monoxide in the upper atmosphere or the details of a new economic trade agreement with other nations is probably minimal. However, if the objectives utilized to appraise and create alternatives in such situations are stated in terms meaningful to the public, and they should be, then the public can have a meaningful role in providing the value judgments necessary to create and appraise those alternatives. We do, however, need useful procedures to obtain and synthesize values of the public in order to contribute to better decision making for the public. Because little effort has been directed to obtain the public's values in a useful format, the potential benefits of the study of this problem are great.

Conflict identification and consensus building

As stated in section 4, there is some evidence to suggest that individuals would differ much less in their value judgments over fundamental objectives than in their value judgments concerning proxy objectives or alternatives. Systematic investigation might indicate opportunities to exploit this greater potential for agreement to construct alternatives preferable to those we now consider. The general problem would be to clearly identify and understand the maximum amount of agreement and to specify the remaining conflict and its basis. It is well understood that one of the most important contributions to "solving a problem" is to understand precisely what the problem is.

Generic value structures

Both with individuals and with organizations, there is a possibility that developing generic value structures could be useful. Some of these generic value structures might pertain to an individual facing several different types of decisions, and others might pertain to several individuals facing the same type of decision such as searching for a job. Because the fundamental objectives hierarchy for an individual for any problem would be the same, it would seem reasonable that the proxy objectives hierarchies for certain types of decisions would be very similar if not identical. It might, for instance, be possible and useful to develop an objectives hierarchy for most of the professional decisions faced by an individual in his or her workplace. To the extent that a particularly unique decision situation presented itself, the decision maker should be able to appraise whether the generic hierarchy was appropriate for that problem.

Fundamental objectives for a firm or organization

It may be an extremely useful exercise to have the executives of a corporation carefully structure their objectives and the utility function over those objectives to indicate the basic reason for the organization's existence. Any decision opportunity or decision problem being addressed in the firm should, of course, only be of interest if it could contribute toward achieving the stated firm values. The firm's objectives would provide a foundation from which any specific objectives hierarchy and associated utility function would be developed for a specific decision situation. Developing such a process so that it would be operational could have significant benefits in terms of better communication and more coordinated decision making.

Legal value structures

On many problems faced by government, the same objectives are found. Rather than to debate the alternatives in each specific situation, which often leads to polarization, it may be useful to legally specify some aspects of the value structure to be consistently used for all decisions of a defined likeness. As an example, it might be desirable to have a governmental guideline for the value trade-off between economic costs and statistical fatalities. That guideline may state, for instance, that a cost of $1.5 million is indifferent to the loss of one statistical life in highway safety decisions. With such a guideline, the discussion on any particular problem would focus on the possible consequences with better consequences as indicated by the value structure. Such process could lead to more efficient communication and more lives saved with less cost. Related to the problem of a legal value structure, some research may address "legal probability distributions" such as for the dose–response effects of various pollutants on health.

Ethical value issues

Moral philosophers and ethicists have certainly dealt in depth with value structures. A key concern of their discipline is to prescriptively suggest how one should act in an ethically appropriate manner. But the contributions that ethicists have made have rarely been integrated with the operational study and use of values for decision making. The potential benefits of such integrations would likely be worth the effort.

Communication and education about values

Perhaps the most important contributions that the study of values might make is to improve the communication and education about values. This communication would be between individuals, between organizations, between an individual and the government, and even between an individual's own feelings and his or her thoughts. The distinctions between fact and value judgments would provide a useful basis to improve communication. A knowledge of the interrelationships among fact and value judgments and the dependence of one upon another would clarify understanding. Education about the appropriate role of value judgments, and indeed the legitimacy of including value judgments in important decision processes, could contribute to elevating the discussion on many important issues. With decision making, there is no such thing as the completely scientific or objective approach. We can strive for systematic, responsible, and justified decision processes, but values – which are not scientific – are an essential part and should be, as well as must be, included.

7. CONCLUSIONS

There are four related topics in this paper. One concerns the role of structuring thinking around values for decision problems and the recognition of decision opportunities. The second concerns procedures that have been useful in quantifying value structures from individuals and organizations. The third concerns the creation of desirable alternatives using values. The fourth concerns the development of a discipline for the integrated study of values.

The reason for an interest in any decision situation is that individuals or organizations have values and they feel their values could be better achieved by carefully considering alternatives and making decisions thoughtfully. We suggest that the use of values to characterize decision situations may contribute to the recognition of situations as decision opportunities rather than decision problems. Structuring values appropriate for the situation can lead to the identification of creative alternatives to better achieve that which is desired. Several suggestions that may assist in this thought process are discussed. The value-focused approach is contracted to the alternative-focused approach to deal with decision situations. The former is an example of constraint-free thinking, whereas the latter is constrained thinking. Both are complements, but constraint-free thinking is often currently excluded in processes involving decision situations. It is often relegated to the subconscious. By bringing it to the conscious level and spending effort thinking about our values, we should be able to have a positive effect on the quality of our decisions and perhaps the quality of our lives.

In thinking of guidelines that have been useful in quantifying values, it is important to begin with the objectives of the assessment procedure. One objective is, of course, to specify a utility function or a value function that can be directly useful in the appraisal of alternatives. But a more important objective is to better understand the decision situation, which could lead to identification of better alternatives, better communication, better use of data, and hopefully better decision making. Because of the second objective, many of the key tricks of the assessment trade have to do with making the individal feel comfortable and enthused about participating in the assessment process. This is done by making the individual recognize his or her key role and by making small, insightful contributions during the process of assessment. Also, to put assessees at ease, it is important to indicate that they will have the first option to see any written material on the assessment and that they have full authority to make any changes or stop any further communiation representing their values. Finally, another very useful device in the assessment process is simply to ask the question "why?" and follow lines of thinking to identify the more fundamental values which are important to the decision maker and to illustrate the reasoning he or she is utilizing.

At the current time, aspects of values are studied from prescriptive, descriptive, and normative perspectives. Values are studied in psychology, law, management, philosophy, engineering, medicine, and the arts. There is, unfortunately, little integration between the contributions made from the different perspectives and in the different fields. Because of the crucial role the values play in our society and in our individual lives, it would seem that an integrated study of values would offer significant intellectual material and rewards for scholars and potential contributions to both the professional and personal lives of citizens.

NOTE

This work was supported by Office of Naval Research Contract No. N00014-84-K-0332 and National Science Foundation Grant SES-8520167. Any opinions, findings, conclusions, or recommendations expressed in this publication are those of the author and do not necessarily reflect the views of the Office of Naval Research or the National Science Foundation.

REFERENCES

Bell, David E. (1982). "Regret in decision making under uncertainty," *Operations Research*, 30, 961–81.
(1985). "Disappointment in decision making under uncertainty," *Operations Research*, 33, 1–27.
Dyer, J. S., and Sarin, R. K. (1979). "Measurable multiattribute value functions," *Operations Research*, 27, 810–22.

Farquhar, P. H. (1977). "A survey of multiattribute utility theory and applications." In *Multiple Criteria Decision Making*, eds. M. K. Starr and M. Zeleny. Amsterdam: North-Holland/TIMS Studies in the Management Sciences, vol. 6, pp. 59–89.

Fishburn, P. C. (1970). *Utility Theory for Decision Making*. New York: Wiley.

Fryback, D. G., and Keeney, R. L. (1983). "Constructing a complex judgmental model: an index of trauma severity," *Management Science*, 29, 869–83.

Gardiner, P. C., and Edwards, W. (1975). "Public values: multi-attribute utility measurement for social decision making." In *Human Judgment and Decision Processes*, eds. M. F. Kaplan and S. Schwartz. New York: Academic Press.

Keeney, R. L. (1980). "Equity and public risk," *Operations Research*, 28, 527–34.

(1981a). "Measurement scales for quantifying attributes," *Behavioral Science*, 26, 29–36.

(1981b). "Analysis of preference dependencies among objectives," *Operations Research*, 29, 1105–20.

Keeney, R. L., and Raiffa, H. (1976). *Decisions with Multiple Objectives*. New York: Wiley.

Keeney, R. L., and Robilliard, G. A. (1977). "Assessing and evaluating environmental impacts at proposed nuclear power plant sites," *Journal of Environmental Economics and Management*, 4, 153–66.

Keeney, R. L., and Wood, E. F. (1977). "An illustrative example of the use of multiattribute utility theory for water resource planning," *Water Resources Research*, 13, 705–12.

Raiffa, H. (1982). *The Art and Science of Negotiation*. Cambridge: Harvard University Press.

Raiffa, H., Schwartz, W., and Weinstein, M. (1978). "Evaluating health effects of social decisions and programs." In *EPA Decision Making*. Washington, D.C.: National Academy of Sciences.

Sicherman, A. (1982). "Decision analysis computer program." In *Decision Framework for Technology Choice – With the Case Study of One Utility's Coal/Nuclear Choice*, vol. II. Palo Alto, California: Electric Power Research Institute Report on Project 1433-1.

Tversky, A., and Kahneman, D. (1974). "Judgment under uncertainty: heuristics and biases," *Sciences*, 185, 1124–31.

(1981). "The framing of decisions and the psychology of choice," *Science*, 211, 453–8.

V

AREAS OF APPLICATION

22

BEHAVIOR UNDER UNCERTAINTY AND ITS IMPLICATIONS FOR POLICY

KENNETH J. ARROW

A key tool in the modern analysis of policy is benefit–cost analysis. Though its origin goes back to the remarkably prescient paper of Dupuit (1844), its theoretical development came much later, after the "marginal revolution" of the 1870s, and its practical application really dates only from the period after 1950. The underlying theory is that of the notion of economic surplus, to which, after Dupuit, such major figures as Marshall, Pareto, Hotelling, Allais, and Debreu have contributed: for a remarkable synthesis, see Allais (1981).

Without going into technical details, the essential steps in the actual calculation of a surplus depend on using choices made in one context to infer choices that might be made in different contexts. If we find how much individuals are willing to pay to reduce time spent in going to work by one method, e.g., buying automobiles or moving closer to work, we infer that another method of achieving the same saving of time, e.g., mass transit or wider roads, will be worth the same amount. Frequently, indeed, we extrapolate, or interpolate; if it can be shown that the average individual will pay $1,000 a year more in rent to reduce his or her transit time by 30 minutes, we infer that a reduction of 15 minutes is worth $500. This is all very much according to Dupuit's reasoning; he would value an aqueduct by the amount that individuals would be willing to pay for the water to be transported in it (and vice versa, if the opposite inference is useful).

The assumption that choices made under different conditions are consistent with each other is then essential to the practice of benefit–cost analysis. The elaboration of these consistency conditions leads to the rationality postulates of standard economic theory. In the usual formulation, we postulate that all choices are consistent with an ordering, a transitive and complete relation, and both our theory and our practice are based on this assumption. We know, of course, that even with these assumptions there are ambiguities in the inferences that can be drawn from empirical observations to policy choices, mostly because of the so-called income effects, a point on which Walras already criticized Dupuit. But, in this chapter, I will not be concerned with this last set of issues.

We now have a new kind of benefit–cost analysis, namely, benefit–risk

497

analysis. The risk of a disutility is itself a cost and a proper subject for measurement along with the direct costs of the usual resource-using type. Similarly, a reduction in risk is to be counted as a benefit. This is true even if individuals are risk neutral, since we would still want to count the expected value of the risk; in the presence of risk aversion, there is still an additional cost or benefit, as the case may be.

Our current interest in risk–benefit analysis has been largely stimulated by concern with health hazards. In terms of public attention, though not in actuality, it is the risks associated with the operation of nuclear power plants that have appeared at the forefront. At a fundamental level, the issues in benefit–risk analysis are not different from those in more familiar welfare comparisons. Again, willingness to pay either for benefits (reduced risks) or to avoid costs (increased risks) is a crucial element. Again, it can in principle be measured by seeking out comparable situations. Thus, if air pollution control results in decreased probability of death, then one way of measuring the benefit is to find out what individuals are willing to pay to decrease this probability in other contexts. A standard method is to compare wages in industries with different occupational risks. After controlling for other factors, we find that in general hazardous occupations have higher wage rates. In equilibrium, this means that workers are indifferent at the margin between the two occupations at the given wage levels. Hence, the difference in wages can be regarded as compensation for the difference in probability of death. (Needless to say, I am ignoring many obvious complications, for example, the risks of nonfatal injury.) This provides a measure of willingness to pay for reduced probability of death, to be used in evaluating the reduction in risk due to air pollution (or automobile safety measures or anything similar).

The similarity in principle can be accepted to justify similarity in practice provided we accept some theory of rationality in individual behavior under uncertainty, which is precisely what is frequently questioned. It is this theme, the implications of current research on decision making in the presence of risk for benefit–risk analysis, that I want to pursue here.

It is necessary to call attention to one important matter on which the analogy to the case of certainty is necessarily loose, that is, the establishment of probability judgments. Benefit–cost analysis under certainty of course requires not only measures of willingness to pay but also measures of the costs of alternative policies. The analogue under uncertainty is measurement of the probabilities of different possible outcomes for each possible policy. Thus, we need the probability of death associated with each possible level of atmospheric pollution or for each possible siting and design of nuclear reactors.

Now no probability can, strictly speaking, be known from a finite sample. In many cases, the evidence is very limited indeed, so that this condition is a practical as well as a theoretical limitation. In many of the most difficult situations, those with high risks but very low probabilities, such as the possibility of a nuclear core meltdown, the evidence on the relevant uncertainty is extremely small. It may all be indirect.

This raises a new and philosophically difficult problem of rationality. Just as we need some kind of rationality hypotheses for measuring willingness to pay, under uncertainty as under certainty, we need rationality hypotheses about probability judgments. These are usually supplied in theory by the theory of subjective probabilities and applications of Bayes's theorem. But what if individuals do not make their probability judgments in this manner?

One last orientation is needed. Who is doing the benefit–risk analysis? I want to ignore all the additional complications due to the difficulties of social choice, so I will suppose that there is a representative individual. Equally, however, I do not want to reduce the solution to the uninteresting proposition that the individual should do what he or she wants. Instead, I will suppose that the analyst is a professional adviser to the individual. Both the client and the economist expect that the latter will have something to contribute by way of clarification, even though ultimately it is the client's interests that are to be served – but the client's interests as properly interpreted, not mere expression of first thoughts.

A little intellectual history will be helpful. In 1952, at a conference on the foundations of risk bearing held by the Centre National de la Recherche Scientifique of France, Allais (1953), and I (Arrow, 1953) presented independently formulated models incorporating risk bearing into the theory of general equilibrium (Allais had also presented his theory a year earlier at a meeting of the Econometric Society). As a good Paretian, Allais followed the lead of his earlier work on welfare economics (Allais, 1945) and perceived and expressed the welfare optimality that necessarily underlies any general competitive equilibrium. This is an essential first step in a benefit–risk analysis. Properly applied, it can be used to derive the shadow prices which yield the first approximations to the appropriate measures of surplus.

There are several differences between Allais's model and mine, most not very relevant to the present discussion. One that was much discussed at the conference later turned out to be irrelevant. In my paper, I assumed that individuals maximize expected utility. I accepted the Bernoulli (1738) theory as it had been updated by von Neumann and Morgenstern (1947) and by Savage (1954). Allais, as is well known, subjected that theory to very strong attack. His own view amounted to a general ordinalist position: there was an ordering of probability distributions, not necessarily linear in probabilities. This position had been advanced earlier by Hicks (1931), though he had done little with it.[1]

A few years later, Gerard Debreu (1959, chapter 7) showed that the two models could be synthesized. A theory of general equilibrium in contingent contracts did not require the Bernoulli hypothesis; it was consistent with any utility function over the outcomes. Debreu also extended the theory of paths over time, in which the uncertainties are realized successively.

Policy analysis with regard to risk, as in the case of certainty, is necessitated by failures of the competitive mechanism, that is, externalities and public goods. An individual living near a nuclear plant cannot buy safety for himself or herself alone; only collective safety can be obtained. Similarly, air pollution cannot for well-known reasons be obtained without collective action; no assignment of property rights will permit the market to achieve an optimal allocation. We use the general equilibrium model to simulate a market; what would individuals be willing to pay at the margin for changes in the externalities if they could be implemented as commodities?

I will consider four doubts about rational behavior in the presence of uncertainty which have arisen from recent empirical research and ask about their implications for the practice of benefit–risk analysis: (1) questions about the expected utility theory; (2) miscalculations of probabilities; (3) preference reversals; and (4) framing.

THE EXPECTED UTILITY HYPOTHESIS

To be concrete, let us consider the expected utility hypothesis applied to policies aimed at affecting mortality. To bring out the essence, I consider only the simplest possible case. A living individual receives a utility from consumption if alive but zero utility if dead. Let,

p = probability of survival,

U = utility,

c = consumption.

Then expected utility is,

$$pU(c). \tag{1}$$

We may think of some policy which increases p but requires resources and therefore reduces c. The willingness to pay (WTP) is then the slope of the curves on which (1) is constant, that is, the amount of consumption that an individual is willing to give up per unit probability of survival while keeping expected utility constant. We see easily that,

$$\text{WTP} = U(c)/pU'(c). \tag{2}$$

This expression has the dimensions of consumption per unit life and therefore can be and is frequently referred to as the "value of life." However, it is not what an individual would pay for the certainty of life as against the certainty of death; it is a marginal evaluation of a small change in the probability of life. Since what an individual would pay for the certainty of life is limited by initial wealth, the WTP is apt to be a good deal larger.

Suppose the Bernoulli hypothesis is false, but individuals are rational in the weaker sense of Allais and Hicks: there is an ordering of probability distributions. In the present simple context, this means that there is a utility function which depends on c and p (and is defined only up to monotone transformations):

$$U(c, p). \tag{3}$$

Again, there is a trade-off between the two variables,

$$\text{WTP} = U_p/U_c. \tag{4}$$

When a real benefit–risk analysis is done, what data are used? Suppose, as suggested above, that willingness to pay is estimated from the wage differentials to be found in riskier jobs, as in Thaler and Rosen (1976) or Viscusi (1979). Now, the probability of survival for one more year (which is what is to be compared with annual wages) depends on many factors, of which occupational safety is only one and not a major one. The observed risk differential is therefore small, so that the observed ratio of wage differential to risk differential is really a measure of (4). In fact, when one looks closely, the empirical material made no real use of the Bernoulli hypothesis as embodied in (1) and (2).

What in fact is gained by the stronger expected utility hypothesis? It is really the ability to extrapolate over large changes in p. But in practice, any feasible policy, whether in nuclear power safety, biomedical research, or occupational safety, will have only a relatively slight effect on the probability of survival over a year or other relevant period. Therefore, the strength of the Bernoulli hypothesis is never employed in practice.

The argument amounts to saying that even a general utility functional for probability distributions, if differentiable, can be regarded as approximately linear in the probabilities, if we are not considering large changes in them. This is precisely the idea so beautifully and richly developed by Machina (1982).

I cannot however, leave this subject without another restatement of the Allais problem. It is hard to believe that the paradox will occur when the alternatives are laid out in a sufficiently transparent fashion. Let us introduce a more specific temporal structure.

Suppose there are 3 time periods. At time 0, there is a chance move: it yields a payment of 1 monetary unit with probability .89. If the complementary event occurs, then at time 1 the subject is offered a choice. He or she can take 1 unit (with certainty), to be paid at time 2, or go on to time 2 and face a gamble yielding 2.5 with probability 10/11 and 0 with probability 1/11. At time 1, the possibility of an immediate payment of 1 with termination is now in the past, and there can be no question but that the individual faces and considers only the second gamble, as against certainty. Presumably, the individual will usually choose the gamble. Now suppose at time 0, the individual is asked: *if* the complementary event were to occur at the chance move coming up, *would* you choose the certainty or the gamble? This is clearly the same decision as in the first story; it requires only a certain imagination. Yet, in this form, a hypothetical choice of certainty amounts to choosing 1 with certainty as against a distribution of 2.5 with probability .10, 1 with probability .89, and 0 with probability .01.

In other words, all that is required is understanding a hypothetical choice and calculating probabilities correctly.

Now it may be that rendering the decision tree transparent may be all that is involved, in which case it suggests that the real issue is one of framing, a point to which I will return below.

MISCALCULATION OF PROBABILITIES

A more serious problem than the nonlinearity of the utility function is the calculation of the probabilities to be used in estimating the risk. There are two issues here. One is not deep conceptually; it is simply that an individual will in general simply not possess all the information available to society as a whole. The probabilities used should of course be conditional on all the information available, if the information can be assembled at a cost which is negligible compared with the improved expected benefits. Hence, there is an externality with regard to information gathering. Therefore, if the information is assembled, the expert opinion should be used to form probabilities. Presumably, any rational individual would agree to this and would voluntarily defer, as he or she does to a physician or other professional.

This observation does create some problems, not at the normative level but at that of interpreting observed choice behavior as a measure of willingness to pay to avoid risks. What is relevant is the ratio of wage difference to difference in probability of death or injury as perceived by the individuals involved. If they act not on the probabilities as estimated by a national collection of statistics but on those estimated by themselves from much more limited data, it is the latter probabilities that should be used as a divisor. There is considerable theoretical and empirical evidence in the case of occupational hazards that individuals are influenced by their own experiences (Viscusi, 1979, chapters 4 and 13). This is consistent with the view that they have little knowledge of general injury rates and therefore condition their probabilities heavily on their own experiences.

A deeper question is raised by the well-known observations, mostly by psychologists, that, even in situations where Bayes's theorem is clearly applicable, individuals do not use it correctly; for reports on such studies, see Tversky and Kahneman (1974). In most of their experiments, too little weight was given by subjects to the prior information; individuals were overly influenced by the current data. This result is consistent with other studies in different fields. Eddy (1980) showed that physicians, in relying on diagnostic tests, did not take adequate account of the underlying prevalence of the disease in forming their judgments. Thus, if a test gave a probability .9 of detecting cancer if it were there and a probability .9 of a negative response if there were no cancer, it would be regarded as highly reliable. Yet the prevalence of cancer is only about .1, which is thus the prior probability of cancer in a random choice from the population. A simple application of Bayes's theorem shows that the probability of cancer, given a positive response on the test, is .5, far less than most physicians would believe.

The misuse of Bayes's theorem is at least compatible with the evidence for volatility in the securities and futures markets. Since the value of a long-lived bond, stock, or futures contract is ultimately dependent upon a great many events which will occur in the future, it should be unresponsive to any particular piece of new information. These markets, however, are notoriously volatile, with large movements in a single day. This has been argued many times for the future markets; for a summary of the evidence, see Cagan (1981). A very rigorous analysis for the bond and stock markets (Shiller, 1979, 1981) has shown the incompatibility of observed behavior with rational expectations models, at least in a simple form. For more extended discussion of these misperceptions, see Arrow (1982).

The extent to which the average person exaggerates the risks in a possible accident to nuclear power plants is of course well known. (I hasten to add that I am not an unreserved admirer of nuclear power. The risks to the plant itself, as exemplified by the Brown's Ferry and Three Mile Island accidents, plus the costs of construction, themselves increased by safety precautions, make the economics of nuclear power very doubtful. Indeed, the main case *for* nuclear power is the social costs of coal-fired power plants in the form of atmospheric pollution caused by combustion and carbon dioxide effects on the world's climate.)

What is the normative or policy implication of this propensity to irrational judgments about uncertainty? Here, I feel strongly we must invoke the appropriate role of the expert. I have postulated a relation of professional to client, and it is certainly in judgments of reality and probability that this professional concern is most appropriate. The normative judgment may and should respect the utility functions (linear or nonlinear) of the public being advised, but it should certainly use probability judgments based both on the maximum of information and the maximum of correct statistical and probabilistic logic.

The two problems discussed thus far, the more general ordinal theory of choice among probability distributions as against the expected utility hypothesis and the miscalculation of probabilities, have been made much of by those, for example at the 1983 conference on decision making, who think of themselves as revolutionaries against an established (though rather recently established) orthodoxy. Beware! These arguments are those of the moderate revolutionaries, the Girondins or the Mensheviks. The cognitive psychologists have found evidence for worse traps; if the implications are as they seem, it is hard to see how any form of benefit–risk analysis can survive.

PREFERENCE REVERSAL

So far, transitivity has been unquestioned; and transitivity is essential to any type of benefit–cost analysis: the substitution of compensations for costs or risks depends essentially on the (usually unstated) transitivity of indifference. I have not checked the literature, but I believe that experiments do not verify transitivity fully even in the case of certainty. It was for this· reason that economists and psychologists developed notions of stochastic orderings (see, e.g., Davidson and Marschak, 1959). But experimental studies of choice under uncertainty have revealed what at the present appear to be a less remediable form of intransitivity.

I refer to the well-known phenomenon of preference reversal, first identified by Lichtenstein and Slovic (1971). Suitably chosen pairs of gambles can be found with the following characteristics: When subjects are asked to choose between the two, they express a preference for one. But when asked to state the amount of money which, if given with certainty, would be indifferent to each gamble, the amounts chosen are in opposite order to the expressed preferences.

This result is so upsetting, indeed to almost any theory of choice under uncertainty, that the experiments were carefully replicated by Grether and Plott (1979). They varied the experiments in ways designed to test various explanations (e.g., cost of information processing) which would preserve transitivity. Not only were the original results confirmed, but no simple rational explanation could be found.

This work does seem to be a major barrier to the use of risk–cost trade-offs from one area in measuring benefits and costs in another. I can only offer some observations derived from earlier work in consumer demand theory as a partial solution.

The comparisons in the preference reversal experiments are global or long-range rather than local. The identification of certainty equivalents requires comparison of two alternatives, one risky, one certain, which are far from each other in an reasonable metric. This distinction was considered also in the theory of consumer's choice under certainty; it is the essence of what has been called the integrability problem. There are many variations in the literature. One is the proposed theory advanced by Hicks and Allen (1934) and Georgescu-Roegen (1936): At each point in commodity space, there is a local indifference map (hence, transitive and complete ordering), but it is an additional assumption that the local indifference maps integrate into a global indifference map permitting indifference judgments across large differences in alternatives.

The very meaning of optimality and therewith the meaning of a benefit–risk analysis as a basis for policy is in principle undermined if comparisons are only local. One might conceivably have a series of local improvements which cycle.

In practice, though, it could be argued, though not with entire conviction, that the possibilities of paradox do not really arise. As we have already argued with relation to policies which affect the probability of death, any feasible changes are apt to be small. Hence, only the local indifference maps are relevant. In that case, the theoretical possibility of cycling will not be realized. To put the matter another way, the willingness-to-pay data used in benefit–risk analysis do not really measure comparison of gambles with certainties. Rather, they compare gambles with small differences in probabilities and stakes. Therefore, the preference reversal phenomenon need not occur in the choices which are the basis for benefit–risk analysis.

The most damning criticism of risk–benefit analysis from experiments is the evidence for what Tversky and Kahneman (1981) have called "framing." An element of rationality, so obvious to the analyst as to pass almost unnoticed, is its *extensionality*, to use the language of logic. That is, if a choice is to be made from a set of alternatives, the choice should depend only on the membership in the set and not on how the set is described. If I have to choose which night of next week I will go to a place, it should not matter if each alternative is labeled by the day of the week or the numbered day of the month. If my budget permits me to divide $1,000 between housing costs and other expenditures, my alternatives can be identified indifferently in terms of either of the two kinds of costs.

Yet the lesson of the framing experiments is precisely that these invariances do not hold. How the choice question is framed affects the choice made.[2] Let me draw a dramatic illustration from a paper on the choice of medical therapy by McNeil, Pauker, Sox, and Tversky (1982). McNeil and some of her colleagues have had a program, which economists and decision theorists should applaud, of letting the patients' values affect medical decision making. In this study, a comparison was being made between two therapies, surgery and radiation therapy, for the treatment of certain forms of cancer. A therapy defines a probability distribution of length of survival. In general, surgery has a positive risk of mortality during the operation, for which there is no counterpart in radiation therapy, but it has a longer expected survival even when this risk is taken into account. Different groups of individuals, including a group of physicians, were presented with the probabilities of survival during treatment, for one year, and for five years for each of the two therapies. With these data, 84% of the physicians preferred surgery, 16% radiation therapy. Then another group was presented with the same data presented differently: the probabilities of dying at each stage were given instead of the probabilities of survival. At each stage, the probability of dying is 1 minus the probability of survival, so the two formulations are not merely logically equivalent but can be transformed into each other by a trivial calculation. Yet the proportion of physicians choosing surgery over radiation therapy dropped from 84% to 50%.

I leave the implications of framing for benefit–risk analysis as an open problem. Economists would tend to argue that the choices made in the market, where the stakes to the individual are high, reflect the correct choice of frame. But this is probably too complacent a view. It may well be true that the individual makes different trade-offs in contexts which, to the analyst, appear to be identical. But this is a deep topic for further study.

NOTES

First published in B. P. Stigum and F. Wenstøp (eds.) (1983). *Foundations of Utility and Risk Theory with Applications*. The Netherlands: Reidel, 19–32.

1 In the development of his specific general equilibrium model, Allais assumed that all distributions were normal, and therefore individuals were assumed to order distributions according to their means and variances. However, I take this to be a particular application, not the underlying general principle.

2 The rest of this paragraph is drawn, with slight modification, from Arrow (1982).

REFERENCES

Allais, M. (1945). *Économie pure et rendement social*. Sirey, Paris.

(1953). "Généralisation des théories de l'équilibre économique général' et du rendement social au cas de risque," in *Économétrie*, Colloques Internationaux de Centre National de la Recherche Scientifique, XL, Paris, pp. 81–109.

(1981). *La Théorie génerale des surplus*. Institut des Sciences Mathematiques et Economiques Appliquées, Paris.

Arrow, K. J. (1953). "Rôle des valeurs boursières pour la répartrition la meilleure des risques," in *Économétrie*, Colloques Internationaux du Centre National de la Recherche Scientifique, XL, Paris, pp. 41–7.

(1982). "Risk perception in psychology and economics," *Economic Inquiry*, 20, 1–9.

Bernoulli, D. (1738). "Specimen theoriae novae de mensura sortis," *Commentarii academiae scientiarum imperiales Petropolitanae* 5, 175–92.

Cagan, P. (1981). "Financial future markets: is more regulation needed?" *Journal of Future Markets*, 1, 169–90.

Davidson, D., and Marschak, J. (1959). "Experimental tests of a stochastic decision theory," in C. W. Churchman and P. Ratoosh (eds.) *Mathematical Models of Human Behavior*. Dunlap and Associates, Stamford, Conn. Reprinted in J. Marschak, *Economic Information, Decision, and Prediction*, Volume I, pp. 133–71. Reidel, Dordrecht, The Netherlands, and Boston, Mass., 1974.

Debreu, G. (1959). *Theory of Value*. Wiley, New York.

Dupuit, J. (1844). "De la mesure de l'utilité des travaux publics," *Annales de ponts det Chaussées*, 2ième Série, 8.

Eddy, D. (1980). *Screening for Cancer: Theory, Analysis, and Design*. Prentice-Hall, Englewood Cliffs, N.J.

Georgescu-Roegen, N. (1936). "The pure theory of consumers' behavior," *Quarterly Journal of Economics*, 50, 545–93.

Grether, D., and Plott, C. (1979). "Economic theory of choice and the preference reversal phenomenon," *American Economic Review*, 69, 623–38.

Hicks, J. R. (1931). "The theory of uncertainty and profit," *Economica*, 11, 170–89.

Hicks, J. R., and Allen, R. G. D. (1934). "A reconsideration of the theory of value," *Economica*, 1, 52–76.

Lichtenstein, S., and Slovic, P. (1971). "Reversal of preferences between bids and choices in gambling decisions," *Journal of Experimental Psychology*, 89, 46–55.

Machina, M. (1982). "'Expected utility' analysis without the independence axiom," *Econometrica*, 50, 277–324.

McNeil, B. J., Pauker, S. G., Sox, Jr., H. C., and Tversky, A. (1982). "On the elicitation of preferences for alternative therapies," *New England Journal of Medicine*, 306, 1259–62.

Savage, L. J. (1954). *The Foundations of Statistics*, Wiley, New York.

Shiller, R. J. (1979). "The volatility of long-term interest rates and expectations models of the term structure," *Journal of Political Economy*, 87, 1190–213.

(1981). "Do stock prices move too much to be justified by subsequent changes in dividends?" *American Economic Review*, 71, 421–36.

Thaler, R., and Rosen, S. (1976). "The value of saving a life," in N. Terleckyj (ed.), *Household Production and Consumption*. National Bureau of Economic Research, Washington, pp. 265–98.

Tversky, A., and Kahneman, D. (1974). "Judgment under uncertainty: heuristics and biases," *Science*, 185, 1124–31.

(1981). "The framing of decisions and the psychology of choice," *Science*, 211, 453–31.

Viscusi, W. K. (1979). *Employment Hazards: An Investigation of Market Performance*. Harvard University Press, Cambridge, Mass.

von Neumann, J., and Morgenstern, O. (1947). *Theory of Games and Economic Behavior*, 2nd edition, Princeton University Press.

23

THE RELEVANCE OF QUASI RATIONALITY IN COMPETITIVE MARKETS

THOMAS RUSSELL AND RICHARD THALER

Smart
My dad gave me one dollar bill
'cause I'm his smartest son,
And I swapped it for two shiny quarters
'cause two is more than one!

And then I took the quarters
And traded them to Lou
For three dimes – I guess he don't know
That three is more than two!

Just then, along came old blind Bates
And just 'cause he can't see
He gave me four nickels for my three dimes
And four is more than three!

And I took the nickels to Hiram Coombs
Down at the seed-feed store,
And the fool gave me five pennies for them,
And five is more than four!

And then I went and showed my dad,
And he got red in the cheeks
And closed his eyes and shook his head –
Too proud of me to speak!

Shel Silverstein
Where the Sidewalk Ends
Copyright © 1974 by Snake Eye Music, Inc.
New York: Harper & Row, 1974
(Reproduced with permission of the publisher)

Economists generally attribute considerable rationality to the agents in their models. The recent popularity of rational expectations models is more an example of a general tendency than a radical departure. Since rationality is simply *assumed*, there is little in the literature to suggest what would happen if some agents were not rational. This is surprising in light of the accumulating evidence that supports Herbert Simon's view that man should be considered at most boundedly rational. In fact, Kenneth Arrow concludes his recent review of this evidence as follows: "I hope to have made a case for the proposition that an important class of intertemporal markets shows systematic deviations from individual rational behavior and that these deviations are consistent with evidence from very different sources." (1982, p. 8).

In this chapter we start to explore the implications of irrationality for economics. We begin by defining what we mean by rational, and what departures from rationality we think are most likely. We then consider what happens if rational and less than fully rational agents (whom we call quasi rational) interact in competitive markets. We show that the knee-jerk reaction of some economists that competition will render irrationality irrelevant is apt only in very special cases, probably rarely observed in the real world. Our analysis highlights the important roles played by arbitrageurs and entrepreneurs. We find that, perhaps counter to intuition, more competition can actually make things worse by leaving no possibility of a profit to an entrepreneur who offers education or information.

RATIONALITY, QUASI RATIONALITY, AND FRAMING

Suppose two individuals face the same budget set, but choose different consumption bundles. What could be the reason? Three distinctly different reasons can be identified: (1) the individuals have different tastes (utility functions); (2) the individuals have different information; (3) one of the individuals has made a mistake. In this chapter we are primarily concerned with behavior of the third type, so we need a method of modeling mistakes.

There is no place for mistakes in the conventional economics framework. In part, this is because of the difficulty of identifying nonrational (by which we mean non-utility-maximizing) behavior. Consider, for example, the observation of a single purchase. The prices that an agent faces determine a budget hyperplane, and any point on that hyperplane that the agent chooses supports some indifference surface. Thus any chosen point can be consistent with maximization.

Suppose we examine more than one expenditure. Is it possible, on the basis of a *series* of expenditures, to characterize these acts as rational or nonrational? Defining rational now to mean maximizing for a single,[1] increasing concave utility function, the answer is a qualified yes. If the actions contain within them a violation of the weak axiom of revealed preference (which is to say, that we observe both *a* chosen when *b* is affordable, and *b* chosen when *a* is affordable), then it can be concluded that no fixed increasing strictly concave function is being maximized. Typically economists have looked for violations of the weak axiom in the choices made by agents confronted with different budget sets. Unfortunately, as Hal Varian (1982) has shown, the price income data of the real world seldom oblige by providing other than nested budget sets, so much of the time violations of the weak axiom are simply not possible.

Another way in which, in principle, one could seek violations of the weak axiom is to present the agent with the same budget set, but presented in different ways. Then his choice must not change. This hypothetical test was first suggested by the inventor of the technique of revealed preference, Paul Samuelson (1983). Samuelson considered the following problems. Suppose that we confront an agent with an income–price vector (Y, p) and observe the choice x. Now confront the agent with the income–price vector (mY, mp) where m is a positive constant. Unless the consumer again chooses x, the weak axiom is being violated. The reason is simple. By multiplying both income and prices by m we do not change the budget set. Thus any choice $y \neq x$ at (mY, mp) violates the axiom.

The same approach has been used more recently by cognitive psychologists to demonstrate simple violations of rationality. In a remarkable series of experiments, Daniel Kahneman and Amos Tversky (1979, 1981) have shown that subjects presented with the same problem (budget set) described in different ways repeatedly change their responses. Kahneman and Tversky call such victories of form over substance "framing" effects.

The violations which Kahneman and Tversky find are not only prevalent, they are systematic. That is to say, depending on how the problem is framed, it can be predicted whether the agent will choose x or y. We propose calling any such regular yet nonrational behavior *quasi rational*. Quasi-rational behavior will include some actions that can be considered mistakes in the classification scheme described above. To incorporate such mistakes in a model of a competitive market, an extra feature has to be added to the characterization of consumer behavior. The extra feature captures the consumer's process of translating raw information into a perceived budget set.

Suppose, then, that we think of agents as being given not budget sets but the ingredients from which they can construct a budget set. Call this the information set I. Assume that the individual constructs the budget set B from I using a mapping which we call F so that $B = F(I)$.[2] Once the agent has B, we know from standard duality theory that maximizing choices can be represented as the appropriate derivatives of an indirect utility function U defined on B. With the approach suggested here, U is actually defined on I so that we have $U(F(I))$ as the integral of the maximizing choices.

What is the nature of F? It may have subjective elements but F is not entirely subjective. It should, for example, conform to the laws of mathematics. Thus, if I is a sample drawn from some population with replacement, then F should not depend on the order in which the observations are drawn or recorded. In some cases, the mapping from I to B will be so obvious that we would expect no one to get it wrong. Kahneman and Tversky call such mappings *transparent*. The cases of interest are those where the mapping is more complex or, as they say, *opaque*.

There is no shortage of evidence documenting human judgments which fail to satisfy rational objective standards. In many cases (see Kahneman, Paul Slovic, and Tversky, 1982) these lapses seem to be associated with the use of a rule of thumb (i.e., the representativeness heuristic, and the availability heuristic) in which the decision maker sometimes focuses on irrelevant aspects of the information set in constructing his budget set.

This suggests a useful distinction between correct and incorrect mappings. We label the correct (or set of correct)[3] mapping F^* and any incorrect mappings F'.[4] We now have the apparatus to characterize all three reasons referred to earlier why choices (under the same budget set) may diverge: (1) differences in I; (2) differences in U; or (3) differences in F. Those choices consistent with an indirect utility function $U(F^*(I))$ are considered rational while those based on any other mapping, F', are considered quasi rational. The term quasi rational has been chosen to capture both the rational maximizing that is suggested by the systematic regularities shown in the experimental data (subjects do not choose at random) and the inconsistencies with the axioms of rational choice.

The existence of the mapping F is not completely foreign to economics. In expected utility theory, for example, the agent has a preference function over consequences but chooses acts. A mapping F from acts to consequences is needed to construct the budget set. In a subcase of this, portfolio theory of the Markowitz mean-variance type, investors observe the prices of assets but have preferences over the mean and variance of returns. Again a mapping F is needed to construct the relevant budget set. Indeed in financial economics the implication of heterogeneity in F is an ongoing area of investigation (Joram Mayshar, 1983; Robert Jarrow, 1983). We are here assuming not just heterogeneity in F, but the existence of a correct and incorrect F. As we shall see, however, some of the structure is identical. Finally, even in decision making under certainty, the new economic theory of the consumer of Kelvin Lancaster (1966) and Gary Becker (1965) in which consumers have preferences over characteristics but purchase market goods, requires a mapping from goods to characteristics in order to construct the budget set.

The existence of the mapping F enables us to characterize *in principle* even a single choice as nonrational. Suppose we give a consumer information concerning two choices, x and y, and that, under the true mapping F^*, x and y are identical but y is cheaper. If an individual buys x, that is nonrational. Nevertheless, it is virtually impossible to classify an act as nonrational *in practice* because of the difficulty in controlling for differnces in tastes $U(.)$, or in information I.

This suggests precisely the role of the laboratory experiment. By controlling for tastes and information it is possible to identify F, and in this way conclude that the behavior is indeed nonrational. It is true that, for every real world example of quasi-rational behavior we can offer, rationality cannot be ruled out. This, however, in no way rules it in. At the present state of our knowledge, it seems we must allow the possibility that some behavior is quasi rational. Nevertheless, with few exceptions, economists have tended to ignore the work of the cognitive psychologists and have continued to investigate markets with only rational agents. Why is the experimental work given so little attention? Economists have generally been critical of these results for the following reasons:

(1) "Much of the research is based on hypothetical questions. Thus respondents have little incentive to respond properly." These critique has been examined by David Grether and Charles Plott (1979) and by Grether (1980) in their replications of work by psychologists. In both studies the quasi-rational behavior was at least as strong in a condition with monetary incentives as in a condition with purely hypothetical questions. Thus while skepticism of hypothetical questions may be reasonable, the evidence about quasi rationality cannot be attributed solely to this problem.

(2) "The experiments are done in the laboratory." While this statement is true, there is other evidence of irrational behavior outside of the lab. For example, Howard Kunreuther *et al.* (1978) found irrational factors to be very important in determining who would buy government-subsidized flood insurance.

(3) "In the real world, people will learn." There are two responses to this critique. First, the subjects have not yet learned to choose according to our normative theories, otherwise one would not obtain the reported experimental results. Secondly, as Hillel Einhorn and Robin Hogarth (1978) have emphasized, many situations will not provide feedback in a way that will facilitate learning. Without well-structured feedback, learning may be negligible.

(4) "Economists are interested in aggregate behavior and these individual errors will wash out when we aggregate." Since the errors that have been identified are systematic (i.e., in a predictable direction), this statement is just wrong. However, there is a more subtle version of this idea.

(5) "Markets will eliminate the errors." While this statement is sometimes made, it is not clear by what mechanism markets will eradicate irrational choices. While it has been argued that evolution will eventually eliminate firms that choose improperly, there is no such process at work for individuals. So far as we know, quasi rationality is rarely fatal.

In summary, there is a large body of experimental evidence suggesting that humans make judgments and decisions in a way that can be characterized as quasi rational. This evidence cannot be dismissed easily. It therefore seems prudent to begin to inquire about the workings of markets in which some agents are quasi rational. Do the quasi rationals affect prices? Does a competitive market protect or exploit the quasi-rational segment? What roles do arbitrageurs and entrepreneurs play? It is to these questions we now turn.

MARKETS WITH QUASI-RATIONAL AGENTS

We will investigate competitive markets with two kinds of agents, rational and quasi rational. To capture the quasi-rational behavior, we use an extended Lancastrian model of consumption. Consumers purchase goods in the market but derive utility from the characteristics the goods possess rather than from the goods *per se.* There is an objective mapping from goods to characteristics. The rational consumers perceive this mapping. The quasi rationals perceive a different incorrect mapping.[5]

Model 1: the basic model[6]

We begin by considering the simplest possible model which includes both rational and quasi-rational agents and allows competitive behavior. We make the following assumptions.

Preferences. All individuals are assumed to have the same preferences[7] over two characteristics:

$$U = C_1^{1/2} + C_2. \tag{1}$$

We concentrate our attention on characteristic 1, C_1, so that characteristic 2, C_2, should be thought of as an aggregate of all other characteristics. We assume that all individuals have the same income Y, and that this income is high enough for C_2 to be bought.

The objective characteristics technology. Characteristic 1 is contained in two goods, g_1 and g_2, and only in these goods. Characteristic 2 is contained in the aggregate good g_3 and only in g_3. By Walras's law we need only consider equilibria in the markets for g_1 and g_2. We assume

$$g_1 = C_1; \quad g_2 = \beta C_1 \tag{2}$$

is the true consumption technology relating quantities of characteristics to quantities of goods. Note that, by saying $g_2 = \beta C_1$, we mean that to obtain one unit of C_1 we must purchase β units of g_2.

The quasi-rational mapping. Quasi-rational agents believe that the relationship in (2) is actually

$$g_1 = C_1; \quad g_2 = \gamma C_1 \quad \gamma \neq \beta. \tag{3}$$

The number of agents. L agents are rational, M quasi rational.

Supply. There is a fixed supply of goods 1 and 2, $\bar{g}_1, \bar{g}_2$.

Demand. Let P_i = price of good i, $i = 1, 2, 3$. Let P_{ci} = price of characteristic i, $i = 1, 2$. Normalize prices by setting $P_3 = P_{c2} = 1$. Then as a function of P_{c1}, the price of characteristic 1, demand for characteristic 1 can be written as

$$D_{C1} = \frac{1}{(2P_{c1})^2}. \tag{4}$$

If good 1 is bought, the price per unit of characteristic 1 is $P_{C1} = P_1$. If good 2 is bought, $P_{C1} = P_2\beta$. Obviously buyers will buy C_1 at what seems to them to be the lower price. Thus rational demands D^R are given by

$$D_1^R = (1/(2P_1)^2, 0, t/(2P_1)^2)$$
$$D_2^R = (0, \beta/(2\beta P_2)^2, (1-t)/(2P_1)^2)$$

as

$$P_1 < \beta P_2, \quad P_1 > \beta P_2, \quad P_1 = \beta P_2,$$

where t is an arbitrary scalar $0 \leqslant t \leqslant 1$. Quasi-rational demands for goods 1 and 2 are the same with β replaced with γ.

Now we have

Proposition 1. A necessary condition for an equilibrium to be a rational equilibrium is that

$$P_1^* = \beta P_2^*.$$

Proof: Unless this condition is satisfied, rational individuals will not buy both goods.

From this we may deduce

Proposition 2. Let $\gamma < (>)\beta$. Then a necessary condition for an equilibrium to be a rational equilibrium is that

$$M/L \leqslant \gamma \bar{g}_2/\beta^2 \bar{g}_1 \quad (M/L \leqslant \bar{\beta} g_1/\bar{g}_2).$$

Proof: Let $\gamma < \beta$. Then at any rational price pair $P_1^q = P_2\beta$ quasi rationals will not buy good 1. Clear the market in good 2 using only quasi-rational demand. Then

$$M\gamma/(2\gamma P_2^*)^2 = \bar{g}_2$$

so that

$$P_2^* = M/4\gamma\bar{g}_2.$$

For rationality we must have

$$P_1^* = \beta P_2^* = \beta\sqrt{M/4\gamma\bar{g}_2}.$$

At this price total demand for good 1 is given by

$$L/\beta\sqrt{M/4\gamma\bar{g}_2}.$$

We will fail to have a rational equilibrium if this is less than the total supply of good 1, i.e., if

$$L\gamma\bar{g}_2/\beta^2 M < \bar{g}_1,$$

from which the inequality in the proposition follows.

Now let $\gamma > \beta$. Then the quasi rationals will not buy good 2. Repeating the argument we see that we must have rational demand for good 2 greater than or equal to $\bar{g}_2$ from which the inequality follows. QED.

Note that, in this example, when $\gamma > \beta$ the degree of error does enter the condition for rationality. On the other hand, when $\gamma < \beta$, the condition does not involve γ. Why is there this asymmetry?

In the model we have assumed that the quasi rationals make an error in evaluating only good 2. When they do not buy this good, as when $\gamma > \beta$, this error cannot affect the outcome. This result is quite general. When there are more characteristics than goods, errors in evaluating goods which are not bought cannot affect the outcome.

Note also that, although the quasi linear utility function is itself quite special, the presence of γ in the conditions for rationality does not depend in any vital way on the special nature of this function. In general when $\gamma < \beta$, proposition 2 will look like

$$L\beta P_2(M, y, \bar{g}_2, \gamma) \geq \bar{g}_1,$$

where P_2 is the price which clears the market for good 2 when only the quasi rationals buy it. Obviously P_2 in general depends on γ.

Proposition 2 states that a rational equilibrium will not obtain if there are "too many" quasi-rational consumers. The next proposition follows directly.

Proposition 3. There exist equilibria which are not rational equilibria.

This result demonstrates that the existence of markets is not sufficient to eliminate the effect of quasi-rational behavior. This market, however, has two special features which help sustain the quasi rationality: (1) the only way to trade characteristics is to trade goods; (2) there are no short sales. Both of these features are important and are analyzed in turn.

Markets for characteristics

One way in which characteristics could be traded directly is if they could be "stripped" from the goods and sold separately. This may or may not be feasible. For example, it is possible to disassemble an automobile and sell all of its parts, but it is not possible to disassemble and sell its relevant characteristics such as ride, handling, fuel economy, comfort, etc. An extreme case of interest is where characteristics can be decomposed costlessly.

Proposition 4. If characteristics can be decomposed and marketed costlessly, then a rational equilibrium will obtain.

Proof: Suppose $\gamma > \beta$. Then if equilibrium were not rational, $P_1 > P_2\beta$. But this would mean that P_{C1} to the quasi rationals who buy good 1 is greater than P_{C1} to the rationals who buy good 2. Thus the law of one price does not hold in characteristics, yielding an incentive for the rationals to buy good 2, strip it of its CX_1, repackage C_1 in good 1 and sell it at a profit. (There is likewise an apparent incentive for the quasi rationals to repackage in reverse, but we assume this will immediately reveal the true relationship between goods and characteristics, and so will not occur.) The action of the rationals will thus drive up the price until $P_1 = \beta P_2$.

In goods markets the cost of characteristics stripping is determined by production technology. In asset markets, however, characteristic stripping is not so much a matter of technology as it is the number of markets and cost of using the markets. For example,[8] with a low-cost futures market in Treasury bills, a six-month Treasury bill can be stripped of its three-month component by selling a three-month futures contract in the bill. This means that the price of three-month T-bills and the combination of one six-month T-bill and one three-month future T-bill cannot get far out of line, even if financial officers of corporations have a preference for simple contracts such as three-month bills and are willing to pay a premium for such contracts.

Costless characteristics repackaging *de facto* sets up a market in characteristics so that the law of one price in characteristics must hold. In the absence of this market, a market in goods is not, in general, a substitute for a market in characteristics.

Short selling

In goods markets it is not generally feasible to take a short position. Markets are just not organized in a way that allows a speculator to borrow and sell Chrysler automobiles or Heinz ketchup in the expectation of a future drop in price. Short selling is permitted in some financial markets, however, and so to extend our analysis to include those markets we explore the ramifications of permitting short sales.

Proposition 5. Short selling will guarantee that the equilibrium is rational provided: (a) within the time space that g_1 and g_2 are traded, there exists a time T^* such that after T^* the true relationship between characteristics and goods is known to everyone; (b) only the rationals sell short.

Proof: Again assume $\gamma > \beta$. Then, if the equilibrium is not rational, $P_1 > P_2\beta$. But, at time T^*, $P_1 = P_2\beta$. Thus short selling by the rationals will be profitable and will force P_1 into equality with $P_2\beta$.

The two extra conditions are necessary to ensure that an equilibrium exists and that short selling is riskless.[9] If the quasi rationals sell short, and if $P_1 = P_2\beta$, they will believe g_2 is overvalued and will wish to sell it short. Thus no equilibrium will exist. The assumption that only rationals sell short is not unreasonable if rationality is associated with professional market participants.

It might be called the Marshallian view based on the following from Alfred Marshall:

> The private purchaser of railway shares may know nothing [about its prospects, the ability of its management, and the propriety of its accounts], but he buys with the confidence that all such points have been scrutinized by many keen men with special knowledge, who are able and ready to "bear" the stock if they find it in any weak spot, which . . . had not been allowed for in making up its value. (cited in Mayshar, 1983, pp. 126–7, fn. 25)

The condition that the true mapping be revealed is necessary to create a pure arbitrage opportunity (some chance of gain, no chance of loss). If characteristic stripping is impossible, then knowledge of the true mapping between goods and characteristics is not sufficient to create an arbitrage opportunity. Only if the quasi rationals become informed can the correct price be assured.

Of course, in most nonfinancial markets, characteristic stripping is not costless and short selling is impossible. In these situations (within model 1) quasi rationals do influence prices, and the rational price equilibrium need not obtain.

Production

Up to now we have been assuming that both goods are in fixed supply. To allow for production we will consider three cases: increasing costs, constant costs, and decreasing costs. Formal proofs follow the same lines as above so we just present the results.

Increasing costs. If both goods are produced with technologies involving increasing marginal costs, then the results of the previous section are qualitatively the same. A rational equilibrium can obtain as long as the number of quasi rationals in the economy is small enough.

Constant marginal costs. The constant marginal cost case is a knife-edge situation. Competition assures that price equals marginal cost so both goods can only coexist if the ratio of marginal costs is exactly equal to β. The size of the two groups of consumers is irrelevant.

Decreasing marginal costs. When both goods are produced with economies of scale, then a rational equilibrium can occur with both goods existing. Also, if the quasi rationals are large enough in number and the goods are close enough in efficiency cost, then the quasi rationals can lead to the wrong good being produced. The rationals in this case recognize that it will be cheaper for them to join the quasi rationals than to buy their preferred (*ex ante*) good.[10]

Comparison with results in finance

The models of fixed supply presented so far are very close in structure to a class of models in financial economics first introduced by John Lintner (1969).

In these models, individuals have different beliefs concerning the mean and variance of assets. The reasons for these different beliefs are not investigated so there is no counterpart to our notion of rationality and quasi rationality, but still the market is composed of individuals with different beliefs, and this assumption might be expected to produce similar results.

In an important sense, however, our results are quite different. In the financial models *à la* Lintner, market prices reflect all beliefs. For that reason Lintner himself found the extension of the model to heterogeneous beliefs basically uninteresting, since everything that was true for homogeneous individuals now became true for the "the market." In the models we discuss, market prices may give zero weight to the beliefs of one class of agents. Why the difference? The reason hinges on special assumptions made in the financial literature which prevent the financial system from breaking up into subsystems. Because assets are assumed to be joint normally distributed and agents are assumed to have exponential utility functions, all individuals hold all assets. For that reason, asset prices reflect all beliefs. In our model, because there are more goods than characteristics and because the technology is linear, it is possible for rational agents completely to escape the influence of quasi-rational agents by specializing in consumption of the good(s) which the quasi rationals cause to be underpriced. It is precisely this force that can restore rationality to the market. Obviously a necessary condition for this to occur is that there are more goods than characteristics. As the finance examples make clear, this is not sufficient. If, for any reason, all goods are bought by all agents, quasi rationals must influence prices. Thus the examples we discussed earlier are actually biased toward the result that market prices will be fully rational, since they permit rational agents to form their own subeconomies.

AN EXAMPLE

As we emphasized in the introduction, it is generally not possible to prove that any act or set of actions is generated by quasi-rational behavior. Differences in tastes and/or information can rarely be ruled out completely. Nevertheless, we present here some data from a market where the law of one price (for characteristics) is violated. While a plausible quasi-rational explanation can be given, as usual rational-based explanations can also be made. Our purposes, therefore, are just to give an example of how a market might turn out when a quasi-rational rule of thumb is widely used, and to use the example to address some other theoretical issues.

Table 23.1. *Real costs of dishwashing liquid*

Group	Number of brands in the group	Average price	Efficiency factor	Real cost
A	8	1.97	1.0	1.97
B	6	1.60	1.4	2.24
C	19	.97	2.7	2.61
D	2	.72	4.7	3.36

Source: Consumer Reports, July 1984, p. 413.

Dishwashing liquid

In 1981 Consumers Union (CU) conducted a study of the price and efficiency of dishwashing liquids. The study was replicated in 1984 with very similar results. We will present the more recent data. Thirty-five brands of dishwashing liquids were tested for their ability to wash dishes. Few differences among brands were discovered on most dimensions, but wide variation was found on the number of dishes a given quantity of the brand could wash. This "dishes washed per squirt" measure was called an efficiency factor. Brands were placed into four groups according to their efficiency factor. Brands in the top group were arbitrarily given an efficiency factor of 1.0. By multiplying the nominal price of the brand by the efficiency factor, a "real cost" was calculated. If the law of one price holds for the characteristic "dishes washed," then the real cost of each brand should be about the same.

Table 23.1 presents CU's results. As can be seen, the law of one price fails to hold. There is a clear negative relationship between the nominal selling price and the real cost. The most expensive brands are usually the best buys. There may, of course, be other characteristics, such as kindness to hands. However, CU found little difference on these dimensions. Furthermore, the most expensive brands are likely to have more of *all* the (positive) characteristics so adding more characteristics would probably strengthen the results.

We think the most plausible explanation for this finding is that some consumers confuse the mapping from price per bottle to price per dish washed. It is well known in marketing that many consumers have a general tendency to buy either the cheapest brand or the most expensive brand. This tendency represents a shopping strategy that greatly reduces decision-making costs at the supermarket. It may well be *rational* to use such a strategy. It would take so long to fully analyze every decision for a single week's family shopping expedition that some simplifying strategies must be used. In cases where quality or taste is easy to judge, a family may learn to make specific alterations to their general strategy ("Don't buy generic cola"). In other cases, such as the dishwashing liquid, a family would have to do some fairly sophisticated testing to determine that its usual "buy cheap" strategy was (in this case) inappropriate.

Since this market has remained stable over the last few years (and probably for much longer), it becomes interesting to ask why the inefficient brands survive. We will consider four forces that could push the (characteristics) market back into equilibrium: arbitrage, entry, education, and tied sales.

Arbitrage and entry

Arbitrage would be possible if one could profitably buy the expensive brands, dilute them, and sell the diluted product as a cheap brand. However, there is no reason to think this is possible. Entry into the "no frill," generic dishwashing liquid market is relatively free. There are unlikely to be profits to be made by entering this market. The high real cost of these brands probably represents the high fixed cost of packaging and distribution. Literally buying the high-priced brands off the shelf and diluting them for resale is surely an unprofitable venture, and, since the data do not necessarily imply extraordinary profits in any segment, entry alone cannot be expected to solve the problem.

Education

One of the high-price/low-cost brands of dishwashing liquid has, from time to time, run an advertising campaign that stresses the true economy of their brand relative to the low-cost "so-called bargain brands." This is an example of a firm trying to educate the quasi-rational segment. Whenever a consumer can be educated at a cost that is less than his potential gain from switching to the efficient product, a profit opportunity exists. However, ironically, this education will not take place if the market is truly competitive. With perfect competition, no one seller can charge a premium above marginal cost and so there is no incentive to pay the costs of education. Only if there is some monopolistic element, such as brand names, will there be a potential return to education. Even then, the educator runs the risk that the education will not be brand specific, so other high-cost brands may be able to free ride at the educator's expense.

Tied sales

Jerry Hausman (1979) has done a careful study of consumer purchases of air conditioners. He finds, much as in the dishwashing liquid example, that more expensive air conditioners are better buys because they are generally more energy efficient. He reports that the average purchase implies a discount rate of 25% after considering utilization rates and energy costs. Furthermore, the implicit discount rates vary systematically with income. Purchases by low-income households imply discount rates of 27%, 39%, and 89% in the three lowest income classes in Hausman's sample. These rates are all much higher than the prevailing borrowing rates (around 18% on most credit purchases) at that time.[11]

Hausman discusses several possible solutions to the apparently inefficient purchases being made. One is of particular interest here:

> Another possible type of market solution would be to have utility companies purchase appliances and lease them to their customers. Presumably utilities would be willing to engage in such activity, since they could borrow money to finance the more energy-efficient appliances and then charge a rental rate which would leave the consumer better off. Utilities could develop expertise in choosing the optimal efficiency model in terms of climate and intended utilization and help their customers make a better choice. (p. 51)

While Hausman's idea is along the right lines, it may not go far enough. What the utility would have to do to be sure of getting optimal choices is to rent the air conditioners with the utility costs included in the rental. Only by tying the sale of the air conditioner services with the purchase of the electricity could the possibility of quasi-rational choices be ruled out. Of course, other problems such as monitoring utilization might prevent such an arrangement from succeeding. Nevertheless, the theoretical point of interest here is that only by creating a market in the ultimate consumption commodity (the characteristics in the model) can the seller guarantee rational choices.

It is interesting to compare this conclusion with that made by Richard Posner in a similar case:

> The leverage theory (of tie-in sales) held that if a seller had a monopoly of one product, he could and would monopolize its indispensable complements as well, so as to get additional monopoly profits. Thus, if he had a patented mimeograph machine, he would lease the machine at a monopoly price and also require his lessees to buy the ink used in the machine from him and charge them a monopoly price for the ink. This procedure, however, makes no sense as a matter of economic theory. The purchaser is buying a service, mimeographing. *The pricing of its components is a mere detail*; it is, rather, the total price of the service that he cares about. If the seller raises the price of one component, the ink, the purchaser will treat this as an increase in the price of the service. If the machine is already being priced at the optimal monopoly level, an increase in the price of the ink above the competitive level will raise the total price of the service to the consumer above the optimal monopoly level and will thereby reduce the monopolist's profits. (1979, p. 929, emphasis added)

Posner, of course, explicitly assumes rational consumers. He says that to do otherwise would be "inconsistent with the premises of price theory." But, if even some consumers are quasi rational, then the way the prices of the various components of a good are framed is no longer a "mere detail." Indeed, framing effects in particular, and quasi rationality generally , open the possibility that repackaging goods via tie-in sales and other similar devices can increase both consumer welfare and monopoly profits. Thus the "Chicago" position on tie-in sales (to permit them) may be right, though for the wrong reasons.

CONCLUSION

When we assume that consumers, acting with mathematical consistency, maximize utility, therefore, it is not proper to complain that men are much more complicated and diverse than that. So they are, but, if this assumption yields a theory of behavior which agrees tolerably well with the facts, it must be used until a better theory comes along. (George Stigler, 1966, p. 6)

There are two possible justifications for the use of maximizing models in applied microeconomics. As Stigler suggests above, one justification is that the models are good predictors. This is the usual "as if" position. The alternative justification is that markets guarantee that only rational behavior can survive. Our reading of the psychology literature referred to earlier suggests that the first justification is frequently violated. Deviations from maximizing behavior are both common and systematic. The implication of the current paper is that the second justification will rarely apply, except (perhaps) in some highly efficient financial markets. Where does that leave us?

First of all, our analysis suggests that research on individual decision making is highly relevant to economics whenever predicting (rather than prescribing) behavior is the goal. The notion that individual irrationalities will disappear in the aggregate must be rejected. However, as Stigler implies, the neoclassical theory will not be abandoned until an acceptable (superior) alternative is available. Such theories will have to be explicitly descriptive rather than normative. The usual approach in economics is to solve for the optimal solution to a problem, and then to *assume* the agents in the model chose accordingly. Thus the model is supposed to be simultaneously normative and descriptive. A model such as Kahneman and Tversky's (1979) prospect theory abandons any claim to normative value. It simply tries to describe human behavior. Thaler and H. M. Shefrin's 1981 self-control theory as saving is in a similar spirit. Both theories seem to fit the data well. It is worth mentioning that both of these models are still basically maximizing. Quasi rationality does not imply random choice.

In the absence of such behaviorally motivated alternative theories, one intermediate step can be taken. A standard practice in applied work is to use the theory to impose restrictions to the empirical estimates. The estimates are then forced to satisfy the restrictions. In the absence of evidence to support the *assumption* that the theory describes behavior, a simple precaution is to do the estimates in an unconstrained fashion whenever that is possible. For example, Grether gave subjects in an experiment a Bayesian revision task in which they *should* equally weight the (given) prior odds and likelihood ratio. He then estimated how they *did* combine the data and found that the subjects on average overweighted the likelihood ratio. The model he estimated would outperform an alternative model that assumed proper Bayesian revision. Until better theories are developed, such a theoretical estimation procedures seem appropriate.

Our analysis also has implications for the use of evolutionary arguments in economics. In a review of Richard Nelson and Sidney Winter's 1982 book on this subject, Michael Spence says that "markets discipline agents and modify their behavior." This statement is clearly true for agents within firms, but has limited applicability to individuals acting as consumers or investors. In fact, the more efficient the market, the *less* discipline the market provides. In a fully arbitraged market, all goods (assets) yield the same characteristics per dollar (returns), thus individuals can choose in any manner without penalty. Only in less than fully efficient markets is there any penalty to quasi rationality.

NOTES

The first version of this chapter was presented at a conference at Cornell University sponsored by the Center for the Study of the American Political Economy. Thaler wishes to acknowledge and thank the Alfred P. Sloan Foundation for financial support. We have received helpful critical comments from Sherwin Rosen, Joachim Sylvestre, Rex Thompson, and Hal Varian. The usual disclaimer applies. The first published version appeared in *The American Economic Review*, 75 (1985), 1071–82. It was revised for this book.

1 The word single is crucial, since if tastes are allowed to change, or if a taste for "variety" is permitted, then virtually any set of actions can be rationalized.
2 The language used here promises more than it delivers. The use of such terms as mapping and information sets does not mean that we have a mathematically rigorous theory of this process, and is meant to be suggestive only.
3 We need not be concerned here with whether F^* is unique. It is sufficient for our analysis that we be able to identify some incorrect mapping F'.
4 The mixture of subjectivity and required consistency appears also in the subjective theory of probability. It is discussed in very clear terms by Bruno de Finetti (1977).
5 A similar notion is used in Douglas Auld (1972) and Claude Colantoni *et al.* (1976).
6 This section has benefited from the helpful comments of Keith Berry.
7 It might be thought that it would be easier to work this example with a Cobb–Douglas utility function. However, it is easy to show that, if we combine Cobb–Douglas preferences with the simple linear consumption technology we are about to introduce, the demand for goods is independent of the technical coefficients. This result is not robust so we work with a less common but more general class of utility function.
8 This example is discussed in Edwin Elton *et al.* (1982).
9 In the finance literature on arbitrage pricing, these two conditions appear as: (1) all investors agree on the state representation; (2) all investors agree on probability zero events.
10 A similar problem is analyzed by John Haltiwanger and Michael Waldman (1985). They call increasing costs congestion and decreasing costs synergy.
.11 Air conditioners are rarely purchased by the very poor so most buyers probably have access to at least installment-buying-type credit.

REFERENCES

Arrow, Kenneth (1982). "Risk perception in psychology and economics," *Economic Inquiry*, 20, 1–9.

Auld, Douglas (1972). "Imperfect knowledge and the new theory of demand," *Journal of Political Economy*, 80, 1287–94.

Becker, Gary S. (1965). "A theory of the allocation of time," *Economic Journal*, 75, 493–517.

Colantoni, Claude S., Davis, Otto, A., and Swaminuthan, Malati (1976). "Imperfect consumers and welfare comparisons of policies concerning information and regulation," *Bell Journal of Economics*, 7, 602–18.

Einhorn, Hillel J., and Hogarth, Robin M. (1978). "Confidence in judgment: persistence in the illusion of validity," *Psychological Review*, 85, 395–416.

Elton, E., Gruber, M., and Rentzler, J. (1982). "Intra day tests of the efficiency of the Treasury bills futures market," Working Paper no. CSFM-38, Columbia Business School.

de Finetti, Bruno (1977). *Theory of Probability*, vols. 1, 2. London: Longmans.

Grether, David (1980). "Bayes rule as a descriptive model: the representativeness heuristic," *Quarterly Journal of Economics*, 95, 537–57.

Grether, David., and Plott, Charles (1979). "Economic theory of choice and the preference reversal phenomenon," *American Economic Review*, 69, 623–38.

Haltiwanger, John, and Waldman, Michael (1985). "Rational expectations and the limits of rationality: an analysis of heterogeneity," *American Economic Review*, 75, 326–40.

Hausman, Jerry (1979). "Individual discount rates and the purchase and utilization of energy-using durables," *Bell Journal of Economics*, 10, 33–54.

Jarrow, Robert (1983). "Beliefs, information, martingales and arbitrage pricing," Working Paper, Cornell Graduate School of Management.

Kahneman, David, and Tversky, Amos (1979). "Prospect theory: an analysis of decision under risk" *Econometrica*, 47, 263–91.

—— (1981). "The framing of decisions and the psychology of choice," *Science*, 211, 453–8.

Kahneman, Daniel, Slovic, Paul, and Tversky, Amos (1982). *Judgment Under Uncertainty: Heuristics and Biases*, Cambridge University Press.

Kunreuther, Howard *et al.* (1978). *Disaster Insurance Protection: Public Policy Lessons*, New York: Wiley & Sons.

Lancaster, Kelvin J. (1966). "A new approach to consumer theory," *Journal of Political Economy*, 74, 132–57.

Lintner, John (1969). "The aggregation of investors' diverse judgments and preferences in purely competitive markets," *Journal of Financial and Quantitative Analysis*, 4, 347–400.

Mayshar, Joram (1983). "On divergence of opinion and imperfections in capital markets," *American Economic Review*, 73, 114–28.

Nelson, Richard, and Winter, Sidney (1982). *An Evolutionary Theory of Economic Change*, Cambridge: Harvard University Press.

Posner, Richard (1979). "The Chicago school of antitrust analysis," University of Pennsylvania *Law Review*, 127, 925–52.

Samuelson, Paul A. (1983). *Foundations of Economic Analysis*, Cambridge: Harvard University Press.

Stigler, George (1966). *The Theory of Price*, New York: Macmillan.

Thaler, Richard, and Shefrin, H. M. (1981). "An economic theory of self-control," *Journal of Political Economy*, 89, 201–2.

Varian, Hal R. (1982). "The nonparametric approach to demand analysis," *Econometrica*, 50, 945–73.

24

HOW SENIOR MANAGERS THINK

DANIEL J. ISENBERG

It is not enough to have a good mind.
The main thing is to use it well.
René Descartes

Jim LeBlanc phoned Steve Baum, who formerly worked in his division, to ask about the CEO's new corporate task force on quality control that wanted to meet with Jim. Jim, the head of the industrial equipment division of Tanner Corporation, thought that Steve, now director of technology, could help him figure out why the task force wanted to meet with him in two weeks.

"It's because you're doing so damn well down there, boss!" Steve replied.

"Gee, thanks. By the way, Steve, what's the agenda for Singer's staff meeting for next week?" (Singer was the president and Jim's boss.)

"Well, we're going to talk about the reorganization and look at the overhead reduction figures for each division. Then Singer's going to report on last week's executive committee meeting and his trip to Japan."

"How did it go?"

"His telex from Osaka sounded enthusiastic, but he just got in last night and I haven't seen him yet."

"Well," said Jim, "I guess we'll just have to see, but, if you hear something, call me right away because if Osaka comes through I'm going to have to hustle to get ready, and you know how Bernie hates to shake it. Now, about the task force.."

In the space of three minutes, Jim LeBlanc got a lot done. In addition to collecting critical information about a task force that the CEO, with unusual fanfare, had personally commissioned one month ago, he also began to plan his approach to the upcoming staff meeting. He decided *not* to try to get a presentation by his marketing people on opportunities in the Far East on the agenda. Sensing that Singer *was* optimistic about the Osaka trip, Jim decided that he should get his people ready for the possibility that the deal would materialize, which meant pulling engineers off another project for a while.

What were the thinking processes that allowed Jim to get so much done so pointedly and so rapidly? What was going on in his mind during his conversation

525

with Steve? How, given the incomplete and uncertain information that Steve gave him, did Jim conclude that the Japan deal was imminent?

For the past two years I have studied the thought processes used by more than a dozen very senior managers while on the job.[1] The managers that I studied ranged in age from their lower 40s to their upper 50s, in managerial experience from 10 to 30 years, and in current job tenure from 4 months to 10 years. Their companies ranged from $1 billion divisions in *Fortune* "100" companies to $10 million entrepreneurial companies just beginning to take hold in the marketplace. Company products included low- and high-technology goods, and markets ranged from rapidly expanding to precipitately deteriorating. All but two of the executives were responsible for the overall performance of their business units. As all had been frequently promoted throughout their careers and were considered excellent performers across the board, they were a representative sample of today's successful business executives.

Two findings about how senior managers do *not* think stand out from the study. First, it is hard to pinpoint if or when they actually make decisions about major business or organizational issues on their own. And, secondly, they seldom think in ways that one might simplistically view as "rational", i.e., they rarely systematically formulate goals, assess their worth, evaluate the probabilities of alternative ways of reaching them, and choose the path that maximizes expected return. Rather, managers frequently bypass rigorous, analytical planning altogether, particularly when they face difficult, novel, or extremely entangled problems. When they do use analysis for a prolonged time, it is always in conjunction with intuition.

Let me make myself clear. Obviously, decisions *do* get made in organizations and these *are* frequently justified by data and logic. In particular, when viewed retrospectively over a long time period, effective executives often appear quite rational. Yet when studying their concurrent thinking processes, being "rational" does not best describe what the manager presiding over the decision-making process thinks about nor *how* he or she thinks.

I have a fourfold purpose in this article. First, I want to present a more accurate and empirically grounded description of what goes on inside the minds of senior managers. (See the insert on the good and bad news about cognition.) Secondly, I hope to offer a more accurate description of managerial thinking that should help provide a beginning language for talking about these elusive mental phenomena. Thirdly, I hope that this language will also help to relieve some managers of the inconsistency between their view of how they are "supposed to" think and the thinking processes that, through experience, they have learned are actually quite effective. Fourthly, I want to take advantage of successful senior managers' experiences to explore the managerial implications of their thinking processes.

WHAT SENIOR MANAGERS THINK ABOUT

Senior managers tend to think about two kinds of problems: how to create

Some good and bad news about cognition

Although the study of cognition is not new, in the past 30 years the popularity and practical importance of the "cognitive sciences" have increased dramatically, adding to our knowledge of the capabilities and limitations of the human mind. The news is both "good" and "bad" in terms of our accuracy as judges and decision makers.

Some good news

The good news is that each of us possesses a wide range of cognitive capabilities, including many that even the most powerful computers cannot match. For all intents and purposes the long-term storage capacity of the human memory is unlimited, capable of storing perhaps trillions of bits of information. Furthermore, much of this memory is almost immediately accessible.

The human mind is also capable of performing very complicated simulations such as giving directions to someone on how to get to an office from an airport or rehearsing an upcoming meeting. We are also capable of making huge inferential leaps with rarely a hitch. Try interpreting the following sentences: "The manager prepared the forecast using an accepted inflation estimate. He knew that it was imprecise but figured that it was better than no projection at all." Who is "he"? What is "it"? What does "projection" refer to? We know what these sentences mean, yet to interpret them correctly required the reader to make a number of inferences, which he or she usually makes with unhesitating accuracy.

Finally, we are capable of using our unlimited memory, our rapid retrieval system, and our unconscious rules of inference to attain extremely high levels of skill, such as playing chess, analyzing stocks, conducting performance appraisals, or speaking a language. These skills do not come easily, requiring years of experience and many thousands of hours of practice. Nevertheless, when we use them we compress years of experience and learning into split seconds. This compression is one of the bases of what we call intuition as well as of the art of management.

Some bad news

The same cognitive processes that underlie our greatest mental accomplishments also account for incorrigible flaws in our thinking. For instance, we easily believe that salient events occur more frequently than they really do: for example, despite the fact that dozens of examples exist where missed budgets did not lead to the termination, managers interpret Sam's being fired for not making a budget as "There is a good chance that division heads who do not meet budgeted profit objectives will get axed."

A second family of flaws arises from our overconfidence in our own expertise at making complex judgments. Various cognitive biases, such as the "hindsight bias," our retrospective confidence in judgments that we hesitated about making at the time ("I *knew* it wouldn't work when she first proposed it"), and our tendency to search for confirming but not for conforming evidence of our judgments, conspire to exaggerate that belief.

And, finally, research, has shown that when presented with data, we are not very good at assessing the degree of relationship among variables – even though this skill is critical for successful management. Unless the relationships are very obvious, we tend to rely on preconceptions and perceive illusory correlations.

A number of excellent books on human cognition are in print. For a nontechnical discussion of the good news, Morton Hunt's *The Universe Within* (New York: Simon & Schuster, 1982), is a good starting place. A more technical discussion of human cognition is Stephen K. Reed's *Cognition: Theory and Applications* (Brooks/Cole, 1982). A somewhat technical but very comprehensive presentation of the bad news can be found in Daniel Kahneman, Paul Slovic, and Amos Tversky's edited volume, *Judgment Under Uncertainty: Heuristics and Biases* (Cambridge University Press, 1982).

effective organizational processes and how to deal with one or two overriding concerns, or very general goals. These two domains of thought underlie the two critical activities that John P. Kotter found general managers engaged in: developing and maintaining an extensive interpersonal network, and formulating an agenda.[2]

A focus on process

The primary focus of on-line managerial thinking is on organizational and interpersonal processes. By "process" I mean the ways managers bring people and groups together to handle problems and take action. Whether proposing a change in the executive compensation structure, establishing priorities for a diverse group of business units, consolidating redundant operations, or preparing for plant closings, a senior executive's conscious thoughts are foremost among the processes for accomplishing a change or implementing a decision: "Who are the key players here, and how can I get their support? Whom should I talk to first? Should I start by getting the production group's input? What kind of signal will that send to the marketing people? I can't afford to lose their commitment in the upcoming discussions on our market strategy."

During the first months of his tenure, one area general manger I studied asked all of his business unit management teams to evaluate their own units. Subsequently, the area manager and his staff spent a day or more with each team discussing the whole area, each business unit within it, and how the two interrelated. Although he was concerned with the substance of the business-unit priorities, uppermost in his mind was a series of process concerns: How could the review process help managers be increasingly committed to their goals? How could the process help managers to become increasingly aware of the interdependencies among business units? How did his business unit managers use their people in reviewing their business units? How much management depth existed in the units?

In addition to thinking about organizational processes, successful senior managers think a lot about interpersonal processes and the people they come in contact with. They try to understand the strengths and weaknesses of others, the relationships that are important to *them*, what *their* agendas and priorities are.

For example, the CEO of a small high-technology company spent over an hour with his personnel director, a woman he rated as having performed excellently so far and whom he saw as having great potential although still inexperienced. At the time of the discussion, the CEO was considering adopting a new top-management structure under which the personnel director would report to another staff member rather than directly to him.

The CEO exlained the proposed change to the personnel director, pointing out that it was not definite and that he was soliciting her reactions. Managers' "maps" of people provide them with guides to action. In this case, because of his sense of the personnel director's needs, the CEO slowed the reorganizing process so that the people who reported to him could deal with the various issues that arose.

The CEO elaborately described to me his awareness of the personnel director's concern at being new and at being a woman, and her desire to be in direct contact with him. He also understood her worry that, if she reported to someone lower than him, people would perceive that the new personnel function was not very important and she would lose power.

The overriding concern

The stereotypical senior executive pays a great deal of attention to the strategy of the business, carefully formulates goals, lays out quantified and clear objectives, and sets about to achieve these objectives in the most efficient way. Whereas senior executives certainly attend to specific strategies and objectives some of the time, in their day-to-day reality specific objectives lurk in the background, not in the forefront of their thoughts.

Approximately two-thirds of the senior managers I studied were preoccupied with a very limited number of quite general issues, each of which subsumed a large number of specific issues. This preoccupation persisted for anywhere from a month to several years and, when in effect, dominated the manager's attention and provided coherence to many of his or her chaotic and disorganized activities.

The general manager of one large division of an automobile company, for example, used the word "discipline" over a dozen times in the course of a two-hour interview. For him, this concept embodied his deep concern for creating order and predictability in a division that, in his view, had become too loose before he took it over. His concern for discipline appeared in a number of diverse actions – strongly discouraging his subordinates' fire-fighting mentality, criticizing their poor preparation for corporate reviews, introducing rigorous strategic planning, encouraging time management, putting out a yearly calendar with divisional and corporate meetings printed on it, publishing agendas for many of these meetings up to a year in advance, and, by keeping recent reports in the top draw of his desk, forcing himself to review frequently the division's activities and performance.

Regardless of its substance, the overriding concern weaves its way in and out of all the manager's daily activities, at times achieving the dimensions of an all-consuming passion.

After his first 100 days in office, an area general manager described his experience turning around a subsidiary in these words:

> The personal cost of achieving our top priorities has been huge. I dropped all outside activities. Now I have a feeling of just having emerged, like a chap who's been taken up by a surf wave and rolled. Suddenly he comes up and can look at daylight again. It has been like a single-minded rage or madness. At the end of the 100 days, somehow I have awakened. It was overwhelming.

Of course senior managers do think about the content of their businesses, particularly during crises and periodic business reviews. But this thinking is always in close conjunction with thinking about the process for getting *others* to think about the business. In other words, even very senior managers devote most of their attention to the tactics of implementation rather than the formulation of strategy.

HOW SENIOR MANAGERS THINK

In making their day-by-day and minute-by-minute tactical maneuvers, senior executives tend to rely on several general thought processes such as using intuition; managing a network of interrelated problems; dealing with ambiguity, inconsistency, novelty, and surprise; and integrating action into the process of thinking.

Using intuition

Generations of writers on the art of management have recognized that practicing managers rely heavily on intuition.[3] In general, however, people have a poor grasp of what intuition is. Some see it as the opposite of rationality, others use it as an excuse for capriciousness, and currently some view it as the exclusive property of a particular side of the brain.

Senior managers use intuition in at least five distinct ways. First, they intuitively sense when a problem exists. The chief financial officer of a leading technical products company, for example, forecast a difficult year ahead for the company and, based on a vague gut feel that something was wrong, decided to analyze one business group. "The data on the group were inconsistent and unfocused," he said after doing the analysis. "I had the sense that they were talking about a future that just was not going to happen, and I turned out to be right."

Secondly, managers rely on intuition to perform well-learned behavior patterns rapidly. Early on, managerial action needs to be thought through carefully. Once the manager is "fluent" at performance, however, and the behavior is programmed, executives can execute programs without conscious effort. In the words of one general manager:

> It was very instinctive, almost like you have been drilled in close combat for years and now the big battle is on, and you really don't have time to think. It's as if your arms, your feet, and your body just move instinctively. You have a preoccupation with working capital, a preoccupation with capital expenditure, a preoccupation with people, and one with productivity, and all this goes so fast that you don't even know whether it's completely rational, or it's part rational, part intuitive.

Intuition here refers to the smooth automatic performance of learned behavior sequences. This intuition is not arbitrary or irrational, but is based on years of painstaking practice and hands-on experience that build skills. After a while a manager can perform a sequence of actions in a seamless fabric of action and reaction without being aware of the effort.

A third function of intuition is to synthesize isolated bits of data and experience into an integrated picture, often in an "aha!" experience. In the words of one manager: "Synergy is always nonrational because it takes you beyond the mere sum of the parts. It is a nonrational, nonlogical thinking perspective."

Fourthly, some managers use intuition as a check (a belt-and-suspenders approach) on the results of more rational analysis. Most senior executives are familiar with the formal decision analysis models and tools, and those that occasionally use such systematic methods for reaching decisions are leery of solutions that these methods suggest that run counter to their sense of the correct course of action.

Conversely, if managers completely trusted intuition, they would have little need for rigorous and systematic analysis. In practice, executives work on an issue until they find a match between their "gut" and their "head." One manager explained to me, "Intuition leads me to seek out holes in the data. But I discount casual empiricism and don't act on it."

Fifthly, managers can use intuition to bypass in-depth analysis and move rapidly to come up with a plausible solution. Used in this way, intuition is an almost instantaneous cognitive process in which a manager recognizes familiar patterns. In much the same way that people can immediately recognize faces that were familiar years ago, administrators have a repertoire of familiar problematic situations matched with the necessary responses. As one manager explained:

> My gut feel points me in a given direction. When I arrive there, then I can begin to sort out the issues. I do not do a deep analysis at first. I suppose the intuition comes from scar tissue, getting burned enough times. For example, while discussing the European budget with someone, suddenly I got the answer: it was hard for us to get the transfer prices. It rang a bell, then I ran some quick checks.

By now it should be clear that intuition is not the opposite of rationality, nor is it a random process of guessing. Rather, it is based on extensive experience both in analysis and problem solving and in implementation, and, to the extent that the lessons of experience are logical and well-founded, then so is the intuition. Further, managers often combine gut feel with systematic analysis, quantified data, and thoughtfulness.

It should also be clear that executives use intuition during *all* phases of the problem-solving process: problem finding, problem defining, generating and choosing a solution, and implementing the solution. In fact, senior managers often ignore the implied linear progression of the rational decision-making model and jump opportunistically from phase to phase, allowing implementation concerns to affect the problem defining and perhaps even to limit the range of solutions generated.

Daniel J. Isenberg

Problem management

Managers at all levels work at understanding and solving the problems that arise in their jobs. One distinctive characteristic of top managers is that their thinking deals not with isolated and discrete items but with portfolios of problems, issues, and opportunities in which (1) many problems exist simultaneously, (2) these problems compete for some part of his or her immediate concern, and (3) the issues are interrelated.

The cognitive tasks in problem management are to find and define good problems, to "map" these into a network, and to manage their dynamically shifting priorities. For lack of a better term, I call this the process of problem management.

Defining the problem

After learning of a state health organization threat to exclude one of their major products from the list of drugs for which the state would reimburse buyers, top executives in a pharmaceutical company struggled to find a proper response. After some time, the managers discovered that the relation problem was not the alleged drug abuse the availability of the drug on the street caused. Rather, the problem was budgetary: the health services department had to drastically reduce its budget and was doing so by trimming its list of reimbursable drugs. Once they redefined the problem, the pharmaceutical executives not only could work on a better, more real problem, but also had a chance to solve it – which they did.[4]

In another case, a division general manager discovered that, without his knowledge but with the approval of the division controller, one of his vice presidents had drawn a questionable personal loan from the company. The division manager told me how he defined the problem: "I could spend my time formulating rules to guide managers. But the real fundamental issue here was that I needed to expect and demand that my managers manage their resources effectively." Although he recognized the ethical components involved, he chose to define the problem as concerned with asset management rather than cheating. Because asset management was an issue the division frequently discussed, the manager felt that it was more legitimate and efficacious to define the problem in this way.

Making a network of problems

By forming problem categories, executives can see how individual problems interrelate. For instance, a bank CEO had a "network" of at least 19 related problems and issues that he was concerned about. Among these were: establishing credibility in international banking, strengthening the bank's role in corporate banking, increasing the range of financial services and products, being prepared to defensively introduce new products in response to competitors' innovations, developing systems to give product cost information, reducing operational costs, standardizing branch architecture, and utilizing space efficiently.

The bank CEO classified these problems in terms of broad issue categories. He found that many were related to the issue of expanding and broadening the bank's competence beyond consumer banking in which it was already firmly established. A second overarching issue was standardization of the bank's many branches with regard to architecture, physical layout, accounting systems, and so on.

Having an interrelated network of problems allows a manager to seize opportunities more flexibly and to use progress on one problem to achieve progress on another, related issue. The bank CEO likened himself to a frog on a lily pad waiting for the fly – the problem or issue – to buzz by. Having a mental network of problems helped him to realize the opportunities as they occurred.

Choosing which problem to work on

Although managers often decide to work on the problem that seems to offer the best opportunities for attack, determining which problems they ought to tackle can be hard. As one manager commented:

> I have to sort through so many issues at once. There are ten times too many. I use a number of defense mechanisms to deal with this overload – I use delaying actions, I deny the existence of problems, or I put problems in a mental queue of sorts. This is an uncomfortable process for me. My office and responsibility say I need to deal with all of these issues, so I create smoke or offer some grand theory as my only way to keep my own sanity. One of the frustrations is that I don't want to tell my people that their number one problems have lower priorities than they think they should get.

In my observations, how managers define and rank problems is heavily influenced by how easy the problems are to solve. Very shortly after perceiving that a problem exists, managers run a quick feasibility check to see if it is solvable. Only if they find it is solvable will they then invest further energy to understand its various ramifications and causes. In other words, managers tend not to think very much about a problem unless they sense that it is solvable. Contrary to some management doctrines, this finding suggests that a general concept of what is a possible solution often precedes and guides the process of conceptualizing a problem.

Thus, the two stages of problem analysis and problem solving are tightly linked and occur reiteratively rather than sequentially. By going back and forth between these two cognitive processes, managers define the array of problems facing them in terms that already incorporate key features of solutions and that thus make it easier for them to take action.

One outcome of this process is that managers have an organized mental map of all the problems and issues facing them. The map is neither static nor permanent; rather, managers continually test, correct, and revise it. In the words of one CEO, the executive "takes advantage of the best cartography at his command, but knows that that is not enough. He knows that along the way he will find things that change his maps or alter his perceptions of the terrain. He trains himself the best he can in the detective skills. He is endlessly sending out patrols to learn greater detail, overflying targets to get some sense of the general battlefield."

Tolerating ambiguity

The senior managers that I observed showed an ability to tolerate and even thrive on high degrees of ambiguity and apparent inconsistency. As one top executive said:

> I think ambiguity can be destroying, but it can be very helpful to an operation. Ambiguities come from the things you can't spell out exactly. They yield a certain freedom you need as a chief executive officer not to be nailed down on everything. Also, certain people thrive on ambiguity, so I leave certain things ambiguous. The fact is we tie ourselves too much to linear plans, to clear time scales. I like to fuzz up time scales completely.

Because demands on a manager become both stronger and more divergent as responsibility increases, the need to tolerate apparent ambiguity and inconsistency also increases. For example, the top manager has to deal with stakeholders who may have adversarial roles. By responding positively to one set of demands, the managers automatically will create other conflicting sets of demands.

The reason I have called the inconsistency "apparent" is that senior managers tend to have ways of thinking that make issues seem less inconsistent. For example, the president of a leading high-technology company was considering whether to exercise or forgo an option to lease land on which to build expensive warehouse space for one of the divisions at the same time as the division was laying off workers for the first time in its history. "To spend a half million dollars on keeping the land and building warehouse space while the plant is laying off people looks terrible and makes no sense," he said, "but, if next year is a good year, we'll need to be in a position to make the product."

Perceiving and understanding novelty

The managers I observed dealt frequently with novel situations that were unexpected and, in many cases, were impossible to plan for in advance. For example, one division general manager found himself with the task of selling his division, which was still developing a marketable product. In response to its shareholders, the corporation had shifted its strategy and thus decided to divest itself of the fledgling division. How should the general manager look for buyers?

If buyers were not forthcoming, would the corporation retain a stake to reduce the risk to potential new partners? How should he manage his people in the process of selling? Should he himself look for a new position or commit himself to a new owner? These were some of the unique questions the division head faced while selling his own division, and there was no industry experience to give him clear answers.

In general, the human mind is conservative. Long after an assumption is outmoded, people tend to apply it to novel situations. One way in which some of the senior managers I studied counteract this conservative bent is by paying attention to their feelings of *surprise* when a particular fact does not fit their prior understanding, and then by highlighting rather than denying the novelty. Although surprise made them feel uncomfortable, it made them take the cause seriously and inquire into it – "What is behind the personal loan by my vice president of sales that appears on the books? How extensive a problem is it?" "Why did the management committee of the corporation spend over an hour of its valuable time discussing a problem three levels down in my division?" "Now that we've shown the health services department beyond a reasonable doubt that this drug is not involved in drug abuse, why don't they reinstate it on the list?"

Rather than deny, downplay, or ignore disconfirmation, successful senior managers often treat it as friendly and in a way cherish the discomfort surprise creates. As a result, these managers often perceive novel situations early on and in a frame of mind relatively undistorted by hidebound notions.

WHAT TO DO ABOUT THINKING

Having looked at the inner workings of the managerial mind, what insights can we derive from our observations? Literally hundreds of laboratory studies demonstrate that the human mind is imperfectly rational, and dozens of additional articles, offering arguments based on every field of study from psychology to economics, explain why.[5] The evidence that we should curtail our impractical and overly ambitious expectations of managerial rationality is compelling.

Yet abandoning the rational ideal leaves us with two glaring problems. First, whether managers think in a linear and systematic fashion or not, companies still need to strive toward rational action in the attainment of corporate goals, particularly in their use of resources. Secondly, we still need to spell out what kinds of thinking processes are attainable and helpful to senior managers.

Program rationality into the organization

Of course, rationality is desirable and should be manifest in the functioning of the company. One alternative to the vain task of trying to rationalize managers is to increase the rationality of organizational systems and processes. Although organizational behavior is very completely rational, managers can design and program processes and systems that will approach rationality in resource allocation and employment.

Decision support systems are one source of organizational rationality. These generally computerized routines perform many functions ranging from providing a broad and quantitative data base, to presenting that data base in easily understandable form, to modeling the impact of decisions on various financial and other criteria, to mimicking expert judgment such as in the diagnosis and repair of malfunctioning equipment or in oil field exploration.

Another rational process that many businesses employ is strategic planning. Nonrational or partly rational managers can devise, implement, and use a plan that systematically assesses a company's strengths and weaknesses, logically extrapolates a set of its competencies, proposes a quantitative assessment of environmental constraints and resources, and performs all these tasks in a time-sequenced, linear fashion.

Of course, companies have used rational systems for information gathering, strategic planning, budgeting, human resource planning, environmental scanning, and so forth for a long time. But I see these systems not only as useful but also as a necessary complement to a manager's apparent inability to be very systematic or rational in thought.

But is it possible for imperfectly rational managers to design even more perfectly rational systems? The answer is a qualified yes. There is evidence, for example, that with help people can design systems that are better than they are themselves at making judgments.[6] Creating organizational systems to improve on their own behavior is not new to managers. In order to still hear the beautiful sirens yet prevent himself being seduced by the music and throwing himself into the sea, Ulysses ordered his men to block their own ears with wax, bind him to the mast, and tighten his bindings if he ordered them to let him go. Although Ulysses begged his sailors to release him, they obeyed his original orders and Ulysses succeeded in both hearing the sirens and surviving their perilous allure.[7]

Programming rationality into the organizational functioning is important for another reason: rational systems free senior executives to tackle the ambiguous, ill-defined tasks that the human mind is uniquely capable of addressing. Many senior managers today face problems – developing new products for embryonic markets, creating new forms of manufacturing operations, conceiving of innovative human resource systems – that are new to them and new to their companies and that they can deal with only extemporaneously and with a nonprogrammable artistic sense. In fact, it may even seem paradoxical that managers need to create rational systems in order to creatively and incrementally tackle the nonrecurrent problems that defy systematic approaches.

Hone intellectual skills

In the literature on managerial behavior there is disagreement as to how much or how often senior managers engage in thoughtful reflection. Many executives that

I studied do make time for in-depth thinking, sometimes while they are alone, sometimes with their peers or subordinates, and sometimes in active experimentation.

Furthermore, most senior managers I studied constantly maintain and sharpen their intellectual abilities in order to better analyze their current or past experiences. Rigorous thinking is a way of life for them, not a task they try to avoid or to expedite superficially.

These senior managers read books outside their fields, engage in enthusiastic discussions of political and economic affairs, attend academic lectures and management seminars, and tackle brain teasers such as word problems, chess, and crossword puzzles. One company president I studied is a regular theatergoer who can discuss Shakespearean and contemporary plays at great length, while another often immerses himself in classical music and allows ideas about difficult work-related issues to float around in his consciousness. These activities are valuable not only for their content but also for the thinking processes that they establish, develop, and refine. Whether managers indulge in such "blue sky" irrelevant activities at work or outside, they are developing critical mental resources that they can then apply to problems that arise in their jobs.

Think while doing

One of the implications of the intuitive nature of executive action is that "thinking" is separable from acting. Since managers often "know" what is right before they can analyze and explain it, they frequently act first and think later. Thinking is inextricably tied to action in what I call thinking/acting cycles, in which managers develop thoughts about their companies and organizations not by analyzing a problematic situation and then acting, but by thinking and acting in close concert. Many of the managers I studied were quite adept at using thinking to inform action and vice versa.

Given the great uncertainty of many of the management or business issues that they face, senior managers often instigate a course of action simply to learn more about an issue: "We bought that company because we wanted to learn about that business." They then use the results of the action to develop a more complete understanding of the issue. What may appear as action for action's sake is really the result of an intuitive understanding that analysis is only possible in the light of experience gained while attempting to solve the problem. Analysis is not a passive process but a dynamic, interactive series of activity and reflection.

One implication of acting/thinking cycles is that action is often part of defining the problem, not just of implementing the solution. Frequently, once they had begun to perceive the symptoms, but before they could articulate a problem, the managers I studied talked to a few people to collect more information and confirm what they already knew. The act of collecting more data more often than not changed the nature of the problem, in part because subordinates then realized that the problem was serious enough to warrant the boss's attention.

Managers also often acted in the absence of clearly specified goals, allowing these to emerge from the process of clarifying the nature of the problem.

Yet how often do managers push their subordinates to spell out *their* goals clearly and specify *their* objectives? A creative subordinate will always be able to present a plausible and achievable goal when pressed, but in the early stages of a tough problem it is more helpful for managers to provide a receptor forum in which their people can play around with an issue, "noodle" it through, and experiment. Sometimes it will be necessary for managers to allow subordinates to act in the absence of goals to achieve a clearer comprehension of what is going on, and even at times to *discover* rather than achieve the organization's true goals.

Manage time by managing problems

All managers would like to accomplish more in less time. One of the implications of the process of mapping problems and issues is that when a manager addresses any particular problem, he or she calls a number of related problems or issues to mind at the same time. One byproduct is that a manager can attain economies of effort.

For example, when working on a problem of poor product quality, a division manager might see a connection between poor quality and an inadequate production control system and tackle both problems together. To address the issues, she could form a cross-functional task force involving her marketing manager, who understands customers' tolerance for defects. (One reason for bringing him in might be to prepare him for promotion in two or three years.) She might intend the task force to reduce interdepartmental conflicts as well as prepare a report that she could present to corporate headquarters.

Managers can facilitate the process of creating a problem network in many ways. They can ask their staff to list short- and long-term issues that they think to be addressed, consolidate these lists, and spend some time together mapping the interrelationships. Or they can ask themselves how an issue fits into other nonproblematic aspects of the company or business unit. How does product quality relate to marketing strategy? To capital expenditure guidelines? To the company's R&D center with a budget surplus? To the new performance appraisal system? To the company's recent efforts in affirmative action? To their own career plans? Managers should never deal with problems in isolation. They should always ask themselves what additional related issues they should be aware of while dealing with the problem at hand.[8]

Some suggestions

A number of suggestions on how managers can improve their thinking emerge from my study of senior managers' thought processes:

Bolster intuition with rational thinking. Recognize that good intuition requires hard work, study, periods of concentrated thought, and rehearsal.

Offset tendencies to be rational by stressing the importance of values and preferences, of using imagination, and of acting with an incomplete picture of the situation.

Develop skills at mapping an unfamiliar territory by, for example, generalizing from facts and testing generalities by collecting more data.

Pay attention to the simple rules of thumb – heuristics – that you have developed over the years. These can help you bypass many levels of painstaking analysis.

Do not be afraid to act in the absence of complete understanding, but then cherish the feelings of surprise that you will necessarily experience.

Spend time understanding what the problem or issue is.

Look for the connections among the many diverse problems and issues facing you to see their underlying relationships with each other. By working on one problem you can make progress on others.

Finally, recognize that your abilities to think are critical assets that you need to manage and develop in the same way that you manage other business assets.

NOTES

Among the many people who have helped my research I want to single out Paul Lawrence and John Kotter. I also extend thanks to the corporate managers who have given freely of their time and ideas. Miriam Schustack made very helpful comments on a previous version of this chapter. First published in *Harvard Business Review, November–December* (1984), 80–90.

1 In studying these dozen executives, I conducted intensive interviews, observed them on the job, read documents, talked with their colleagues and, in some cases, subordinates, and engaged them in various exercises in which they recounted their thoughts as they did their work. I also reported my observations and inferences back to the managers to get feedback. I spent anywhere from 1 to 25 days studying each manager (the mode was two and a half days in field interviews and observation).

2 John P. Kotter, *The General Managers* (New York: Free Press, 1982).

3 See, for example, Chester I. Barnard, *The Functions of the Executive* (Cambridge: Harvard University Press, 1938); also Henry Mintzberg, "Planning on the left side and managing on the right," *HBR*, July–August 1976, 49.

4 See my study, "Drugs and drama: the effects of two dramatic events in a pharmaceutical company on managers' cognitions," Working Paper no. 83-55 (Boston: Harvard Business School, 1983).

5 Some of Herbert A. Simon's classic work on bounded rationality and "satisficing" is collected in *Models of Thought* (New Haven: Yale University Press, 1979). More recently, Amos Tversky, Daniel Kahneman, and other psychologists have described the mechanisms producing imperfect judgment and nonrational choice. See, for example, Daniel Kahneman, Paul Slovic, and Amos Tversky, eds., *Judgment Under Uncertainty: Heuristics and Biases* (Cambridge University Press, 1982).

6 Louis R. Goldberg, "Man vs. model of man: a rationale, plus some evidence, for a method of improving on clinical inferences," *Psychological Bulletin*, 73 (1970).

7 Jon Elster, *Ulysses and the Sirens: Studies in Rationality and Irrationality* (Cambridge, Mass.: Harvard University Press, 1979).

8 For an interesting application of these ideas to a different leadership setting, see my chapter "Some hows and whats of managerial thinking: implications for future Army leaders" in *Military Leadership on the Future Battlefield* (New York: Pergamon Press, 1984).

25

PROBLEMS IN PRODUCING USABLE KNOWLEDGE FOR IMPLEMENTING LIBERATING ALTERNATIVES

CHRIS ARGYRIS

Social scientists have become increasingly concerned with their possible responsibility to question and to change the status quo (Dahrendorf, 1958; Deutch and Hornstein, 1975; Habermas, 1972; Lazarsfeld and Rietz, 1975; Mitroff and Kilman, 1978; Moscovici, 1972). A need for research on "liberating alternatives" is being expressed. Examining this literature, one finds a dearth of research on how to implement the "liberating alternatives" suggested by the social scientists.

Implementation has often been considered "applied" or "practical," thereby delegating it to the domain of vocational activities, a domain that scientists rarely have supported. Recently, however, a recognition has developed that there are very powerful intellectual issues in moving from ideas to action (Lindblom and Cohen, 1979). It is the purpose of this paper to explore some of the "individual" factors that will make implementing liberating alternatives difficult.

The paper contains two interrelated arguments. Individuals, acting as agents for various kinds of organizations, must do the actual implementing. They bring to this task theories of action (probably learned early in their lives) which when used correctly will be *counterproductive* to implementing liberating alternatives. While acting, individuals are unaware of the counterproductivity of their actions. The unawareness is due to their culturally learned theories of action. The word "individual" above was placed in quotes because although individuals may do the implementing, the theories of action in their heads – the theories that they will use – are, I suggest, examples of massive socialization processes.

The second argument is that social scientists have a theory of action about conducting empirical research called *the scientific method*. The basic features of the scientific method as a theory of action are similar to the individual theories of action I have just suggested are counterproductive to implementing liberating alternatives. It is therefore unlikely that social scientists using the scientific method theory of action will produce usable knowledge about implementing liberating alternatives. Hence, it is necessary to develop research methods that maintain the normal science criterion of disconfirmability and simultaneously lead to the production of usable knowledge about implementing liberating alternatives.

The equivalent to liberating alternatives in the perspective that Donald Schön and I (Argyris and Schön, 1974, 1978) have suggested is the concept of double-loop learning. Learning may be defined as occurring under two conditions. First, learning occurs when an organization achieves what is intended; that is, there is a *match* between its design for action and the actual outcome. Secondly, learning occurs when a *mismatch* between intention and outcome is identified and corrected; that is, a mismatch intention and outcome is identified and corrected; that is, a mismatch is turned into a match.

Organizations do not perform the behavior that produces the learning. It is individuals acting as agents of organizations who produce the behavior that leads to learning. Whenever an error is detected and corrected without questioning or altering the underlying values of the system (be it individual, group, intergroup, organizational, or interorganizational), the learning is single-loop. The term is borrowed from electrical engineering or cybernetics where, for example, a thermostat is defined as a single-loop learner. The thermostat is programmed to detect states of "too cold" or, "too hot," and to correct the situation by turning the heat on or off. If the thermostat asked itself such questions as why it was set at 68 degrees, or why it was programmed as it was, then it would be a double-loop learner.

Single-loop and double-loop learning are diagrammed in figure 25.1. Single-loop learning occurs when matches are created, or when mismatches are corrected by changing actions. Double-loop learning occurs when mismatches are corrected by first examining and altering the governing variables and then the actions. Governing variables are the preferred states that individuals strive to satisfice when they are acting. These governing variables are *not* the underlying beliefs or values people espouse. They are the variables that can be inferred, by observing the actions of individuals acting as agents for the organization, to drive and guide their actions.

Figure 25.1 Single- and double-loop learning.

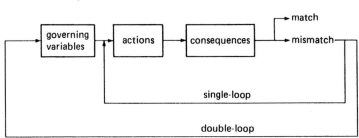

The diagram indicates that learning has not occurred until a match or a mismatch is produced. From our perspective, therefore, learning may *not* be said to occur if someone (acting for the organization) discovers a new problem or invents a solution to a problem. Learning occurs when the invented solution is actually produced. This distinction is important because it emphasizes that, while uncovering problems and inventing solutions are necessary, these are not sufficient to create the conditions required for organizational learning.

Let us begin by describing an instrument useful for diagnosing the theories of action people use to deal with double-loop issues. Although the instrument focuses on interpersonal issues, it can be modified (as we shall see) to study group, intergroup, and organizational issues.

THE *X–Y* CASE

Respondents are given a short case of how a superior (*Y*) attempted to communicate to a subordinate (*X*) that his job performance was unacceptable, that it had to be changed, and that he (*Y*) would be willing to help *X* make the change. The instrument consists of several sentences taken from the transcript of an actual dialogue between a Mr *X* and a Mr *Y* (see figure 25.2). Only Mr *Y*'s statements are included.

Next, they are asked to respond to three questions, mailing their responses directly to the researcher. The questions they are asked to answer and the format they are asked to use are:

A. Questions
1. What is your reaction to (or your diagnosis of) the way *Y* helped *X*?
2. What advice, if any, would you give *Y* to improve his performance when helping individuals like *X*?
3. Assume that *Y* met you in the hall and asked, "What did you think of the way I handled *X*?" How would you respond?

Figure 25.2

1. *X,* your performance is not up to standard (and moreover . . .)
2. You seem to be carrying a chip on your shoulder.
3. It appears to me that this has affected your performance in a number of ways. I have heard words like "lethargy," "uncommitted," and "disinterested" used by others in describing your recent performance.
4. Our senior professionals cannot have those characteristics.
5. Let's discuss your feelings about your performance.
6. *X,* I know you want to talk about the injustices that you believe have been perpetrated on you in the past. The problem is that I am not discussing something that happened several years ago. Nothing constructive will come from it. It's behind us.
7. I want to talk about you today and about your future in our system.

B. *Format* – please write your response to these questions in the following format.

Your thoughts and feelings	*What you and Y said*
(Give in this column the thoughts	*Me*: (write what you would say)
and feelings you had during the	*Y*: (write what you expect *Y*'s
sessions but which you did not	response would be)
communicate.)	*Me*: (write your response to this)
	Y: (write *Y*'s response)
	etc.

The results presented below have been obtained from approximately 1,000 respondents in executive programs or in field settings within private and public organizations. The respondents included males and females of various ages and professions as well as minorities and people of several different cultures (in Europe, South America, India, and the United States). The results are reported in detail in Argyris (1982a, b).

RESPONDENTS DIAGNOSE *Y*'S ACTIONS AS INEFFECTIVE

The first findings always generated by the case is that all the respondents evaluate *Y*'s impact on *X* as negative and ineffective (see figure 25.3 for their comments). They do not believe that *Y* created conditions for learning. A few in every group (never more than 20 %) believe that *Y* communicated to *X* that he had to change, but that *Y* could have communicated this more effectively. For example, sixteen top executives of a very large corporation evaluated *Y*'s behavior toward *X* as in figure 25.3.

A second finding is that the responses can be ordered into a causal sequence:

> *If Y* behaves in ways that can be described as insensitive, judgmental, intimidating, *then X* will probably feel misunderstood, prejudged, disregarded, and hence, will react defensively.

A third finding is that most respondents predict second and third order causal consequences. They predict that, if *Y* continues to behave toward *X* as he does, both will feel that the situation is uninfluenceable; that the best one can hope for is that civility will prevail; that the only solution is for the company to set a deadline by which *X* must improve; and, finally, that *Y* will probably have to be tough with *X*.

Early in our research, Schön and I were troubled by the lack of variance in responses. We believed that results with so little variance probably indicated flawed instruments and analysis as well as poor theory. We now believe that these findings are indeed valid. They can be explained by a theory that is empirically disconfirmable. This perspective proposes that the low variance is an example of massive socialization where most people are taught to reason in the same way and to create similar meanings (as described below). They use the same theory of action.

543

PARTICIPANTS' RESPONSES ARE ALSO COUNTERPRODUCTIVE

If it is true that most individuals use the same theory of action, then all our respondents should, when trying to help others, use the same actions that they evaluated as counterproductive when used by *Y*. If this hypothesis is true, given the opportunity our respondents would behave the same way as did *Y*, even though they asserted that *Y*'s actions were counterproductive.

In order to test this hypothesis, we first identify a puzzle before the respondents. If they attempted to help *Y* by telling him what was in their diagnostic frame (figure 25.3), they would be using with *Y* the same causal theory

Figure 25.3

Y's action strategies

Y's comments have a strong power tone to them; they smell of conspiratorial knowlege.

Y gives no sign of interest or compassion.

Y sets up *X* to give only answers *Y* wants to hear.

Y comes across as a blunt, uncaring executioner of the firm's policy decision with regard to *X*.

Y makes it abundantly clear that he does not want to be bothered with *X*.

Y is insensitive to *X*'s feelings.

Y waits too long to listen to *X*.

Y does not give *X* a chance to respond. He pays lip service to hearing *X*'s side.

Y is too blunt, direct, one-sided.

Y cuts off *X*.

Y communicates the seriousness of the situation from the company's point of view.

At no time does *Y* appear to communicate that he and the firm genuinely want *X* to have a second chance.

Impact on X

Makes *X* feel defensive, rejected.

Makes *X* defend his past performance aggressively.

Y will feel prejudged, "loaded deck."

X is not likely to relax and learn.

X is left with no room for constructive exploration.

Totally demoralizes *X*; makes *X* feel inferior.

X is placed in a no-win situation.

Impact on learning

Inhibits learning on part of both individuals.

X will probably look for another job.

that they judged counterproductive when Y used it with X. For example, if they were forthright, they would have to tell Y that he was "blunt" or "insensitive." Such meanings can be experienced by the recipient (in this case, Y) as blunt and insensitive.

Typically, the respondents are initially surprised by the inconsistency. There is usually a period of defending their diagnosis. To date, most individuals eventually agree that, if they acted forthrightly, they would produce the inconsistency identified by the researchers.

About this time, many begin to argue that they would not state what was in their diagnostic frame directly. They would "ease in." Put simply, they would ask Y questions which, if he answered correctly, would make him aware of their evaluation of him (i.e., of what they were hiding). Most clients refer to their scenarios to illustrate easing in. Others role-play this approach. In all cases so far, the participants evaluate the easing in as manipulative or judgmental or irritating. The point is that the participants themselves evaluate the easing-in approach as creating defensiveness.

For example, here are five different executives' opening sentences with possible interpretations of their impact on Y as given by fellow executives in the group.

Executive said	*Y could have thought*
1. It's hard to say from just reading your notes. I guess I would like to hear a little about how X reacted.	1. What is he driving at? Why does he want to focus on X's reaction?
2. What do you think he was thinking?	2. How do I know what X was thinking? I told him that X didn't say much. What is he driving at?
3. Do you suppose there might have been a way to let him know you meant it when you said he had to "shape up or ship out"?	3. I did let him know I meant it. If he didn't believe me, that's more his problem than mine.
4. Do you mean that his attitude in the meeting was as negative as the attitude people assert he has on the job?	4. Couldn't you tell that he was pretty unresponsive? What is he driving at? Does he believe that X's attitude was better?
5. Perhaps if you could persuade him to open up about it, he might get it off his chest.	5. The last thing I want to do is open up past wounds . . . oh, these bleeding hearts!

We may now add two more generalizations to the first three described above. When individuals are asked to communicate threatening information with the view of helping others, they will most likely use an easing-in approach which is as counterproductive as the forthright approach. Individuals who use the forthright or the easing-in approaches will tend to be unaware of the counterproductive features of these approaches.

Let us pause for a moment to make explicit what has so far been tacit about the researcher–subject relationship. The subjects are no longer subjects, and the researcher is no longer a researcher. The researcher has begun to confront the subjects with major gaps and inconsistencies in their reasoning processes and actions. The respondents do not take such feedback lightly. They respond with feelings ranging from surprise to bewilderment, shame, frustration, and anger. It is unlikely that individuals will expose themselves to such a dialogue for the sake of research. There must be a payoff for them if they are to continue a process that will become more painful before it becomes less so (Argyris, 1982a).

The point is that empirical research that attempts to get at the factors that inhibit liberating alternatives will probably not only have to be a genuine learning experience for those participating but a liberating one at that. Subjects must be seen as clients, clients, who are being helped to double-loop learn. The researchers are more interventionists than researchers because they will have to be able to design learning experiences that the clients believe are worthwhile. This means that the researchers must have models of alternative worlds as well as models and skills that will enable the clients to move from here to there. We will return to these requirements again.

REASONING PROCESSES THAT PRODUCE COUNTERPRODUCTIVITY

Let us examine the reasoning processes that clients use when they produce the actions described above.

The responses clients produced (figure 25.3) may be ordered on a hierarchy or ladder of inference. Some appeared to be relatively close to what was in the transcript. For example, "Y cut X off" and "Y used hearsay data." Other comments contained meanings that were not easily connected to the transcript. For example, evaluations such as "Y exerted too much control," "Y was blunt," and "Y was judgmental, accusatory, and negative," or attributions such as "Y sought to frighten X" and "Y intended to protect himself."

The ladder of inference (see figure 25.4) begins with what the actors consider to be the relatively directly observable data on which they will base their diagnosis and actions (rung 1). The second rung is the cultural meanings that the actors believe are embedded in the data of the first rung, meanings which are commonly understood by all participants. The third rung of the ladder is the meaning the actors impose to produce their respective diagnoses.

For example, the first sentence in figure 25.2, "X, your performance is not up to standard," is on rung 1. The culturally understood meaning (rung 2) might be that X's performance was not acceptable. A culturally understood meaning is one inferred as the result of socialization in a given culture. The third rung is the meaning that the individual imposes on the cultural meaning. For example, some respondents inferred that Y was being judgmental, insensitive, blunt etc.

The ladder of inference describes the reasoning processes individuals use whenever they are trying to understand the effectiveness of any human actions, whether at the individual, group, organizational, or interorganizational level (Argyris, 1982a). For example, a class of 120 governmental professionals and administrators were asked to read a book-length case that described the relationships among Secretary Califano (HEW), Secretary Marshall (Labor), their respective policy teams and President Carter and his White House staff as they tried to define a new welfare policy (Lynn and Whitman, 1981). They were then asked to evaluate the effectiveness of the case actors at any level they wished. An analysis of their transcribed responses indicates that the class developed the following diagnoses (Argyris, 1982a). These statements are relatively direct quotations taken from the class tapes, and have been confirmed by the members.

(1) There were working groups with entrenched positions, unwilling to change, much disagreement and miscommunication, a failure to confront the real issues.

(2) There was Califano who was "Washington-hip," who let things boil; smart enough to know that if he accepts responsibility, he also will get in trouble; who, having a secret agenda, acted as a trial lawyer; who learned from Lyndon Johnson to humiliate his staff.

(3) There were the classic power struggles. The players were heads of agencies, born to win. Ambitious men want to win. If they lose, they lose their own respect and the respect of their staff. Everyone is looking out for Number One. People's self-esteem is wrapped up in game-playing.

(4) There was the Washington culture which supported the mentality of throwing money at problems and simultaneously taking care of constituents. Also, there was the underlying tension between the culture of the "Georgia hicks" and the "Washington sophisticates."

These comments evidence the same causal reasoning as in the $X–Y$ case:

If individuals, groups, or intergroups behave in accordance with 1–4 above, then there will be:

hardening of positions
intergroup rivalries
mistrust
distancing from the responsibility of confronting process issues;

which in turn will lead to:

escalating error
undiscussability of the counterproductive features in settings where they are occurring)
(discussability among friends or cliques)
acting as if there is nothing undiscussable and as if one cannot discuss that undiscussability.

Figure 25.4 Ladder of inference.

4	Researcher's imposed meanings
3	Respondent's imposed meanings
2	Culturally understood meanings of data
1	Relatively directly observable data

Under these conditions, people will tend to believe:

(1) It is unlikely that these patterns can be changed. The situation is typical, that is, it is hopeless and uninfluenceable.

(2) It is rational for the actors to continue to state their respective positions and to be diplomatic about the way they resist. For example:

Remaining courteous but uninfluenceable.

Act as if you are influenceable but don't give in lest you be seen as a traitor to your group.

If you do get upset, have a drink with the others and make up.

Let the chairman be responsible for dealing with the process issues.

(3) Whatever set of factors they select as causal, the way to deal with the problem is to have a strong leader. One person has to be in charge. But:

Washington sophisticates know better than to take charge in such a situation.

(4) Create a deadline, because groups will eat up all the time that you give them. But:

Giving groups deadlines places them under pressure. They can use that pressure to excuse their ineffectiveness.

If time and space were available, it would be possible to show that individuals, acting as agents of organizations, use the same reasoning processes when dealing with threatening problems such as investment policies or technical performance of project teams studying long range strategy issues (Argyris, 1982a).

What is counterproductive about these reasoning processes? First, individuals usually do not illustrate their evaluations or attributions. The recipients will hear the imposed attributions (rung 3) but they have no idea how the communicators arrived at their judgments. Secondly, individuals usually do not test publicly for the validity of their attributions or evaluations. They appear to act as if they imposed meanings (rung 3 – "Y was blunt," "Califano is a Washington sophisticate") are concrete and obvious. Thirdly, they design easing-in approaches to prevent or circumvent defensive reactions. Often these approaches produce defensive reactions anyway but the recipients (who are reacting with an easing-in approach) do not communicate the defensiveness they feel. Fourthly, the lack of feedback makes the players unaware of their impact on others. There are second- and third-order consequences illustrated by the $X–Y$ and the Califano cases. For example, the first four features lead to misunderstandings and mistrust, and these lead to third-order consequences such as escalating error.

It is these counterproductive features that will make it unlikely that liberating alternatives will be produced of the type described at the outset. A study that shows that a universe of trust and risk-taking was produced while dealing with double-loop issues would confirm our position. More importantly, it would disconfirm the theory that we use to explain the above results. Let us turn to a brief description of our explanation and the theory behind it.

AN EXPLANATION OF THE $X-Y$ RESULTS

A possible answer to the question of why there is so little variance in the reasoning processes and actions of the respondents is that all individuals must distance themselves from the relatively directly observable data in order to design and manage their actions. It is not possible to react without first extracting from whatever occurs and organizing one's reality. This is what is meant by "constructing or enacting reality." High levels of inference are necessary because they make possible on-line management of reality. In this connection, one is reminded of Simon's view (1969) that the environment is more complex than the human mind can deal with directly, and of Miller's (1956) work which states that the human mind may be able to process, at a given moment, seven (plus or minus two) units of information. Beyond this number, new and more abstract concepts are needed which subsume the lower-level units of information. The work of both men suggests that there is a hierarchy of concepts which makes it possible to organize, make sense out of, and enact reality.

However, there is nothing in their work that requires this hierarchy of concepts to be attributions or evaluations that are not illustrated or tested. That is, it may well be true that the human mind must use concepts requiring high levels of inference from the raw data. But why must individuals use concepts that contain such a high probability for miscommunication? And why do individuals use such concepts when they advise others not to do so? And why, in many cases, do they do so when they are simultaneously advising others not to do so (e.g., "The trouble with you is that you are putting the other person down")?

MODEL I THEORY-IN-USE

A second cause of the results may be discovered if we focus on the meaning the actors' imposed meanings (rung 3) have for effectiveness. That is, we now impose our meanings (rung 4) on those imposed by the actors. In so doing, we are asserting that a theory exists that explains the rung 3 meanings *and* that individuals must have this theory in their heads; they must be programmed with it.

Donald Schön and I have proposed a theory of action perspective which assumes that human beings design their actions (Argyris and Schön, 1974, 1978). Since it is not likely they can design complex actions *de novo* in every situation, individuals must hold theories about effective action which they bring to bear on any given situation. We suggest that there are two kinds of theories of action. The first are espoused theories. The advice that the respondents gave to Y were aspects of espoused theories of effective action. But, as we have seen, few respondents acted congruently with those espoused theories. Moreover, most of them seemed to be unaware of the gap between their espoused theory and their actions. Such discrepancies are not new in social science.

The theory of action perspective does not stop there. It suggests that the unawareness is designed. It suggests that the incongruence is designed. It suggests, in other words, that human beings must have a theory of action that they use to produce all these difficulties. We call this type of theory their theory-in-use. If we can make explicit the theory-in-use, then we can explain, predict, and have the basis for changing these findings.

We have created a model of the theory-in-use that most individuals appear to us to use. A model I theory-in-use has four governing variables, or values, for the actor to satisfice: (1) strive to be in unilateral control, (2) minimize losing and maximize winning, (3) minimize the expression of negative feelings, and (4) be rational. Along with the governing variables are a set of behavioral strategies such as (1) advocate your views without encouraging inquiry (hence, remain in unilateral control and hopefully win), and (2) unilaterally save face – your own and other people's (hence, minimize upsetting others or making them defensive).

These governing variables and behavioral strategies form a master program which influences the diagnostic and action frames that individuals produce. Hence, when *Y* behaved as he did, he violated the governing variable of not eliciting negative feelings and the behavioral strategy of unilaterally protecting others and one's self. Such actions would not assist *Y* to win because winning, in this case, was defined as helping *X* change his attitude.

This theory-in-use, which we call model I, is held by all of the individuals studied so far (Argyris and Schön, 1974, 1978; Argyris, 1976a, b, 1980). It is our hypothesis, yet to be confirmed directly, that model I is learned through socialization. Model I individuals are able to behave according to model I, the opposite to model I, or an oscillating model I (i.e., *A* unilaterally controls *B*, and then *B* does the same to *A*, etc.) The behavioral strategies, once learned, are highly skilled. "Highly skilled" means that the action achieves its objectives. Although complex, it is performed effortlessly; actions are produced so fast they appear automatic.

We may now hypothesize that the respondents enacted the diagnostic frames that they did because they were being consistent with model I, and being so made it possible for them to make recommendations and take action. But, being programmed with model I theory-in-use, they also made unillustrated attributions and evaluations; they saw no reason to test their attributions and evaluations because they believed they were true. They were unaware of the many inferences that were embedded in their reasoning processes because, according to their model I theory-in-use, everything they thought and said was not only true, it was obvious and concrete. But the reason that it was obvious and concrete is that they had learned throughout life (i.e., in socialization) that most people would agree with them. This expectation was confirmed by the data in this case.

FACTORS THAT INHIBIT ORGANIZATIONAL DOUBLE-LOOP LEARNING

If it is true that all these consequences are due to highly skilled and programmed, and hence automatic, reactions, then it follows that individuals will carry these skills into *any* social system, be it a private or public organization, family, school, union, hospital, and so on. If it is also true that individuals who act as agents for systems do the learning, then they will necessarily create conditions within the systems that inhibit double-loop learning. This prediction should not be disconfirmed, even if individuals are placed in systems where the internal environmental conditions encourage double-loop learning and the external environmental conditions are at least benign.

Does this mean that we are predicting that organizations should not be observed to produce double-loop learning? The answer is yes. Does this mean that organizations should not be observed changing their underlying values and norms? The answer is yes for those values that are related to how human beings deal with each other. The answer is "not necessarily" for organizational policies. Double-loop changes in substantive areas may occur but *not* because the present participants detected and corrected errors (which is our definition of learning). The changes could occur by fiat or unilateral imposition. For example, the Pentagon Papers may be viewed as a beginning act of double-loop learning about organizational policies and practices. Those chosen to write them had the technical skills and access to the relevant information required to accomplish the task. But these inquiries were ordered by the top. Indeed, the case could be made that there were participants who held the views eventually described in the documents, but those views, previous to McNamara's edict, were undiscussable, and their undiscussability was undiscussable. Did the Defense Department learn how to deal with undiscussables and their undiscussability? I would venture the answer is no.

But at the core of this management information system were several interpersonal values, such as "valid information is a good idea." The difficulty was that (as is the case in most organizations) the theory-in-use about valid information tends to be that valid information is a good idea when it is not threatening. The moment any substantive or technical information is threatening, our model I theories-in-use are automatically engaged.

When the requirements of our model I theories-in-use are contrary to the technical requirements, a conflict occurs. The predisposition of the participants is to hide the clash, yet play the model I political games that they have learned to "cover themselves." They will, in effect, violate the formal technical requirements and conceal the fact that they are fighting them.[1] If successful, they will create a situation where the executives on top and the staff in charge of the management information systems will not know about the games, the camouflage of the games, or the camouflage of the camouflage.

Elsewhere we have tried to show how these features will necessarily have to occur in any organization whose participants are programmed with model I (Argyris and Schön, 1978). We suggest that human beings programmed with model I theory-in-use will create and impose a 0–I learning system on any organization in which they participate.

Briefly, we attempted to identify the cognitive features of information that would tend to facilitate and inhibit the production of error. We hypothesized the following continua:

Conditions that enhance the probability of error	Conditions that enhance the probability of learning
Information is:	Information is:

vague——————————————————concrete
unclear——————————————————clear
inconsistent——————————————————consistent
incongruent——————————————————congruent
scattered——————————————————available

When individuals programmed with a model I theory-in-use strive to solve difficult and threatening problems with available information that has features that approximate the left end of these continua, they will create conditions of undiscussability, self-fulfilling prophecies, self-sealing processes, and escalating error. These conditions act to reinforce vagueness, lack of clarity, inconsistency, and incongruity, which in turn reinforce the use of model I (i.e., people strive harder to be in unilateral control, to minimize losing and maximize winning, etc.).

At the same time, these conditions tend to create win–lose groups and intergroup dynamics, with competitiveness dominating over cooperation, mistrust overcoming trust, and unquestioned obedience replacing informed dissent. They also lead to the coalition groups and the organizational politicking that have been described by Allison (1971), Bacharach and Lawler (1980), Baldridge (1971), Cyert and March (1963), and Pettigrew (1973).

Under these conditions, it is difficult to see how structural and policy changes will lead to double-loop learning. In order for this to occur, individuals must be able to alter their theories-in-use and to neutralize the 0–I learning system while simultaneously, and probably under stress, they act according to a new theory-in-use. Unless they alter the model I features, they will use their automatic, highly skilled model I responses. But how are they to alter their automatic responses when this is all they can produce, when these responses are organizationally reinforced and culturally sanctioned?

Schön and I have described elsewhere models II and 0–II which combined would create liberating alternatives so that double-loop learning could occur. To date, we have never been successful in helping individuals produce model II actions by making it organizationally and culturally acceptable to do so. For example, whenever clients attend a conference to learn model II behavior, they presumably enter a (temporary) organizational and cultural setting where model II actions and 0–II learning systems are rewarded. Moreover, they are embedded in a context where none of the everyday task pressures exist. Yet they are unable to produce model II actions and an 0–II learning system even though they wish to do so (Argyris, 1982a). Such a change requires changes in the reasoning processes, in the skills used, and hence in the theory-in-use. This is possible but only after instruction and practice (Argyris, 1982a).

The underlying hypothesis is: The automatic reasoning processes that lead to escalating error on the one hand and difficulty in creating liberating alternatives on the other, are caused by individuals (1) holding a model I theory-in-use (2) who are embedded in a 0–I learning system which in turn is embedded in cultures that support models I and 0–I.

The coverage of the hypothesis is broad, and intendedly so. Simultaneously, it is easily falsifiable. All one has to do· is present a case where individuals programmed with model I theories-in-use, and embedded in 0–I learning systems (in any social organization), dealt with a double-loop learning systems (in any social organization), dealt with a double-loop threatening issue (excluding the exceptions noted above) in such a way that errors did not escalate.

IMPLICATIONS FOR RESEARCH METHODOLOGY OF PRODUCING
LIBERATING ALTERNATIVES

The most central feature of our research is that individuals inhibit genuine liberating alternative worlds of the kind we described earlier because they are programmed to do so. Their sense of competence and confidence in themselves is created by the model I theories-in-use and the 0–I double-loop learning systems in which they are embedded. Both of these are counterproductive to double-loop learning. The second central feature is that individuals tend to be unaware of this fact.

Researchers will therefore be dealing with subjects who will in all likelihood be unable to provide valid responses about their actions and their theories-in-use even if they wish to do so. Moreover, they will tend to be unaware of this possibility.

Elsewhere I have suggested that the theory-in-use of rigorous empirical research is model I. For example, the governing variables of rigorous research are for the researcher to be in unilateral control, to define the purpose of the research, to design out as much as possible feelings that may distort responses, to control the time perspective, to define unilaterally the task to be performed, and if necessary to deceive the subjects as to the true purpose of the research.

These consequences are not unfamiliar to human beings. To them, this is what life is all about. The difficulty occurs when we wish to conduct research to produce knowledge about universes that are contrary to models I and 0–I. How, for example, will knowledge be produced about models II and 0–II when the technology we use is model I and when researchers are admonished not to produce normative models of universes that do not exist?

I have reviewed a wide range of empirical research from the fields of social psychology, sociology, political science, and organizational theory whose authors purport to inform the public about how to create features of alternative universes, and have found almost all of these alternatives to be consistent with model I. In a few cases where it appeared the researchers were studying model II phenomena, the research was limited to espoused theories and not in theories-in-use. Unfortunately (in my opinion), there were even cases where the researchers appeared to advise the public to act in a manipulative, unilaterally controlling manner in order to reduce the injustice of the present world (Argyris, 1980).

I am suggesting that these findings cannot be ignored if we, as social scientists, are going to help provide liberating alternatives. I also realize that it is not going to be easy to devise appropriate research methods.

Permit me to make one point clear. It will not do to devise research methods that skirt the important issues of causality and disconfirmability. We must always be concerned about knowing the extent to which we are knowingly or unknowingly kidding ourselves or others. Our research results must be refutable, indeed even more strongly than is acceptable under present standards, because they may be used by human beings under difficult, threatening conditions, and where they may have little unilateral control over others.

EMPIRICAL RESEARCH FEATURES PRODUCING KNOWLEDGE ABOUT DOUBLE-LOOP ISSUES

The first criterion for empirical research is that it must differentiate between actions, espoused theories, and theories-in-use. The questionnaire and interviews most frequently used in research may be valid for espoused theories. Conversations (taped or recollected) are the basis for inferring theories-in-use.

The $X-Y$ case is an example of a simple instrument that can be used for studying and producing double-loop changes.

1. The respondents are able to identify a problem in everyday life that, in their view, is important to their effectiveness, one which requires knowledge and skills they wish to improve.
2. The respondents are asked to describe the strategy they intend to use to solve the problem, and the reasons behind that strategy. This provides insight into their espoused theories of action.
3. The respondents then write a scenario of what they said (or would say) when dealing with the problem. On the left-hand side of the page, they write any thoughts or feelings they had but did not communicate to the other person(s). This gives data to infer any discrepancies between espoused theory and action. In our case, it also makes it possible to infer their theory-in-use.

When participants are asked to generate cases from their own experience using the $X-Y$ format, the cases give insight into the issues that they presently consider important. Such cases also identify the knowledge and skills they seek to improve (and, by implication, those which they do not); their espoused theories of action; their theories-in-use; discrepancies between espoused theory, behavior, and theory-in-use; their awareness of such discrepancies; their criteria for effective performance; the way they deal with others; their self-censoring mechanisms; and the second-order consequences such as self-fulfilling prophecies, self-sealing processes, and escalating error.

When such cases are generated in a group of people from the same organization, the cases produce rich data about the organizational learning conditions – to what degree they facilitate or inhibit the identification and correction of error. And the cases produce a great deal of data on group conformity, group competitiveness, intergroup rivalries, interorganizational rivalries, and the games people play to protect themselves and survive in the organization.

The second requirement of empirical research is that more attention should be paid to producing models of alternative worlds, including the intervention which could actually enact the new models in the "real" world. Basic research about alternatives must combine a description of the world as it is with models of the world as it might be, and should include information about how to get from here to there. This combination cannot be decomposed into sequential action. For instance, developing the $X–Y$ case required a theory about what was dysfunctional about models I and 0–I. Confronting clients with their inconsistencies required reasoning and skills that were derivable from normative models of action and system (models II and 0–II) that do not exist in the present world.

Embedded in the idea of decomposition is also the assumption that descriptive knowledge will result in usable knowledge; that usability accrues simply because description does; that if you know enough of the truth quantitatively, you will eventually learn the truth about effectiveness. Not necessarily so. Elsewhere I have indicated that the most certain fact about empirical knowledge in organizational research is that it is rarely cumulative or additive (Argyris, 1980).

Embedded in the first two requirements for empirical research is a third, namely, that basic research in this field must be concerned about effectiveness. Valid propositions about effectiveness, in turn, require normative criteria, hence, we are back to the requirement of normative models of what the world might be.

We may now identify another reason why truth about the world as it is may not teach us the best way to be effective. When they are acting, people use different theories of action, different definitions of rigor, and different concepts of validity than when they are acting in order to reflect or inquire. We saw a significant difference between the diagnoses and advice people gave in the $X–Y$ case and the later case scenarios and interactions in which they were involved, creating actors. The same phenomena have been observed in everyday organizational life (Argyris and Schön, 1978; Argyris, 1982a). These differences are informed by different theories of action: the advice by the espoused theory, the action by the theory-in-use. Espoused theories are idealizations; theories-in-use are presumed to represent the actual propositions being used.

A fourth requirement of empirical research is related to the kinds of propositions that are needed. If knowledge is to be used to create liberating alternatives, then the propositions must be usable not only to describe them but to create them. Most normal science propositions describe (usually quantitatively) the empirical relationship between variables. Such propositions do not tell the actor how to create the *a* and *b*. If the variables were trust and public testing, and we assume for a moment a positive linear relationship between them, the actors would not be able to use such a proposition to create trust and public testing. Worse yet, if the research above is correct, most people who believed the proposition would also believe that they could produce it. Our research would predict that this is highly unlikely and that they would be unaware of that.

If actors are to be able to produce the actions, they require propositions that are retrievable, usable, and do not produce consequences counterproductive to those predicted in the proposition when correctly used. We are only beginning to understand the form such propositions take. The statement "There is a curvilinear relationship between *a* and *b*" cannot be used by actors in real time conditions. To do so would require measurement of such intangibles as trust and risk-taking in order to assess where the two variables are on the curve at the present time. How does one interrupt an interaction in order to measure trust and risk-taking? Hand out an instrument? Ask the actors? Does either strategy make it likely the answer could be distorted? If so, what are the covert strategies? How would one overcome the self-fulfilling prophecies we saw people create when they were using easing-in strategies?

Speaking of easing-in strategies, a way to state the proposition so that the actor can create it is to say: Ask questions which, if the receivers understand and answer correctly, will enable them to realize what you are hiding in your diagnostic frame. Or, if you intend to communicate an attribution, illustrate it and state it so that it can be tested publicly. Propositions would also be required about how to test ideas publicly. Model II would suggest stating the illustrated attribution and asking others to confirm or disconfirm it.

These theory-in-use propositions do not contain the precision required by the normal science paradigm. But they can be used to produce the intended consequences because they combine sloppiness with accuracy. It is difficult for many of us to believe that rigor might well be achieved by combining sloppiness with iterative learning in order to eventually produce accurately the consequences that we intend. Often we generate explanatory maps that are rigorous and complete, that we admit may not be usable by individuals, and we degrade the maps that they do use.

For example, let us review Naylor, Pritchard, and Ilgen's (1980) recent treatise of human behavior in organizations. Examining the systematic, schematic presentation of their theory (p. 24), one is impressed by their attempt to present an ideal map of the relevant variables and their interrelationships, and also by the complexity of this map. The authors are aware of this, and periodically they pause to give comments such as this:

Unfortunately there is an increasing body of evidence indicating that people do not utilize the cognitive system in its pure, or theoretically most effective, sense. They tend instead, for one reason or another, to use degraded versions of the system. These degraded judgmental strategies are often simpler ways of dealing with the making of judgments, and are based upon rules, or principles, of simplification that may be intuitively appealing or "logical" to the individual but which may or may not be effective substitution strategies for the entire "pure" process.   (p. 110)

What is the evidence that this is a degraded decision tactic? Can it not be an elevating one? I believe their answer would be that the process is degraded because people do not behave according to the authors' ideal descriptive model.

Note the reasoning. Scholars who develop a rigorous, descriptive model – one which probably has not been empirically tested – assert that their model is the correct one; that people would act consistently with it if only they were truly rational (a tacit normative position). The increasing evidence that people do not act consistently with such scholarly models they explain by asserting people degrade their reasoning.

I would like to suggest an alternative hypothesis. People upgrade their reasoning by using heuristics because they have developed vague rules of use that produce accuracy. As Von Neumann (1958) noted years ago, the human mind's effectiveness may be the result of being able to tolerate noise, whereas computers require a more precise calculus and conditions of minimal noise. Is it not possible that theory-in-use human rationality means coupling precise sloppiness or vagueness with accuracy?

There is also the issue of retrievability of knowledge. Much empirical knowledge is in a form that makes it difficult to store and retrieve under real time conditions. For example, Stogdill (1974) has written a handbook about leadership which contains hundreds of generalizations. How is a leader to use this knowledge? Say he is in a meeting where he sees competitiveness among the subordinates, dependence on him, and group conformity. Will he suddenly stop and refer to the handbook? Even if he did, the knowledge is probably scattered throughout several chapters.

Elsewhere I have suggested that Lewin's (Lewin, Lippitt, and White, 1939) topological maps may provide insight into how to package knowledge so that it is retrievable and usable. For example, Lewin's concept of gatekeeper would help the leader explain all the above observations as well as provide a way to discuss the issues with the subordinates (Argyris, 1980).

The fifth and final requirement returns to the important issue of disconfirmability. As we have seen in the $X–Y$ case, knowledge is ordered by actors as well as researchers by the use of a ladder of inference. The first rung is relegated to the relatively directly observable data, such as actual conversations, and includes a great deal of variance. The cultural meanings embedded in their words (rung 2) also vary, but not as widely. The same is the case for the individual meanings that the actors impose (rung 3).

DISCONFIRMABILITY OF PROPOSITIONS

We also found that there was almost no variance in the meaning that we imposed on the client's meanings. All used model I action strategies such as unillustrated attributions and evaluations or advocacy with neither inquiry nor testing. We explained this lack of variance by saying that everyone studied to date held the same theory-in-use.

This suggests that social scientists should focus on predicting the theory-in-use meanings people produce and not on predicting to rungs 1, 2, and 3. The predictions would not be about the actual words but the theory-in-use meanings of these words. The empirical research would have to focus on all the rungs of the ladder but the predictions would be about the theory-in-use meanings.

For example, a theory of action perspective predicts that if the respondents are programmed with model I theories-in-use, then what they will write in their diagnoses, say to each other during their discussion, and say in any setting where they are dealing with threatening double-loop issues, will be consistent with model I and 0–I and not with other theories-in-use.

Such a perspective will permit the testing of propositions that contain anecdotal or conversational data. Now a single sentence (or a single case) can be shown to be an illustration of predictable features of theory. The test is rigorous in the sense that an *a priori* prediction can be made as to what meanings will and will not be imposed by the respondents.

We are suggesting that the creation of one sentence, of several sentences, or a thousand sentences is a complicated design act that is informed by a theory-in-use; that there is nothing random about the meanings individuals impose. If we are trying to predict what meanings individuals will or will not include, we must begin with the relatively directly observable data (rung 1) and work up to the predicted imposed meanings (rung 3).

We are then able to state propositions such as the following:

If individuals faced with a threatening double-loop problem use a model I theory-in-use, then:
(a) They will communicate the threatening issues either directly, or by easing in, or in a combination of both approaches.
(b) They will produce the above with model I behavior strategies (e.g., unillustrated evaluations and attributions, advocacy with no inquiry).
This will lead to second-order consequences such as misunderstandings, self-fulfilling prophecies, and self-sealing processes.

Those descriptive propositions can also be formulated in terms of the rules the actors use in their respective theories-in-use. For example:

Whenever I believe what I have to say will make the other person defensive, I should ask those questions through which, if he answers them correctly, he will realize what I am hiding (easing-in).
Whenever the other person reacts defensively, interpret that as evidence that my diagnosis is correct and continue the easing-in approach. Do no test publicly the

attribution that the other person is reacting defensively – act as if I do not hold such an attribution.

These findings, whether stated as descriptive propositions or rules for action, are hypothesized to hold whether individuals are reacting to an experiment or to a real-life situation; whether the issues are substantive or interpersonal (they only have to be double-loop and threatening); or whether they gain insight into their impact or not.

Moreover, tests of these propositions can be conducted without the usual fear of individuals either knowingly or unknowingly distorting the data. According to our theory, a model I respondent can only produce a model I or opposite-to-model I meanings. The prediction should not be disconfirmed, even if the respondents are aware of the prediction and then intend to disconfirm it. For example, elsewhere I have presented illustrations where individuals who are programmed with model I, who choose to reduce the dysfunctional aspects of model I, who describe new actions they intend to take, are then told that they will not be able to produce these actions (Argyris, 1982a). This prediction is usually flatly rejected by the participants. "If we choose to change our actions, we can do so" is their view. They then work alone, or in groups, to produce new actions. Once they feel they have produced them, they share them with their fellow respondents, who invariably score the "new" actions as consistent with model I, hence confirming our prediction (Argyris, 1982a).

Similar predictions can be made for the organizational context. For example, a group of officers experienced a one-day seminar with the X–Y case. At the end of the day, they identified an area in their business where their learning was directly applicable, namely, the periodic evaluations of top professionals. We predicted that, even though they and their subordinates had been exposed to new concepts, they had not learned to translate the new ideas of performance evaluation from espoused theory to theory-in-use. Since the officers and subordinates wanted to continue to learn, all agreed to have the sessions taped, and invited me to attend as observer. All the sessions began with model I interactions. I was asked to help them reflect on their actions with the intent of changing them. After several sessions, the clients began to act more competently. Those who did learn to produce model II behavior have continued to use it (over a four-year period), not only in performance evaluations but whenever threatening messages are being communicated (Argyris, 1982a).

Another situation involved top management and the issue of whether to spend time and effort to learn to reason differently – that is, to learn model II – or to put that same effort into the establishment of a new financial system. Management opted for the latter. Later interviews with the officers confirmed that all those who had pushed for the financial change agreed that the model I competitive, self-protective games continued. Indeed, some feared that it would now be even more difficult to overcome such elements because they were so intertwined with the management information system being used.

SUMMARY

We have described a research methodology that combines inquiry and learning, one where the respondents are subjects *and* clients. It is a methodology that can be used not only to study features of the universe as it is but also to study and to create alternative universes. The propositions are directly usable. They make it possible to go beyond the status quo to create alternative universes. The research setting includes a learning environment for teaching navigation from the present to the alternative universe. The propositions are publicly testable and disconfirmable in real-life settings as well as in the learning environment. Indeed, the tests are tougher than those accepted by normal science because people are acting in real situations where they are vulnerable. And the propositions can be integrated into elegant theories, that is, theories that require a minimum number of axioms and concepts for maximum comprehension.

NOTE

1 It may also be possible for individuals to fight the management information system by going outside the organization. An example is the federal law that greatly reduced the requirement of PPBS.

REFERENCES

Allison, Graham T. (1971). *Essence of Decision: Explaining the Cuban Missile Crisis.* Little Brown, Boston.

Argyris, Chris (1976a). *Increasing Leadership Effectiveness*, Wiley-Interscience, New York.

(1976b). "Single- and double-loop models in research on decision-making," *Administrative Science Quarterly*, 21.

(1980). *Inner Contradictions of Rigorous Research.* Academic Press, New York.

(1982a). *Reasoning, Learning, and Action: Individual and Organization.* Jossey-Bass, San Francisco.

(1982b). "Why individuals and organizations have difficulty double-loop learning," in Paul S. Goodman (ed.), Jossey-Bass, San Francisco.

Argyris, Chris, and Schön, Donald (1974). *Theory in Practice.* Jossey-Bass, San Francisco.

(1978). *Organizational Learning.* Addison-Wesley, Reading, MA.

Bacharach, Samuel B., and Lawler, Edward J. (1980). *Power and Politics in Organizations.* Jossey-Bass, San Francisco.

Baldridge, J. V. (1971). *Power and Conflict in the University: Research in the Sociology of Organizations.* Wiley, New York.

Cyert, Richard M., and March, James G. (1963). *A Behavioral Theory of the Firm.* Prentice-Hall, Englewood Cliffs, NJ.

Dahrendorf, R. (1958). "Out of Utopia: towards a reorientation of sociological analysis," *American Journal of Sociology*, 64, 115–27.

Deutch, M., and Hornstein, H. A. (1975). *Applying Social Psychology.* Laurence Erlbaum, Hillsdale, NJ.

Habermas, J. (1972). *Knowledge and Human Interests.* Heinemann, London.

Lazarsfeld, P. F., and Rietz, J. G. (1975). *An Introduction to Applied Sociology.* Elsevier, Amsterdam.

Lewin, K., Lippitt, R., and White, R. K. (1939). "Patterns of aggressive behavior in experimentally created social climates," *Journal of Social Psychology*, 10, 271–301.

Lindblom, Charles E., and Cohen, David K. (1979). *Usable Knowledge: Social Science and Social Problem-solving.* Yale University Press, New Haven.

Lynn, Laurence E. Jr., and Whitman, David de F. (1981). *The President as Policymaker: Jimmy Carter and Welfare Reform.* Temple University Press, Philadelphia.

Miller, G.A . (1956). "The magical number seven, plus or minus two: some limits on our capacity for processing information," *Psychological Review*, 63, 81–97.

Mitroff, Ian I., and Kilman, Ralph H. (1978). *Methodological Approaches to Social Science.* Jossey-Bass, San Francisco.

Moscovici, S. (1972). "Society and theory of social psychology," in J. Israel and H. Tajfel (eds.) *The Context of Social Psychology.* Academic Press, New York, 17–68.

Naylor, James C., Pritchard, Robert D., and Ilgen, Daniel R. (1980). *A Theory of Behavior in Organizations.* Academic Press, New York.

Pettigrew, A. M. (1973). *The Politics of Organizational Decision Making.* Tavistock Publications, London.

Simon, Herbert A. (1969). *The Sciences of the Artificial.* MIT Press. Cambridge, MA.

Stogdill, R. M. (1974). *Handbook of Leadership.* Free Press, New York.

Von Neumann, J. (1958). *The Computer and the Brain.* Yale University Press, New Haven.

26

ON THE FRAMING OF MEDICAL DECISIONS

BARBARA J. MCNEIL, STEPHEN G. PAUKER, AND AMOS TVERSKY

The analysis of medical practice as a decision-making process underscores the proposition that the choice of a therapy should reflect not only the knowledge and experience of the physician but also the values and the attitudes of the patient (McNeil, Weischselbaum, and Pauker, 1981). But if patients are to play an active role in medical decision making – beyond passive informed consent – we must find methods for presenting patients with the relevant data and devise procedures for eliciting their preferences among the available treatments. However, the elicitation of preferences, for both patients and physicians, presents a more serious problem than one might expect. Recent studies of judgment and choice have demonstrated that intuitive evaluations of probabilistic data are prone to widespread biases (Kahneman, Slovic, and Tversky, 1982), and that the preference between options is readily influenced by the formulation of the problem (Tversky and Kahneman, 1986).

In a public health problem concerning the response to an epidemic, for example, people prefer a risk-averse strategy when the outcomes are framed in terms of the number of lives saved and a risk-seeking strategy when the same outcomes are framed in terms of the number of lives lost. The tendency to make risk-averse choices in the domain of gains and risk-seeking choices in the domain of losses is a pervasive phenomenon that is attributable to an S-shaped value (or utility) function, with an inflection at one's reference point (Kahneman and Tversky, 1979, 1984). As a consequence, equivalent descriptions of the same options could give rise to different preferences, contrary to the invariance principle of normative decision theory.

To investigate the effect of framing on the choice between therapies we presented people with a hypothetical choice between two treatments for lung cancer: surgery and radiation therapy (McNeil, Pauker, Sox, and Tversky, 1982). The participants received statistical data regarding the effectiveness of the two therapies at three different points in time: immediately after treatment, after one year, and after five years. These data indicated that surgery offers a higher life expectancy than radiation, but it entails much greater risk of immediate death.

All the participants received the same information, but for half of them the data were framed in terms of mortality, whereas for the second half the data were framed in terms of survival. This minor variation in the formulation of the problem had a dramatic effect on people's choices: the percentage of respondents who favored radiation therapy rose from 18 % in the survival frame to 44 % in the mortality frame! Evidently, the advantage of radiation therapy over surgery looms larger when stated as a reduction of the risk of imminent death from 10 % to 0 % rather than as an increase from 90 % to 100 % in the rate of short-term survival. Surprisingly, this effect was no smaller for experienced physicians or for statistically sophisticated business students than for a group of clinic patients. Furthermore, the effect was hardly reduced when the treatments were not identified as surgery or radiation, and were merely labeled *A* or *B*.

The present article describes two studies that extend the analysis of the framing of medical decisions. In the first study, we compare the effect of the mortality/survival frames to a mixed frame that includes both formulations. In the second study, we turn to genetic counseling and investigate people's willingness to forgo pregnancy (i) when the outcomes are described in positive or negative terms, and (ii) when the risks are presented in a conditional or an unconditional form. The implications of the studies are discussed in the final section.

STUDY 1: LUNG CANCER

This study was conducted to investigate the effect of a mixed frame in the choice between surgery and radiation therapy for lung cancer. The following background material was provided in a written form. Each respondent received one of the three formats.

Surgery for lung cancer involves an operation on the lungs. Most patients are in the hospital for two or three weeks and have some pain around their incisions; they spend a month or so recuperating at home. After that, they generally feel fine.

Radiation therapy for lung cancer involves the use of radiation to kill the tumor and requires coming to the hospital about four times a week for six weeks. Each treatment takes a few minutes and during the treatment, patients lie on a table as if they were having an X-ray. During the course of the treatment, some patients develop nausea and vomiting, but by the end of the six weeks they also generally feel fine.

Thus, after the initial six or so weeks, patients treated with either surgery or radiation therapy feel about the same.

Format S (for survival):

Of 100 people having surgery, 90 will live through the surgery, 68 will be alive at the end of the first year, and 34 will be alive at the end of 5 years.

Table 26.1. *Percentage of respondents who favor radiation over surgery under three different formats*

Format	American sample	Israeli sample	Total
Survival (S)	16% (87)	20% (126)	18%
Mortality (M)	50% (80)	45% (132)	47%
Mixed (MS)	44% (223)	34% (144)	40%

Of 100 people having radiation therapy, all live through the treatment, 77 will be alive at the end of the first year, and 22 will be alive at the end of 5 years.

Format M (*for mortality*):

Of 100 people having surgery, 10 will die during the treatment, 32 will have died by 1 year, and 66 will have died by 5 years.

Of 100 people having radiation therapy, none will die during treatment, 23 will die by 1 year, and 78 will die by 5 years.

Format MS (*for mortality and survival*):

Of 100 people having surgery, 10 will die during treatment and 90 will live through the treatment. A total of 32 people will have died by the end of the first year and 68 people will be alive at the end of the first year. A total of 66 people will have died by the end of 5 years and 34 people will be alive at the end of 5 years.

Of 100 people having radiation therapy, none will die during the treatment (i.e., all will live through the treatment). A total of 23 will have died by the end of the first year and 77 will be alive at the end of the first year. A total of 78 people will have died by the end of 5 years and 22 people will be alive at the end of 5 years.

The subject population consisted of 390 participants in postgraduate courses in the Department of Radiology at the Brigham and Women's Hospital and Harvard Medical School. In addition, we administered the questionnaire to a group of 402 medical and science students at the Hebrew University in Jerusalem, Israel.

The results are summarized in table 26.1, which presents the percentage of respondents who prefer radiation to surgery under all three formats. (Sample sizes are given in parentheses.) The results may be summarized as follows. First, the American and the Israeli subjects exhibited the same pattern of responses. Secondly, the contrast between the survival and the mortality frame replicates the finding reported in McNeil et al. (1982). Thirdly, the mixed frame (MS) produced intermediate results, as expected. The overall percentage of respondents who favored radiation over surgery was 47% in the mortality frame, 18% in the survival frame, and 40% in the mixed frame. It is noteworthy that the mixed frame is closer to the mortality frame than to the survival frame. Evidently, the mortality data have more impact than the survival data even in a direct comparison.

STUDY 2: GENETIC COUNSELING

Genetic counseling is a particularly important context for the study of patients' preferences (Pauker, Pauker, and McNeil, 1981). Our study focuses on the decision of whether or not to become pregnant in the face of a specified risk of an abnormal child. We presented normal volunteers with a hypothetical case of pregnancy involving a risk of a serious cardiac abnormality. Each participant responded to one of four formats, described below, that differ in the formulation of the risk.

Format A (for abnormal):

Assume that you (your spouse) are *not* pregnant but that you are considering having a child. Imagine that a new painless test has become available. It is done on blood drawn from a vein and will indicate the chance that a pregnant woman will have either a normal child or one with a major abnormality of the heart. If the baby has the abnormality, s/he will need two open-heart operations – one at 6 months of age and another at age 4 or 5 years. All such children have reduced exercise tolerance and are likely to have serious heart disease later.

Consider now that the screening test has been performed and shows that the chance that you will have a child with this heart abnormality either now or in any future pregnancy is 5%. Additional diagnostic tests to refine this estimate are not available now nor will any be available in the future even if you (your spouse) become pregnant at a later date.

Format N (for normal):

The second format was identical except that the probability of an abnormality was replaced by the probability of a normal child. It read "the chance that you will have a child without this problem either now or in the future is 95%."

Format AN (for abnormal and normal):

The third format included both complementary probabilities. It read "the chance that you will have a child with this heart abnormality either now or in any future pregnancy is 5%; hence, the chance that you will have a child without this problem is obviously 95%."

The fourth format, denoted C/A, expresses the 5% chance of a cardiac abnormality as a 10% chance of a genetic defect and an even chance of a cardiac abnormality conditional on the presence of the defect.

565

Format C/A (conditional/abnormal):

Assume that you (your spouse) are *not* pregnant but that you are considering having a child. Imagine that a new painless test has become available. It is done on blood drawn from a vein and will indicate the chance that a pregnant woman will have either a normal child or one with some abnormality.

Consider now that the screening test has been performed and shows that there is a 10% chance of a genetic defect. If you have the defect, then there is:

– 50% chance that the defect will be consequential and the child will have a major abnormality of the heart. In this case, the baby will need two open-heart operations – one at 6 months of age and another at age 4 or 5 years. All such children have reduced exercise tolerance and are likely to have serious heart disease later.

– 50% chance that the defect is inconsequential, in which case the child will not have the above problem in the heart.

Additional diagnostic tests to refine this estimate are not available now nor will any be available in the future even if you (your spouse) become pregnant at a later date. Hence, it is impossible before birth to determine if the potential defect is consequential or inconsequential.

Each of the above formats was followed by four possible responses and the participant was asked to check one of them:

I would go ahead and get pregnant
I would probably go ahead and get pregnant
I would probably *not* go ahead and get pregnant
I would *not* get pregnant

The subject population consisted of 321 men who were taking part in postgraduate courses in the Department of Radiology at the Brigham and Women's Hospital and Harvard Medical School, and 325 women from a variety of sources (League of Women Voters, members of the Boston Women in Health, physiotherapists at a local hospital, secretaries and technologists at the Department of Radiology at the Brigham and Women's Hospital, and a few women radiologists participating in postgraduate courses in radiology.)

Each individual answered two questions: one of the four problems described above and one problem (in a different format) from a parallel set of problems involving a less severe cardiac abnormality that occurs 10% of the time. The order of presentation was counterbalanced. Because the results from the two sets were essentially the same, the data were combined.

The results are summarized in table 26.2, which presents the percentage of participants who said that they are (definitely or probably) against pregnancy. (Sample sizes are given in parentheses.) As in previous work, the framing of the data had a marked effect on people's choices. In general, most respondents (83%) favored pregnancy despite the risk. However, 23% of the respondents chose to avoid pregnancy in the negative format that specifies the probability of an abnormal child, as compared with only 15% who chose to avoid pregnancy in

Table 26.2. *Percentage of respondents who chose to avoid pregnancy under four different formats*

Format	Women	Men	Total
Normal (N)	13% (96)	17% (150)	15% (246)
Abnormal (A)	22% (115)	23% (106)	22% (221)
Mixed (AN)	14% (219)	28% (224)	21% (443)
Conditional (C/A)	35% (203)	41% (158)	38% (361)

the positive format that specifies the (complementary) probability of a normal child. The difference is statistically significant, $p < .05$ by a sign test. The same pattern was observed for both men and women. Furthermore, 38% chose to avoid pregnancy in the conditional format (C/A); significantly more than in the other formulations.

As can be seen in table 26.2, men and women responded similarly with two notable exceptions. First, men were slightly more risk averse in all conditions. Second, men and women reacted differently to the mixed frame. Women treated the mixed frame like the positive one, whereas men treated it much like the negative frame.

DISCUSSION

The present demonstrations illustrate the impact of framing on medical decision making. As predicted, pregnancy in the face of risk was more attractive in the positive frame than in the negative frame, and least attractive in the conditional frame. We also found an interesting and unexpected difference between men and women. Women generally favored pregnancy more than the men and interpreted the mixed frame more positively than the men. This observation suggests the intriguing hypothesis that people interpret mixed or ambiguous frames in a selective fashion that is consistent with their values and/or beliefs. In the lung cancer problem, we found again a marked difference between the mortality and the survival frame with a mixed frame in an intermediate position.

What are the implications of these findings for medical decision making in general and for the elicitation of patients' preferences in particular? The present results show that even the most elementary normative principles cannot be taken as descriptively valid. Although the information presented to all participants was the same, their responses vary widely depending on the format. To ensure reasonable decisions, serious consideration must be given to the framing of the problem, and this raises the thorny question of what is the "right" way to frame the data and the decision. Should we look at public policy decisions in terms of lives saved or in terms of lives lost? Should we think of the outcomes of treatments in terms of survival rates or mortality rates? There does not seem to be a simple answer to these questions. The fact that different formulations lead to

Barbara J. McNeil, Stephen G. Pauker, and Amos Tversky

different results suggests that neither formulation alone is entirely adequate. The mixed frame may be more helpful because it calls attention to both the positive and the negative aspects of the outcome. More generally, we suggest the use of alternative frames as a form of sensitivity analysis. A person may wish to examine the problem from different perspectives, using different frames. If both the positive and the negative formulation, say, lead to the same decision, the person may feel that his or her preferences are reasonably robust. On the other hand, if different frames elicit different preferences, additional thinking and analysis are recommended.

NOTE

This study was supported, in part, by a grant from the Henry J. Kaiser Family Foundation.

REFERENCES

Kahneman, D., and Tversky, A. (1979). Prospect theory: an analysis of decision under risk. *Econometrica*, 4, 263–91.

(1984). Choices, values, and frames. *American Psychologist*, 39, 341–50.

Kahneman, D., Slovic, P., and Tversky, A. (eds.) (1982). *Judgment Under Uncertainty: Heuristics and Biases*. New York: Cambridge University Press.

McNeil, B. J., Pauker, S. G., Sox, H. C., and Tversky, A. (1982). On the elicitation of preferences for alternative therapies. *New England Journal of Medicine*, 306, 1259–62.

McNeil, B. J., Weischselbaum, R., and Pauker, S. G. (1981). Speech and survival: tradeoffs between quality and quantity of life in laryngeal cancer. *New England Journal of Medicine*, 305, 982–7.

Pauker, S. G., Pauker, S. P., and McNeil, B. J. (1981). The effect of private attitudes on public policy: prenatal screening for neural tube defects as a prototype. *Medical Decision Making*, 1, 103–14.

Tversky, A., and Kahneman, D. (1986). Rational choice and the framing of decisions. *The Journal of Business*, 59, Part 2, 251–78.

27

WHETHER OR NOT TO ADMINISTER AMPHOTERICIN TO AN IMMUNOSUPPRESSED PATIENT WITH HEMATOLOGIC MALIGNANCY AND UNDIAGNOSED FEVER

JONATHAN E. GOTTLIEB AND STEPHEN G. PAUKER

CASE DESCRIPTION

JP is a 52-year-old man with a history of mixed histiocytic–lymphocytic lymphoma of the stomach, diagnosed in 1975. He was treated with surgical excision and postoperative radiotherapy and had no clinical evidence of recurrence five years later. In the spring of 1980, four months prior to the present admission, he developed fatigue and pallor. Hematologic evaluation resulted in the diagnosis of acute myelogenous leukemia.

On the day of admission, the patient developed fever and chills. Physical examination was remarkable only for a temperature of 39°C and general pallor. Laboratory evaluation revealed a hemoglobin level of 8.5 g per deciliter, a white blood cell count of 35,000 per cubic centimeter with 35% myeloblasts, and a platelet count of 108,000 per cubic centimeter. Tobramycin and ticarcillin were administered. Subsequently, two blood cultures were positive for *Staphylococcus epidermidis*; oxacillin was also administered. On the second hospital day, antileukemic therapy with cytosine arabinoside and daunorubicin was begun. Cotrimoxazole was given prophylactically.

After an initial defervescence, the patient developed severe dysphagia and recurrent fever. Barium swallow suggested the presence of esophageal ulcers, consistent with, but not diagnostic of, *Candida* esophagitis. At that time, all other clinical and laboratory data failed to disclose a source of infection. The patient's white blood cell count during this episode was 6,000 per cubic centimeter with 8% polymorphonuclear leukocytes, 50% lymphocytes, and 40% blast forms.

With the presence of continued fever after 10 days of broad-spectrum antibiotics, without an apparent source of infection and with continued granulocytopenia, the patient likely had *Candida* esophagitis and, quite possibly, had a disseminated fungal infection. Without any documentation of systemic mycosis, however, there was much disagreement about whether or not to

569

administer systemic amphotericin therapy, with its attendant severe side effects. A consultation was requested from the Division of Clinical Decision Making to better clarify the risks and benefits of the different management options.

THE PROBLEM STATED

The decision facing the clinicians is whether or not to begin therapy with amphotericin B *at this time*. The choice between administering and withholding amphotericin for presumed disseminated fungal infection is difficult. Arguments in favor of using the drug include the reasonable likelihood of the presence of fungal disease, the efficacy of therapy, and the dire consequences of untreated infection. Arguments against using the drug include the almost universal toxicity of amphotericin, including renal dysfunction, and the lack of conclusive evidence of fungal disease in this patient.

If one were certain that the patient had systemic mycosis, then there should be no hesitation in administering amphotericin. Similarly, if one were certain that fungal disease was not present, use of the drug should be precluded. Thus, the physician must consider how certain (or uncertain) of the presence of fungal disease one must be before administering amphotericin. Unfortunately, further tests that would provide an improved estimate of the likelihood of fungal disease are not available. Furthermore, a delay in beginning therapy would markedly increase mortality if fungal disease were present.

SUMMARY OF AVAILABLE DATA

Incidence of fungal infection

Infection is a common consequence of current therapy for leukemia [1]. Patients typically receive several drugs, often resulting in profound pancytopenia for several weeks. During this period of granulocytopenia, patients are susceptible to infection with a variety of usual and unusual organisms [2, 3]. In leukemic patients followed over a relatively long period of time, infection accounts for 70% of deaths, whereas 25%–30% of infectious episodes result in death [4–6]. Causative organisms include gram-negative bacteria (*Pseudomonas*, *Klebsiella*, *E. coli*), staphylococcal species, fungal organisms (*Candida*, *Phycomycetes*), viruses, and *Pneumocystis*. Most infections documented by culture are due to bacterial organisms; thus, early empirical therapy with broad-spectrum antibiotics is often employed. The advent of more potent antineoplastic regimens has resulted in a steady rise in the number of fungal infections in this group of patients [7–11]. Approximately 25%–30% of deaths in patients suffering from leukemia are associated with deep fungal infection [10, 12–14]. The rate of antemortem diagnosis of disseminated fungal infection, however, remains only 15%–40% [15, 16]. Thus, many potentially treatable fungal infections are not identified clinically and often contribute to early mortality in patients receiving potent chemotherapeutic programs.

Whether or not to administer amphotericin

The present challenge is to identify those patients with leukemia and granulocytopenia who have clinical signs of infection and who actually have systemic mycoses without laboratory documentation. Serological tests are being developed for this purpose, but interlaboratory variations, low sensitivity, and low specificity make such tests not generally useful at present [17–19].

Efficacy of therapy

A recent study examined all febrile episodes in granulocytopenic patients receiving immunosuppressive therapy for leukemia and after transplantation [6]. Overall, there was a 60% chance of surviving the febrile episode; 42% of patients had the infection documented clinically or bacteriologically. All received broad-spectrum antibiotics. Another study examined the records of patients with autopsy or laboratory evidence of deep fungal infection [10]. Seven of 42 patients with *Candida* infection were treated with amphotericin. Of these, none died of fungal infection, although one patient who had undergone renal transplantation demonstrated evidence of disseminated candidiasis at autopsy. Of 35 patients who were not treated with amphotericin, 16 died of disseminated fungal infection and 14 others demonstrated evidence of deep organ involvement at autopsy. That group was, however, dissimilar to the patient under discussion here with respect to underlying disease, immunosuppressive therapy, and the degree of granulocytopenia.

A recent prospective, randomized study examined the course of febrile granulocytopenic patients with cancer who had been receiving broad-spectrum antibiotics for more than seven days and who did not have documentation of infection [20]. All 15 patients treated with amphotericin recovered without sequelae (the median duration of neutropenia was 26 days), whereas four of the 18 patients treated with antibiotics alone developed evidence of disseminated fungal infection.

Complications of amphotericin therapy

Data regarding complications of amphotericin are more sparse. Fever, chills, nausea, headache, and phlebitis occur in almost 90% of patients who receive the drug [21]. Renal dysfunction [22], including a decrease in glomerula filtration rate, renal tubular acidosis [23, 24], and impaired urinary concentrating ability [25, 26] occurs in over 80% of patients. While some permanent impairment of renal function occasionally persists following cessation of therapy, symptomatic renal failure is rare [27]; most patients have full recovery of renal function. Other side effects, such as anemia and thrombocytopenia, are transient and usually not of long-term clinical significance [21]. Deaths from amphotericin administration occur only rarely and are due to anaphylaxis, hepatic necrosis, or, indirectly, to electrolyte disturbances. Precise estimates of the risk of death from amphotericin therapy are unavailable, but such events appear exceedingly rare [28].

571

Jonathan E. Gottlieb and Stephen G. Pauker

Remission and survival in adult non-lymphocytic leukemia

Before the advent of therapy with anthracycline antibiotics and the pyrimidine nucleoside cytosine arabinoside, the remission rate in acute myelogenous leukemia was low and life expectancy was short; fever than 25% of patients entered remission [29]. With current chemotherapeutic protocols, the initial remission rate has increased to 59%–78% [30]. Average duration of remission ranges from 6 to 12 months in different studies. With the achievement of secondary remissions, with or without maintenance chemotherapy, average survival ranges from one to two years [31, 32]. For patients who do not achieve remission, average survival is about 3.5 months, essentially unchanged from that of untreated patients [31, 32].

ANALYSIS OF THE DECISION

Assumptions

In formulating this decision in an analytic framework, we shall make several explicit assumptions:

1. The patient may or may not actually be suffering from a disseminated fungal infection. The likelihood of such infection can be expressed as a probability.
2. If the patient has such an infection, administering amphotericin will be beneficial and will lower the mortality rate from fungal infection.
3. If the patient does not have a fungal infection, administering amphotericin will not increase mortality since fatal toxicity almost never occurs.
4. All patients who receive amphotericin therapy will suffer short-term side effects from the drug. If the patient succumbs to granulocytopenia, such side effects will be ignored, but if the patient survives the acute episode, such side effects will result in a diminution of the quality of life for the period of time that the drug is administered.
5. A patient surviving the acute episode may or may not achieve a remission of leukemia. Whether or not such a remission occurs will determine the patient's expected survival. Providing the patient survives the granulocytopenia episode, the leukemic remission rate is independent of both the presence of fungal infection and the administration of amphotericin.
6. If the patient survives the granulocytopenic episode, there will be no long-term sequelae or quality-of-life adjustments related to the presence or absence of fungal infection.
7. Recovery from granulocytopenia is incorporated into the analysis only to the extent that it modifies the likelihoods of dying from fungal or nonfungal infection. If the granulocytopenia resolves, the mortality from the fungal infection will be low and will not be affected by treatment with amphotericin. In that case, improved cell-mediated immunity would be the major factor that would determine recovery.

572

Structure of the analysis

The decision will be presented by the decision trees [33] shown in figures 27.1 and 27.2. The square node at the left of figure 27.1 denotes the decision whether or not to administer amphotericin. The upper branch of that node denotes the option of administering the drug and the lower branch denotes the option of withholding that therapy. In either case, fungal infection may, in fact, be either present or absent, as denoted by the circular nodes at the right of figure 27.1. Those circular, or chance, nodes reflect the actual state of the world which is not under the control of either the physician or patient and which is not affected by whether or not therapy is administered. Thus, in both cases, we represent the probability that fungal disease is present as P and the probability that fungal disease is absent as $(1 - P)$.

The consequences of each management strategy in the presence and absence of fungal disease are represented by the decision trees in figure 27.2. The upper tree describes the course of events if fungal disease is present. In that case, the patient may die during this episode of granulocytopenia from either fungal or nonfungal infection. These outcomes are denoted by the first two branches of the chance node on the left. Both events result in the same consequence, short-term mortality, and both are assigned the utility UDIENOW, as shown in the upper two boxes at the right margin of the figure. If the patient does not receive amphotericin, then the probability of death from fungal infection is denoted as F. If amphotericin is administered, then the likelihood of death from fungal infection is diminished. The symbol E denotes the efficacy of amphotericin, varying from zero (i.e., no effect on mortality) to one (i.e., all deaths from fungal infection prevented). Thus, if amphotericin is administered, the probability of death from fungal infection is $F(1 - E)$.

Figure 27.1 Initial branches of decision tree. The square node denotes the decision whether or not to administer amphotericin. The circular nodes represent the chance that disseminated fungal infection is present. The probability P of fungal disease is not affected by the choice of therapy. Each of the four branches at the right leads to one of the two trees in figure 27.2.

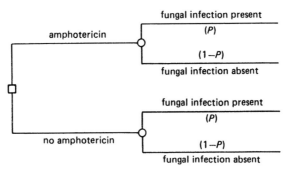

The probability of dying from nonfungal infection is denoted as N. Since that probability is assumed to be independent of the fungal mortality rate, the probability of dying from nonfungal infection is either $N(1 - F[1 - E])$ or $N(1 - F)$, depending on whether or not amphotericin is administered. The probability of surviving the granulocytopenia is therefore either $(1 - N)(1 - F[1 - E])$ or $(1 - N)(1 - F)$, again depending on whether or not amphotericin is administered. In figure 27.2, this complex expression is simply denoted by the symbol *.

If the patient survives the granulocytopenic episode, he may or may not achieve a remission from his leukemia, as denoted by the chance node on the right. The probability of remission is denoted as R. If remission is achieved, the utility is the expected survival of such patients and is denoted by the symbol UREMIT, as shown in the third box from the top at the right edge of the figure. If amphotericin is administered, this expected survival is "quality adjusted" to account for the universal toxic side effects of the drug. This quality adjustment is performed by subtracting the factor TOX from the expected survival. As shown by the lower branch of the chance node on the right, if remission is not achieved, the utility or expected survival is denoted as UNOREMIT; if amphotericin was

Figure 27.2 Consequences of management strategies. The upper tree shows the potential outcomes in the presence of fungal infection; the lower tree shows the possible outcomes if fungal infection is absent. Each circular node denotes a chance event. The expressions in parentheses at each branch denote the probability of that branch occurring. The symbol "(*)" stands for the expression "$((1 - N)(1 - F))$ *or* $((1 - N)(1 - F[1 - E]))$". The symbols in the boxes at the right denote the utilities of the various outcomes. When two alternative probabilities or utilities are shown, the first pertains to withholding amphotericin whereas the second pertains to administering the drug. For details, see text.

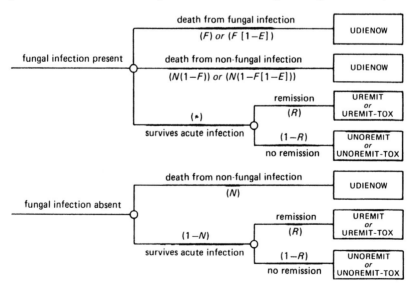

Table 27.1. *Probabilities of chance events*

Event	Symbol	Baseline value[a]
Efficacy of amphotericin (probability of curing[b] fungal infection with treatment)	E	0.50
Fungal mortality rate (probability of dying with untreated fungal infection)	F	0.95
Nonfungal mortality rate (probability of dying from nonfungal infection during this episode of granulocytopenia)	N	0.20
Probability of fungal disease	P	0.30
Remission rate (probability of achieving remission from leukemia)	R	0.60

[a] Best estimate based on available literature and expert opinion.
[b] Cure is defined as preventing an expected death from fungal infection; thus, the fungal mortality rate in patients treated with amphotericin is $F(1 - E)$.

administered, the quality-adjusted survival is UNOREMIT − TOX. In this analysis, all utilities are expressed as "quality-adjusted months of expected survival."

The somewhat simpler lower tree in figure 27.2 corresponds to the consequences of either administering or withholding amphotericin when fungal infection is actually absent. In that case, the outcome "death from fungal infection" does not appear, but the tree is otherwise analogous to the upper tree in the figure. In this simpler case, the probability of death from acute infection is N and the probability of surviving the granulocytopenia episode is simply $(1 - N)$.

Probabilities and utilities

The definitions of the symbols for the various probabilities used in the decision tree are summarized in table 27.1. To our knowledge, there are no prospective studies dealing with the efficacy of amphotericin in this setting. Most clinicians involved with the care of this patient agreed that amphotericin would be less than completely efficacious and estimated that on average its use would allow the patient to recover from fungal infection half of the time. Thus, we have assigned a baseline value of 0.5 to the variable E.

The mortality of untreated fungal disease in similar patients is unknown, but such infections are widely regarded as highly fatal. Before the advent of amphotericin, they were nearly universally fatal. We have used a value of 0.95 for the baseline probabilities of death due to untreated fungal disease in this patient (F). The incidence of fatal nonfungal infections was calculated by subtracting the general incidence of fatal fungal infection (approximately 12%, as described in table 27.1) from the mortality rate of patients with febrile granulocytopenic episodes, that is, 30%–40%. Thus, we used a figure of 0.2 for the baseline probability of death from nonfungal infection N.

The likelihood of fungal disease in this patient (P) is difficult to estimate. As quoted above, approximately 40% of similar patients die during the febrile episode. Moreover, approximately 30% of all patients who die of leukemia have evidence of disseminated fungal disease at autopsy. Clinicians involved in this patient's care estimated the likelihood of fungal disease to be 0.3, which is $2\frac{1}{2}$ times the likelihood calculated by multiplying the chance of death (40%) by the chance of disseminated fungal infection at autopsy (30%). This estimate is not unreasonable in light of the prior treatment with broad-spectrum antibiotics and the evidence of *Candida* esophagitis.

The remission rate R in acute nonlymphocytic leukemia has increased dramatically during the past decade and currently is at least 60%. Although that value might be adjusted downward in this case because of the patient's age and prior history, the clinicians involved in his care felt that a value of 0.6 was still appropriate.

The baseline probabilities presented above were taken from the literature and were then modified or supplemented by the opinions of the experienced clinicians involved in this patient's care. As will be demonstrated below, each of these estimates was subjected to sensitivity analysis, and none were found to be sufficiently close to the break-even or threshold point to substantially affect the decision.

Expressions for the utilities that describe each potential outcome are summarized in table 27.2. As described above, utilities are expressed as expected months of quality-adjusted survival. Favorable responses to antileukemic therapy are associated with remissions which last from 12 to 24 months; we used 18 months to represent the utility of achieving remission (UREMIT). Average survival before the advent of effective chemotherapy was only 3.5 months; we used that value for the utility of not achieving remission (UNOREMIT). Episodes of granulocytopenia usually last from 20 to 40 days. We assumed that the mean duration was 30 days and that patients who die during the episodes will, on average, die halfway through the average episode. Thus, we used 0.5 months for the baseline utility of dying of infection (UDIENOW). Since the quality of life of those patients who eventually die of granulocytopenia is already quite low due to their septic state, we chose not to further diminish that utility by adjusting for the additional toxic effects of amphotericin.

Amphotericin toxicity rarely results in death. Although its use is associated with nearly universal morbidity, one must estimate just how severe that morbidity is. Based on the opinions of experienced clinicians, we initially assumed that the quality of life during amphotericin therapy would be diminished by 50%. Since therapy with that drug typically lasts for six weeks, we used half of that value, or 0.75 months, as the quality adjustment for amphotericin toxicity (TOX).

Table 27.2. *Utilities of outcomes*

Outcome	Symbolic representation	Baseline value (in quality-adjusted months)[a]
Death from infection	UDIENOW	0.50
Remission, no amphotericin, surves fungal infection	UREMIT	18.00
Remission, amphotericin, survives fungal infection	UREMIT – TOX	$18 - 0.75 = 17.25$
Remission, no amphotericin, fungal infection absent	UREMIT	18.00
Remission, amphotericin, fungal infection absent	UREMIT – TOX	$18 - 0.75 = 17.25$
No remission, no amphotericin, survives fungal infection	UNOREMIT	3.50
No remission, amphotericin, survives fungal infection	UNOREMIT – TOX	$3.5 - 0.75 = 2.75$
No remission, no amphotericin, fungal infection absent	UNOREMIT	3.50
No remission, amphotericin, fungal infection absent	UNOREMIT – TOX	$3.5 - 0.75 = 2.75$

[a] Best estimate based on available literature and expert opinion; quality adjustment is made by subtracting TOX from expected survival, where TOX reflects the side effects of amphotericin.

Calculation of expected utilities

Having structured the decision and having assigned probabilities and utilities to each chance event and to each outcome, we now calculate the expected or average utility for each of the two management plans – administering and withholding amphotericin. The principles of decision analysis [33–40] state that the option with the higher expected utility should be selected. For each chance node, the expected utility is calculated to be the sum of the branchwise products of probability and (expected) utility. For example, consider the lower tree in figure 27.2 and assume that amphotericin is *not* administered. In that case, the expected utility of the chance node at the right is R times UREMIT plus $(1 - R)$ times UNOREMIT or, rearranging terms, UNOREMIT + R(UREMIT – UNOREMIT). Similarly, the expected utility of the chance node at the left of this tree is N times UDIENOW plus $(1 - N)$ times the previously calculated expected utility of the chance node at the right, or N(UDIENOW) + $(1 - N)$ (UNOREMIT + R[UREMIT – UNOREMIT]). In a similar manner, the expected utilities of administering amphotericin and withholding the drug are calculated by folding the tree back from right to left.

Using the baseline values specified in tables 27.1 and 27.2, we find that the expected utility of administering amphotericin is 8.0 quality-adjusted months of survival, whereas the expected utility of withholding the drug is only 7.2 quality-adjusted months. Thus, administering amphotericin would appear to be the preferred course of action in this patient, with an expected gain of 0.8 quality-adjusted months of survival. That relatively small gain represents an improvement of 0.8/7.2, or 11%, for this patient. If no quality adjustment is made for amphotericin toxicity, then the expected survival with amphotericin therapy would be 8.5 months whereas the expected survival without such therapy would remain 7.2 months, a gain of 1.3 months, or 18%, in life expectancy.

Sensitivity analysis

One of the most powerful decision-analytic techniques is sensitivity analysis, by which one examines the impact that changes in various assumptions will have on the decision. If each of the assumptions (e.g., each of the probabilities and utilities in tables 27.1 and 27.2) is independent of all other assumptions, then it is reasonable to vary each parameter by itself, assuming all other parameters to be fixed at their baseline or "best guess" values. On the other hand, if several assumptions might be interdependent, or if it seems important to examine the trade-off between specific gains and losses, then it is best to examine several variables at once.

In the initial sensitivity analyses presented below, we shall assume that the various probabilities presented in table 27.1 are independent of one another, and we shall therefore present a variety of one-way sensitivity analyses. Each analysis is performed by varying the value assigned to a particular parameter, holding all others constant. For each new value assigned to that parameter, the expected utility of each management option is recalculated to determine if the variation altered the relative values of the two options. The simplest way to understand such sensitivity analyses is to view them in graphical form.

In figure 27.3, we examine the effect of changes in the efficacy of amphotericin as a treatment for disseminated fungal infection. In that figure, the horizontal axis depicts all possible efficacies E, ranging from zero (no efficacy, mortality from fungal infection not affected by therapy) to one (perfect efficacy, no treated patients die of fungal infection). The vertical axis depicts the expected utility in quality-adjusted months of survival. The solid line represents the option of administering amphotericin and the broken line represents the option of withholding that therapy. The rule of selecting the strategy with the higher expected utility translates into the graphical rule of selecting the higher of the two lines. The baseline assumption was that the efficacy of amphotericin was 0.5. As can be seen on the graph, that assumption corresponds to an expected utility of 8.0 for amphotericin and one of 7.2 for no amphotericin. The graph clearly demonstrates that administering amphotericin is the preferred alternative as long as the efficacy of the drug is greater than 0.17, that is, as long as it is greater than 17% effective in preventing death from fungal infection. The value of 0.17 is called the *threshold* [35, 40] value for the efficacy of amphotericin. At the threshold, either strategy would result in the same expected utility. Note that the broken line corresponding to withholding amphotericin therapy is horizontal, that is, the efficacy of amphotericin has no effect on the prognosis of patients *not* given the drug.

Figure 27.4 presents a sensitivity analysis of the probability of death from untreated fungal infection. The format is identical to that of the previous figure except that the horizontal axis now depicts the fungal mortality rate F. The

Figure 27.3 Effect of variations in efficacy. A one-way sensitivity analysis of the relation between drug efficacy E and expected utility. The solid line corresponds to the plan of administering amphotericin and the broken line corresponds to withholding the drug.

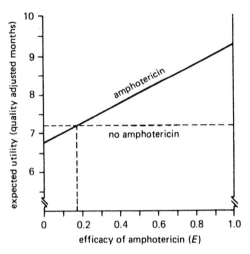

Figure 27.4 Effect of variations in the fungal mortality rate. A one-way sensitivity analysis of the relation between fungal mortality F and expected utility. The format is the same as in figure 27.3.

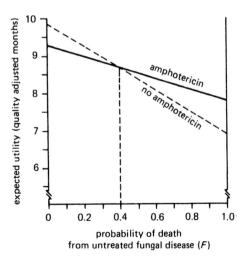

baseline value of that variable was 0.95, and at that value amphotericin therapy is clearly preferred. As can be seen in the figure, amphotericin therapy is the preferred alternative unless the probabilities of death from untreated fungal disease is below 0.4. Although not pictured here, an analogous series of calculations based on varying the probability of dying from nonfungal infection N demonstrated that the nonfungal mortality rate has no effect on the decision if any patients service such infections. In other words, as long as there is any chance of not succumbing to nonfungal infection, the preferred strategy is to administer amphotericin.

The effect of varying the probability of fungal infection P is illustrated in figure 27.5. At the baseline value of 0.3, amphotericin is the preferred choice and remains so unless the probability of fungal disease is below 0.13. The range of clinical estimates of the probability was between 25% and 75%, all well above the calculated threshold.

The likelihood of achieving remission from leukemia and the expected duration of such remissions are examined in figure 27.6. Figure 27.6a demonstrates that administering amphotericin is the preferred choice unless the probability of achieving remission is below 0.1. Figure 27.6b demonstrates that amphotericin therapy remains the better strategy unless the expected duration of survival in patients achieving remission falls below six months. The baseline values for these parameters were 0.6 and 18 months, respectively. Furthermore, it can be demonstrated that administering amphotericin is the preferred choice as long as the life expectancy of patients surviving granulocytopenia is greater than 5 months compared to the baseline calculated value of 12.2 months, that is, UNOREMIT + R(UREMIT − UNOREMIT), or $3.5 + 0.6(18 − 3.5)$.

Figure 27.5 Effect of variations in probability of fungal infection. A one-way sensitivity analysis of the relation between the probability of fungal infection P and expected utility. The format is the same as in figure 27.3.

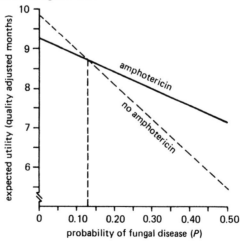

The analysis of the effect of variations in UREMIT on the decision demonstrates that utilities as well as probabilities can be subjected to sensitivity analysis. Figure 27.7 demonstrates a sensitivity analysis of the effect of variation in another utility variable, the quality-of-life adjustment for drug side effects (TOX). At the baseline value of 0.75 months, administering amphotericin is clearly the preferable option. Withholding the drug is not preferable until the quality cost of toxicity exceeds 1.9 months. Since the average drug course is only six weeks, or 1.5 months, the quality of the life during drug administration must be worse than death to preclude using the drug.

The results of each of the nine possible one-way sensitivity analyses are summarized in table 27.3 as the threshold value for each variable. As can be seen in that table, no baseline value is sufficiently close to its associated threshold for reasonable variations to affect the decision. Our conclusion that amphotericin therapy is warranted seems quite solid.

In considering whether or not to administer amphotericin to this patient, one is, in effect, balancing the efficacy of amphotericin therapy against its toxicity. We shall examine the joint effect of variations in these parameters by performing a two-way sensitivity analysis, as shown in figure 27.8a. Any combination of drug efficacy E and drug toxicity (TOX) will correspond to a unique point in that graph. The region above the curve corresponds to all combinations of efficacy and toxicity for which amphotericin therapy would be preferable. The area below the curve corresponds to all combinations of efficacy and toxicity for which

Figure 27.6 Effect of variations in the probability and expected duration of remission. (a) One-way sensitivity analysis of the relation between the probability of achieving remission R and expected utility. (b) One-way sensitivity analysis of the relation between the expected duration of a remission (UREMIT) and expected utility. The formats are the same as in figure 27.3.

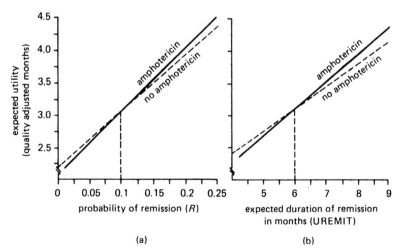

(a)   (b)

581

the drug should be withheld. The curve demonstrates that there is an almost linear trade-off between gains in efficacy and increases in drug toxicity. The baseline values of 0.75 and 0.5 for toxicity and efficacy, respectively, correspond to a point well within the amphotericin region.

The size of the area above the curve will be influenced by variations in other assumptions of the analysis. One can create families of curves corresponding to variations in other parameters and in so doing can perform three-way sensitivity analyses. Two such analyses are presented in figures 27.8b and 27.8c. Figure

Table 27.3. *Sensitivity analyses*

Variable	Represents	Baseline value	Threshold value
Probabilities			
E	Efficacy of amphotericin	0.50	0.17
F	Fungal mortality rate	0.95	0.40
N	Nonfungal mortality rate	0.20	1.00
P	Probability of fungal disease	0.30	0.13
R	Remission rate	0.60	0.10
Utilities (months)			
UDIENOW	Time to death from infection	0.50	7.7
TOX	Quality lost from side effects	0.75	1.9
UREMIT	Expected survival with remission	18.00	6.0
UNOREMIT	Expected survival with no remission	3.5	*a*

a No threshold exists; decision unchanged for any value of this variable.

Figure 27.7 Effect of variations in the severity of drug toxicity. A one-way sensitivity analysis of the relation between the diminution in the quality of life due to amphotericin side effects (TOX) and expected utility. The format is the same as in figure 27.3.

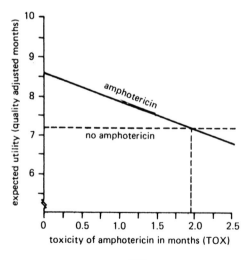

27.8b shows the effect of variations in the probability of fungal disease P. With likelihoods of fungal infection higher than our baseline assumptions of 0.3, the area above the curve increases; with lower likelihoods, it decreases. The line labeled $P = 0.1$ corresponds roughly to the assumptions that fungal disease is no more prevalent in granulocytopenic patients than in all patients dying with leukemia. Even if that highly unlikely assumption were true, the efficacy of amphotericin would only need to exceed 57% to justify administering the drug. Figure 27.8c demonstrates the effect of variations in the probability of dying from untreated disease F. Given our baseline assumption about efficacy and toxicity, amphotericin therapy would still be indicated if the fungal mortality rate were only 50%.

These additional sensitivity analyses lend further support to the robustness of the conclusion that therapy with amphotericin is the preferred course of action in this febrile, granulocytopenic patient, although there is no conclusive evidence of disseminated fungal infection.

COMMENTS

The extensive analysis presented here firmly favors the use of amphotericin in this patient, whose likelihood of having systemic fungal infection was estimated to be

Figure 27.8 Trade-off between drug toxicity and drug efficacy. (a) Two-way sensitivity analysis of the threshold relation between the severity of drug toxicity (TOX) and the efficacy of drug therapy E. The area above the curve corresponds to those combinations of these two factors for which administering amphotericin would be the preferred choice. (b) Three-way sensitivity analysis, including the effect of variations in the probability of fungal infection P. (c) Three-way sensitivity analysis depicting the effect of variations in the fungal mortality rate F. For details, see text.

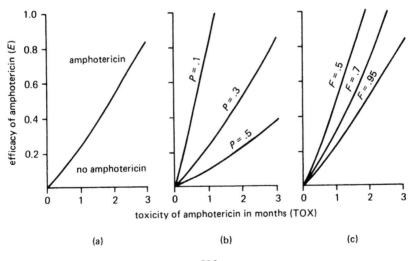

30% although no documentation of such infection was available. The threshold probability of fungal infection above which amphotericin should be administered was calculated to be 0.13. As an approximate bedside technique, the clinician could make similar calculations using the equation for the therapeutic threshold [35]. That equation states that the threshold probability should be equal to $1/((B/C) + 1)$, where B is defined as the net benefit of treating patients having disease (i.e., administering amphotericin to patients having systemic mycosis) and C is defined as the cost of treating patients without disease.

Based on the data presented in tables 27.1 and 27.2, we can estimate the cost of treatment C to be 0.75 months. Among patients with fungal infection, survival will increase from 0.5 months to 18 months if remission is achieved (60% of patients) and will increase from 0.5 months to 3.5 months if remission is not achieved (40% of patients). Thus the benefit of therapy might be as high as $17.5 \times 60\%$ plus $3 \times 40\%$, or 11.7 months. The efficacy, however, is estimated to be only 50%; thus, the benefit is at most half of that value, or 5.85 months. Furthermore, 20% of patients surviving fungal infection will succumb to nonfungal infections, lowering the benefit to 80% of 5.85, or 4.68 months. Finally, all treated patients will suffer amphotericin toxicity (a quality loss of 0.75 months), making the net benefit only 3.93 months. Thus, the threshold is roughly $1/((3.93/0.75) + 1)$, or 0.16, agreeing quite well with the more detailed calculation. Such a bedside analysis would have demonstrated that this patient, who had a 30% chance of systemic fungal infection, should be treated with amphotericin.

We shall now consider the effect of other assumptions that we made on the decision. We assumed no long-term morbidity or mortality of fungal infection. In fact, fungal infection can result in long-term morbidity and mortality because of the possibility of recurrence, chronic organ by dysfunction, and so forth. This effect would cause a greater reduction in quality-adjusted survival in the untreated branch, and therefore would only reinforce our conclusion to use amphotericin. We also assumed no mortality due to amphotericin. In the event of circumstances in which there will be a decrease in survival (such as a high likelihood of precipitating end-stage renal failure), the drug-associated mortality would have to approach 11% before our conclusion would be affected. Many assumptions were inherent in our derivation of the probabilities and utilities from the literature. Although we have not attempted to justify those estimates in detail, they are in keeping with the clinical impressions of the experienced clinicians caring for this patient.

Although the general class of granulocytopenic patients with leukemia who remain febrile after receiving broad-spectrum antibiotics and who have no documented fungal infection might benefit from amphotericin, our limited data do not adequately support such a broad recommendation. The high likelihood of *Candida* esophagitis in this patient distinguishes him from that general group. All other things being equal, however, if the likelihood of fungal infection is greater than 10%–15%, then amphotericin therapy may well be beneficial. Certainly amphotericin is a highly toxic drug with imperfect efficacy; however, we believe that, in this patient and ones similar to him, the potential benefit of its use outweighs its complications.

NOTE

Supported in part by training grant T15LM07027 from the Computers in Medicine program of the National Library of Medicine, by grant 1P41RR01096 from the Division of Research Resources and grant 1P01LM03374 from the National Library of Medicine. Dr Pauker is the recipient of Research Career Development Award 1K04GM00349 from the Institute of General Medical Sciences, National Institutes of Health, Bethesda, Md.

First published in *Medical Decision Making*, 1 (1981), 75–93.

REFERENCES

1. Sickles, E. A., Young, V. M., Greene, W. H., and Wiernik, P. H. (1973). Pneumonia in acute leukemia. *Ann. Inter. Med.* 79:528–34.

2. Baker, R. D. (1962). Leukopenia and therapy in leukemia as factors predisposing to fatal mycoses. *Am. J. Clin. Pathol.* 37:358–73.

3. Bodey, G. P. (1966). Fungal infections complicating acute leukemia. *J. Chronic Dis.* 19:667–87.

4. Hersh, E. M., Bodey, G. P., Nies, B. A., and Freireich, E. J. (1965). Causes of death in acute leukemia. *JAMA* 193:105–9.

5. Schimpff, S. C., Young,, V. M., Greene, W. H., Vermeulen, G. D., Moody, M. R., and Wiernik, P. H. (1972). Origin of infection in acute nonlymphocytic leukemia. *Ann. Intern. Med.* 77:707–14.

6. Stuart, R. K., Braine, H. G., Lietman, P. S., Saral, R., and Fuller, D. J. (1980). Carbenicillin–trimethoprim/sulfamethoxazole versus carbenicillin–gentamicin as empiric therapy of infection in granulocytopenic patients. *Am. J. Med.* 68:876–85.

7. Silver, R. (1963). Infections, fever and host resistance in neoplastic diseases. *J. Chronic Dis.* 16:677–701.

8. Gruhn, J. G., and Sanson, J. (1963). Mycotic infections in leukemic patients at autopsy. *Cancer* 16:61–72.

9. Schumacher, H. R., Ginns, D. A., and Warren, W. J. (1964). Fungus infection complicating leukemia. *Am. J. Med. Sci.* 247:313–23.

10. Hart, P. D., Russell, Jr, E. R., and Remington, J. (1969). The compromised host and infection: II. Deep fungal infection. *J. Infect. Dis.* 120:169–92.

11. Eilard, T., and Norrby, R. (1978). Clinical diagnosis of systemic fungal infections. *Scand. J. Infect. Dis. (suppl.)* 16:15–22.

12. Krick, J. A., and Remington, J. S. (1976). Opportunistic invasive fungal infections in patients with leukaemia and lymphoma. *Clin. Haematol.* 5:249–310.

13. Mirsky, H. S., and Cuttner, J. (1972). Fungal infection in acute leukemia. *Cancer* 30:348–52.

14. Bennett, J. E. (1978). Diagnosis and management of candidiasis in the immunosuppressed host. *Scand. J. Infect. Dis (suppl.)* 16:83–6.

15. Gaines, J. D., and Remington, J. S. (1973). Diagnosis of deep infection with *Candida*. A study of *Candida* precipitins. *Arch. Inter. Med.* 132:699–702.

16. Edwards, J. E., Lehrer, R. I., Stiehm, E. R., Fischer, T. J., and Young, L. S. (1978). Severe candidal infections. *Ann. Intern. Med.* 89:91–106.

17. Filice, G., Yu. B., and Armstrong, D. (1977). Immunodiffusion and agglutination tests for *Candida* in patients with neoplastic disease: inconsistent correlation of results with invasive infections. *J. Infect. Dis.* 135:349–57.

18. Glew, R. H., Buckley, H. R., Rosen, H. M., Moellering, R. C., and Fischer, J. F. (1978). Serologic tests in the diagnosis of systemic candidiasis. *Am. J. Med.* 64:586–91.

19. Holmberg, K. (1978). Serological diagnosis of systemic candidiasis and invasive aspergillosis. *Scand. J. Infect. Dis. (suppl.)* 16:26–32.

20. Pizzo, P. A., and Robichaud, K. (1980). Treatment and prevention of fungal infection in cancer patients. In Nelson, J. D., and Grassi, C., eds. *Current Chemotherapy and Infectious Disease.* Washington DC, Am. Soc. Microbiol. 1432–3.

21. Meade III, R. H. (1979). Drug therapy reviews: clinical pharmacology and therapeutic use of antimycotic drugs. *Hosp. Pharmacy Forum of N. Engl. Med. Center Hosp.* 8:1–9.

22. Medoff, G., and Kobayashi, G. S. (1980). Strategies in the treatment of systemic fungal infections. *N. Engl. J. Med.* 302:145–55.

23. McCurdy, D. K., Frederic, M., and Elkinton, J. R. (1968). Renal tubular acidosis due to amphotericin B. *N. Engl. J. Med.* 278:124–31.

24. Douglas, J. B., and Healy, J. K. (1969). Nephrotoxic effects of amphotericin B, including renal tubular acidosis. *Am. J. Med.* 46:154–63.

25. Utz, J. P., Bennett, J. E., Brandriss, M. W., Butler, W. T., and Hill II, G. J. (1964). Amphotericin B toxicity. *Ann. Inter. Med.* 61:334–54.

26. Norrby, R., and Eilard, T. (1978). Treatment of opportunistic systemic mycoses. *Scand. J. Infect. Dis. (suppl.)* 16:59–64.

27. Butler, W. T., Bennett, J. E., Alling, D. W., Wertlake, P. T., Utz, J. P., and Hiil, G. J. (1964). Nephrotoxicity of amphotericin B: early and late effects in 81 patients. *Ann. Intern. Med.* 61:175–87.

28. Meade III, R. H. (1979). Antifungal agents. In Miller, R. R., and Greenblatt, D. J., eds. *Handbook of Drug Therapy.* New York, Elsevier–North Holland, 159–74.

29. Rodriguez, V., Hart, J. S., and Freireich, E. J. (1973). POMP combination chemotherapy of adult acute leukemia. *Cancer* 32:69–75.

30. Dabich, L. (1980). Adult acute nonlymphocytic leukemia. *Med. Clin. North Am.* 64:683–704.

31. Henderson, E. (1980). Acute myelogenous leukemia. In Williams, W. J. *et al.* eds., *Hematology.* New York, McGraw-Hill, 830–41.

32. Clarkson, B. (1980). The acute leukemias. In Isselbacher, K., *et al.* eds., *Principles of Internal Medicine.* New York, McGraw-Hill, 1620–30.

33. Raiffa, H. (1968). *Decision Analysis.* Reading, Mass., Addison-Wesley.

34. Lusted, L. B. (1968). *Introduction to Medical Decision Making.* Springfield, Ill., Charles C. Thomas.

35. Pauker, S. G., and Kassirer, J. P. (1975). Therapeutic decision making: a cost-benefit analysis. *N. Engl. J. Med.* 293:229–34.

36. Kassirer, J. P. (1976). The principles of clinical decision making: an introduction to decision analysis. *Yale J. Biol. Med.* 49:149–64.

37. Weinstein, M. C., and Fineberg, H. V. (1980). *Clinical Decision Analysis.* Philadelphia, W. B. Saunders.
38. Pauker, S. G., and Kassirer, J. P. (1978). Clinical application of decision analysis: a detailed illustration. *Semin. Nucl. Med.* 8:324–35.
39. Barza, M., and Pauker, S. G. (1980). The decision to biopsy, treat, or wait in suspected herpes encephalitis. *Ann. Intern. Med.* 92:641–9.
40. Pauker, S. G., and Kassirer, J. P. (1980). The threshold approach to clinical decision making. *N. Engl. J. Med.* 302:1108–17.

28

THE EFFECTS OF PRIVATE ATTITUDES ON PUBLIC POLICY: PRENATAL SCREENING FOR NEURAL TUBE DEFECTS AS A PROTOTYPE

STEPHEN G. PAUKER, SUSAN P. PAUKER, AND BARBARA J. MCNEIL

Although screening programs for neural tube defects (NTDs) are routine and cost-effective in Great Britain [1–6] their potential use in the United States has been hotly debated [7–13]. In this chapter we report the attitudes of 338 prospective patients seeking genetic counseling about the use of amniocentesis for prenatal diagnosis. We have integrated these attitudes with the expected accuracy and complications of a comprehensive screening program for NTDs and have estimated the proportion of these prospective parents who would benefit from a maternal serum alpha-fetoprotein (AFP) screening program. Thus, we have addressed perhaps the most critical problem related to the decision of whether or not to institute an AFP screening program: "What are the implications of the attitudes of prospective parents toward the desirability of a large-scale screening program for the prenatal detection of NTDs?" In a larger sense, we are addressing a prototypical problem for many policy analyses: How can the personal attitudes of individual members of society be integrated into decisions affecting the medical care of society as a whole [14]?

METHODS

Summary of screening plan. Figure 28.1 summarizes the policies analyzed in this paper. Maternal serum AFP concentration is measured at a gestational age between 16 and 18 weeks. If the concentration of AFP is above a predetermined level (typically either 2.5 times the median or two standard deviations above the mean), the serum test is repeated. If the AFP concentration in the second sample is also elevated, the woman is informed that she is at increased risk of carrying a fetus affected by an NTD. The couple is offered an ultrasonic examination to verify the gestational age and to detect twins or fetal death. If ultrasound demonstrates a gestational age consistent with the observed AFP concentration, twins, or fetal death, the evaluation stops. On the other hand, if ultrasound offers no explanation for the elevated AFP level, then one of two policies may be followed. The first (policy A in figure 28.1), which corresponds to the current

British screening program [2–4] and to a similar program in New York State [7], offers amniocentesis to every woman whose ultrasonic examination reveals neither an error in gestational dating nor the presence of twins or fetal distress. The recently proposed [9] second policy (policy B in figure 28.1) assumes that ultrasound can detect some NTDs, and hence elective abortion can be offered to the couple if either anencephaly or meningomyelocele is demonstrated. Under this policy, if ultrasound does not demonstrate an NTD, the couple is offered amniocentesis. If amniotic fluid AFP concentrations are shown to be normal, the evaluation stops; if the levels are elevated, the couple is counseled about elective abortion. Under either policy, the couple's decision regarding amniocentesis is difficult because of the risk of miscarriage of a normal pregnancy.

Overview of the analysis. The desirability of a screening program can be measured by the degree to which the target population will accept the results of

Figure 28.1 Flow diagram of screening program considered in this analysis.

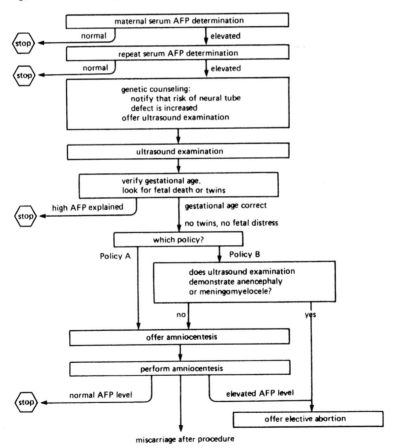

589

screening and proceed to further diagnostic or therapeutic evaluation. In the context of prenatal screening for NTDs, the proportion of parents who would proceed with amniocentesis is one measure of the desirability of the program. Each couple's decision would be based on both objective and subjective data. The objective data include the chance of having an affected child and the risk and accuracy of amniocentesis. The subjective data are the couple's attitudes toward elective abortion and toward miscarriage occurring as a complication of amniocentesis.

In this chapter, we used decision analysis to integrate the objective and subjective data and to determine whether amniocentesis would be appropriate for an individual. The analysis was repeated for each prospective parent and the results were tallied so that we could determine the proportion of such parents who would accept amniocentesis if a screening program demonstrated them to be at increased risk of having a child affected by an NTD.

Assumptions of the analysis. To calculate the probability of NTDs, we have made the following assumptions:

1. The incidence of NTDs in the United States is one per 1,000 births. Of the affected children, 60% will have meningomyelocele and 40% will have anencephaly [15].

2. Closed defects constitute 10% of all NTDs – the defects are covered by sufficient skin to prevent leakage of AFP into amniotic fluid or maternal serum. Thus, maternal serum levels will be normal and these fetuses will not be identified by the screening program [16].

3. A positive screening result is defined as *two* elevated serum AFP levels; screening provides a sensitivity of 85% and a specificity of 96% [1–4, 7–10].

4. Ultrasound reveals an error in the estimated gestational age or the presence of twins in 50% of women with two elevated AFP levels [1–4, 7–10].

5. Ultrasound has a sensitivity of 95% in detecting anencephaly and 75% in detecting meningomyelocele [17]. The specificity of ultrasound is 100% in detecting these defects [9]. These assumptions were used in the analysis of policy B.

6. The excess miscarriage rate in women having second trimester amniocentesis is 0.5%, a compromise between the rates reported in the United States [18, 19] and the far higher rate reported in Great Britain [20, 21].

7. Elevation of amniotic fluid AFP levels has a sensitivity of 95% and a specificity of 99% in detecting NTDs in women identified by elevated serum AFP levels [16, 22].

8. The attitudes toward abortion of prospective parents participating in a screening program for NTDs can be approximated by the attitudes of parents seeking genetic counseling for a variety of reasons, most commonly about their risk of having a child affected by Down's syndrome [23].

Sensitivity analysis. Recognizing the potential limitations of the data upon which the above assumptions were based, we performed several sensitivity analyses by repeating all our calculations using three different sets of assumptions. First, we assumed that the accuracy of the serum screening program for detecting NTDs could be adversely affected in a large-scale program such that the sensitivity might be as low as 70% and the specificity as low as 90%. Second, in analyzing policy B, we considered that the sensitivity of ultrasound in detecting meningomyelocele might be as low as 0% or as high as 90%. Finally, we assumed that the results of amniotic fluid AFP determinations might not be independent of maternal serum AFP levels [3]. If the two tests are interdependent, then the sensitivity and specificity of amniotic fluid AFP testing could be lower than we had assumed. In the absence of data regarding the degree of dependence, we repeated the analysis under the assumption that the sensitivity of amniotic fluid AFP levels in detecting the NTDs might be as low as 85% and the specificity as low as 95%.

Attitudes of prospective parents. Several attitudes are important in this analysis: first, the attitudes of prospective parents toward an elective abortion; secondly, their attitudes toward a miscarriage induced by diagnostic amniocentesis; and finally their attitudes toward the birth of a defective child. These attitudes were placed on a scale [23, 24] from zero to 100, where zero implied no burden (i.e., the birth of a normal child) and 100 was defined as the burden of an affected child. To assess the attitudes of the individual parents on this scale, we asked prospective parents seeking genetic counseling at the Harvard Community Health Plan questions such as: "At what chance of a pregnancy's producing a severely deformed child would you prefer elective abortion to the risk of having a live-born child affected by that deformity?" The minimum chance at which they would still prefer abortion was used as a measure of the burden of abortion relative to the burden of an affected child. An analogous question was used to assess the burden of a miscarriage induced by amniocentesis. Since none of the 338 prospective parents felt that the burden of miscarriage was greater than the burden of elective abortion [24], we made the conservative assumption in this analysis that the burden of a procedure-related miscarriage is as severe as the burden of an elective abortion. Thus, a screening program that appears desirable under this assumption would certainly be desirable for prospective parents for whom the burden of miscarriage would be less than the burden of elective abortion.

Analysis. We first used Bayes' rule [25] and data on the reliability of serum screening and ultrasound to calculate the chance of carrying a fetus affected by an NTD. We then examined the effect on that likelihood of lower sensitivities and specificities for these tests. Finally, we used the distribution of the attitudes of prospective parents to estimate the proportion of people facing the amniocentesis decision for whom amniocentesis would be the logical choice [23, 24].

591

RESULTS

Attitudes toward abortion. On a scale in which the birth of an affected child is given a burden of 100 and the birth of a normal child is given a burden of zero, the perceived burden of elective abortion was quite variable. As shown in figure 28.2, for example, 167 of the 338 parents interviewed (49 %) felt that the burden of an abortion would be low – 20 % or less of the burden of an affected child. In contrast, 32 (9 %) felt that the burden of abortion would be high – at least 80 % of the burden of an affected child. Over 75 % felt that the burden of abortion would be less than half the burden of an affected child. The mean assessed burden of abortion was 33 % of the burden of an affected child, and the standard deviation was 31 %. There was no significant difference between the attitudes of the 15 parents seeking counseling for NTDs and the 323 parents seeking counseling for chromosomal disorders.

The likelihood of an NTD after two elevated maternal serum AFP levels. The chance of a fetus's being affected by an NTD, after two elevated maternal serum AFPs, varies from 1 % to over 5 %, depending on the false-positive and false-negative rates that can be achieved in a large-scale screening program (see figure

Figure 28.2 Attitudes toward elective abortion of 338 prospective parents seeking genetic counseling. The horizontal axis displays their assessments of the burden of abortion expressed as a percentage of the burden of an affected child. The shaded bars denote the number of parents who assessed the burden of abortion at various values. The vertical axis and the heavy curve show the cumulative percentage of parents who assessed the burden of abortion to be below various values.

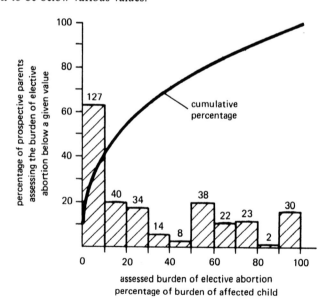

592

28.3). Our best estimates of those error rates (i.e., 4% and 15%, respectively) suggest that women having two elevated serum AFP levels would face a 2% risk of bearing an affected fetus. Even if the false-positive and false-negative rates were 8% and 30%, respectively (values twice as high as our best estimates, and a most unlikely occurrence, based on the experience in Great Britain [2, 3, 4]), women at "high risk" would still have a 1% risk of bearing an affected fetus. Thus, the women identified by serum screening would have nearly 20 times the risk of bearing children with NTDs as would women from the general population.

The likelihood of an NTD after ultrasonic examination. Ultrasonic examination can provide alternative explanations of elevated serum AFP concentrations (e.g., incorrect estimation of gestational age or the presence of twins) and can detect the presence of some NTDs. For clarity, we shall consider these two types of information separately. After either an incorrectly estimated gestational age or the presence of twins has been excluded, the chance of an NTD is roughly doubled. Thus under policy A the chance of a woman with elevated

Figure 28.3 Revised likelihood of neural tube defects (NTDs) as a function of the false-positive and false-negative rates of screening – where a positive result means *two* elevated maternal serum alpha-fetoprotein (AFP) levels. The false-positive rate is shown on the abscissa. Each curve corresponds to a different false-negative rate, i.e., 0%, 15%, and 30%. The incidence of NTDs is assumed to be 1 per 1,000. The arrow in the lower left corner of the figure indicates the best estimates of the error rates and revised probability of a detect.

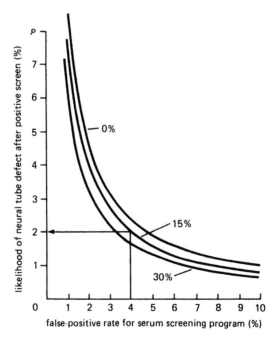

serum AFP carrying a fetus affected by an NTD is about 4% after the ultrasound examination. On the other hand, when data regarding the ability of ultrasound to detect the presence of an NTD are considered (policy B), the likelihood of an NTD after a negative ultrasound examination is quite different. For example, if an NTD is *not* determined by ultrasound, then the likelihood of an affected fetus is diminished, and, if the fetus is affected, the lesion will most likely be a meningomyelocele. The less sensitive ultrasound is in detecting meningomyelocele, the higher the likelihood of that defect after a negative ultrasound examination (figure 28.4). In the extreme case, in which ultrasound is assumed incapable of detecting meningomyelocele, the likelihood of an affected fetus would be 2.4% after a negative ultrasonic examination. In the average case (75% sensitivity), the likelihood of an affected fetus would be 0.7%.

The amniocentesis decision. Assuming that ultrasound cannot reliably diagnose an NTD and that amniocentesis is required before counseling about elective abortion (policy A), our analysis suggests that 86% of the prospective parents interviewed should, on the basis of their personal attitudes toward abortion, proceed with amniocentesis if they have two elevated maternal serum AFP levels and if ultrasonic examination verifies the gestational age and fails to

Figure 28.4 Relation between the sensitivity of ultrasound in detecting meningomyelocele and the likelihood of an affected fetus if the ultrasonic examination is negative. The sensitivity of ultrasound in detecting anencephaly is held constant at 95% and the specificity of ultrasound is assumed to be 100%. The arrow indicates the best estimate of the sensitivity of ultrasound and is used in subsequent calculations.

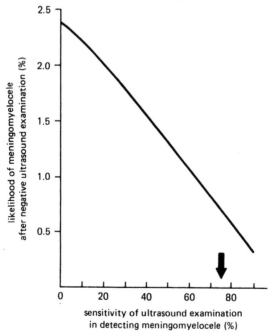

sensitivity of ultrasound examination in detecting meningomyelocele (%)

demonstrate twins or fetal death. On the other hand, assuming that ultrasound can reliably diagnose some NTDs (policy B), the analysis suggests that a smaller proportion of parents should elect amniocentesis because of the decreased likelihood of meningomyelocele after a negative ultrasonic examination. For example, assuming that ammniotic fluid and maternal serum AFP are independent and that ultrasound has a sensitivity of 75%, the analysis suggests that 63% of the parents interviewed should, on the basis of their personal attitudes, proceed with amniocentesis (figure 28.5, solid line). If the sensitivity of ultrasound is lower, this percentage will be higher. In contrast, if serum and amniotic fluid AFP levels are not independent, then the information provided by amniocentesis is less valuable since it would, in part, duplicate the data provided by maternal serum levels. Assuming the sensitivity of ultrasound is 75% in detecting meningomyelocele, the analysis suggests that 42% of the parents interviewed should proceed with amniocentesis (figure 28.5, broken line). Again, if the sensitivity of ultrasound is lower, this percentage will be higher.

DISCUSSION

Public policy decisions concerning large-scale medical programs usually involve analyses of several different types of information, such as expected health

Figure 28.5 Relation between the sensitivity of ultrasound in detecting meningomyelocele and the proportion of prospective parents who should accept amniocentesis, based on their personal attitudes toward abortion. Serum and amniotic fluid AFP levels are assumed to be independent for the relation summarized by the solid line, but dependent for the relation summarized by the broken line. The heavy arrow indicates the best estimate of the sensitivity of ultrasound.

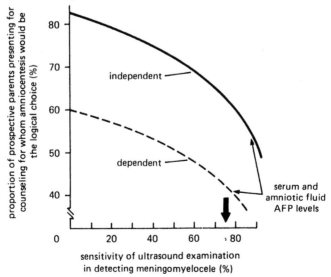

benefits, risks, financial cost, and available resources. Frequently, the information available at the time of decision making is scanty or totally lacking. Nonetheless, decisions must be made. In this chapter, we have analyzed a current controversy in medicine in several countries – whether or not to institute a large-scale screening program for the prenatal detection of neural tube defects. Unlike most other such analyses, however, we have considered not the usual benefits and costs but rather patients' attitudes toward various outcomes. We have shown that the attitudes toward elective abortion of prospective parents who have sought genetic counseling are consistent with the implicit assumptions of a prenatal screening program and that many couples can be expected to accept such a program and to benefit from it on a personal level. If this were not the case, then all questions relating to costs, risks, and benefits of such a program would be moot. In effect, then, we have integrated social choice and individual values [14].

Because only a small number of patients request genetic counseling about the prenatal diagnosis of NTDs, the attitudes of a group of parents counseled about a variety of diseases, particularly Down's syndrome, were used. If Down's syndrome were viewed as a more severe malformation than meningomyelocele, then the use of those data might result in an underestimate of the burden of elective abortion relative to the burden of a child affected by meningomyelocele. Such a systematic error could result in an overestimate of the proportion of parents who would accept amniocentesis. The close agreement between our projections and data derived from interviewing the parents of children affected by spina bifida argues against that bias, however. In a study of 167 such families, Hsia *et al.* [26] found that 78% felt that amniocentesis should be offered to people at risk.

Because the prospective parents interviewed sought genetic counseling about prenatal diagnosis, they could well represent a select group whose attitudes toward abortion might be more liberal than those of the general population. On the other hand, if we had used data from individuals not actually considering amniocentesis, those data could have been faulted because such individuals might provide less thoughtful answers than would prospective parents in need of making a decision. In this study, we opted to use the attitudes of a group of parents who were actually facing the decision.

It is difficult to anticipate the accuracy of a large-scale program, but our assumptions about the sensitivity and the specificity of maternal screening, ultrasonic examination, and amniocentesis fit nicely with the estimates and observations of screening programs in other countries [1–4] and the few research programs currently active in the United States [7, 8]. The sensitivity analysis of laboratory accuracy (figure 28.3) and the rather convex shape of the cumulative attitude curve (figure 28.2) both suggest that the acceptability of a screening program will not be tightly coupled to even moderate decreases in laboratory accuracy.

In general, whenever possible in this analysis we have made conservative assumptions regarding benefits. Thus, our estimates of the proportion of prospective parents who would benefit from an NTD screening program should be conservative. For example, we have not considered the use of amnioscopy, amniography, or repeat amniocentesis to eliminate the few false positives remaining after the demonstration of elevated or borderline amniotic fluid AFP levels. The availability of these additional tests would improve the diagnostic accuracy in pregnancies at "extremely high risk" and thereby make the screening program more attractive to prospective parents but, of course, more costly to society. By not including these procedures in our analysis, we have both followed the plan of the British program and introduced additional conservative biases into our analysis. Thus, our conclusion that amniocentesis would be acceptable to substantial numbers of parents should be quite robust.

NOTE

Supported in part by the National Institute of General Medical Sciences through Research Career Development Awards 1K04 GM 00349 (SGP) and K04 GM 00194 (BJM), the Division of Research Resources (grant 1P41 RR 01096), and the National Library of Medicine (grant 1P04 LM 03374). First published in *Med. Decision Making*, 1 (1981), 103–14.

REFERENCES

1. Brock, D. J. H., Bolton, A. E., and Monaghan, J. M. (1973). Prenatal diagnosis of anencephaly through maternal serum alpha-fetoprotein measurement. *Lancet* 1:923–6.
2. United Kingdom Collaborative Study on Alpha-Fetoprotein in Relation to Neural Tube Defects (1977). Maternal serum alpha-fetoprotein measurements in antenatal screening for anencephaly and spina bifida in early pregnancy. *Lancet* 1:1323–47.
3. United Kingdom Collaborative Study on Alpha-Fetoprotein in Relation to Neural Tube Defects (1979). Amniotic fluid alpha-fetoprotein measurement in antenatal diagnosis of anencephaly and open spina bifida in early pregnancy. *Lancet* 2:651–62.
4. Wald, N. J., Cuckle, H. S., Boreham, J., Brett, R., Stirrat, G. M., Bennet, M. J., Turnbull, A. C., Solymar, M., Jones, N., Bobrow, M., and Evans, C. J. (1979). Antenatal screening in Oxford for fetal neural tube defects. *Br. J. Obstet. Gynaecol.* 86:91–100.
5. Chamberlain, J. (1978). Human benefits and costs of a national screening programme for neural tube defects. *Lancet* 2:1293–7.
6. Hagard, S., Carter, F., and Milne, R. G. (1976). Screening for spina bifida cystica: a cost–benefit analysis. *Br. J. Prev. Soc. Med.* 30:40–53.
7. Macri, J. N., Haddow, J. E., and Weiss, R. R. (1979). Screening for neural tube defects in the United States: a summary of the Scarborough conference. *Am. J. Obstet. Gynecol.* 133:119–25.
8. Milunsky, A., Alpert, E., Neff, R., and Frigoletto, F. D. (1980). Prenatal diagnosis of neural tube defects. IV: Maternal serum alpha-fetoprotein screening. *Obstet. Gynecol.* 55:60–6.

9. Goldberg, M. F., and Oakley, G. P. (1979). Prenatal screening for anencephaly–spina bifida: some epidemiologic projections for a national program. In Porter, I. H., and Hook, E. B., eds. *Service and Education in Medical Genetics*. New York, Academic Press, 55–67.

10. Macri, J. N., Weiss, R. R., and Libster, B. (1979). Maternal serum alpha-fetoprotein screening for neural tube defects: structure and organization. In Porter, I. H., and Hook, E. B. eds. *Service and Education in Medical Genetics*. New York, Academic Press, 221–35.

11. Sanders, C., chairman (1979). Third meeting, National Council on Health Care Technology, December 12–13, Washington D.C.

12. Nadler, H. L., and Simpson, J. L. (1979). Maternal serum alpha-fetoprotein screening: promise not yet fulfilled. *Obstet. Gynecol.* 54:333–4.

13. Haddow, J. E., and Macri, J. N. (1979). Prenatal screening of neural tube defects. *JAMA* 242:515–16.

14. Arrow, K. J. (1963). *Social Choice and Individual Values*. 2nd edn. New York, Wiley.

15. Center for Disease Control (1979). Temporal trends in the incidence of birth defects – United States. *Morbidity Mortality Weekly* 28:401–2.

16. Milunsky, A., and Alpert, E. (1976). Prenatal diagnosis of neural tube defects. I: Problems and pitfalls: analysis of 2,495 cases using the alpha-fetoprotein assay. *Obstet. Gynecol.* 48:1–5.

17. Birnholz, J. C., Finberg, H. J., Greenes, R. A., *et al.* (1979). Ultrasound detection of major congenital anomalies. Scientific program, 65th Scientific Assembly and Annual Meeting (Atlanta, Ga., Nov. 26–30, 1979), Radiology Soc. NA, p. 379.

18. NICHD National Registry for Amniocentesis Study Group (1976). Mid-trimester amniocentesis for prenatal diagnosis. *JAMA* 236:1471–6.

19. Golbus, M. S., Loughman, W. D., and Epstein, C. J. (1979). Prenatal diagnosis in 3,000 amniocenteses. *N. Engl. J. Med.* 300:157–63.

20. Medical Research Council Working Party on Amniocentesis (1978). An assessment of the hazards of amniocentesis. *Br. J. Obstet. Gynaecol.* 85 (suppl 2):1–41.

21. Galjaard, H. (1976). European experience with prenatal diagnosis of congenital disease: a survey of 6,121 cases. *Cytogenet. Cell Genet.* 16:453–67.

22. Milunsky, A., and Alpert, E. (1976). Prenatal diagnosis of neural tube defects. II. Analysis of false positive and false negative alpha-fetoprotein results. *Obstet. Gynecol.* 48:6–12.

23. Pauker, S. P., and Pauker, S. G. (1979). The amniocentesis decision: an explicit guide for parents. In Epstein, C. J., Curry, C. J. R., Packman, S., Sherman, S., and Hall, B. D., eds. *Risk, Communication, and Decision Making in Genetic Counselling, Part C of Ann. Review of Birth Defects, 1978*. National Foundation – March of Dimes. Birth Defects Original Article Series XV:5C, New York, Alan R. Liss, pp. 289–324.

24. Pauker, S. P., and Pauker, S., G. (1977). Prenatal diagnosis: a directive approach to genetic counseling using decision analysis. *Yale J. Biol. Med.* 50:275–89.

25. Raiffa, H. (1968). *Decision Analysis*. Reading, Mass., Addison-Wesley.

26. Hsia, Y. E., Leung, F., and Carter, L. L. (1979). Attitudes toward amniocentesis: surveys of families with spina bifida children, 1974, 1977. In Porter, I. H., and Hook, E. B., eds. *Service and Education in Medical Genetics*. New York, Academic Press, pp. 303–21.

29

DISCUSSION AGENDA FOR THE SESSION ON MEDICAL DECISION MAKING

MILTON C. WEINSTEIN (moderator), AND
HARVEY V. FINEBERG, BARBARA J. MCNEIL, AND STEPHEN G. PAUKER

and

MINUTES OF A GROUP DISCUSSION ON CLINICAL DECISION MAKING

ROBERT J. QUINN, rapporteur

DISCUSSION OUTLINE: DESCRIPTIVE/PRESCRIPTIVE/NORMATIVE INTERACTIONS IN MEDICAL DECISION MAKING

A. Issues relating to values and preferences

Valued consequences that are typically reflected in formal models of medical decision making include the following:

survival (length of life)
quality of life
  symptoms
  physical function
  social function

1. Are preferences regarding these attributes fixed or labile? How do they change with age, physical status, mental status, interactions with physicians? Prescriptively or normatively, how does one deal with the existence of "multiple selves"? Is the prescriptive solution more complicated than just trying to assess the uncertainty about future preferences, and then take expectations across all possible future utility functions? If perfectly or imperfectly knowable, should future preferences substitute for present preferences in decisions with future consequences?

599

    Examples: labor and anesthesia (Christensen–Szalanski)

              smoking and addictive behaviors

              myopia, ignorance, or uncertainty about old age

              euthanasia (Schelling)

2. Are some preference functions normatively "better" than others? When is it appropriate for the physician to intervene to try to change patients' preferences?

   What are the ethical implications for informed consent?

   Example: a couple's desire to have a baby at home, under the care of a midwife

3. Issues in assessing utilities for health outcomes: Assuming that preferences are stable and measurable, what is the best way to measure them? While proper von Neumann–Morgenstern utility functions may be the prescriptive goal, are there other means to that end that are more reliable or acceptable than using lottery techniques, e.g., category scaling, magnitude estimation? What are the trade-offs between normative validity and practical considerations, recognizing that numbers derived from a category scale are not assessed by the "theoretically correct" method, but observing the empirical fact that they are easier for many people to use? Other methodologic issues in utility for health outcomes:

   How to model time preference? How to deal with health states worse than death?

   Examples: Torrance studies using time-trade-off (indifference mapping) methods

                 Bush studies using category scaling

                 Theoretical papers on optimality of different functional forms (Plishkin–Shepard–Weinstein)

                 Empirical papers on differences in results between methods (Torrance; Read–Quinn *et al.*)

4. What do we make of the observed framing effects observed in medical settings? Is there some underlying instability in the preference structure such that the way the question is asked *affects* the preferences expressed by patients? Or do these inconsistencies represent errors that people should be encouraged (taught) to avoid? Or are there legitimate psychological consequences from thinking of health outcomes in different ways? How can you tell which responses represent the patient's "true" preferences, or is this even a meaningful question?

   Examples: McNeil–Tversky–Pauker–Sox study of framing Llewellyn–Thomas *et al.* study of anchor effects

5. Are there psychological consequences of medical decisions that have normative (or at least prescriptive) status, such that patients would want to take them into account explicitly?

   Consequences: Regret/blame (Bell; Quinn–Weinstein)

                    Disappointment

Examples: Anxiety
Cognitive dissonance (Akerlof–Dickens)
Preservation of optimism
Appendicitis
Diagnostic test ordering (Berwick–Weinstein; Sox; Sackett)
Errors of omission vs. commission (Brett)

6. How should the value of diagnostic information be measured? Is the EVSI/EVCI model adequate? Does test information have value (medical or nonmedical) to patients, independent of its use by physicians? Does test information have value (medical or nonmedical), independent of its ability to affect subsequent decisions (by physician or patient)? Can information have negative value? Are "Ulysses" effects real in medicine?
Example: Ultrasound in pregnancy (Berwick–Weinstein)

7. Whose values are reflected? Patient? Doctor? Family? Whose values *should be* reflected? How is the principal–agent paradigm played out in medical care? How *should* the interaction between doctor and patient be structured?

8. How do physicians cope with conflicts between the interest of the patient at hand and the collective societal interest? How *should* they cope with them?
Examples: Immunizations carrying some risk (e.g., polio, pertussis)
Costly technologies (e.g., expensive tests, organ transplants)

B. Issues relating to beliefs and probabilities

1. Is Bayesian analysis helpful to physicians? Is it even feasible, given the problems in estimating the requisite conditional probability distributions and prior probabilities? Are other models of diagnosis (i.e., posterior probability estimation) more suited to the decision-making style of physicians, e.g., regression or discriminant analysis?

2. Do physicians' errors in manipulating probabilities have practical consequences, or do physicians tend to rely on "clinical judgment" to reach the best decision despite limited ability to deal with probabilities? (Reference: Berwick–Fineberg–Weinstein study of MD quantitative skills.) Do limits on physicians' ability to manipulate probabilities have any practical importance for the health outcomes for patients?

3. Where *do*, and *should*, probability estimates come from? How *do* physicians synthesize information from diverse sources (e.g., randomized trials, observational studies, data banks, uncontrolled published series of patients, personal experience, intuition)? How *should* information from these sources be combined?

4. Do randomized trials have limits in applicability to decision making? How can randomized trials be justified by a Bayesian?

5. Is it helpful for physicians to quantify probabilities? Can they be trained to be good probability assessors? Is the practice of medicine suited to the

decision-analytic ideal of discussing probabilities apart from values (with other physicians, as in rounds, or with patients)?

C. Issues relating to conceptions of choice

1. Physicians are taught in most medical schools, first to make a diagnosis, then to give the treatment appropriate for that diagnosis. Decision analysis teaches us to think systematically about the sequence of testing decisions (i.e., information acquisition) and treatment decisions, and views the "diagnosis" as a superfluous, possibly misleading, objective. Which model *should* they apply? What are the implications for medical education, e.g., training emphasis on differential diagnosis vs. problem-solving?
2. Should physicians think of the decision-making process as an algorithm or as an active problem-solving process? Can, or should, they be expected to reanalyze (i.e., optimize) each individual case? Do physicians satisfice?
3. Is there a useful concept of a "close call" or "toss-up" in medical decision making, where the decision analysis shows a small or unstable advantage to one strategy, and the physician should be encouraged to disregard the result and revert to intuition? What is the role of sensitivity analysis? What is the role of explicit judgmental probability distributions in situations where no learning about those distributions is possible?
4. Whose decision is it, the physician's or the patient's? Who is the principal and who is the agent? Is the physician a consultant or an agent? What is the *best* conception of this dyad?

EXTRACTS FROM PLENARY DISCUSSION FOLLOWING MEDICAL PAPERS

Krantz:
I'm impressed with this work, but I'm concerned about how to treat probabilities about which we are not very confident. The standard procedure involves performing a sensitivity analysis, and that is necessary, of course; but it seems that we need a more systematic way of discounting questionable probabilities in important problems like this one.

Pauker:
I agree that the problem you raise is a critical one, but in clinical use of decision analysis I think it's imperative that the patient understand what is going on. The statistical methods used must be fairly simple, so that everybody involved has a reasonable understanding of the analysis.

Pratt:
Steve, in cases such as the one you've presented here, have discussions with patients helped in alleviating the later experience of anxiety, regret, and other emotional side effects of the type we've been talking about?

Pauker:

As to post-decisional regret, I don't know whether or not analysis helps. For one thing, it is not clear what should be classified as evidence of regret. Consider, for example, a patient who elects not to undergo amniocentesis and later gives birth to a Down's syndrome child. If the mother feels now that she made the right decision at the time, should her anguish over the outcome of her decision be considered regret? The matter of pre- and post-decisional anxiety is different: analysis clearly creates acute anxiety in patients facing decisions about amniocentesis and other procedures. My feeling is that it is better for the patient to feel anxiety in the office, where it is somewhat manageable, than at home.

Thaler:

I'd like to make a brief comment on the normative–prescriptive–descriptive issue. Let's say that analysis of two alternative medical treatments has been performed, and one treatment has a much higher expected utility. The analysis allows one to feel better if a bad outcome follows from the choice of the alternative with the higher expected uility. Regret, therefore, has a big role in prescriptive and descriptive analysis; but, because we can purge ourselves out of it, regret has no business in normative models.

Slovic:

I think, though, that we have to consider the possibility that involving the patient in a decision analysis might exacerbate feelings of post-decisional regret. Decision analysis, by searching for an optimal or "right" decision, gives emphasis to the notion that one can also make a wrong decision, thus raising anxieties and setting the stage for regret. In many important medical decisions, the probabilities and utilities may be so ill-defined that the patient would be better off concentrating on the various qualitative arguments, pro and con, of each option in order to construct a convincing justification for the decision. The existence of such a justification would probably form a "buffer" for regret, thus helping the patient bear the consequences better than if the choice had been based on a decision analysis.

Schelling:

I have several questions related to the quantification of values in the medical problem presented this morning. First, is it valid to use that patient's value function for another patient faced with the same decision? What if the other patient had not had the advantage of having experienced both the transplant and hemodialysis, as is likely? How are their values likely to differ? And if both patients' values are assessed, which should be used: the person-specific but less informed values, or the "substitute" values that are more informed by experience? Should the latter set of values be shown to other patients as a way of "teaching" them the effects of experience or would this lead to unwanted bias?

Pauker:

The developers of health status indices would answer your first questions by stating that one can profitably use the value of an "average" person to make decisions for others. However, this may be more appropriate for public health resource allocation and other decisions for large groups of people. For specific clinical decisions, the use of one value function can lead to large and frequent errors – each case is different enough that you'd want to analyze it separately.

As to your last question, I'm not in favor of showing to a patient the results of another's value assessment. In general I think it's not a good idea to pollute the thinking the patient is doing about his or her own values.

With regard to the question of where we should go from here in medicine, I believe that we will see some kinds of mechanisms instituted to deal with difficult clinical decisions. If we in the field of decision analysis do not press our influence now, by default those mechanisms will resemble the ways clinical choices are made at present. I think that the time is now in medicine.

Fineberg:
It occurs to me that much of the debate about the theoretical validity of decision analysis is far separated from the "real world" of clinical decision making. The old prescriptions such as "First do not harm" and so on simply do not go far enough in modern medicine, and *any* improvement in aids to decision making would be a giant step forward.

Pauker:
I believe that the most important issues surrounding the use of decision analysis in medicine will be questions related to informed consent and the appropriate level of patient participation in decision making.

Kahneman:
I'm worried about the possible "responsibility costs" to patients of their going through the analysis and playing a greater role in making decisions. Take one of the worst imaginable outcomes: a patient develops melausoma after following the course of action indicated by an analysis in which he or she plays an active role. One can imagine that patient feeling much worse about that decision than if he or she had simply followed doctor's orders. I'm concerned that two or three hours in a decision analysis isn't enough to educate patients and inoculate them against feelings of regret and self-blame that could result.

Pauker:
The question is, how can one quantify perceived regret and incorporate that into the analysis?

Kahneman:
Well, we might predict in any case that the risks of regret would be higher following an "out-of-character," exceptional procedure, whether you're talking about the medical treatment or the decision-making procedure used to select that treatment.

Fineberg:

An important question is how much a physician could find out in advance, through interacting with a patient, how sensitive that patient would be to regret and similar concerns. It would be critical for the physician also to realize the difference in psychological involvement between doctor and patient; while the decision may be critical for the patient, it may well be run-of-the-mill for the doctor.

Shafer:

If I could take a devil's advocate position, as I did yesterday, what would be the result if two different types of analyses were performed on the same patient? If one analytical method were Ward's [Edwards] and one Ralph's [Keeney] or if they used different values on two parameters, would it make a difference? Based on yesterday's discussion, one might say that, yes, it probably would, but it is the *process* of performing the analysis that is most important. In today's discussion on the other hand, the *outcome* of the medical decision seems more important.

Edwards:

Decision analysts in most areas of application would never argue that it is proper for them to make decisions for their clients. In medicine, on the other hand, it is not clear in all cases just who should be the decision maker. As Milt Weinstein noted, the situation is more complex, and the roles of decision maker and decision analyst become confounded.

Weinstein:

There are many models of interaction between the doctor, patient, and decision analyst or other third party. One is that the third party gathers information about outcome probabilities from the doctor, information about values from the patient, performs an analysis and recommends a decision. But, even without a decision analyst, there is still the question of who the decision maker should be; the patient may not always be in a position to make the best decision.

Thaler:

I will volunteer my own opinion, which is also consistent with some of Danny Kahneman's comments, that sometimes the physician knows best and should make the decision for the patient.

Meyer:

The distinction between decision maker and decision analyst is, to some extent, an artificial one. In any important medical decision, a group of people is involved; the task of some may lean more toward consenting to decisions rather than stating possible courses of action, but all share the goal of making peace with their collective action. A related point is that substantive and process problems are interdependent in medicine as in business management. An important problem is the meta-decision of how to both frame the "theory of the clinical case" and structure the decision process. When the new process arrived at through this meta-decision is routinized, substantive problems such as the experience of regret may no longer arise, and it may be easier for all to live with their decision.

Kaplan:

This discussion brings to mind an important difference between legal and medical decision making. In the law, a person's actual degree of guilt does not change simply because a jury returns the verdict of "guilty" or "not guilty." In medicine, on the other hand, the Heisenberg principle applies: the analysis can affect the outcome. Because mind and body are interrelated, telling a patient of all possible risks actually may cause the recovery period to be longer and more painful. In addition, unexpected variables or new technologies may be discovered after the analysis, causing another kind of regret and perhaps new physical effects. The point is, although decision analysts try to look at the whole story, there really is no whole story.

Zeckhauser:

I believe that, in trying to help patients by using decision analysis, Steve Pauker and his colleagues are doing the right thing. Given the medical cases in my experience, the potential help from analytical procedures is enormous, and the responses from the patients involved have shown that the procedures are like Ralph Keeney's wood bridges – basically sound. Also, the analysis itself seems to help reduce feelings of regret and guilt. I'd be interested to know if people here disagree strongly with this, based on different experiences.

Weinstein:

A large problem is that it's difficult to construct an experiment to confirm or disprove the benefits of decision analysis, particularly if validational criteria include not only lives saved or reduced pain and suffering, but also more elusive phenomena such as regret.

Schelling:

Ralph Keeney and Ward Edwards typically are consulted by clients who are not at that time under a great deal of stress. This factor can't be any less important in medicine. For example, consider the case in which a man is kept alive in a comatose condition for an extended period of time. We find deciding very difficult in this man's case, perhaps because so few of us give much thought to that problem beforehand, while we are conscious, healthy, and free from stress. Consider the number of hours in a lifetime spent thinking about life insurance; we should devote at least as much time to discussing, perhaps with our physicians but certainly with our attorneys, the circumstances under which we are allowed to die. If agreements are drawn up after careful thought and planning, there may be more of a presumption that the comatose already *have* answered the important questions. More generally, the point is that we should encourage patients to think about their utilities when neither they nor their physicians are under great stress.

Fineberg:
It is important to distinguish between a patient's a priori discussion of how he or she would want to decide later, and a patient's a priori request that a subsequent change of mind be ignored. The latter presents problems, because there are three sets of values to bear in mind: how the patient feels now, how the patient wants to feel later, and how the patient predicts he or she will feel later. There is no clear moral basis upon which a physician may choose one of those sets of values. Even the patient has no way to choose among them.

Schelling:
That's not true for me; if my physician won't promise to "pull the plug" under certain circumstances, I'll help it myself before I am sick enough to need someone's help.

Argyris:
I would want Steve Pauker to help me with a medical decision as long as he doesn't see decision analysis as the key issue. Any analytical method is a component tool in the larger task of patient management, which is, and probably should be, a multifaceted, sloppy process. What we may need is a formal theory of "rigorous sloppiness."

Pauker:
A problem is that the validity of decision analysis may not be testable unless we concentrate on concrete outcome measures such as years of life. A second problem we've been discussing is whether the decision analyst's client would more properly be the doctor or the patient. In the real world, the physician is also the analyst. But, if we don't think that's appropriate, maybe teaching decision analysis to physicians is a bad idea.

Fischhoff:
As decision analysts, we should look at some of the side effects of plying our trade in medicine, business, and other fields. We often change the definition and structure of problems we tackle, partially by presenting ourselves as knowing something that others don't; we often change our clients' attitudes towards themselves, sometimes making them take more responsibility for their choices and actions; and we can change the nature of social relationships, whether between doctor and patient or among the executives of a corporation. We must remain aware of these changes and think hard about whether or not they are beneficial.

Perhaps one of the most important questions is how far a decision analyst can take a patient before the decision is outside the patients' range of knowledge and control. That is, at what point does the patient lose an intuitive grasp of the problem, increasing the danger of manipulation by the analyst? It may be that analyses should follow parallel "top–down" and "bottom–up" tracks. The "top–down" approach would start with a decomposed problem structure, axiomatic treatment of values, and so on and derive meaningful, critical trade-offs from the analytical model; in the other track, the "bottom-up" approach would lead the patient up from a holistic intuitive understanding of the problem. One would have more confidence in the analysis if the two tracks produced a single result.

Pratt:

I would argue that, especially for tough decisions, it may be better to make choices for the patients rather than put them through the analysis. I admit that there's the chance of manipulating the patient, but one would hope that physicians would do so only in good faith. Of course, there will be questions about what "good faith" means in practice. We should recognize, though, that these questions are relevant to medical decision making without decision analysis. As in the old joke about looking for keys under the street lamp, we should look for problems with all types of doctor–patient interaction.

Pauker:

John, I disagree with the contention that patients should not undergo a decision analysis for tough decisions; close calls are precisely when the physician should *not* have major input. Abortion decisions are among the toughest, and utilities differ from patient to patient – no one policy is appropriate.

Pratt:

But, to find out if amniocentesis is called for, you need to decide about abortion. Physicians should spare patients that decision.

Pauker:

An easy way out of that one is possible only if amniocentesis is not called for; in that case, don't perform it. Otherwise, there's no way to spare the patient from both decisions and the possible feelings of guilt.

Luce:

I have several comments related to this general discussion. First, looking back, I'm glad that I wasn't held to some past predications I made about my later preferences. Secondly, we need alternatives to the von Neumann–Morgenstern model, which is not very useful in dealing with uncertainty (as opposed to risk) in decision problems. Finally, I think we should concentrate on an intermediate form of decision aid for physicians: one in which the main goal is getting information relevant to the problem in front of the doctors. Isn't that the primary function of decision trees? Attempts to go beyond that are just too problematic.

Zeckhauser:

The exchange between John Pratt and Steve Pauker raises two separate issues: one involves the virtues of decision analysis, while the other is the question of who does the analysis. We shouldn't reject decision analysis because we assume it will involve the patient more and lead to unwanted side effects such as "responsibility costs." The use of decision analysis does not have to take away the physician's current decision-making role. I'll concede the point about manipulating the patient, but that happens now. Analysis would help doctors do just what they're doing today, but a little bit better.

Meyer:

In listening to the type of work Steve Pauker and colleagues are doing, it seems clear that the traditional roles of doctor and patient are not terribly useful. Rather the doctor and patient both face a problem, and they must resolve it jointly. This joint problem solving, it seems to me, is not helped by the old idealization in which specific people are assigned to particular decision-making roles.

Bell:

I'm struck by the fact that today we've been talking less about the outcomes of decisions than about the effects of the decision-making process. One of those effects that we haven't talked much about is the possibility that the physician who tries to assess a patient's utilities might be thought insensitive by the patient. It may be that you can't learn what it's like to have a medical decision analysis performed on you by performing them on others. Perhaps all decision analysts should be required to undergo the kind of analysis they'll be performing on others.

Argyris:

It think it would be helpful to us "fools" if we made tapes of ourselves trying to analyze the decisions of others. I also believe that some of the problems we observe in our clients – overconfidence in and premature commitment to courses of action, attempts to manipulate superiors, and adherence to various other personal agendas – are difficult to tackle with single-loop control systems like decision analysis. To combat these phenomena, the decision analytic approach recommends measures such as tracing the relationships between deadlines and each decision, stating assumptions explicitly, and so on. All of those suggestions will influence single-loop behavior, but none will change overconfidence, advocating personal agendas, etc. The people who do those things will find new and creative ways of doing them long after the recommendations have been put into place. Decision analytic models require a world that believes in valid information; the problem is, the world wants valid information only when it isn't threatening, and often decision analysis, done well, is threatening.

Keeney:

Problems such as hidden agendas actually make me more of an advocate of decision analysis, certainly for public decisions and also for some medical ones. I'd just as soon not have some people in Washington spend $10 billion to prevent four identifiable fatalities so they can move up the ladder. Nor do I want to be in the situation Milt Weinstein described and have my chance of dying doubled because somebody doesn't want either feelings of guilt or liability losses. To the degree that the analysis can make it more difficult for somebody to base decisions on these hidden values, I find it very useful.

Another point I wanted to raise relates to the issue of decision-making roles and how they're influenced by the use of decision analysis. As Steve Pauker said this morning, one of the main purposes of decision analysis is to provide insights. Individuals interested in a decision problem can obtain important insights from a decision analysis that did not identify a specific decision maker, but rather examined different viewpoints represented by analyst-supplied utility functions and descriptions of consequences.

Kahneman:

Following up on this question of the usefulness of decision analysis, I'd like to know if, when you're just given the problem in bare outline, there are cues one can use to determine if decision analysis is going to pay off. That is, what is the sensitivity of the decision to decision analysis? We might agree, for instance, that, if the decision is going to involve a close call, we may not want to do the analysis.

Argyris:

Well, for economic reasons at least. Decision analysis certainly requires a substantial investment of time and money. What I'd like to know is whether or not one could construct a pretest to see if the analysis is worth the investment, rather like the analysis within decision analysis of what information is worth getting. Are there any signs that could alert one to the fact that the decision one would have made initially would be flipped by analysis? I think the advantage of being able to focus only on those types of problems would be worth a considerable research effort to look for those signs.

Edwards:

An operationalization of your question, Danny, is: When should a decision analyst choose to withdraw from conducting an analysis? Clearly there are conditions under which one would. For me, one of those conditions is the existence of hidden agendas; it's just never clear what one can do about them. That's probably an idiosyncrasy of mine, since I've heard Ralph say exactly the opposite ...

Keeney:

I just don't understand how you ever work, if you always avoid hidden agendas [laughter]. I don't think I can always detect them, but I think it's possible to reduce their influence by making the analysis explicit.

Meyer:

If I understand Danny's comment correctly, there is a longstanding procedure to address the questions you are discussing. As Ron Howard described in his "proximal decision analysis" paper, the idea is simply this: the analyst gets point estimates for all outcome dimensions, including the uncertain ones, and then a quick and dirty decision analysis is performed using those point estimates, to see if alternate strategies seem to be close or not; secondly, a sensitivity analysis is carried out, and, if alternate strategies remain close over a reasonable range of inputs, then one obviously is dealing with what Milton referred to as a "close call." So I believe that, yes, one can answer that question with a relatively easy, low-cost procedure.

Edwards:
That's where I wouldn't withdraw, because one of the main functions of decision analysis is to create new options. Close calls are interesting, but mainly because they invite you to consider the problem, and possible solutions, more carefully and creatively.

Pauker:
I'm bothered a bit by this discussion about close calls. I've been interested in this area for a couple of years, and one conclusion I've come to is that a close call can be an important, positive outcome of an analysis. Sometimes it can be a welcome relief to know that it doesn't make one bit of difference which course of action one takes. Also, there often are a few dimensions, such as dollar cost, which do not enter the decision unless "all else is equal"; identifying a decision as a close call therefore allows the legitimate consideration of those variables in the analysis.

Tversky:
With regard to the matter of close calls, I think we are faced with a dilemma. That is, people are not likely to trust an analysis if it results in a close call. They are likley to place much more confidence in a recommendation if the results are clear, but in that case a quick-and-simple analysis may be sufficient.

Kahneman:
But there may also be the "miracle cases," where you do the analysis and end up believing with great confidence in an alternative that you would not have chosen when you began. In these cases even a brief analysis is quite valuable.

Raiffa:
I've been in cases where at the outset the decision appeared to be a close call, but after analysis one alternative came out as clearly superior. I've also been in cases where initially alternative *A* appeared better than alternative *B*, but after very little analysis it emerged that *B* was clearly better than *A*. The point is that it's easy to come up with instances of reversals between one's intuitive impressions and the results of analysis.

Argyris:
I'm still not certain why you would want to avoid doing the analysis if you knew it were going to be a close call. If I found myself in that situation, I would tell the decision maker, be it an individual or organization, that the decision looks like a close call, but the process of going through the analysis can be valuable in and of itself. My experience, and Steve's also, I think has been that the decision analyst cannot collect information about values without putting the patient through a terribly important learning experience.

Kahneman:

The background to my initial question was in part the notion that one of the effects of the analysis was raising the responsibility of the patient, which may make some consequences harder to bear. I'm deeply concerned about ethical issues surrounding analysis which involve patients to a great extent without information about them, or otherwise taking into account, these responsibility costs. It may be worthwhile to undertake the meta-decision analysis of whether or not to perform a complete analysis if the benefits are not likely to outweigh these costs.

Keeney:

I have two final points about close calls. One, you may have a close call between alternatives *A* and *B* in an analysis, but alternative *C* may drop out and that's useful information. Secondly, where there are sequential decisions, a close call between *A* and *B* at the beginnings of the sequence assumes that everything else is done "optimally." Thus, although the initial *A/B* decision is "conditionally" close, there may be a lot of insights from the analysis for secondary decisions that may or may not be close.

Tversky:

In the late fifties and early sixties, there was a great deal of excitement about axiomatic decision theory and the Bayesian approach to uncertainty that appear to provide a logical basis for a normative theory of decision making. Many felt that this work could serve as a descriptive theory as well, but in any event we seem to have a solid foundation for building the technology of decision analysis. In the sixties and seventies, we accumulated evidence of the descriptive shortcomings of these models, showing that value and beliefs are more biased and labile than many people had thought.

Now we must try to strike a balance between two extreme positions. On the other hand, we shouldn't carry on as usual with decision analysis, ignoring the large systematic errors and illusions. There is good reason to believe that the effects of framing (e.g., these observed in the judgments of physicians) are common in decision analysis. They should be taken into account. On the other hand, we should not overreact to the lability of preferences and conclude that decision analysis cannot be used to help. In fact, it could be argued that the psychological research shows that people need a great deal of help, and formal training. Rather than abandoning decision analysis, we should try to make it responsive to the complexities and the limitations of the human mind.

We should also be aware of the inherent incompleteness of decision analysis. We must question whether first-order outcomes, such as dollars and lives, adequately represent the consequences of a decision, and whether second-order outcomes, such as regret, should be formally introduced. If so, we must confront the problem of how to trade off regret for dollars, which is especially difficult because regret – like other second-order outcomes – is highly reactive and frame dependent.

INDEX

Abelson, R. F., 127
abortion, 592–3
accuracy, 148–9, 150
acquisition, *see* information acquisition
actions: action-outcome connections, 135–6; concurrent, 153; conflict in, 132–4; fairness of, 176–7; *see also* tasks
active memory, 320
additivity, 471; additive psychological effects, 378–9
adjustments: judgment and, 161–2
advantage: cumulative, 102, 103
AFP screening, 588
agenda setting, 116
Allais, Maurice, 83, 89, 93, 181, 183–4, 215–16, 499, 501
alpha-feroprotein screening, 588
alternatives: coordinated, 485–6; creation using values, 482–8; desirable, 483–4; individual preferences for group action, 485; liberating, *see* liberating alternatives; one-sided bargaining, 484–5; value-focused thinking, 486–8
ambiguity, 93; conflict of interest, 41–2; global, 45; goal, 134; necessary cost, 45; sensible action and, 49; toleration, 534
amniocentesis, 588, 594
amphotericin therapy: analysis structure, 573–5; assumptions, 572; available data, 570–2; complications, 571; efficacy, 571; expected utilities calculation, 577–8; fungal infection incidence, 570–1; probabilities and utilities, 575–7; remission rate for non-lymphocytic leukemia, 572; sensitivity analysis, 578–83; statement of problem, 570

anchoring, 161–2, 402
applications: benefit-risk analysis, 497–507; competitive markets, 508–24; medical decisions, *see* medical decisions; senior management thinking, 525–39
arbitrage, 520
Argyris, Chris, 540–61, 607, 609, 610, 611
Arrow, Kenneth J., 497–507
artificial intelligence, 72, 347
aspiration level, 126
assessment procedures, *see* elicitation
attention, 136; as scarce resource, 72–4; information acquisition and, 127
attributes, 470–2, 473; proxy and fundamental, 475–6; single-attribute utility functions, 471; *see also* multi-attribute theory
auctions, 379–81
augmentation: political nature of, 46; principle, 104, 110
automobile emissions, 73–4
availability, 125
awareness, circle of, 67

backward induction, 376
bargaining, 466; chips, 177; framing and, 177; loss aversion and, 177; one-sided, 484–5
base rates, 123–4, 300
Bayes, Rev. Thomas, 78
Bayes theorem, 68, 291; misuse, 502–3
Bayesian conditioning, 269–70
Bayesian language, 242–5; semantics, 243–5; syntax, 245

613